Living & Working in CANADA

• A Survival Handbook •

David Hampshire
&
Sally Jennings

Survival Books • London • England

First published in 1999
Second Edition 2003
Third Edition 2006
Fourth Edition 2009

Survival Books Limited
26 York Street, London W1U 6PZ, United Kingdom
+44 (0)20-7788 7644, +44 (0)870-762 3212
info@survivalbooks.net
www.survivalbooks.net

British Library Cataloguing in Publication Data
A CIP record for this book is available from the British Library.
ISBN: 978-1-905303-64-9

Printed and bound in India by Ajanta Offset

Acknowledgements

My sincere thanks to all those who contributed to the successful publication of this fourth edition of *Living and Working in Canada*, in particular, Joe & Kerry Laredo for updating, Peter Read for editing, Lilac Johnston for proof-reading, Di Tolland for photo selection and DTP, and Jim Watson for the cover design, cartoons and maps. Also a big thank you to the many people who contributed to this and previous editions, including Michelle Snow, Frank Berto, Bill Burnett, Diane Compton, Leslie Daniels, Marshall E. Drukarsh, Dan Hoffman, Diane Kerne, Brian Kilgore, Ian Nicholson, Brenda McManus and all the members of Compuserve's 'Canada' forums.

Finally, a special thank-you to all the photographers (see page 382) – the unsung heroes – whose beautiful images add colour and bring Canada to life.

What readers & reviewers have said about Survival Books:

'If you need to find out how France works then this book is indispensable. Native French people probably have a less thorough understanding of how their country functions.'

Living France

'It's everything you always wanted to ask but didn't for fear of the contemptuous put down. The best English-language guide. Its pages are stuffed with practical information on everyday subjects and are designed to compliment the traditional guidebook.'

Swiss News

'Rarely has a 'survival guide' contained such useful advice – This book dispels doubts for first-time travellers, yet is also useful for seasoned globetrotters – In a word, if you're planning to move to the US or go there for a long-term stay, then buy this book both for general reading and as a ready-reference.'

American Citizens Abroad

'Let's say it at once. David Hampshire's Living and Working in France is the best handbook ever produced for visitors and foreign residents in this country; indeed, my discussion with locals showed that it has much to teach even those born and bred in l'Hexagone – It is Hampshire's meticulous detail which lifts his work way beyond the range of other books with similar titles. Often you think of a supplementary question and search for the answer in vain. With Hampshire this is rarely the case. – He writes with great clarity (and gives French equivalents of all key terms), a touch of humour and a ready eye for the odd (and often illuminating) fact. – This book is absolutely indispensable.'

The Riviera Reporter

'A must for all future expats. I invested in several books but this is the only one you need. Every issue and concern is covered, every daft question you have but are frightened to ask is answered honestly without pulling any punches. Highly recommended.'

Reader

'In answer to the desert island question about the one how-to book on France, this book would be it.'

The Recorder

'The ultimate reference book. Every subject imaginable is exhaustively explained in simple terms. An excellent introduction to fully enjoy all that this fine country has to offer and save time and money in the process.'

American Club of Zurich

'The amount of information covered is not short of incredible. I thought I knew enough about my birth country. This book has proved me wrong. Don't go to France without it. Big mistake if you do. Absolutely priceless!'

Reader

'When you buy a model plane for your child, a video recorder, or some new computer gizmo, you get with it a leaflet or booklet pleading 'Read Me First', or bearing large friendly letters or bold type saying 'IMPORTANT - follow the instructions carefully'. This book should be similarly supplied to all those entering France with anything more durable than a 5-day return ticket. – It is worth reading even if you are just visiting briefly, or if you have lived here for years and feel totally knowledgeable and secure. But if you need to find out how France works then it is indispensable. Native French people probably have a less thorough understanding of how their country functions. – Where it is most essential, the book is most up to the minute.

Living France

A comprehensive guide to all things French, written in a highly readable and amusing style, for anyone planning to live, work or retire in France.

The Times

Covers every conceivable question that might be asked concerning everyday life – I know of no other book that could take the place of this one.

France in Print

A concise, thorough account of the Do's and DONT's for a foreigner in Switzerland – Crammed with useful information and lightened with humorous quips which make the facts more readable.

American Citizens Abroad

'I found this a wonderful book crammed with facts and figures, with a straightforward approach to the problems and pitfalls you are likely to encounter. The whole laced with humour and a thorough understanding of what's involved. Gets my vote!'

Reader

'A vital tool in the war against real estate sharks; don't even think of buying without reading this book first!'

Everything Spain

'We would like to congratulate you on this work: it is really super! We hand it out to our expatriates and they read it with great interest and pleasure.'

ICI (Switzerland) AG

Important Note

Canada is a vast and diverse country with many faces and numerous ethnic groups, religions and customs, and continuously changing rules and regulations, particularly with regard to immigration, social insurance, Medicare, education and taxes. Each province and territory also has different laws and regulations, encompassing a wide variety of fields. We cannot recommend too strongly that you check with an official and reliable source (not always the same) before making any major decisions or taking an irreversible course of action. However, don't believe everything you're told or read – even, dare we say it – herein!

Useful addresses, websites and references to other sources of information have been included in all chapters and in **Appendices A** to **C** to help you obtain further information and verify details with official sources. Important points have been emphasised, some of which it would be expensive, or even dangerous, to disregard. **Ignore them at your peril or cost!**

NOTE

Unless specifically stated, the reference to any company, organisation or product in this book doesn't constitute an endorsement or recommendation. None of the businesses, products or individuals recommended in this book have paid to be mentioned.

Contents

15. LEISURE 253

16. SPORTS 269

17. SHOPPING 289

Authors' Notes

- Times are shown using am (ante meridiem) for before noon and pm (post meridiem) for after noon. Most Canadians don't use the 24-hour clock. All times are local, so check the time difference before making inter-province or international telephone calls (see **Time Difference** on page 331).

- All prices are in Canadian dollars, unless otherwise stated, and don't generally include goods and services tax (GST) or provincial sales tax (PST) – see **Sales Tax** on page 292. Prices should be taken as estimates only, although they were (mostly) correct at the time of publication.

- His/he/him also means her/she/her – please forgive us ladies. This is done to make life easier for both the reader and the authors, and isn't intended to be sexist.

- British English is used in this book, although Canadian words that differ significantly from British English are indicated in brackets. Canadian spelling is a confusing mixture of British and American English, although most spelling in this book is British English (or should be).

- Warnings and important points are shown in **bold** type.

- The following symbols are used in this book: ☎ (telephone), 🖹 (fax), 💻 (Internet) and ✉ (email).

- Lists of **Useful Addresses**, **Further Reading** and **Useful Websites** are contained in **Appendices A**, **B** and **C** respectively.

- For those unfamiliar with the metric system of **Weights & Measures**, Imperial conversion tables are shown in **Appendix D**.

- A map showing the provinces and territories and their capital cities is inside the back cover.

Introduction

Whether you're already living or working in Canada or just thinking about it – this is THE BOOK for you. Forget about those glossy guide books, excellent though they are for tourists; this amazing book was written especially with you in mind and is worth its weight in maple syrup. Furthermore, this fully revised and completely re-designed 4th edition is printed in full colour. ***Living and Working in Canada*** is designed to meet the needs of anyone wishing to know the essentials of Canadian life – however long your intended stay, you'll find the information contained in this book invaluable.

General information isn't difficult to find in Canada; however, reliable and up to date information specifically intended for foreigners living and working in Canada isn't so easy to find, least of all in one volume. Our aim in publishing this book is to help fill this void, and provide the accurate, comprehensive and practical information necessary for a relatively trouble-free life. You may have visited Canada as a tourist, but living and working there is a different matter altogether. Adjusting to a different environment and culture and making a home in any foreign country can be a traumatic and stressful experience – and Canada is no exception.

Living and Working in Canada is a comprehensive handbook on a wide range of everyday subjects and represents the most up-to-date source of general information available to foreigners in Canada. It isn't, however, simply a monologue of dry facts and figures, but a practical and entertaining look at life in Canada.

Adjusting to life in a new country is a continuous process, and although this book will help reduce your 'beginner's' phase and minimise the frustrations, it doesn't contain all the answers (most of us don't even know the right questions to ask). What it will do, is help you make informed decisions and calculated judgements, instead of uneducated guesses and costly mistakes. **Most importantly, it will help you save time, trouble and money, and repay your investment many times over!**

Although you may find some of the information a bit daunting, don't be discouraged. Most problems occur only once and fade into insignificance after a short time (as you face the next half a dozen!). Most foreigners in Canada would agree that, all things considered, they love living there. A period spent in Canada is a wonderful way to enrich your life, broaden your horizons, and with any luck (and some hard work), also please your bank manager. I trust ***Living and Working in Canada*** will help you avoid the pitfalls of life in Canada and smooth your way to a happy and rewarding future in your new home.

Good luck!

David Hampshire & Sally Jennings

May 2009

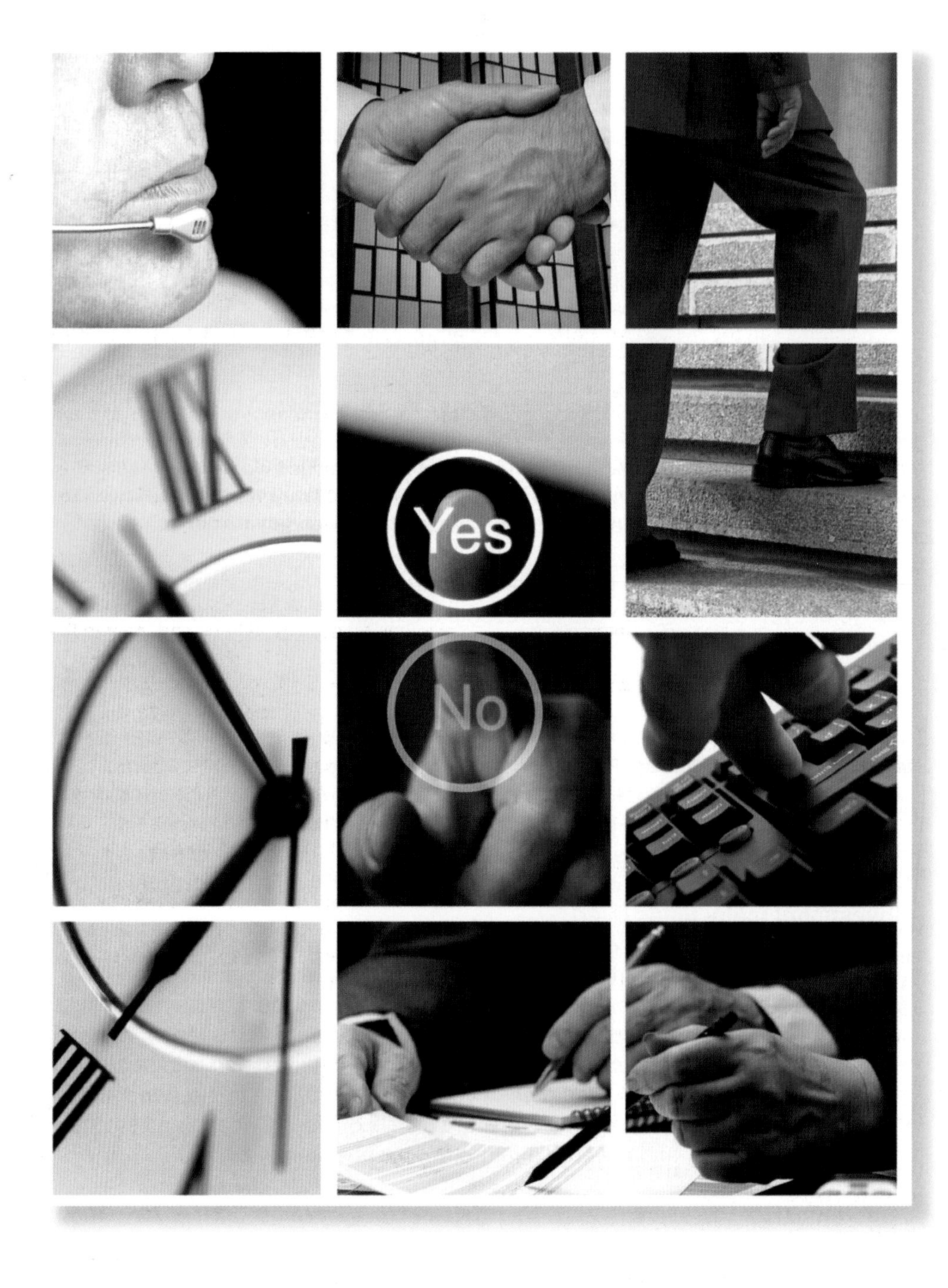
Yes
No

1. FINDING A JOB

The main problem facing those wishing to work in Canada isn't usually finding a job, but obtaining a work permit or being accepted for immigration. Described by the United Nations as 'the best country in the world in which to live', thanks to its high standard of living and quality of life, Canada wants to remain 'top dog' and is therefore fairly selective regarding immigrants (and is becoming more so). In addition to requiring immigrants to be in good health and of good character (i.e. with no criminal record), Canada also wants people who are hard-working and well educated, with training and experience. The largest class of immigrants, described as 'skilled workers', is decided by a points system that's heavily weighted towards those with high-level qualifications and work experience in jobs deemed to be in demand by the federal government.

Canada is a nation of immigrants and many Canadians can trace their ancestors back to foreign settlers within five or six generations (less in the west). Some 30 per cent of the 33.6mn population has British or Irish ancestry and around 25 per cent French ancestry (a figure that's steadily decreasing). Successive waves of immigration in the first half of the 20th century brought large numbers of Chinese, Ukrainians, Dutch, Scandinavians, Portuguese, Greek, Scots, Italians and Poles. The second half of the century saw an influx of immigrants from Asia (particularly Hong Kong, India, China and Taiwan – over 1mn Canadians are of Chinese descent), which have comprised some two-thirds of migrants in recent years.

In the early 21st century, immigration from Iran, Iraq, Syria and Egypt is growing rapidly. Early immigrants tended to head for the wide open spaces of the prairies to obtain land, but most now go to Toronto and the other large cosmopolitan cities. The major Canadian cities have the largest Chinese communities outside China, e.g. over 40 per cent of Toronto's population and 35 per cent of Vancouver's are immigrants (many of them recent).

Canada's birth-rate is falling and immigration is necessary to maintain the population at its current level. The country also has an aging workforce and, prior to the recession in 2008-09, was facing a severe skilled worker shortage. Nevertheless, as a percentage of the total population, immigration (at around 230,000 annually plus approximately 200,000 temporary immigrants) has recently fallen below the rate it reached in the early '90s. More importantly, the Canadian government decided that the immigration system wasn't providing the 'right' type of immigrants – those who would boost the country's economy. For these reasons, immigration legislation was revised in June 2008 (see **Chapter 3**).

> Like most other developed countries, Canada has a problem with illegal immigrants, but it isn't nearly as severe as in the US.

The Economy

Until the recession hit in 2008, Canada had been increasing its exports and changing from its previous pattern of exporting raw materials to selling high-value finished products such as telecommunications equipment, car parts and other transport equipment. The greatest growth has been in the western provinces, particularly in oil and gas rich Alberta, which has long shaken off the effects of a national energy programme in the '80s that siphoned off $60bn from Alberta to provide cheap energy for Ontario and Quebec.

Calgary, once called Cowtown because of its extensive ranching (as Toronto was Hogtown), has become a boom-town and houses the headquarters of some of the leading players in high-tech industries, plus many oil companies (the west end of town is known as the Oil Patch). British Columbia, richly endowed with natural resources including mineral reserves and timber, has benefited from the Pacific Rim economies, aided by the influx of wealthy Asian immigrants (one-third of BC's exports go to Asian markets).

Vancouver has been dubbed 'Hollywood North' due to the fact that US studios film there all year round to take advantage of the mild weather, and because it's cheaper and has lower taxes than the US (Toronto is also a popular film venue). British Columbia, Manitoba and Quebec have thriving aerospace industries. In recent years the provincial government of Quebec has pumped money into Montreal to develop a multimedia complex, and Ottawa is becoming known as Canada's 'Silicon Valley'. The rich new Hibernian oil field off Newfoundland promises a boom in the eastern maritime provinces.

In the country brand index (💻 www.countrybrandindex.com) survey conducted by FutureBrand, Canada was in second place in 2008; the top ten countries were Australia, Canada, the USA, Italy, Switzerland, France, New Zealand, the United Kingdom, Japan and Sweden. Countries are ranked across 30 distinct categories, providing a perspective on strengths, weaknesses and opportunities.

Recession

Since experiencing a severe recession in the early '90s, there was a strong recovery in the Canadian economy, particularly in the last decade or so; and until 2007 the economy was booming, when the effects of a slowdown in the US economy (some 80 per cent of exports are to the US) began to impact on Canada. Like most other countries, Canada succumbed to the global recession in the fourth quarter of 2008, although it wouldn't officially be in recession until April 2009 (a recession is commonly defined as two consecutive quarters of negative GDP growth, and there was growth in the third quarter of 2008).

In April 2009, there was no doubt that Canada was in a severe recession, with unemployment at over 10 per cent in some provinces and rising. The country was faced with a financial perfect storm of a sputtering US economy, tumbling oil and commodity prices, and falling domestic demand. Canada's economy contracted at an annualised rate of 3.4 per cent in the fourth quarter of 2008, and in the first-quarter of 2009 by a projected 4.8 per cent.

Although the government was forecasting that Canada would make a strong recovery and would come out of the recession in better shape than many other countries, it was obvious from the conflicting forecasts that no-one knows how deep or prolonged the recession will be – and whether it could turn into a depression – and when growth would return, although most analysts were predicting sometime in 2010.

Business confidence was at an all-time low in spring 2009, with sales and investment expected to remain low for 'the forseeable future'. Most businesses expect to cut back on employment and equipment investment amid declining sales over the next year, indicating a weak outlook for the Canadian economy. A drop in domestic demand has caused labour shortages to decline to a record low level. Nevertheless, Canada is expected to weather the recession better than many other western countries.

EMPLOYMENT PROSPECTS

Finding a job is – or should be – the number one priority for anyone emigrating to Canada. Unless you have an income from investments or considerable savings, you'll need to find employment at the earliest opportunity, preferably even before you set foot in Canada. Firstly, you must ensure that Canadian employers will accept your qualifications (see below) and work experience, and that you'll be able to find work – any kind of work – until your ideal job becomes available.

Before deciding to migrate to Canada, or applying for a visa, you need to answer a number of questions. For example, are your qualifications sufficient to practice your profession or trade in Canada? Is there a Canadian licensing authority for your profession or trade and can you meet their requirements? If not, what do you need to do? Is there any demand in Canada for your particular skills, and if so, where?

Many immigrants initially have difficulty finding employment. A recent study revealed that even university-educated immigrants aged 25 to 54 are less likely to be employed than their Canadian-born counterparts, irrespective of the country where they obtained their degree. Employment rates do, however, vary according to where immigrants obtained their university degree, with those educated in Western countries generally having higher employment rates than those educated elsewhere. However, the gap in employment rates between degree-holding immigrants and Canadian-born employees narrows the longer an immigrant had been in Canada.

There are a number of reasons why immigrants, particularly those who have arrived more recently, have difficulty finding employment. These include problems with foreign credential recognition, language barriers, comparability of educational attainment, and a lack of Canadian work experience and knowledge of the Canadian labour market.

Some migrants, even from developed countries such as the UK and US, are shocked to discover that they need to take extra exams to work in Canada. A further blow many newcomers face is to be offered a job at the bottom of the career ladder, after leaving more senior positions in their home countries. The consolation is that, if you're highly capable in your job, once you have a little Canadian experience, advancement can be rapid. Bear in mind the following when seeking employment in Canada:

- One quarter of recent degree-qualified migrants are working in jobs that don't require tertiary qualifications.
- After three years in Canada, only around half of degree-qualified migrants have jobs that are relevant to their degrees.
- The average salary for new, degree-qualified, male migrants aged 25 to 54 is generally around a third less than for the average male Canadian.

You should be focused on moving somewhere where your skills are needed. As far as climate goes, most people prefer to move to British Columbia (e.g. Vancouver); but will you be able to get a job there? The vast majority of immigrants choose to settle in Ontario, British Columbia or Quebec; however, don't overlook the less popular provinces and cities, such as Alberta, Manitoba, the Atlantic provinces, and cities such the capital Ottawa, Hamilton and Winnipeg. Your 'ideal' location – at least initially – should be somewhere where you'll be able to get a job and the all-important Canadian work experience to add to your résumé. Despite the recession, long-term job prospects are good in Canada, which is facing a severe skills shortage and has an aging population. Many sectors are experiencing labour shortages including information technology, the food service industry, healthcare (the country has a huge shortfall of doctors and nurses), and skilled workers in a wide range of professions and trades.

JOB MARKET

Manufacturing's share of the job market has been shrinking for decades and now only some 15 per cent of Canadian workers are employed in manufacturing, the most important sector of which is the automotive industry. The federal government estimates that around 75 per cent of the workforce is employed in service industries such as banking, insurance, education and a vast civil service. Among the occupations most in demand (in addition to those listed above) are information technology experts, health care specialists such as occupational therapists and physiotherapists, technical sales staff for computers, semi-conductors and instrumentation, and communications experts. Industries that are expected to show no growth in the next decade include clothing, pulp and paper, textiles, fishing and tobacco, while slow-to-moderate growth is predicted for the retail and wholesale trades, and the printing and publishing industries.

Working conditions in Canada are governed by legislation designed to ensure that employees are treated fairly and equitably. The federal Employment Equity Act ensures that employers take concrete steps to improve the employment situation of women, those with disabilities, aboriginal peoples and members of visible minorities. The federal government operates a Federal Contractors Programme to ensure that employment equity programmes are implemented by employers wishing to do business with the federal government, and also ensures that provincial and municipal governments comply by enforcing equity programmes within their workforces. The three levels of government employ around 1.5mn people or some 10 per cent of the total workforce.

The government Working in Canada website (💻 http://workingincanada.gc.ca – select Working in Canada from the menu) has a 'Working in Canada Tool' which is designed to help you decide where to live and work. The tool can be used to produce a report on job descriptions, wages, skill requirements, language training and job opportunities, based on your occupation and the location where you wish to live. Human Resources and Skills Development Canada (💻 www.hrsdc.gc.ca) publishes an abundance of information about employment trends and job prospects in Canada, as does Statistics Canada (💻 www.statcan.gc.ca).

Unemployment

Canada's unemployment rate fell to a 35-year low of 6 per cent in January 2008, since when it has risen again and in April 2009 was 8 per cent (the highest for seven years). As in other first world countries, Canada has not escaped the recession and almost 275,000 jobs were lost in the first three months of 2009. (for the latest figures, see Statistics Canada, 💻 http://www40.statcan.ca/l01/cst01/lfss01a-eng.htm).

The unemployment rate in March 2009 for the ten provinces (the Northwest Territories, Nunavut and the Yukon are excluded) is shown below:

Unemployment Rate March 2009

Province	Unemployment Rate
Alberta	5.8
British Columbia	7.4
Manitoba	5.1
New Brunswick	9.5
Newfoundland & Labrador	14.7
Nova Scotia	8.9
Ontario	8.7
Prince Edward Island	11.5
Quebec	8.3
Saskatchewan	4.7

(source: Statistics Canada)

In recent years, unemployment has been more likely to result in long-term job loss than previously, and many white-collar workers, particularly those seeking middle management positions, often make dozens of job applications without success. Increasing worldwide competition is squeezing everyone, and Canadian companies are as keen to

you're expected to work, and burn-out is common among managers and executives who often work long days. The two- or three-week annual holidays hardly compensate for the effort expended. Key employees routinely give up breaks and take work home, and it isn't unusual for them to be called at home or even when on holiday (vacation).

Don't be misled by the informality and casual atmosphere or dress in many companies – most Canadian employers have their eye firmly fixed on the bottom line.

reduce costs and increase productivity as those in other countries, which has led them to cut their workforces.

Construction and manufacturing are the hardest-hit sectors of the Canadian economy in the latest recession (some 500,000 manufacturing jobs have been lost since 2002 alone). In terms of gender, women have enjoyed the greatest increases in employment in recent years, e.g. during 2008 the increase in jobs for women aged 25 and over (around 100,000) was twice that of men in the same age group (50,000), while youth employment showed little growth.

A budget in January 2009, which included a stimulus package and tax reductions, was designed to create around 200,000 jobs.

Specialisation

Although specialisation has brought many Canadians greater rewards, it has seriously inhibited their freedom to change jobs. Over the next decade it's estimated that 80 per cent of new jobs will require more than a high school education, and most employers will require workers with a high degree of specialisation and training. Increasing specialisation and unemployment has encouraged (or forced) many people to turn to self-employment and start small businesses.

Work Ethic

Canadians work hard, but less frenetically than Americans. Work is seen as an important part of life, but not the only thing life has to offer. However, the higher you rise, the harder

QUALIFICATIONS & SKILLS

The most important 'qualification' for working in Canada is the ability to speak English fluently (see **Language** on page 39). If English isn't your mother tongue, but you have a degree or a certificate from a recognised educational establishment in an English-speaking country, this usually presents no problems. However, applicants from non-English speaking countries or backgrounds may need to take a language proficiency test, such as the International English Language Testing System (IELTS) examination. (French-speaking applicants may need to take a *test d'évaluation de français* or TEF.)

Once you've overcome this hurdle, you need to establish whether your trade or professional qualifications and experience will be recognised in Canada. While you may be well qualified in your own country, you may need to pass further professional examinations or trade tests to satisfy Canadian standards. You need to establish whether or not your qualifications will be recognised in the Canadian province to which you intend to move before making any plans to emigrate to Canada. Details are available from the Canadian Information Centre for International Credentials/CICIC (💻 www.cicic.ca/404/recognition-of-professional-qualifications.canada). Your qualifications may be accepted as they are and you may be required to take additional examinations before you can practice your occupation in Canada. Note that Canada doesn't readily accept professional or trade qualifications obtained overseas, even from developed countries, and many immigrants must take additional examinations or re-train in order to obtain local certification.

Most individuals who plan to settle permanently and work in Canada will need to know the 'value' of the education, training, and experience they have acquired outside Canada. Broadly speaking, qualifications recognised by professional and trade bodies overseas are recognised in Canada. However, recognition may vary depending on the country where the qualification was earned and the particular province in Canada, and in some cases foreign qualifications aren't recognised by Canadian professional and trade associations or employers. All academic qualifications should also be recognised, although they may be given less prominence than equivalent Canadian qualifications, depending on the country and the educational establishment where they were obtained.

The procedures for evaluating and recognising qualifications earned outside Canada depend on whether you wish to enter an occupation or pursue further studies, whether your chosen occupation is regulated (i.e. controlled by provincial and territorial – and sometimes federal – law, and governed by a professional organisation or regulatory body) or non-regulated, and the province/territory where you intend to settle.

The regulatory body governing a profession or trade has the authority to set entry requirements and standards of practice; to assess applicants' qualifications and credentials; to certify, register, or license qualified applicants; and to discipline members of the profession or trade. Requirements for entry, which may vary from province to province, usually consist of examinations, a specified period of supervised work experience, language competency and other criteria. If you want to work in a regulated occupation and use a regulated title, you must have a licence or certificate or be registered with the regulatory body for your occupation. Some occupations are regulated in some provinces and territories, but not in others.

Some 20 per cent of Canadians work in regulated occupations (i.e. professions and trades), such as electrician, engineer, medical doctor (MD), plumber, physiotherapist and veterinarian. The system of regulation is intended to protect the health and safety of Canadians by ensuring that professionals and tradesmen meet the required standards of practice and competence. As a general rule, if your chosen occupation is regulated, the recognition of qualifications is determined by the appropriate provincial or territorial regulatory body, while for a non-regulated occupation, recognition is normally at the discretion of the employer.

A 'non-regulated' occupation is a profession/trade for which there's no legal requirement or restrictions on practice with regard to licences, certificates or registration. The vast majority (around 80 per cent) of occupations in Canada fall into this category. For some non-regulated occupations, certification or registration with a professional body is available on a voluntary basis, whereas for other non-regulated occupations there's no certification or registration. In general, applicants for non-regulated occupations must demonstrate to a prospective employer that they possess the experience and training required for the job. Even when an occupation isn't regulated, employers can still require applicants to be

registered, licensed or certified with the relevant professional association.

You should be aware that the recognition process may be different in each province and territory and for each profession/trade. It can be a time-consuming process (up to twelve weeks); therefore it's important that you obtain all the information necessary and the specific requirements before undertaking an assessment. The fee levied by credential evaluation and qualification agencies varies from around $80 to $175 for a basic evaluation, plus an additional $200 for a detailed evaluation (if applicable).

The contact details of the assessment or evaluation service for regulated occupations in each of the provinces and territories are listed on the Canadian Information Centre for International Credentials' (CICIC) website (🖳 www.cicic.ca/404/recognition-of-professional-qualifications.canada).

☑ SURVIVAL TIP

Whatever kind of job you're looking for, whether temporary or permanent, part- or full-time, always take proof of your qualifications, training and experience to an interview, plus copies of references and a current résumé/CV (see page 33).

When leaving a job in Canada, you should ask for a written reference (one isn't usually provided automatically), particularly if you intend to look for further work in Canada or you think your work experience will help you to obtain employment overseas.

EMPLOYMENT & JOB SERVICES

Government employment services in Canada are provided by Service Canada (SC), which was created in 2005 to improve the delivery of government programmes and services to Canadians, by making access to them faster, easier and more convenient. Service Canada offers access to a wide range of Government of Canada programs and services for citizens through over 600 SC centres (including youth centres), community offices and scheduled outreach sites across the country, plus call centres and the internet. It also operates a Job Bank, which is an invaluable resource for job seekers (Job Bank, Employment Information Services, Service Canada, 140 Promendade du Portage, Phase IV, 5th Floor, Box 511, Hull, QC K1A OJ9, 🖳 www.jobbank.gc.ca).

Self-help kiosks in job centres provide updates on the job market and allow you to find out which occupations and job categories are in demand, the skills required and the training opportunities or services available to help you find work. Service Canada Centres also operate computerised Job Banks containing vacancy listings in the local area and across the nation, to help you match your skills and experience to specific jobs. You can select the jobs that are of interest and obtain more information from staff, who can also arrange interviews.

Service Canada employs counsellors who can test applicants' occupational aptitudes and interests, help them make career decisions, and channel them into appropriate training programmes through screening and referral services. Many non-profit community agencies offer counselling, career development, skills training and job placement services, generally targeted at 'disadvantaged' groups such as women, youths, minorities, the disabled, ex-offenders and older workers.

Many communities have career counselling, training, placement and support services for both the employed and unemployed. Programmes are sponsored by a range of organisations, including unions, churches, social service agencies, non-profit organisations, local businesses and vocational rehabilitation agencies,

TRAINING & EDUCATION

Canadian employers respond well to job applicants who are in the process of improving their skills by undergoing training and further education; in fact, continually upgrading your skills is expected. Many adult Canadians attend night school or complete online courses to gain additional qualifications and enhance their job prospects. The Public Canada Service Agency (300 Laurier Avenue West, Ottawa, ON K1A OR3, ☎ 1-800-622 6232, 🖳 www.psagency-agencefp.gc.ca) works with government agencies and the unions to ensure that Canada has a modern, well trained public service (which is a huge employer in Canada with around 1.5mn employees).

A good source of assistance in finding occupational training for new immigrants is the Canada Employment and Immigration Union (National Office, Suite 1004, 233 Gilmour Street Ottawa, ON K2P 0P2, ☎ 613-236-9634, 🖳 www.ceiu-seic.ca) or the Service Canada Centres mentioned above. SC Centres can match job seekers with a vast array of local sources of career development training available from colleges, universities, school boards, private trainers, and other community agencies. Provinces have primary responsibility for the direction, monitoring and administration of training programmes, each of which has a government body responsible for training, education and apprenticeships.

For comprehensive information about training and education, see the government websites, Job Futures (🖳 www.jobfutures.ca/en), Canada's national career and education planning tool, and Training and Careers (🖳 www.jobsetc.gc.ca/eng). In the January 2009 budget, the Government allocated $8.3bn for its Canadian Skills and Transition Strategy. This includes extra support for people who have lost their jobs, including enhancements to Employment Insurance (see **Chapter 13**) and more funding for skills and training development to help Canadians get better jobs, while giving Canada a more flexible, knowledgeable workforce and a competitive edge in the global economy.

EMPLOYMENT AGENCIES & CONSULTANTS

Employment agencies and consultants flourish in major cities and towns in Canada. Most large companies engage agencies and consultants to recruit staff, particularly executives, managers, professional employees and temporary office staff (temps). Many agencies specialise in particular trades, professions or fields, e.g. computing, accounting, publishing, advertising, banking, insurance, sales staff, secretarial and office staff, bilingual people, catering, teaching, health professionals, engineering and technical, nursing, industrial recruitment, construction, temporary workers and domestics, while others deal with a range of industries and positions. Agencies may handle permanent or temporary (e.g. less than 90 days) jobs or both.

Many agencies, often calling themselves 'executive counsellors' or 'executive search' consultants (head-hunters), cater for the lucrative executive market. Head-hunters are extremely influential and although many companies and managers consider it unethical to lure away a competitor's top staff, most are happy to use their services. Critics claim that this encourages job-hopping, forces up salary levels and diminishes corporate loyalty. Employment agencies must usually be licensed by provincial or municipal authorities.

Agency fees for permanent positions are usually equal to three months' gross salary or 25 per cent of the gross annual salary and are paid by employers. Many agencies state in their advertisements that their services are 'fee paid', meaning that the employer pays for the agency's services, not the applicant. Some agencies act as employers, hiring workers and contracting them out to companies for an hourly rate. Employees are paid either an hourly rate (with weekly wages) or receive a monthly salary. This may include paid federal and provincial holidays and annual vacation after a qualifying period (like a regular job), but may receive no benefits such as medical insurance.

Temporary employment agencies usually take a percentage of employees' wages as their commission, e.g. 10 per cent, or charge as much as the first two or three weeks' salary. Wages are usually negotiable, therefore you should drive a hard bargain and ask for more than you're willing to accept. In cities, good temps are hard to find, so you may have a lot of bargaining power. Shop around different agencies to get an idea of the general rates of pay and fees.

Temporary agencies traditionally deal with workers such as office staff, domestic help, nurses and other medical services, security guards, cleaners, labourers and industrial workers. More recently, some agencies have begun to specialise in finding work for self-employed people on a contract basis, e.g. computer professionals, nurses, technicians and engineers. Before you sign on with an agency, check that they're government-approved (to the appropriate ISO standard) and therefore 'certified' to provide staff for lucrative short-term government contracts, which are common in Canada. Typical of such agencies is Spherion (🖳 www.spherion.ca).

For the larger picture, you can obtain a copy of the *Canadian Directory of Search Firms* (Mediacorp Canada Inc.) that lists over 2,500 search firms and 4,000 recruitment specialists in Canada by occupation, geographical area and those with offices in the US, Europe and Asia (as well as Canada). This book is available through *Canada Employment Weekly* (🖳 www.mediacorp.ca). Alternatively, you can contact the Association of Canadian Search, Employment and Staffing Services/ACSESS (2233 Argentia Road, Suite 100, Mississauga, Ontario, L5N 2X7, ☎ 1-888-232 4962 or ☎ 905-826 6869, 🖳 www.acsess.org) and ask for a list of agencies specialising in your field. Some of Canada's largest employment agents are listed in the table below:

Canadian Employment Agencies

Name	Website
Adecco Employment Services	www.adecco.ca
Beresford Blake Thomas	www.bbtworldwide.com
Calian	http://bts.calian.com/en/career_jobs
David Aplin Recruiting	www.aplin.com
Design Group Staffing	www.dg.ca
Drake International	www.drakeintl.com
Eagle Professional Resources	www.eagleonline.com
Express Personnel Services	www.express.com/ca
FEP Search Group	www.fepsearchgroup.com
Human Resources Jobs	www.humanresourcesjobs.ca
Hunt Personnel	www.hunt.ca
Kelly Services	www.kellyservices.ca
Maizis & Miller Consultants	www.maizisandmiller.com
Manpower	www.manpower.ca
Manpower Professional	www.manpowerprofessional.ca
Office Jobs	www.officejobs.com
Quantum Management Services	www.quantum.ca
Randstad Canada	www.randstad.ca
Spherion Staffing Solutions	www.spherion.ca
Team Recruiter	www.teamrecruiter.com
Technogenie Resources	www.technogenie.com
Télé-Ressources	www.teleressources.com
The 500 Staffing Inc.	www.the500.com
The People Bank	www.thepeoplebank.com
WW Work	www.wwwork.com

The headhunters directory (🖳 www.headhuntersdirectory.com/canada.htm) provides links to headhunters, executive recruiters, executive search firms, employment, staffing and personnel agencies in each province, and a list of links to placement agencies are provided on the Jobbank website (🖳 www.jobbank.gc.ca – Finding a Job/Other job sites). A list of the leading Canadian job websites and job boards is on page 33.

CONTRACT JOBS

It's possible to find contract work in Canada in many occupations, particularly in computers, aerospace and electronics. Contractors are usually employed on the same general terms as permanent employees, but at higher salaries. Contracts are usually for a minimum of one year (although open-ended contracts are also common) and may be extended for up to six years. If you wish to withdraw from a contract you should note that penalties can be severe and may include repayment of relocation expenses, visa charges and air fares.

Teacher exchange positions are available (usually for an academic year from August to August) through the League for the Exchange of Commonwealth Teachers (LECT, Queens Road, Reading RG1 4BS, UK, ☎ +44-118-902 1171, 🖳 www.lect.org.uk) or through the Society for Educational Visits and Exchanges in Canada (300-950 Gladstone Street, Ottawa, ON K1Y 3E6, ☎ 613-727 3832, 🖳 www.sevec.ca). You shouldn't experience difficulty in obtaining the necessary visa if you have skills that can provide an economic benefit to Canada, but you need a firm job offer before applying for a visa.

Contract jobs are available through employment agencies, some of which specialise in providing contract workers. Many contract jobs are for technical specialists, although there's also a strong market in providing cleaning, catering, maintenance and manual workers. Some companies specialise in supplying contract staff to major companies, many of who are increasingly contracting out non-core support work, from cleaning to computing, rather than hiring full-time employees.

Professional contractors (or freelancers) often work from home. The potential for home-based work in Canada is huge, especially in the computer industry, which is keen to capitalise on the number of people (particularly women) wishing to work part-time from home. The International Homeworkers Alliance (IHA, 143 Main St E, Hamilton, ON L8N 1G4, ☎ 905-521 9888, 🖳 www.homeworkers.org) provides listings of work-at-home opportunities. You pay a membership fee to join and a small monthly maintenance fee to view company lists and must contact companies directly to arrange work.

You should be aware that there are many scams posing under the umbrella of offering jobs to homeworkers, typical of which is one claiming that you can earn $1 a time for putting a piece of paper in an envelope (called 'stuffing'). You pay around $50 for the 'kit' that consists of a booklet listing various companies who may need envelope stuffers, only one of which pays $1 a time, but expects you to buy the envelope and get the piece of paper printed out of your fee. If in doubt, check offers with a Better Business Bureau.

PART-TIME JOBS

Part-time jobs are available in most industries and professions, and are common in offices, bars, shops, factories, cafes and restaurants. Often, part-time workers are poorly paid, and rates are usually around (or even below) the minimum wage (see below) for non-skilled workers, depending on the local unemployment rate and labour market. Part-time employees often have no protection from exploitation by employers, although some large companies provide part-time employees with the same benefits as full-time employees. Some companies operate a job-share scheme, where two or more people share the same job. Part-time jobs are also available through employment agencies (see above).

TEMPORARY & CASUAL WORK

Temporary and casual work, legal and illegal, is available throughout Canada. However, visitors (or anyone without a work visa) should be wary of working illegally (see page 39). One of the big attractions for itinerants is that casual workers are often paid cash in hand at the end of each day's work. There are temporary employment agencies in most towns and cities. If you're seeking a full-time job but cannot find one in your profession or trade, a temporary job can often be a stepping-stone to a permanent position, as many employers use them as trial periods. A temporary job also allows you to get your 'foot in the door' and to learn about other openings within a company that you may prefer or be better suited for.

Short-term contract jobs include temporary office jobs available through specialist agencies and the usual range of menial jobs such as gardening or farm work, bar and restaurant jobs, and commission-only selling. For information about temporary jobs, contact the Association of Canadian Search, Employment and Staffing Services (6835 Century Avenue, Mississauga, ON L5N 2L2, ☎ 905-826 6869, 💻 www.acsess.org).

HOLIDAY & SHORT-TERM JOBS

In view of the necessity for prospective employers to prove that there's no unemployed Canadian citizen or immigrant visa holder available to fill a job (see **Chapter 3**), it isn't possible (legally) to enter Canada on a visitor's visa and then seek work, whether full- or part-time. Young people wishing to take holiday jobs or longer temporary employment in Canada find it easier to do so through organisations that specialise in 'gap' employment between secondary school and university or after university but before taking a full-time job.

The book *Summer Jobs USA* (published by Peterson's) contains some jobs in Canada. Most jobs listed are in summer camps and are for unskilled positions such as waiting-staff, cleaners and gas jockeys (pump attendants). Many specify non-smokers only and prefer college students, while some require certified skills in first-aid and life saving. Where the job is for the whole summer season, training is usually provided at the beginning of the season. Airfares may also be paid if you work the whole summer.

Service Canada (💻 www1.servicecanada.gc.ca – select 'Employment for Youth and Students' from the menu) provides information about a number of programs for youth and students, including Canada Summer Jobs (an initiative of the Summer Work Experience program) and the National Research Council (NRC) Summer Employment Program.

VOLUNTARY WORK

The minimum age limit for voluntary (volunteer) work in Canada is 15 to 18 (depending on the province) and most organisations require fluent English or French. Special qualifications aren't usually required and the minimum length of service varies from one month to one year (often there's no maximum length of service). Handicapped volunteers are also welcomed by many organisations. Voluntary work is (not surprisingly) unpaid, although meals and accommodation are usually provided, and some organisations also pay a small amount of pocket money. However, this is usually insufficient for out-of-pocket living expenses (entertainment, drinks, etc.), therefore you must ensure that you bring enough money with you.

☑ SURVIVAL TIP

A voluntary job (even for a half day a week) can be a useful way for you to obtain Canadian experience to help secure a full-time position, particularly if you can obtain a volunteer position within an organisation where you can showcase your skills.

It's essential before travelling to Canada for any voluntary work that you check whether you're eligible and whether you're permitted to enter the country under the existing immigration and employment regulations. You may be required to obtain a visa (see **Chapter 3**); check the documentation required with a Canadian embassy or consulate well in advance of your planned visit. The usual visa regulations apply to voluntary workers and your passport must be valid for at least one year.

International workcamps provide an opportunity for people from many countries to live and work together on a range of projects, such as building, conservation, gardening and community projects. Camps are usually run for two to four weeks between April and October. Usually workers are required to work an eight-hour, five-day week and the work can be physically demanding. Accommodation is usually shared with your fellow slaves and is basic. Most workcamps consist of 10 to 20 volunteers from several countries, with English and/or French the common languages. Volunteers generally pay a registration fee and their own travelling costs to and from the workcamp, and may also be expected to contribute towards the cost of board and lodging. An application to join a workcamp should be made through the appropriate recruiting agency in your home country.

There are many organisations that can help you find voluntary work in Canada, including the following:

- **British Universities North America Club** (BUNAC, 16 Bowling Green Lane, London EC1R 0QH, UK, ☏ +44 20-7251 0215, 💻 www.bunac.org) operates a reciprocal exchange system called SWAP. It helps you obtain the necessary work permits, but won't find you a job (although it provides lists of suitable jobs).
- **The Canadian Red Cross** (170 Metcalfe Street, Suite 300, Ottawa, ON K2P 2P2, ☏ 613-740 1900, 💻 www.redcross.ca).
- **Centre for International Mobility** (PO Box 343, FIN-00531 Helsinki, Finland, ☏ +358-207 868 500, 💻 www.cimo.fi) has a few exchange places in conjunction with the International Association for the Exchange of Students for Technical Experience (IAESTE) in Canada.
- **Charity Village** (💻 www.charityvillage.com – see 'Contact Us' for further contact information) is Canada's supersite for the non-profit sector, with 3,500 pages of news, jobs, resources, how-to articles, volunteer and event listings, educational opportunities, and much more.
- **Connect Youth** (British Council, 10 Spring Gardens, London SW1A 2BN, UK, ☏ +44 -20-7389 4030, 💻 www.britishcouncil.org/connectyouth) organises exchange schemes with other countries.
- **The Council on International Educational Exchange** (CIEE, 300 Fore Street, 3rd Floor, Portland, ME 04101, US, ☏ 1-800-40 STUDY or ☏ 207-553 4299, 💻 www.ciee.org) runs a programme called Internship Canada with the Canadian Student Federation for undergraduates or 'gap' year students with a firm offer from a university. CIEE has offices in Australia, China, France, Germany, Italy, Japan, Spain, Taiwan and the UK.
- **Lattitude** (formerly GAP, 44 Queen's Road, Reading, Berkshire RG1 4BB, UK, ☏ +44-118-959 4914, 💻 www.lattitude.org.uk) places gap year students with volunteer projects in Canada.

- **Peace Brigades International** (☏ 613-237 6968, 💻 www.pbicanada.org) seeks volunteers willing to help with promoting non-violence and protecting human rights.
- **Volunteer Canada** (353 Dalhousie Street 3rd Floor, Ottawa, ON K1N 7G1, ☏ 1-800 -670 0401 or 613-231 4371, 💻 www.volunteer.ca) acts as a national umbrella organisation on behalf of volunteer bureaux and centres in all provinces and territories. It maintains a list of local volunteer bureaux and centres which match volunteers with opportunities.

There are also numerous organisations operating in individual provinces and cities such as 💻 www.benevolat.gouv.qc.ca (Quebec), www.govolunteer.ca (BC and Alberta), www.volunteeralberta.ab.ca (Alberta), www.volunteerbridge.ca and www.volunteertoronto.on.ca (both Toronto).

TRAINEES & WORK EXPERIENCE

A number of countries have organised career development programmes with the International Association for the Exchange of Students for Technical Experience (IAESTE, 💻 www.iaeste.org). The aim of the programme is to enable participants to gain practical experience for a maximum of 18 months in Canada and other participating countries. IAESTE also provides on the job training in Canada to full-time foreign university/college students in technical fields such as agriculture, architecture, computer science, engineering, mathematics, and natural and physical sciences.

Applicants should be aged 19 to 30 and have completed two or preferably three years in a technical major. Applications must be made by 10th December in your country of citizenship to gain acceptance for the following summer. Training periods are up to 18 months, although the majority are for 8 to 12 weeks during the summer. The IAESTE programme is also available to Canadian students in over 50 countries.

For further information ask your college or university for the address of IAESTE in your home country or contact them via their website (💻 www.iaeste.org). In most countries there are government agencies handling educational exchanges and training in Canada, e.g. in the UK it's the Central Bureau for Educational Visits and Exchanges (see 💻 www.britishcouncil.org/new).

NANNIES & AU PAIRS

Canada doesn't have an official scheme for au pairs, although it does have a Live-In Caregiver Program, which allows care providers to work in Canada when there aren't sufficient Canadian residents to fill the available positions. Live-in caregivers are individuals who are qualified to provide care in private homes without supervision, for children, the elderly and those with disabilities. Live-in caregivers must live in the private home where they work in Canada.

Service Canada works with employers who wish to engage live-in caregivers, while Citizenship and Immigration Canada (see **Chapter 3**) works with foreign live-in caregiver applicants. Live-in caregivers can receive a work permit for up to three years if they meet programme requirements, and there are special conditions which allow a foreign live-in caregiver to apply for permanent residency after working in Canada for two years.

Applicants under the Live-In Caregiver Program must:

- Have successfully completed the equivalent of a Canadian high school education.
- Have six months of full-time training in a classroom setting or twelve months of full-time paid employment, including at least six months of continuous employment with one employer in a field or occupation related to the job you're seeking as a live-in caregiver.
- Be able to speak, read and understand either English (or French, if applicable) at a level that allows you to work independently in a home setting. For example, it's important as a caregiver to be able to contact emergency services if necessary and to understand the labels on medication.

You must be provided with a written employment contract which defines your job duties, hours of work, salary and benefits. The contract also reinforces your employer's legal responsibilities to you.

For further information, see the Citizenship and Immigration Canada website (www.cic.gc.ca/english/work/caregiver/index.asp) or the Human Resources and Skills Development Canada website (www.hrsdc.gc.ca/eng/workplaceskills/foreign_workers/ei_tfw/lic_tfw.shtml).

> Canada has a number of student work programmes (see page 68) for citizens of the UK, Ireland, Sweden and Finland. To qualify you must be a full-time student at a university or similar recognised post-secondary institution in your country of citizenship, be aged between 18 and 30, and provide an unconditional letter of acceptance or a letter confirming that you've recently graduated.

WORKING WOMEN

For many years, discrimination in Canada prevented women from competing equally with men and from entering male-dominated professions. However, in the last few decades, women have succeeded in breaking down the barriers and now officially compete on equal terms with men for education, professional training, employment, leadership positions and political power. Women still encounter some prejudice, however, and resistance and some inequalities exist, not least in salaries. Despite laws prohibiting job discrimination on the basis of sex and requiring equal pay for equal work, women's pay is still 15 to 30 per cent lower than men's for some full-time jobs. However, the situation is changing rapidly and there are ever more women in high-ranking professional jobs.

Professional women are common in Canada and have more equality than their counterparts in most other countries, although some find it difficult (or impossible) to reach the top ranks of their professions. The main discrimination against professional women isn't salary but promotion prospects, as some companies and organisations are reluctant to elevate women to important positions. Generally, the closer women get to the top, the more they're resented, although this is changing. Around 40 per cent of corporate managers are women, with most of those holding high positions employed in federal and provincial government jobs, although many are also self-employed or work in the health sciences. Nevertheless, you're likely to come across women in top positions in all walks of life in Canada.

There are increasing pressures on women to seek employment to supplement the family income, and women constitute around 45 per cent of the labour force. Some 60 per cent of women work either full- or part-time and they make up around 65 per cent of part-time workers, although many would prefer full-time work. Status of Women Canada (SWC, MacDonald Building, 123 Slater Street, 10th Floor, Ottawa, ON K1P 1H9, ☎ 613-995 7835, www.swc-cfc.gc.ca) is the federal government agency responsible for promoting gender equality and the full participation of women in Canada's economic, social, cultural and political life. Contact SWC for information and fact sheets about its programmes and services.

As a means of circumventing prejudice and low wages, many women have turned to self-employment and over a third of business start-ups in recent years have been owned by women. Women-owned businesses have increased at twice the rate of male-owned businesses in the last decade and provide employment for nearly 2mn Canadians and create new jobs at a faster rate than the national average.

JOB HUNTING

When looking for a job in Canada, you should contact as many prospective employers as possible, either by writing, telephoning or just dropping off a résumé (CV). Whatever job you're seeking, it's important to market yourself appropriately for the kind of job you're after. For example, the recruitment of executives and senior managers is handled almost exclusively by consultants, who advertise in the national newspapers such as *The Globe & Mail* and interview all applicants before presenting their clients with a shortlist. At the other end of the scale, jobs requiring little or no previous experience (such as store clerks) may be advertised in local newspapers or store windows, and the first able-bodied applicant may be offered the job on the spot. You'll need a résumé/CV (see below) for any job application.

If you're willing to look beyond the attractions of living in a major city such as Toronto, Vancouver or Montreal (which attract some 75 per cent of all migrants), and head somewhere more off the beaten track, such as the Atlantic provinces of New Brunswick, Nova Scotia and Prince Edward Island, or even less 'fashionable' cities such as the capital Ottawa or Winnipeg, you may have more success. Outside of the major cities there's less competition for jobs and a slower pace of life, which may suit those who wish to escape the rat race. Taking a position in a less popular town or province can also help you get a foot on the ladder in your preferred job sector and gain valuable Canadian experience.

When writing for a job, you should address your letter to the Human Resources Department and include your curriculum vitae and copies of references and qualifications. Writing for jobs from abroad is usually the least successful method of securing employment in Canada, as Canadian employers aren't allowed to employ people from outside the country unless they can prove that there's no Canadian citizen or immigrant visa holder available for the job.

As well as the usual methods of job seeking, there are many Canada-specific resources for job seekers, some of which are listed below.

- Service Canada (see page 23) mainly handle non-professional skilled and unskilled jobs, particularly in industry, retailing and catering. Service Canada centres are an excellent resource for job-seekers, as they provide counselling and publications on job search techniques, interviewing tips, résumé/CV writing and many other topics. They can also direct job-seekers to local job finding clubs which provide a free, three-week programme to assist people with their job search, including facilitators and coaches and the use of computers, faxes and photocopiers. See also 💻 www.servicecanada.gc.ca (see **The WORK place** for links to resources).
- Visit internet job search engines such as All Canadian Jobs (💻 www.allcanadianjobs.com), Canada Jobs (💻 www.canadajobs.com), Eluta (💻 www.eluta.ca) and the federal government Job Bank (💻 www.jobbank.gc.ca). For further information, see The Internet below.
- The Canadian Career Development Foundation (119 Ross Avenue Suite 202, Ottawa, ON K1Y ON6, ☎ 613-729 6164, 💻 http://ccdf.ca) is a charitable foundation that's 'committed to advancing the understanding and practice of career development'. It aims to improve access for Canadians to quality career services.
- Canadian local and major city newspapers have 'Job Opportunities' or 'Help Wanted' sections on most days, although most advertisements appear on Saturdays. Service Canada also has a direct link to the 'help wanted' ads in the major Canadian newspapers (💻 www1.servicecanada.gc.ca/eng/ns/lmi/workplace/jobs/help/help.shtml). Jobs are also advertised in professional journals and trade magazines. Most newspapers can be accessed online via 💻 www.world-newspapers.com/canada.html (search by province) and 💻 www.onlinenewspapers.com/canada.htm (listed A-Z by town/city).

- International and national recruiting agencies acting for Canadian companies. These companies chiefly recruit executives and key managerial and technical staff, and many have offices worldwide and throughout Canada. Some Canadian companies appoint consultants to handle overseas recruitment in certain countries.
  Contact employers directly via their own websites, particularly companies and organisations in your field or which routinely employ people in your profession or trade. This is an excellent way to discover the 'hidden' job market; that is, jobs that haven't been advertised and which are often filled by word of mouth.
- If your professional qualifications are recognised in Canada, you can write to Canadian professional associations for information and advice (addresses can be obtained from Canadian Chambers of Commerce). Most professionals, e.g. in medicine, engineering and law, must be licensed by individual provinces.
- Subscribe to job newsletters and digests such as *Canada Employment Weekly* (💻 www.mediacorp.ca).
- Most provinces publish civil service 'job opportunity' newspapers. If you're in Canada and have a computer, many job opportunities are advertised on computer networks. Look for 'Community Nets' and 'Freenets' in major cities, such as 💻 www.craigslist.com.
- Networking (getting together with like-minded people to discuss business) is a popular way to make business and professional contacts in Canada. Networking can also be done via the internet, when it's termed e-networking.

- Many good business contacts can be made among expatriate groups. Newcomers to Canada frequently find that ethnic business and professional associations are a good source of job information.

Many books are written for those seeking employment in Canada, including *The Canadian Job Directory* and *The Canada Student Employment Guide*, both by Keven Makra (Guidance Centre), *How to Find a Job in Canada* by Efim Cheinis & Dale Sproule (Oxford University Press), *Career Focus Canada: A Personal Job Search Guide*, by Helene Martucci Lamarre & Karen McClughan (Pearson Education Canada), *Career Directory 2007: Canada's 100 Best Employers for College and University Graduates*, by Karen Chow & Richard Yerema (Mediacorp) and the *Canadian Summer Job Directory* (Sentor Media).

The Internet

The internet has rapidly become the number one resource for finding employment, both in Canada and elsewhere. Websites include mainstream (High Street) and internet-dedicated employment agencies (temporary, contract and full-time); professional head-hunters; job boards where employers and jobseekers can place ads; companies advertising vacancies on their own websites; and Canadian government and provincial government sites. Most websites are in English and French.

The main internet job resources include:

- Job boards, which include 💻 www.allstarjobs.ca, www.canjobs.com, www.eluta.ca, www.monster.ca, www.thecanadianimmigrant.com/jobboard and www.workopolis.com. For other job boards, see the boxes below.
- The government Job Bank website, 💻 www.jobbank.gc.ca.
- For careers in the federal public services, see the website of the Public Services Commission of Canada (💻 http://jobs-emplois.gc.ca/index-eng.htm). For a comprehensive list of job opportunities in public organisations, see 💻 www.jobbank.gc.ca – Finding a Job/Other job sites.

General Job Websites

www.allcanadajobs.com
www.bestjobsca.com
www.canadausemployment.com
www.careerbeacon.com
www.careerbuilder.ca
www.careerclick.com
www.jobboom.com
www.jobhawk.com
http://jobport.ca
www.jobshark.ca
www.plusjobs.ca
www.wehire.ca

Industry and Area-specific Job Websites

www.albertajobcentre.ca – Alberta
www.brainhunter.com – IT & engineering
www.bcjobs.ca – British Columbia
www.cooljobscanada.com – hospitality & tourism
www.educationcanada.com – education
www.edujobscanada.com – education
www.extremejobs.ca – travel & tourism
www.handicapemploi.com – jobs for disabled workers
www.hcareers.ca – hospitality careers
www.hospitalitycareers.ca – hospitality
www.jobloft.com – retail, food & hospitality
www.mediajobssearchcanada.com – media
www.sapphireca.com – IT staff
www.socialworkjobs.ca – social workers
www.technogenie.com – technical positions
www.workwest.ca – western Canada
www.yuwin.ca – Yukon WorkinfoNETwww.wehire.ca

Lists of industry-related job websites and websites by province are also provided on the Job Bank website (💻 www.jobbank.gc.ca – see Finding a Job/Other job sites).

RÉSUMÉS & INTERVIEWS

Your résumé (usually written 'resume' in Canadian English) or curriculum vitae (CV) is of vital importance when looking for employment in Canada, particularly when jobs are thin on the ground and applicants are a dime a dozen. Never forget that the purpose of your résumé is to obtain an interview, not a job, and it must be written with this in mind. This means that it must be individually tailored to each job application (along with your cover letter).

Think of your résumé as a advertisement or brochure for your time and skills, and try to see it from a prospective employer's point of view. Would you stand out against the competition (the other candidates) and would the manager want to talk to you about a possible job? Employers may scan a résumé for just 30 seconds to decide whether to consider an applicant and may even use an automated scan to short-list candidates. Your résumé is your first contact with a prospective employer and should be designed to open the door to an interview.

A résumé is a 'snapshot' of your education/ qualifications, skills and experience, and must:

- be written with the employer's interests in mind
- be targeted for a particular job or organisation
- be honest without embellishment
- provide a clear demonstration of your skills, abilities and achievements
- clearly indicate what you offer the employer
- be professional in appearance
- be word-perfect with no spelling or grammar mistakes
- be no more than two or three A4 pages in length

If you aren't up to writing a good résumé, you can employ a professional résumé writer who can turn your humdrum working life into an epic of which Indiana Jones would be proud. Professional help will also ensure that your résumé adheres to a strict code of ethics (i.e. so you won't lose your job later for over-embellishing your life story) and some writers guarantee that a résumé is in the proper form for the region and industry where you're looking.

There are also many websites that can help, such as CV Tips (💻 www.cvtips.com/cv_writing.html), Work Bloom, résumé writing resources (💻 http://workbloom.com/resume-center.aspx) and also the Service Canada Job Bank (💻 usually.jobbank.gc.ca/intro_eng.aspx) which has a Résumé Builder feature.

Bear in mind that résumés must be in the standard Canadian format, which isn't the same as in other countries. If your résumé isn't in the correct format or doesn't contain the correct information, it's likely that it will be discarded.

In addition to a good résumé, employers may require the names of a number (e.g. three) of personal or professional referees, who they'll contact (usually by telephone, so there's no incriminating documentation of any 'candid' remarks).

Job interviews should never be taken lightly in Canada, where interviewing and being interviewed for a job is a science, and creating a good impression can make the difference between being on the ladder of success or in the unemployment (or soup kitchen) queue. Dress smartly, even if the job is shovelling muck. The secret is in preparation, so do your homework on prospective employers and try to anticipate every question you may be asked (and then some) and rehearse your answers. Most employers expect you to know something about the company, its products or services, and general reputation in the press – all information you can research in your local library. Some employers require prospective employees to complete aptitude and other written tests.

You may be asked to show proof of your immigration status or your eligibility for the appropriate visa, and you may also be required to sign a release authorising the employer to run a credit check (which could be done in your previous country of residence), even for jobs that don't directly involve money or finance. Interviews should always be followed up immediately with a letter, confirming your interest in (and suitability for) the job, and thanking the interviewer for his or her time and interest (it pays to be obsequious when job hunting!).

There are numerous books dealing with everything from writing a compelling résumé to how to answer (or field) questions during an interview, including *Best Canadian Resumes*, Sharon Graham (Ontario Institute for Studies), *Knock 'em Dead Resumes* by Martin Yate (Adams Media Corporation), *The Only Resume and Cover Letter Book You'll Ever Need*, Richard Wallace (Adams Media), and *101 Great Answers to the Toughest Interview Questions*, Ron Fry (Delmar Learning).

SALARY

It can be difficult to determine the level of salary you should receive in Canada, particularly for professional and executive appointments, where salaries and benefits are rarely quoted in job advertisements (except for sales appointments, when the fanciful salaries quoted can be ignored). On the other hand, 'Help Wanted' small advertisements in local newspapers may state salaries. Service Canada centres (see page 23) can also provide information on local wage rates. Usually salaries are negotiable and it's up to you to ensure that you receive the level of salary and benefits commensurate with your qualifications and experience (or as much as you can get). If

Minimum Hourly Wages by Province (April 2009)

Province	Minimum Hourly Wage
Alberta	$8.40
British Columbia	$8.00
Manitoba	$8.50
New Brunswick	$7.75
Newfoundland & Labrador	$8.00 (increasing to $10 by July 2010)
Northwest Territories	$8.25
Nova Scotia	$8.10 (increasing to $9.65 by October 2010)
Nunavut	$10.00
Ontario	$8.75 (increasing to $10.25 by March 2010)
Prince Edward Island	$8.00
Quebec	$8.50
Saskatchewan	$8.60 (increasing to $9.25 by May 2009)
The Yukon Territory	$8.58

you have friends or acquaintances working in Canada, ask them what an average or good salary would be for your particular trade or profession.

Minimum hourly wages, which apply to full- and part-time workers, are fixed by each province and vary according to the state or territory – although they are all low! See the table above for the rates in April 2009.

Salaries in some companies and professions (particularly for government employees) are decided by national pay agreements between unions and employers. Salary reviews vary between 6 and 18 months, depending on the employer. When negotiating your salary, bear in mind that benefits and employment protection provided by Canadian employers are less than in many other western countries. Canadian jobs come with fewer fringe benefits than those in most European countries and may not include a company pension, although an increasing number of Canadian companies now provide company pensions.

The average Canadian weekly earnings was $801.24 in October 2009, an increase of 3 per cent over the previous year. However, wage increases vary according to the sector and region. For example, between October 2007 and October 2008, earnings increased by 8.8 per cent in accommodation and food services; 4.5 per cent in health and social assistance; 3.5 per cent in educational services; 1.8 percent in the retail trade, and only 1.7 percent in manufacturing. Average weekly earnings (by province and industry) are shown in the tables below:

Average Weekly Earnings by Province (October 2008)

Province	Average Weekly Earnings
Alberta	$889
British Columbia	$778
Manitoba	$728
New Brunswick	$741
Newfoundland & Labrador	$749
Nova Scotia	$699
Ontario	$831
Prince Edward Island	$655
Quebec	$755
Saskatchewan	$766

(source: Statistics Canada)

Average Weekly Earnings by Industry (October 2008)

Industry	Average Weekly Earnings
Accommodation & Food Services	$354
Arts, Entertainment & Recreation	$479
Construction	$1,024
Educational Services	$871
Finance & Insurance	$1,019
Forestry & Logging	$1,033
Health Care & Social Services	$743
Information & Cultural Industries	$998
Management (companies)	$895
Manufacturing	$962
Mining, Oil & Gas	$1,483
Professional, Scientific & Technical	$1,053
Public Administration	$974
Real Estate, Rental & Leasing	$720
Retail Trade	$500
Transportation & Warehousing	$825
Utilities	$1,183
Wholesale Trade	$948

(source: Statistics Canada)

Salaries vary considerably for the same job in different regions of Canada and are generally higher in major cities, e.g. Toronto and Montreal, and in remote areas such as the north of Canada (you need some incentive to spend most of the year buried under snow). For example, a junior office worker may earn less than $20 per hour in Fredericton (New Brunswick) and Winnipeg (Manitoba) but over $30 in Banff, Calgary and Drumheller (Alberta).

Also bear in mind the local cost of living. For example, although salaries are much higher in Toronto and Vancouver than they are in Newfoundland, but so is the cost of living, and the extra salary might not compensate sufficiently (even though a secretarial job in Newfoundland may pay only $20,000, while a big city secretary can earn over $30,000).

Further details of Canadian salaries can be found on 💻 www.livingin-canada.com/work-salaries-wages-canada.html.

With the exception of executives, salary rises in recent years have barely matched inflation and wage growth is non-existent for many low-paid workers. Most salary increases for blue-collar workers come from working longer hours. Salaries for non-executive staff have actually fallen (relative to the cost of living) in the last few decades.

The Economic Research Institute website (💻 www.erieri.ca) contains a number of assessment tools including a salary assessor that allows you to compare the salaries of over 5,500 positions in Canada and the US.

SELF-EMPLOYMENT & STARTING A BUSINESS

Many Canadians and immigrants have an ambition to start their own business. Entrepreneurs are respected and encouraged in Canada and no stigma is attached to business failure, which often spurs people to even greater efforts. Provincial governments often see self-employment as a growth area of the economy and encourage such enterprise. Even during the bleakest years of the recession in the early '90s, over 700,000 new businesses opened their doors, over half of which were sole proprietorships or small businesses with no more than a few employees.

Although many self-employed people come from the ranks of the unemployed, the majority leave secure and well-paid jobs to go it alone. As employers have increasingly been replacing full-time employees with freelancers, consultants and outside contractors in recent years, self-employment has become a necessity for many people, rather than an option. HRSDC (💻 www.hrsdc.gc.ca) produces a list of business opportunities expected to expand in the next decade, which currently includes retirement homes in small towns, personal and home security systems, home office products and services, health foods and specialist travel for the elderly.

Whatever people may tell you, starting your own business isn't easy (otherwise most of us would be doing it) and it requires a lot of hard work (self-employed people generally work much longer hours than employees); a sizeable investment and operating funds (most businesses fail due to lack of capital); good organisation (e.g. bookkeeping and planning); excellent customer relations (in Canada the customer is always right – even when he's wrong!); and a measure of luck (although generally the harder you work, the more 'luck' you'll have). Bear in mind that around two out of three new businesses fail within three to five years and that the self-employed must provide their own pension plans and don't qualify for employment insurance and workers' compensation.

The key to buying or starting a successful business is exhaustive research, research and yet more research (plus innovation, value and service). Bear in mind that choosing the location for a business is even more important than the location for a home. Many business consultants advertise in the Canadian and foreign press (see **Appendix B**) and offer everything from sandwich bars to motels, laundrettes (laundromats) to restaurants. Always thoroughly investigate an existing or proposed business before investing a cent.

Service Canada operates a self-employment programme on behalf of Human Resources and Social Development Canada (HRSDC) for individuals who are eligible for Employment Insurance (see **Chapter 13**). The programme includes income and entrepreneurial support while you develop and implement your business plan. For information, see 💻 www1.servicecanada.gc.ca.

Business Visas

For foreigners, one of the main attractions of buying a business in Canada is that it offers an easier method of obtaining a visa, as the Canadian government is keen to encourage foreign entrepreneurs. You must demonstrate that you have sufficient funds available to start a business and provide for your family for a reasonable period. In practice, this usually means at least $300,000. It isn't mandatory to use a specialist business immigration lawyer, but doing so usually helps smooth the process. Always obtain a quotation in writing and shop around a number of immigration lawyers (but check their credentials and references), because fees can run into thousands of dollars depending on the amount of work involved.

If you invest in a suitable business before you arrive in Canada, you're usually given an unconditional visa, otherwise you receive a conditional visa that requires you to have a business in operation (with at least one Canadian employee) within two years. For further information, see **Chapter 3**.

Business Structures

There are four kinds of business structure you can choose if you're self-employed: a sole proprietorship, partnership (general and limited), joint-venture or corporation. Due to the ever-changing and complex tax laws, you should consult a tax expert before deciding on the best one for you. You must also decide whether to buy an established business, a franchise or start a new business from scratch. When buying an existing business, always employ a licensed business broker (buyer's broker) to advise you on the purchase.

Franchises have a much higher success rate than other start-up businesses. For information contact the Canadian Franchise Association (5399 Eglinton Avenue West,

Suite 116, Toronto, ON M9C 5K6, ☏ 1-800-665 4232 or 416-695 2896, 💻 www.cfa.ca), which sets voluntary standards for members operating in Canada. The CFA provides an information package of franchise opportunities entitled *Investigate before Investing*, and holds regular information seminars for prospective franchisees. *Canadian Business Franchise Magazine* (💻 www.franchise.org) focuses on particular franchises and contains articles that answer many of the usual questions from prospective franchisees (it also lists franchises for sale).

Professional Advice

Before investing in a business in Canada, it's essential to obtain professional and legal advice. If you aren't prepared to do this, you shouldn't even think about starting a business in Canada (or anywhere else for that matter). Engaging the services of a business and investment consultant is usually the wisest course, although the quality of advice and service varies. Few foreigners are capable of finding their way through the web of legal requirements and regulations without expert advice, not to mention federal, provincial and local laws and regulations.

The purchase of a business must be conditional on obtaining visas, licences, permits and any loans or other funding required. While it's much easier to buy an existing business than start a new one, you must investigate thoroughly the financial status, turnover and value of a business (obtain an independent valuation). It's also important to engage an accountant at the earliest opportunity.

Information

Many local, provincial and federal government agencies and departments provide information and advice about starting and running a business. The best place to start is the local provincial office of Canada Business, which is a co-operative of federal business departments, provincial government associations, and academic and research organisations. Canada Business provides a wide variety of business counselling regarding finance, accounting, record keeping, business start-up and management, taxes, marketing, sales promotion, advertising, retailing, manufacturing, and sales and service businesses. You can find their local address in the blue section of *White Pages* or refer to their website (💻 www.canadabusiness.ca).

Note that in some provinces the name of the organisation includes the name of the province, e.g. Canada-Ontario Business Service Centre (COBSC). The Business Development Bank of Canada (💻 *www.bdc.ca/en/home.htm)* provides not only loans and venture (or 'vulture' if you're a cynic) capital, but also provides counselling services for existing and proposed small businesses.

There are many business magazines published in Canada, which you can subscribe to via Magazines Canada (💻 http://magazinescanada.ca/consumer/listing.php?id=3).

There are numerous useful organisations for those planning to start a business in Canada, both official and unofficial, including the following:

Useful Websites

Name	Website
Business Development Bank of Canada	www.bcd.ca
Canadian Association of Family Enterprise (CAFE)	www.cafecanada.ca
Canada Business	www.canadabusiness.ca
Canadian Chamber of Commerce	www.chamber.ca
Canadian Federation of Independent Business	www.cfib.ca
Industry Canada	www.ic.gc.ca
Invest in Canada	www.investincanada.gc.ca
Location Canada	www.locationcanada.com
Retail Council of Canada	www.retailcouncil.org

Provincial & Territory Websites

Province/Territory	Website
Alberta	www.albertacanada.com
British Columbia	www.welcomebc.ca
Manitoba	www.gov.mb.ca
New Brunswick	www.gnb.ca/immigration
Newfoundland & Labrador	www.hrle.gov.nl.ca/hrle/immigration
Nova Scotia	www.novascotiaimmigration.com
Northwest Territories	www.gov.nt.ca
Nunavut	www.gov.nu.ca
Ontario	www.ontarioimmigration.ca
Prince Edward Island	www.giv.pe.ca/immigration
Quebec	www.immigration-quebec.gouv.qc.ca
Saskatchewan	www.immigrationsask.gov.sk.ca
The Yukon Territory	www.immigration.gov.yk.ca

There are also many provincial government and business organisations regarding economic development, trade and investment. The official provincial government websites above also provide information about business opportunities.

ILLEGAL WORKING

There are no official statistics regarding illegal immigrants in Canada, with estimates anywhere between 40,000 and 120,000. However, it's acknowledged that tens of thousands of people work illegally in Canada, mostly in 'transient' jobs such as bartenders, waiters and waitresses, nannies and servants, farmworkers (particularly during fruit and vegetable harvests), the fishing industry and construction, where workers are often paid partly or wholly in cash. In order to get a job in Canada, an employee must have a social insurance number (SIN) that's issued to Canadians and legal immigrants.

It's strictly illegal for foreigners to work in Canada without a visa or official permission and if you work illegally with false documents the consequences will be even more serious.

If you're tempted to work illegally you should be aware of the pitfalls, as the black economy is a risky business for both employers and employees. Harbouring or employing alien labour, e.g. a housekeeper, isn't an offence under the criminal code of Canada, but you can be charged under the Immigration Act and face a stiff fine. Foreigners caught working illegally are fined and deported and refused entry into Canada for five years. Illegal immigrants have no entitlement to federal or company pensions, no employment or accident insurance, and no benefits.

LANGUAGE

One of the most important qualifications for anyone planning to live or work in Canada is a good command of one (or both) of the two 'official' languages, English and French (although some ethnic groups seem to get along fine without speaking either). Around 60 per cent of the population are native English speakers and some 25 per cent French speakers. Despite the efforts of the federal government to encourage everyone to learn and use both languages, barely 15 per cent of Canadians speak English *and* French, and one in six (over 5m) Canadian residents grew up speaking a language other than English or French.

English is by far the most important language, and you usually need to speak, read and write it well in order to get around in Canada; e.g. dealing with government officials, motoring, using public transport, shopping, and to understand and hold conversations with the people you meet. English proficiency is particularly important if you have a job requiring a lot of contact with others, speaking on the phone and dealing with other foreigners, many of whom speak their own 'dialect' of English.

French is mostly spoken in Quebec, where it's the first language, although there are also large numbers of French speakers in New Brunswick, which is officially bilingual, Ontario and Manitoba. French proficiency is essential in Quebec, where many people (particularly government officials) refuse to speak anything other than French and may refuse to speak to you if you don't speak French to them (although they're more accommodating with Americans and Britons than with Canadians). If you already speak fluent French as it's understood in France, you may take a while to adjust to the Canadian version, although they won't have any difficulty understanding you. Canadian French (called *Québécois*) in Quebec, where it's also known as joual) isn't, for the most part, the French spoken in France and can be unintelligible, even to a Parisian.

It's important for foreign students to have a good command of English or French (as applicable) because they must be able to follow lectures and take part in discussions in the course of their studies. This may also require a wider and more technical or specialised vocabulary. For this reason, most colleges and universities won't accept students who aren't fluent in English (French in Quebec), and most require prospective students to take a Test of English/French as a Foreign Language (TOEFL/TOFFL). If you wish to improve your English or French before starting work or commencing a course of study in Canada, there are language schools throughout the country (see page 154).

If you already speak English fluently, you probably won't have too much trouble understanding Canadians, although if you don't speak with a Canadian, American or BBC accent, they may have trouble understanding you. Those who speak English with a European, Australian, New Zealand or South African accent find that most Canadians are incapable of distinguishing between their accents.

Most Canadians and Britons understand each other most of the time, although there are inevitably occasions, particularly during your first few months in Canada, when small misunderstandings may cause bewilderment, amusement or embarrassment. Most differences are found in the rich assortment of slang and colloquialisms, and most cities, regions and ethnic groups have their own idioms. Written Canadian English is closer to British English than American English and the differences are usually less obvious in the written word.

Around 15 per cent of Canadians speak neither English or French as their first language, including many immigrants, some native Americans (e.g. Cree, Ojibwa, Iroquois) and the Inuit (Inuktitut). Canadians use many words adapted from the various native (e.g. Inuit and First Nations) languages, such as igloo, parka, muskeg (a level swamp or bog) and kayak. The name Canada itself is a corruption of the word *kanata*, a Huron-Iroquois word for village or small community.

Canada has also given the world many words and phrases, including kerosene, puck, bushed, toque and black ice. For further information, consult the *Gage Canadian Dictionary* and *A Concise Dictionary of Canadianisms.*

2. EMPLOYMENT CONDITIONS

Employment conditions (or 'employment standards' as it's called in Canada) in Canada are largely dependent on individual contracts and an employer's general employment terms. Most are negotiated between employers and employees through collective bargaining agreements (e.g. with unions), civil service rules and industry practices. However, federal and provincial laws govern certain aspects of employment standards, including general holidays, annual vacation, hours of work, minimum wages, layoff procedures and severance pay – which can therefore vary from province to province.

The rights and responsibilities of around 12,000 businesses and 840,000 of their employees (around 10 per cent of the Canadian workforce) are defined by the Canada Labour Code. The following sectors are largely federally regulated:

- Banking;
- Marine shipping, ferry and port services;
- Air transportation, including airports, aerodromes and airlines;
- Railway and road transportation that involves crossing provincial or international borders;
- Canals, pipelines, tunnels and bridges (crossing provincial borders);
- Telephone, telegraph and cable systems;
- Radio and television broadcasting;
- Uranium mining and processing;
- Businesses dealing with the protection of fisheries as a natural resource;
- First Nations activities;
- Federal Crown corporations;
- Private businesses necessary to the operation of a federal act.

If you work in any other sector, the employment standards that regulate your conditions of work are defined by your provincial or territorial Ministry of Labour.

Government employees (around 10 per cent of the total workforce) usually have considerably better job protection and legal rights than employees of private companies. Employees in the private sector can lose their jobs with as little as two weeks' notice and, unless you've been working for an employer for at least three months, you won't be entitled to any redundancy (severance) pay. Even after five years' service, you're only entitled to a paltry ten days' pay. Consequently, Canadian employers are more likely to lay off workers when business is bad. On the other hand, you may also quit your job at any time for any reason, although it's usual to give two weeks' notice.

Job titles are important in Canada because they define an employee's status and the perks that go with a job. All large Canadian corporations and employers have a strict hierarchy, including the federal civil service, which, despite attempts to simplify it, has over 4,000 job classifications, each with its own pay range. Employee benefits provided by medium and large firms are generally much better than those provided by small businesses. When negotiating your terms of employment for a job in Canada, the checklists at the end of this chapter will prove useful.

Although it's rare, an employer may ask a credit bureau (see **Credit Rating** on page 231) for a report on an employee, but must inform him of this. Private employers are permitted to have dress or 'grooming' codes, although public employers have less freedom to limit their employees' freedom of expression. Employers are, within limits, entitled to ask about an employee's lifestyle; however, this mustn't conflict with federal and provincial laws regarding discrimination (see below).

For further information about employment standards in Canada, see 💻 www.hrsdc.gc.ca/eng/labour/employment_standards/index.shtml.

For a directory of contact addresses for work-related organisations in each of Canada's provinces and territories, see 💻 www.naalc.org/french/pdf/canada.pdf.

EMPLOYMENT CONTRACT

If you're offered a job in Canada, it's wise to have a comprehensive and legally watertight written contract detailing your terms of employment. However, foreigners are often dismayed to find that most Canadian employers don't automatically provide contracts, except for executives, professionals (such as university professors), engineers and professional athletes. A written contract of employment should contain all the terms and conditions that have been agreed between you and the employer, including those discussed in this chapter. Before signing a contract, you should know exactly what it contains. If your knowledge of English (or French) is imperfect, you should ask for a translation.

Your employment is usually subject to satisfactory references being received from your previous employer(s) and/or character references. In the case of a school-leaver or student, a reference is usually required from the principal of your last school, college or university. For certain jobs, a pre-employment medical examination is required and periodic examinations may be a condition of employment, e.g. when good health is vital to the safe performance of your duties. If you require a permit to work in Canada, your contract may contain a clause stating that 'the job contract is subject to a permit being granted by the Canadian authorities'. For all jobs, you must have a Social Insurance Number (see page 213).

Employees with a contract must be notified in writing of any changes in their terms and conditions of employment. If you don't receive a written copy of your employer's general terms and conditions that apply to all employees, generally the federal and provincial minimum legal requirements apply.

Complaints

If you feel that your employer has broken the employment standards laws, you can file a complaint. However, you need to be aware that there may be time limits for filing and that complaints can take a long time to be resolved. In some provinces their are convoluted procedures to be followed before you can file a formal complaint, while in others complaints can be refused if employment standards staff believe that there are other ways to try to resolve the problem before a formal complaint can be filed. For example, in British Columbia a worker must first use a Self-Help Kit to try to solve a problem, otherwise the complaint won't be accepted, and in Prince Edward Island workers must first try to resolve the issue with their employer, including recovering wages or other entitlements they're owed.

Union members are covered by collective agreements that usually contain more comprehensive protection than those provided by employment laws, and members have access to a grievance procedure and union representation when their rights are violated. On the other hand, with the exception of Quebec, non-union workers aren't provided with free legal assistance at complaint hearings.

PLACE OF WORK

Unless your employment contract states otherwise, your employer can change your place of work (whether you like it or not) but must provide you with accommodation close to the new workplace. Some companies warn you that you may occasionally be required to work at other company locations, but you should have this clarified before accepting a position.

SALARY & BENEFITS

Negotiating an appropriate salary is just one aspect of your remuneration package, which may consist of much more than what you receive in your pay cheque. Many companies offer a range of fringe benefits for executives, managers and key personnel, and it isn't unusual for executives to increase their annual salaries dramatically through profit-sharing, stock options and bonuses. When discussing salary with a prospective employer, you should take into consideration the total salary package, including commission, bonuses and benefits. Your starting salary should be stated and overtime rates, bonus rates, planned increases and cost-of-living rises should also be included.

Salaries are usually paid by cheque or direct deposit to a bank account (but can be paid in cash) every two weeks for hourly-paid workers and bimonthly or monthly for salaried workers. You must receive an itemised pay statement (or wage slip) detailing all deductions, either with your pay cheque or when your salary is paid into a bank account.

Minimum hourly wages (that apply to both full and part-time workers) are set by each province, although under certain conditions, lower minimum wage rates can be paid, e.g. to apprentices, disabled workers and full-time students. Minimum wages also don't apply to certain categories of worker, e.g. sales personnel working on commission, many farm workers, casual baby-sitters, and employees of seasonal amusement and recreational establishments.

Salaries are usually reviewed once or twice a year, depending on your position and the industry. Annual increases may be negotiated individually by employees, by an independent pay review board or by a union (called collective bargaining).

Commission & Bonuses

Your salary may include commission or bonus payments, calculated on your individual performance (e.g. based on sales) or your employer's profits. Bonuses may be paid regularly (e.g. monthly or annually) or irregularly. Some employers in Canada pay employees an annual bonus (usually in December) and some limited companies may offer employees free shares. When a bonus is paid, it may be stated in your offer of employment, in which case it's obligatory. In your first and last years of employment, an annual bonus is usually paid pro rata if you don't work a full calendar year.

Some employers operate an annual voluntary bonus scheme, based on an employee's individual performance or the company's profits (a profit-sharing scheme). If you're employed on a contract or freelance basis for a fixed period, you may be paid an end-of-contract bonus.

Expenses

Expenses paid by your employer may be listed in his general terms and conditions. These may include travel costs from your home to your place of work, when travelling on company business or for training or education. Most companies pay a mileage allowance to staff who are authorised to use their private cars on company business (but make sure that business use is covered by your car insurance). Companies without a company restaurant or canteen may pay employees a lunch allowance.

Education & Training

If you need to improve your English or French, language classes may be paid for by your employer. If it's necessary for you to learn a foreign language (other than English or French) to do your job, the cost of language study should be paid by your employer. The education and training provided by your employer may be stated in his general terms and conditions.

It's in your interest to investigate courses of study, seminars and lectures that you feel would be of benefit to you and your employer. Many employers give reasonable consideration to a request to attend a part-time course during working hours, provided you don't make it a full-time occupation! They may offer to pay for your courses if you contract to stay with them for a certain number of years.

In addition to relevant education and training, employers must provide the essential tools and equipment for a job (although this is open to interpretation).

> It's compulsory for companies to provide relevant and adequate safety and health training for all employees (see **Health & Safety** on page 56).

Company Cars

Few Canadian employers provide company cars as fringe benefits. Even when a car is essential for your job, your employer will expect you to provide your own car, for which you're paid a mileage allowance when using it on company business. Using your car for business will affect your insurance if it's registered in the 'pleasure use' category. If a company car is provided, check what sort of car it is, whether you're permitted to use it privately, who pays for the fuel for private mileage and whether private use affects your tax position. A company may provide you with a free parking space downtown, which can be expensive if you have to pay for it yourself.

TRAVEL & RELOCATION EXPENSES

Your relocation expenses to Canada (or to a new job in another region of Canada) depend on your agreement with your employer, and may be detailed in an employment contract or your employer's general terms and conditions. If you're hired from outside Canada, your air ticket (or other travel expenses) to Canada may be paid for by your employer or his agent. You can usually claim any additional travel costs, e.g. the cost of transport to and from airports. If you change jobs within Canada, your new employer may pay your relocation expenses when it's necessary for you to move house. Don't forget to ask, as they may not offer to pay (it may depend on how desperate they are to employ you). If you have to pay the moving expenses there's a small benefit in that they are tax deductible.

An employer may pay a fixed relocation allowance based on your salary, position and size of family (e.g. $10,000), or may pay the total cost of moving house irrespective of the amount. The allowance should be sufficient to move the contents of an average house and you must normally pay any excess costs yourself. Your employer may ask you to obtain two or three removal estimates when he's liable for the total cost of removal. Generally you're required to organise and pay for the removal yourself. Your employer usually reimburses the equivalent amount in Canadian dollars after you've paid the bill, although it may be possible to get him to pay the bill directly or make an advance payment.

Ensure that the relocation package is adequate and if you leave the employer

before a certain period elapses, ask whether you're required to repay a percentage of the cost (or the full cost if you break a contract).

Relocation expenses paid by your employer aren't considered to be a taxable benefit. However, you cannot claim increased housing costs following a transfer as a deductible expense. See also **Relocation Consultants** on page 94.

WORKING HOURS

With some variations (depending on the type of industry in which you're employed), the standard working day is eight hours and the standard working week 40 hours. Where collective agreements exist, additional hours are paid at overtime rates (see below). In manufacturing, the average working week (with paid overtime) is 50 hours. Many Canadian executives and managers work long hours, which is essential if they want to succeed – generally the higher the position a person holds, the longer the hours he works.

Typical office hours are 8 or 9am to 4 or 5pm with a lunch break of between 30 and 60 minutes. Under federal law, employees must have a meal break of at least 30 minutes for every five hours worked and the time between starting and finishing work mustn't be more than 12 hours.

When you're paid by the hour, if you arrive at work and find there's nothing to do, your employer must pay you for at least two hours. If there's less than a full day's work to do, you must be paid for at least four hours. Most Canadian employers allow paid time off during working hours to visit a doctor or dentist.

Flexible Hours

Many Canadian companies operate flexible working hours, which are becoming more popular because of the different time zones (see page 331), particularly among office workers. (Phone calls to distant offices need to be carefully planned; for example, someone in Montreal has to wait until 11am to call someone in Vancouver at 8am, and the person in Vancouver has to call the person in Montreal before 2pm local time to be sure of catching him before he leaves the office.) It's traditional to start work earlier in the west in order to solve the time problem of dealing with the east.

A flexible working schedule normally requires employees to be present between certain hours, e.g. 10am to noon and 2pm to 4pm. Employees may make up their required working hours by starting earlier than the required 'core' time, reducing their lunch break or by working later. Smaller companies may allow employees to work as late as they like, provided they don't exceed the legal maximum permitted daily working hours (see above).

Overtime

Hourly-paid employees who work more than a certain number of hours must be paid at the official overtime rate, which varies from province to province. In most provinces, the overtime rate is equivalent to one-and-a-half times the employee's standard rate of pay. However, in New Brunswick, Newfoundland and Labrador the overtime rate is one-and-a-half times the **minimum wage**. In most provinces and territories the maximum number of hours that may be worked per day before overtime rates apply is eight, while the maximum weekly hours are usually 40, except for Alberta, New Brunswick and Ontario (44), and Nova Scotia and Newfoundland (48).

For daily overtime you normally receive time-and-a-half for the first three hours and double-time for hours worked in excess of 11 (12 in British Columbia). When overtime is calculated weekly, you receive time-and-a-half for the first eight hours in excess of the above limits and double-time for the ninth and any subsequent hours. You must have 32 consecutive hours free from work each week, but your employer can ask you to work during this time provided he pays you double-time, i.e. twice the standard hourly rate.

An employer can give employees time off in lieu of extra hours worked (called 'banking time' in Canada) instead of paying overtime, by mutual agreement. This compensatory time is on a 'one-for-one' basis, e.g. if you work five extra hours this week, you can work five hours less next week. As a cost-cutting move, some companies are starting to require time off in lieu and eliminating overtime altogether.

Employees who aren't covered by overtime rules include agricultural workers, live-in household workers, taxi drivers and employees of bus and coach companies, railways and airlines. Many white-collar employees, e.g. executives, managers, administrators and professionals, who earn 'ample' salaries, aren't covered by overtime laws even when they're employed in covered industries. Employees who earn at least half of their salary in commission are also excluded from overtime pay rules, although they must receive a minimum rate of pay. Overtime work is voluntary and you cannot be forced to do it.

HOLIDAYS & LEAVE

Annual Holidays

All workers must receive (and take) at least two weeks' paid holiday (vacation) per year, and those who leave a job before taking their holiday must receive payment in lieu. Some companies may offer three weeks' paid holiday from the outset and it may be negotiable – it may depend on how keen they are to hire you. You may not be granted the full two weeks if you join a company after their 'vacation year' has started, but you're usually allowed some days pro rata after you've worked for a few months. Holiday entitlement is calculated on a pro rata basis (per completed calendar month of service) when you don't work a full calendar year.

This miserly holiday allowance will come as a severe blow to Europeans and other foreigners who are used to receiving four to six weeks' paid annual leave (the average in Canada is 12 days per year compared with 25 in France and 30 in Germany). Teachers and others employed in some private educational establishments may be surprised to discover that there's no paid Easter holiday of one or two weeks and the long summer holiday period is often unpaid, so that it may be necessary to find work in summer school.

After three or five years' employment with one company, your official paid holiday entitlement usually rises to three weeks. Thereafter, each year of employment normally raises your annual holiday entitlement by one or two days, therefore it can take you eight years before you're entitled to four weeks' paid holiday per year.

Many companies provide anniversary-year bonus holidays, such as an extra week after 10 or 20 years' service (yippee!).

Your annual holiday entitlement usually depends on your profession, position and employer, and some employers have more generous schemes based on your length of service. White-collar employees usually become eligible for longer holidays after a shorter term of service than blue-collar workers and senior managers may be entitled to additional annual holiday (but have no time to take it!). Most employers require annual holiday to be taken within the year in which it's earned, but some allow a portion to be carried over to the next year. If you want to extend your holiday, you may be able to take unpaid holiday.

Employees also receive holiday pay of 4 per cent of their wages (calculated on their salary during the preceding year) in their first six years of employment and 6 per cent in the following years.

Before starting a new job, check that any planned holidays will be approved by your new employer. This is particularly important if they fall within your first 6 or 12 months. Holidays may usually be taken only with the prior permission of your manager or boss and in many companies must be booked up to a year in advance.

If you resign your position or are given notice, employers must usually pay you in lieu of any outstanding holiday.

> Foreign embassies and consulates in Canada usually observe all Canadian national and local holidays in addition to their own national holidays.

National & Provincial Holidays

When Canadians talk about a 'holiday' they mean a national (federal or provincial) holiday and not annual or school holiday, which is called vacation (as in the USA). The federal government designates seven days as national holidays, shown in the table below preceded by an asterisk (*). You're entitled to be paid for these days provided that you earn wages on 15 of the 30 days prior to the holiday (unless you're paid the minimum wage, in which case this doesn't apply). Individual provinces designate their own additional holidays, as shown below. Banks, post offices, public schools, offices and most businesses are usually closed on national and provincial holidays.

Employees who must work on national holidays are entitled to be paid time-and-a-half for the first 11 hours and double time for hours worked in excess of 11, plus a day off in lieu. There are exceptions to this rule for certain employees, including those employed in petrol stations, hospitals, restaurants, continuously operating plants, amusement parks, seasonal industries (excluding the construction industry) and domestic services, who are paid the normal rate but must be given another (paid) day off in lieu.

The three main national holidays are Canada Day (which celebrates Canada's creation as a dominion), Labour Day (which honours Canadian workers) and Thanksgiving (which commemorates the first harvest of European settlers). Many holidays are celebrated by federal law on Mondays in order to create three-day weekends for federal employees and many provinces also schedule provincial holidays on Mondays. When a holiday falls on a Saturday or Sunday, another day is usually granted to employees. If a holiday, such as Christmas Day, falls on a Sunday, banks and most shops close the following day.

Other holidays may include extended holiday plans, such as the period between Christmas and New Year's Day, local holidays (e.g. provincial national days), 'floating' holidays (e.g. your birthday, which some employers grant as a holiday) and days off for sickness, funerals, etc. (see **Compassionate & Special Leave** below). Floating holidays may be decided by the employer or individual employees. Other holidays don't need to be paid days, but most employers pay for them. For example, many companies give employees a full paid holiday on Christmas Eve and some also on New Year's Eve.

The following days are national holidays and are observed by most Canadians,

National Holidays

Date	Holiday
*1st January	New Year's Day
*March/April	Good Friday
March/April	Easter Monday
*Monday before 25th May	Victoria Day – Queen Victoria's birthday (not observed in Quebec)
*1st July	Canada Day (previously Dominion Day), the anniversary of the creation of the Dominion of Canada in 1867 – in Newfoundland, it's Memorial Day, which commemorates the loss of almost the entire Newfoundland Regiment on this day in 1916 at the Battle of the Somme
*first Monday in September	Labour Day (usually marks the 'end of summer')
*second Monday in October	Thanksgiving Day
11th November	Remembrance Day – The signing of the armistice of World War I, in which many Canadian soldiers fell in Flanders. As in the UK, people wear poppies and observe two-minutes' silence at 11am. Not a full-day holiday for all Canadians
*25th December	Christmas Day
26th December	Boxing Day

although only those marked with an asterisk are statutory holidays (table above).

In addition to national holidays, there are also the following provincial holidays:

Provincial Holidays

Province	Holiday
Alberta	Third Monday in February – Alberta (or Family) Day
	First Monday in August – Heritage Day
British Columbia	First Monday in August – British Columbia Day
Manitoba	First Monday in August – Civic Holiday
New Brunswick	First Monday in August – New Brunswick Day
Newfoundland	Nearest Monday to 17th March – St Patrick's Day
	Nearest Monday to 23rd April – St George's Day
	Nearest Monday to 27th June – Discovery Day
	Nearest Monday to 10th July – Orangemen's Day
Northwest Territories	First Monday in August – Civic Holiday
Nova Scotia	First Monday in August – Natal Day
Nunavut	First Monday in August – Civic Holiday
Ontario	First Monday in August – Civic Holiday
Prince Edward Island	First Monday in August – Natal Day
Quebec	24th June – Saint-Jean-Baptiste Day
Saskatchewan	First Monday in August – Civic Holiday
The Yukon Territory	Third Monday in August – Discovery Day

Compassionate & Special Leave

Most Canadian companies provide paid leave on certain occasions only, e.g. military leave, leave to attend the funeral of a family member ('bereavement days') and leave for jury duty, although smaller companies are generally more flexible. An employer must allow an employees time off for jury duty but isn't required to pay them (and the amount paid to jurors by the courts is derisory). A person selected for jury duty cannot be fired. Other special leave is usually limited to a number of days per year, e.g. three.

The grounds for compassionate leave may be listed in your employer's general terms and conditions. An employer isn't required to allow employees time off work for religious observance, although he's required to accommodate religious beliefs to a certain extent.

Whether or not you're paid for time off work or time lost through unavoidable circumstances (e.g. public transport strikes, car breakdowns and bad weather) depends on your employer and whether you're paid hourly or are a salaried employee. The attitude to paid time off in Canada also depends on your status and position. Executives and managers, who often work much longer hours than officially required, usually have more leeway than blue-collar workers. Some public-sector employers allow employees to take sabbaticals and may even continue to pay them a percentage of their salary; this is, however, exceptional, although usual at universities.

Pregnancy

Time off work for sickness in the early stages of pregnancy is usually given without question but usually isn't paid or is deemed to be sickness (see below). Pregnant women are entitled by law to 17 weeks' unpaid pregnancy leave. After giving birth, the mother is entitled to 35 weeks of unpaid maternity leave and fathers are entitled to 27 weeks' unpaid paternity leave, although parents aren't usually permitted to take their leave simultaneously.

An employer cannot refuse to employ or fire a woman because of a pregnancy (or for any reason connected with pregnancy or childbirth), force her to take maternity leave or fail to honour her reinstatement rights after a pregnancy. A mother is entitled to her previous job (or a similar job) with no loss of wages, fringe benefits or seniority – as is a father after paternity leave. The law requires employers to treat pregnancy and childbirth as a temporary disability, and health insurance plans must cover these conditions if they include temporary disabilities. A pregnant or nursing mother cannot be required to work overtime.

For further information, see 🖳 www.labour.gc.ca (maternity).

Sickness or Accident

You're usually required to notify your employer as soon as possible (i.e. within a few hours of your normal starting time) of sickness or an accident that prevents you from working. Failure to do so may result in loss of pay. You're required to keep your boss or manager informed about your illness and when you expect to return to work. For periods of up to seven days, you must usually provide a written statement of why you were absent on your return to work, although some employers require a doctor's certificate. If you're away from work for more than seven days, you must obtain a doctor's certificate.

INSURANCE

Social Insurance

Social insurance includes benefits for the unemployed, the aged, the disabled and those with low incomes. Social insurance contributions are compulsory for most Canadian residents and are deducted from salaries by employers. For further information, see **Social Insurance** on page 213.

Health Insurance

Canada has a national health insurance scheme (Medicare) funded by the Ministry of Health and administered by provincial governments. Health cover is free in most provinces, although in some members must make a monthly contribution. Medicare doesn't cover all health services and many people take out private insurance (called extended health cover), which may be paid by your employer, to cover non-insured hospital and other medical expenses.

> ☑ **SURVIVAL TIP**
>
> **Migrants aren't eligible for Medicare for their first three months in Canada and should purchase private health insurance to cover their families during this period. For more information, see Health Service on page 197 and Health Insurance on page 217.**

Compensation Insurance

Canada provides state benefits to workers for work-related injuries and illnesses through the Workplace Compensation Board (WCB). Payments are 85 per cent of your net pay before the injury or illness, less any earnings after the injury/illness, up to an annual maximum sum which varies depending on the province and is amended annually (it's generally around $50,000). The WCB also pays other costs related to a workplace injury or illness, including healthcare costs, transport and clothing. Workers are entitled to compensation for job-related injuries irrespective of whether they were at fault. If a worker dies as a result of an accident, his dependants receive the benefits.

During the first two years, benefits are paid every two weeks, after which they're paid monthly. If a benefit is still being claimed after six years, it's made permanent and you may be entitled to a lump sum payment of up to 10 per cent of the annual benefit. A worker claiming such benefits is required to co-operate fully with the WCB in his rehabilitation and is expected to return to work as soon as possible.

Employment Insurance

State employment insurance provides workers and their families with a weekly income for a limited period when they're unemployed through no fault of their own, e.g. due to sickness, layoffs, plant closures or natural disasters. There are mandatory employer and employee contributions to the employment insurance fund. For further information, see **Employment Insurance** on page 217.

Sick Pay & Disability Benefits

Sick leave is usually paid in full for a fixed number of days a year (annual sick leave plans) and employees are often permitted to carry over and accumulate unused sick leave from year to year (usually there's a maximum number of days). Sick pay is more commonly provided for white-collar employees than for blue-collar workers.

Short-term benefits in the event of an illness or accident are covered under the employment insurance scheme (see above), while long-term disability insurance (LTD) is provided under the Canada Pension Plan (CPP). However, workers are eligible for this benefit only if they've been contributing to the CPP for four of the last six years and benefits are rarely sufficient to meet your financial commitments. Private LTD insurance typically replaces 50 to 60 per cent of income and usually begins after six months of disability and continues for a specified number of months or until retirement age, depending on your age at the time of the disability.

Private LTD insurance is more commonly provided for white-collar workers than blue-collar workers. Employees are usually required to contribute towards the cost of private LTD insurance and there are usually service requirements of between a month and a year before you become eligible. You should therefore find out whether you're covered under a private disability plan through your employer. Private sickness plans commonly have a service requirement, e.g. three months, before new employees become eligible for benefits. Short-term sickness and accident benefits usually continue for a maximum of 26 weeks (six months) and pay around two-thirds of your salary. Some employees are eligible for an immediate disability pension under their company pension plan (see below).

For further information about disability benefits and insurance, see **Disability Insurance** on page 221.

RETIREMENT & PENSIONS

The Human Rights Code prohibits employers from fixing a mandatory retirement age and makes compulsory retirement illegal. Therefore, those wishing to continue working into their dotage can do so (provided they're still capable), although an employer can always decide to make them redundant! Nevertheless, 65 is the normal retirement age and a gold watch the usual retirement gift.

Many Canadian companies provide an employee pension plan that tops up the federal pension scheme, Canada Pension Plan/CPP (see page 222), called the Quebec Pension Plan or QPP in Quebec. Your contributions to both CPP and a company top-up scheme are deducted from your gross salary, and vary depending on your age and your employer's pension fund. Some employers don't operate their own pension scheme, but contribute to a private Registered Retirement Savings Plan (RRSP) or Life Income Fund.

See **Private Pension Plans** on page 222 for more information.

UNION MEMBERSHIP

Around 4mn workers in Canada are union members, most of whom are employed in government, education, manufacturing, and health and social services. There are hundreds of unions in Canada, most of which are affiliated to the Canadian Labour Congress (CLC, 2841 Riverside Drive, Ottawa, ON KIV 8X7, ☏ 613-521 3400, 🖳 http://canadianlabour.ca), which has over 3mn members. The two public sector unions, the Canadian Union of Public Employees (CUPE) and the National Union of Public and General Employees (NUPGE), are the largest unions in Canada.

Unions remain strong in traditional industries such as manufacturing and transport, but have little influence in the service, finance and retailing sectors.

Under the Labour Code administered by the Ministry of Labour, employees have the right to form, join or assist labour unions; to bargain collectively through representatives of their own choosing on wages, hours and other terms of employment; and to engage in concerted activities for the purpose of collective bargaining or other mutual aid or protection, such as striking to secure better working conditions. However, employees also have the right not to join a union if they don't wish to do so.

Collective bargaining systems operate under the Industrial Relations and Disputes Investigation Act, one of the provisions being that a union that gains the support of a majority of the workers in a bargaining unit can obtain federal or provincial certification, making it the legal bargaining agent for that unit. Employers must agree to collective bargaining once certification has been obtained. Some provinces have supplementary rules regarding unions and collective agreements. Certain employees such as farm workers, domestic servants of a family and managers have no rights to collective bargaining. Where union contracts are in place, the law prohibits work stoppages during the term of a collective agreement, and if any disputes arise they must be settled through an established grievance procedure or arbitration.

Information about Canadian unions is published in the *Directory of Labour Organisations in Canada* available from Human Resources and Skills Development Canada (140 Promenade du Portage, Phase IV, Hull, QC K1A 0J9, 🖳 www.hrsdc.gc.ca).

OTHER CONDITIONS

Acceptance of Gifts

With the exception of those in the public sector, employees are normally permitted to accept gifts of a limited value from customers or suppliers, e.g. a bottle of whisky or small gift at Christmas. Generally any small gifts given and received openly aren't considered a bribe or unlawful (although if you do business with someone else in the following year, don't expect a 'bribe' next Christmas). Most Canadian companies forbid the acceptance of any gifts of substance and cash payments are totally out of the question (if you accept a real bribe, make sure it's a large one and that you have a secret bank account!). You should declare any gifts received to your immediate superior, who will decide what should be done with them. Some Canadian bosses pool gifts and share them among all employees.

Confidentiality & Changing Jobs

If you disclose confidential company information, either in Canada or overseas (particularly to a competitor), you're liable for instant dismissal and may also be prosecuted. You may not take any secrets or confidential information (e.g. customer mailing lists) from a previous employer, but you may usually use any skills, knowledge and contacts acquired during his employ. You may not compete against a former employer if there's a valid, binding restraint clause in an employment contract. An employment contract may contain a clause defining the sort of information that the employer considers to be confidential, such as customer and supplier relationships and details of business plans.

If there's a confidentiality or restraint clause in an employment contract that's unfair, e.g. it inhibits you from changing jobs, it's probably invalid in law. If you're in doubt, consult a lawyer who specialises in company law and ask about your rights. If you're a key employee, you may have a legal binding contract preventing you from joining a competitor or starting a company in the same line of business as your employer (and in particular enticing former colleagues to join your company), although this will be valid for a limited period only.

Discipline & Dismissal

Most large- and medium-sized companies have comprehensive grievance and disciplinary procedures which must be followed before an employee can be suspended or dismissed. Some employers have disciplinary procedures whereby employees can be suspended with or without pay, e.g. for breaches of contract. Employees can also be suspended (usually with pay) pending investigation into an alleged offence or impropriety. Disciplinary procedures usually include verbal and official written warnings, and are to protect employees from unfair dismissal and to ensure that dismissed employees cannot (successfully) sue their employers. If you have a grievance or complaint against a colleague or your boss, there may be an official procedure to be followed in order to obtain redress. If an official grievance procedure exists, it may be detailed in your employer's general terms and conditions.

Caution

In general, employers can terminate employees' employment at any time without justification and, unless the employee has a contract, he's entitled to little or no compensation.

Unlike employers in most European countries, Canadian employers aren't liable for high redundancy payments and are more likely to lay off workers when business is bad. Dismissal is common among executives and managers, particularly for older employees, and is generally accepted as a fact of life. Companies often have a high turnover of senior executives and a shake-up at the top often works its way down the management ladder.

Many provinces have exceptions to the 'instant dismissal' rule for private employees, e.g. in cases where employees refuse to perform an act that violates public policy or where dismissal violated an oral assurance of job security or a 'just cause' policy. In these cases, employees can sue for wrongful dismissal. Employees of federal, provincial and local governments are covered by civil service laws and can be dismissed for 'just cause' only. In Canada, you cannot be fired within a certain period of falling ill or before or after giving birth, provided that you intend to return to work.

Where formal discharge and disciplinary procedures exist, company policy may state that an employee be given notice before he can be fired, in which case he may have a legal right to notice (see **Probationary & Notice Periods** below).

If you've worked at a job for over one year that isn't subject to a collective bargaining agreement and you believe you've been unlawfully dismissed, you should contact the Provincial Ministry of Labour or a labour law attorney to find out whether you have grounds for a wrongful dismissal lawsuit. An employee can file a complaint with a government inspector if he feels his dismissal was unjust, and an adjudicator from the Ministry of Labour will investigate the complaint. If the dismissal is found to be unjust, the employee is entitled to reinstatement with back pay.

If you're temporarily laid off, your employer must tell you two weeks before the job ends or pay you extra money if you've been employed for longer than six months. Although it varies according to the province, you can usually be laid off for up to 13 weeks in any 20-week period without having your employment terminated.

When you leave a full-time job, your employer must give you a 'record of employment', without which you cannot apply for (un)employment insurance.

Discrimination

It's illegal to discriminate against employees in Canada on grounds of sex, race, national origin, skin colour, pregnancy, age (except in the Yukon), religion, marital status, sexual orientation, physical handicap or weight. It's also illegal for employers or trade unions to discriminate against or retaliate against anyone who wants to join, not join or quit a trade union (see **Union Membership** on page 53). Job advertisements are permitted to specify such characteristics of applicants only when they're an essential requirement – called a 'bona fide occupational qualification' – e.g. for a job as a female fashion model.

Women doing identical jobs as men, with equal skill, effort and responsibility and similar working conditions, are legally entitled to the same salary and terms of employment. Employers cannot offer better benefits to male employees, for example, they aren't permitted to have different pension plans for each sex.

There's also protection from discrimination against the elderly and companies are prohibited from forcing active workers aged 65 and over to retire. In fact, there's no longer a mandatory retirement age in Canada (see www.labour.gc.ca and www.hrsdc.gc.ca).

Due to the threat of legal action by employees and rejected job applicants, large employers are careful not to discriminate against prospective employees. Despite the strict legislation, however, it's acknowledged that discrimination is widespread and it's almost impossible to prove discrimination on the grounds of sex and extremely difficult on the grounds of race or other factors. If you believe that you've been the victim of employer discrimination, you should contact the local provincial Human Rights Commission or the Canadian Human Rights Commission (National Office, 344 Slater Street, 8th Floor, Ottawa, ON K1A 1E1, ☎ 613-995 1151, 💻 www.chrc-ccdp.ca). As with most issues in Canada, there are lawyers who specialise in discrimination and employee-employer disputes.

Not only are there laws against discrimination, there's also a federal Employment Equity Act, which requires employers to take steps to improve the employment situation of women, the disabled, native Americans and other minority groups. Federal and provincial government departments and other large 'public' employers such as police forces have taken the lead, operating what's known as a policy of 'affirmative action' (imported from the US). Furthermore, the Federal Contractors Programme requires that all employers who do business with the government operate their employment policies on the same basis. This policy has caused resentment among non-minorities, who see themselves as victims of 'reverse discrimination'.

For further information about employment discrimination laws, see 💻 www.naalc.org/migrant/english/pdf/mgcanemd_en.pdf, and for information about Canada's employment equity, see 💻 http://en.wikipedia.org/wiki/employment_equity_(canada).

Health & Safety

Work-related injuries are a major problem in Canada, where some 5 per cent of the male and 2 per cent of female workers suffer injuries at work each year, according to the Association of Workers' Compensation Boards of Canada. (There were almost 1,000 work-related deaths in Canada in 2006.) The commonest causes of industrial injuries are motor vehicles, electrical hazards such as power lines, ladders, scaffolding and roofs (particularly on construction sites), toxic chemicals, and violent crime in the retail sector.

Canada has strict laws regarding worker safety and health, and in some provinces you have the right to refuse to do unsafe work without fear of being fired.

Unsafe work may include working without proper protective clothing and equipment such as helmets or boots, or working with tools on which you haven't been trained. For more information about what work you can refuse to do and the procedures you must go through (stating why you think the task is unsafe, inspecting what you think is unsafe with your supervisor, calling a Health and Safety inspector, etc.), contact your local HRDC labour office or the Canadian Centre for Occupational Health and Safety (☎ 1-800-668 4284 or 905-570 8094, 💻 www.ccohs.ca).

Smoking Laws

Smoking in indoor (and in some cases, outdoor) workplaces and public places is banned in all territories and provinces, although some jurisdictions allow specific exemptions to the smoking ban. Smoking may also be banned in vehicles when children are present, which in Nova Scotia applies to anyone under the age of 19! Some provinces allow smoking in specially-ventilated rooms, while other don't. Many provinces also ban the retail display of tobacco products (the so-called 'shower curtain' law).

In British Columbia, for example, smoking is banned in all public spaces such as restaurants, pubs and private clubs, offices, malls, conference centres, sports arenas, community halls, government buildings and schools, and within a three-metre radius of doors, open windows and air intakes.

Long-service Awards

Most large companies present their employees with long-service awards after a number of years, e.g. 15, 20 or 25 years. These are usually in the form of a gift such as a clock presented to employees by senior management. Periods of absence, e.g. maternity leave, usually count as continuous employment when calculating your length of service.

Medical Examination

Canadian employers rarely require prospective employees to have a pre-employment medical examination. A medical may, however, be required for employees over a certain age (e.g. 40) or for employees in particular jobs, e.g. where good health is of paramount importance for reasons of safety. Thereafter a medical examination may be necessary periodically, e.g. every one or two years, or may be requested at any time by your employer. Medical examinations may also be required as a condition of membership of a company health, pension or life insurance scheme. Some companies insist on employees having regular health screening, particularly senior managers and executives. Employers are usually required to pay for mandatory medical exams.

Federal law allows employers to require applicants to take medical exams or drug tests, provided that they keep the results confidential, although many provinces regulate drug testing. It's rare for employers to require existing and prospective employees to take a drug test; if they do, this cannot be administered until a conditional offer of employment has been made. Although uncommon, another test that can be required for jobs related to government work and national or company security is a lie detector test.

Most job advertisements (particularly for government positions) will specify clearly the physical labour that is required on the job, including weights to be lifted, and the proportion of activity to sedentary work.

Part-time Job Restrictions

Many Canadian companies don't mind full-time employees working part-time (i.e. moonlighting) for another employer, unless it's one in the same line of business or the work interferes with your full-time job. Any restrictions should be included in your employment contract.

Probationary & Notice Periods

For some jobs there's an official probationary period of from one or two weeks for hourly-paid employees and up to three months for salaried employees. Unless your contract or your employer's terms and conditions states otherwise, once you've been employed for more than three months your notice period is two weeks. If your contract or employer's terms and conditions specifies a different notice period, its length may depend on your method of payment, your job and your length of service.

Employees in the private sector who have worked for less than three months may lose their job without notice and for any reason or none at all; employees with less than three months' service may also quit a job without notice and for any reason. Once you've worked for three months, two weeks' notice is required by either party. Exceptions are employees covered by a collective bargaining agreement and those with contracts containing other conditions.

Where formal discharge and disciplinary procedures exist, company policy may state that an employee be given notice before he can be fired, in which case he may have a legal right to notice. See also **Discipline & Dismissal** above.

> ☑ **SURVIVAL TIP**
>
> **If you're fired and your employer insists that you leave right away, he must pay you for the notice period, plus any outstanding holiday and sick leave.**

Redundancy Pay

If you're employed in a volatile business, particularly in an executive or managerial position, it's important to have adequate financial compensation in the event of redundancy (severance) or dismissal written into your contract or, at the very least, to have a good understanding of what you're entitled to. Executives may have a clause in their contracts whereby they receive a generous 'golden handshake' if they're made redundant, e.g. after a take-over. Without a compensation clause, you're entitled to your normal notice period only, i.e. two weeks or one month, or payment in lieu of notice.

An employer must give redundancy pay if there are collective bargaining agreements or contracts that provide redundancy benefits. The law in some provinces requires redundancy pay under certain conditions, while in others employees must usually rely on their employer's benevolence. Some companies wishing to reduce their workforce may offer employees voluntary redundancy payments (pay-outs) or early retirement. Minimum redundancy terms vary, but the following usually applies:

Redundancy Terms

Period of Employment	Entitlement
Up to three months	None
Between 3 and 12 months less one day	One week's pay
Between 12 and 36 months less one day	Two weeks' pay

In British Columbia, employees receive one week's pay after three months' employment, two weeks' pay after one year, and three weeks' pay after three years' employment, plus one week's pay for each additional year of employment up to a maximum of eight years. In all provinces, you may also be entitled to be paid in lieu of any holiday and days off for sickness or compassionate leave owed you, plus a refund of your contributions to company pension plans.

Many companies provide counselling for people who are made redundant, e.g. on job prospects and job hunting, benefits, retirement, retraining and self-employment. Redundancy pay doesn't affect your eligibility to claim employment benefit. If possible, you should ensure that you receive a cheque for the total redundancy package and all paperwork before leaving employment.

CHECKLISTS

When negotiating your terms of employment for a job in Canada, the checklists below will prove useful. The points listed under **General Positions** apply to most jobs, while those listed under **Managerial & Executive Positions** may apply to executive and top managerial appointments only.

General Positions

Salary

- Is the total amount of the salary adequate, taking into account the cost of living?
- Is it linked to inflation?
- Does it include an allowance for working (and living) in an expensive region or city (e.g. Toronto) or a remote area (e.g. in the Yukon or Nunavut, where workers often receive a 'hardship' allowance)?
- How often is the salary reviewed?
- Does the salary include commission or bonuses (see page 45)?
- Is overtime paid or time off granted in lieu of any extra hours worked (see page 47)?
- Is the total salary (including expenses) paid in Canadian dollars or is the salary paid in another country (in a different currency) with expenses for living in Canada?

Relocation Expenses

- Are relocation expenses or a relocation allowance paid?
- Do relocation expenses include travelling expenses for all family members?
- Is there a maximum limit and, if so, is it adequate?
- Are you required to repay your relocation expenses (or a percentage) if you resign before a certain period has elapsed?
- Are you required to pay for your relocation in advance (this may run into thousands of dollars)?

- If employment is for a fixed period, will your relocation expenses be paid when you leave Canada?
- If you aren't shipping household goods and furniture to Canada, is an allowance paid to buy furniture locally?
- Do relocation expenses include the legal and estate agent's fees incurred when moving home?
- Does the employer engage the services of a relocation consultant (see page 94)?

Accommodation

- Does the employer pay for temporary accommodation (or pay a lodging allowance) until you find permanent accommodation?
- Is subsidised or free, temporary or permanent accommodation provided? If so, is it furnished or unfurnished?
- Must you pay for utilities such as electricity, gas and water?
- What does accommodation cost?
- If accommodation isn't provided by the employer, is assistance in finding suitable accommodation given? What does it consist of?
- While you're living in temporary accommodation, does your employer pay your travelling expenses to your permanent home? How far is it from the place of employment?
- Are your expenses paid while looking for local accommodation?

Working Hours

- What are the weekly working hours?
- Does the employer operate a flexible working hours system (see page 47)? If so, what are the fixed (core) working hours?
- How early must you start? Can you carry forward any extra hours worked and take time off at a later date (or carry forward a deficit and make it up later)?
- Are you required to clock in and out of work?
- Can you choose to be paid for overtime or take time off in lieu of time worked?

Part-time or Seasonal Work

- Is part-time or seasonal work (e.g. during school terms) possible?
- Are flexible working hours or (partial) working from home permitted?
- Does the employer have a job-sharing scheme?
- Are extended career breaks permitted with no loss of seniority, grade or salary?

Holiday Entitlement

- What's the annual holiday (vacation) entitlement? Does it increase with service (see page 48)?
- What are the paid national and provincial holidays (see page 50)?
- Is free air travel to your home country or elsewhere provided for you and your family and, if so, how often? Are other holiday travel discounts provided?
- Is paid or unpaid maternity/paternity leave provided (see page 51)?

Insurance

- Is health insurance provided for you and your family? What does it include (see page 217)? It's important to ensure that all members of your family are fully insured before you set foot in Canada.
- Is free life insurance provided?
- Is accident or any special insurance provided by your employer?

- For how long is your salary paid if you're ill or have an accident (see **Disability Insurance** on page 221 and **Sick Pay & Disability Benefits** on page 52)?

Company Pension

- Is there a company pension scheme (see page 211) and, if so, what's your contribution?
- Are you required or permitted to pay a lump sum into the pension plan in order to receive a full or higher pension?
- What are the rules regarding early retirement?
- Is the pension transferable and do you receive the company's contributions in addition to your own if you resign? If not, does the employer contribute to a private pension plan?
- Is the pension linked to the inflation rate?
- Do the pension rules apply equally to full and part-time employees?

Employer

- What are the employer's prospects?
- Is his profitability and growth rate favourable?
- Does he have a good reputation?
- Does he have a high staff turnover and has he laid off a high percentage of workers in recent years?

Women

- What's the employer's policy regarding equal promotion opportunities for women?
- Is paid maternity leave provided?
- How many women hold positions in middle and senior management or at board level?

Education & Training

- What initial or career training does the employer provide?
- Is training provided in-house or externally; does the employer pay for training or education abroad, if necessary?
- Does the employer have a training programme for employees in your profession (e.g. technical, management or language)? Is the employer's training recognised for its excellence (or otherwise)?
- Are free or subsidised English or French lessons provided for you and your spouse (if necessary)?
- Does the employer pay for a part or the total cost of non-essential education, e.g. a computer or language course?
- Does the employer pay for day release to attend a degree course or other study?

Other Conditions

- What are the promotion prospects?
- Does the employer provide a free nursery (crèche) for children below school age or a day care centre for the elderly?
- Is a free or subsidised employee restaurant provided? If not, is a lunch allowance paid? Is any provision made for shift workers, e.g. breakfast or evening meals?
- Is a travelling allowance paid from your Canadian home to your place of work?
- Is free or subsidised parking provided at your workplace?
- Are free work clothes, overalls or a uniform provided? Does the employer pay for the cleaning of work clothes (both factory and office)?
- Does the employer provide perks such as inexpensive home loans, interest-free loans or mortgage assistance? An inexpensive home loan can be worth thousands of dollars a year.
- Is a company car provided? What sort of car? Can it be used privately and, if so, does the employer pay for the fuel? Who pays for insurance, servicing and repairs?
- Does the employer provide fringe benefits or subsidised services such as in-house banking, credit union membership, car discount scheme, travel discounts, employees' discount shop or product discounts, sports and social facilities or club membership, fitness centre, subsidised theatre tickets, shopping services, shoe repairs, laundry or cleaning service, car servicing, on-site kindergarten or elementary school, and adult education?

- Do you have a written list of your job responsibilities?
- Have your employment conditions been confirmed in writing?
- If a dispute arises over your salary or working conditions, under the law of which country is your contract (if applicable) interpreted?

Managerial & Executive Positions

- Is private schooling for your children paid for or subsidised? Does the employer pay for a boarding school in Canada or another country?
- Is the salary indexed to inflation or protected against devaluation and cost-of-living increases? This is particularly important if you're paid in a foreign currency that fluctuates wildly or could be devalued.
- Are you paid an overseas allowance for working in Canada?
- Is rent-free accommodation provided?
- Are paid holidays provided (perhaps in a company-owned house or apartment) or 'business' conferences in exotic places?
- Are all costs incurred by a move to Canada reimbursed? For example, the cost of selling your home, employing an agent to let it for you or storing personal effects?
- Does the employer pay for domestic help or contribute to the cost of a cleaner or cook?
- Does the employer provide profit-sharing or stock options (which may be worth more than your annual salary)?
- Is a car provided, perhaps with a chauffeur?
- Are you entitled to any miscellaneous benefits, such as club memberships, free credit cards, or tickets for sports events and shows?
- Is there an entertainment allowance?
- Is extra compensation (e.g. a 'golden handshake') paid if you're laid off or dismissed? This could be important in Canada's volatile job market!

Entrées
Visas
Departures/
IMMIGRATION CANADA
ADMISSION
08 JUL 2009
A.I. EDMONTON I.A.
3421
EXPIRATION
CUSTOMS
DOUANES
1057

3.
PERMITS & VISAS

Some 20 per cent of Canadian residents are foreign-born, which ranks the country among those with the highest immigrant share of the population, along with Switzerland and Australia. Annual immigration is up to around 260,000 a year (in 2007 it was 236,760) and over 250,000 people a year also take Canadian citizenship. Before the recession hit in late 2008, Canada was expected to welcome between 240,000 and 265,000 new permanent residents in 2009, although it's now (spring 2009) expected to be fewer. Nevertheless, the demand for qualified workers in Canada is growing, and by 2012, immigration is projected to account for all the country's labour force growth (Canada's population grew by its highest quarterly growth rate for 18 years in the third quarter of 2008).

Only holders of an immigrant visa or a work permit may work in Canada, including informal work in a household as a nanny, au pair or mother's helper. An immigrant visa gives you the right to live and work in Canada (and change jobs freely) on a permanent basis, and to apply for Canadian citizenship after three years' residence. Work permits are issued for specific jobs only and aren't transferable between jobs, but in certain circumstances they can be extended. Before a work permit can be issued, apart from making you a job offer in writing, a prospective employer must prove that there are no unemployed Canadian nationals or immigrant visa holders who can do the job.

Immigration to Canada is dealt with by Citizenship and Immigration Canada (CIC), which is the government department responsible for the processing of foreigners entering Canada and those seeking permanent residence. The Department maintains offices throughout Canada and in Canadian High Commissions, embassies and consulates abroad. Entry into the country is strictly controlled and anyone who doesn't comply with visa requirements can be fined, jailed or deported. Canada restricts the entry of undesirables and misfits and anyone who's considered to be a threat to the health, welfare and security of Canada, by requiring certain applicants to undergo a medical examination and all applicants to produce a police certificate declaring that they don't have a criminal record.

The information you provide in support of your application to enter Canada for any purpose is collected under the authority of the Immigration Act, and protected and accessible only under the provisions of the Privacy Act and the Access to Information Act.

Canada doesn't have an annual immigration quota but sets annual targets, which can be exceeded if there are an exceptional number of high-quality applicants; conversely, in years when there are fewer applicants, officials may be more lenient regarding marginal applications. The targets can also be reduced when unemployment increases and the demand for workers falls, as it did in 2009.

Note that, as in many areas of life in Canada, the immigration rules for the province of Quebec are different from the rest of Canada; for information, see 💻 www.immigration-quebec.gouv.qc.ca/en.

This chapter outlines the legislation in late 2008, following the changes to the 2001 Immigration and Refugee Protection Act (IRPA) made by the Budget Implementation Act, 2008, which took effect in June 2008. These were, according to the Minister of Citizenship and Immigration, designed to make the system 'fairer and more responsible, ensuring a balance between the economic, family reunification and refugee protection goals of Canada's immigration system'. However, they were criticised as cloaking discrimination against 'undesirable' immigrants.

Further information is available from the Citizenship and Immigration Canada website (💻 www.cic.gc.ca), including a plethora of links to sites operated by immigration lawyers, licensed recruitment and employment professionals, and general 'expatriate' sites (see **Appendix C**). A good starting place for immigrants is the Canadian government's 'Going to Canada' website (💻 www.goingtocanada.gc.ca); the 'Entry Requirements' and 'Working in Canada' tools on the home page provide links to everything you need to know in order to visit, live or work in Canada.

Note that immigration is a complex subject and that the information contained in this chapter is intended as a general guide only. You shouldn't base any decisions or actions on the information contained herein without first confirming it with an official and reliable source, such as a Canadian High Commission, embassy or consulate. See also **Canadian Citizenship** on page 307.

2008 Changes to Immigration Act

Until June 2008, all applications for immigration had to be dealt with in the order submitted, delaying the approval of priority applicants and preventing the government from reacting quickly to labour shortages. The principal aim of the changes was to 'more closely match the skills of newcomers with Canada's labour shortages and shorten the time it takes for skilled workers to immigrate to Canada'. This was achieved by:

- Removing the obligation of CIC to process all applications and allowing it to return 'unsuitable' applications (and refund the corresponding application fees) without processing them, therefore reducing the backlog of unprocessed applications and speeding up the processing of 'suitable' applications;
- Giving the Minister of Citizenship and Immigration the authority to prioritise certain skills and occupations according to labour market needs.

The new regulations were made effective retrospectively and have applied to all applications since 1st March 2008.

> While migrants are invariably warmly welcomed in Canada, newcomers should be aware that immigration is a sensitive issue and a minority of Canadians would like to see immigration numbers reduced or frozen, primarily due to the failure of the infrastructure in the major cities to keep pace.

VISITORS

In the words of its brochures, 'Canada welcomes visitors to share its unique history, culture and magnificent scenery' and receives over 35mn visitors each year. A visitor is defined as 'a person who enters Canada for a temporary purpose, such as a tourist', but he must still be of good health and have no (major) criminal convictions. All visitors admitted to Canada are permitted to stay for a maximum of six months, unless otherwise notified in writing by an examining officer. The date that you must leave Canada is stamped in your passport, although extensions are possible in certain circumstances.

Many non-resident foreigners, including certain citizens of the UK, require a 'temporary resident visa' (hereafter referred to simply as a 'visa'), which costs $75 for a single entry visa and $150 for a multiple entry visa. A full list of countries and territories whose citizens require a visa in order to enter Canada as visitors can be found at 💻 www.cic.gc.ca/english/visit/visas.asp.

Those who don't require a visa include:

- Citizens of Andorra, Antigua and Barbuda, Australia, Austria, Bahamas, Barbados, Belgium, Botswana, Brunei, Czech

Republic, Cyprus, Denmark, Estonia, Finland, France, Germany, Greece, Hungary, Iceland, Ireland, Israel (passport holders only), Italy, Japan, Korea (Republic of), Latvia (Republic of), Lithuania, Liechtenstein, Luxembourg, Malta, Mexico, Monaco, Namibia, the Netherlands, New Zealand, Norway, Papua New Guinea, Poland, Portugal, St Kitts and Nevis, St Lucia, St Vincent, San Marino, Singapore, Slovakia, Solomon Islands, Spain, Swaziland, Sweden, Slovenia, Switzerland, the United States, and Western Samoa;

- British citizens and British Overseas Citizens who are re-admissible to the UK;
- Citizens of British dependent territories who derive their citizenship through birth, descent, registration or naturalisation in one of the British dependent territories of Anguilla, Bermuda, British Virgin Islands, Cayman Islands, Falkland Islands, Gibraltar, Montserrat, Pitcairn, St. Helena, or the Turks and Caicos Islands;
- Anyone holding a British National (Overseas) passport issued in Hong Kong;
- Anyone who has obtained an alien registration card (green card) or can provide other evidence of permanent residence in the US;
- Anyone holding a valid Special Administrative Region passport issued by the Government of the Hong Kong Special Administrative Region of the People's Republic of China;
- Anyone holding a passport or travel documents issued by the Holy See.

You need a full passport to enter Canada – including Americans after 1st June 2009 – and if it's close to its expiry date, it's wise to renew it before leaving for Canada.

VISAS

There are three types of visa in Canada:

- **Single entry visa** – normally allows you to enter Canada only once, but can be used for repeat entries from the US or Saint-Pierre and Miquelon during the time validated for your stay in Canada, provided you don't enter another country. A single-entry visa is normally valid for six months.
- **Multiple entry visa** – allows you to enter Canada as many times as you wish for the time validated for your stay in Canada.
- **Transit visa** – required if you'll be in Canada for 48 hours or less on your way to another country.

To enter Canada as a visitor, whether or not you require a visa, you must have the following:

- A passport valid for at least three months from the date of your intended arrival in Canada;
- Sufficient money to support yourself and your dependants during your stay;
- Private medical insurance for the duration of your stay.

As in the US, possession of a visa isn't a guarantee of entry into the country; although unlike the US, Canada rarely refuses anyone with a visa or work permit (with the attached 'record of landing') unless their circumstances have changed since it was issued. For example, the holder of a visa may have got married or divorced since it was granted. The authorities don't mind you changing your circumstances, but they expect you to inform them in plenty of time.

As a visitor, you must not work while you're in Canada – unless you have a work permit (see below).

Visa Applications

In some countries, visa applications can be submitted in person to the immigration section of a Canadian High Commission, embassy or consulate, and a visa issued while you wait. Applications are processed on a first-come, first-served basis. It's therefore wise to arrive early (check opening times in advance). Routine applications submitted by post or courier should take six working days to process. On the rare occasion when an interview is necessary (see below), you should receive notification within six working days.

It's recommended that postal applications are sent by registered post and that the self-addressed return envelope is registered. Applications may be submitted by private courier, in which case the courier should be paid in advance for the return of your documents.

You should allow at least a month for a visa application to be processed.

Forms & Documentation

Visa application forms are available in most countries from the Immigration Division of a Canadian High Commission, embassy or consulate. You can write to, phone or call at these offices to obtain application forms and check your occupation for eligibility. As well as a set of application forms, you'll be provided with a comprehensive guide to completing them, a form for requesting a police clearance certificate, and a list of approved doctors for the medical examination (see below). You can photocopy the forms if you need extra copies for your spouse and dependants. You must submit a form for each of your dependant children (i.e. those aged under 22 and unmarried), even though they may not intend to accompany you at this stage (the assumption is that they may decide to follow you later). You don't pay a fee for non-accompanying dependants at this stage.

You need to provide proof of your identity, marital status, education and employment through documents such as your passport, marriage or divorce papers, birth certificates for all family members, military records, examination passes and professional memberships, and a record of employment. You shouldn't send the originals of these with the application forms, but send photocopies instead. However, you should be prepared to produce the originals if requested. If there's insufficient space on the forms to provide full details, you should attach separate sheets of paper. This applies particularly to information about you and your spouse's occupations, as the more detail you give the easier it is for the immigration officials to compare these against the thousands of occupations listed in the National Occupational Classification (NOC — see page 74).

The completed forms must be returned with two passport-size photographs, a passport valid for the length of your stay, evidence of your immigration status in your country of residence (if it isn't the country of your birth), details of your travel plans, proof of funds available for your visit and evidence that you're employed. All documentation must be in English or French or be accompanied by a certified translation in either of these languages (see 💻 www.cic.gc.ca for the latest information).

When completing the forms, bear in mind that you're more likely to be refused a visa if you're discovered to have lied than if your circumstances aren't 'perfect'. On the same premise, you can be refused entry when you arrive in Canada if any of your circumstances (such as getting married or divorced or having additional children) have changed since your application and you haven't informed the immigration authorities.

Using a Professional

When applying for an immigrant visa, it's sometimes wise to employ the services of an experienced immigration attorney (lawyer) or immigration consultant. Whether you need professional help will depend on the individual case, although the procedure can be complicated and the rules and regulations change frequently. Many visa applications are rejected because the paperwork is incorrect, e.g. the wrong information was provided, a form wasn't completed correctly or the wrong visa application was made. A lawyer or consultant can also inform you about all the options (both federal and provincial/territory) open to you and which would be the most likely to succeed.

Bear in mind when someone makes an application on your behalf, you must check that the information provided is correct in every detail. If an application is rejected (for any reason), the chances of being granted a visa by appealing or reapplying are less likely, so it's vital to get it right first time. There are many immigration attorneys and consultants in Canada and abroad, some of whom specialise in certain categories of immigrants. Attorneys' fees depend on the complexity of the case and range from around $300 for a simple consultation to $5,000 to $10,000 for a complex application involving a lot of work.

You should engage an attorney or consultant who's a member of the professional organisation, the Canadian Association of Professional Immigration Consultants (CAPIC, 245 Fairview Mall Drive, Suite 602, Toronto, ON M2J 4T1, ☎ 416-483 7044, 💻 http://capic.ca), who has been highly recommended or who has a good reputation, because incompetent and dishonest consultants aren't unknown. Always ensure that you know exactly how much you must pay and the exact services you'll receive in return. If you wish to appeal successfully against a refusal to grant a visa, you probably need to engage the services of an immigration attorney. Attorneys have the right to attend immigration interviews with you, but consultants don't.

▲ Caution

Bear in mind that nobody, however much you pay them, can guarantee that an application will be approved.

Medical Examination

If your projected stay in Canada is for less than six months, you generally don't require a medical examination. If you're planning to stay for longer than six months and have been living for more than half of the previous year in a 'designated country/territory', you must undergo an examination.

Designated countries/territories include the following: Afghanistan, Algeria, Argentina, Azerbaijan, Bahamas, Bahrain, Bangladesh, Belize, Bolivia, Bosnia, Brazil, Bulgaria, the Canary Islands, China, Colombia, Croatia, Dominican Republic, Estonia, French Guiana, Gambia, Georgia, Guinea, Guyana, Haiti, Honduras, Hong Kong, India, Indonesia, Iran, Iraq, Kenya, Korea (North or South), Latvia, Libya, Macao, Madeira, Malaysia, Mexico, Morocco, Mozambique, Nigeria, Oman, Pakistan, Panama, Peru, Philippines, Romania, Russia, Saudi Arabia, Serbia, Singapore, South Africa, Taiwan, Ukraine, Venezuela, Vietnam and Zimbabwe. For a full list of designated countries/territories, see 💻 www.cic.gc.ca/english//information/medical/dcl.asp.

If you require a medical examination, this can add several months to your visa application processing time.

Interviews

An interview isn't always necessary and if you're called for one you shouldn't assume that it means you're going to be turned down (immigration officials are far too busy to be bothered with applications that they feel must be refused). The main purpose of an interview is to decide how many points to award under the personal suitability and language categories (see below), and even then, only if your points total is marginal. Your spouse and dependant children must attend the interview with you and although interviews are informal, you must be able to demonstrate a mature approach to immigration. You should expect to be asked about your education and your current job, as well as how you intend to find somewhere to live, find a job, educate your children and other matters.

It helps to mention that you've made contingency plans in case it takes longer than expected to find a job, and also that you have been reading Canadian newspapers and books on the Canadian way of life. You may be tested on your language ability if neither English nor French is your mother tongue. You should take with you the originals of all your supporting documents (e.g. passport, education certificates, job references, etc.) and evidence of your financial situation (e.g. bank statements).

STUDENTS

Every year, over 100,000 students come to Canada to study. Most require a study permit, but you don't require a permit for the following:

- a course of study of six months or less;
- a minor child already in Canada, provided you have legal status in Canada other than visitor status;
- your family or staff if you're a foreign representative in Canada.

A study permit is issued for a limited time (generally the duration of the course of study) and usually applies to a specific course in a specific educational institution. A study permit is usually issued if the applicant has an acceptance letter from a Canadian educational institution and sufficient funds to pay for their tuition and living expenses. Medical examinations and police clearance certificates are sometimes required by applicants. A temporary resident visa may be required if a student is a citizen of a country that requires such a visa to enter Canada.

Applicants wishing to study in Quebec require approval from the government of Quebec and must renew their status annually; for information, see www.immigration-quebec.gouv.qc.ca/en (click on 'Foreign students' from the menu).

The fee for a study permit is $150.

☑ SURVIVAL TIP

Citizenship and Immigration Canada advises that it takes at least six months to gather the information and documents required to apply for a study permit for Canada, and to plan and prepare for a move to Canada as an international student.

Working as a Student

Students are usually issued a study permit only if they have sufficient funds to support themselves, although students are permitted to work in Canada:

- On campus without a work permit;
- Off campus with a work permit;
- In co-op and internship programmes, where work experience is part of the curriculum, with a work permit;
- In a post-graduation work programme for one or two years, related to the field of study, with a work permit.

The spouse/common-law partner of foreign students is allowed to work in Canada while the partner studies.

Student Work Programmes

Canada has a number of student work programmes for citizens of the UK, Ireland, Finland and Sweden. To qualify you must be a full-time student at a university or similar recognised post-secondary institution in your country of citizenship, be aged between 18 and 30, and provide an unconditional letter of acceptance or a letter confirming that you've recently graduated.

UK & Ireland: Two programmes are currently available. **Programme A** is a student general working holiday (vacation) programme. Students must obtain a written job offer from a Canadian employer stating the salary, period of employment, type of work involved and that the employment is full-time. If the job is an unpaid traineeship, you must provide proof of sufficient funds to cover the work period. You must also provide written confirmation of your return to

studies at the end of the period of employment in Canada. You don't normally require a medical examination unless the employment is in health services, child care or a related occupation. No fee is payable for authorisation. The number of places on this programme is limited and applications are dealt with on a first-come, first-served basis.

Programme B is operated in conjunction with the British Universities North American Club (BUNAC) and Union of Students in Ireland Travel (USIT). An offer of employment isn't required under this programme, but you must provide evidence of $1,000 to take with you ($600 if you have a relative in Canada) and evidence of return transportation home. In the UK you should contact BUNAC (16 Bowling Green Lane, London EC1R 0QH, ☎ +44-20-7251 3472, 🖳 http://validate.bunac.org.uk) and in Ireland USIT (19-21 Aston Quay, O'Connell Bridge, Dublin 2, ☎ +353-1-602 1904, 🖳 www.usitnow.ie). See also Study Overseas (🖳 www.studyoverseas.com/f_canada.htm).

Finland & Sweden: For information regarding Finland you should contact CIMO (PO Box 343, Hakaniemenkatu 2, SF 00531 Helsinki, ☎ +358-9-7747 7033). In Sweden, only the general working holiday programme is available and places are limited, therefore you should apply early. For details contact the International Employment Office (Box 7763, S-103 96 Stockholm, ☎ +46-8-406 5700). There's no student working programme for Denmark or Norway.

TEMPORARY WORK PERMITS

Every year, around 100,000 foreign nationals enter Canada to work. Permanent residents have the right to work in Canada but most other people require a temporary work permit, which can sometimes be extended.

A job offer from a Canadian employer is usually required before a permit is issued but in some circumstances, 'open' permits are issued, which aren't employer-specific. Applicants must also have a Labour Market Opinion (LMO) letter issued by Human Resources and Skills Development Canada (HRSDC, see 🖳 www.hrsdc.gc.ca/eng/workplaceskills/foreign_workers/ei_tfw/lmi_tfw.shtml), confirming that the proposed employment won't adversely affect Canadian workers.

Work permits may be granted without an HRSDC letter in the following circumstances:

- Under international agreements, e.g. the North American Free Trade Agreement (NAFTA);
- If the work would bring significant cultural, economic or social benefit to Canada;
- As part of reciprocal agreements Canada has with other countries, e.g. teacher and youth exchange programmes;
- In the case of students studying in Canada in order to meet course requirements;
- To the spouses/common-law partners of work permit and, in some cases, study permit holders;
- For some types of charitable or religious work.

The processing time for temporary work permit applications varies greatly, depending on the processing office. The process and documents required for a temporary work permit in the province of Quebec are different; see 🖳 www.immigration-quebec.gouv.qc.ca/en (click on 'Temporary workers' from the menu).

The fee for a temporary work permit is currently $150.

RESIDENTS

The Canadian government grants 'permanent residence visas' to immigrants in various categories, including a new 'Canadian

Experience Class' . Using a points system, applicants are assessed according to various factors to determine whether they and their dependants are likely to establish themselves successfully – socially as well as economically – in Canada. The selection rules particularly favour applicants with government-approved job offers.

Those who obtain a permanent residence visa (landed immigrant) can live and work anywhere in Canada, can enjoy a lot of the benefits of Canadian citizenship, may apply for citizenship after three years, and can sponsor family members for Canadian permanent resident status.

Permanent Resident Card

Since 2002, all permanent residents have been issued with a Permanent Resident Card. Cards are usually issued for five years (although in some cases it's just one year) and you must ensure that you apply for a new card at least two months before your current card expires. A new card (whether the old one has expired or been lost, damaged or stolen) costs $50.//

Categories

There are five principal categories (also referred to as 'classes' and 'programs') under which you can apply for permanent resident status, as follows (the numbers in brackets indicate the likely target numbers of immigrants in each category for 2009):

- **Skilled workers & professionals (70,000)** – for people who want to settle and work in Canada (outside Quebec);
- **Canadian experience class (12,000)** – a new category for people who have recent Canadian work experience or who recently graduated in Canada;
- **Investors, entrepreneurs & self-employed people (13,000)** – for people who want to start a business in Canada;
- **Provincial nominees (22,000)** – for those nominated under the Provincial Nomination Program (PNP) by one of Canada's provinces or territories to settle and work there;
- **Family class (9,000)** – for family members of permanent residents or citizens of Canada.

These five categories are discussed in detail in the sections below. There are two further categories, which aren't considered here: Quebec-selected skilled workers (28,000), i.e. people selected by the Quebec government to settle and work in Quebec, and those in the Refugees and Humanitarian class (35,000), who must demonstrate 'a well-founded fear of persecution in their native land'.

The Canadian federal government Client Application Status service allows you to check the status of your immigration application via the internet at http://canadaonline.about.com/cs/immigration/a/immstatus.htm. Details are updated weekly.

Skilled Workers & Professionals

Applicants in this category are assessed on a series of factors (see below). Each factor is allotted a maximum number of points (see below) and to qualify you must score at least 67 points overall. However, even if you reach the number of points required, Canadian visa officials have the discretion to refuse your application (although this is unusual).

- **Education** – up to 25 points;
- **Language skills** – up to 24 points;
- **Experience** – up to 21 points;
- **Age** – up to 10 points;
- **Arranged employment** – up to 10 points;
- **Adaptability** – up to 10 points.

As well as scoring at least 67 points overall, applicants must demonstrate that they have sufficient funds to support themselves and their dependants after their arrival in Canada. Applicants and their dependants must also undergo medical examinations and security clearances as part of the immigration process. Those planning to live in Quebec are subject to different selection criteria (see 💻 www.immigration-quebec.gouv.qc.ca/en).

You can take a self-assessment test on the CIC website (💻 www.cic.gc.ca/english/immigrate/skilled/assess/index.asp), which will help you determine whether you meet the requirements of a skilled worker immigrant. If you're married or in a common-law relationship, both partners should take the test to see who scores the most points – the person with the most points should apply as the principal applicant. The test is only to give you an idea of whether you'll qualify and is for your private use only (CIC doesn't keep a record of the results). If you want to keep a record, you can print or save the results from your computer.

If your occupation is on the list of 38 high demand occupations published by the federal government, you don't need a job offer to apply. The list of occupations is shown on the CIC website (💻 www.cic.gc.ca/english/immigrate/skilled/apply-who-instructions.asp#list).

Education

Points are awarded as follows:

University Degree

Number of Points	Level of Education
25	PhD or master's degree and at least 17 years' full-time or full-time equivalent study
22	Two or more university degrees at the bachelor's level and at least 15 years' full-time or full-time equivalent study
20	A two-year university degree at the bachelor's level and at least 14 years' full-time or full-time equivalent study
15	A one-year university degree at the bachelor's level and at least 13 years' full-time or full-time equivalent study

Trade or Non-university Certificate or Diploma

Number of Points	Level of Education
22	A three-year diploma, trade certificate or apprenticeship **and** at least 15 years' full-time or full-time equivalent study
20	A two-year diploma, trade certificate or apprenticeship and at least 14 years' full-time or full-time equivalent study
15	A one-year diploma, trade certificate or apprenticeship and at least 13 years' full-time or full-time equivalent study
12	A one-year diploma, trade certificate or apprenticeship and at least 12 years' full-time or full-time equivalent study
5	Secondary school educational credential

Language Skills

Points are awarded for proficiency in English and French (the four elements of language proficiency are listening, reading, speaking and writing). If you speak both languages, you should take the Language 1 test in whichever you're more proficient in, and the Language 2 test in the other.

Number of Points	Proficiency in Language 1
16	high
8	moderate
4 to 8	basic
0	none
	Proficiency in Language 2
8	high
8	moderate
4 to 8	basic
0	none

Experience

This is the most important of the selection criteria, because if you score no points under this section your application will invariably be refused. Points are awarded for experience as follows:

Number of Points	Experience
21	Four years or more
19	Three years
17	Two years
15	One year

Age

Points are awarded as follows:

Points	Age of Applicant
0	16 or less
2	17
4	18
6	19
8	20
10	21 to 49
8	50
6	51
4	52
2	53
0	54 or older

Arranged Employment

If you have a validated job offer, you score up to ten points.

Adaptability

You can score points on more than one of the following criteria up to a maximum of ten:

Points	Adaptability
3 to 5	Spouse's or common-law partner's education
5	Minimum of one year of full-time authorised work in Canada
5	Minimum of two years of full-time authorised post-secondary study in Canada
5	Points received under the Arranged Employment factor
5	Family relationship in Canada
0	Informal job offer in Canada

Settlement Funds

As well as scoring sufficient points, applicants in the Skilled Workers & Professionals category must satisfy the assessing officer that they have sufficient funds to settle in Canada **if they don't already have pre-arranged employment in Canada.** The funds must be transferable and be over and above any debts or other obligations the applicant has.

The settlement funds required in spring 2009 (they are reviewed annually) were as follows:

Number of Family Members	Funds Required
1	$10,833
2	$13,486
3	$16,580
4	$20,130
5	$22,831
6	$25,749
7 or more	$28,668

Canadian Experience Class (CEC)

In September 2008, the Canadian government introduced a new immigration category for workers and graduates with Canadian work experience. Unlike the other immigration categories, the Canadian Experience Class (CEC) focuses on the applicant's Canadian work experience, taking into account experience with Canadian society and knowledge of the Canadian labour market, as well as language skills. It should allow a larger number of skilled trades people to immigrate permanently to Canada who previously lacked the formal education required to qualify under the Skilled Workers category. Individuals applying for permanent residence through this new immigration category will be able to apply within Canada while continuing to work.

The creation of the CEC isn't expected to increase the total number of permanent residents admitted to Canada; in fact, CIC projections show that there will be approximately 15 per cent fewer skilled workers admitted. Instead, resources will be shifted from the processing of applications at missions abroad to 'in-land' processing. It should also remove the requirement for many students and temporary workers to apply for work permit renewal, which has been one of the causes of the processing backlog.

The CEC is limited to those who:

- Have legally entered Canada;
- Have work experience defined by the National Occupational Classification (NOC) Levels of 0, A and B (see below);
- Have at least moderate proficiency in one of Canada's two official languages documented by IELTS and/or TEF;
- (Recent graduates of Canadian post-secondary institutions), have completed at least two years post-secondary study and at least 12 months work experience in Canada after graduation (but within the two years preceding the CEC application) and exclusively in NOC Skill Levels 0, A or B;
- (Work permit holders), have at least a secondary school diploma, trade certificate

or apprenticeship plus two years of full-time work experience in Canada in NOC Skills Levels 0, A or B, acquired within the three years prior to the CEC application.

No proof of funds is required. For information about the National Occupational Classification (NOC), see below.

National Occupational Classification (NOC)

The National Occupational Classification (NOC) is the official Canadian government classification system of occupations maintained by Human Resources and Skills Development Canada (HRSDC). The NOC is the authoritative resource on occupational information in Canada and contains over 30,000 job titles organised under 520 occupational group descriptions. It's used daily by thousands of people to compile, analyse and communicate information about occupations, and to understand the jobs found throughout Canada's labour market. The NOC describes the duties, skills, aptitudes and work settings for occupations, and is also the foundation for labour market statistics and career information.

Only occupations in skill type 0, skill level A or B, of the NOC are considered for Canadian immigration purposes.

For further information about the NOC, see www5.hrsdc.gc.ca/noc/english/noc/2006/welcome.aspx). A list of the NOC occupations that qualify for immigration are shown on the Canreach website (www.canreach.com/noc.asp).

Investors, Entrepreneurs & the Self-employed

Formerly the 'Business Class', this category is intended to promote Canada's economic and employment development by attracting immigrants with business experience, entrepreneurial skills and venture capital. It also seeks to expand Canada's business opportunities overseas by attracting immigrants who are familiar with foreign markets and doing business abroad.

Bear in mind that it can take a long time to obtain a visa under the Investors, Entrepreneurs & the Self-employed category.

As its new name indicates, the category has three sub-categories, as follows:

- **Investor** – For those with a net worth of at least $800,000, who have managerial experience and are willing to make a secured passive investment of $400,000 for five years.
- **Entrepreneur** – For those with a net worth of at least $300,000, who are willing and able to establish, invest in or buy a business in Canada which will create or maintain employment in Canada.
- **Self-employed** – For those with the relevant experience who are willing and able to support themselves and any dependants as a self-employed artisan, athlete or farmer.

As well as meeting the criteria for the individual category under which you plan to apply, you must also score 35 points on the Business category points test. Applicants must also pass medical and 'security' checks.

If you know where you want to live and work in Canada, the 'Working in Canada Tool' (http://workingincanada.gc.ca/welcome.do?template=cic&lang=en) can provide you with useful information regarding local demand for the services you offer, and typical wages; any local restrictions or regulations that might affect you; details of training opportunities available; and a list of sources of further information and advice.

Provincial Nominees

To apply for a work permit under the Provincial Nomination Program (PNP), you must be nominated by a Canadian province or territory and have the necessary skills, education and work experience to make an immediate economic contribution. Applicants aren't assessed on a 'points' basis and the program, which includes provisions for skilled workers in specific categories and business investment immigration, is designed to meet the economic and social needs of individual provinces and territories. Many provincial employment programs provide more flexibility in their selection criteria than federal programs, and therefore PNPs give applicants more opportunities.

Before submitting an application under the program, you must receive a Provincial Nomination Certificate from the province. After a successful nomination, a separate application must be made to Citizenship and Immigration Canada (CIC) for an immigration (permanent resident) visa. You must pass a medical examination and security checks, and show that you have enough money to support yourself and your dependants on arrival.

Because the criteria for provincial nomination are determined by the individual provinces and territories, they vary from province to province and can change without notice. The provinces and territories currently participating in the programme are shown in the box below:

Further information about the PNP scheme can be found at www.cic.gc.ca/english/immigrate/provincial/index.asp, including links to the participating provinces' and territories' websites (click on 'Who can apply' from the above website and then the province name), where the process is explained and you can download application forms.

Family Class

As its name suggests, the family class caters for Canadian citizens and permanent residents wishing to be joined by close relatives including a spouse, common-law partner or conjugal partner 16 years of age or older; an unmarried dependant child under the age of 22; a parent or grandparent; a brother, sister, nephew, niece, grandchild who's an orphan, unmarried and under 18 years of age; or any other relative where the sponsor has none of the above relatives or family members, in Canada or abroad.

The citizen or permanent resident acts as the 'sponsor' to the applicant(s) and as such must demonstrate his financial ability (see below) to support them.

Dependent Child

To qualify as a dependant child you must be:

- Under 22 and unmarried on the date the application for sponsorship is

PNP Websites

Province/Territory	Website Address
Alberta	www.alberta-canada.com/pnp
British Columbia	www.aved.gov.bc.ca/provincialnominee
Manitoba	www2.immigratemanitoba.com/browse/howtoimmigrate/pnp
New Brunswick	www.gnb.ca/immigration/index-e.asp
Newfoundland/Labrador	www.nlpnp.ca
Nova Scotia	www.gov.ns.ca/econ/nsnp
Ontario	www.ontarioimmigration.ca/english/pnp.asp
Prince Edward Island	www.gov.pe.ca/immigration/index.php3?number=1014385
Saskatchewan	www.immigrationsask.gov.sk.ca
The Yukon Territory	www.immigration.gov.yk.ca/ynp_overview.html

submitted (and still unmarried when you arrive in Canada); or

- Of any age or marital status and financially dependent on your parents as a result of being a full-time student; or
- Unable to support yourself due to a mental or physical disability.

Financial Ability

The following figures are the minimum incomes required by sponsors for 2009:

The following must be deducted from the total family income:

- Workmen's compensation board payments, except for permanent disabilities;
- Welfare payments from municipal or provincial sources;
- Payments from any source for employment training or any social or welfare benefits that aren't fixed and continuing;
- All debts.

Size of Family	Minimum Income Required
1 (the sponsor)	$21,666
2	$26,972
3	$33,159
4	$40,259
5	$45,662
6	$51,498
7	$57,336
Each additional person	$5,838

The total must exceed the values listed above. Note that the Quebec government has different income standards.

VISA FEES

You're required to pay a fee when you lodge a visa application, some of which are listed in the box opposite. The fees shown were correct at the time of publication, although they are liable to change; you can check the current fees before submitting a visa application at 💻 www.cic.gc.ca/english/information/fees/fees.asp.

In addition to the above, all applicants except dependant children of a principal applicant or sponsor, children being adopted or orphaned brothers, sisters, nieces, nephews or grandchildren, must pay a 'right of permanent residence' fee (RPRF) of $490.

If non-accompanying dependants change their mind and decide to join you, their fees must be paid at that time. Refunds of visa fees aren't made if someone decides not to come to Canada, but the right of permanent residence fee is refundable for someone who decides against immigration or whose application is refused.

All fees are payable when an application is submitted and must be made by banker's draft or cashier's cheque (personal cheques aren't accepted). Some immigration offices accept cash (check in advance), when you should take your application to the office in person and obtain a receipt. Fees should generally be paid in Canadian dollars,

although some offices may accept local currency (check in advance and inquire what the procedure is regarding the exchange rate).

For further information about visa fees for immigration and citizenship services, see www.cic.gc.ca/english/information/fees/fees.asp.

RETIRING IN CANADA

Canada doesn't have a separate immigration category for retirees. If you don't require a visitor's visa (see page 81) to enter Canada you can usually remain for up to six mon formality (it may also be possible to an extension). However, if you wish to retire permanently in Canada, you'll need to qualify for permanent residence, e.g. under the family class or an independent immigration category. In practice, most foreign retirees in Canada lived and worked in Canada before their retirement, or have children or grandchildren there.

Many retirees spend six months a year in Canada, for example, many Americans spend the summer in Canada and the winter in the southern USA.

Permanent Residence Visa Application Fees

Category/Type	Fee
Investor, Entrepreneur & Self-employed	
Principal applicant	$1,050
Family member of the principal applicant aged 22 or older or under 22 and a spouse or common-law partner	$550
Family member of the principal applicant aged under 22 and not a spouse or common-law partner	$150
Family Class	
Sponsorship application	$75
Principal applicant	$475
Principal applicant if aged under 22 and not a spouse or common-law partner	$75
Family member of the principal applicant aged 22 or older or under 22 and a spouse or common-law partner	$550
Family member of the principal applicant aged under 22 and not a spouse or common-law partner	$150
Other Categories	
Principal applicant	$550
Family member of the principal applicant aged 22 or older or under 22 and a spouse or common-law partner	$550
Family member of the principal applicant aged under 22 and not a spouse or common-law partner	$150

4. ARRIVAL

On arrival in Canada your first task will be to negotiate immigration and customs. Fortunately this presents few problems for most people. If you're a US citizen or permanent US resident you don't require a passport or visa to enter Canada, but you should carry identification papers that establish your status (if not a passport, your driver's licence or an ID card with your photograph, or if you're a naturalised US citizen, your naturalisation certificate). Permanent US residents should carry their green card. With the exception of certain visitors, most people wishing to enter Canada require a passport with a visa (see Chapter 3 for information).

If you stop in Canada in transit to another country, you may be required to go through Canadian immigration and customs at your first port of entry.

It's wise to obtain some Canadian dollars before arriving in Canada, as this saves you having to change money on arrival (although $US are widely accepted). You may find it more convenient to arrive on a weekday rather than at a weekend, when offices, banks and shops may be closed.

In addition to information about immigration and customs, this chapter contains a list of tasks that must be completed before or soon after arrival in Canada, and includes suggestions for finding local help and information.

ARRIVAL/DEPARTURE RECORD

Before you arrive in Canada by air or sea, the airline or shipping company will give you a landing card (officially called a 'traveller declaration card') which must be completed in pen in block capitals in English or French. If you don't have an address in Canada, it's often wise to enter the name of a hotel in an area or city where you're heading or write 'touring', rather than leave it blank. If you enter Canada by road from the US there's no form to complete, but you may be asked where you've come from, your destination in Canada, how long you're planning to stay and whether you have anything to declare.

Many non-immigrant visas are of the multiple-entry kind that allow you to enter and leave Canada as often as you wish during its validation period. However, the period that you're allowed to remain also depends on the expiration date of your passport. If you have a valid multiple-entry, non-immigrant visa and obtain a new passport, retain your old passport and take it with you when travelling to Canada, as the visa remains valid. You must never remove a visa from your old passport, as this will invalidate it.

All visitors admitted to Canada are permitted to stay for a maximum of six months, unless otherwise notified in writing by an examining officer.

IMMIGRATION

When you arrive in Canada, the first thing you need to do is go through Canadian Immigration. This is divided into two sections,

'Canadian Residents' and 'Non-Residents'; make sure you join the correct line. Canadian immigration officials are usually friendly and polite, but if you encounter one who isn't, you should remain polite and answer any questions in a direct and courteous manner, however personal or irrelevant you may think they are. Immigration officers have the task of deciding whether you're permitted to enter Canada and have the necessary documentation, including a visa if required. Present the following to the immigration officer, as applicable:

- Your passport (plus an old passport if it contains an unexpired visa);
- Your completed 'traveller declaration card'.
- You may also be asked for the following:
- Evidence of private medical insurance to cover the duration of your stay (this is rarely requested but you're strongly advised to have private medical insurance as Canada doesn't provide free medical or hospital treatment for visitors);
- Evidence that you have sufficient money to support yourself and your family for the duration of your stay (as above, you're rarely asked for this, but you could be).

You should also have any documents or letters to hand that support your reason for visiting Canada. After entering Canada with an immigrant visa, your passport is stamped to show that you're a permanent resident. You're permitted to travel abroad and re-enter Canada by showing this passport stamp. If you enter Canada from certain countries you may be required to have an immunisation certificate, therefore you should check the requirements in advance at a Canadian High Commission, embassy or consulate before travelling. An immigration officer can decide to send you for a routine health check before allowing you to enter the country.

Clearing immigration during a busy period can take a long time, therefore it's advisable to be prepared – if you need to catch a connecting flight you should allow two to three hours. Among the most notorious entry points for delays are Toronto and Vancouver airports. Immigration queues (line-ups) are shorter at smaller airports, although you may have little choice of entry point.

▲ Caution

If a foreign visitor (including US citizens) has been convicted of a criminal offence abroad, which includes drunk driving offences, he can be barred from entering Canada.

CUSTOMS

If you travel to Canada by air or sea, you'll be given a *Customs Declaration* form (E311) to complete by the airline or shipping line. Hand the completed form to the customs officer at your port or frontier of entry. The head of a family may make a joint declaration for all members residing in the same household and travelling together.

There are no restrictions on the amount of money you may take into Canada, in Canadian or foreign currency (or take out when you leave). However, if you're carrying over $10,000 (in cash, securities or negotiable instruments), you should inform a customs official when you arrive. Failure to do so could result in penalties, seizure and/or prosecution.

Canadian ports and international airports operate a system of red and green 'channels', as is common in Europe. Red means you have something to declare and green means that you have nothing to declare, i.e. no more than the customs allowances, no goods to sell, and no prohibited or restricted goods. If you're certain you have nothing to declare, go through the 'green channel', otherwise go through the red channel. Even when you go through the green channel you may be stopped, your customs declaration form inspected, and you may be asked to open your bags. There are stiff penalties for smuggling.

A list of items you're bringing in is useful for short-stay visitors and essential for long-stay visitors or migrants, although the customs officer may still want to examine your bags. If you're required to pay duty, it must be paid at the time goods are brought into the country. Import duty may be paid:

- In cash in Canadian dollars only;
- By Canadian dollar travellers' cheques;
- By personal cheque (with the necessary identification) for amounts of $500 or less, drawn on a bank in Canada and made payable to 'Canada Border Services Agency';
- Via major credit cards, e.g. MasterCard and Visa.

If you're unable to pay on the spot, customs will keep your belongings until you pay the sum due. This must be paid within a certain period, noted on the back of your receipt. Postage or freight charges must be paid if you want your belongings sent on to you.

If you're discovered trying to smuggle goods into Canada, customs may confiscate them, and if you hide them in a vehicle, boat or plane, they can impound that also! If you attempt to import prohibited items, you may also be liable to criminal charges or deportation. If you have any questions regarding the importation of anything into Canada, contact the customs representative at a Canadian High Commission, embassy or consulate. For information about personal exemptions, see **Duty-free Allowances** on page 303. Temporary visitors driving across the Canadian border from the US should be aware that although you don't need to pay any import duty on the vehicle, you may not lend it to a Canadian while you're there, unless it's to share the driving on a long trip.

The Canada Border Services Agency publishes various brochures, including *I Declare* and *Settling in Canada*, available from www.cbsa-asfc.gc.ca.

Visitors

If you're a visitor to Canada, you can bring your belongings to Canada free of duty and tax without declaring them to customs provided that:

- They're brought in with you and are for your personal use only;
- They're kept in Canada for no longer than six months in a 12-month period;
- You don't sell, lend, rent or otherwise dispose of them in Canada;
- They're exported either when you leave Canada or before they've been in Canada for more than six months, whichever occursfirst.

Permanent & Temporary Residents

When you enter Canada to take up permanent or temporary residence, you can usually import your personal belongings duty- and tax-free. This applies to one shipment only and you cannot go back to your country of origin and bring or ship in another load of duty-free belongings. Any duty or tax payable depends on where you've come from, where you purchased the goods, how long you've owned them, and whether duty and tax has already been paid in another country. The requirement is that goods should have been 'owned, possessed and used' before your arrival in Canada, and it helps to have sales receipts and registration documents (if they haven't been used, you may need to pay duty unless they're wedding gifts from a wedding within three months after your arrival).

Items defined as 'personal and household effects' include antiques and family heirlooms, appliances, boats and their trailers, books, furniture, furnishings and linen, hobby tools and other hobby items, jewellery, musical instruments, private collections of coins, stamps or art, silverware, private aircraft, and holiday (vacation) trailers (but not trailers for permanent residence). They also include vehicles, provided that they'll be used only for non-commercial purposes.

If you're coming to live in Canada and are sending your household goods unaccompanied, you must provide customs with a detailed list of everything being shipped and its value. Items of high individual value, such as works of art, antiques or jewellery, should have a recent valuation certificate. A person emigrating to Canada may bring professional equipment such as books and tools of trade, occupation or employment. Canadian High Commissions, embassies and consulates provide a free information package and a sample inventory list.

You must produce two copies (preferably typed) of a list of the goods you plan to bring in as settler's effects, showing their value, make, model and serial number (where applicable). Keep another copy for yourself. This list should be divided into two parts: one marked 'Annexe A, Goods in Possession' (those that you have with you) and the other marked 'Annexe B, Goods to Follow'. The customs officer completes form B4, *Personal Effects Accounting Document*, based on the information you provide, allocates a file number and provides a receipt copy that you must show when you collect any unaccompanied goods.

You'll be asked by customs officials whether you packed the goods yourself or had them packed for you and whether anyone else may have had access to them since they were packed. Where relevant, removal companies provide documentation certifying that your goods were sealed by them, but you should be aware that if you admit that anyone other than a removal company packed or had access to your belongings, they'll be subject to a full customs inspection for which you must pay. Copies of form B4 can be obtained from customs offices and completed in advance to speed up the process. It's unnecessary to employ a broker or agent to clear your belongings through customs, as you can do this yourself after your arrival in Canada or you can authorise someone to represent you.

There's no time limit on receiving 'goods to follow', but you must collect them up to 40 days after the completion of form B4 (see above). This means that you can ask the carrier to hold your shipment until you've arranged permanent storage/accommodation for it and know where you want the goods sent. They're held in bond until you produce the forms to clear them. Imported goods mustn't be sold, lent, rented or otherwise disposed of in Canada within one year of their importation or of your arrival (whichever is later) without customs authorisation.

Seasonal Residence

If you're a non-resident of Canada and inherit, receive, buy or rent (on a minimum three-year lease) a permanent structure in Canada for use as a seasonal residence, you may claim certain items as duty-free imports for the purpose of furnishing that residence. Portable or mobile homes don't qualify for these exemptions, nor do certain 'construction' items such as electrical or plumbing fixtures, windows, doors and other items designed for permanent installation in a building.

The Canada Border Services Agency publishes a brochures for newcomers entitled *Settling in Canada*, available on their website www.cbsa-asfc.gc.ca/publications/pub/rc4151-eng.html.

Returning Residents

If you're a Canadian resident returning from abroad, you must complete form E24, *Personal Exemption Customs Declaration*, on which you declare articles acquired abroad and in your possession at the time of your return, including:

- Articles you've purchased abroad;

- Any gifts that were given to you while abroad, including wedding or birthday presents;
- Articles purchased in duty-free stores;
- Repairs or alterations made to any articles taken abroad and returned;
- Items you're bringing into Canada for another person;
- Goods you intend to sell or use in your business.

Returning residents may bring into Canada personal belongings of Canadian origin free of duty without proof, provided that they're clearly marked as made in Canada (they'll be labelled in English and French). Foreign-made personal articles taken abroad are dutiable when they're brought into Canada, unless you have proof of prior possession, such as a purchase receipt. Items such as watches, cameras, tape recorders, computers and other articles that can be readily identified by a serial number or permanent markings, can be registered with customs before leaving Canada.

Customs officers list your valuables and their serial numbers on a wallet-sized card, *Identification of Articles for Temporary Exportation* (form Y38), provided you show them to a customs officer and attest that you acquired them in Canada or lawfully imported them. They won't register jewellery on this form and suggest that you carry an appraisal report with a signed and dated photograph of each item together with the bill of sale and, if relevant, proof that duty has been paid. If you take an item of jewellery out of Canada and change it in a way that increases its value, it's no longer considered the same item and duty must be paid on it (this also applies to motor vehicles).

Household effects and tools of a trade or occupation taken out of Canada are allowed in duty-free when you return, provided they're properly declared and registered. All furniture, carpets, paintings, tableware, linens and similar household furnishings acquired abroad may be imported free of duty, provided they've been used abroad by you for not less than one year or were available for use in a household where you were resident for one year. The year of use needn't be continuous nor does it need to be the year immediately preceding the date of importation. Items such as clothes, jewellery, photographic equipment, tape recorders, stereo components and vehicles are considered to be personal articles, and cannot be imported free of duty as household effects. The exemption doesn't include articles placed in storage outside the home or articles imported for another person or for sale.

Restricted Goods

Some items may not be imported into Canada or are subject to restrictions, including the following:

- All weapons must be registered when you arrive in Canada. Restricted items are: modified weapons of any kind, semi-automatic and automatic weapons (although some semi-automatic weapons with short barrels are allowed), sawn-off guns and rifles, switchblades, some martial arts' weapons, mace and pepper spray (pepper spray isn't actually illegal, but it's illegal to bring it into the country), blowguns, crossbows, replica firearms and replacement ammunition magazines. Be warned that if you include firearms of any sort in your household effects, the whole shipment is likely to be held for inspection on arrival. For further information, see the website of the Canada Border Services Agency (💻 www.cbsa-asfc.gc.ca).
- Explosives, ammunition and fireworks all require authorisation and permits. For more details contact Natural Resources Canada (580 Booth, Ottawa, ON K1A 0E4, ☎ 613-995 0947, 💻 www.nrcan.gc.ca).

☑ SURVIVAL TIP

Medicines & Syringes

If you're carrying prescription medicines, they should be clearly identified and carried in the original packaging with a label stating what they are and that they're being used under prescription. It's wise also to carry a copy of your prescription and the phone number of your doctor. Diabetics and others who need to bring syringes with them should also have evidence of their medical condition.

- Automobiles, motorcycles and boats are all permissible import items, but vehicles must conform to regulations regarding safety standards and emissions, and must bear a compliance label to that effect. For full details contact Transport Canada (330 Sparks Street, Tower C, Place de Ville, Ottawa, ON K1A 0N5, ☎ 613-990 2309, 💻 www.tc.gc.ca).
- Goods subject to import controls such as certain clothing, handbags and textiles. For further information contact the Export and Import Permits Bureau, International Trade Canada (💻 www.dfait-maeci.gc.ca).
- Meat, dairy products, and fresh fruit and vegetables. Certain food items may be imported from the US, although the limits are low (usually around two days' worth of edibles).
- Agricultural and horticultural products, including seeds, fertilisers, pest control products and plants.
- Some animals and plants that are classified as endangered species may not be imported dead or alive, nor any product made from their fur, feathers, skin or bone (including internal organs sold in some countries as medicine).

Even if you have a permit, all restricted goods must be declared and presented to a customs officer.

You're permitted to take your domestic pets into Canada, but they must be accompanied by a certificate of good health. Dogs and cats require proof of vaccination against rabies. For the specific regulations regarding your home country or previous country of residence, the best place to start is with companies that specialise in shipping animals abroad. See also **Pets** on page 326.

Caution

Although they aren't restricted, video cassettes and DVDs can arouse suspicion in customs officials, who may think they contain pornographic material.

FINDING HELP

One of the biggest difficulties facing new arrivals in any country is how and where to obtain help with day-to-day problems, e.g. finding a home, schools, insurance requirements and so on. This book was written in response to that need (and also because the authors need to earn a living!). However, in addition to the comprehensive information provided in this book, you also require detailed *local* information. Although the general principles of the law and many other aspects of daily life in Canada are broadly the same throughout the country, each province has its own laws and ways of doing things.

Migrants who don't have a job or relatives in Canada may wish to be met on arrival by a friendly face and there are number of organisations and individuals who perform this service for a fee, some of which advertise in publications such as Canada News (see **Appendix B**) in the UK. Citizenship and Immigration Canada (CIC) have 'A Newcomer's Introduction to Canada' section on their website (💻 www.cic.gc.ca/english/resources/publications/index.asp – click on 'newcomers') with links to programs for newcomers, plus a list of key immigrant-serving organisations across Canada.

An excellent service for newcomers is the volunteer-run 'Host Program' funded by CIC to provide friendship to new immigrants. Volunteers are carefully matched to immigrants and share their time and friendship during an immigrant's critical first few months, helping with banking, grocery shopping, finding services, schools, and showing newcomers how to use the transit systems and unfamiliar household appliances.

You can contact the local host programme via the following addresses:

- **Alberta:** Calgary Catholic Immigration Society (3rd Floor, 120-17th Avenue SW, Calgary, AB T2S 2T2, ☎ 403-262 2006, 💻 www.ccis-calgary.ab.ca).
- **British Columbia:** Immigrant Services Society (# 501, 333 Terminal Avenue, Vancouver, BC V6A 2L7, ☎ 604-684 2561, 💻 www.issbc.org).
- **Manitoba:** International Centre of Winnipeg (2nd Floor, 406 Edmonton Street, Winnipeg, MB R3B 2M2, ☎ 204-943 9158, 💻 www.international-centre.ca).

- **New Brunswick:** Multicultural Association of Fredericton (123 York Street, Fredericton, NB E3B 3N6, ☏ 506-454 8292, 🖳 www.mcaf.nb.ca).
- **Newfoundland:** Association for New Canadians (144 military Road, PO Box 2031, St John's, NL A1C 5R6, ☏ 709-722 9680, 🖳 www.anc-nf.cc).
- **Nova Scotia:** Metropolitan Immigrant Settlement Association (Suite 201, 7105 Chebucto Road, Halifax, NS B3L 4W8, ☏ 902-443 2937, 🖳 www.misa.ns.ca).
- **Ontario:** Catholic Immigration Centre (219 Argyle Avenue, Ottawa, ON K2P 2H4, ☏ 613-232 9634, 🖳 www.cic.ca), Culturelink (160 Springhurst Avenue, 3rd Floor, Toronto, ON M6K 1C2, ☏ 416-588 6288, 🖳 www.culturelink.net) or the Community Development Council Durham (Social Development Council of Ajax/Pickering, 134 Commercial Avenue, Ajax, ON L1S 2H5, ☏ 905-686 2661, 🖳 www.cdcd.org).
- **Prince Edward Island:** PEI Association for Newcomers to Canada (25 University Avenue, Suite 400, Holman Building (4th Floor), Confederation Court Mall, PO Box 2846, Charlottestown, PE C1A 8C4, ☏ 902-628 6009 🖳 www.peianc.com) provides assistance to government-sponsored refugees.
- **Saskatchewan:** Regina Open Door Society (1855 Smith Street, Regina, SK S4P 2N5, ☏ 306-352 3500, 🖳 www.rods.sk.ca).

In **Quebec**, the *Ministère de l'Immigration et des Communautés culturelles* is organised into different regions, each with a local *Carrefour d'intégration* office that works with the immigrant-serving organisations to help newcomers adapt to life in Quebec.

Obtaining information isn't usually a problem as there's a wealth of information available in Canada on every conceivable subject. However, without these information services you may discover that finding up-to-date information, sorting the truths from the half truths, comparing the options available and making the correct decisions are difficult, particularly because most information isn't usually intended for foreigners and their particular needs.

You may find that your friends, colleagues and acquaintances can help because they're often able to proffer advice based on their own experiences and mistakes. But take care! Although they mean well, you may receive as much false and conflicting information as accurate (not always wrong, but possibly invalid for your particular province/territory, community or situation).

Canadians are renowned for their friendliness and you should have no trouble getting to know your neighbours and colleagues, who will usually be pleased to help you settle in. In most communities there are local volunteer services designed to meet a range of local needs that can direct you to a variety of free or inexpensive local services.

Libraries (see page 266) are a mine of local information. Besides keeping reference works, phone directories, local guidebooks, maps, magazines and community newspapers, they distribute useful leaflets and brochures regarding local clubs and organisations of every description. Library staff are helpful at providing information and answering queries, and may even make phone calls for you.

Town halls, police headquarters (the police are usually helpful), visitors bureaux, tourist offices and chambers of commerce, some of which have multilingual staff, are also good sources of free maps and local information. Some large companies have a department or staff dedicated to assisting new arrivals or use a relocation company (see page 94) to perform this task. Relocation magazines are published in many areas (contact local chambers of commerce or estate agents for information).

There are expatriate and ethnic clubs and organisations in most areas. These may provide members with detailed local information regarding all aspects of living in Canada, including housing costs, schools, names of doctors and dentists, shopping information and much more. Many clubs produce fact sheets, booklets, newsletters and run libraries, and most also organise a variety of social events including day and evening classes, ranging from cooking to English or French-language classes. There are numerous social clubs in most towns, whose members can help you find your way around (see page 262).

Many countries have consulates in the main cities, most of which maintain a wealth of local information about everything from doctors to social organisations. Many businesses (e.g. banks) produce books and leaflets containing useful information for newcomers, and local libraries and bookstores usually have books about the local area (see also **Appendix B**). Other ways to meet people include enrolling in a day or evening class, joining a local church or temple and, if you have school-age children, taking part in the activities of the local parents' advisory council.

CHECKLISTS

Before Arrival

The following checklist contains a summary of the tasks that should (if possible) be completed before your family's arrival in Canada:

- Obtain a visa, if necessary, for yourself and all your family members (see **Chapter 3**). Obviously this *must* be done before your arrival in Canada.
- Make sure that you have any necessary permits for yourself and your personal and household effects, e.g. car, firearms and pets.
- Visit Canada before your move to compare communities and schools, and arrange schooling for your children (see **Chapter 9**).
- Find temporary or permanent accommodation and buy a car. If you purchase a car, arrange insurance (see page 181) and register it in the province where you'll be resident (see page 174).
- Arrange for the shipment of your personal and household effects.
- Arrange travel insurance for yourself and your family.
- Arrange health insurance for your family (see page 52). This is essential if you won't be covered by Medicare or your Canadian employer.
- Open a bank account in Canada and transfer funds (you can open an account with many Canadian banks from abroad).
- Obtain an international driver's permit (if your current licence isn't written in English or French).
- Obtain an international credit card or two, which will be invaluable in Canada.
- Obtain as many credit references as possible, e.g. from banks, mortgage companies, credit card companies, credit agencies, companies with whom you've had accounts, and references from professionals such as lawyers and accountants; in fact, anything that will help you establish a credit rating.

☑ SURVIVAL TIP

Assemble and take with you all your family's official documents, including birth certificates, driver's licences, marriage certificate, divorce papers, death certificate (if a widow or widower), educational diplomas, professional certificates, school records, student ID cards, employment references, curriculum vitae, medical and dental records, bank account and credit card details, insurance policies (plus records of no-claims' allowances) and receipts for any valuables. You will also need a number of passport-size photographs, particularly for school-age children.

After Arrival

The following checklist contains a summary of the tasks to be completed after arrival in Canada (if not done before arrival):

- On arrival at a Canadian airport or port, hand your passport, record of landing and other documents to the immigration official.
- Hand your Traveller Declaration Card (provided on the ship or aircraft) or, if your goods are being shipped separately, a *Personal Exemption Customs Declaration* (form E24), to the customs officer and if you're importing more than your personal exemption (see above), provide a list.
- If you haven't bought a car in advance you may wish to rent one (see page 193) for a week or two, as it's almost impossible to get around in Canada without one (but avoid renting a car at an airport, which is the most expensive option).
- Register immediately for Provincial Health Insurance (Medicare), because cover isn't backdated to when you arrive in the country but begins from when you apply.
- Do the following within the few weeks following your arrival (if not done before):
  - Apply for a social insurance card (SIN) from your local social insurance office (see page 213).
  - Open a cheque account at a local bank (they print cheques while you wait) and give the details to your employer (see page 233).
  - Arrange schooling for your children (see **Chapter 9**).
  - Register with a local doctor (see **Chapter 12**).
  - Arrange whatever insurance is necessary, such as health, car, household and third party liability (see **Chapter 13**).

Vancouver, BC

5.
ACCOMMODATION

In most areas of Canada, accommodation isn't difficult to find, depending of course on what you're looking for and whether you wish to rent or buy. There are, however, a few exceptions, such as large cities (e.g. Toronto, Montreal and Vancouver) and their suburbs, where good accommodation is in high demand and short supply, and rents can be high. Rents and the cost of property in different regions and cities vary enormously, with property in the most expensive areas costing as much as ten times what it does in the cheapest areas. Accommodation usually accounts for between 35 and 50 per cent of the average Canadian family's budget – in Toronto and other major cities, 20 per cent of families spend half of their income on housing.

Three-quarters of Canadians live in urban areas with over 400 people to the square kilometre, most in a bungalow, house or flat (apartment). Some two-thirds of Canadian families own their own homes, compared with around 70 per cent in the UK, 55 per cent in France and 40 per cent in Germany. It's estimated that around 2mn Canadians live in mobile home units, which are popular with first-time buyers. In addition, many well-off Canadians own a second (vacation) home, usually a cabin in the back country, where they can hunt or fish in the summer. Skiing enthusiasts may own a property (or a timeshare) in one of the top ski resorts such as Banff, while those who can escape Canada's harsh winters (e.g. retirees – known as snowbirds) often have apartments or mobile homes in the warm southern US states, particularly Florida and Arizona.

Canadians are very mobile, moving home on average every 2.5 years. Not surprisingly, many are anxious that buying a home won't restrict their mobility (companies often want staff to move from one end of the country to the other) and that they'll be able to sell for a profit when they move on.

TEMPORARY ACCOMMODATION

On arrival in Canada, you may find it necessary to stay in temporary accommodation for a period before moving into a permanent home or while waiting for your furniture to arrive. If friends, relatives or your employer haven't made arrangements for you, it's best to book into temporary furnished accommodation when you first arrive. This allows you time to explore the various local communities before making a long-term commitment. In most medium-size cities, you can expect to pay between around $600 and $900 per month for a small apartment, between around $800 and $1,200 for a townhouse, and well over $1,500 for a detached home. In the central areas of major cities (e.g. Toronto, Vancouver and Montreal) you can pay over $2,000 per month just for an apartment.

Some companies provide rooms, self-contained apartments or hostels for employees and their families, although this is usually for a limited period only. If you're hired from abroad or your employer is transferring you to Canada, you're usually provided with temporary accommodation until you find a permanent home. In many cities and suburbs there are 'corporate' hotels, which are hotels that have been renovated and converted to serviced apartments and are rented on a weekly basis.

In most major cities there are long-stay 'corporate' apartments and condominiums, such as Premiere Suites (💻 www.

premieresuites.com), who operate nationwide, and Glen Grove Suites (🖳 www.glengrove.com) in Ontario, which also provide leisure and sports facilities for guests. In most areas, particularly in the major cities, self-contained furnished apartments are available with their own bathrooms and kitchens (see **Self-catering** below). Although expensive, apartments are more convenient and usually less expensive than a hotel or motel room, particularly for families (considerable savings can be made by preparing your own meals). Another advantage is that you can usually rent an apartment on a weekly or monthly basis and you aren't required to commit yourself to a long period. Another option is to rent a holiday home for a period; see 🖳 www.canadavacationrentals.ca (or type 'vacation rentals in xxxx' into a search engine such as Google, where 'xxxx' is the city or region where you're looking).

Single people and married couples (without children) may be able to find temporary accommodation in hostels, such as those provided by the Young Men's Christian Association (YMCA) and Young Women's Christian Association (YWCA), both of which have hostels throughout Canada. Alternatively, in most areas it's possible to rent a furnished room or bed & breakfast accommodation for a short period. Information about hotels, motels, bed and breakfast, self-catering, hostels, dormitories and YMCA/YWCAs is provided below (see also 🖳 www.caa.ca, the website of the Canadian Automobile Association, which maintains a list of hostels in Canada).

Hotels

The quality and standards of Canadian hotels vary considerably, from superb international luxury establishments (some with hundreds of rooms) to seedy and rundown back street hovels (called flophouses), where you're unlikely to find a bedtime mint on your pillow. Canada doesn't have as many private family hotels as Europe, although delightful 18th and 19th century inns, lodges and historic hotels can be found in the east, particularly in the area around the St. Lawrence seaway and the Maritime Provinces. A full listing of these can be found in Fodor's *Canada's Great Country Inns*.

Advertised room rates don't include goods and services tax (GST) and provincial taxes (PST – see page 244), so ask for the room rate inclusive of taxes. Many hotels have reduced rates at weekends (during the week they're full of business people) or lower Sunday to Thursday rates if they're in popular weekend resorts; some have reduced rates in winter during the off season. Many hotels in summer resorts, particularly in the Maritime Provinces, are closed during the winter, i.e. from October to May, and those that remain open usually have greatly reduced rates.

The following table provides a rough guide to the minimum rates for a double room in Canada, although in the major cities and resorts during the high season you can easily pay up to double the rates shown:

Class	Stars	Price
Luxury	4/5	$225+
First class	3	$175+
Mid-range	2	$120+
Economy	none/1	$60+

During off-peak periods, or at any time when room occupancy is low, you can usually haggle over room rates, which are often fluid and based on what the market can bear. Always ask about discounts and special rates. Among the many discount categories that may be available are family, group, foreign visitor, students, senior citizens, youth hostel members, YMCA/YWCA members, plane/train/bus pass holders, rental car users, CAA or other auto club members, government or airline employees, and military and corporate rates (which may be granted to anyone with a company identification or business card). If you're from outer space, ask about special rates for extraterrestrials.

Many hotel chains have periodic special offers, such as a four-for-one programme, where up to four people can stay in a double room for the price of a single. The major hotel chains usually allow children under 12 to stay free when sharing their parents' room, plus free continental breakfast. If you're seeking a low-cost bed, look for accommodation described as student, budget, economy, no frills, rustic, basic or European-style rooms, all of which are euphemisms for inexpensive and basic. In major cities such as Toronto, there are long-stay hotels, some of which cater for women only. Rates vary and may be under $50 per night for weekly rates, depending on the facilities available. You can also find budget hotels on the internet (e.g. 💻 http://budgethotels.com).

Most hotel chains have toll-free reservation numbers (listed in the *Yellow Pages*) and any hotel in a chain can make reservations for you at other hotels in the chain. Some chains provide free phones at airports (and free shuttle buses) and main railway stations. When booking a hotel, you should always have a reservation confirmed in writing either by email or fax. A deposit may be required when booking if you don't use a credit card.

A reservation guaranteed by a major credit card will be kept all night; otherwise, a room is usually held until 6pm only (4pm in major resorts). If you plan to arrive later than this, inform the hotel in advance. You must usually cancel a reservation held with a credit card guarantee or an advance deposit 24 or 48 hours before your confirmed arrival date. You can usually check in as late as you wish, while checkout is normally by 11am or noon. You aren't required to produce your passport or any ID when registering at a hotel in Canada, although you may need a credit card for extra charges.

Resort hotels are common in Canada, many of which were owned and operated by the Canadian Pacific Railway (now by Fairmont Hotels), although some of these (particularly those in busy tourist resorts) can be expensive. Resort hotels provide a range of private facilities including golf courses, tennis courts, horseback riding trails, bike and hiking paths, swimming pools and ocean or lake beaches. Always check whether the use of sports facilities and other activities is included in room rates, otherwise it can add around $50 per day to the cost. If you plan to stay at a resort hotel for a number of days, you may be quoted 'American Plan' (AP), which includes all meals (full board), 'Modified American Plan' (MAP), which includes breakfast and lunch or dinner (half-board) or 'European plan' (no meals). With AP and MAP you're expected to pay for meals whether you take them or not.

Canadian hotel websites include the Canadian Hotel Guide (💻 www.canadianhotelguide.com), Canada Hotel Experts (💻 www.canadahotelexperts.com), Choice Hotels (💻 www.choicehotels.ca) and Purely Canada (💻 www.purelycanada.com).

Motels

Motels (motor hotels, also called 'motel lodges' and 'motor inns') can be found on highways throughout the country. They offer guests a clean and comfortable no-frills room for a reasonable price, and generally offer standard rates and facilities throughout the country (although some offer facilities such as swimming pools and saunas). Motels are generally better, cleaner and safer than inexpensive downtown hotels. Rates are quoted per room rather than per person and are usually quoted for single occupancy with a charge for each additional person. This means that for families and other groups able to share rooms, costs are reduced considerably. Motel room rates range from $45 to $100 per night, with the more expensive being in resorts or remote areas in high season. Motels offer a range of discounts (see above, under **Hotels**).

The motel business is highly competitive and rates vary depending on local competition and the season. Most motels have neon signs outside stating 'vacancy' or 'no vacancy' and often quote their rates on billboards, although those *without* neon signs or on roads bypassed by new freeways are often cheaper, particularly during mid-week. Motels don't usually have restaurants, room service or provide breakfast, although family restaurants, fast food outlets, cafes and bars are usually located nearby (and may offer discounts to motel guests). Sometimes breakfast is available through room service, although it's generally expensive. If a motel has a restaurant, it's usual to pay for each meal separately, rather than charge them to your bill (as is usual in hotels). It's normal to pay in advance when you check in at a motel and you must sometimes pay a key deposit of around $5 and possibly a deposit for a TV remote control.

Many motels furnish all their rooms with two double beds (queen or king size) or a double bed and two singles (twin beds). Additional fold-up camp beds (cots) can usually be provided. Some motels have suites with more than one bedroom sharing the same facilities (intended for families or groups), which are self-catering rooms with a small kitchenette. If you're travelling as a family or group, ask how many people a room accommodates and whether there's a surcharge for additional people. Most motels (and hotels) don't charge for children under 12 sharing their parents' room, or will provide a cot in the parents' room for a small extra charge.

Motel rooms are usually fairly similar with little individuality or character. All rooms have TV (often with cable TV and pay-per-view films), a private bathroom (with towels and washcloths/flannels), phone, air-conditioning and heating, and possibly a fridge. Motels often provide washing machines and dryers, vending machines for drinks and sweets, while ice is usually available from a machine in the lobby.

Unlike the US, many motels in Canada are independently owned and run, although there are a number of franchises and chains. The largest and cheapest nationwide chains of motels include Days Inn with around 65 locations, Super 8, Travelodge, Howard Johnson's and Comfort Inns with over 50 locations, plus smaller chains such as Accent Inns (which has five motels in British Columbia). If you're staying at a chain motel, the receptionist will book you a room at other motels in the chain. Most chains also have a toll-free booking number (call the toll-free information directory on ☎ 1-800-555 1212 or see 💻 www.canadatollfree.ca). The Canadian Automobile Association (💻 www.caa.ca) publishes booklets containing a list of approved motels and their rates, and all motel chains publish directories containing directions, maps, facilities, addresses, telephone numbers and email addresses.

Bed & Breakfast (B&B)

Bed and breakfast (called *Gîte du Passant* in Quebec; B&B in the west) accommodation, often referred to as 'inns', is popular in Canada, particularly in small towns and holiday (vacation) centres. Standards and prices vary considerably, from a reasonable $75 for a single to $250 (on a par with a luxury hotel) for a double, depending on the location and the season. A private bath isn't always included, so check when booking. In Toronto and other major cities, B&B helps owners pay their mortgages, and is a reasonably affordable way of staying downtown.

> The breakfast part of B&B may vary from a roll and coffee or tea (i.e. continental breakfast), to a full cooked meal with many courses (in some parts of Canada they take breakfast *very* seriously), so check in advance.

Many B&Bs offer other meals, picnic baskets, transportation, tours, and worthwhile free services ranging from bike loans to the use of libraries, saunas, Jacuzzis/hot tubs, gardens, tennis courts and swimming pools.

There are some regional associations that inspect and approve B&Bs, but mostly it's a buyer beware situation. A wealth of B&B guides are published, including *The Annual Directory of American and Canadian Bed & Breakfasts* by Tracey Menges (Rutledge Hill Press), *The Canadian Bed & Breakfast Guide* by Gerda Pantel (Penguin Books), *The Western Canada Bed & Breakfast Guide* by Sarah Bell (Gordon Soules Book Publishers) and *Atlantic Canada Bed and Breakfast* (Formac Publishing).

B&Bs in Canada can be rented via official agencies or reservation organisations, or you can make a booking yourself by telephoning the numbers shown in guide books, B&B directories, the *Yellow Pages* or online directories. There are a number of online B&B directories, including Bed and Breakfast Canada (🖳 www.bbcanada.com) and the Western Canada Bed and Breakfast Innkeepers Association (🖳 http://bcbandb.com). Most B&B associations also have websites listing B&Bs in their area.

Self-catering

Self-catering apartments, houses, bungalows and condominium (condo) apartments are common throughout Canada, particularly in cities and mountain (e.g. ski) resorts. However, they don't always accept children, so check in advance. Apartment hotels are usually owned by a company and are designed for short-term rentals, whereas condominium apartments have individual private owners who let their apartments through management companies. Accommodation usually consists of a studio (bachelor's) or a one or two-bedroom apartment, with a fully-equipped kitchen or kitchenette and a private bathroom with a shower.

Some condo complexes provide the same facilities as hotels, such as a lobby, lounge, coffee shop and restaurant, while others provide no services. Condos usually have double beds, fully-equipped kitchens with a dishwasher, all linen, a washer and drier (or shared facilities), TVs, and often air-conditioning and room telephones. Most resorts have a daily maid service. Other amenities may include swimming pools, tennis courts, golf courses, saunas, barbecue grills, and grocery and other stores within the complex. When choosing self-catering accommodation, check the minimum and maximum rental periods, furnishings and equipment level, whether pets are allowed, sports and social facilities, local beaches, public transport, nearby stores, maid and baby-sitting services, and anything else of importance to you. Apart from serviced condos and hotel apartments, most self-catering accommodation doesn't provide a maid or cleaning service, although local services can usually be arranged.

The cost of a one-bedroom condo in a first class complex starts at around $100 per night for two adults and may be no more than $150

per night for four adults. Children under 12 may be accommodated free of charge when sharing an apartment with their parents. A good quality two-bedroom apartment costs between $125 and $150 per night and accommodates up to six people. Weekly and monthly rates usually reduce the per day cost considerably. An apartment is often a good choice for a family; it's cheaper than hotel rooms, provides more privacy and freedom, and you're able to prepare your own meals when you please.

Condo apartments can be rented through travel agents and are often included as part of fly-drive packages. Some discount travel organisations (plus the CAA and credit card companies) provide savings of up to 50 per cent on hotels, condos and other rental accommodation. Book as early as possible, particularly during holiday (vacation) periods, and avoid national holidays when everything is booked up months in advance. Most guide books list agencies and organisations providing self-catering accommodation, and many establishments advertise in the travel and property sections of newspapers.

See also **Temporary Accommodation** above.

Hostels, Dormitories & YMCAs/YWCAs

For those travelling on a tight budget, one way to stretch limited financial resources is to stay in hostels, which may include an historic city building to an old lighthouse or log cabin. Most hostels recognise International Youth Hostel Federation (IYHF) membership, although there are far fewer hostels in Canada than, for example, in Europe. Hostelling

International-Canada is affiliated to the IYHF and has around 70 locations. While everyone is welcome, members pay a reduced rate for accommodation and other programmes available through individual hostels. Non-Canadian guests must be members of the youth hostel association in their own country or purchase a 'welcome stamp' for each night's stay.

Contact Hostelling International-Canada (205 Catherine Street, Suite 400, Ottawa, ON K2P 1C3, ☏ 613-237 7884, 💻 www.hihostels.ca) for a list of hostels and membership details. Hostelling International members may receive discounts for restaurants, museums and transportation (which includes rental cars, buses, ferries and airlines). Rates vary but are usually from around $30 per night for a bunk in a single-sex dormitory with four beds, although private rooms are sometimes available.

Other Canadian hostelling organisations include the Canadian Hostelling Association (1600 James Naismith Drive, Gloucester, ON K1B 5N4, ☏ 613-748 5638) and Backpackers Hostels Canada, which has hostels, retreat centres, residences, homes, inns and hotels, costing from $25 per person, per night. Backpackers Hostels publishes a guidebook to hostels in Canada available from Backpackers Hostels Canada (☏ 1-888-920 0044 or 807-983 2042, 💻 www.backpackers.ca).

Some hostels limit stays, e.g. to three nights, and it's wise to book in advance, particularly during holiday periods or in large cities. Some allow non-members to stay for a small extra charge so that they can experience hostel life before becoming members. Youth hostels provide separate dormitories (e.g. 8 to 16 beds) for males and females. All hostels require guests to buy or rent (for around $1) a sheet sleeping bag (sleep sack) consisting of two sheets sewn together or provide their own. Most require guests to share light domestic duties and don't provide meals, but usually have cooking facilities. There's often a curfew around 10pm and alcohol, smoking and drugs are prohibited. However, Canadian hostels are generally more relaxed than their European counterparts. A variation on youth hostels is the home hostel, which is a private residence with the same rates as a hostel.

Other inexpensive city accommodation can be found at Young Men's Christian Association (YMCA, 💻 www.ymca.ca) and Young Women's Christian Association (YWCA, 💻 www.ywcacanada.ca) hostels. Two-thirds of Ys are mixed (coed) and accept women and families, while the rest are for men only. Room rates for Ys located in cities range from around $45 to $55 for a single and $50 to over $100 for a double room with a private bathroom. It's usually necessary to reserve a room and pay in advance, for which there's a reservation fee. Most Ys offer cheaper weekly rates and some offer economy packages which include room, half-board (breakfast and evening meal) and excursions. Many Ys have swimming pools, gyms and other sports facilities. For further information, contact YMCA Canada (42 Charles Street East, 6th Floor, Toronto, ON M4Y 1T4, ☏ 416-967 9622, 💻 www.ymca.ca).

Another place to stay in university cities during holiday times is on a university campus. Rooms are open to all, although bona fide students are given preference, with rates around $35 per room. The major drawback is that campuses may be some way from the city centre and the rooms are basic, although you can use the university's sports facilities. It's recommended to book rooms in advance through a university's accommodation office.

RELOCATION CONSULTANTS

If you're fortunate enough to have your move to (or within) Canada paid for by your employer, he may arrange for a relocation consultant to handle the details. Services provided by relocation companies usually include house hunting (rent or purchase), shipment of furniture and personal effects, reports on schools, area information dossiers, orientation tours, plus miscellaneous services such as financial counselling, home marketing, spouse counselling and assistance after arrival.

> Relocation consultants' services are expensive and can run into thousands of dollars per day, although most people consider it money well spent (particularly if their employer is footing the bill!).

Fees can vary considerably, so if you're paying the bill, obtain a number of quotations and compare the services provided. Most large property companies have relocation divisions, and many offer a free relocation service to individuals.

If you just wish to look at properties for rent or sale in a particular area, you can make appointments to view properties through estate agents (see page 101) in the area where you plan to live, and arrange your own trip to Canada. However, make *absolutely certain* that agents know exactly what you're looking for, and obtain property lists in advance. Local realtors are invariably helpful and will drive you round to see houses for sale. They are also a mine of information on current local conditions.

Relocation guides are published in many areas and cities, and contain house prices, guides to neighbourhoods, employment prospects, school scores, maps, entertainment information and public services details. Information is also available from local chambers of commerce and estate agents. A series of regularly updated relocation guides for various Canadian cities (Montreal, Ottawa, Toronto and Vancouver) and provinces (Alberta) is available from Moving To Magazines (💻 www.movingto.com). They also publish magazines for Saskatchewan, Southwestern Ontario and Winnipeg, although these are currently out of print due to a lack of advertising.

CANADIAN HOMES

Depending on the province, Canadian homes are built in a range of architectural styles including ranch, contemporary, Victorian, French manor and English Tudor. In addition to single-family detached homes and apartments, you can choose from a wide range of townhouses. Homes include single (bungalow) and two-storey, split- and multi-level houses. The average size of a detached single-family home is around 1,500ft^2 (139m^2) and for new single-family homes is over 1,800ft^2 (167m^2). A bonus is the basement, which isn't counted in the square footage. Whereas land values constitute a large part of the cost of a home in many countries, building plots in Canada are relatively inexpensive and extensive prefabrication helps reduce building costs.

Kitchens in modern Canadian homes are usually large with an eat-in dining area, plenty of counter space, built-in cupboards, dishwashers, waste disposal units, and possibly laundry facilities and/or a pantry. Kitchens in older homes may not have been modernised, although most Canadian homes contain a profusion of labour-saving devices. Cookers or stoves, which may be electric or gas, don't usually have grills but broilers, which are larger than European grills and located in the top of the oven; and therefore you cannot bake or roast and grill at the same time unless you have a double-oven stove. Most Canadians use a separate toaster.

There's usually no facility for warming plates on Canadian ranges. Canadian refrigerators are frost-free, huge (big enough to withstand a supermarket strike for at least a year), and side-by-side models usually have water and ice-cube dispensers.

Most Canadian bathrooms contain baths (tubs) with a diverter valve on the taps to allow you to switch to a shower attachment; many homes also have a separate shower room or an en suite shower or bathroom to the master bedroom. Most modern two- or three-bedroom family homes have two full bathrooms. Canadian baths tend to be small, uncomfortable and not very deep (most Canadians prefer to shower), and bathrooms seldom contain a bidet. Canadians also have what are called half-bathrooms (or a half-bath), which isn't a bath for babies, but a room *without* a bath. It usually contains a toilet and washbasin, and possibly a shower. Modern homes usually have a downstairs toilet. Canadian showers supply water in torrents, rather than the trickle common in many countries.

In many parts of Canada, particularly affluent middle class suburbs in the major cities, many homes have outdoor or indoor heated swimming pools. If you have a pool, it will need a lot of attention such as filling, emptying, cleaning, filtering, chlorinating, etc., although there are companies that will look after it for you (you can pay someone to do almost anything in Canada). Many homes also have hot tubs or Jacuzzis. A hot tub is usually located outside the house where the climate is favourable (such as western British Columbia) and consists of a large, usually square wooden or fibreglass tub containing hot water, the temperature of which is thermostatically controlled. Hot tubs accommodate a number of people and are intended as a relaxation rather than a bath. A Jacuzzi is installed inside a home and has jets like a whirlpool bath.

Houses and apartments have light fittings in all rooms, which are included in the sale, together with window and floor coverings. Few homes have curtains (drapes) because windows are fitted with shades or blinds to keep out the sun. Modern houses tend to be carpeted in the bedrooms with hardwood floors in living rooms; polished wooden floors are common in older homes. Most have large fitted wardrobes (closets), plus other standard features such as smoke and security alarms.

Most modern houses have ultra-efficient heating and new houses usually include thermal insulation and double- or triple-glazing. Older houses may have single glazing with detachable storm windows. Windows and doors in all areas usually have screens to keep out flies, mosquitoes and other insects during summer, although storm windows may need to be removed to fit them. Modern Canadian homes have separate living, dining and family rooms (often used as a playroom for children), a study (den), bar, cellar or basement (useful for storage), and maybe a utility or laundry room, which tends to be in the basement.

The area at the back of the house is called the yard rather than the garden; as well as plants and a place for children to play, it will almost certainly have a barbecue. Most Canadian houses have a paved or covered outdoor area such as a terrace, patio, deck or porch (often screened to keep out bugs). Homes are built either of brick or have a wooden (or more recently, steel) frame with an outer surface that may consist of wood, brick, stucco, cedar shingles or a 'siding' of wood, aluminium (plain or painted) or vinyl, which is popular because it's maintenance-free. Roofs are made of 'shakes' (overlapping thin slices of wood) or tiles (shingles) made of asphalt, cedar, pine or other wood.

☑ SURVIVAL TIP

If you're staying for less than two years, you're usually better off renting a home than buying because it takes around three years to amortise the costs of purchase.

BUYING A HOME

Before committing yourself to buying a home in Canada, you should consider renting (see below) for a period, e.g. six months, or at least until you know exactly what you want to buy and where you want to live. It isn't unusual for newcomers to uproot themselves after a relatively short period and move to another region – or even return home! Having said that, most newcomers will want to get on the housing ladder as soon as possible, not least because buying a home costs no more than renting and is generally an excellent long-term investment.

Canada has a wide range of properties (see below), both old and new, and property prices are generally lower than in other western countries, particularly for those coming from Western Europe. Most new detached homes in Canada are built to order by developers, who are also the builders. Townhouses and apartments are usually part of large complexes and are often ready to move into, and, if you buy while they're being built, you may be able to choose the porcelain, paint, carpet, and fixtures and fittings. Whether you're buying a new or used property, you can usually haggle over the price, but be careful how you do it. People who come from countries where haggling involves making disparaging remarks about the property can have a hard time when dealing with Canadians, who may take it as a personal insult.

The 'experts' (i.e. inspectors) say that you should always have a house inspection (survey) on a resale house, although most people don't bother with houses under around 15 years old. Some experts even recommend an inspection on a new property with a warranty, as some builders use short cuts and inferior products that can lead to problems later. Before buying a new condo you should speak to people who have already purchased one in the same development, as problems are commonplace (owners are usually happy to share their gripes!).

If you're planning to buy an older condo, you're advised to contact the condominium committee and request the minutes from their last two years' meetings, their budget and any other records they'll provide. In this way, you can check whether there are any regular complaints (e.g. about noise), how much money is in the contingency fund (if any), and whether there are any structural problems or renovations that you'll be required to pay for. You may also be advised to have a radon test if a property is located in an area susceptible to high levels of radon (a naturally occurring radioactive gas that can cause cancer). A pre-purchase inspection costs from around $250 and for a little more, some inspectors will produce a video film of their findings, in addition to a written report.

In some provinces, an owner must disclose any significant defects when selling a property. If he fails to do so, you have a good chance of receiving damages if you sue. All claims must be made within a limited period. Always use a certified inspector who's a me
Canadian Association of Home a
Inspectors (CAHPI, PO Box 1371
ON K2K 1X6, ☎ 1-888-748 2244 or 613-839 5344, 💻 www.cahpi.ca) or another professional organisation.

There are many books published about buying property in Canada, including the *Home-buyer's Guide for Canadians* and *Buy & Sell Recreational Property in Canada*, both by Geraldine Santiago (Self-Counsel Press). Free property booklets and magazines listing properties for sale are published in most regions (many are available in local editions) and distributed via local estate agents, stores, restaurants, supermarkets, bookstores and libraries. There are also numerous property websites, including 💻 www.propertysold.ca, www.realestatecanada.com, www.realtor.ca and www.royallepage.ca.

One of the biggest problems for people moving to Canada in recent years hasn't been buying a home, but selling their existing home abroad for a good price, particularly in the UK and US.

Canada Mortgage & Housing Corporation

The Canada Mortgage and Housing Corporation (CMHC) is Canada's national housing agency, committed to helping Canadians (and migrants!) access a wide choice of quality, affordable homes, while making vibrant, healthy communities and cities a reality across the country. CMHC works to enhance Canada's housing finance options, assist Canadians who cannot afford housing in the private market, improve building standards and housing construction, and provide policymakers with the information and analysis they need to sustain a vibrant housing market in Canada. CMHC also provides mortgage loan insurance that enables you to buy a home sooner with as little as a 5 per cent down payment.

The CMHC provides a wealth of information and assistance to homebuyers (see 💻 www.cmhc-schl.gc.ca/en/co) and renters (see below) and should be your first stop before buying or renting a home in Canada. It even has a special section for newcomers (💻 www.cmhc.ca/newcomers) with information in eight languages.

Types of Property

The following types of property are widely available in Canada:

- **Condominium** or **Apartment:** A flat (apartment), usually located in a city or resort where building land is expensive. May be relatively low-rise, e.g. four floors in small towns or suburbs, or high-rise in the downtown area of major cities. In many cities, old warehouses have been converted into huge studio apartments, known as 'artist studios' or lofts, consisting of a single vast room of up to 1,000ft^2 (around 100m^2).
- **Townhouse:** A terraced (row) house on two or more levels (sometimes also called 'split-level'), attached to other units, with private entrances and (usually) an integral garage. Townhouses are sometimes part of a condominium-type development.
- **Duplex:** One building built as two separate houses with private entrances, either side-by-side (called 'semi-detached' in the UK) or top and bottom. If there are four units, it's called a fourplex.
- **Bungalow and Bi-level:** Although a bungalow normally has only one floor, they may also have a basement, part of which is often used as a family recreation room. In a bi-level, the main floor is raised so that the basement area has windows above ground level.
- **One-and-a-half Storey:** A bungalow with a pitched roof that has one or more rooms in it, called a 'chalet bungalow' in some other countries.

- **Standard Two-Storey:** Detached house, possibly with a garage, standing on its own plot of land. It normally has a basement and two or three bedrooms.
- **Executive Home:** A detached house on a larger plot of land, with at least four bedrooms, two bathrooms, study, laundry room, family or recreation room, attached two-car garage, and possibly a swimming pool and/or tennis court, and anything else you fancy if you're prepared to pay for it.
- **Mobile Home:** The other end of the scale from an executive home, a mobile home is anything from a small to large single-level home, designed to be transported on a trailer, although they're rarely moved. They're found in special 'mobile home' sites on blocks, and are connected to utility services and mains sewerage. They're a cheap option for homebuyers and renters.

There's also the classic log cabin in the country on its own piece of land ('acreage'), which is the typical dream home for many immigrants. Estate agents love people who want to buy one of these – they know they'll be screaming to sell it and move back to the city after a couple of winters of being snowed in and having their sewerage system back up because it's minus 40 degrees and everything has frozen solid! It's wise to postpone this dream until you've spent a couple of winters in Canada in a town, rather than in the wilderness.

Property Prices

Property prices in Canada grew by around 10 per cent a year between 2002 and 2007, since when prices have fallen overall, with buyers becoming scarcer due to the precarious economy, spiralling unemployment and a lack of financing. However, although there's a slump, the market remains relatively stable and there's no crash (and no sub-prime lending crisis). In fact, in 2009 houses were more affordable than previously, due to lower prices and lower mortgage repayments.

Sales were down 31 per cent in February 2009, compared with a year previously, and average prices had fallen 9.2 per cent. Prices fell most in British Columbia, Alberta and

Ontario, although in around half the regions they were higher, including most Atlantic provinces; e.g. prices in Newfoundland & Labrador were up 25 per cent. There were still plenty of homes for sale, but the number on the market was almost 11 per cent lower than in February 2008. Sales fell by 17 per cent in 2008, and most analysts were predicting a fall in 2009 of around 10 per cent, followed by a recovery in 2010.

Canada's highest house prices are found on the west coast, in British Columbia (BC), which enjoys the country's mildest weather. As in other countries, prices are higher in the cities than in rural areas; Vancouver (BC) has by far the most expensive housing, followed by Victoria (BC), Calgary, Toronto and Edmonton. Housing is more affordable in the Atlantic Provinces, Quebec and Manitoba.

Average prices in the provinces and in the main cities in March 2009 are shown in the tables below. The statistics (rounded up or down to the nearest $1,000) are compiled monthly from the sale of existing properties sold through the Multiple Listing Service (MLS), and are provided by the Canadian Real Estate Association (CREA, 💻 www.crea.ca/public/news_stats/statistics.htm).

A Home Buyer's Plan introduced in 1992 allows first-time buyers to withdraw up to $25,000 from their Registered Retirement Savings Plan (RRSP – see page 215) to use as a down payment on their first home.

Fees

In addition to the cost of a property, you should be aware of other costs:

- Property purchase tax or land transfer fees are from 0.5 to 2 per cent of a property's total value (excluding Alberta, rural Nova Scotia and Saskatchewan);
- Goods and services tax (GST) is payable on new homes and in some regions, provincial sales tax (PST) is also payable (see page 244). Both taxes are normally included in the quoted price. Depending on the cost of the home, this is refundable to first-time buyers in some provinces;
- Inspection and survey fees;
- Legal fees;
- Registration fees for the deeds and mortgage;

Average Price by Province/City (A-Z)

Province	Average Price
Alberta	$328,000
British Columbia	$426,000
Manitoba	$205,000
New Brunswick	$152,000
Newfoundland & Labrador	$198,000
Northwest Territories	$306,000
Nova Scotia	$189,000
Ontario	$292,000
Prince Edward Island	$148,000
Quebec	$210,000
Saskatchewan	$229,000
The Yukon Territory	$219,000
Canada – Average	$289,000

Average Price by City (A-Z)

City	Average Price
Calgary, AB	$372,000
Edmonton, AB	$309,000
Fredericton, NB	$161,000
Halifax, NS	$230,000
Hamilton, ON	$263,000
Montreal, QC	$255,000
Ottawa, ON	$288,000
Quebec City, QC	$199,000
Regina, SK	$246,000
St John's, NL	$159,000
Saskatoon, SK	$267,000
Toronto, ON	$362,000
Vancouver, BC	$531,000
Victoria, BC	$441,000
Winnipeg, MB	$211,000

- Property insurance (you must have fire insurance to obtain a mortgage;
- Property tax (see page 247);
- Mortgage application fees and possibly legal fees associated with a mortgage. If you don't have the standard 25 per cent deposit and qualify for a 'CMHC-insured' mortgage (see page 239), you must also pay for an insurance policy to cover the risk to the lender. If the mortgage company wants an appraisal (survey and price) on the property, you must also pay for this;
- Vendor's adjustments. This is the 'unused' portion of pre-paid expenses such as real estate tax, utilities, and annual maintenance fees for condominiums and other 'community' homes;
- Utility connection fees.

Holiday Homes

Every weekend during the summer, southern Ontarians depart in droves from Toronto to their second homes in what's known as 'cottage country' – Muskoka (don't call it 'the Muskokas' – only outsiders do this), while those from southern Quebec go to the Laurentians, Vermont, Lake Champlain or Plattsburgh (a small city in upstate New York's Lake Champlain Valley). During the winter, they still go to their country cottage to snowmobile, when local gas stations are as likely to be filling snowmobiles as cars.

The most popular areas for holiday (vacation) homes are the country areas of Ontario and Quebec, and the mountains and lakes of Alberta and British Columbia. Canadians who enjoy the outdoor life often buy or rent a cabin, trailer or houseboat somewhere in the backwoods for the summer; or an apartment, condominium or timeshare in one of the popular ski resorts in the winter. Renting is done through an agency and, depending on the size of the property, can range from $50 to $250 per day. Lower monthly rates are usually available.

From a legal viewpoint, Canada is one of the safest countries in the world in which to buy a holiday home. There are few traps for the unwary, and property and planning laws are much stricter than in most European countries. Non-residents' rights as property owners are the same as those of Canadian citizens. For safety, however, you should always do business with an established company or a real estate agent with a good reputation. If you're a foreign resident, bear in mind that with a visitor's visa you can only remain in Canada for a maximum of six months per year (see **Chapter 3**). If you buy or inherit a seasonal residence in Canada, you can bring furniture and personal effects into the country duty-free.

Many developers offer a furnishing package (or 'turn key' service) that includes all furniture, electrical apparatus, linen and miscellaneous items for an inclusive 'special' price, which is designed for buyers who are planning to let their homes. A typical furniture package for a three-bedroom property costs $12,000 to $15,000 and is generally better value than buying items individually (but check because the value varies). Furnishings must be financed separately and cannot be included in a mortgage.

Part-ownership Schemes

If you don't wish to invest in buying a property outright, you may wish to investigate part or holiday ownership schemes such as shared ownership, where a number of buyers own shares in a property-owning company; part-ownership between family, friends or even strangers (some companies offer this option), a holiday property bond, or even timesharing. Timesharing in Canada doesn't have the dreadful reputation that it has earned in Europe, although it isn't as good value as part-ownership.

ESTATE AGENTS

Some 90 per cent of people in Canada buy and sell their homes through estate agents (realtors), who must be licensed by local property boards. Estate agents are increasingly doing business via the internet. In most provinces, real estate brokers and their sales people must be registered under the province's Real Estate and Business Brokers Act (REBBA). A typical example is Ontario, which requires sales people to be permanent residents of Canada over 18 years of age, to be employed by a registered broker and to have passed written examinations. Registration must be renewed every two years. Most estate agents belong to three bodies: the national Canadian Real Estate Association (CREA, 200 Catherine Street, 6th Floor, Ottawa, ON K2P 2K9, ☎ 613-237 7111, 💻 http://crea.ca), the provincial association and a local board, e.g. in a city.

Unlike other countries, where most agents are engaged by the seller, estate agents in Canada act for the buyer as often as the seller and can, in some circumstances, act for both. Under CREA rules, members are required to disclose in writing (to all parties concerned) who they're working for. There are three types of agency:

- Vendor's agent, where the estate agent works for the vendor and must inform him of anything he knows about a buyer (like the maximum price you're prepared to pay for a property – so don't mention this if you hope to do a deal);
- Purchaser's agent, where the estate agent works exclusively for the buyer and must disclose anything known about the vendor;
- Dual agent, when the estate agent works for both parties.

Most agents are self-employed and pay a percentage of their commissions and a desk fee to the agent where their licence is held. The standard commission may be negotiable, with agents usually earning anywhere between 3 and 7 per cent commission. Where buying and selling agents are involved, they split the commission.

The other main difference between estate agents in Canada and many other countries is that Canada has a national computerised Multiple Listing System (MLS) which contains details of all properties for sale. Therefore, it isn't necessary to traipse around a number of estate agents to see what properties they have for sale. You can simply engage an agent to act for you as a purchaser and find suitable properties on the MLS.

> Many agents are mortgage brokers who are affiliated to mortgage providers, and it's normal practice for them to pre-qualify you for a mortgage before they start showing you properties.

When an agent has shown you a home that you wish to buy, he immediately writes up a purchase contract. He then contacts the seller's agent and asks when he can present an offer. The purchase contract is drawn up with the time usually left open until an hour or two after the agreed presentation time, after which it becomes void. The buyer's agent then presents the offer to the seller and the seller's agent, and may wait while the owner discusses the offer with his agent; if the offer is acceptable the deal is signed on the spot and a deposit cheque paid into the trust (escrow) account of the seller's agent. Trust accounts are protected by an insurance scheme approved by the local real estate board. If the offer is unacceptable, the prospective buyer may make a counter offer, which is re-presented to the vendor. In theory you can go back and forth indefinitely, but in practice it's usually no more than once or twice.

There may be conditions in an offer that must be satisfied by a set date, otherwise the contract is void. The most common conditions of the purchase are a satisfactory home inspection and finance being obtained, but there can be others, e.g. subject to the vendor finding another house by a set date or to the buyer selling his home. These conditions are valid for a limited period only and once waived, the contract is legally binding on both parties. Therefore, within a few hours of finding a home you like, it can legally be yours.

Less than 10 per cent of homes sold in Canada are sold directly by owners without using an agent or broker. When an owner is selling his own home, he usually holds an 'open house' at weekends when the public can inspect it without making an appointment. If successful, an owner is likely to save thousands of dollars in agent's fees, part or all of which he may pass on to the buyer. It's particularly recommended when you're selling an attractive home at a realistic price.

However, if you're buying directly from a vendor, you should always use the services of a lawyer, an appraiser and a home inspector before going ahead with a deal. Some people (mostly lawyers) say that you should use a lawyer to check the contract, even if you're using a licensed estate agent. Most estate agents use standard contracts that have been approved by their provincial associations in which there's a clause stating that the agent must use due diligence, honesty and integrity. If you wish, you can have a 'subject to lawyer's approval' clause added to a contract for safety.

RENTAL ACCOMMODATION

Renting a home in Canada has become increasingly popular in recent years across the country, particularly among migrants, many of whom have been unable to sell their homes abroad, and those waiting to see whether prices have hit the bottom before taking the plunge. In any case, it's advisable to rent for a period (e.g. six months) before buying for a number of good reasons, not least so that you have time to research exactly where and what to buy, but also because many people uproot themselves after a short period and move to another region of Canada or even return home.

> ☑ **SURVIVAL TIP**
>
> **Before committing yourself to a long-term rental, sight unseen, it's advisable to rent a temporary apartment or house for a period, so that you can inspect a long-term rental property 'in the flesh' before committing yourself to renting it.**

Renting allows you to become familiar with the weather, the amenities and the local people, and to meet other migrants who have made their home there and ask them about their experiences. Not least, it also gives you plenty of time to look around for a permanent 'dream' home at your leisure. The wrong decision regarding location is one of the main causes of disenchantment among migrants; buying a home will also tie you down, and, if you do decide to uproot yourself within a short period, will result in considerable additional expense.

Rental accommodation is freely available in most areas, although the choice and cost of rental property varies wildly, depending on the city or region. Renting is generally the best solution for anyone planning to remain in Canada for a limited period, say less than two years. Rental property can be found within a few weeks in most areas; in others, it can take much longer and you may have to compromise on what you're looking for. In major metropolitan areas, finding an apartment or house that suits your needs and your budget may be difficult, and you may be forced to live out of town and commute.

Most property in Canada is rented unfurnished and you may have difficulty in finding a furnished apartment or house. Furnished apartments in Canada are usually equipped with essentials only, which include a stove (range), refrigerator (or fridge/ freezer) and basic furniture. Some linen (e.g. bed, bath and table) may also be supplied. Unfurnished apartments usually have a stove and a refrigerator or fridge/freezer. Most property is centrally heated; with apartments, this may be from a communal boiler where the rent includes your heating costs. Most modern apartment blocks have a communal laundry room with coin-operated washing and drying machines. Apartments and houses in modern urban developments usually have their own washing machines and dryers. Luxury apartment developments may have swimming pools, Jacuzzis, hot tubs, saunas, heated spas, racquetball and tennis courts, and a fully-equipped health club or fitness centre, all of which are 'free' to tenants (the landlord pays for them in his annual condo fees). Cable TV and the internet may be included in the rent.

Single people, particularly the young and students, may find it difficult to secure affordable accommodation. Studio, bachelor and efficiency apartments are all fancy names for a one-room apartment in which you live, sleep and eat, with a separate kitchen and tiny bathroom. Single people can save money by sharing accommodation. This is common in all areas and costs between around $300 and $500 per month in a city. Advertisements ('room to share') for roommates are found in most newspapers, in free 'singles' newspapers and magazines, and on notice boards, e.g. at universities. It's also possible to rent furniture (a student package starts at around $50 per month).

There are numerous property rental websites in Canada, including 🖳 www.canadahomeguide.ca, www.canadarentals.net, www.canadianresidentialrentals.com, www.gscrentals.com, www.rentbc.com (includes 'dedicated' websites for other provinces – scroll down the page) and www.rentalproperties.ca.

If you're a tenant, landlord or property manager, the Canada Mortgage and Housing Corporation (CMHC, 🖳 www.cmhc-schl.gc.ca/en/co/reho) provides information about tenant and landlord rights, responsibilities and rental practices across the country. For information about your legal rights and obligations regarding renting in each province and territory, see 🖳 www.cmhc-schl.gc.ca/en/co/reho/yogureho/fash/index.cfm.

Rental Costs

Rental costs vary considerably, depending on the size, number of bedrooms, the quality of a property and its furnishings (if applicable), its age and the facilities provided. Most importantly, rents depend on the neighbourhood and the region of Canada. The rent for similar properties in different parts of the country can vary by as much as 1,000 per cent! As a rule, the further a property is from a large city or town, public transport or other facilities, the less expensive it is. Average rental costs for unfurnished apartments and houses range from $450 per month for a bachelor studio, $550 to $700 for a one- to two-bedroom apartment, $650 to $950 for a two- to three-bedroom townhouse and $850 to $1,600 for a three- to four-bedroom detached house, with an overall average of around $650 per month.

Leases are usually for a fixed period of 12 months, so unless you're sure that you want to stay that long, it's better to remain in temporary accommodation until you've found a place you really like. Many immigrants commit themselves to a year's rental and then regret it when they find a property they want to buy, feeling they've wasted what could have been part of the deposit on a home. Bear in mind that if you want to be able to leave at short notice, you should sign an agreement that allows you to give 30 days' notice; otherwise, you must find someone to sub-let from you (if it's permitted). Leases can always be broken for a fee. Furnished rentals range from $1,200 per month for a small apartment, $1,600 for a two-bedroom apartment with a full kitchen, $1,800 for a two- to three-bedroom townhouse and in excess of $2,000 for a detached family home. In metropolitan areas such as Toronto and Vancouver and even their outer suburbs, you can expect to pay $3,000 or more per month just for an apartment.

It's possible to find less expensive, older apartments and houses for rent, but these are generally small and don't offer the conveniences of a new property. You can also find 'heritage' houses and apartment buildings which are old, restored properties, although these are much sought after and therefore more expensive than modern homes. If you like a property but think the rent is too high, you should try to negotiate a reduction or ask the agent to put your offer to the owner. Check the cost of extras such as maintenance, which may include grass-cutting, window-washing, leaf-removal and snow-removal (if a house has a sidewalk, you're normally responsible for clearing it of snow). Sometimes rents may include heating, air-conditioning, gas cooking and hot water, but not electricity.

The laws concerning rental accommodation vary from province to province and even from city to city. To check your rights, contact the non-criminal division of the local legal aid society, which may be able to put you in touch with a tenants' rights coalition or association in your area. There are also a number of books available, including *Landlord/Tenant Rights in British Columbia* by David Lane & Roneen Marcoux, the *Rental Form Kit for BC* and *Landlord/Tenant Rights in Ontario* by Ron McInnes (published by Self-Counsel Press).

MOVING HOUSE

If you're moving to Canada from abroad, it usually takes from four to eight weeks to have your personal effects shipped, depending on the distance and route. It's advisable to obtain at least three written quotations and (if possible) some recommendations before committing yourself. Moving companies (or movers) usually send a representative to carry out a detailed estimate. Most international companies charge by the cubic foot or metre, while local companies may charge by the number of boxes and their weight. Most pack your belongings and provide packing cases and special containers, although this is naturally more expensive than packing them yourself. Ask how they pack fragile and valuable items, and whether the costs of packing cases, materials and insurance (see below) are included in the quotation. If you're packing yourself, most shipping companies will provide packing crates and boxes.

Whenever possible, it's best to have your own container rather than share one. There are enough potential hazards (one immigrant's most sentimental possessions were smashed when a car was put into the container on top of their box) without adding the unpacking and re-packing of the container, as each family's possessions are loaded and unloaded.

For international moves, it's best to use a shipping company that's a member of a professional association such as the International Federation of Furniture Removers (FIDI), the Overseas Moving Network International (OMNI) or the Association of International Removers Ltd. Members usually subscribe to an advance payment scheme that provides a guarantee. When a member company fails to fulfil its commitments to a customer, the contract is completed at the agreed cost by another company or your money is refunded. Make a complete list of everything to be shipped and give a copy to the shipping company. Don't include anything illegal (e.g. guns, bombs, drugs or pornographic material) with your belongings as customs checks can be rigorous and penalties severe. Give your shipping company a phone number and an address in Canada (plus email, if applicable) through which you can be contacted.

Caution

You should fully insure your belongings with a well-established insurance company during shipment or while in storage – warehouses have been known to burn down!

Around 50 per cent of all moves result in some damage to possessions (water damage is common during international moves). Don't use the moving company's insurance policy because this may limit their liability to a paltry sum. It's advisable to make a photographic or video record for insurance purposes of any valuables shipped.

If your stay in Canada is for a limited period only, it may be wise to leave your most valued possessions at home (e.g. with relatives or friends), particularly if their insured value wouldn't provide adequate compensation for their loss. If you bring them, you should pack them in your personal baggage or ship them by air. If there are any breakages or damaged items, these must be noted and listed before you sign the delivery bill. If you need to make a claim, be sure to read the small print because claims must often be made within a limited period, sometimes within a few days. Always send claims by registered post.

For house moves within Canada you can rent a van or lorry (truck) by the hour, half-day or day (see 💻 www.uhaul.com). Many transport companies also sell packing boxes in various sizes, and rent or sell removal equipment (trolleys, straps, etc.) for those who feel up to doing their own move. See also the checklists in **Chapter 20** and **Customs** on page 329.

What to Take With You?

If you're staying in Canada for a prolonged period or plan to become a permanent resident, you need to decide what personal and household items to take and how to ship them. What you actually take is obviously a personal decision, but in many cases it's better to store, give away or sell bulky items in your home country, and buy replacements when you arrive in Canada. For example:

- Clothing. If you come from a warm or hot country, bear in mind that Canada has long, very cold winters (except in Vancouver, where it's mild but wet). While you need some summer clothes, taking too many may mean that most languish in a wardrobe for nine months of the year, so there's little point in paying to ship them.
- TVs and videos made for any country other than Canada and the US won't work in Canada because the transmission standards are different (see **Chapter 8**).
- Electrical items that operate on a 220-240V system, rather than Canada's 110V system (see below).
- Furniture can easily be replaced in Canada, either new or second-hand. Take into account the cost of shipping and insurance (and possibly storage while you look for somewhere to live) versus the cost of replacement.
- Beds and bedding. Bed sizes are different in Canada from those in Europe and many other countries. When your bed linen needs replacing, you won't be able to replace it locally and may need to buy new beds; therefore you may as well do it at the start and save the cost of shipping them.

- Cars and other motor vehicles. Canadian safety and exhaust emission standards are high and you must bring any imported vehicles up to these standards before you can use them on Canadian roads. If you're coming from the UK or another country where you drive on the left, your vehicles won't be suitable for Canada where they drive on the right.

In the end it comes down to whether you can bear to be without certain possessions, and the cost of buying replacements in Canada compared with the cost of shipping and storing them (possibly less than you can gain by selling them before you go). Bear in mind that the bulk of your effects may not arrive until several weeks after you do, and then may be held in storage for customs checks; therefore you should ensure that the things you need to live for the first few weeks or months are sent by air (including your children's favourite toys).

KEYS & SECURITY

When moving into a new home, particularly in a burglary-prone urban area, it's often wise to replace the locks (or lock barrels) as soon as possible and fit high security (double cylinder or deadbolt) locks, because there could be many keys in circulation for the existing locks. However, if you're renting, you need to obtain the permission of the owner or landlord, who may forbid it (he'll certainly want a key). If you own your home, you may wish to have an alarm system fitted, as it's usually the best way to deter thieves and may also reduce your homeowner's insurance premium.

Most outside doors, particularly apartment doors in major cities, are fitted with a peephole and chains so that you can check the identity of a visitor before opening the door. Inside doors often have locks that are operated by pressing and/or twisting a button on the centre of the doorknob or by pushing or twisting the knob itself (these locks should be replaced if found on outside doors because they aren't secure). All external doors should be lockable from the inside as well as the outside.

No matter how secure your door and window locks, a thief can usually obtain entry if he's determined enough, often by simply smashing a window (although you can fit external steel security blinds). You can, however, deter thieves by ensuring that your house is well lit, even (or particularly) when no one is at home, when it's wise to leave a TV or radio on (a timer switch can be used to switch radios, TVs and lights on and off randomly). Most security companies provide home security systems connected to a central monitoring station. When a sensor, e.g. smoke or forced entry, detects an emergency or a panic button is pushed, a signal is sent to a 24-hour monitoring station. Remember, prevention is better than cure because those who are burgled rarely recover their belongings. Police recommend that you display alarm/security company stickers even if you have no alarm.

If you lock yourself out of your apartment (or car), there may be a local locksmith on emergency call, day and night; although if it's past midnight, it may be more economical to break a window to gain entry to your home (but difficult if you live on the 39th floor!). If you vacate a rented house or apartment for an extended period, it may be obligatory to notify your building superintendent, agent or insurance company, and to leave a key with the superintendent or agent in case of emergencies. Fire prevention is also an important aspect of home security, and it's sensible to install smoke detectors in all rooms and keep a fire extinguisher handy (these should be provided by your landlord if you're renting).

UTILITIES

Electricity, gas and water companies in Canada are called 'utility' companies, and are owned by private companies, local municipalities or the provincial government (there are also co-operatives in some rural areas). Canada produces around 15 per cent of its electricity from nuclear power plants in Ontario, Quebec and New Brunswick. Utility companies are monopolies, therefore provincial governments have established public utility or public service commissions (PUCs or PSCs) to set rates and regulate their operation in accordance with provincial law. In some regions you may be billed for electricity and gas (and/or water) by the same utility company on one bill, although each utility is itemised separately.

If you're renting a property, your water may be included in your rent. You should apply in person to utility companies to have your electricity, gas or water service switched on (take proof of ownership or a lease, plus a photo ID, such as a driver's licence, and a bill addressed to you at the address). A security deposit is necessary if you're a new customer, which is equal to an average monthly bill (based on the previous owner's/tenant's usage). A deposit may be returned (without interest) when you've been billed for a number of consecutive billing cycles, e.g. eight, or have paid most bills before the penalty due date in the past year or so. When moving into a property, there's a 'start-up' fee (usually $25) to switch on the service and read the meter, which is included in your first bill. You must contact your electricity, gas and water companies (usually at least 48 hours in advance) to get a final meter reading and bill when vacating a property.

Electricity and gas meters are read and customers billed monthly in most areas, although in some areas bills may be sent out every two or three months; the number of billing days is shown on the bill. If the meter reader is unable to read your meter, you'll receive an estimated bill, which is usually annotated with 'EST', 'Avg' or 'A'. A utility company may send a revised bill based on a meter reading provided by the householder. You're given 30 days to pay a bill before it becomes overdue. If you miss paying a bill (or your payment arrives after the due date), it's added to your next bill and you may be charged a late payment penalty, e.g. 5 per cent of the outstanding amount. If you don't pay a utility bill, you eventually receive a 'notice of discontinuation of service', when you should pay the bill within the period specified, e.g. 15 days, even if you dispute the amount. Utility companies offer an 'equal payment plan', where your annual energy costs are spread evenly throughout the year. This helps to manage the high heating costs in winter.

Most utility companies publish a number of useful booklets explaining how to conserve energy, e.g. through improved insulation, and reduce your bills. Most utility companies perform a free home energy conservation survey, and private companies will conduct a more in-depth audit (most utilities also offer rebates and financing for the purchase of new energy-efficient appliances). Some provinces have proposed deregulation of electricity supplies, which has led to a scam where people calling themselves 'energy brokers' or 'energy aggregators' approach residents and offer future discounts for signing up with them. Contracts appoint the broker as the agent in purchasing electricity at unspecified prices for a period (e.g. five years or longer), which isn't recommended.

Most provinces have 'utility consumer advocates' who are public officials and who handle consumer problems concerning utilities. To find out whether your province has one, contact the Consumers Council of Canada (1910 Yonge Street, 4th Floor, Toronto, ON M4S 1Z5, ☏ 416-483 2696, 💻 www.consumerscouncil.com).

Electricity

The electricity supply in Canada is 110/120 volts AC, with a frequency of 60 hertz (cycles). Every resident, whether in an apartment or a house, has an electricity meter. This is located either in the basement of an apartment block or outside a house, where it can be read when you aren't at home. When you buy a new property, there's a 'new meter charge' (connection fee) of around $10. In many areas, electricity is charged at peak and slack period (off-peak) rates at different times of the day and different seasons (usually summer and winter).

> Electricity costs vary with the area, e.g. from 3¢ to 8¢ per kilowatt-hour (KWH or KWHR). There's also a bimonthly 'demand charge' (service fee) of around $10.

It's possible to operate electrical equipment rated at 240 volts AC with a converter or a step-up transformer to convert it to 110 volts AC, although generally it isn't worth bringing electrical appliances to Canada that aren't rated at 110 volts AC. Some electrical appliances (e.g. electric razors and hair dryers) are dual-voltage and are fitted with a 110/240 volt switch. Check for the switch, which may be inside the casing, and make sure it's switched to 110 volts before connecting it to the power supply. Most newcomers buy new electrical appliances in Canada, which are of good quality and reasonably priced. Shop around before buying expensive appliances as prices vary considerably (also check the comparison tests in consumer magazines).

An additional problem with some electrical equipment that isn't made for the North American market is that the frequency rating is designed to run at 50 hertz (Hz) and not Canada's 60Hz. Electrical equipment without a motor is generally unaffected by the increase in frequency to 60Hz (except TVs). Some equipment with a synchronous motor may run okay with a 20 per cent increase in speed; however, automatic washing machines, ranges, electric clocks, record players and reel-to-reel tape recorders are unusable in Canada unless they're designed for 60Hz operation. To find out, look at the label on the back of the equipment; if it says 50/60Hz, it should be okay. If it says 50Hz, you might try it anyway, but first ensure that the voltage is correct as outlined above. If the equipment runs too slowly, seek advice from the manufacturer or the retailer.

The standard Canadian mains plug has two flat pins (live and neutral) plus an optional third pin (earth). It's possible to buy adapters for many foreign plugs, but it's more economical to change plugs. All appliances sold in Canada are fitted with a moulded two-pin plug that runs off any outlet in the country. Some electrical appliances are earthed, which means they have a three-core wire and are fitted with a three-pin plug. If you need to fit a plug, the colour coding is usually white (neutral), black (live) and green (earth).

Caution

Always make sure that a plug is correctly and securely wired because bad wiring can prove fatal. Never fit a two-pin plug to a three-core flex.

In some Canadian homes, there are no switches on wall sockets. Electrical appliances should be fitted with their own on/off switches. Light switches operate in the opposite way to some other countries, where the UP position is ON and the DOWN position is OFF (some switches may operate from left to right). The ON position may be indicated by a red spot on the switch. Standard and other lamps often have two or three-way bulbs that provide two or three levels of brightness (e.g. bright, medium and dim). Often lamp switches (or knobs) must be turned in a clockwise direction or pushed and pulled. Electric light bulbs have a standard size screw fitting for all lamps and sockets, which may be different from other countries. Bulbs for older appliances or foreign appliances (e.g. sewing machines) may not be available in Canada, so you should bring a few spares with you.

Most Canadian apartments and all houses have their own fuse boxes. If a fuse blows, first turn off the mains switch. This may be on the consumer unit or on a separate switch box nearby. Fuses in modern homes and homes with modern wiring are usually of the circuit breaker type; when a circuit is overloaded, it trips to the OFF position. Switch off the main switch and open the circuit breaker box. After locating and remedying the cause of the failure (if possible), just switch the circuit breaker to the ON position. Close the circuit breaker box and switch on the main switch. Most electricity companies will service your major electrical appliances, e.g. heating or air-conditioning systems, and some provide service contracts.

If you have a suitable roof for solar panels or live away from the centre of a town and have room for a wind generator or have a nearby stream, you may be able to generate some of your own electricity. These are intended as supplementary systems as they don't generate sufficient power to run the heavy-duty appliances installed in most modern homes. They can, however, provide back-up systems in times of power outages and will reduce your electricity bills.

Gas

Gas (usually natural) is available in most Canadian cities. The same company may supply you with gas and electricity, when you receive one bill for both, with gas and electricity costs itemised separately. Gas is available in all but the remotest areas of Canada, although most modern houses are all-electric and aren't connected to the gas supply. When you buy a new property, there's a 'new meter charge' (connection fee) of around $25. Outside cities and in remote areas, gas may be supplied in bottles. Gas is usually billed by the gigajoule and usually costs $5 to $7 per gigajoule. If you rent an apartment, your gas consumption may be included in your rent.

Gas leaks are extremely rare and explosions caused by leaks even rarer (although often devastating and therefore widely reported). You can install a carbon dioxide gas detector that activates an alarm when a gas leak is detected.

Water

In many areas, you don't receive a water bill as the cost is included in local property taxes; while in others there's a charge, and each building or apartment has its own water meter, where you're billed each month or quarter for the water you use. Bills may include a meter charge, e.g. $10 per month. Water rates are 30¢ to 60¢ per cubic metre and typical monthly

water bills are $25 per month for a one-bedroom apartment, $70 for a 2,000ft² (186m²) house and around $225 for a four-bedroom, four-bathroom house with a hot tub.

Some provinces occasionally have restrictions on the use of water during the summer months, e.g. for swimming pools, washing motor vehicles or watering gardens, when there may be bans between sunrise and sunset. Canadians usually drink water straight from their house supply, although some people find the taste of purifying chemicals (e.g. chlorine) unpleasant, and prefer to drink bottled water. Householders in many areas fit filters to cold-water taps used to provide water for drinking or cooking. It's generally safe to drink water from rivers, lakes, wells and streams in rural and country areas, but not in the high country, where water may carry giardiasis, known as beaver fever or backpackers' diarrhoea.

Canadian taps can be complicated for the uninitiated and may be fitted with a variety of strange controls, e.g. one common design is operated by a handle that works on a universal joint arrangement, where an up-and-down movement controls the flow and a left-to-right movement the temperature; in Canada the left tap is generally for hot water. When there are separate hot and cold water taps in a shower, both taps may turn in the same direction or in opposite directions; check them before scalding or freezing yourself. Where a shower and bath are combined, a lever or knob is commonly used to convert the flow from bath to shower and vice versa. Most Canadian baths and washbasins have a single mixer spout. Sometimes taps must be pulled or pushed rather than turned, and a lever may also control the plug.

Before moving into a new home in Canada, you should inquire where the main stop-valve or stopcock is, so that you can turn off the water supply in an emergency. If the water stops flowing for any reason, you should ensure that all taps are closed to prevent flooding from an open tap when the supply starts again.

Good insulation (for walls, roof and water pipes) is essential in Canada. You can use electrical heat tracing wire to warm pipes in winter and can also fit a freeze alarm (costing less than $100), which will call a user-selected phone number when the inside temperature drops below 45°F (7°C). In winter, it's advisable to leave the central heating on a low setting (e.g. 55°F/13°C) when you're absent from home, and leave a tap (faucet) on an outside wall dripping a little to avoid freezing. If a pipe freezes or bursts you must shut off the water immediately. When you're away, it's also advisable to have a friend or neighbour check your home regularly to ensure that the heating is working and that the pipes haven't frozen.

HEATING & AIR-CONDITIONING

In most of Canada, winters are very cold and central heating is essential. However, it can also get very hot in summer, so all modern office buildings and about a third of private homes have air-conditioning. Around half of Canadian homes are heated by piped natural gas and another third by electricity. The rest have oil storage tanks or wood stoves (mostly in rural areas where there are no utility lines). Heating bills vary depending on your usage and the size of your home, but you can expect to pay at least $200 per month in winter. Modern homes often have a combined heating and cooling (air-conditioning) system that's thermostatically controlled. Many homes are fitted with ceiling fans, particularly in bedrooms. When using air-conditioning, all windows and outside doors should obviously be closed. You may find that some air-conditioners are noisy and you need to switch them off at night to get to sleep. Air-conditioners can be rented during the hottest months of the year.

If you live in an apartment block, heating is centrally controlled and is turned on in the autumn and off in the spring. Apartment buildings in some cities must, by law, be heated to specified minimum temperatures during the coldest months. If you live in an apartment in a building with a centrally controlled heating system, you may have no control over room temperatures, apart from turning individual radiators on or off, although most radiators are fitted with a gauge with low, medium and high settings. In some apartment buildings, the cost of heating and air-conditioning is included in your rent. If you're required to pay for heating/cooling separately, check the average monthly cost.

Central heating dries the air and may cause your family to develop coughs and other ailments. Those who find the dry air unpleasant can increase the indoor relative humidity by adding moisture to the air with a humidifier, vaporiser, steam generator or even a water container made of porous ceramic. Humidifiers that don't generate steam should be disinfected occasionally.

5¢
CANADA
POSTES-POSTAGE
BRITISH COLUMBIA 1858-1958 COLOMBIE-BRITANNIQUE
POSTES
CANADA
POSTAGE
WHOOPING CRANE
GRUE BLANCHE
5¢
1955

6. POSTAL SERVICES

Canada Post is a Crown corporation operating some 7,000 post offices and postal outlets and delivering mail to over 13mn addresses. Post offices and post boxes in Canada are denoted by a red sign bearing the words 'CANADA POST – ***POSTE CANADA*****' and the logo of a white wing motif on a red background. Around 20 per cent of post offices are operated by Canada Post, while the rest are run by private individuals (called postal outlets) from businesses such as convenience shops, gift shops, pharmacies, and university book and stationery shops. Many post offices also offer fax, electronic mail and telegram services. In Canada, letters and parcels are called mail (post), which is mailed (posted) in a mailbox (which also refers to the box outside a home where letters are deposited), and delivered by a mail carrier (postperson).**

The Canadian postal service is reliable, but neither cheap nor fast. Canada Post's delivery standards for letter post are one to three days for local letters, three days within a province and four days between provinces. Unless you pay for special services, next day delivery is rare (even within a city) and it isn't uncommon for ordinary letters to take five or six business days to get from a rural collection point to their destination. Canada Post says this is because post has to go to a main sorting office and they don't seem to think it odd that US Mail, which covers the same vast distances, manages to deliver 75 per cent of 'over 600 miles' (965km) post within its target of three days. Delivery between major cities is generally faster than to small towns and a letter travelling between major cities (e.g. Toronto and Vancouver) is usually delivered faster than a letter posted to a small town in a neighbouring province – but don't bank on it! Not surprisingly, fax and electronic mail (e-mail) are popular in Canada.

The post office operates a domestic guaranteed express post service (priority courier), as do private companies such as DHL, Emery World-wide, Federal Express, Greyhound Courier Express, Loomis, Purolator and UPS (who also provide express international parcel services). Companies guarantee next-day delivery for domestic express items sent before a certain time of day and provide a money-back guarantee if the promised delivery times aren't met. Pick-up services are provided by the post office and private companies.

As in the US, there are several nationwide companies such as Mail Boxes, Etc. offering most postal services except letter delivery. Services include a post box service, post-hold, post forwarding, stamps, envelopes, postcards, packing supplies, air shipping/receiving, postal metering, postal money orders, telegrams, cablegrams, fax, copy service and other business services.

If you have a complaint about any aspect of the postal service or post fraud, you should contact your local post office or postal outlet and complete a complaints form. If you don't receive satisfaction, you should contact Canada Post's Customer Service (☎ 1-866-607 6301) and if that fails, the Office of the Ombudsman (PO Box 90026, Ottawa, ON K1V 1J8, ☎ 1-800-044 198).

Information about Canada Post's services is provided in a range of leaflets available from post offices, particularly the *Canada Postal Guide*, which can be ordered via ☎ 1-800-565 4362 or 1-866-607 6301, or online 💻 www.canadapost.ca. For information about telegrams and fax, see page 129 .

BUSINESS HOURS

Post office hours in Canada are usually from 10am to 5pm, Mondays to Fridays and main post offices in major towns don't close at lunch times. In rural areas and small towns, post offices may have restricted and varied business hours, and may open any time between 8 and 9.30am until between 2 and 5pm Mondays to Fridays, or may open for a few hours each morning only and perhaps a few hours on Saturdays and Sundays, e.g. when located in a retail outlet that's open. Some central post offices in large cities provide self-service facilities 24/7, where you'll find stamp and change machines, scales, tables of postage rates and post boxes large enough to accept parcels. All post offices are closed on Sundays and national holidays. It's wise to avoid post offices at lunch times and after 4pm when offices send their mail.

On 30th April, the last day on which Canadians can file their tax returns, main post offices remain open until midnight to date stamp tax returns (if you owe tax and are a day late filing, you're charged interest!). Post offices should be avoided at all costs during the week leading up to this date! (Although this practice is changing as these days many people now file their income tax returns online.)

LETTERS

Canada Post provides just one class of letter post, but there are two sets of rates: one for standard letters and one for non-standard and oversize letters.

Standard Letters

Maximum dimensions are 245mm x 156mm x 5mm (postcards 235mm x 120mm), with a maximum weight of 50g. Rates are:

Weight	Canada	US	Other countries
Up to 30g	$0.54	$0.98	$1.65
30 to 50g	$0.98	$1.18	$2.36

mail boxes

Non-standard Letter Post

Maximum dimensions are 380mm x 270mm x 20mm, with a maximum weight of 500g. Rates are:

Weight	Canada	US	Other countries
Up to 100g	$1.18	$1.96	$3.90
100 to 200g	$1.96	$3.40	$6.80
200 to 500g	$2.75	$6.80	$13.60

PARCELS

Canada Post's parcel rates vary widely depending on three principal factors: first, their size and weight; second, their destination and the originating post office; and third, the desired speed of delivery.

Parcels are divided into two main categories, 'light' and 'heavy', and three sub-categories, 'small', 'medium' and (you've guessed it) 'large', according to their weight and size. The maximum weight of parcels to most countries is 30kg, although it's only 10kg or 14kg to some. The services provided are summarised below.

All parcels must be securely wrapped. Postal outlets sell a variety of packaging products, including tape, envelopes, padded envelopes, boxes, tubes, wrapping paper and cushioning material.

Private parcel delivery services are operated by companies such as Federal Express, Loomis, Purolator and United Parcel Service (UPS). These companies provide a next-day air parcel service within Canada, and international document and parcel services to hundreds of countries and territories worldwide. Parcels can also be sent via postal, business and communication services, which have offices nationwide.

There are too many possible parcel rates to list here, but to obtain a price for a particular parcel you can use the 'Find a Rate' tool on the Canada Post website (💻 www.canadapost.ca).

Domestic Parcels

Three services are available (slowest to fastest):

- **Regular:** for delivery in 'as little as two days' (i.e. two days or more!), with free delivery confirmation if paid for online;
- **Xpresspost:** for guaranteed delivery the next day or the day after (depending on the origin and destination), with delivery confirmation and insurance for up to $100;
- **Priority:** for guaranteed next-morning delivery, with delivery confirmation and insurance for up to $100.

US Parcels

Six services are available (slowest to fastest):

- **Small Packet USA Surface:** for delivery of items weighing less than 1kg in six days or more with insurance for up to $100;
- **Expedited Parcel USA:** for delivery in six days or more, with delivery confirmation and insurance for up to $100;
- **Small Packet USA Air:** for delivery of items weighing less than 1kg in four days or more with insurance for up to $100;
- **Light Packet USA:** for delivery of items weighing less than 500g in four days or more (depending on the origin and destination);
- **Xpresspost USA:** for guaranteed delivery in three to five days (depending on the origin and destination), with delivery confirmation and insurance for up to $100;
- **Priority Worldwide:** for guaranteed delivery by noon the next business day, with delivery confirmation and insurance of up to $100.

Worldwide Parcel Services

Seven services are available to destinations other than Canada and the US (slowest to fastest):

- **International Parcel Surface:** for delivery in four to six weeks, with insurance for up to $100;
- **Small Packet International Surface:** for delivery of items weighing less than 2kg in four to six weeks with insurance of up to $100;
- **International Parcel Air:** for delivery in six days or more with insurance for up to $100;

- **Small Packet International Air:** for delivery of items weighing less than 2kg in six days or more with insurance of up to $100;
- **Light Parcel International:** for delivery of items weighing less than 500g in four days or more;
- **Xpresspost International:** for guaranteed delivery in four days or more, with delivery confirmation and insurance of up to $100;
- **Priority Worldwide:** for guaranteed delivery in two or three days, with delivery confirmation and insurance of up to $100.

Customs Declaration

Parcels sent to addresses outside Canada must be accompanied by a customs declaration form. Requirements in most countries are met by using an adhesive form C1, which is a combined customs and dispatch note. If the item being sent is of 'no commercial value' (NCV), you should write this on the customs form under 'value'. Forms are available from post offices.

GENERAL INFORMATION

Note the following when sending letters and parcels in Canada:

- You should affix airmail labels (available free from post offices) to all international airmail. Alternatively you can write or stamp '*PAR AVION* – BY AIRMAIL' in the top left corner.
- You can collect post from any post office in Canada through General Delivery (called *Poste Restante* in most other countries). Post should be addressed as follows: Name, c/o General Delivery, town, province and postal code (if known). General delivery post is kept at a town's main post office (if there's more than one) and is returned to the sender if it's unclaimed after 14 days. Therefore when sending post via general delivery always put a return address on the envelope. Identification is necessary for collection and some post offices ask for two forms of identification, e.g. passport, social insurance card, driver's licence or a credit card.

- If you have post sent to you at a temporary private address in Canada, you should have it addressed c/o the regular occupants. Otherwise the postman may return it to the sender (he *knows* you don't live there). If a letter cannot be delivered, it's returned stamped 'return to sender', 'not deliverable as addressed', 'moved not forwardable' or something similar. All post sent in Canada should have a return address in case it cannot be delivered (you can have a name and address stamp made).
- Post boxes are red, with white lettering and look like waste bins on grey legs. Most post boxes have a flap with a handle (which may be invisible from the top of the box) that you pull back to open the slot where post is deposited. There are also post boxes at railway stations, airports and in hotel lobbies. These are often simply a slot in a wall marked 'CANADA POST'. Post is also collected from private homes, post offices and businesses.

  In some suburbs and rural areas there may be no post boxes because post is collected by the postman when he does his rounds. In some areas, particularly where there are large houses with long driveways, houses have delivery/collection boxes situated at the end of the drive. These have a small flag (a metal arm) that's raised to indicate to the postman that there's post to be collected. In apartment blocks there are usually rows of post boxes in the foyer or entrance hall.

  In the suburbs there's one delivery/collection a day only, while in city centres there may be a number of collections per day, with the last at around 6pm or earlier at weekends. In most rural areas there's one delivery per day, either in the morning or mid-afternoon, excluding Sundays and holidays. In some remote rural areas there's no post delivery service and all post must be collected from local postal outlets. In new suburban subdivisions there may be no door-to-door post delivery service. Instead there's what's called a 'superbox' (although there's nothing 'super' about it) at the end of the street with individual locked boxes to which all post is delivered.

In most areas (over 4,600 locations) you can rent a postal box (PO box), which is a locked compartment in a post office or postal outlet. Postal boxes come in various sizes, from small to XX-large, with rents from around $125 to $650 per year.

- When you receive post from overseas on which duty is payable, the duty may be collected by the postal service, along with customs clearance and delivery fees on dutiable items. For packages containing dutiable articles, the customs officer will attach a Customs Invoice (E14) showing the rate of duty and the amount to be paid.
- Most post in Canada is sorted by machine, which is expedited by the use of full and correct postal addresses and codes. Each character of the postal code has its own significance. The first three characters of the postal code (known as the forward sortation area/FSA) identify a particular geographical area. The first character (always a letter) designates a province or a territory within a province. The second character (always a number) denotes whether the post is to go to an urban or rural location. The third character of the code (always a letter) further defines the destination, e.g. in an urban code it identifies a postal station or city post office, and in a rural code a group of post offices in a geographic area. The last three characters of the code (known as the local delivery unit/LDU) help to direct post to a specific location such as a city block, a large business, an office building or a community in a rural destination. The postal code follows the province name or initials (and doesn't precede it as in many other countries), as shown in the example below:

René le Phew
9753 Gold Rush Avenue, Apt 999
Noname City, YT T7F 6R4
Canada

Addresses in rural areas may be of a different sort, either a post office box address, where people have their own locked box in the lobby of a post office, or a 'rural route' address such as RR#3, S45 C67. These consist of a number of locked boxes at the side of the road, where the RR number refers to a route taken by the postman, the S refers to the site of the block of boxes and the C refers to the individual box (compartment) belonging to an individual. Delivering to boxes reduces the travelling done by postmen, but not by those to whom the post is addressed!

If you don't know your postal code or want to find someone else's, you can consult the *Postal Code Directory*, available at all main post offices or you can obtain a copy from the National Philatelic Centre, Canada Post (75 St Ninian Street, Antigonish, NS B2G 2R8, ☏ 1-800-565 4362). You can also find postal codes on the Canada Post website (💻 www.canadapost.ca).

When postal codes were established, the following two-letter province and territory abbreviations were also introduced and are the beginning of the code:

Postal Abbreviations

Province/Territory	Abbreviation
Alberta	AB
British Columbia	BC
Manitoba	MB
New Brunswick	NB
Newfoundland and Labrador	NL
Northwest Territories	NT
Nova Scotia	NS
Nunavut	NU
Ontario	ON
Prince Edward Island	PE
Quebec	QC
Saskatchewan	SK
The Yukon Territory	YT

- Stamps can be purchased in books of 10, 25 and 50, or in rolls of 100 from vending machines located in or outside post offices, airports, bus and railway stations, drugstores, banks, newsstands and hotels. Many post offices have self-service machines where stamps, stamp booklets, express post stamps, postcards, stamped envelopes and stamp pins are available, some of which may accept up to $20 bills. Stamp machines accept ATM 'cash' cards.

- If you send an item of post with insufficient postage it's returned to you for the collection of postage. When there's no return address on the item (which is written in the front top left corner in Canada) it's forwarded to the addressee for the collection of postage due plus an administrative charge (called a 'deficient postage fee').
- Domestic money orders can be purchased from post offices for any value from 1¢ to $999.99 for a flat fee of $4.95. International money orders can also be purchased in Canadian dollars, US dollars and British pounds, but although the maximum value in dollars is $999.99, as for domestic orders, the maximum in sterling is a mere £100. Costs vary according to the destination, e.g. $4.95 to the US, $5.50 to the UK and $6 to other foreign destinations. To find out if a postal Money Order has been cashed, or for enquires regarding a lost or destroyed postal Money Order, call 1-800-563-0444.
- Another way of sending money securely is by 'MoneyGram', which is available from over 1,100 post offices in Canada to some 152,000 destinations in more than 180 countries.
- Literature for the blind weighing up to 7kg (15.4lbs) can be sent free within Canada, to the US and to other international destinations. You must write 'Literature for the Blind' where the stamp is normally affixed (in the top right-hand corner on the front of the envelope or parcel).

Like many countries, Canada Post provides services for philatelists. Post offices sell first-day covers, stamp collecting kits, and sets of commemorative and special stamps. Canada Post also publishes *The Postal Service Guide to Canadian Stamps*. For information, contact the National Philatelic Centre (Canada Post, 75 St. Ninian Street, Antigonish NS, B2G 2R8, ☎ 1-800-565 4362 or 1-902-863 6550, 💻 www.canadapost.ca).

Canada Post (a post office with a heart!) volunteers reply to letters addressed to Santa Claus, although they're unlikely to send you a Ferrari. The address is Santa Claus, North Pole, Hoh Oho, Canada.

> Canada Post offers a fee **epost** service, which allows you to view, pay and manage your bills online. For information, see 💻 www.epost.ca/main/en/more_about_epost.shtml.

VALUABLES & IMPORTANT DOCUMENTS

Canada Post provides a number of services for the delivery of valuables, and important documents and letters:

- **Registered Post** – If you need verification that an item has been received or require proof of posting, domestic post can be registered, which is often used to send legal documents, financial statements and important letters. Proof of posting, delivery confirmation (an official stamped receipt is provided at the time of posting) and information on the delivery status of the item are available by calling a toll-free number. Registered post costs $7.50 plus postage and includes indemnity against loss up to $100.
- **Security Registered Post** – If you need additional security or insurance you can use security registered post, which is available for domestic post, US post, international letters and parcels, and literature for the blind. This service provides proof of posting and delivery confirmation (the addressee's signature is obtained on delivery and may be returned to the customer with an acknowledgement of receipt card if this option is chosen). Additional security is provided by special handling and insurance of up to $5,000 in Canada (costing $1.05 per $100 insurance), plus a toll-free number (☎ 1-888-550 6333) to check the delivery status (which can also be done via the Canada Post website). The weight limit for domestic security registered post is 30kg and the cost is determined by the weight, size and destination of the item.
- **Insurance** – Insurance can be purchased in conjunction with COD, Priority Courier,

Xpresspost, Expedited Parcel Service, Regular Parcel Service, Registered and Delivery Confirmation. Fragile and perishable items can be insured for loss but not against damage. The insurance limit depends on the destination, e.g. $5,000 for registered post within Canada and $1,000 for surface and air parcels to the US.

- **Collect on Delivery (COD)** – COD (called 'cash on delivery' in some other countries) is a domestic service for post for which an amount is due to the sender up to $1,000. COD items can be insured for up to $1,000.
- **Advice of Receipt** – The advice of receipt (AR) service provides you with the signature of the addressee. An AR card or label is purchased at the time of posting or (in some cases) up to two years after an item has been sent. When purchased at the time of posting, the AR card or label is attached to the item. A signature is obtained from the addressee on delivery and the card is returned to the sender, thus providing delivery confirmation. When purchased after posting, the card is sent to the postmaster, superintendent or manager of the delivery office, where the addressee's signature is obtained from the AR card. Acknowledgement of receipt costs $1.50 at the time of posting. To the US and other international destinations, AR can be used only with registered post at the time of posting.

CHANGE OF ADDRESS

Before you move home you should complete a 'request for redirection of post' form available at postal outlets. You receive a free change of address kit including free postcards (as many as you want) to notify correspondents of your new address. Whenever possible, notify your post office at least one month before you move and be sure that the effective date is entered on notification forms (the change of address usually takes 10 to 14 days to become effective, but it's wise to allow longer). The service is available for a six-month period for residential and business addresses, and can be extended provided that the extension is requested before the expiry date. There's no limit to the number of times it can be extended, but the current rate must be paid each time.

Permanent redirection of post costs $39 for six months or $69 for a year if your move is within the same Canadian province, $45 or $80 if you move to another province and $110/196 if you move abroad. When the period expires, post is returned to the sender (including international post), therefore you need to remember to give all your correspondents your new address well in advance. Publishers of periodicals usually need at least six weeks' notice to effect a change of address. If you complete a change of address form, your junk post (which earns Canada Post millions of dollars a year) will automatically follow you as Canada Post sells its mailing list (including redirection of post forms) to companies.

You can also request a 'temporary redirection of post' for a fee of $36 for up to three months and $12 per month thereafter within the same province, $42 + $14 to another province or $69 + $23 to an address abroad (including the US). If you're going to be away from your home for a short period, you can use the 'Hold Mail' service. The fee is $7.50 per week for a minimum of ten business days (i.e. two weeks). Delivery is made on the 'resume service' date indicated on the card.

If you receive post that isn't addressed to you, you have two choices of what to do with it (the third is to throw it away, which is illegal!). You can send it on to the addressee by crossing out your address, writing the correct address and dropping it in a post box without a stamp. Or, if you don't know the new address, you can cross out the address and write 'address unknown' and drop it in a post box (it's returned to the sender). If you going to be away from home for an extended period, it's advisable to have your mail redirected to a relative or friend who can open it and inform you of anything of importance requiring your attention (mail can also be scanned and forwarded by email).

7. TELECOMMUNICATIONS

Canadian geography and population distribution have always required effective communication systems; with a relatively small population spread over 6,000km (3,728mi) from sea to sea, communications are one of the major threads holding Canada together. Not surprisingly, Canada has one of the world's best telephone services which utilises satellite communications, national data networks, cellular telephony, optical fibre networks, cable TV and virtually universal internet access. Since the creation of Canada's domestic satellite system, telecommunications has been at the forefront of the country's scientific and industrial policies, and it's the government's policy to make Canada the most connected country in the world.

Canadians are among the most habitual telephone users, making more calls than people in almost any other country. Almost all Canadian households have at least one fixed-line phone and most people also have a mobile phone. Since the telecommunications industry was deregulated in 1994, increased competition in the long-distance market has resulted in much lower call rates and Canada has one of the most modern and cheapest (for local and long-distance calls) telephone systems in the world.

Canadian telecommunications are regulated by the Radio-television and Telecommunications Commission (CRTC, ☎ 819-997 0313 or 1-877-249-2782, 💻 www.crtc.gc.ca).

Telephone Companies

There are over 50 telephone companies in Canada. The major companies, which offer mobile phone, internet and television services, as well as fixed telephone services, include:

- Bell Aliant (💻 www.aliant.ca) – created in 2006 and covering practically the whole country;
- Bell Canada (💻 www.bell.ca) – Canada's largest communications company, covering all the main population areas;

> Canada's Consumer Complaints Board website (💻 www.complaintsboard.com) has a page 'dedicated' to complaints against Bell Canada – for overcharging, 'awful service', and even 'scams and cheating'.

- Cogeco (💻 www.cogeco.ca) – covers Ontario and Quebec;
- MTS Allstream (💻 www.mts.mb.ca) – covers only the Winnipeg area;
- NorthwesTel (💻 www.nwtel.ca) – covers northern British Columbia, Northwest Territories, Nunavut and the Yukon;
- Rogers Telecom (💻 www.rogers.com) – covers the whole country;
- Sasktel (💻 www.sasktel.com) – covers Saskatchewan;
- Shaw Communications (💻 www.shaw.ca) – covers the whole country;
- Télébec (💻 www.telebec.com – in French) – covers Quebec only;
- Telus (💻 www.telus.com) – the second-largest operator, covering the whole of western Canada.

INSTALLATION & REGISTRATION

Homes in Canada (new and old) are invariably wired for telephone services and many homes have points (phone jacks) in almost every room, although you should check the number and type of points in advance. If you need additional wiring or points you can have it done by your phone company, a contractor or you can do it yourself. Installation of one point plus wiring should take around half an hour and cost around $50. There's a fee of around $100 for installing a line if a new property doesn't have one and a connection fee of around $50 if a property already has a line (plus the cost of any additional points). To have a phone connected, contact a local phone company (their numbers are listed in telephone directories). You usually need to provide:

- Your name, full address, social insurance number (if you have one; if not, your passport number) and your previous address;
- The type of monthly service you require, your choice of long-distance company, how you would like your directory listing to appear or whether you would like an ex-directory (unlisted) number.

Unless you're a previous customer, have a credit history with Visa or MasterCard or can prove that you own your home, you must pay a $200 deposit with your first bill, which is refunded with interest after one year, or you must find a co-signer (guarantor) with an account with the phone company who will be responsible if you abscond without paying the bill. You're given a number when you apply.

CHOOSING A TELEPHONE

All phones used in Canada must be approved by the Canadian Radio-Television and Telecommunications Commission (CRTC), which is indicated by the 'CRTC registration number' shown on a label fixed to the base or back of a phone.

Renting phones from a phone company isn't expensive (e.g. from around $5 per month), although most Canadians buy their phones (they can also be purchased from phone companies via monthly payments). The price of a phone usually depends on the quality of its construction (the most important attribute), country of origin, and, not least, its features. A standard one-piece phone (with the keys on the handset) costs around $20, while an all-singing, all-dancing, multi-function model costs from $100 to $300.

If possible, you should test phones before buying or buy from a retailer who provides a money-back guarantee. It's also wise to check the warranty period (usually one year) and its terms before making a purchase. The latest phones have a cordless infrared keyboard and allow you to store names and numbers, access telephone banking, send and receive emails, and access interactive services – in fact, you need no longer get out of bed! For reports and ratings of the various telephones (and many other products) available, visit the Consumer Reports website (💻 www.consumerreports.org).

USING THE TELEPHONE

All phone dials and push buttons in Canada are marked with letters and numbers, so you just dial the number or press the key corresponding to a letter. Using a telephone in Canada is much the same as in any other country, with a few Canadian idiosyncrasies. When you make a call you hear either a regularly repeated long buzzing tone, which indicates that the number is ringing, or a rapidly repeated series of short buzzes, which indicates that the phone is busy (in use). When you pick up the receiver you hear the dial tone or, if you have voicemail (the phone company's answering service) and have new messages, you hear a series of beeps (e.g. three) followed by a pause (repeated).

Telephone numbers consist of a three-digit area code (123), a three-digit exchange code (456) and a four-digit subscriber number (7890), usually written as 123-456 7890. An area code may cover a city, a portion of a province or an entire province. Canada uses the same code system as the US and area codes for Canada and the US are shown on maps in telephone directories. New codes are being introduced as existing numbers have been exhausted by the growth of mobile phones, fax machines, computer modems and pagers. The area codes in Canada are as follows:

Area	Code(s)
Alberta North	780
Alberta South	403
British Columbia	250
Newfoundland & Labrador	709
New Brunswick	506
Northwest Territories	867
Nova Scotia	902
Manitoba	204
Montreal	514
Nunavut	867
Ontario	519, 705, 807 & 905
Ottawa	613
Prince Edward Island	902
Quebec	418, 450 & 819
Saskatchewan	306
Toronto City	416
Vancouver	604
The Yukon Territory	867

If you're making a call to a number within your local service area, you dial the seven-digit number only (except in British Columbia and Ontario, where you have to dial ten digits). When making a call to another area code, you dial 1 + area code + the seven-digit telephone number. Local calling and service areas are shown in telephone directories.

Provinces are served by local phone companies such as Bell Canada, which are regulated by provincial and federal agencies. For long distance, e.g. inter-province and international calls, independent long-distance phone companies such as AT&T, Intel and Sprint are available. Most areas are served by several long-distance companies, although some areas have only one. Your local provincial phone company is your long-distance carrier by default and if you want to use another company, you must make arrangements with them.

All phone companies provide special services for those with disabilities including hearing and speech-impaired customers, who are exempt from certain charges. Special handsets are available for the blind (with a nodule on the figure 5) and extra large key pads for the partially sighted. Telephones fitted with a flashing light, loud ring, a built-in amplifier or an inductive coupler (for those with behind-the-ear hearing aids) are available for the hard of hearing. A number of companies and organisations provide a Telecommunications Device for the Deaf (TDD) or teletype (TTY) line. These typewriter-like devices permit hearing or speech-impaired people to communicate over phone lines. Ask your phone company about TDD services.

Most phone companies provide message-taking services (voicemail) that can be less expensive (around $3 per month) and more efficient than having your own answering machine (costing from around $50 to $125). Message features usually include timed messages, the ability to receive messages when you're on another call, and to save and erase messages selectively.

TOLL-FREE NUMBERS

Toll-free numbers are indicated by the codes 800, 888, 877 and 866, and are provided by businesses, organisations and government agencies in Canada (and the US). Many organisations and businesses list these numbers in all correspondence, advertisements and on all documentation, and they're usually listed in directories alongside ordinary numbers. Most toll-free numbers are for long-distance callers only and must be prefixed with a '1' (a local number is usually provided for local callers). Toll-free numbers can be accessed from outside North America, although calls aren't free. Sometimes toll-free numbers are given as letters to make them easier to remember, e.g. 1-888-VIA PREFER for VIA Rail.

For information about toll-free numbers, call national toll-free directory assistance (☎ 1-800-555 1212) or see 💻 www.canadatollfree.ca).

INFORMATION & ENTERTAINMENT NUMBERS

Don't confuse toll-free numbers with 900 information or entertainment numbers, which are expensive. Information numbers provide information on a wide range of subjects, including health, weather, road conditions and sports, while entertainment numbers include music lines, chat lines, competitions, horoscope or dial-a-prayer lines. These numbers are often used by fraudsters who make offers that seem too good to be true (they are!), e.g. 'guaranteed' credit or cash loans at low rates. Bear in mind that companies with these numbers often make their living entirely from the income generated by calls. The longer they can keep you on the line and the more times they can induce you to call, the more money they make. Some information provided by information and entertainment numbers is also available free via public service numbers (see page 131).

> **▲ Caution**
>
> Be wary of any advertisements that fail to disclose the cost of calls or make it difficult for you to determine the total cost.

The use of information/entertainment numbers is a multi-million dollar growth industry. Charges usually range from around $2 to $10 per minute, averaging around $5, although some lines are very expensive. Children and guests may make calls to these numbers using someone else's phone and run up thousands of dollars in bills (psychic and sex lines are among the most popular). Most phone companies offer a blocking option that allows you to block calls to 900 and other numbers from your home or office number (you can also block long-distance calls). If you have a complaint about a 900 number, you should contact the Canadian Radio-Television and Telecommunications Commission (☎ 1-877-249 2782, 💻 www.crtc.gc.ca) or write to the Secretary General (Ottawa, ON K1A 0N2).

CUSTOM & OPTIONAL SERVICES

All phone companies provide a range of extra services called custom calling or optional services, most of which require a touch-tone phone that provides faster dialling plus access to a range of computerised services. Custom calling or optional services include call answer, call waiting, three-way calling and call forwarding, which can be ordered individually or as part of a package. Services cost from around $4 a month for one service to around $10 for three. Alternatively, you can choose a package that includes the most popular custom calling services.

OPERATOR SERVICES

To speak to the operator you dial 0. All operators speak English and many also speak French (if you want a French-speaking operator you'll be connected to one). The operator provides a number of services and can help you in an emergency. If you're trying to make an urgent call and the number is continuously busy, you can ask the operator to interrupt the conversation (there's a fee, e.g. $5). When the operator is making a connection, you should ask whether you're connected rather than 'through' to your number because 'through' means finished in Canada (also a line is said to be 'busy' and not 'engaged'). Also bear in mind that to 'phone' means to 'call' in Canada.

Whenever possible you should dial direct. Operator assisted calls are expensive unless you're unable to obtain a number due to a fault. If you dial correctly and get the wrong number, report the fault (see your telephone book for the number). The faulty call should be credited to your bill or, if you're using a payphone, you should be allowed a free call. Operators don't give out private telephone numbers and to find a number you need to call Directory Assistance on 411. A charge of around 50¢ is added to your telephone bill. Certain types of call can be made only through the operator, including the following:

Collect Calls

A collect (reverse charge) call is where the party being called agrees to pay for the call. Dial '0' followed by the area code and the number you wish to call. When the operator answers, tell him you wish to make a collect call and give your name, and you'll be put through as soon as the party accepts the call.

Conference Calls

You can talk with several people in different locations simultaneously via a conference call, provided that the phone has a 'conference call' or 'link' button. Desktop video-conferencing (DVC) is also possible via personal computers, where the person talking can be seen by other parties (as with a videophone). There's a special charge for these services, depending on the area and the phone company.

Person-to-person Calls

The operator will try to obtain the required person for you and you pay for the call only when you reach him – useful when making a long-distance or international call.

Third-number Calls or Bill-to-a-third-number

You can make a call from another phone and bill it to your own or another number, provided that there's someone at home to verify that the charges are acceptable.

Time & Charge

When making a long-distance call you can ask the operator to tell you its duration and cost.

CHARGES

As in most other countries, telephone charges are invariably 'packaged' by the major companies so that it's virtually impossible to calculate how much individual calls are costing, or to compare charges between telephone companies. Many offer 'free' local calls or a set monthly fee, e.g. $25 per month, including all local and a limited number of long-distance and/or international calls.

Detailed comparisons between the packages offered by the various companies can be found on http://1010phonerates.com.

If you're going to be away from your home for at least a month, you can usually save on line rental by asking your phone company to temporarily suspend your service.

BILLING & PAYMENT

Telephone bills are sent out monthly. Bills usually contain several pages and include a list of itemised calls and monthly charges for special services and equipment rentals. At the bottom of the bill, there's usually a perforated payment return portion that must be included with your payment. Local and long-distance calls (if billed by the same company) are itemised with the date, time, place, area and number called, rate, number of minutes and cost. Bills are sent by your local phone company and don't include charges for long-distance calls if you use a separate company. If you have any questions about your bill, the number to call is shown on the bill.

In addition to call charges, bills may contain a subscriber line charge, goods and services tax (GST), provincial sales tax (PST), line maintenance fee and long-distance charges. Service charges are billed one month in advance. Where applicable, telephone line installation and connection fees are included in your first bill. Payment can usually be made in person at a phone company office, at authorised payment agencies, on the internet or by post (a return envelope is included with your bill).

Your regular monthly bill is usually sent on the same day each month and is overdue when payment isn't received by the 'due by' date printed on the bill. Payments received after the due date are shown as the balance on the next bill. If payment isn't received by the due date, you may be sent another bill advising suspension of your service if it isn't paid within a certain period, e.g. seven days. You may also be charged a 'late payment' fee, e.g. 1.5 per cent of the amount due. If your service is suspended you must pay the amount due plus a reconnection fee (e.g. $50) and it may also be necessary to pay a deposit.

INTERNATIONAL CALLS

Most private phones in Canada permit International Direct Dialling (IDD), which allows calls to be dialled to over 190 countries and collect (reverse charge) calls to be made to around 140 countries. To make an international call, you dial the international access code (011), the country code (e.g. 44 for Britain), the area code *without* the first zero, and finally the subscriber's number. For example, to call the number 7123-4567 in central London (area code 20), England (country code 44) you dial 011-44 20-7123 4567. The reason you don't get the operator after dialling the first 0 of 011 is that there's an automatic delay after you dial 0, during which time you can dial additional numbers.

When making a person-to-person, collect call (not accepted by all countries), calling card or billing to a third number international call, dial 01 instead of 011, followed by the country code, city code and number. The operator comes on the line and asks for details, such as the name of the person you're calling or your calling card number. If you cannot dial an international call directly, you must dial 00 and go through the international operator, when the cost is the same as dialling yourself. If you ask the operator to connect you when it's possible to dial yourself, the call is much more expensive.

Calls to the US cost little more than domestic calls and substantial savings can be made by calling during off-peak periods. International calls have different times for off-peak calls, depending on the country called. Charges vary considerably and are constantly changing (although when using a calling card, the same fee is usually charged 24/7).

Long-distance phone companies compete vigorously for overseas customers and offer Canadian citizens and residents calling cards, which allow you to bill calls made in Canada and abroad to a credit card or your home or business phone bill. However, you're better off using a pre-paid calling card, which can be used to make both national and international calls (some cards can also be used to access the internet). Billions are sold annually by gas stations, convenience stores, delis, highway rest areas and numerous other outlets, including online. The cost of making international calls with calling cards varies, but is from as little as a few cents per minute, although you also need to check connection costs.

The only drawback is that you need to enter a lot of digits to make calls. Also bear in mind that calls from mobile and public phones with calling cards (and calls to mobile phones from land lines) are MUCH more expensive than calls made from land lines to land lines. There are a number of sites where you can compare and buy cards, including www.callingcards.com, www.justdial.ca and www.webstel.com.

Canada subscribes to the Home Country Direct service that allows you to call a special number giving you direct and free access to a bilingual operator in Canada. The operator connects you to the number required and also accepts calling card and reverse charge (collect) calls. For information about the countries served by the Home

Country Direct service call ☎ 1-800-CALL ATT and ask them to send you a Canada Direct wallet card.

PUBLIC TELEPHONES

Public phones or payphones are still plentiful in cities and towns, airports, railway and bus stations, hotel and office building foyers, bars and restaurants (many provide cordless phones), post offices, libraries and other public buildings, shops, department stores and drugstores, laundrettes (laundromats), shopping centres (malls), petrol stations and at motorway service stations. Most public phones are usually in working order. There are no public phone offices in Canada and all long-distance and international calls must be made from payphones, many of which provide little shelter from noise and the elements (some public phones have a 'LOUD' button to increase the volume). Because local calls are free to subscribers, some shopkeepers allow you to make a local call from their phone.

> ☑ **SURVIVAL TIP**
>
> **Before using a payphone, read the operating instructions, which vary from area to area and company to company (payphones are operated by a number of private companies).**

Some payphones are 'dial tone first', which means you get a dial tone before you insert any coins. Coins are inserted only after you've dialled and are connected. These phones allow you to dial an emergency number (or the operator, directory assistance or a toll-free number) when you have no coins. With other payphones, you must insert the minimum call fee before you get a dial tone (even when calling an emergency service), although the fee is returned automatically if it's a free call. If you've inserted coins and there's no reply, you simply replace the receiver to get your money back. Public phones in major airports have a screen on which instructions can often be displayed in English, French, German, Spanish and possibly other languages (e.g. Cantonese in Vancouver).

The cost of a local call from a payphone is 50¢ ($1 if you're paying by credit or calling card) for a three-minute call. Payphones may accept only nickels (5¢), dimes (10¢) and quarters (25¢) and don't give change. Off-peak rates also apply to payphones. You can also make toll-free calls from payphones. Direct dial calls from payphones also benefit from off-peak discounts, but are more expensive than calls from private phones.

Charges for long-distance calls from payphones are set by the company that services the phone. When you make a call from a payphone, check the dialling instruction card on the phone to see which long-distance company services the phone. If you wish to use a long-distance company other than the one assigned to the payphone, you must first dial the number 1 followed by the code for your preferred provider. Some payphones provide fast access to long-distance carriers by pushing a single button and allow you to bill calls to a credit card. After you've dialled the number and before the call is connected, the operator tells you the charge for connection (usually $2.50). Insert this amount and be prepared to pay more when requested. If you're making an international call, you require a huge pile of quarters. After you've deposited the correct amount, the call is connected. As with local calls, your coins are returned if there's no answer. Payphones usually have directories that are attached in various ingenious ways. You can also obtain free directory assistance by dialling 411. For directory assistance for toll-free numbers, dial ☎ 1-800-555 1212.

The cost of long-distance calls from hotel rooms, either direct-dialled or via the hotel switchboard, is usually very high due to surcharges (and a hotel's exclusive deal with a phone company). To save money, use a payphone in the lobby. Local calls usually cost around 75¢ from a hotel room, although they may be free from a motel (which may be indicated by a 'free local calls' sign on the phone).

Many phone companies issue payphone cards for various values such as $5, $10, $20 and $50, and some also issue long-distance calling cards. Before buying a card, check to see whether it's restricted to domestic calls or allows you to make calls abroad. In major tourist or transport centres, payphones accept credit cards. Some companies make a surcharge for calling-card calls. Payphone cards can also be used to make international calls to Canada from overseas.

DIRECTORIES

Telephone directories (commonly referred to as phone books) contain a wealth of information about telephone services, using telephones, area codes and a time zone map, international city codes, call rates, emergency numbers, service numbers, toll-free numbers, repair services, establishing or changing services, local service options, customer calling services, customer rights, phone safety, billing and payment, directory assistance, area and long-distance calling, dialling instructions and operator assistance. Other information often includes a calendar of events, local information and maps, public transportation, leisure and sports, parks, shopping, community services and postal codes. Emergency numbers are usually listed inside the front cover of both white and *Yellow Pages*. Some directories include nuclear emergency information, and a first aid and survival guide.

Directories are divided into sections, e.g. general information, *White Pages* (subscribers' numbers), blue pages (local, provincial and federal government offices), *Yellow Pages* (business listings) and green pages (coupons). *Yellow Pages* are indispensable in Canada and list subscribers under a business or service heading (in alphabetical order). Local 'Yellow Page' directories are also published in some areas. You can order extra copies of any white or *Yellow Pages* published by your local phone company by completing a pre-paid card in your local directory, but you may have to pay for them. Directories for provinces other than the one where you live can also be ordered (for a fee) and can also be consulted in public libraries. Both white and *Yellow Pages* can also be accessed via the internet (www.whitepages.ca and www.yellowpages.ca).

In most areas, white and *Yellow Pages* are published annually by Area Code, e.g. 416 (Toronto) or 604 (Vancouver). Telephone directories, including *Yellow Pages*, are available in bars, restaurants, hotel lobbies, main post offices and public reference libraries, some of which also have foreign directories. National directories listing businesses, colleges and universities, associations and organisations, international organisations and travel resources (resorts, car rentals, hotels and motels, etc.) are also available.

With your basic telephone service, you receive a listing in the *White Pages* of your local telephone book; business customers also receive a free listing in the *Yellow Pages*. Two people with the same family name can have both their first names listed and you can purchase additional listings for around $1 per month.

▲ Caution

It isn't advisable for women to list their first names in telephone directories, which could attract obscene phone calls.

Anyone can get an ex-directory (non-listed) number in Canada for a fee of around $1 per month (a rare occasion when you must pay **not** to have something). This means that your number isn't included in the directory, but is available through directory assistance. For an additional fee (e.g. $2 per month), you can have a non-published number, which means your number is also unavailable through directory assistance. Bell Canada customers (and others) can include their e-mail and internet addresses in the *White Pages* for a small monthly fee.

In all areas, you dial 411 for local directory assistance (inquiries) or information. Often numbers are given by recorded messages and repeated, so be ready to write them down. The operator will help you in an emergency (the emergency number is 911 in all cities). Residential customers pay for all calls to directory assistance, usually around 75¢ per call, while calls from payphones are free. With certain phones such as a Vista 350 or 450 screenphone, you just press a key and speak the name of the person or company whose number you require (the number can also be dialled automatically).

MOBILE PHONES

Mobile (cell) phones are as widely used in Canada as elsewhere in the world and, as with fixed-line services, there's a plethora of companies to choose from. Among Canada's largest mobile phone companies are Rogers Wireless (www.rogers.com), Canada's largest mobile provider, Bell Mobility (www.bell.ca), Telus Mobility (www.telusmobility.com), Fido (www.fido.ca), now owned by Rogers, Solo Mobile (www.solomobile.ca), Koodomobile (www.koodomobile.com) and Virgin Mobile (www.virginmobile.ca).

The 3G and digital networks covers over 95 per cent of the population, including all the major population centres and corridors, but not the all of the remote northern regions (operators provide coverage maps). If you live or work in a remote area, such as the Northwest Territories, Nunavut or the Yukon, you should ensure that a company's coverage includes that area (if applicable). Canada subscribes to the GSM digital network (see www.gsmworld.com), which allows the same phone to be used in over 200 countries worldwide.

Buying a mobile telephone is a minefield, as not only are there many networks to choose from, but numerous call charges, connection fees, insurance, monthly subscriptions and tariffs. Before buying a mobile, shop around and compare telephone charge rates, installation and connection charges, prices and features, and rental charges. Comparisons between mobile phones and mobile phone service providers, including costs, can be found on www.cellphones.ca and useful advice is also provided by Canadian Content (www.canadiancontent.net/mobile).

Mobile phones are sold by specialist phone shops, and department and chain stores which have arrangements with service providers or networks to sell airtime contracts (along with telephones). Don't rely on getting good or impartial advice from retail staff, some of whom know little or nothing about telephones and networks (the difference between Clint Eastwood and a mobile phone seller is that Clint isn't a real cowboy). Retailers advertise in magazines and newspapers, where a wide range of special offers is promoted.

Calls to and from mobile telephones, including calls made from fixed-line telephones, are much more expensive than calls between fixed-line telephones, and calls to 800 numbers aren't free from mobile telephones. Contract arrangements typically cost $10 or $15 per month, with varying amounts of 'free' calls.

Canada offers a wealth of options for those who don't wish to sign up to an expensive mobile phone contract and travellers who wish to make calls overseas from Canada and calls to Canada from overseas. If you have an overseas mobile phone (which must be unlocked) you can replace the SIM card with a Canadian card and buy pre-paid (or pay-as-you-go) credits as and when required.

If you choose a pre-paid phone without a contract, you can 'top up' your credit at post offices, department stores, supermarkets, convenience stores and mobile phone shops. Pay-as-you-go top-up cards are available in denominations of $15 (sometimes expires after 30 days), $25 (60 days) and $50 (60 days), although you may simply be given a receipt with an activation number on it. There's no charge for receiving calls, as there is with some contracts (particularly for international and mobile-to-mobile calls). Pre-paid mobile services abound and are offered by most mobile phone companies.

TELEGRAMS & FAX

Those of a nostalgic bent will be pleased to know that it's still possible to send a telegram within Canada (costing from around $20) and from Canada to over 200 other countries (e.g.

$20 + $1 per word to the UK). See 💻 www.telegrams.ca for information.

Facsimile (fax) machines are also widely used in Canada, where there are public fax bureaux in most cities and many hotels provide fax services (e.g. fax machines in foyers and in-room in some hotels) for public use. Faxes can be sent from a payphone-type machine and credit card operated machines found in public places throughout Canada, e.g. airports and railway stations. You can also send and receive faxes via a computer.

INTERNET

Canadians are among the world's biggest users of the internet and the country is a world leader in e-commerce – not surprising given its size and the sparseness of its population. Some 85 per cent of the population (28mn people) regularly use the internet, over half via a broadband (DSL) connection, which is available to over 95 per cent of Canadians (many use wireless technology).

The most popular sites in Canada are the major international ones, such as Google, Yahoo and MSN. Facebook is the dominant social network (much more popular than MySpace), while Kijiji (💻 http://toronto.kijiji.ca) is a close rival in popularity to Craigslist. The most popular native Canadian sites are those of the major Canadian news companies, which maintain an extensive web presence. According to a 2008 report by comScore, the most popular Canadian sites are those of Quebecor Media, principally Canoe.ca, followed closely by the sites of CTVglobemedia, which includes globe and mail (💻 www.theglobeandmail.com) and CTV.ca.

There are literally hundreds of internet service (or access) providers (ISPs) in Canada, offering dial-up access from just $5 per month and broadband access from $15. Most telephone service providers also provide internet access (see the list on page 121), which can be 'bundled' with fixed and mobile phone, television and radio services to simplify your life, if not save you money.

For information about how to choose an ISP, see Industry Canada (💻 www.ic.gc.ca/eic/site/dir-ect.nsf/eng/h_uw00367.html). Canadian ISP.com (💻 www.canadianisp.ca) allows you to search for an ISP by province/territory, while with Broadband Market (💻 www.broadbandmarket.ca) you can compare over 50 broadband ISPs and choose the best price/service combination.

Travellers are well-catered for in Canada, where internet cafés and coffee shops (from around $2 to $5 an hour) are common in the major cities, and libraries also provide internet access. There are also many coffee shops, restaurants, malls and libraries offering free wireless internet access. You can find wifi hotspots in an area or city via 💻 www.wi-fihotspotlist.com/browse/ca and 💻 www.wififreespot.com/can.html.

Internet Telephony

If you have a broadband internet connection, you can make long-distance and international phone 'calls' for free (or almost-free) to anyone with a broadband connection. Voice over internet protocol (VOIP) is the latest technology which is reshaping the telecoms landscape and may eventually make today's telephone technology (both land lines and mobile networks) obsolete. The leading company in this field is Skype (💻 www.skype.com) with over 50mn users, while another major player is VOIP (💻 www.voip.com). There are also other companies in the market.

All you need is access to a local broadband provider and a headset (costing as little as $15) or a special phone, and you're in business. Calls to other computers anywhere in the world are free, while calls to landlines are charged at a few cents a minute. The downside is that lines are prone to interference and sudden disconnections.

EMERGENCY NUMBERS

The national emergency number in Canada is 911 for police, fire and ambulance emergencies, plus coastguard, cave and mountain rescue services. Emergency phone numbers for all other emergency-type organisations (e.g. rape crisis, Samaritans, etc.) are listed inside the front cover of telephone directories. There are also local emergency numbers that you should make a note of and keep in a prominent place near your phone(s). If you're calling from a payphone, the local emergency number is usually shown on the phone dial. Emergency 911 calls are free from all phones, including payphones (no money is required). If you don't know the number or get no reply from 911, call the operator (dial 0) and ask for the emergency service you require. If you have a shared line that's required for an emergency call, you'll be told by the operator and must hang up immediately.

☑ SURVIVAL TIP

When making an emergency call, don't hang up but let the emergency person end the conversation because they may have important questions or instructions about what you should do until help arrives. If you're unable to remain on the line, tell the operator the nature of the emergency, the exact location where help is required and your phone number.

In addition to the above emergency services, in most areas there are special local crisis hotlines for help and advice regarding missing children, youth crises and runaways, child abuse, battered women, deaf contact (or an emergency teletypewriter for the deaf), eye traumas, alcoholics anonymous, animal bites, poison advice, crime victims, gays and lesbians, health, rapes, suicide prevention, VD clinics, Aids and drug abuse. These numbers are usually listed in local directories. See also **Emergencies** on page 200 and **Counselling** on page 207.

PUBLIC SERVICE NUMBERS

There are no longer any national service numbers (e.g. for the weather) in Canada as provided in many other countries, because the internet has taken over, although some private companies offer these services via 900 numbers. Public service numbers are listed in telephone directories, e.g. in a 'Self Help Guide', which may include arts, leisure and recreation, consumer problems, children's services, disabled services, discrimination, education, services for the elderly, employment, financial services, health, information/referral services, landlord/tenant services, legal services, pollution, taxes, transportation, veterans' services, voter information, weather and welfare. In most areas, consumer information services (often free) may be provided by local Better Business Bureaux.

All provinces provide a range of toll-free hotlines offering a wide variety of information including education, health, consumer and welfare information, where bilingual (English/French) information specialists are often available to answer your questions. Some communities have a local 'special event telephone line', where residents can make community announcements.

8. TELEVISION & RADIO

Most Canadian households have at least one television (TV) and over 70 per cent have two or more. The average Canadian family watches between around 21 and 26 hours of television per week, depending on which survey you read. Despite the competition from TV, cinema, DVDs and computer games, radio flourishes in Canada and has a growing audience; the average Canadian listens to the radio for around 14 hours per week. Radio and TV programmes (terrestrial and cable/satellite) are listed in daily newspapers, many of which provide free weekly programme guides.

TELEVISION

A TV is an essential part of Canadian life and even the most modest motel or hotel boasts a colour TV in every room (so that you can follow the hockey wherever you go!). Airports and bus stations may have coin-operated TVs built into the arms of chairs, and bars, clubs, restaurants, dance halls and even laundrettes have TVs.

The TV industry and programming in Canada is strongly influenced by the US and the majority of programmes are produced in the US (every bit as banal as you may have heard). In many homes, TV rivals family and religion as the dispenser of values and is often referred to as the 'plug-in drug' or the 'third parent'.

The pervasive influence of the US on Canadian TV has led the Canadian government to mandate that all Canadian TV stations must devote a certain percentage of air-time each day to Canadian-produced programmes. Private TV licensees must generally achieve an annual Canadian content level of 60 per cent, measured over the broadcast day, and 50 per cent overall during the peak evening hours (7-11pm). Stations owned by the Canadian Broadcasting Corporation (CBC) must have 60 per cent Canadian content at all times (it broadcasts 90 per cent Canadian content during prime time). Canadian pay TV services also have Canadian programming requirements. However, due to cross-border terrestrial transmissions, cable and satellite, it's estimated that less than 40 per cent of what Canadians watch is Canadian content. The French commercial networks air significantly more Canadian content than their English counterparts.

Most Canadians receive their TV service through some sort of multichannel platform, such as cable or satellite TV, as opposed to antenna-based terrestrial TV. If you watch a lot of TV then you'll find it's worthwhile (essential?) to subscribe to cable or satellite TV, which provides access to hundreds of channels. Many programmes are broadcast in high definition (HD) format which offers greatly improved picture and sound quality (for which you'll need an HD television). If you have an analogue TV and receive HD terrestrial (over-the-air) broadcasts, you'll need a set-top converter box.

There's no TV licence fee in Canada and with the exception of some government grants received by CBC, Canadian TV is financed by advertising. The more people who watch a particular programme, the more advertising costs, which results in fierce competition between stations to produce hit programmes that increase their daily ratings. Programmes that receive poor ratings are often axed at the drop of a hat. Some programmes, particularly sports broadcasts, are actually produced by one or more advertisers.

The Canadian Radio-Television and Telecommunications Commission (CRTC, www.crtc.gc.ca) oversees Canadian TV and radio standards.

Standards

The standards for TV reception in Canada aren't the same as in most other countries (except the US). The Canadian transmission standards are NTSC and ATSC, which are different from the PAL standard used in most of Europe. TVs and video and DVD recorders that aren't manufactured for the NTSC/ATSC standard won't function in Canada, although dual-standard TVs are available. DVD (and video) recorders manufactured for non-Canadian markets cannot be used to record or play back NTSC-standard DVDs and videos.

The cost of a TV varies considerably, depending on its make, screen size, features and, not least, the retailer. Wide-screen plasma and LCD high definition TVs (HDTVs) are widely available and relatively inexpensive, e.g. from around $250 for a budget 22in HDTV up to $2,000-3,000 for a 40in HDTV from a top manufacturer. In most apartments there's no need to fit a private aerial (antenna) as all large buildings have a master aerial on the roof for terrestrial stations and most are wired for cable.

In spring 2009, cable and satellite channels were broadcasting in high definition, but relatively few via terrestrial stations were in HD. It isn't necessary to have a converter box to receive HD TV broadcasts via cable or satellite on analogue TVs (although you won't enjoy the enhanced picture and sound of HDTV), as the equipment provided by cable/satellite already converts the signal to analogue if necessary. However, if you want to record HD broadcasts you'll require an HD video recorder. If you have an analogue TV and receive HD terrestrial (over-the-air) broadcasts, you'll need a set-top converter box.

Digital Switch

Analogue TV broadcasting will cease on 31st August 2011, after which you'll need either a digital TV or a 'converter' box for an analogue TV. (US broadcasts switched to digital in February 2009.)

Stations & Programmes

Canada has four nationwide TV networks, some with regional subsidiaries, as follows:

- CBC Television, owned by the Canadian Broadcasting Corporation (CBC, www.cbc.ca), broadcasts in English, French and Aboriginal languages (in northern Quebec and Labrador) and incorporates CBC North, a publicly-owned network operating in northern Quebec and Labrador;
- Canadian Television Network (CTV, www.ctv.ca), a private network owned by CTVglobemedia, with a subsidiary called CTV Northern Ontario;
- Global (www.globaltv.com), a private network owned by Canwest and broadcasting in English;
- Télévision de Radio-Canada (www.cbc.radio-canada.ca), usually referred to as Radio-Canada or SRC and owned by CBC, broadcasting in French.

In addition, there are several regional stations, including TVA (a private network owned by Quebecor Media and based in Quebec, but available nationwide via cable), broadcasting in French. Another station is APTN, whose programming focuses on Aboriginal subject matter, broadcasting in three territories in English, French and various Aboriginal languages, and available nationwide via cable and satellite. Other ethnic and multicultural services, serving one or more cultural groups (outside of the two official languages) are also growing in strength. Four terrestrial TV stations, CFMT and CJMT in Toronto, CJNT in Montreal and CHNM in Vancouver, air multicultural programming in a variety of languages, while Telelatino airs programming in Italian and Spanish on basic cable.

Other regional networks include A (British Columbia, Ontario and the Atlantic coast), Citytv (Alberta, BC, Manitoba and Ontario), E! (Alberta, BC, Ontario and Quebec) and Great West Television (BC), and two religious stations, Crossroads Television System (Alberta and Ontario) and Joytv (BC and Manitoba), all broadcasting in English; TQS

(Quebec) in French; and Omni Television (Alberta, BC and Ontario) in various languages.

Networks compete vigourously for the 'best' (or rather, most popular) programmes and sports events. Toronto is the media capital of Canada and the major networks all have their head offices there. In addition to the national and regional networks, there are over 100 licensed commercial TV stations available on cable. Local stations also show their own local news, sports and other broadcasts, which are sometimes surprisingly amateurish affairs.

Despite the high proportion of Canadian-made programmes, most are every bit as bad as programmes made in the US, particularly those made by small stations with even smaller budgets. Even the programmes made by CBC can be pretty bad, particularly the poorly disguised clones of popular US programmes, such as *Street Legal* (*LA Law*), *North of 60* (*Northern Exposure*), *Degrassi* (*Saved by the Bell*) and *Side Effects* (*St. Elsewhere*). However, not everything is rubbish and Canadian TV has its own annual awards for the 'least worst' TV programmes, called a Gemini (TV's equivalent of the Oscar). Among the most successful recent series are the comedies *Corner Gas* and *Little Mosque on the Prairie*, the drama *Da Vinci's Inquest*, and the reality series *So You Think You Can Dance Canada*.

Cultural programming (often British) is provided by the commercial-free Public Broadcasting Service (💻 www.pbs.org) out of the US (available via cable and satellite) and provincial channels, such as Knowledge in BC or Access in Alberta. BBC World and BBC Prime are available on cable.

Swearing is permitted on Canadian TV, although pornography isn't available on terrestrial or cable TV. Where applicable, programmes have a warning displayed at the beginning of each segment stating that it contains coarse, disturbing or graphic material, and 'viewer discretion is advised' (which means the kids will all be watching in their rooms!).

One big difference between TV in Canada and the US is the news. Unlike the US, Canadian TV shows international news and doesn't descend into meaningless sensationalism (not much anyway!) or sound bites. The Canadian Broadcasting Corporation is an excellent source of news, taking its lead from the BBC and doing a good job of living up to its standards.

Most TV stations are on the air 24/7 and most programmes (with the exception of sport and some political coverage) are broadcast at the same time each day, irrespective of the time zone. Because Newfoundland is half an hour ahead of the rest of Atlantic Canada (see page 331), the phrase 'half an hour later in Newfoundland' has become part of the Canadian lexicon. If a programme is shown at 8pm in Atlantic Canada, it's then broadcast an hour later in central Canada, where it's again 8pm, and so on across the country. Some British Columbia sports events may start early to hit prime time in Toronto or start at the normal time in British Columbia, which gets them on the air in late evening in Ontario.

TV programmes (including cable) are listed in major daily newspapers, many of which publish free weekly TV guides, and in the *TV Times Canada* magazine (with a circulation of 1.3mn). An online TV guide is available from 💻 www.tvguide.ca (among others).

Cable Television

Around 75 per cent of Canadian households subscribe to cable TV, which offers hundreds of channels and is available in most large towns and cities, where many homes have access to more than one cable company. Despite increased competition from DTH satellite services (see below), cable still dominates the pay TV market in Canada (any station that's available on satellite – and most are – can be carried by any Canadian cable system). Most cable TV companies also offer cable telephone and broadband internet services.

> ☑ **SURVIVAL TIP**
>
> **Cable TV is a minefield in Canada with a wide range of services offered by different cable providers – with any luck you'll have only one option, which will the solve the tricky problem of which company to choose.**

Ask your neighbours or estate agent which company supplies your local cable TV service and obtain their rates and options. The main cable TV operators in Canada are Rogers Cable (🖳 www.rogers.com) and Shaw Communications (🖳 www.shaw.ca), while others include Bell Canada (🖳 www.bell.ca), Cable Axion (🖳 www.axion.ca), Cogeco (🖳 www.cogeco.ca), Eastlink (🖳 www.eastlink.ca), Persona (🖳 www.persona.ca), Telus TV (🖳 www.telus.com) and Videotron (🖳 www.videotron.com). A list of all Canadian cable TV providers is available at 🖳 http://tv.about.com/od/canadiancableproviders.

Most apartments, condos and townhouses have cable included in the rent or at least have a cable hook-up. All you need do is call and tell the cable company your address and they'll switch it on and send you a bill. Modern TVs are 'cable ready' and no cable converter box is required. To receive pay-per-view programmes you need to pay a deposit and obtain a descrambler from your cable company. When there's a pay-per-view programme that you want to watch, such as a movie or sports event, you call your cable company and they unscramble it for you (and charge the fee to your account).

Cable TV is usually available in hotels, motels and even in some YMCAs and youth hostels (although some hotel pay-per-view films are expensive). Most cable stations broadcast 24/7 and offer hundreds of channels. Although there are some general entertainment cable TV channels, many are dedicated to a particular genre, including movies, sports, religion, comedy, local events, news, financial news, shopping, children's programmes, weather, health, music (rock, country) and foreign-language programmes, e.g. Spanish or Mandarin. English soccer-addicted expats will be glad to hear that Fox Sports World Canada offers comprehensive coverage of English Premiership soccer matches.

The cable channels available in a city or locality depend on the franchise agreement with the local municipality, although the most popular channels are usually available throughout the country. Cable companies charge an installation fee of around $40 and provide a basic cable service for a flat fee of around $20 per month ($30-50 for digital services), plus premium subscription stations which average another $10 to $20 per month. The average subscriber pays around $35 per month. Most companies provide a preferred or plus service, which is an expanded basic service. You will also need a receiver box (called a digital terminal for digital TV) which cost from around $100 and can also be rented from around $3 per month from cable TV companies.

A typical cable package includes all the local terrestrial Canadian stations, ABC, NBC, CBS and Fox from the US, CBC and CTV dedicated news channels and CNN and CNBC news channels from the US, some US-based cable channels such as Arts and Entertainment, Canadian cable stations such as Women's Television Network, and some cross-breeds such as Bravo, which shows some US Bravo shows and Canada-only Bravo programming. Canada has two cable sports channels that buy some programming from ESPN and other sports programmers in the US.

If you have cable you can receive the US Public Broadcasting System (PBS), which will be of particular interest to expatriate readers (e.g. the British). PBS output includes comedy (British sitcoms are popular), children's programmes (e.g. *Sesame Street*), drama, documentaries, discussion programmes, excellent science and nature features, live music and theatre, and anything that's generally too 'highbrow' for the national networks. However, as a result of lack of funding, the PBS network is forced to broadcast many low-budget, narrow-interest programmes and canvasas biannually (twice a year) for sponsorship and donations.

If you make a donation to PBS they may send you gifts, such as a John Cleese T-shirt if they're running a Fawlty Towers marathon or a CD of a symphony if they're showing an orchestral performance.

Satellite Television

There are many TV satellites positioned over North America serving Canada and the US. Many satellite transmissions are broadcast exclusively for local cable TV companies, who pass the satellite signal through their cable network to subscribers. Every hotel, bar and club has a satellite dish (if it doesn't have cable) that's mainly used to show sports events (some show a number of ballgames simultaneously on different TVs).

However, a growing number of people are buying satellite dishes for home use, particularly in remote rural areas where homes cannot be connected to a cable system. Digital dishes with a 1.5m dish cost around $200 and can receive TV stations from around the world. Alternatively, some companies provide a 'free' dish if you sign up to view selected programmes for a period.

'Direct-to-home' (DTH) technology, using high-powered transmitters, has recently extended the coverage of satellite broadcasting. There are two DTH service providers in Canada, each offering a variety of programme packages with up to 500 channels: Bell Canada (www.bell.ca) and Star Choice (www.starchoice.com), now owned by Shaw Direct. As a result of competition and increased subscriptions, prices for DTH equipment have dropped significantly to less than $200 for equipment and installation, and monthly subscription rates now start from $20 or less.

Contracts between the satellite owners, programmers and local cable TV companies are exclusive, so direct reception of the satellite signal is illegal. Satellite owners' attempts to scramble signals (using sophisticated encryption) have had little effect and black market pirate devices are quickly on the market and sold through advertisements in magazines such as *Popular Mechanics*.

If you have a large motorised satellite dish you may be interested in the *World Radio TV Handbook* (WRTH Publications), which provides information about stations worldwide.

The reception of US DTH programmes in Canada is illegal, although decoding equipment is available and it's estimated that up to a million Canadians access US satellite TV programmes.

DVDs & Videos

You can buy practically anything on DVD in Canada, where there's a huge market in educational, training and sports DVDs. New DVDs sell for between around $20 and previously viewed videos (old rentals) of recent releases cost around $6 to $12. Videos and DVDs of movie classics cost between $6 and $10. The best place to buy videos and DVDs is from a mail-order service such as Cinemail or Zip (see below), which may offer new members special introductory deals.

Many DVD stores are open from around 9am until midnight or even 2am, seven days a week. To rent a DVD you must be a member, for which stores require ID and proof of your address. If you're aged under 18, a parent is required to be a guarantor. Rental charges are usually around $1 to $5, depending on the movie rating and local competition. For example, Blockbuster rent new releases for $3.99 for two days and $5.99 for seven days. You can also rent Blue-ray DVDs, which offer

higher quality than regular DVDs, for an extra dollar or two (but you need a Blue-ray DVD player).

The standard rental period is usually one day for new releases and three days for regular movies. Most stores will rent you several old releases for a few days for a single price, e.g. 'five flicks, five days, five bucks' or 'seven movies, seven days, $7'. Each of the major DVD franchises offers different incentives to keep its clientele coming back. Blockbuster boasts that any new release you want (selected titles of course) will be in stock, otherwise your next rental is free. Classic and educational videos and DVDs can also be rented from public libraries.

The main DVD rental chains include Blockbuster (🖳 www.blockbuster.ca – the largest), Cinemail (🖳 www.cinemail.ca), Rogers Video (🖳 www.rogersvideo.ca), and Zip (🖳 www.zip.ca). Rogers and Blockbuster don't stock 'blue' movies but what they term 'adult' movies, although some privately owned stores do (the minimum age limit for renting adult movies is 18). Many video stores sell food such as ice-cream bars, ice-lollies, sweets and popcorn (watching movies is hungry work).

Some large chains also rent playstations, with a large range of games. The rental is usually around $13 for three days, plus the cost of the game rental, typically $6 for three days. You must also make a deposit of $150 to $200 in cash or with a credit card for the playstation. This is a relatively inexpensive way to check whether a child (and you!) will get good value from games before forking out hundreds of dollars to buy a system.

☑ SURVIVAL TIP

DVDs may be encoded with a region code, restricting the area of the world in which they can be played. The code for North America is 1, while discs without any region coding are called all-region or region 0 discs. However, you can buy all-region DVD players and DVD players can be modified to be region-free, allowing the playback of all discs. (see 🖳 www.regionfreedvd.net and www.moneysavingexpert.com/shopping/dvd-unlock).

RADIO

Radio reception is good in most parts of Canada, including stereo reception, which is excellent in all but the most mountainous areas (where you're lucky to receive anything). Canada has about 500 local radio stations and in major cities you generally have a choice of about 50 stations, although in remote areas you may be able to receive only a few stations.

Local stations generally stick to a bland commercial format with little originality, although they're a good source of information about local news, entertainment, and road and weather reports. Although most stations are commercial, advertising on radio is a lot less obtrusive than on TV. Many radio stations are highly specialised and include a variety of foreign language stations and non-commercial stations run by colleges, universities and public authorities. Stations are classified as AM (or medium wave) or FM (VHF, often stereo), and a few broadcast simultaneously on both wavebands; frequencies are quoted in kHz (AM) or MHz (FM). Canadian radio stations are identified by their call sign: a four letter designation that begins with 'C.'

Canadian music stations can be highly specialised, offering easy-listening, country and western or rock. Interestingly, the mix is changing, as many listeners have abandoned music stations for talk radio. Part of the problem is poor sound quality on AM, therefore stations are turning to formats that don't require quality sound (three-quarters of Canadians have CD players in their homes or cars, which may have something to do with this). The situation may improve as more people switch to digital radio (see below), which provides better sound quality and is also immune to interference from static or echoes. Those with cable TV can subscribe to an FM stereo service in most areas, which improves FM reception on your stereo receiver.

If you're looking for serious radio, you need to tune to CBC radio (🖳 www.radio.cbc.ca), which is government subsidised at a cost of around 8¢ per day for each Canadian. CBC offers primarily news and public affairs programming (patterned on BBC Radio) in

English and French, plus a 24-hour cable news service in both languages, a Northern service in eight Aboriginal languages, and Radio Canada International (RCI), a short-wave radio service broadcasting around the world in seven languages. CBC, which started broadcasting in 1937, has been called the 'ribbon of reason' that holds Canada together (just as the railway was once the 'ribbon of steel').

CBC has five radio channels: Radio 1 (arts), Radio 2 ('serious' music), Radio 3 (popular music), Galaxie (continuous music) and Radio Canada International/RCI (news). It also offers a satellite service, called Sirius, which allows you to listen to broadcasts on the other channels. Radio Canada (🖳 www.cardio-canada.ca) is Canada's principal French station.

Avid radio listeners may be interested in the *World Radio TV Handbook* (WRTH Publications).

Digital Radio

Canadian radio stations are rapidly switching to digital audio broadcasting (DAB), especially in Montreal, Ottawa, Toronto and Vancouver, but universal conversion has been delayed by a federal review of radio broadcasting.

The DAB transmission system currently used in Canada isn't compatible with the hybrid HD RadioTM digital radio technology being used by some US AM and FM radio stations. No Canadian stations are yet transmitting digital signals using HD RadioTM; however, this may change should the US system be found capable of meeting part of Canada's future DAB needs. Similarly, digital receivers used to access satellite pay radio services, such as Sirius (🖳 www.siriuscanada.ca/en) and XM Radio (🖳 www.xmradio.ca), aren't capable of receiving the free local DAB services offered by Canada's broadcasters.

9. EDUCATION

Canada spends around 7 per cent of its GDP on education and has a diversified education system, with public and private schools ('school' usually refers to everything from kindergarten to university) at all levels operating alongside one another. Around 15 per cent of Canadians have a university degree, over 25 per cent a diploma from a post-secondary education institution and around 50 per cent graduate from high school. However, although very few Canadians are illiterate in the sense of not being able to read and write, almost 15 per cent have had only a primary education and a surprisingly high proportion have only marginal literacy skills (although most of these are new immigrants, with limited English- or French-language skills). For example, they cannot use a weather chart to calculate temperature differences, cannot decipher a simple graph or use a bus schedule.

Full-time education is compulsory in all provinces and includes the children of foreign nationals permanently or temporarily resident in Canada. Compulsory schooling in Canada usually commences at the age of four to seven and continues until the age of 16 in all provinces except for New Brunswick and Ontario, where it's 18. Although the typical Canadian receives 13 years of education, the average is lower in rural areas and small towns, and higher in metropolitan areas. Perhaps not surprisingly, native Americans have lower levels of schooling than others and some 55 per cent have no high school diploma and fewer than 5 per cent are university graduates.

Education in Canada is the responsibility of individual provinces and districts, therefore standards and requirements vary considerably from province to province and district to district. However, the federal government provides financial support for post-secondary education, adult occupational training and tuition in the two official languages. It's also responsible for educating native Americans, Armed Forces personnel and their families, and inmates of prisons and other penal institutions.

Education in public primary and secondary schools is free, but parents must pay 'student fees' of between $5 and $100 per term for extra-curricular classes such as music and art. Most students attend public schools, although some 5 per cent attend private fee-paying schools, some of which are church-sponsored, parochial schools (usually Roman Catholic, although in some cities there are others, such as Muslim schools). Most public schools are mixed (co-educational) day schools. Private schools include day and boarding schools and are mostly mixed, although some are single sex. With the exception of some private schools, all education in Canada is non-denominational.

Formal education in Canada comprises three levels: elementary, secondary and higher education. Vocational training, adult education and special schools or classes (e.g. for gifted or handicapped children) also form part of the education programme in most provinces. Foreign families resident in Canada for a limited period may prefer to send their children to a private international school, where the organisation and curriculum are similar to that of public schools, although the administration differs. In recent years, many parents concerned about a decline in public education have turned to private schools. Although the cost of private education is high, many parents consider it an acceptable price to pay, particularly if the result is a bachelor's or master's degree from a prestigious university. With the exception of most private and some parochial schools, school uniforms are rare in Canada.

The language of instruction in most Canadian schools is English, the exception being Quebec where it's primarily French, although in some communities classes are provided in both languages. For children of *Québécois* citizens who attend an English primary school, there's a publicly-supported English school system where English is the language of instruction. All other schools in Quebec teach in French and most children attend French schools, irrespective of the language spoken at home.

> There are 'French immersion' programmes (to encourage bilingualism) in schools in all provinces, which provide an alternative education for students whose parents wish them to be taught in French. French immersion programmes are most popular in the Maritimes and least popular in British Columbia.

Each year some 30,000 migrant children enter Canada speaking neither English or French and must start their education in special language units or special schools. If your children don't speak English or French fluently, enquire whether English or French as a Second Language (ESL/FSL) classes are available or whether study is available in other languages. In some major cities children can be taught in foreign languages, e.g. in Vancouver some schools teach in Cantonese, Japanese, Korean and Punjabi (children often go to Saturday school to learn the native language of their parents).

Many provinces and communities provide schools or special classes for children with special educational needs, including those with emotional and behavioural problems, moderate and severe learning difficulties, communication problems, partial hearing or physical handicaps. There are also private schools in Canada catering for gifted and talented children, and most public schools have 'gifted and talented' programmes.

An excellent overview of the Canadian education system is provided by Wikipedia (http://en.wikipedia.org/wiki/education_in_canada).

PUBLIC OR PRIVATE SCHOOL?

Before making any major decisions about your children's education, it's important to consider their individual ability, character and requirements. This is of particular importance if you're able to choose between public and private education, when the following points should be considered:

- How long are you planning to stay in Canada? If you're uncertain, it's probably best to assume a long stay. Due to language and other integration problems, enrolling a child in a Canadian school (public or private) with a Canadian syllabus is only recommended for at least one year, particularly for teenage children.
- Bear in mind that the area where you choose to live will affect your choice of public schools. It's usually necessary to send your child to the public school that serves the area where you live, which is why homes within the catchment area of desirable schools are in demand and more expensive. It's difficult and may be impossible to get your child accepted at a public school in another area if the school is full. In some cities (e.g. Edmonton) parents can send their children to any school in the city and in Manitoba parents can choose any school in the province, provided places are available.
- Do you know where you're going after Canada? This may be an important consideration regarding your children's schooling. How old are your children and what age will they be when you plan to leave Canada? What future plans do you have for their education and in which country?
- What educational level have your children reached now and how will they fit into the

Canadian public school system or a private school? The younger they are, the easier it will be to place them in a suitable school.

- If your children don't speak English or French, how do they view the thought of studying in one of these languages? Are they willing to take ESL or FSL classes? Does the school offer a good programme? Alternatively, is schooling available in Canada in their mother tongue?
- What are the school hours and the school holiday (vacation) periods? How will they affect your family's work and leisure activities?
- Is religion an important consideration in your choice of school? About a quarter of public schools are Roman Catholic 'separate' (i.e. denominational) schools and many private schools are also maintained by religious organisations.
- Do you want your children to attend a mixed (co-educational) or a single-sex school? All public schools in Canada and the majority of private schools are mixed.
- Should you send your children to a boarding school? If so, should it be in Canada or in another country?
- What are the secondary and higher education prospects for your children in Canada or another country? Are Canadian examinations or qualifications recognised in your home country or the country where you plan to live after leaving Canada?
- Do the schools under consideration have a good academic record? What percentage of high school pupils go on to higher education? Other important indicators are the school dropout rate, the average daily attendance rate, the expenditure per pupil (including textbooks) and the average teacher salary.
- How large are the classes? What is the teacher-student ratio?

Obtain the opinions and advice of others who have been faced with the same decisions and problems as yourself and collect as much information as possible before making a decision. Speak to the principals and teachers of schools on your shortlist. Finally, most parents find that it's beneficial to discuss the alternatives with their children before choosing a school.

PUBLIC SCHOOLS

There's no federal school system in Canada. Education is controlled at the provincial level by each province's Ministry or Department of Education (see the table below). State-funded provincial schools are called either public or 'separate' (e.g. Roman Catholic) schools and although anyone can attend either, they're generally split along religious denomination lines. Public schools are the responsibility of provincial departments of education and funded mainly from local and provincial taxes, with some federal funds. Practices and policies regarding education (public and private) vary depending on the province, and each province determines their education policy in accordance with provincial laws. The Minister of Education is responsible for setting policy relating to educational affairs, such as the allocation of provincial and federal funds, certification of teachers, textbooks and library services, provision of records and educational statistics, and setting and enforcing the term of compulsory education.

One of the unique aspects of the Canadian public school system is the amount of decentralisation and the degree to which schools are run by local school authorities. Each province is divided at the local level into school districts governed by a superintendent and a locally elected school board (or board of education) that decides instructional policies, hires teachers, purchases equipment and generally oversees the day-to-day running of schools. Most schools have Parents Advisory Councils (PACs) that mainly concern themselves with raising money to buy equipment such as computers, video surveillance, emergency lighting, playground equipment, and school buses for children with special needs.

Teacher qualifications and standards vary from province to province. All provinces require teachers to have a licence or certificate to teach in public elementary and secondary schools, although the actual requirements for teacher certificates are set by provincial education departments. All provinces require a bachelor's degree for teaching elementary grades and most require a bachelor's degree as the minimum preparation for teaching in secondary schools, while a few insist on five years' study or a master's degree. Parents are encouraged to participate in their child's education and schools are constantly seeking volunteer 'teaching assistants' to help with reading, art and special projects.

The websites of the province/territory Ministries or Departments of Education are shown in the table below:

Choosing a Public School

For most Canadian parents, one of the most important (if not *the* most important) criterion when choosing a new neighbourhood is the reputation of its schools. This is often measured by the number of students schools send to the best Canadian universities (statistics are provided by all schools). In recent years there's been an ongoing debate about school choice, which varies considerably depending on the city or province, e.g. in Edmonton (Alberta) parents can send their children to any school in the city and in Manitoba parents can choose any school in the province (provided there are spaces available).

However, in most areas it's necessary to send your child to the public school that serves the area where you live and it's difficult to get your child accepted at a public school in another area. For this reason, homes within the catchment area of desirable schools are in demand and more expensive. If you plan to send your child to a public school, you should make enquiries about the quality of local schools before deciding where to live. Often the more expensive property is in a neighbourhood, the better

Provincial/Territory Education Departments

Province/Territory	Website
Alberta	http://education.alberta.ca
British Columbia	www.gov.bc.ca/bced
Manitoba	www.edu.gov.mb.ca
New Brunswick	www.gnb.ca/0000/index-e.asp
Newfoundland & Labrador	www.ed.gov.nl.ca/edu
Northwest Territories	www.gov.nt.ca/agendas/education/index.html
Nova Scotia	www.ednet.ns.ca
Nunavut	www.gov.nu.ca/education/eng/index.htm
Ontario	www.edu.gov.on.ca
Prince Edward Island	www.gov.pe.ca/education
Quebec	www.meq.gouv.qc.ca
Saskatchewan	www.education.gov.sk.ca
The Yukon Territory	www.education.gov.yk.ca

the local public schools. Relocation guides are published in many cities and regions, which include profiles of local schools and comparative scores for different grades. Many communities take pride in the quality of their local public school system, which is crucial in maintaining property values.

The quality of public schools varies considerably from province to province and community to community, and although some are poor, most are excellent. Where schools are well-run, well-supported and well-funded by the local community, the quality of public education rivals any in the world and can offer opportunities seldom available in many other countries. Even at schools where average standards are low, students who take full advantage of the opportunities afforded receive an excellent education.

For information about schools in a particular area, contact the local district school board (information is usually available from the local council website).

Organisation

Most children start school before the age of six, when compulsory schooling usually begins, either in a nursery school or a kindergarten (see **Pre-school Education** below). The maximum 13 years of formal elementary and secondary education covers education from the ages of 5 to 18, divided into increments called grades (kindergarten and grades 1 to 12). Children usually start in kindergarten at the age of five and advance one grade per year until reaching grade 12 at age 18. Occasionally a student must repeat a grade due to prolonged absence or low marks, but this is rare.

In most provinces, a child can legally quit (drop out of) school at 16, but this is generally discouraged and the majority of students stay at high school until they reach the age of 18.

Elementary and secondary education together are sometimes referred to as 'K12' – Kindergarten through to Grade 12.

Usually a pupil has one teacher for all major subjects during his first six years of schooling (elementary) and a different teacher for each subject during the last six grades in junior and senior high schools.

An excellent comparison of the grade structure by province is provided by Wikipedia (🖳 http://en.wikipedia.org/wiki/education_in_canada).

Registration

At elementary and secondary levels, students usually attend a public school close to their home. If you have a preference for a particular public school or school district, it's usually necessary to buy or rent a property in that area (see **Choosing a Public School** above), although you can request that your child attends a school outside your area (called 'cross-boundary'). It's quite normal for Canadians to ask an estate agent to find them a home in a particular school district. All schools prefer children to start at the beginning of a new term (semester), although this isn't mandatory.

Parents should enquire at a school district's central office or Board of Education to find out which school their child will be assigned to and the documents required for registration. Usually you need to produce proof of residence, an immigration record of landing, a passport, a birth certificate

School Grades

Age	Grade	School
2 to 5	-	Pre-school or Kindergarten
6 to 11	1 to 6	Elementary
12 to 14	7 to 9	Junior high
15 to 18	10 to 12	Senior high

(or a certified copy) and details of your child's medical history, including immunisations and tuberculin screening (see **Health** below). It's also necessary to provide past scholastic records, including a school report from your child's last school. This is used to assign students to a class or grade and should be as detailed as possible, with samples of essays, projects and examinations.

Many towns provide transport to school (buses), although it may be provided for certain schools or ages only, and may depend on the distance, e.g. there may be a school bus only when the distance from your home to school is over 2 or 2.5 miles. Some towns provide buses for children in special education only.

Terms & School Hours

The school year in Canada usually runs from the first week of September until the end of June (ten months) and is divided into periods or quarters (terms/semesters). There are a few year-round schools and some have a school year that runs from mid-August to the end of May. School holiday dates are published by schools well in advance, thus allowing parents plenty of time to schedule family holidays during official school holidays. It isn't advisable to take a child out of school when he should be taking examinations or during important course work assignments.

The school day in elementary schools is usually from 8.30am to 3 or 3.30pm, with an hour for lunch. There are also usually two 15-minute breaks (recesses) to allow students to let off steam between classes (and to allow teachers to find the aspirin). In high schools, hours are usually from 8.30am until 3.30pm, with one early afternoon a week. Extracurricular activities and sports are scheduled after school hours. Lessons in public schools are held from Mondays to Fridays and there are no lessons on Saturdays or Sundays.

Canada also has what it calls 'semestered high schools', where instead of the standard eight subjects being taught throughout the year, four subjects are taught each term, with one long lesson (usually 70 minutes) on each subject each day. This system is thought to give a better understanding of each subject and to be more suitable for pupils who find it difficult to cope with eight subjects each week. However, when students haven't done a subject such as maths (math) for a term, it can cause some headaches picking it up again and a lot of time may be spent in revision.

Health

In most provinces, school children must be immunised against a range of diseases before starting school. These may include polio, DTP (diphtheria, tetanus and whooping cough) and MMR (measles, mumps and rubella or German measles). Tuberculosis screening may also be necessary. Most schools have full- or part-time nurses (who may cover a number of schools) or at the very least staff trained in administering first-aid. Special medical checks (physicals) are necessary to take part in some sports activities. Dental checks aren't carried out at schools, but many schools promote a dental health week. Health education is provided in elementary and secondary schools, including sex education and graphic explanations of the perils of drugs and smoking (which are combined with community programmes). In many communities, volunteer ambulance corps members teach children about safety and accident prevention.

Pre-school Education

Pre-school education embraces all formal and informal education before the age of five (when compulsory schooling starts). It includes tots and toddler programmes, play school, nursery school and kindergarten. Attendance at school for children under five years of age isn't compulsory in Canada, where pre-schools and nursery schools are private. However, kindergarten is part of the public school system and is compulsory for children aged five on 1st September, when they'll start at the beginning of the school year in September.

There are various kinds of pre-schools in Canada, including non-profit co-operative schools, church-affiliated schools, local community schools, private schools and Montessori schools. A co-operative school is usually the least expensive because parents work voluntarily as teachers' aides alongside professional teachers. Church-affiliated schools are usually attached to religious centres and may include religious education (it isn't always necessary for children to follow the same religion as the school). Private schools are the most expensive and vary considerably from small home-run set-ups to large custom-built schools.

A number of private nursery schools in Canada use the Montessori method of teaching, developed by Dr. Maria Montessori in the early 1900s. Montessori is more a philosophy of life than a teaching method and is based on the firm belief that each child is an individual with unique needs, interests and patterns of growth. Some Montessori schools have 'pre-school' (for children aged two and a half to six years) and elementary levels (ages 6 to 12).

Nursery school is highly recommended for all children, particularly those whose parents don't speak English or French as their mother tongue.

After a few years in nursery school, a child is integrated into the local community and well prepared for elementary school (particularly when English or French isn't spoken at home). Parents can also make friends in the community through pre-school contacts.

Elementary School

Children must start school on 1st September following their fifth birthday. The first years of compulsory schooling in Canada are called elementary or primary school. Elementary school is usually mixed and is attended until age 11 (grades 1 to 6), when students go on to a junior high school (grades 7 to 9). In some districts, students attend elementary school until age 13 (up to grade 8) before attending a senior high school (grades 10 to 12).

The elementary school curriculum varies with the organisation and educational aims of individual schools and local communities. Promotion from one grade to the next is based on testing and a child whose performance is poor may be required to repeat a year, while a gifted child may be allowed to skip a year. Elementary schools provide instruction in the fundamental skills of reading, writing and maths, as well as history, geography, crafts, music, science, art, and physical education (phys ed. or gym). French and 'foreign' languages, which used to be taught only at high schools, are now introduced during the last few years of elementary school in some areas and, if you wish, your child can enter an 'early French immersion programme' at kindergarten or grade 1 level. For more information contact the local branch of the 'Canadian Parents for French' programme.

Secondary School

Secondary education in Canada is for children aged from 12 to 18 (grades 7 to 12). It generally takes place in a high school that may be divided into junior and senior high (held in separate buildings or even at separate locations). Junior high is for those aged 12 to 14 (grades 7 to 9) and senior high for ages 15 to 17 (grades 10 to 12). In Quebec, students attend high school for grades 7 to 11 and then transfer to a general and vocational college (*collége d'enseignement général et professionnel/CEGEP*) for a further two or three years. Like elementary education, secondary education is mixed.

Secondary schools may specialise in academic or vocational streams or the arts; all include some kind of 'streaming' system that's designed to prepare students for a vocational or community college or university. Mandatory or 'core' curriculum subjects must be studied for a prescribed number of years or terms, as decided by each province. These generally include English (French), maths, general science, health, sport (physical education) and social studies or social sciences (which may include Canadian history and government, geography, world history and social problems). In addition to mandatory subjects, students choose optional subjects (electives) that will benefit them in the future.

Electives usually comprise around half of a student's work in grades 9 to 12. Around the ninth grade, students receive career guidance counselling as they begin to plan their careers and select subjects that will be useful in their chosen fields. Counselling continues throughout the senior high school years and into college. Larger schools may offer a selection of elective courses aimed at three or more levels: academic, vocational and general. Students planning to go on to college or university elect courses with an emphasis on academic sciences (biology, chemistry, physics), higher mathematics (algebra, geometry, trigonometry and calculus), advanced English or French literature, composition, social sciences or foreign languages.

The vocational programme may provide training in four fields: agricultural education which prepares students for farm management and operation; business education which trains students for the commercial field; home economics which prepares students for home management, child care and care of the sick; and trade and industrial education, which provides training for jobs in mechanical, manufacturing, building and other trades. Students interested in entering business from high school may take typing, book-keeping, computer studies or 'business' English or French.

School sports are popular in Canada, although most take place outside school hours (extracurricular). Team sports have a high profile at high school and being 'on the school team' is more important to many students than being top of the class. Students who excel at sports are often referred to disparagingly as 'jocks', implying that they're too stupid or lazy to succeed at their academic work. However, if a student's grades don't reach the required level he's likely to be barred from taking part in team sports until his grades improve (and he's constantly monitored). High school sport is central to school activities and the ceremony that goes with college sport is also found at high-school level.

In addition to sports, many other school-sponsored activities take place outside school hours, including science and nature clubs, musical organisations (e.g. band or choir), art and drama groups, and language clubs. Most high schools have a student-run newspaper and a photographic darkroom is often available. Colleges and universities place considerable weight on the achievements of students in high school extracurricular activities, as do Canadian employers. High schools are important social centres and participation in school-organised social events, such as school dances and the first hockey game of the season, is widespread.

Examinations & Grades

When a student enrols in a public school, a 'record file' is opened for him (which follows him throughout his school years) and there's a continuous evaluation system throughout all grades. Students are marked on each essay (paper), exam and course taken in each subject studied throughout their 13 years of education (grades K to 12). The following grading system is used in high schools throughout Canada:

Grading Classification

Grade	Classification	Percentage
A	Excellent	90 to 100
B	Good	80 to 89
C	Average/fair	70 to 79
D	Poor	60 to 69
F	Fail	Below 60

All grades are internal and are in relation to the general standard achieved at a particular school, which usually makes it difficult to compare standards in different schools and provinces. Marks depend on a range of criteria, including a student's performance in tests given at intervals during the year, participation in class discussions, completion of homework assignments, and independent projects. Students receive a report card at least twice per year (in some districts it may be up to six times a year), which shows their grades in each subject they're studying.

High school students who need to make up for lost time after illness (or idleness) can attend special 'cramming' summer courses at learning centres run by private companies such as the Sylvan Learning Centre, which has centres in most large towns in Canada (☎ 1-800-EDUCATE, 💻 http://tutoring.

sylvanlearning.com/index.cfm), and Kumon (☏ 1-800-222 6284, 💻 www.kumon.com), who specialise in maths and reading. High schools divide their curriculum into 'advanced', which prepares students to go to university, or 'general', which prepares students to go to a community college or trade school.

High school students take the General Educational Development (GED) Diploma before completing high school, which is the recognised entrance qualification for admission to a Canadian university (mature students aged 25 or over can take GED 'equivalency exams' if they haven't passed the GED).

PRIVATE SCHOOLS

There are private fee-paying schools in all cities in Canada serving a wide range of needs and educating around 5 per cent of Canadian children. Private schools include single-sex schools, schools sponsored by religious groups, schools for students with learning or physical disabilities, and schools for gifted children. Some private schools place the emphasis on sports or cater for students with artistic talent in art, drama, dance or music. There are also schools emphasising activities such as outdoor living or which adhere to a particular educational philosophy, such as Montessori and Waldorf schools. Although most Canadian private schools prepare students for entry to a Canadian college or university, some international schools prepare students for the International Baccalaureate (IB) examination. Some private schools teach exclusively in a foreign language, e.g. Cantonese, follow traditional curricula and prepare students for examinations set by examining boards in their 'home' country.

Private schools are organised like public schools (see page 143), although the curricula and approach differ considerably. They range from nursery schools to large day and boarding schools, from experimental and progressive schools to traditional institutions, and include progressive schools with a holistic approach to a child's development and schools with a strict traditional and conservative regime, and a rigid and competitive approach to learning. School work in private schools is usually rigorous and demanding, and students often have a great deal of homework and pressure. Many parents favour this competitive 'work ethic' approach and expect their offspring to work hard to justify the expense.

Fees vary considerably depending on a variety of factors, including the age of students, the reputation and quality of the school, and its location (schools in major cities are usually the most expensive). Fees aren't all-inclusive and additional obligatory fees are payable, plus fees for optional services. Unless you're rich or someone else is paying, you usually need to start saving before you have any children, although there are some federal tax breaks. Some schools offer payment plans to attract new students.

In addition to tuition fees, most private schools solicit parents for contributions (some schools are quite aggressive and verbal in their requests). For example, parents might have to pay an extra $5,000 to the theatre fund in order for their children to attend a school. Most schools provide scholarships for gifted and talented students, although they may be restricted to children from poorer families or ethnic minorities. Some schools have large endowments, enabling them to take any students they wish, irrespective of their parents' ability to pay.

Private schools provide a broad-based education and generally offer a varied approach to sport, music, drama, art and a wide choice of academic subjects, e.g. some schools offer horse-riding or skiing during school hours or unusual subjects such as speleology (the scientific study of caves). Due to their small classes, teachers in private schools are able to provide students with individually-tailored lessons and tuition, rather than teaching on a production-line system. Private schools may employ specialist staff, e.g. reading specialists, and tutors to help with maths and other subjects. Most also offer after-school programmes, sports teams, clubs, enrichment programmes and tutorial classes. However, private schools may not have the broad resources of public schools, such as an extensive library.

When making an application, you should do so as far in advance as possible. It's usually easier to gain entry to the first grade than to get your child into a later grade, where entry is more limited. Entry may be facilitated for foreign children as many schools consider it an advantage to have a wide selection of foreign students. Gaining entrance to a prominent private school is difficult, particularly in major cities, and you can never guarantee that a particular school will accept your child. Although many nursery and elementary schools accept children on a first-come, first-served basis, the best and most exclusive schools have a demanding selection procedure and many have waiting lists. Therefore you shouldn't rely on enrolling your child in a particular school and neglect other alternatives.

Before enrolling your child in a private school, make sure that you understand the withdrawal conditions in the school contract, particularly if you plan to stay in Canada for a limited time only. Before sending your child to a particular private school, irrespective of its reputation, you should consider carefully your child's needs, capabilities and maturity. For example, it's important to ensure that a school's curriculum and regime are neither too strict nor too liberal for your child.

Directories of private schools are available in most reference libraries in Canada, from the provincial Ministry of Education and from the Canadian Association of Independent Schools (12 Bannockburn Avenue, Toronto, ON M5M 2M8, ☎ 416-780 1779, 💻 www.cais.ca).

HIGHER EDUCATION

Higher education in Canada is often referred to as post-secondary education, and refers to study beyond the secondary school level and usually assumes that a student has undertaken 13 years of study and has a General Educational Development (GED) diploma. Students must usually take a University Transfer Course at a college for one year before attending a university. Mature students aged over 25 are also admitted to these courses, whether or not they have a GED, but must take GED 'equivalency exams'.

For students who don't go to university, post-secondary education continues at community colleges, which are low-fee colleges with one to three-year programmes in a range of practical and para-professional skills, ranging from graphic design to nursing, taught under the broad categories of Arts, Business, Health Services, and Science and Technology. For information and a list of colleges contact the Association of Canadian Community Colleges (200-1223 Michael Street N, Ottawa, ON K1J 7T2, ☎ 613-746 2222, 💻 www.accc.ca).

Over 40 per cent of Canadian high school graduates go on to some sort of higher education. There are three main levels of higher education in Canada: undergraduate

studies (bachelor's degree), graduate studies (master's degree) and postgraduate studies (doctorate). Canada has 77 universities and 146 community colleges, with a wide variety of admission requirements and programmes. The total annual university enrolment is around 600,000 full-time and some 250,000 part-time students, over half of whom are female; around 30,000 are overseas students. However, although an increasing number of students obtain degrees, many are unable to find jobs in their preferred field and end up in dead-end jobs that don't require higher education (such as retail).

The academic standards of colleges and universities vary greatly, and some institutions are better known for the quality of their social life or sports teams than for their academic achievements. Establishments range from vast educational 'plants', offering the most advanced training available, to small intimate private academies emphasising personal instruction and a preference for the humanities or experimentation.

Tuition fees increased dramatically in the '90s and have more than doubled since 1990. Some universities offer programmes that are completely funded by student fees, e.g. Queen's University in Kingston (Ontario) charges well over $50,000 for its two-year Master of Business Administration (MBA) programme. Normally, however, fees for Canadian citizens for most courses are in the region of $4,000 to $5,000, but specialised courses such as dentistry and medicine can cost up to $15,000. Foreign students must pay up to three to four times these amounts. In recent years, many foreign students have become residents in order to reduce their tuition fees.

☑ SURVIVAL TIP

You can check current tuition fees, as well as other costs, grants and scholarships, at www.canadian-universities.net.

The cost of living can vary considerably from area to area and is, not surprisingly, highest in the major cities. Health insurance is essential and compulsory, although students may be automatically enrolled in the university health insurance plan. Many families participate in savings and investment schemes to finance their children's college education. In 1998, the government introduced several new schemes to help fund education, including enhancements to Registered Education Savings Plans (RESP), which are savings schemes to fund post-secondary education with tax-breaks.

The money in a RESP isn't taxed until a student starts to draw on it and because most students are on low incomes, the tax payable is far less than it would otherwise have been. If the designated student doesn't go on to post-secondary education, another child can be named or the funds in the plan can be transferred to the parent/grandparent's own Registered Retirement Savings Plan (RRSP). Other plans include one that allows adults to withdraw money from their RRSPs without paying tax, provided they spend the money on their own education, and a ten-year 'Canadian Millennium Scholarship' scheme to help needy students fund their higher education. A useful book describing these schemes is *Head Start – How To Save For Your Children's or Grandchildren's Education* by Gordon Pape & Frank Jones (Stoddart Publishing).

Many students obtain part-time employment to finance their studies, during term-time and summer breaks (foreign students should check in advance whether their visa allows such employment), while others receive grants, scholarships and loans to help meet their living expenses. Scholarships are awarded directly by universities as well as by fraternal, civic, labour and management organisations. Although public universities don't usually provide financial aid to foreign students, it's possible to obtain a scholarship or partial scholarship for tuition fees from a private university.

The federal government runs the Canada Student Loans Program, which may also pay some of your fees and living expenses (see www.hrsdc.gc.ca/en/learning/canada_student_loan/index.shtml for details). Canada Access Grants are available for students from low-income families and those with permanent disabilities. For further details, see www.

hrsdc.gc.ca/en/learning/canada_student_loan/grant2.shtml or the website of the appropriate provincial government.

Entry qualifications for Canadian colleges and universities vary considerably; generally the better the university (or the better the reputation), the higher the entrance qualifications. Some specialist schools, such as law schools, have a standard entrance examination. Usually overseas qualifications that qualify students to enter a university in their own country are taken into consideration. It's also necessary for mature students returning to full or part-time college education to provide diplomas or certificates showing the education level they've attained, otherwise they must take basic tests. Whatever your qualifications, each application is considered on its merits. All foreign students require a thorough knowledge of English (French in Quebec) and those who aren't of English (or French) mother tongue must take a TOEFL/TOFFL test (see below). Contact individual universities for details of their entrance requirements.

Applications must be made to the Director of Undergraduate Admissions at colleges and universities. If you plan to apply to highly popular colleges and universities, such as those in Toronto, you must apply in August (or autumn) for admission in the following autumn term (August/September), although it's recommended to start the process 18 months in advance. For less popular universities, the latest a foreign student can apply for September admission is March of the same year, as overseas applications usually take at least six months to process. The number of applicants each university receives per available place varies considerably depending on the university. You would be wise not to make all your applications to universities where competition for places is at its fiercest (unless you're a genius). It's best to apply to three universities of varying standards, e.g. speculative, attainable and safe.

All colleges and universities have a huge variety of societies and clubs, many organised by the students' union or council, which is the centre of campus social activities. Canadian universities usually have excellent sports facilities and some provide full academic scholarships to athletes.

There are many books that provide information about Canadian universities and colleges, including University Planning for Canadians for Dummies by Caryn Mladen, David Rosen & Pat Ordovensky (John Wiley) and *MacLean's Guide to Canadian Universities* (also available on their website 💻 www.macleans.ca/universities).

> The Canadian Information Centre for International Credentials (💻 www.cicic.ca/392/admission-to-universities-and-colleges-in-canada.canada) provides comprehensive Information for students educated abroad applying for admission to Canadian universities and colleges.

Many provincial departments of higher education have a toll-free 'education hotline' where you can obtain information about all aspects of higher and further (adult) education. You can also contact the Association of Universities and Colleges of Canada (350 Albert Street, Suite 600, Ottawa, Ontario K1R 1B1, ☎ 613-563 1236, 💻 www.aucc.ca). Another useful organisation for overseas students is the bi-lingual Canadian Bureau for International Education (CBIE, 💻 www.cbie.can), which promotes the special interests of the international learner, both foreigners studying in Canada and Canadians studying abroad, through educational exchanges, scholarships, training awards and internships, technical assistance in education and other related services.

There are many internet sites that provide information about Canadian universities and colleges, including 💻 www.schoolfinder.com and www.uwaterloo.ca/canu/index.html.

ADULT & FURTHER EDUCATION

Adult and further education generally refers to education undertaken by adults of all ages after leaving full-time study, and often after years or even decades of intervening occupation. It doesn't include degree courses taken at college or university directly after

leaving high school, which come under higher education (see above). It also excludes short day and evening classes, e.g. those held at community colleges and usually termed 'continuing education' (although there's often a fine distinction between further and continuing education). Further education includes everything from basic reading and writing skills for the illiterate to full-time advanced, professional and doctoral degrees at university. On many university campuses, more students are enrolled in adult and further education courses than in regular degree programmes.

Adult education courses may be full or part-time and are provided by colleges, universities, community colleges, technical schools (which may use the facilities at elementary and high schools), trade schools, business schools, and elementary and high schools. Courses are also provided by private community organisations, government agencies, job training centres, labour and professional organisations, private tutors and instructors, business and industry, industrial training programmes, museums, clubs, private organisations and institutes, correspondence course schools and educational TV programmes.

Typical of these classes are those offered under the auspices of the Forum for International Trade Training (FITT) for people who want training and a qualification (e.g. the Certified International Trade Professional/ CITP diploma) in import and export skills. FITT provides workshops for small and medium-sized businesses, and also sponsors and monitors training at universities and colleges throughout Canada. For further information, contact FITT (30 Metcalfe Street, Ottawa, ON K1P 5L4, ☎ 1-800-561 3488 or 613-230 3553, 💻 www.fitt.ca).

Each year thousands of students attend further education courses at universities or community colleges, many of which are of short duration and job-related. They're scheduled in the evenings, at weekends and during the summer recess. Lecturers may be full- or part-time faculty members or professionals practising in the fields in which they lecture. Students generally aren't required to take a minimum number of courses per semester or to take courses in succeeding semesters. You can register in a formal vocational programme or simply take a course for pleasure. The most popular fields in adult education are accounting, business administration and management, education, engineering, fine and applied arts, health professions, information technology (IT), language, literature, physical education, psychology and religion.

The federal government underwrites the cost of basic adult education, so that older students, particularly members of minority groups, can go back to school for the rudiments of an education they failed to get as children, e.g. in reading, writing, maths, history and geography. Many cities and provinces also offer career, vocational and continuing education programmes in public schools, including English and French as a Second Language (ESL/FSL) classes. Adult education also gives students the opportunity to complete their high school studies, which in some cities can be undertaken in Cantonese and other languages.

Many further education courses are of the open learning variety, where students study mostly at home. Correspondence colleges, most of which are private commercial organisations, offer literally hundreds of academic, professional and vocational courses, and enrol many thousands of students each year. Quebec operates a scheme called *Télé-Université* (💻 www.teluq.uquebec.ca, in French), a subsidiary of the University of Quebec, for those wishing to pursue higher education at home using multimedia equipment.

LANGUAGE SCHOOLS

If you don't speak English (or French if you're planning to live in Quebec) fluently or you wish to learn another language, you can enrol in a language course at numerous language schools in Canada. There are English-language schools in all cities and large towns, although the majority, particularly those offering intensive courses, are in the major cities. Many adult and further education institutions provide English courses and many Canadian universities offer summer and holiday English and French-language courses. Colleges and universities often run an English Language Programme, which is a pre-academic, English-as-a-Second-Language (ESL) programme for students whose native language isn't English.

Obtaining a working knowledge of or becoming fluent in English while living in Canada is 'relatively easy' (if learning any language can ever be called easy!) because you're constantly immersed in the English language (except in Quebec) and have the maximum opportunity to practise. However, if you wish to speak English fluently, you'll probably need to take lessons. It's usually necessary to have a recognised qualification in English or pass a Test of English as a Foreign Language (TOEFL) in order to be accepted at a college or university in Canada. Foreigners who wish to study English full-time can enrol at one of the many English-language centres at Canadian universities.

Most language schools offer a variety of classes depending on your current language ability, how many hours you wish to study per week, how much money you want to spend and how fast you wish to learn. Courses vary in length from one week to six months and cater for all ages. Full-time, part-time and evening courses are offered by most schools, and many also provide residential courses. Fees at a community college are around $250 to $350 for ten weeks (two classes per week of three to four hours). Residential courses (often with half-board, consisting of breakfast and an evening meal) usually offer excellent value. Bear in mind that if you need to find your own accommodation, particularly in a major city, it can be *very* expensive. Language classes generally fall into the following categories:

Language Class Categories

Category	No. hours per week
Compact	10 to 20
Intensive	20 to 30
Total immersion	30 to 40

Course fees vary considerably (usually calculated weekly) depend on the number of hours tuition per week, the type of course, and the location and reputation of the school. Expect to pay $150 to $200 per week for a compact course and around $250 per week for an intensive course providing 20 to 30 hours of language study. Half-board accommodation usually costs about $200 to $300 extra per week (or more in large cities). It's possible to enrol at a good school for an all-inclusive (tuition plus half-board accommodation), four-week intensive course for as little as $450 per week. Total immersion or executive courses are offered by many schools and usually consist of private lessons for a minimum of 30 or 40 hours per week, with fees running to $2,500 or more per week. Not everyone is suited to learning at such a fast rate (or has the financial resources!).

Some immigrants are eligible for free federal government sponsored classes called Language Instruction for Newcomers to Canada (LINC – see box below). Other low-income students may have their fees paid or part-paid by provincial governments, although there's often a waiting list for classes. In some areas, immigrant settlement agencies, community groups and churches provide free or low-cost language classes.

Whatever language you're learning, don't expect to become fluent in a short period unless you have a particular flair for languages or already have a good command of a language. Unless you desperately need to learn a language quickly, it's better to space your lessons over a long period. Don't commit yourself to a long course of study (particularly an expensive one) before ensuring that it's the correct one for you. Most schools offer a free introductory lesson and free tests to help you find your appropriate level. Many language schools offer private and small group lessons. It's important to choose the right course, particularly if you're studying English to continue with full-time education in Canada and need to reach a minimum standard or gain a particular qualification.

You may prefer to have private lessons, which are a faster but more expensive way of learning a language. The main advantage of private lessons is that you learn at your own speed and aren't held back by slow learners or dragged along in the wake of the class genius. There are advertisements for English teachers in local newspapers. You can also place an advertisement for a private teacher in local newspapers and magazines, on shopping mall notice boards, at town halls, libraries, universities and schools, and through your (or your spouse's) employer. Your friends, colleagues or neighbours may also be able to recommend a private teacher. For further information regarding languages in Canada, see **Language** on page 39.

The Canadian government provides a free (English or French) 'Language Instruction for Newcomers to Canada' (LINC – 💻 www.cic.gc.ca/english/resources/publications/welcome/wel-22e.asp) programme (called the English Language Service for Adults/ELSA in some provinces). It offers both full- and part-time classes for all migrant adults, not just the person looking for work (some centres also provide free transportation and child care while you attend classes).

totem poles

tram (streetcar), Toronto, ON

10. PUBLIC TRANSPORT

Like their neighbours in the US, Canadians aren't enthusiastic about public transport and when not flying they prefer to drive. Public transport varies from excellent to adequate in the major cities, but is poor in country areas where you almost always need your own transport. In cities, modern integrated transport systems allow travellers to transfer from one kind of public transport to another on a single ticket, completing their journeys quickly, inexpensively and safely.

With a few exceptions, such as the luxury express coach service between Calgary and Edmonton, long-distance bus services leave much to be desired, and the train service is no longer what it was in the days before the airlines took over, when it was the only way to travel (unless you were prepared to use a horse, canoe or dog-sled). With over half the population living in the area around the Great Lakes and the St Lawrence lowlands, most of whom only venture beyond the urban areas for holidays (vacations), there isn't much call for train travel other than in the tourist season. Even the famous cross-Canada train, *The Canadian*, which used to leave Montreal for Vancouver each day, now starts from Toronto and runs only three days per week.

The one area of public transport where Canada really excels is air travel, where Canadians enjoy among the most comprehensive and cheapest services in the world (only the US does it better). Trains and cars just cannot compete over long distances, e.g. it takes around five days to drive from Toronto to Vancouver, but you can fly in just five hours.

There are reduced fares on public transport for children, youths, students and senior citizens in most areas, and some local services are subsidised by provincial and local governments. Regular travellers can save money by buying blocks of tickets or monthly passes. Many cities and towns provide 'park and ride' services, where inexpensive or free parking is combined with low-cost public transport into town centres. A restricted public transport service is provided on federal holidays, including Christmas Day, and on New Year's Eve most public transport in major cities is free from 6pm until 2am, to discourage people from drinking and driving.

There's a wealth of travel websites for Canada and you can also book online directly with most transport companies, including bus, rail and airline operators. You can also book via a travel agent who's a member of the Association of Canadian Travel Agents (350 Sparks Street, Suite 510, Ottawa, ON K1R 7S8, ☎ 613-237 3657, 💻 www.acta.ca), which could save you both time and money.

TRAVELLERS WITH DISABILITIES

Canadian public carriers under federal jurisdiction (railways, ferries and airlines either based in Canada or other scheduled and chartered carriers using Canadian airports) must ensure that disabled travellers don't 'encounter undue obstacles' when travelling and that their staff have received 'awareness training'. Airlines operating planes with 30 or more seats must provide assistance with embarking and disembarking if they're given 48 hours notice (and ideally, even if they aren't given notice). Some municipal and inter-city buses are equipped with wheelchair-lifts and other services.

Travellers should contact individual carriers for information about their facilities for disabled travellers or contact the Canadian Transportation Agency (CTA, 15 Eddy Street, Gatineau, Quebec, K1A 0N9, ☎ 1-888-222 2592, 💻 www.cta-otc.gc.ca) or the Canadian Paraplegic Association (1101 Prince of Wales Drive, Suite 230, Ottawa, ON K2C 3W7, ☎ 613-723 1033, 💻 www.canparaplegic.org).

TRAINS

The railway was responsible for opening up Canada in the 19th century and played a major role in the development and exploitation of the whole North American continent, although it has been in decline since the '50s and has lost much of its former business to the automobile, air travel and long-distance buses. Having said that, it has undergone something of a revival in recent years, particularly as a relaxed way to view some of the spectacular scenery in the west of the country. Canada's rail network is one of the largest in the world, with 31,000mi (50,000km) of tracks. However, in terms of passenger miles per head of population, it rates well behind other industrialised nations. The fastest and best trains carry freight, which has priority over (and subsidises) the passenger service.

The passenger rail service in Canada is operated by VIA Rail (an independent Crown corporation) and the rolling stock and lines are owned by Canadian Pacific and Canadian National. VIA Rail serves some 480 communities on a network of 8,700mi (14,000km), carrying around 4mn passengers a year and operating some 450 trains a week (around two-thirds in the Quebec City-Windsor corridor). Some 90 per cent of all rail transportation in Canada is on the two main transcontinental routes, with just 10 per cent on the 30 regional railways. Long-distance trains have carriages with swivel chairs (parlour coaches), *couchettes*, bedrooms for two people and single bedrooms (roomettes); and some luxury trains, such as *The Canadian*, have carriages with panoramic windows (dome cars), elegant dining rooms and hot showers. Anxious to share in the new enthusiasm for trains by tourists, VIA Rail is looking at ways to bring its system and services up to date, including privatisation or franchising.

Rail is unable to compete with the low cost and speed of air travel (a 10-hour train journey can usually be accomplished in one hour by air) and the convenience of car travel. Canadian long-distance trains move painfully slowly compared with those in most European countries (but at least they give you a chance of seeing a bear or a moose as you crawl through the Rockies). On some routes there's just one train per day, and late trains are so common on long-distance routes that timetables warn passengers not to book connecting transportation in advance. There are no passenger trains on the islands of Newfoundland and Prince Edward Island and on several routes you must travel part of the way by coach. The rail system is at its best in the Montreal-Windsor corridor, which is hardly surprising because almost half the population lives there (you can connect at Windsor for US Amtrak trains to Detroit and Chicago). Trains are frequent and relatively fast, particularly during the peak commuting hours.

The advantages of long-distance rail travel are the spaciousness of the carriages (cars) and the chance to relax and enjoy the changing landscape. Service is the equal of any railway in the world and you can eat and drink well at what are reasonable prices by international standards. As a means of travel for tourists with plenty of time and a wish to see some of the world's most spectacular scenery, trains provide the best opportunity in Canada for relaxed travel, isolated from the usual hectic pace of life (Canadian trains are God's way of telling Canadians to slow down).

VIA Rail provides special accommodation for wheelchair-bound passengers (indicated by a wheelchair symbol on the outside of carriages) on most trains, including specially designed sleeping accommodation and bathrooms on overnight trains. Wheelchair symbols in the timetable show which stations are accessible to passengers with special needs, and have hydraulic wheelchair lifts and platforms at train

level. Wheelchairs are available on request at most stations, although disabled, elderly and other passengers requiring special assistance should notify VIA Rail by phone 24 hours before their departure. Passengers requiring special meals should give 48 hours' notice, as should those who require medications to be stored at low temperatures. Passengers who require assistance in attending to their personal needs (e.g. eating, medical care or personal hygiene) must travel with an escort, who's given a free seat.

Seeing eye and hearing-guide dogs may ride in passenger carriages, but other household pets (such as dogs and cats) must travel in baggage cars in cages that allow them to stand. Cages can be purchased at most stations and VIA Rail reserves the right to refuse to transport animals in unsuitable cages. Customers are responsible for feeding and exercising their animals, and there's a charge of between $10 and $40 per animal.

For further information about VIA Rail services, contact Customer Relations (VIA Rail Canada Inc., PO Box 8116, Station 'A', Montreal, PQ H3C 3N3, ☏ 1-800-681 2561, 🖳 www.viarail.ca). The *National Timetable* booklet (available from any VIA Rail station) contains information about all VIA Rail's long-distance routes, sleeping accommodation and travel advice. VIA Rail stations, offices and approved travel agents also provide information about package tours, connections with other train services and buses, hotel reservations, car rental and other travel-related matters.

In addition to the VIA Rail system and local rail services, there are a number of scenic narrow gauge railways in Canada, including the White Pass & Yukon Route Railroad (☏ 1-800-343 7373, 🖳 www.wpyr.com). In the east, the South Simcoe Railway (🖳 www.southsimcoerailway.ca) in Ontario uses 1920s carriages and an 1890s locomotive from the old Canadian Pacific Railway, while in Quebec the Hull-Chelsea-Wakefield line (☏ 819-778 7246, 🖳 www.steamtrain.ca) employs a 1907 steam locomotive that runs alongside the scenic Gatineau river.

A number of books are published for rail lovers, including *The Trans-Canada Rail Guide* by Melissa Graham (Trailblazer) and *VIA Rail* by Christopher C. N. Greenlaw (Voyageur Press).

Tickets

Train tickets in Canada are either one-way (singles) or round trip (return). You can buy long-distance tickets that allow you to break your journey, which is cheaper than buying separate tickets for each section. Tickets for VIA Rail services should be purchased from a ticket office or agent *before* commencing your journey; however, conductors on trains can issue tickets to extend your journey to any destination on the train's route. You can also buy upgrades for accommodation onboard trains, such as sleeping cars, club service and custom class accommodation (subject to availability).

Paying

You can pay for tickets and accommodation at stations or onboard trains in cash and with credit cards such as American Express (Amex), Diners Club, MasterCard and Visa. Tickets can also be purchased from travel agents or via the internet with a credit card.

Fares

Children under the age of two travel free (provided they don't occupy a seat) and those aged up to 11 receive a 50 per cent discount in economy class and a 25 per cent discount in VIA 1 (1st class) and sleeper classes. Children under eight aren't permitted to travel alone, but children aged from 8 to 11 may travel unaccompanied under certain conditions and with written permission from a parent or legal guardian. Senior citizens over 60 receive a discount, of 10 per cent on all fares and up to 50 per cent on some routes, subject to certain conditions, e.g. advance purchase, restricted periods, limited number of economy class seats, cancellation fees, etc. Full-time students with an International Student Identity Card (ISIC) and youths aged under 18 receive a 40 per cent discount in economy class and up to 50 per cent subject to certain conditions (as above for seniors). Group discounts are also available for parties of 20 or more.

Other discounts are available on specific routes, e.g. Victoria–Nanaimo, and in northern regions you can obtain a 40 per cent reduction on economy class tickets year-round or sleeper class fares during super-saver periods, provided you buy them at least seven days in advance. On the Toronto–Vancouver route you can get a 25 per cent reduction on economy class or 'Silver and Blue' class tickets during off-peak periods and a 40 per cent reduction during super-saver periods by buying tickets at least seven days in advance. On the Montreal–Halifax/Gaspé route or the Quebec City–Windsor corridor, you can get a 40 per cent discount on economy or sleeper class by buying a ticket at least seven days in advance. However, on all the above routes, there's only a limited number of seats available at reduced rates.

Reservations

VIA Rail advises passengers to arrive at a station 30 minutes before the departure time. This, however, is generally necessary only when you need to buy a ticket or have baggage to check. Although you can pay when making a reservation, it isn't necessary and if you don't, you're given a date by which you must pay for tickets. Only the advance purchase of a ticket guarantees a seat. If you're planning to take a long-distance train during the summer or on a federal holiday, it's wise to book well in advance.

You can make reservations up to six months in advance at city railway stations, VIA Rail ticket offices, most travel agents, by phone or through VIA Rail's 'Resernet' internet booking service (💻 www.viarail.ca). When you reserve a seat or sleeper on the internet, you're given a reservation number and a date/time by which you must pay for your ticket, or the reservation is cancelled. If you arrive at a station without a reservation and seats are still available, you're assigned a seat and sold a ticket on the spot.

Refunds

To obtain a refund of an unused ticket, you must submit the ticket with the receipt coupon. Refunds can usually be made at any VIA Rail sales office or at the travel agent that issued the ticket. Where refunds cannot be made immediately, a refund application must be made and the refund is mailed to you. Refunds of a CANRAILPASS and reduced fare tickets are subject to certain conditions. For refunds by post, you must send the original tickets and receipt coupons (not photocopies) to VIA Rail Canada Inc. (Ticket Refunds, Union Station, 65 Front Street West, Room 0119, Toronto, ON M5J 1E7). Send tickets by registered post so that you have proof of delivery.

Canrailpass

The Canrailpass provides 12 days of economy class travel within a 30-day period. Off-peak (1st January to 31st May and 16th October to 31st December) fares in 2009 were $576 for an adult and $518 for a child, youth, student or senior, while peak fares (1st June to 15th October) were $923 for an adult and $831 for a youth, student or senior. You can buy a maximum of three extra days' travel within the 30-day period for $49 for an adult (others $44) in the off-peak season and $79 for an adult (others $71) in the peak season.

At some suburban stations, ticket outlets may be open during peak hours only, outside of which tickets must be purchased on trains. If in doubt, check in advance. Rail ticket machines may be available which accept all coins (except pennies) plus $5, $10 and $20 bills. Monthly tickets can usually also be purchased by post.
For further information, see 🖳 www.viarail.ca/planner/en_cart_canr.html.

Accommodation

VIA Rail accommodation is offered in two classes: economy and first class. The cheapest 'accommodation' is economy class, where you sleep in your seat on overnight trips. Blankets and pillows are distributed to passengers on board eastern overnight trains, but passengers on the western overnight must bring their own or you can buy them on trains. First class includes the overnight 'sleeper class', where you have a private 'bedroom' with a seat that converts to a bed and are provided with bedding and towels. First class passengers can choose their seat at the time of reservation and enjoy the use of payphones (payable by credit card), priority boarding, three-course meals, complimentary aperitif, and a choice of wines with lunch and dinner.

First class is known by different names depending on the route. For example, it's called 'VIA 1' on the rail corridor between Quebec City and Windsor, 'Silver & Blue' class on trains from Toronto west (including *The Canadian*), and 'Easterly' class on the *Ocean* and *Chaleur* trains from Montreal east to the *Gaspé* Peninsula. Halifax Easterly and 'Silver & Blue' trains include a coach with a scenic dome, the Bullet Lounge (where breakfast is served), the Mural Lounge, an art-deco dining carriage, and showers in each sleeping car. Not surprisingly, first class costs over twice as much as economy class.

URBAN TRANSIT SYSTEMS

Canada's major cities have excellent urban and suburban transit systems, where relatively fast and frequent services are available on a mixture of buses, surface and underground (metro/subway) trains, monorails and, in some cities, ferries. Tickets are valid for the whole system or you receive a free transfer that allows you to change from one mode of transport to another. Tickets are singles or multiples or passes for one or more days. Smoking, eating, drinking and playing radios and cassette/CD players aren't usually permitted (except with headphones), and only guide dogs and pets enclosed in acceptable carrying cases are permitted. Bicycles can be taken on some trains, although usually only outside commuting hours.

When a transit system includes buses and trains, fares are the same for both and there are usually discounts for children aged under 14, students, seniors and for tickets purchased in blocks or 'books'. When paying cash you need the exact amount and should keep your ticket as proof of payment until you complete your journey. The choice of public transport in selected cities is shown below:

- **Calgary** has buses and the Calgary Light Rail Transit System known as the 'C-Train' or the 'LRT'. There are express buses during the morning rush hours, on which there's a supplement of 50¢ in addition to the standard fare of $2.50 ($1.50 for children), and books of ten tickets are available for $21 and $13 respectively. You can travel for up to one hour in one direction for the basic fare, changing as often as necessary. Buses generally run around every 20 minutes and the C-Train every few minutes. Schedules and maps are available from Calgary Transit (224-7 Avenue SW, Calgary, ☎ 403-262 1000, 🖳 www.calgarytransit.com).
- **Edmonton** has a Light Rapid Transit (LRT) system with the same fares for buses and trains: $2.50 per ride for adults ($21 for a book of ten tickets), $2.25 for youths and seniors ($18.50 for ten). Schedules and maps are available from Customer Services, Churchill LRT Station (☎ 780-496 1611, 🖳 www.edmonton.ca/transportation).

- **Montreal** has a rapidly expanding underground (*métro*, 💻 www.stm.info) system which is fast, clean and quiet, with 68 stations on four lines in spring 2009, plus an extensive network of buses. Underground tickets are available from booths at stations, which you insert into a slot in the turnstiles to gain access to platforms. Underground and bus tickets are valid on both modes of transport and if you want to transfer to a bus, you obtain a transfer (*correspondence*) ticket from the machine just inside the turnstile. A single journey costs $2.75 (you can buy a strip of six tickets for $12 and there are concessions for certain travellers), a one-day tourist pass $9 and a three-day pass $17. Unlike some underground networks, the Montreal underground is safe at almost any time of day or night.
- **Ottawa** has only one form of public transport available, the bus service, of which there are two systems: the Ottawa-Carleton Regional Transit Commission (☎ 613-741 4390, 💻 www.octranspo.com) with hundreds of routes, and the other in Hull operated by the *Societé de Transport l'Outaouais* (☎ 819-770 3242, 💻 www.sto.ca – in French only!). Transfers between the two systems can be purchased on buses. Fares vary with the route (indicated by a colour code at bus stops) and are shown in the front window of buses. You can buy tickets at newsstands, Shoppers Drug Mart or Pharmaplus stores, or pay the driver in cash, when you must tender the exact fare.
- **Quebec** city has buses only. Maps are available from tourist information booths or from the Commission des Transports de Québec (☎ 1-888-461 2433, 💻 www.ctq.gouv.qc.ca).
- **Toronto** has an interconnecting underground, bus and tram (streetcar) system operated by the Toronto Transit Commission (☎ 416-393 4636, 💻 www.ttc.ca). As in Montreal, the system is fast, safe, clean and relatively quiet, and operates from 6am until 1.30am the next day, from Mondays to Saturdays, and from 9am to 1.30am on Sundays. There's cheap all-day parking at underground stations, but spaces are filled early by commuters. To use the network you need an underground or surface transport token, a ticket or the exact change. To transfer to a bus or tram, you need to ask for a 'transfer' when you buy your underground token. You can buy tickets or tokens at underground entrances or stores displaying the sign 'TTC tickets may be purchased here'. A single fare (one token) is $2.75 for adults ($11.25 for five tokens, $22.50 for ten), $1.85 for students and seniors ($15 for ten tokens) and 70¢ for children aged under 12 ($5 for ten tokens).

  You can also buy a day pass for $9 that's valid for unlimited travel for one person after 9.30am on weekdays or for up to two adults and four children any time at weekends or holidays. For further information, including a *Ride Guide*, ☎ 416-393 INFO or visit 💻 www.city.toronto.on.ca/ttc/fares.htm.
- **Vancouver** has electric and gas-powered buses run by the South Coast British Columbia Transportation Authority (thankfully known as TransLink), SeaBus catamaran ferries and the SkyTrain monorail (which is an inexpensive way to get around urban and suburban Vancouver). Daily services on main routes operate from 5am until 2am the following day, with less frequent 'Owl' services operating on some downtown-urban routes until after 4am. Most buses are wheelchair-accessible.

  Fares are the same on all three systems: $2.50 for a journey within one zone, $3.75 for two zones and $5 for all three zones.

Books of ten tickets cost $19, $28.50 and $38 respectively, with reductions for seniors, students and children. Transfers are free and available on boarding and are valid for 90 minutes for travel in any direction on all modes of transport. Day passes cost $9 (full fare) or $7 (reduced). For further information ☏ 250-382 6161 or visit 💻 www.translink.bc.ca.

- **Winnipeg** has several bus lines serving the metropolitan area and a '99 Flyer' shuttle service for the downtown shopping area (including Chinatown, the library and Forks Market) between 11am and 3.15pm. The standard fare is $2.30 or $20 for ten tickets, and discounts ($1.80/$13.80) are available on all services for children under 17, students and seniors. Schedules and maps are provided in the back of the Winnipeg telephone directory or ☏ 204-986 5700 or visit 💻 www.winnipegtransit.com.

LONG-DISTANCE BUSES

In addition to local buses operating in Canadian cities and their suburbs, Canada has an extensive network of long-distance buses (also called coaches). Long-distance buses are the cheapest form of public transport in Canada and to the US. Although there have been cutbacks in services in recent years caused by increased competition from domestic airlines, long-distance buses continue to survive and even prosper. You can travel almost anywhere in Canada by bus on an extensive network of scheduled routes with good connections. Most small towns away from the major cities have some sort of bus service, but these tend to be infrequent and slow, so for convenience almost everybody has private transport.

A number of companies provide long-distance services, by far the largest of which is Greyhound Canada. Greyhound carries 6.5mn passengers each year and travels to nearly 1,100 towns and cities in Canada. It provides the cheapest option for independent travellers seeking door-to-door transport to small towns, and those that aren't served by Greyhound are usually covered by regional and local bus companies, many of which accept Greyhound bus passes. The largest of these is Acadian Lines (☏ 1-800-567 5151, 💻 www.smtbus.com), which operates throughout the Maritime Provinces.

Bus terminals in major cities offer a host of services and usually have a restaurant; travel agent; ticket, luggage and parcel services; toilets; and left luggage lockers. Bus passes often entitle you to discounts at bus terminal restaurants (although it's usually cheaper to eat away from terminals), nearby hotels, youth hostels and sightseeing tours. Although bus terminals are usually safe places, they're sometimes located in run-down, inner-city areas and aren't the best places in which to spend a lot of time.

> ☑ **SURVIVAL TIP**
>
> **You must usually buy your ticket at a bus terminal or a central office before boarding a bus. Allow plenty of time as there are often long queues (line-ups).**

Tickets aren't generally sold on buses, except in some rural areas and on city (urban) routes. Obtain information about schedules, connections and fares, and confirm them by checking the posted schedules. Always ask for the cheapest available fare, which may not be advertised. Greyhound offers a variety of special fares including companion, family, seniors (60 and over) and a Canada pass.

You can buy open-dated tickets from bus terminals or travel agents in advance, although usually it's unnecessary or even impossible to make a reservation. You can make as many stopovers as you wish, provided the entire journey is completed before your ticket expires (although there may be restrictions with special fares and sightseeing tours). Bus pass coupons must be validated each time they're used, so you should arrive early at terminals to have your ticket stamped. In addition to bus terminals, buses also stop at designated 'flag stops', where you must flag down a bus by waving at the driver.

Fares depend on a number of considerations, including whether you're travelling one-way or round-trip (return), the time of travel and when you're returning. One child under four travels free and other children under four travel at half price, while children aged 5 to 11 travel for half fare when accompanied by an adult. In addition to standard fares, a range of discount and promotional fares is available, although these don't usually apply during holiday periods. The range of tickets available includes one-way, round-trip, supersaver, group discounts, discounts for senior citizens and handicapped travellers (10 per cent discount), excursion and promotional fares.

As with planes and trains, luggage is checked in before boarding a bus. Allow around 45 minutes in cities and 15 minutes in small towns. You should identify your luggage with a name tag and keep your claim check in a safe place. When two buses are running on the same service, make sure your luggage is put on the correct bus, as it isn't unusual for it to end up on the wrong one. You can take a small- to medium-sized bag (you can buy one with a cold pack to keep your lunch fresh) onto the bus, provided it fits in the overhead luggage compartment. Always keep any valuables with you on the bus.

Most long-distance buses have air-conditioning, heating, toilets (absolutely essential when travelling with children), and reclining seats with headrests and reading lamps. The seats are comfortable, with the smoothest ride being in the middle of the bus away from the wheels (the best view, however, is at the front, where you also have the most leg room). Window seats are often cooler than aisle seats, particularly at night when drivers usually turn up the air-conditioning to keep themselves awake. Take a warm sweater, jacket or blanket inside the bus with you, as the powerful air-conditioning is freezing at anytime. If you plan to sleep on a bus, an inflatable pillow or sleeping bag (to use as a pillow, not to bed down in the aisle) is useful. Ear plugs and eye masks are also recommended if you're a light sleeper.

If you use a radio or cassette/CD/MP3 player on a bus, you must wear earphones. Smoking and alcohol are prohibited on all buses and if you're caught having a puff in the restroom, you're ejected from the bus and could be prosecuted by the bus company and the police (there's a fine of up to $500!). If you're travelling across Canada, bear in mind that distances are vast and a coast-to-coast trip takes seven or eight days, with only brief stops at fast food joints or bus terminals every few hours, and no overnight sleep stops or stops for showers (the main consolation is that you don't need to pay to sleep on the bus). Many people provide their own food and drink, so that they can eat at their leisure. On long journeys you may have to get off the bus occasionally for it to be cleaned.

At rest stops, you may have just a few minutes to stretch your legs or grab some food and the driver may drive off without warning if you aren't on the bus!

For information about Greyhound services contact Greyhound Canada Transportation Corporation (877 Greyhound Way SW, Calgary, AB T3C 3V8, ☎ 1-800-661 8747, 💻 www.greyhound.ca). The Brewster bus line (PO Box 1140, 100 Gopher Street, Banff, AB T1L 1J3, ☎ 1-866-606 6700 or 403-762 6700, 💻 www.brewster.ca) operates sightseeing tours in the west, mainly in the Rockies.

TAXIS

Taxis are relatively inexpensive in Canada and are plentiful in most cities (except when it's raining or you have lots of luggage). Taxis are usually easily distinguishable in major cities, e.g. the Yellow Cab Line cabs are painted (surprise, surprise) bright yellow, although there are several companies in most cities so you can expect taxis to come in a variety of colours and styles. The only common feature is a plastic 'Taxi' sign on the roof, which when illuminated means that the taxi is for hire. Taxis can be hailed on the street or you can pick one up at a cab rank outside hotels and railway stations.

There's a minimum charge of around $3 (flag-drop) after which the cost is around $1.50 to $1.75 per kilometre. In addition to what's shown on the meter, you must also pay additional costs such as bridge or ferry tolls and surcharges, e.g. for night and Sunday journeys. Special rates may apply to some destinations, which are usually posted in cabs. Waiting time is charged at $35 to $40 an hour. Most drivers don't like changing anything larger than a $10 or $20 bill, but don't mind keeping the change. With the exception of Quebec, where taxi drivers may refuse to answer you if you don't speak French, most Canadian taxi drivers are courteous and helpful.

At Canadian airports and major rail stations there may be a taxi 'dispatcher'. His job is to get you a taxi, advise you on fares and help prevent you being cheated by bogus cab drivers. At some airports and rail stations, fares to popular destinations are posted on notice boards, while at smaller rail stations there may be a special taxi phone. Minibus shuttle services are also available at most airports; like taxis, they take you exactly where you want to go, but the fare is lower because it's shared with your fellow passengers.

All taxi drivers must hold a chauffeur's licence and a taxi licence from the municipal authority. If you have a complaint about a taxi, note the cab and driver's licence numbers and the name of the taxi company. This information should be listed on the receipt, which must be provided on request.

AIRLINE SERVICES

Canadians have excellent air links to most countries and some 100 airlines transport around 40mn passengers some 55bn miles a year. The two most popular domestic routes, Montreal-Toronto and Vancouver-Toronto, each carry over 1mn passengers a year, and even the short route from Calgary to Edmonton (less than 200mi/320km) carries around half a million passengers per year.

Canada's flag carrier (founded in 1936) and largest airline is Air Canada (🖳 www.aircanada.com), which has a fleet of over 300 aircraft serving some 160 destinations worldwide. In January 2001 it acquired Canada's second-largest carrier, Canadian Airlines, subsequently merging the latter's operations into its own and making it the world's twelfth-largest airline (it's now the eighth-largest by fleet size). In recent years, Air Canada has faced a number of financial difficulties, including filing for

bankruptcy protection in 2003, and like most major airlines was struggling in 2009 (not helped by the global recession). Air Canada is a member of the Star Alliance airline network (🖳 www.staralliance.com).

Other Canadian airlines include the second-largest, Air Canada Jazz (🖳 www.flyjazz.ca – now spun off from Air Canada), one of the largest regional airlines in the world serving 86 destinations in Canada and the US; and Canadian North (🖳 www.cdn-north.com), the country's premier northern airline serving Nunavut and the Northwest Territories from Calgary, Edmonton and Ottawa. The country's main budget airline is WestJet (🖳 www.westjet.com), serving an increasing number of cities across Canada's ten provinces and the US, including Hawaii, the Caribbean and Mexico. Air Canada Jetz (owned by Air Canada) is based in Montreal, from where it operates a premium business service for corporate clients and professional sports teams.

In the north of the country the larger carriers use Boeing 737s (or similar planes) when flying into 'major' airports, although in smaller towns and remote areas the smaller airlines operate seaplanes (float planes) that land on lakes and use skids (rather than floats) when they're frozen. There's also a seaplane service between Vancouver and Victoria.

You should check-in at least an hour before a domestic flight and two hours before an international flight, as some airlines may over-book. Check-in closes 30 to 60 minutes before departure and if you turn up too late you'll find you've been bumped (put on a later flight). Although there are occasionally delays in departure, particularly in winter, in general flights are punctual and you don't spend 'hours' flying around in circles above busy airports waiting to land. Canada is one of the world's safest countries in which to fly and its major airlines have an excellent safety record that's second to none. Smoking on aircraft is banned on all domestic and foreign flights within Canada and is prohibited in airport terminal buildings except for designated areas.

Canada signed an Open Skies agreement with the EU in 2009 (similar to the one with the US signed in 2008) that allows any Canadian or EU carrier to fly freely between any European airport and Canadian airports.

Airports

Canada's leading international airports are Calgary, Edmonton, Gander (Newfoundland), Halifax, Montreal, Toronto, Vancouver and Winnipeg. These are termed 'gateway' airports and act as a hub for Canadian carriers and regional/commuter airlines which operate services to smaller airports. When taking a plane from an international airport in Canada, check in advance which terminal you require. With the exception of Montreal Mirabel airport, which is 34mi (55km) outside town and takes around one hour to reach from the city centre, and Edmonton which is 19mi (30km) outside town and takes 45 minutes to get to, all other major airports can be reached from the city centre in around 30 minutes. St John's, Winnipeg and Vancouver airports are less than 5mi (8km) outside town and can be reached in around 15 minutes. Most airports provide short and long-term parking lots.

Major airports are organised by airline, where each carrier has separate check-in desks, gates, lounges and even exclusive terminals at some airports. Signs at airports are in English and French, and most have information desks and centres with multilingual staff. If you have any problems, inquire at the ticket booth of the airline you're travelling with. Flight departures aren't announced but are displayed on information screens and departure boards, so keep an eye out for your flight.

You may have a long walk to the baggage reclaim area, although major airports have moving walkways. Luggage trolleys (carts) are free at some airports, but need to be rented at others for $1 (this means if you're a foreigner arriving in Canada, you cannot get a trolley unless you've got some Canadian coins!). Most international airports have banks, currency exchanges and cash machines (ATMs), and stamp and travel insurance machines. All international airports have executive and VIP passenger lounges, and publish free passenger information booklets. Major airports also have emergency clinics (and sometimes a dental service), restaurants, bars, gift stores, luggage storage, lost property offices, fax machines, photocopiers, computer rentals and other business services (some even have a massage booth). Duty-free goods are available on cross-border flights with the exception of flights that are pre-cleared to US destinations, e.g. in Vancouver, customs and immigration clearance on US-bound flights is carried out before departure.

Public transport to and from major airports includes buses, taxis, mini-buses (shuttle buses), limousines and sometimes rail services. Often there's a dispatcher whose job is to find you a taxi and advise you on fares. Many hotels and motels provide a courtesy bus service at major airports, although smaller airports may have no bus services at all. A shuttle minibus or mini-van door-to-door 'taxi' service is often provided and can be booked to pick you up at home. Air taxis – helicopters and light aircraft – are available at all major airports and many smaller regional airports. Some airports levy an 'airport improvement fee' (AIF) for departing passengers of anything between $5 and $40.

International Fares

International air fares to and from Canada are among the lowest in the world and have been slashed even further in recent years. When travelling to Canada, particularly from Europe, it's cheaper to travel from a major city (e.g. London), where a wide choice of low-cost fares is available. If you're travelling from London, shop around travel agents and airlines for the lowest fares, and check the travel pages of *Time Out* magazine and British Sunday newspapers such as *The Sunday Times*, or check online (see below). Fares from London can be as low as around £165 Gatwick-Toronto or £400 Gatwick-Vancouver.

One of the best companies for cheap charter (holiday) flights from the UK is Canadian Affair (☏ +44-20-7616 9184 or 604-678 6868, 💻 www.canadianaffair.com), which claims to offer the cheapest UK-Canada flights; in spring/summer 2009 it operated over 60 direct non-stop flights to Canada each week, with departures from nine UK Airports and two Irish airports to eight Canadian destinations.

With the exception of full-fare open tickets, fares depend on the number of restrictions and limitations you're willing to tolerate. These include minimum advance purchase periods, limitations on when you can fly, a minimum and maximum period between outward and return flights, and advance booking of both outward and return flights, with no changes permitted and no refunds (or high cancellation penalties).

The main disadvantage with all discounted tickets is that they're non-refundable and cannot be used on other flights or airlines. Before buying a ticket, carefully check the restrictions. It pays to shop around before buying a ticket because it's easy to pay a lot more than is necessary for an identical service. The cheapest round-trip ticket to/from Canada is usually cheaper than any one-way flight.

The cheapest international flights can usually be found via comparison websites such as 💻 www.kayak.co.uk, www.skyscanner.net and trevelsupermarket.com; and online travel agents such as 💻 www.expedia.com, www.opodo.com and www.travelocity.com, although these don't tend to list budget airline fares. You can also book via a specialist company such as Flight Centre (☏ 1-877-967 5302, 💻 www.flightcentre.ca), who have outlets in Alberta, British Columbia, Halifax, Ontario, Ottawa and Toronto – or via an airline's website (although they are usually more expensive).

Canadian airlines offer a range of flight passes offering discounts and other benefits, e.g. Air Canada offers the Rapidair Flight Pass for travel between Montreal, Toronto and Ottawa, and the City Flight Pass for flights from a range of Canadian cities.

Domestic Fares

Flying is the fastest and most convenient way of travelling in Canada and to the US, which together have the lowest air fares in the world (some even lower than Greyhound buses). Low-cost airlines offer 'no-frills' flights (bring your own sandwiches) and while the seat may not be as wide as on a major carrier, the fares are unbeatable. Like international fares, Canadian domestic fares vary depending on ticket restrictions (see above), and are heavily influenced by the time of day, the day of the week, how far in advance you book your ticket and the season.

There are generally three fare seasons in Canada: high (summer and holiday periods), shoulder (e.g. mid-October around Thanksgiving) and low or off-peak, which is most other times (particularly during school terms). The summer peak season runs from 1st June to 1st September. Christmas and New Year are peak periods for domestic flights, although not usually for international flights. The shoulder season is the Canadian term for a period that's less busy than the high season (such as spring and autumn/fall) and often includes the period immediately before a federal holiday. When planning a flight during a holiday period, book *well* in advance.

One-class economy seating is popular on short domestic flights and many airlines are replacing first class with a better business class. The most expensive fares are open return tickets, for which there are no advance booking requirements, flights can be booked or cancelled at any time (tickets are usually valid for one year). Excursion and discount fares usually apply to round-trip flights only and must normally be purchased in advance, e.g. 7 or 14 days.

With the exception of full-fare tickets, fares are usually non-refundable, although you may be able to change your flight for an additional fee (e.g. $25). On long-haul domestic flights (usually scheduled over one hour), services are much the same as on international flights, with meals, drinks and films (although you must usually pay for alcoholic drinks, films are usually free). Short-haul flights are often economy (coach) class only, while long-haul flights usually have business and economy class compartments. Infants under two years of age travel free on most domestic flights provided they don't occupy a seat. There's a 10 per cent discount for children aged two to 12 and seniors aged 65 or over, but youths (13 and over) must pay full fare. However, a discounted adult fare is often cheaper than a child fare. Many airlines also offer discounts for youths, students and senior citizens.

As a result of deregulation, special promotional fares can be offered at almost any time and there's usually at least one airline offering a promotional flight to where you want to go. Promotional fares or special offers on major routes can make a journey of a thousand miles cheaper than a short hop of a few hundred miles. Many smaller airlines are able to offer inexpensive domestic flights by using little-used airports; and some offer all seats at the same low fare, which may be lower than the lowest fare offered by larger national airlines. Sometimes it's cheaper to buy a round-trip than a one-way ticket, and leave the return trip unused.

You should reserve a seat on a domestic flight. When you book your flight, you're usually allocated a seat number and can check in at the gate if you have carry-on luggage only. If you need to travel on a particular flight, book as early as possible. If you don't have a reservation you can go to an airport and wait for a flight, called 'standby'.

Most airlines routinely over-book flights (when not half-empty) as an insurance against passengers who don't turn up ('no-shows'). This sometimes results in passengers with reservations being 'bumped' (denied a seat) and being forced to travel on a later flight, for which you receive 'Denied Boarding Compensation' (DBC), depending on when the next flight is. (If you aren't given a seat number when you check in – when other passengers have one – you're likely to be a candidate for being bumped.) Compensation may be a sum of money equal to the price of your ticket, a ticket upgrade on the next flight or even a free return ticket to any destination on the airline's domestic network. Airlines sometimes ask for volunteers, who might be offered compensation, e.g. Air Canada sometimes pays up to $300 (although you might have to be pushy to get it), in addition to which you're offered a seat on the next flight (which may be just one or two hours later) or a free re-booking.

Compensation excludes delays or cancelled flights due to an aircraft malfunction or bad weather, which is why airlines often blame bad weather or mechanical failure when they pull a flight that's under-booked or they have too few staff to operate it.

To avoid being bumped, try to check in at least one hour before the scheduled departure time for a domestic flight, and check in by the time specified for an international flight. If you check in late and are bumped, you won't be entitled to claim DBC. One way to ensure you have a seat is to visit an airline office (or some travel agents) and obtain a boarding pass and seat number in advance – with some airlines you can choose your seat when booking on the internet. However, you may still need to confirm your flight online 24 hours before you fly, even when you have been allocated a seat number online!

When the weather is bad in the local area or the area where your flight originates, it's wise to confirm your flight before arriving at the airport. Some airlines recommend that you confirm your flight 24 hours in advance. Although the 'OK' under status on your ticket means that a reservation has been made, a confirmation may still be necessary.

☑ SURVIVAL TIP

Airlines are increasingly putting the onus on passengers to confirm flights, usually online, and if you don't you could be bumped – although they may not tell you that you need to do this.

Nowadays, 'electronic ticketing' is employed by most airlines, whereby you don't receive a ticket or boarding pass. Tickets are typically booked via the internet, when you receive your confirmation by email and can print your receipt or 'boarding pass' (you may also be able to allocate yourself a seat number online). You're given a confirmation number, which is necessary when checking in via a machine at the airport, or you can check in at a desk. If you have no luggage or only hand luggage, you may be able to go directly to the departure gate where you're assigned a seat.

All Canadian airlines operate a bonus 'frequent flyer' or 'mileage club' scheme for regular passengers, where passengers receive free tickets, bonus miles, free upgrades and discounts after travelling a number of miles, e.g. 25,000. Benefits may also include car rental and hotel discounts. Membership of these schemes is free, although you must join online or at the check-in counter before flying. Bonus miles can also be earned by using car rental companies, hotel chains and credit cards affiliated to frequent flyer schemes or by buying certain products ('Air Miles' schemes are operated by independent organisations).

There are several sources of information on frequent flyer programmes including *The Official Frequent Flyer Guidebook* (💻 www.flyerguide.com) containing 600 pages of detailed information, including award charts on over 50 major frequent traveller programmes. It explains in-depth how the different programmes work and shows you how to earn more when you travel. *Inside Flyer* magazine (☎ 1-800-767 8896 within Canada/US or 719-597 8889, 💻 www.insideflyer.com) is a monthly magazine that reports the latest news on frequent flyer programmes. Another excellent travel newsletter and website is the Travel Insider (💻 http://thetravelinsider.info) – sign up for the free weekly newsletter online.

Most Canadian airlines also operate airline clubs for travellers. Membership privileges include the use of private airport lounges, computers and fax facilities, ATMs, showers, cheque-cashing facilities and other special services.

FERRIES

All maritime provinces have ferry services to connect islands to the mainland and with each other. Ferries are a slow means of transportation, which ferry companies are starting to capitalise on by turning their boats into mini cruise ships with dining and private cabins. Rates are per vehicle, inclusive of up to four passengers, or per passenger for those without a vehicle. Reservations are recommended because ferries often run only once per day and if you show up without a booking and the ship is full, you must wait 24 hours for the next one. Make sure you plan to arrive at the ferry terminal well in advance of your departure time, as ferries usually depart exactly on schedule. Attendants park your car on board and you travel (ride) in the passenger compartments. Passengers without vehicles may check in their luggage. Smoking is permitted in designated areas of ships and terminals only, and is strictly prohibited on vehicle decks.

cruise ship, Vancouver, BC

In British Columbia, the BC Ferry Corporation provides daily car and passenger services from Vancouver to Victoria and the Gulf Islands. There's an hourly service, with journeys taking from one and a half hours on a turn-up-and-go basis, although you can also book (advisable on holiday weekends). A cafeteria is available, a children's play area, a small shop and even a quiet reading room with good coffee on some ferries. The service between Port Hardy and Prince Rupert (summer only) is operated on alternate days in each direction, takes 15 hours and it's wise to book (see 💻 www.bcferries.bc.ca for fares and schedules); there's a fare index on the website.

In New Brunswick, toll-free river ferries are part of the highway system and are located mainly on the Lower Saint John and Kennebecasis rivers. Other toll-free services operate between Deer Island and Letete on the mainland. Toll ferries operate between Blacks Harbour and Grand Mana, and between Deer Island and Campobello Island, the latter only in summer. The Marine Atlantic company ☎ 1-800-341 7981, 💻 www.marine-atlantic.ca) operates a daily ferry service from North Sydney (Nova Scotia) to Port aux Basques (Newfoundland), costing from $28 for an adult foot passenger and from $80 for a vehicle. Marine Atlantic also operates ferry services throughout the Atlantic Maritime provinces, and provides a 'Cruising Labrador' service.

Ontario Ferries (☎ 519-724 2115, 💻 www.ontarioferries.com) serves south-western Ontario, including trips to Pelee Island, Leamington, Kingsville, Ontario, Sandusky and Ohio (April to mid-December), and northern Ontario, connecting with Manitoulin Island and the Bruce Peninsula (mid-May to mid-October). In Greater Toronto, the Toronto Parks and Recreation Department operates ferries to the Toronto islands (Centre Island, Ward's Island and Hanlan Point) from Queen's Quay at the end of Bay Street. Schedules vary depending on the season. A round trip costs around $3 for adults, $1.50 for seniors and students, and $1 for children aged under 15. The Maple Leaf ferry runs from the foot of Bathurst Street to the Island Airport (☎ 416-338 0338, 💻 www.toronto.ca/parks).

There are also direct ferry (vehicle and passenger) services between Victoria (BC) and Seattle (WA) in the US, operated by five ferry companies. For example, Victoria Clipper operates a daily catamaran (passenger only) service, taking two to three hours and costing from US$85 single to US$155 return (fares vary according to the time of year).

steamboat, Calgary, AB

11. MOTORING

It's almost impossible to survive in Canada without a car unless you live in the middle of one of the major cities and rarely leave it. Canada is almost 3,000mi (4,827km) from Toronto to Vancouver and around 5,000mi (8,000km) between the Atlantic and Pacific coasts. Once you travel outside the cities, towns are few and far between and, although there are buses, trains and planes, they aren't a lot of use if all you want to do is pop into the nearest town to shop. Canada has more vehicles per head of population than any country in the world except the USA, totalling some 19m, and Canadians buy around 1.5mn new cars each year (most made in the US). Despite this, the average Canadian drives only some 11,000mi (18,000km) per year, with annual running costs for the typical car around $8,000.

Given the number of cars on the roads, there are surprisingly few deaths from vehicle accidents. Quebec has the highest accident rate – in Montreal in particular, local drivers have nerves of steel, excessive confidence and a devil-may-care attitude. The first thing you notice when driving any distance in Canada is that it's a HUGE country. In some regions you can drive for miles without seeing another vehicle, and people living in remote rural areas think nothing of spending several hours behind the wheel to do the weekly shopping. Main roads and city streets are generally kept as straight as possible, and streets in most cities are designed on a grid pattern.

It's wise to avoid rush hours if possible, which vary with the city but are usually between 7 and 9.30am, and from 4 to 6.30pm (small towns usually have shorter rush hours, e.g. 7.30 to 8.30am and 4.30 to 5.30pm). In some cities there are special rules on major thoroughfares during rush hours, where parking is prohibited and lanes may change direction unexpectedly (indicated by overhead lights).

Unlike in most countries, responsibility for the Canadian highway system lies with provincial and municipal authorities and not with the federal government. Therefore traffic laws often vary depending on the province and you shouldn't take it for granted that the road rules in all provinces are the same. Nevertheless, there's general uniformity with respect to road signs and basic rules (they all drive on the right!). Detailed information about road rules in all provinces and territories is provided in the *Digest of Motor Laws*, published annually by the Canadian Automobile Association (CAA, 💻 www.caa.ca – see page 192) in conjunction with the American Automobile Association and issued free to members. All provinces also publish a 'driver's handbook' (highway code), available from local bookshops, driving test centres, driver and vehicle licencing offices, and online from government publication websites.

In general, Canadian road and automobile terms have been used throughout this chapter. Canada uses the metric system of weights and measures, and speed limits and distances are given in kilometres and fuel prices in litres (see **Appendix D** for Imperial conversion tables).

VEHICLE IMPORTATION

If you plan to import a motor vehicle or motorcycle into Canada, either temporarily or permanently, first ensure that you're aware of the latest regulations. Taking a new or relatively new car to Canada from overseas is usually an expensive and pointless exercise. Apart from the bureaucratic hassles, cars can be purchased in Canada far cheaper than in most other countries. All imported cars must meet Canadian regulations, particularly those regarding emissions, unless they're over 15 years old or are being imported temporarily.

Don't assume that motor vehicles manufactured to United States safety standards automatically meet Canadian safety standards. If you import a vehicle, you must ensure that it either complies with Canadian standards or can be modified. If you're in doubt, contact the Registrar of Imported Vehicles (405 The West Mall, Toronto ON M9C 5K7, ☎ 1-888-848 8240, 💻 www.riv.ca). If your vehicle doesn't meet the required safety standards but can be modified, the registrar's representative at your entry point into Canada will charge you a fee to register it and gives you 45 days to comply with the regulations.

☑ SURVIVAL TIP

All petrol (gasoline) sold in Canada is unleaded and, if you're importing a car that requires leaded petrol, you must have it converted to run on unleaded fuel before you can use it in Canada.

There are restrictions on importing a vehicle that wasn't manufactured in the current year from a country other than the United States. A vehicle can be imported provided:

- It's for your personal use;
- You've owned it since it was new;
- You received it as a gift from a friend or relative abroad (you must testify in writing that no money changed hands);
- It's a replacement vehicle imported privately after a vehicle was damaged beyond repair while you were travelling abroad (you must submit a statement from the insurance company and a copy of the police report verifying this);
- You're a returning resident or a former resident of Canada, importing a used or second-hand vehicle after living in another country for at least 12 consecutive months immediately prior to your return to Canada;
- You've been outside Canada for a period of six consecutive months or more and owned the vehicle for at least the same period before you returned to Canada.

If you're entering Canada as a permanent resident, you can include a car in your duty-free allowance (see page 303) provided that it's for your personal use and isn't for commercial purposes. A non-resident can import a car into Canada without paying duty, although if it's sold duty must be paid. Savings can be made when importing some cars and motorcycles into Canada, although generally it isn't worth the time, trouble and expense involved. For further information contact Transport Canada (330 Sparks Street, Ottawa, ON K1A 0N5, ☎ 613-990 2309, 💻 www.tc.gc.ca). The Canada Border Services Agency (see 💻 www.cbsa-asfc.gc.ca for a list of their offices) publishes a pamphlet entitled *Importing a Motor Vehicle Into Canada*.

Imported vehicles may also be subject to provincial or territorial sales tax (see **Sales Tax** on page 292) and safety requirements, therefore you should check with the motor vehicle department of the province or territory to which you're moving. The underside of all vehicles taken into Canada (unless driven over the border from America) must be steam-cleaned or high-pressure washed to remove any soil or other potentially contaminating substances before they're brought into Canada (ideally this should be done immediately before shipping).

VEHICLE REGISTRATION

Vehicle registration rules and fees according to the province. In all provinces you pay a registration fee for your number plates (equivalent to 'road tax' in other countries); in some, you also pay a fee to license the

vehicle, which may vary according to the weight or mass of the vehicle. The registration fee may be a flat fee or may be based on a car's weight or age (or a combination). In most provinces, number plates belong to an individual and not the vehicle, and are transferred to a new car when a car is sold (there's a fee of around $25 to $40, depending on the province). The exceptions are Newfoundland, where the plates remain with the vehicle, and Northwest Territories, where the old plates are scrapped and a new set issued on the sale of a vehicle. In most provinces only the buyer needs to attend the Motor Licence Office, although in Quebec the seller and buyer must both be present. Upon registration you're usually issued with two number plates (only one in Alberta and Quebec), the expiry date (month/year) of which is shown on the rear plate. In some provinces, a vehicle can be registered before entry, although you may require a local address.

Registration fees are normally payable annually. The exceptions are New Brunswick (where you can choose to pay for any period from 1 to 12 months), Saskatchewan (where you can choose any period from 3 to 12 months) and Ontario (where you can pay for two years at a time).

Registration is validated by a sticker affixed to the rear number plate (it's best to remove the old sticker and glue the new one directly to the plate, which makes it more difficult to steal). There are penalties for late renewal and you can be arrested for displaying an expired sticker. Duplicate plates and registration papers are available for a small fee. Most provinces don't refund a proportion of the fee if you surrender the registration before it expires, for example when you're moving to another province, when the whole process must be repeated. Detailed information about vehicle registration is provided by provincial motor vehicle offices and is also contained in the *Digest of Motor Laws* published annually by the Canadian Automobile Association (see page 192).

To register a car you need some or all of the following papers:

- Proof of identity and date of birth (such as a driving licence);
- Proof of ownership, e.g. a bill or certificate of sale showing the purchase price and date, a lease agreement or a Transfer of Ownership Document (TOD) or, for new vehicles, a New Vehicle Information Statement (NVIS);
- Proof of insurance;
- The current registration document;
- A Safety Standards Certificate (see **Safety & Emission Inspection** below);
- Registration authorisation if you aren't the owner of the vehicle;
- A completed vehicle registration application form;
- The registration fee, which may include GST and provincial sales tax.

BUYING A CAR

There are taxes on new and used cars in Canada: GST is charged at 5 per cent in all provinces and PST in certain provinces at the rates shown below. See also **Sales Tax** on page 292.

Tax Levied on New & Used Cars

Province	PST Rate (%)	Total Tax (%)
Alberta	0	5
British Columbia	7	2
Manitoba	7	12
New Brunswick	8	13
Newfoundland	8	13
North West Territories	0	5
Nova Scotia	8	13
Nunavut	0	5
Ontario	8	13
Prince Edward Island	10	15.5
Quebec	7.5	12.875
Saskatchewan	5	10
The Yukon Territory	0	5

All taxes due must be paid at the time of registration.

New Cars

Most new cars sold in Canada are made in North America, with only some 100,000 per year imported from elsewhere. There are no Canadian car manufacturers, although several US and Japanese manufacturers make or assemble cars in Canada. In addition to the wide range of US models, however, most European and Japanese cars are available. US cars have reduced somewhat in size in recent years, although saloons (sedans) and estates (station wagons) are still the size of small trucks. 'Compact' (or 'economy' or 'mid-size') models are around the same size as European family cars. 'Sub-compact' is the name given to small family cars such as the Ford Escort or VW Golf, while open sports cars are called roadsters or convertibles.

Canadian cars have traditionally had a prodigious thirst, although the 'gas-guzzlers' have largely been replaced by smaller 'economy' cars. However, many American cars still handle poorly, are too big for many people and have poor fuel consumption, therefore it's no surprise that an increasing number of Canadians have been changing from American cars to Japanese or European cars.

Many Canadian cars (or cars made for the Canadian market) are liberally adorned with 'idiot' gadgets and buzzers, e.g. those informing you that your seat belt isn't fastened, you've left your lights on or your key is in the ignition. Some cars have combination locks on the doors that can be used to lock or open them when you've locked your keys inside the car (provided you haven't forgotten the combination!).

Air-conditioning is standard on most cars and certainly isn't a luxury in the hotter months, although it decreases power and increases fuel consumption. Most cars are fitted with automatic transmission and power steering. All cars sold in Canada come with driver's and front passenger airbags as standard (many cars are now fitted with up to six or more as standard equipment).

Although comparisons between new car prices in different countries are often difficult (e.g. due to fluctuating exchange rates and the different levels of standard equipment), new cars are cheaper in Canada than in most other countries, despite the high cost of meeting Canada's safety and emission regulations. The list price of practically every vehicle sold in Canada can be found on the *Consumer Reports* website (💻 www.consumerreports.org) and 💻 www.canadiancarprices.com. Lemon Aid Cars (💻 www.lemonaidcars.com) is another useful website.

The dealer mark-up on new cars is much lower than in most other countries and most of a dealer's profit is made on options and selling finance and insurance. The basic or 'sticker' price (e.g. in an advertisement or showroom) may, however, provide little indication of the on-the-road price, which may be thousands of dollars more. Many 'options' may be already fitted to a showroom model and you have to pay for them whether you want them or not (or look elsewhere). Some manufacturers (particularly Japanese) include many 'options' as standard equipment, while others (e.g. German) make you pay heavily for them, and usually have a list of options as long as your arm. You can save a lot of money by buying a car on which 'extras' are standard equipment. Always check that any stated options are in fact present on a car by asking the salesman to show or demonstrate them.

Note that list prices don't include GST or provincial sales tax (see above) and registration (see **Vehicle Registration** above). Many dealers also include a charge, e.g. around $125, for the paperwork associated with buying a car; this is one of the many things you should haggle over. Dealers expect you to haggle, therefore don't be afraid to walk away when the price isn't right. When sales are slow, dealers may offer incentives such as free CAA membership, service discounts, options or special equipment, and a free loan car for up to five days when a repair or service is required. Many manufacturers offer optional extended warranties, which are good value if you do high mileage or plan to keep a car for a long time.

Around half of all new cars purchased in Canada are on lease deals, with over 80 per cent leased from financing companies belonging to car manufacturers. Car leasing is also available from banks. Personal lease deals usually require a deposit (down payment) and monthly payments over a period of between one and five years; there's a standard mileage allowance of 15,000 per year and you can purchase the car outright at the end of the lease period. Whether you're better off leasing or buying depends on your priorities.

If you like to have a new car every two or three years, want its maintenance taken care of and are willing to pay a little more over the long term, leasing is preferable; if you prefer to own your car and are prepared to maintain it yourself, you should buy. If you decide to lease a car, shop around and compare a number of leasing deals, as they vary considerably, depending on the dealer. You may obtain a better deal towards the end of a month, when salesmen are sometimes struggling to meet their targets. All leasing offers stipulate 'qualified buyers only', which means that unless you have an excellent credit rating you won't be eligible.

The CAA (see page 192) and *Consumer Reports* magazine (🖳 www.consumerreports.org) both provide a car 'price printout' service. This lists all standard equipment, every available option and the factory invoice cost of the vehicle. Car magazines regularly publish list and best (offer) prices and also show dealer margins, so you know exactly how much profit a dealer is making.

There are also many consumer magazines (such as *World of Wheels*) and guide books for car buyers with which you can make comparisons until your head spins. These include the annual *Car Buying Guide* (Consumer Reports – 🖳 www.consumerreports.org) and *So...You Wanna Buy A Car* by Bruce Fuller & Tony Whitney (Self-Counsel Press).

Many car dealers pay a 'bird dog' fee of $30 to $150 for referrals. Ask the salesman for his business card, write your name and phone number on the reverse, and tell your friends to give the card to the salesman when they buy a car. You get paid when the deal is finalised ('closed').

Used Cars

Used (also called second-hand, previously owned or 'pre-possessed') cars are good value in Canada, particularly low-mileage cars less than a year old, where the saving on the new price can be as much as 25 per cent. The minute a new car leaves the showroom it's usually worth at least 10 per cent less than the purchase price (unless it's a limited edition model, in which case it may have appreciated). Some models depreciate much faster than others and represent excellent second-hand buys.

Inexpensive second-hand cars can be purchased for as little as $500, although obviously you should be more circumspect when buying a 'wreck' – it must still meet the safety and emission standards. If you want a car for a short period only, an older car reduces your losses if you sell it within a short period. If you don't want a gas-guzzler, Japanese cars are generally among the cheapest and are usually reliable and economical. Old Volkswagens are also good value and it's easy to get them repaired and find spare parts.

Obtaining spares for some imported cars is difficult or even impossible. Also the number and location of dealers for imported cars varies considerably with the province (in some provinces you may find that the nearest dealer is hundreds of miles away). Older, classic, European sports models can be purchased in Canada for much less than in Europe, although their condition is often poor and finding spares and expert mechanics can be difficult. When buying a second-hand car, you should check carefully for rust, as a huge amount of corrosive salt is used on Canadian roads in winter. The best place to buy a secondhand car is BC. Make sure that the vehicle you're buying has adequate cold-weather equipment (i.e. a good heater and an engine-block heater).

Cars with high mileage (e.g. 20,000 per year), particularly cars sold by hire (rental) companies, can usually be purchased for substantially less than the average price and may offer excellent value, provided they've been regularly serviced. However, you should be careful when buying a car with average (e.g. 11,000mi/18,000km per year) or high mileage that's over four years old, as this is the time when it may need expensive repairs. Always check that a car has been regularly serviced (check receipts and service records).

You should be wary if an owner says he does his own servicing, as this may mean it has rarely been serviced. Unless you're an expert, you should take someone with you who's knowledgeable about cars or get a car's major systems checked by a dealer selling the same make. The fee is around $100, which you may be able to recoup many times over if faults are found (provided you still think the car's worth buying).

Excellent sources of information are the *Used Car Buying Guide* (Consumer Reports) and the annual *Lemon Aid* series of books by Phil Edmonston (Dundurn Press, 💻 www.lemonaidcars.com). A 'lemon' is the Canadian (and American) word for anything that doesn't work properly (particularly cars) and the Lemon-Aid guide lists failure-prone models and components.

The price of a used car depends on its make, size, age, condition, the time of year, and the area where it's for sale. Buying a car privately may be cheaper than buying from a dealer, although you won't get a warranty and must usually know what you're doing. You need to get up early to get a good used car in some areas, where used-car brokers (who buy cars and pass them onto dealers) do most of their deals before breakfast! You may get a better deal from a dealer who sells new cars of the make you're looking for, rather than from a used car lot selling used cars only, although the latter may be less expensive. If possible, choose a dealer who has been recommended. You can usually check whether there has been a large number of complaints against a dealer through a local consumer protection agency or Better Business Bureau (💻 www.bbb.org).

When purchasing a car privately, check that the seller owns it through the Personal Property Registration Office in the provincial capital, obtain a bill of sale, the proper registration and copies of all financial transactions. Check the registration month and year on the rear number plate, because if a vehicle is unregistered you could be held responsible for the past year's registration fee. If you're stopped by the police, you must show proof of ownership. The fine for not having the original paperwork is around $25 – photocopies aren't acceptable. If a car is unregistered it's also uninsured and it needs temporary insurance before you can test drive it on a public road.

One of the best places to buy second-hand cars (and to compare prices) is through local newspapers, e.g. the Saturday edition of the *Toronto Globe & Mail*. Free car shopper magazines and newspapers are also published in all areas. Always do your own research in your local area by comparing prices at dealers, in local newspapers and in the national press. Many private sellers are willing to take a considerable drop and you can haggle over the price with most dealers. When buying privately, used cars are usually paid for in cash or with a certified cheque. You can use Auto Trader (💻 www.autotrader.ca) to compare prices across the country and buy used vehicles.

SAFETY & EMISSIONS TESTS

Safety testing regulations vary from province to province. An annual safety inspection is necessary in some provinces, including Nova Scotia, New Brunswick and Prince Edward Island, while in others inspections are required only when a vehicle changes hands, e.g. within seven days of registration. Most provinces require safety inspections for commercial vehicles or buses and coaches, although few require inspections for private cars.

The test inspection includes the operation of lights, wipers, defrosters, horn, driver's seat, seat belts, driver's and passenger's side windows, bodywork, tyres, brakes, suspension, exhaust, and engine and transmission mountings. It doesn't include an evaluation of the performance of the engine or transmission. The prescribed standards can be rather skimpy in some provinces, e.g. Ontario's rules on brake linings are less than those recommended by most manufacturers. The annual test fee is usually a nominal $10 to $25, and cars that pass are issued with a Safety Standards Certificate (SSC).

☑ SURVIVAL TIP

Don't confuse these safety certification inspections with the 'certified' used car programmes run by manufacturers' dealerships, which are more comprehensive and provide a warranty. The CAA provides thorough inspections at approved garages at a cost of around $100 for members or $150 for non-members.

Throughout Canada, all vehicles made since 1990 must have a catalytic converter, but only British Columbia (actually Greater Vancouver and the Fraser Valley only) and Ontario require emissions inspections – the former for vehicles more than six years old, the latter five years. In British Columbia the inspection is called 'AirCare' (💻 www.aircare.ca) and costs $23 (for re-tests and pre-1991 vehicles) or $45; in Ontario it goes by the name of 'Drive Clean' (💻 www.ene.gov.on.ca/en/air/driveclean) and the maximum fee is $35 (you can have two re-tests for $17.50 each after repairs). Test are required annually in Ontario and on 1991 or older vehicles in BC, where vehicles from 1992 or later are tested every two years.

DRIVING LICENCE

The minimum age you can obtain a 'regular', full driving licence (driver's license) in Canada is 16 in all provinces except the Yukon, where it's 15. For commercial vehicles (including tractor-trailers), the age limit is 18 or 19. To obtain a Canadian driving licence, you must pass a test consisting of four parts: knowledge, traffic signs, vision and roads.

Licensing in Canada is by a system called the 'graduated licensing program', run by each province. The rules vary slightly in each province, but in general new drivers are licensed to drive in stages. For example, an inexperienced driver who has passed a written test is allowed to drive during daylight hours only (but not on major roads), provided that he's accompanied by a fully licensed driver. As drivers gain experience, the restrictions are relaxed. Several provinces issue new drivers with probationary licences lasting one or two years only, after which another test must be passed to obtain a full licence. In Nova Scotia, for example, the graduated licensing programme spans 2.5 years, with two stages: a six-month learner phase, followed by a 24-month newly licensed driver phase.

The classes of driving licence issued in Canada are generally as shown in the table below, but check with the province you're moving to as there are variations. (Licences in Ontario are classed by letters rather than numbers and are much more complex.)

You're issued with an interim licence until your new licence is sent to you in around six weeks.

Licences are usually valid for five years, although in some provinces licences for those aged under 18 and over 70 are valid for a shorter period, e.g. one or two years. Most licences expire on the holder's birthday. You must pay any outstanding fines for driving offences before a new licence is issued. Once drivers reach a certain age, e.g. 70, they may need to take an eye test or a driving test. If your licence expires and is allowed to lapse for more than a year, a test may also be mandatory. Licence fees vary considerably depending on the class, but a five-year licence to drive an ordinary passenger car costs around $60.

Depending on the province, tourists and immigrants may drive in Canada for a period of from three to 12 months with a foreign driving licence, although you may also need an International Driving Permit (IDP). Residents must apply for a Canadian licence within a certain period, usually 90 to 120 days, and surrender their foreign licence. Some provinces have a reciprocal licence exchange agreement with other countries that allow you to exchange your foreign licence without taking a driving test. If you take up residence in a provinces or territory where there's no agreement, you must take a written test and a practical road test. In order not to have to go through the graduated licensing program, you must have a letter from the licensing office in your home country showing your driving history for at least the last 18 months, detailing any prosecutions and accidents.

Driving License Classes

Class	Licensed Vehicle(s)
1	Tractor-trailer combination
2	Bus with a seating capacity of more than 24 people (some provinces require endorsements for buses with air-brakes)
3	Vehicles with three or more axles or towing a trailer
4	Taxi, ambulance or bus seating fewer than 24 people
5	Standard passenger vehicles or light trucks
6	Motorcycles or mopeds
7	Learner's category (in some provinces you must state the stage of the graduated licensing scheme you've reached)

In Prince Edward Island, Class 6 is for motorcycles only, mopeds are Class 8 and farm tractors are Class 9.

An application for a driving licence in Canada is usually made to the local motor licence office, although in some provinces driving licences are issued by authorised private agents or local licensing examination stations. In some provinces you can apply by post, while in others you must apply for (and renew) a licence in person at a motor licence office. You must produce the expiring licence or provide other proof of identification, pay any outstanding fines or debts owed to the motor vehicle branch, sign the renewal form, pay a fee and have your photograph taken. Most licences require a photograph (some must be in colour) and often include your social insurance number (SIN – see page 213).

Most provinces operate a points system, where drivers receive penalty points for traffic offences. When you accumulate a certain number of points within a 12-month period, e.g. ten in Ontario, your licence is automatically suspended for a period, e.g. 30 days. When renewing your licence, you must take a written test if you accumulate more than a certain number of points. A driving licence can be suspended, cancelled or revoked. All provinces are members of the Canadian Driver Licence Compact and exchange traffic offence conviction information.

You should carry your foreign licence as well as your IDP when driving in Canada, where a driving licence is the most common form of identification.

CAR INSURANCE

Car insurance (sometimes referred to as 'financial responsibility' insurance) is compulsory throughout Canada and drivers must carry proof of insurance at all times. Non-residents require a 'Non-resident Inter-Provincial Motor Vehicle Liability Insurance Card' (phew!), which shows that you meet the minimum legal 'financial responsibility' requirements throughout Canada (see below).

Insurers must state the level of their financial responsibility, i.e. the maximum amount they'll pay irrespective of how many people are involved in an accident or the amount of property damage caused. Each province sets a minimum financial responsibility level, which is usually $500,000. It isn't difficult to calculate that this could be woefully inadequate, and experts recommend that you have minimum cover of $750,000, depending on your assets. If your liability after an accident exceeds your insurance limit, your assets are used to pay damages, if necessary until you're bankrupt. Liability limits can usually be increased significantly (e.g. to $1m) for a modest additional premium.

Car insurance is relatively expensive in Canada and in some provinces must be purchased through the province's public insurance corporation. Usually, however, you can also buy car insurance from private corporations, independent insurance brokers and your bank's insurance division. Shop around!

There are various levels of car insurance, including:

- **Collision Cover** insures you against damage caused to your own vehicle, irrespective of who was responsible for the damage. Without it, if you're totally at fault in an accident, there's no recompense for damage to your vehicle. Collision cover usually has an excess (deductible), normally $250; the higher the excess, the lower your premium. Whether it's necessary to have collision cover (and comprehensive cover described below) usually depends on the value of your car. Collision cover is required by a lender (auto-loan) or a leasing company.
- **Comprehensive Cover** insures you against loss or damage from fire, theft, vandalism, collisions with animals, storms, water, flood, riots, explosions, earthquakes and falling objects, and includes accidental glass breakage, e.g. from a stone thrown up by another vehicle. It doesn't cover you against accidents involving other vehicles or objects, for which you require collision cover (see above). Comprehensive cover usually has a lower excess than collision cover.
- **Miscellaneous Extra Cover** encompasses a wide range of options, including the cost of a hire (rental) car when your car is being repaired, and towing and labour costs in the event of an accident (also provided by automobile clubs – see page 192). If you frequently use hire cars, you may be interested in a policy that includes a collision (or loss) damage waiver (CDW/LDW) for hire cars. This may also be provided by a credit card company.
- **Extended Medical Cover** is available from some insurance companies, which offer to increase your level of medical cover beyond that provided by your province's cover as a form of protection against abnormally high medical bills. This cover is sometimes offered by employers to their staff as a perk and paid for by the employer.

Many provinces have implemented 'no-fault' schemes, whereby accident victims, irrespective of fault, may claim compensation from their insurers for injuries. These schemes range from 'pure no-fault' (in Quebec and Manitoba), where there are no restrictions on claims, to 'threshold no-fault' (in Ontario and other states), where certain limits are specified, above which lawsuits are permitted. Thresholds can be monetary (e.g. a certain value of medical expenses) or verbal (i.e. a debilitating injury, or loss or impairment of bodily functions, etc.).

In Ontario, for example, seriously injured claimants (and the representatives of anyone killed in a car accident) may sue for pain and suffering (provided that the threshold is met), but not for lost income and other economic losses resulting from an injury. As with similar systems in other countries, the aim is to reduce the involvement of courts and therefore reduce insurance costs and expedite the settlement of claims.

Canadian car insurance is valid in the US and, if you rent a car there, some of the provisions in your Canadian car insurance may also apply to US hire cars, but check in advance.

If you plan to travel in the US with your own car, you should consult your insurance broker, as the lack of free medical care there and the generally litigious nature of Americans ('make my day – injure me and I'll be rich for life') could make an accident horrendously expensive.

Newcomers to Canada may have difficulty obtaining car insurance at a reasonable cost, particularly if they come from the UK or another country where people drive on the 'wrong' side of the road (some insurance companies seem to think that this automatically makes you incapable of driving on the right!). Insurers also require a complete record of your insurance history and no-claims discount, and may not accept evidence that's satisfactory in most other countries, e.g. renewal requests and certificates of insurance for a number of years, which they claim isn't proof that you kept the policies running throughout the year. The maximum no-claims discount for foreigners may be lower than for Canadians (e.g. 40 per cent) on the basis that they're unused to Canadian road rules and roads, and particularly to driving in severe winter weather.

When completing an insurance proposal form, you should ensure that you state any previous accidents or driving offences, or your insurer can refuse to pay in the event of a claim. Drivers who have been banned for drunken or dangerous driving must usually pay at least double the standard premium for three years (even penalty points on your licence can increase your premium). Your insurance company may cancel your policy if you're found guilty of drunken driving, speeding or recklessness resulting in injury or death. See also **Insurance Companies & Agents** on page 211 and **Insurance Contracts** on page 212.

Information about car insurance and car insurance publications are available from insurance companies and the Insurance Bureau of Canada (💻 www.ibc.ca).

SPEED LIMITS

Speed limits can vary considerably with the province or town, e.g. 62mph (100kph) on primary roads, 50mph (80kph) on non-primary roads, 31mph (50kph) or 'as posted' in urban areas, 25mph (40kph) in rural school zones, and 19mph (30kph) in urban school zones. All speed limits are quoted in kilometres per hour.

You're more likely to be stopped for speeding in Canada than in many other countries, particularly on major holiday weekends and in rural areas, where speeding fines often comprise a large proportion of local municipal revenue. In most provinces, non-freeway speed limits are more rigorously enforced than freeway limits and are therefore more widely observed. Speed limits are enforced by police using radar guns, fixed radar traps, marked and unmarked cars, helicopters and light aircraft. An increasing number of authorities (particularly in Alberta and Ontario) have introduced cameras that record a speeder's number plate – the first you know about it is when you receive a ticket in the post (the owner is responsible irrespective of who was driving, unless you can prove that your car was stolen).

As in many other countries, drivers often warn oncoming drivers of radar traps by flashing their headlights, although this is illegal and can result in a fine. It's illegal to posses a radar detector device in a vehicle in Manitoba, the Northwest Territories, Ontario, Quebec and the Yukon, irrespective of whether it's used.

On roads with a 100kph limit, you may receive a warning if your speed is between 100kph and 120kph (75mph), but at 120kph you can be fined around $100 and above 140kph (87mph) around $250.

GENERAL ROAD RULES

The following list includes some of the most common road rules in Canada and some tips designed to help you adjust to driving conditions and avoid accidents. Note, however, that like many things in Canada, some rules vary depending on the province.

- In Canada traffic drives on the right-hand side of the road. It saves confusion if you do likewise! If you aren't used to driving on the right, take it easy until you're accustomed to it. Be particularly alert when leaving lay-bys, T-junctions, one-way streets, petrol (gas) stations and car parks, as it's easy to lapse into driving on the left. It's helpful to display a reminder (e.g. 'think right!') on your car's dashboard.
- When you want to turn left at a junction, you must pass in front of a car turning left coming from the opposite direction, and not behind it (as in some other countries). At major junctions in some cities there are green-arrow signals for left-hand turn lanes. Certain lanes are signposted 'RIGHT LANE MUST TURN RIGHT' or 'EXIT ONLY' and mean what they say. If you get into these lanes by mistake and leave it too late to exit from them, you must turn in the direction indicated.
- Use of a horn is prohibited in some cities and towns and in any case should be used only in emergencies, e.g. to avoid an accident.
- The wearing of seatbelts is compulsory for all car occupants, and adults are responsible for ensuring that anyone under 16 is wearing one. Fines are levied

for violations, the amount of which varies according to the province but is at least $50 and can be hundreds of dollars. In Ontario, not wearing a seatbelt also 'earns' you two licence penalty points (see **Driving Licence** above).
- There's no automatic priority to the right (or left) on any roads in Canada (as there is in many European countries), although generally a turning vehicle must give way to one going straight ahead. 'STOP' signs are red and octagonal; 'YIELD' (give way) signs are an inverted triangle (yellow with black letters). You must stop completely at a stop sign before pulling out from a junction (motorists who practise the 'rolling stop' are a favourite target of traffic cops). Not all junctions have signs. When approaching a main road from a secondary road, you must usually stop, even where there's no stop sign. At a 'YIELD' sign you aren't required to stop, but must give priority to other traffic.
- You must use dipped headlights (low beams) between sunset and sunrise (usually from half an hour after sunset until half an hour before sunrise) in all provinces. Dipped lights must also be

used when visibility is reduced to less than 500ft (150m). Driving with dipped lights during the day is permitted in all provinces, encouraged in some and mandatory in the Yukon. Full beam (high beams) must be dipped when a car approaches within 500ft (150m) or when you're following within 500ft of another vehicle.

- Headlight flashing in Canada usually means 'after you'. As in many other countries, drivers often warn oncoming traffic of potential hazards (including police radar traps) by flashing their headlights (which is illegal). Hazard warning lights (both indicators operating simultaneously) are usually used to warn other drivers of an accident or when your car has broken down and is causing an obstruction, and shouldn't be used when merely illegally parked.
- The sequence of Canadian traffic (stop) lights is usually red, green, yellow, red. Yellow means stop at the stop line; you may proceed only if the yellow light appears after you've crossed the stop line or when stopping may cause an accident. A green filter light (arrow) may be shown in addition to the full lamp signals, which indicates you may drive in the direction shown by the arrow, irrespective of other lights showing. Stop lights are frequently set on the far side of a junction, sometimes making it difficult to judge where to stop, and are also strung across the road rather than located on posts by the roadside. In some suburban areas, there are flashing red lights to indicate a stop light ahead. Driving through (running) red lights is a major cause of accidents in Canada.
- One of the most surprising rules is that in some provinces and cities you may make a right turn at a red traffic light, unless otherwise posted. You must, however, treat a red light as a stop sign and stop before making a right turn. You must also give way to pedestrians crossing at traffic lights. Busy junctions often have signs indicating that turning on a red light isn't allowed (e.g. 'NO TURN ON RED') or is allowed at certain times only. If you've stopped and the motorist behind you is sounding his horn, it probably means that you can turn right. In some provinces, you can also make a left turn on a red light from a one-way street into another one-way street.

▲ Caution

Never assume you can make a turn at a red light – if you do so when it's illegal, you can be heavily fined.

- Always approach pedestrian crossings with caution and don't park or overtake another vehicle on the approach to a crossing. Pedestrians have the right of way once they've stepped onto a pedestrian crossing without traffic lights and you must stop; motorists who don't stop are liable to heavy penalties. In some towns, a pedestrian may indicate that he intends to cross by pointing (arm fully extended) and walking in the direction he plans to go. Where a road crosses a public footpath, e.g. at the entrance to a property or a car park bordering a road, motorists must give way to pedestrians.
- Railroad crossings on public roads are clearly marked, usually with a large 'X' sign (in Ontario they're white with a red border). Some crossings have automatic gates or other barriers and most have red lights that flash when a train is coming. On private roads there may be no barriers or lights, so it's wise to stop and look and listen in both directions before crossing. In heavy traffic, don't attempt to cross until your exit is clear. Never attempt to cross a railway line when the barriers are down or the lights are flashing.
- Be particularly wary of cyclists, moped riders and motorcyclists. It isn't always easy to see them, particularly when they're hidden by the blind spots of a car or are riding at night without lights. When overtaking give them a wide – WIDE berth. If you knock them off their bikes, you may have a difficult time convincing the police that it wasn't your fault; far better to avoid them (and the police).
- Children on pedestrian crossings or getting on or off school buses (usually painted yellow and clearly marked 'SCHOOL BUS') have priority over all traffic. All motorists must stop at least 65ft (20m) from a school bus loading or unloading, indicated by flashing (usually red) lights or 'stop arms'. Vehicles must stop even when a school

bus has halted on the opposite side of the road (children may run across the road) unless the road is divided by a barrier. Motorists must remain stopped until the bus moves off or the driver signals motorists to proceed. **Never pass a school bus with flashing red lights!**

The law regarding school buses is taken very seriously and motorists convicted for the first time of passing a stopped bus are subject to a fine of as much as around $2,000 in Ontario, possible imprisonment or community service, and six penalty points on their driving licence. If you're convicted a second time within five years, the fine could be many thousands of dollars and a further six penalty points, plus a possible six-month prison sentence.

- In some cities (e.g. Toronto) and towns where there are trams (streetcars), you must stop well away from the rear doors when a tram stops in front of you, so that passengers can get off easily and safely – unless there are safety islands in the street at tram stops, in which case it isn't necessary to stop.
- Using a mobile phone while driving is illegal and can result in a fine.
- Certain provinces allow you to use studded tires during the winter months only, while others permit their use all year round. Ontario has banned their use at any time due to the damage they cause to road surfaces that aren't covered with snow.
- Road rules prohibit driving in bare feet, parking on a highway, allowing passengers to ride in the back of a pick-up truck and having an open alcoholic drink can or bottle in your car (even when it's stationary and the ignition is off).
- An unofficial but widely observed practice on Canadian highways is that, if you break down, you indicate this by opening the bonnet (hood) and boot (trunk) of your car, which a passing motorist will interpret as a call for help and may stop to help. In some areas there are emergency phones, but it's usually safer to stay in the car, particularly at night and in winter. (Most people carry mobile phones nowadays which can be used to call automobile clubs or emergency services for assistance.)
- Most road signs in Quebec are in French only, with the exception of Montreal, where motorways (*autoroutes*) and bridges may have dual-language signs.

All provinces publish local rules of the road, e.g. *The Official Driver's Handbook* in Ontario, available from provincial ministries of transport and bookshops.

CANADIAN ROADS

Canada has over 560,000mi (900,000km) of roads and a national main road (highway) system covering around 15,000mi (24,000km), including the longest main road in the world (the Trans-Canada Highway, which stretches 4,859mi/7,820km from St John's in Newfoundland to Victoria in British Columbia). The standard of Canadian roads varies enormously, from twelve-lane 'freeways' in urban areas to gravel or dirt tracks in remote rural areas. Generally Canadian roads have fewer road markings (e.g. reflective studs and lines) than European roads.

Streets in most cities are laid out in a grid pattern (hence the word 'gridlock' for traffic jam), all roads running either north-south or east-west, and you need to know the numbering (or lettering) system so that you can find your way around. It's also useful to know which part of a town or city you want when asking for directions, e.g. uptown, downtown, eastside or westside (descriptions vary with the town).

Most major cities have multi-lane main roads, particularly Toronto,

where the 401 (one of the busiest roads in the world) has between 6 and 18 lanes. Some lanes, known as 'collector' lanes, have exit warnings for towns several kilometres in advance. Main access routes are busy night and day (needless to say, it's best to avoid rush hours). Direction signs may be sparse, inconsistent and poorly placed (most road signs in North America are 'discrete'), and are particularly difficult to read at night in urban areas. Road signs are white (reflective) on a green background and signs for attractions have a blue background.

Suburban roads and motorways are generally well surfaced and maintained, although roads can suffer frost damage in winter, which makes for 'interesting' corrugated surfaces. On gravel roads you should keep your distance from the vehicle in front to avoid flying stones and dust, and slow down and pull over to the right when someone overtakes or when a vehicle comes from the opposite direction. If you're likely to be doing a lot of driving on dirt roads, it's wise to get a mesh 'bug and gravel' screen or plastic film fitted; otherwise you'll be constantly replacing your windscreen (some people also fit screens to their lights and fuel tank). Driving with lights on during the day helps other drivers to see you through thick dust (and anytime in poor visibility).

As you may have discovered already, Canada is a huge country and vast distances look small on maps (unless you have an ENORMOUS map). When estimating journey times, carefully calculate distances and take into account the road quality and terrain. Although it's possible to make good time on major roads (e.g. an average of 60mph/100kph), your speed is greatly reduced on secondary roads, particularly in mountainous areas, where speeds may average just 20 to 30 mph (around 30 to 50kph). Most people reckon on covering between 300 and 400mi (around 500 to 650km) per day (i.e. in six to seven hours), but possibly less when travelling with children (unless you tranquillise them).

There are few toll roads in Canada, although some bridges (e.g. to the US) have tolls. Exceptions include highway 407 in the Greater Toronto area, which has overhead sensors rather than toll collection booths, and a toll road on the Trans Canada Highway between Debert and Oxford in Nova Scotia.

Some roads are referred to by their number, while others are referred to locally by a name, which can be confusing. Multi-lane roads are called freeways, except in Quebec where they're called *autoroutes*. Many freeways have just two lanes in each direction and sometimes the number of the road is changed by adding a '4' to the number, e.g. Highway 1 (the Trans-Canada Highway) changes to '401' when it becomes four lanes around Toronto. Even this major route has some poor surfaces where it goes through unpopulated areas with little traffic.

If you drive in the north or other remote areas, you should take every opportunity to top up your fuel tank (ideally don't let it get below half full) and carry extra fuel in a can. You should also carry a spare tyre, some tools, a shovel, water and food (plus some insect repellent). In country areas, you should lookout for wildlife on the roads; major migration routes are marked by 'deer marker' signs (a black deer on a yellow background), although you should expect to encounter animals at any time of the year, particularly at night when many (nocturnal) animals are active and visibility is poor. Keep your eyes on the edges of the road and be prepared to stop or swerve – hitting a deer or moose can do serious damage to your car (it won't do the deer or moose much good either).

▲ Caution

Animals often stop in the middle of the road at night – it's rather disconcerting to sit in your car with three or four moose staring at you, mesmerised by the lights – and you should try switching your lights off and on and using the horn to move them (although this may only agitate them). You shouldn't get out of the car, as moose and large deer can be dangerous and can move very fast when threatened. If you meet a grizzly bear, it's time to practise driving in reverse – fast!

WINTER DRIVING

With the exception of some parts of southern British Columbia, most of Canada has long, cold, snowy winters. If you need to park your car out of doors in winter (not recommended) the engine can freeze solid if you don't take precautions. It's a common sight in outdoor car parks to see cars left securely locked with their engines running, but most vehicles are fitted with engine heaters that you plug in when you turn the engine off. If you need to leave your car out overnight, you should be prepared to dig it out of a snow-drift in the morning (make sure that you have a shovel and a blanket in the car). You should also be aware that tyres acquire a flat spot after standing in the cold overnight and you need to drive slowly until the air in the tires has warmed up.

Major roads have a mixture of salt and sand spread on them to help prevent vehicles from sliding on ice. Snowploughs clear heavy falls and it isn't uncommon to see them driving two or even three abreast on major roads. In cities, the major roads are cleared first, followed by secondary streets, although it can take a couple of days before they're all cleared. You need 'four-season' radial snow tyres in winter, plus snow chains (rarely) and equipment such as a shovel, traction mats, a bag of sand and a tow-chain (plus a blanket and water) in case you get stuck. You can buy all the necessary equipment in an 'emergency car kit' from a hardware store. If you get stuck in deep snow and cannot get yourself out, don't sit in the car with the engine running (to operate the heater) as it may fill with carbon monoxide and kill you!

The CAA recommends that you carry matches and a candle in an open-topped tin – just one candle burning in a car keeps it reasonably warm. When travelling in country areas in winter, the CAA recommends that you carry a warm coat and other extra clothing, sleeping bags, emergency food such as fruit, chocolate or tinned soup (and a Primus stove), a torch, warning lights or road flares, jump leads, an axe, a fire extinguisher, an ice-scraper and a brush, and some methyl-hydrate for de-icing fuel lines and windows.

If you think all this seems extreme, bear in mind that in January 1998 there was a severe ice-storm in south-east Canada that crippled vast areas of Ontario and Quebec and brought down power lines, and less severe ice (and other) storms are a frequent occurrence.

In spring you should wash your car thoroughly, particularly underneath, and repair any paint chips, otherwise salt from the roads will soon cause rust patches.

TRAFFIC POLICE

Traffic laws in Canada are taken seriously and police strictly enforce the law. The Royal Canadian Mounted Police (RCMP) is responsible for freeways in remote areas, provincial police (known as the *Sureté Québec* in Quebec) operate in rural areas and municipal police in towns. They're particularly hot on the wearing of seatbelts and speeding – most Canadians stick to speed limits. Police have the right to search vehicles if they stop you for a 'valid reason' and if they arrest you they can seize anything in your possession, including your car. However, unless you're breath-tested positive, you're more likely to receive a ticket than be arrested.

If a policeman wants you to stop, he usually drives along behind you flashing his overhead lights (which may be red, blue or yellow or a combination) and possibly sounding his siren. You must pull over and stop as soon as you can, if possible on the hard shoulder. Once you've stopped, stay in your car and let the officer come to you. Keep your hands in view, e.g. on the steering wheel, and don't do anything that could be misconstrued. If you're stopped by an unmarked vehicle, you should ask to see the officer's identification.

Whatever you're stopped for, the officer will ask to see your driving licence and want to see your vehicle registration document and insurance card (you must carry these in the car at all times).

> ☑ **SURVIVAL TIP**
>
> **Don't antagonise an officer or joke with him (they have no sense of humour), as this may lead to a fine, whether you've done anything illegal or not.**

A foreign accent and an apology may get you a warning rather than a ticket. If you're stopped for speeding or another 'minor' offence such as failing to stop at a 'STOP' sign or making an illegal turn, you may get away with a caution. Although some people attempt to bribe a patrolman, e.g. by inserting a $20 note in their licence, this practice isn't recommended.

If you receive a ticket for a motoring offence, you may have the choice of paying a statutory fine or going to court. On-the-spot fines are standard for speeding, failing to carry your licence and not wearing a seatbelt (including passengers). Note also that, if you break the law, you may be 'tagged' (spotted) by the police (but not necessarily stopped) and may receive a summons later. If you're driving a rental car, the rental company receives the summons and may debit a fine from your credit card.

Some provinces accept bail bonds from the CAA (and AAA), while others (such as New Brunswick) don't. If you're stopped for a motoring offence and are bailed to appear in court, you can (where permitted) leave your CAA membership card and a bail bond with the court and leave the province. If you appear for trial, your card and bond certificate are returned to you or the CAA. However, if you choose to forfeit your bond and don't appear for trial, the court notifies the CAA, which then arranges for payment and recovers your membership card from the court. You then reimburse the club for the amount spent on your behalf and your membership card is returned.

MOTORCYCLES

The minimum age for riding a moped (up to 50cc) is 14. For motorcycles over 50cc, the minimum age is 16 in all provinces, although some require parental permission to issue a licence at this age.

Like cars, motorcycles are inexpensive in Canada compared with many other countries. If you want a bike for a short period only, it's probably best to buy second-hand, as you won't need to bear the initial depreciation (most dealers sell new and second-hand bikes). The procedure and legal requirements when buying a bike are much the same as for buying a car (see page 175). It's also possible to rent a motorcycle or moped in most areas. A useful publication is the *Motorcycle Touring International Directory* by Daniel Kennedy (White Horse Press), which lists some 150 guided motorcycle tour companies, many of which have bikes for rent.

Insurance for motorcycles is high and similar to that for cars. The cost of insurance depends on your age (riders aged under 25 pay much more), the type and cubic capacity of your motorcycle, and the length of time you've held a licence. It's wise to have insurance well above the legal minimum (see **Car Insurance** above).

In general, the road rules that apply to cars (see above) also apply to motorcycles; however, there are a few things that apply to motorcyclists only:

- In general, motorcycles registered for use on public roads must meet the equipment requirements in the province in which they're registered, in addition to federal safety standards.
- Carrying proof of ownership, registration and insurance of motorcycles is required in all provinces. A motorcycle driving licence is required, although this may be an authorisation on a car licence; a special moped licence is required in most provinces.
- A crash helmet of an approved design is obligatory for all motorcycle and moped riders and passengers throughout Canada (unless your wear a turban or other headwear for religious reasons). Failure to wear a helmet incurs a fine of around $100.
- In many provinces, a rider is required to wear eye protection, goggles or sunglasses, if a windscreen isn't fitted to a bike.

- Motorcyclists are required to use their headlights (low beam) at all times.
- A strong lock is recommended when parking a bike in a public place.

ACCIDENTS

If you're involved in an accident, the procedure is as follows:

- Stop immediately. If possible, move your car off the road and keep your passengers and yourself off the road. If you're involved in an accident where someone is injured or there's damage costing over $300 to repair, you must remain at the scene until the police have arrived and established what happened. It's a criminal offence to fail to stop at the scene of an accident in which you've been involved.
- Warn other drivers of an obstruction by switching on your hazard warning lights (particularly on freeways). If necessary, e.g. when the road is partly or totally blocked, set flares, turn on your car's dipped headlamps and direct traffic around the hazard. In bad visibility, at night or in a blind spot, try to warn oncoming traffic of the danger, e.g. with a torch at night.
- If anyone is injured, immediately phone for an ambulance, the fire department (if someone is trapped or oil or chemicals are spilled) or the police, or get someone else to do it. There are telephone boxes with a direct line to the local Royal Canadian Mounted Police (RCMP) on some freeways and highways. Use them to request assistance for breakdowns and report hazards and accidents. Give first-aid only if you're qualified to do so. Don't move an injured person unless it's absolutely necessary to save him from further injury and don't leave him alone except to phone for an ambulance. Cover him with a blanket or coat to keep him warm.
- After a minor accident you must remain at the scene until personal details (names and addresses of drivers and vehicle owners, registration and insurance details, etc.) have been exchanged with other drivers or the owners of damaged property. In general, it's recommended to report all accidents immediately to the local police, whether they're called to the scene or not, and to inquire about other reporting requirements (if you fail to report an accident your driving licence can be suspended for a year). Ensure that you obtain a report number from the officer on duty for your insurance company (this should be given to you on a card).
- You mustn't say anything that could be interpreted as an admission of guilt. Don't agree to pay for damages or sign any papers except a traffic ticket (which you must sign) before checking with your insurance company or a lawyer. Let the police and insurance companies decide who was at fault.
- If either you or any other drivers involved decide to call the police, don't move your vehicle or allow other vehicles to be moved. If it's necessary to move vehicles to unblock the road, take photographs of the accident scene if a camera (or camera phone) is available or make a drawing showing the position of all vehicles involved before moving them.
- Check whether there are any witnesses to the accident and take their names and addresses, particularly noting those who support your version of events. If a motorist refuses to give his name, note the registration number. Write down the registration numbers of all vehicles involved

and their drivers' and owners' names and addresses, vehicle registration certificate, licence and insurance details. You must (by law) also give these details to anyone having reasonable grounds for requiring them, e.g. anyone injured or the owner of damaged property. Don't, however, reveal how much insurance cover you have. Note also the names and badge numbers of any police present.

- If you have an accident involving a domestic animal (except a cat) and are unable to find the owner, it must also be reported to the local police. This also applies to certain wild animals, e.g. deer or moose, which are a danger on rural roads, including some freeways.
- If you're arrested by the police, you aren't required to make a statement, even if they ask for one. The best policy is not to say or sign anything until you've spoken to a lawyer.
- You should report all accidents to your insurance company in writing as soon as possible, even if you don't plan to make a claim (but you should reserve your right to make a claim later). Your insurance company will ask you to complete an accident report form, which should be returned as soon as possible. The claims procedure depends on your insurance cover and that of anyone else involved in the accident (see **Car Insurance** above).

Caution

In some areas you should be wary of stopping at what looks like the scene of an accident, e.g. on a deserted highway, as accidents are sometimes staged to rob unsuspecting drivers.

DRINKING & DRIVING

Drunken driving or driving under the influence of drugs, known as 'impaired' driving, is taken very seriously by the police in Canada. You're considered unfit to drive when your breath contains 35 micrograms of alcohol per 100ml, or your blood contains 80mg of alcohol per 100ml. In most provinces you're considered to be driving while intoxicated (DWI) or driving under the influence (DUI) when your blood-alcohol content (BAC) is 0.1 per cent (in some cases it's lower, e.g. 0.08 per cent or even 0.05 per cent for minors). In some provinces, if your BAC is above a certain level, e.g. between 0.05 and 0.09 per cent, you may be charged with 'driving while ability impaired', although this is usually done only after an accident or in a case of reckless or dangerous driving. In some provinces, if the test shows more than 0.05 per cent, you can receive a 24-hour driving ban. In provinces with a progressive licensing system for new drivers (see **Driving Licence** above), the permitted BAC is zero for drivers who haven't completed the programme.

Steep fines and other penalties for drunken driving have been imposed since the late '80s, which has been a powerful deterrent for most people. A first conviction for drunken driving results in a fine (e.g. $250 to $500 for first offenders) and suspension of your licence for a minimum of one year. In some provinces, imprisonment for up to 60 days is mandatory after a first or second offence. In many provinces, offenders must participate in a programme of alcohol education or rehabilitation. If you have an accident while drunk, the penalties are usually more severe, particularly if you cause an injury or death. However, many people believe that the penalties are too lenient and that tougher action is required to deter habitual drinkers from driving. Ontario has taken this seriously and under its Comprehensive Road Safety Act (passed in 1998) three-time offenders face a ten-year driving ban and four-time offenders a lifetime ban. Two-time offenders receive a three-year ban and first offenders a one-year ban.

DUI is predominantly a male crime, but contrary to popular belief the worst offenders aren't young drivers: 60 per cent are in the 25 to 44 age bracket (although this age bracket makes up only some 20 per cent of drivers in Canada).

Random breath tests are permitted in most provinces and traffic police carry breathalyser testing kits. In many provinces, police set up periodic road blocks to check drivers and they may stop drivers as they enter or leave a town. A refusal to take a test results in your driving licence being automatically suspended, e.g. for six months or a year. If you're found to be over the limit, you're arrested on the spot, your licence is taken away and you're held in jail until you appear in court (usually the next day).

The rules regarding alcohol also apply when operating a boat or riding a moped, bicycle or horse; driving under the influence of drugs carries the same penalties as those for drunken driving.

CAR THEFT

Car theft is a huge problem in Canada, where a car is stolen every three minutes, averaging about 400 cars a day or some 150,000 annually. Almost half of those who are caught and charged are aged between 12 and 17. If you're driving anything other than a worthless wreck, you should have your car fitted with an alarm, immobiliser (system interrupter) or other anti-theft device, plus a visible deterrent such as a steering or transmission shift lock.

Many new cars are fitted with deadlocks and sophisticated alarm systems as standard equipment (an alarm or tracker system may also get you a discount on your car insurance). This is particularly important if you own a car that's desirable to car thieves, which includes most new sports and executive cars, which are often stolen by professional crooks to order. A good security system won't prevent someone breaking into your car – which usually takes professional crooks a matter of seconds – or even prevent your car being stolen, but it at least makes it more difficult and may persuade a thief to look for an easier target.

Radios and CD players attract a lot of (the wrong) attention in most cities, particularly in expensive foreign cars. Some drivers put a sign in their car windows proclaiming 'No Radio' (or 'No Valuables', 'Trunk is Empty' and 'Doors Open'), to deter thieves from breaking in to steal them.

When leaving your car unattended, store any valuables (including clothes) in the boot (trunk) or out of sight. This shouldn't be done immediately after parking your car in some areas, where it isn't wise to be seen putting things in the boot. In any case, boots aren't safe unless they're fitted with a protective steel plate or you have a steel safe installed inside the boot.

Don't leave your car papers in your car, as this won't only help a thief to sell it fast, but also hinder its recovery (particularly if you don't have a copy of the papers). If possible, avoid parking in long-term car parks, as these are favourite hunting grounds for car thieves. When parking overnight or when it's dark, park in a well-lit area, which may help deter car thieves.

If your car is stolen (or anything is stolen from it), report it to the police in the area where it was stolen. You can report it by phone, and the police often forward the relevant paperwork to your insurance company, meaning that you don't have to visit a police station. You should also report a theft to your insurance company as soon as possible.

FUEL

All petrol (*gaz* in Quebec) sold in Canada is unleaded and sold by the litre. Three grades of petrol (gas) are available: regular (87 octane), special or mid-grade (89 octane) and premium (92 octane). Premium petrol is typically 10 per cent more expensive than regular and diesel 15-20 per cent cheaper than regular, so it pays to run a diesel car if you do a lot of miles. Fuel prices include a 'gas consumption tax', which varies from province to province (even

in Alberta, where there's no general provincial sales tax, there's a tax on petrol).

Fuel prices are lowest in cities and suburban areas where there's lots of competition, and highest on major roads (prices are often increased at the start of holidays and long weekends) and in rural areas (where the next petrol station may be 100 miles away). The price of petrol also varies with the region, the highest being in the far north and on the east coast, the lowest in the major cities (particularly in the east). Prices in spring 2009 were from around 92¢ for regular gas (75¢ for diesel) in Toronto, and from 98¢ per litre for regular gas (85¢ for diesel) in Vancouver. For current prices in all the provinces and most towns, see 💻 www.gasbuddy.com or www.gasticker.com.

Some city service stations open 24/7, while on major roads, truck stops have the longest opening hours. When motoring in rural areas, however, it's recommended to keep your tank topped up (and check your oil and water frequently), as petrol stations are few and far between and may be closed on Sundays and holidays (many petrol stations are also closed in the evenings and at weekends). It pays to keep a reserve supply in a steel can (plastic fuel containers can break when a car is travelling on uneven roads or may burst at high altitudes and petrol can ignite from a static electricity spark).

The trend is towards self-service stations, but there are some with 'full-serve' pumps, where an attendant fills your car, checks the oil and cleans your windscreen (windshield) free of charge, as well as checking your tyre pressures and radiator water level if asked (it's unnecessary to tip for these services).

When buying fuel, make sure that the pump is reset to zero, particularly if an attendant is filling your car. It's advisable to check your own oil level, as a garage attendant may 'short stick' the dipper so that it doesn't register. Extra services aren't available at 'self-serve' pumps, but the price of fuel may be slightly lower. At many petrol stations you must pay before filling your car, particularly at 24-hour and late night stations in cities. You pay the attendant, e.g. $20, and collect any change after filling your car.

Most petrol stations have toilets (restrooms), sometimes located outside the main building, when it may be necessary to ask an attendant for the key (cleanliness varies). Petrol stations also sell sweets (candy), hot and cold drinks (usually from machines), motoring accessories, cigarettes, newspapers, household goods and various other items.

Fuel saving and general motoring tips are available free from the Natural Resources Canada (580 Booth, Ottawa, ON K1A 0E8, ☎ 613-995 0947, 💻 www.nrcan-rncan.gc.ca).

AUTOMOBILE CLUBS

The main automobile club in Canada is the Canadian Automobile Association (CAA, 💻 www.caa.ca), established in 1913, which has branch offices in all provinces and territories. The CAA acts as an advocate of road safety and is committed to the improvement of Canadian roads, and lobbies federal and provincial governments to enact legislation in the interest of drivers. The CAA's most valuable service to motorists, however, is its emergency roadside assistance – especially during a blizzard! Another popular service is the 'triptik', a free route planning service. For example, if you want to travel from Ottawa to Charlottetown (Prince Edward Island) in two days, the CAA will provide the necessary maps showing the best direct route (highlighted in yellow) and CAA-recommended motels along the way. It will even book the motels for you!

Like many things in Canada, CAA membership deals (both benefits and prices) vary with the province, although they're similar. Typical membership categories and fees are shown below:

- **Basic membership** costs around $65-70 per year and includes a battery boost (when your car won't start), free delivery of fuel (if you've run out), roadside repair (e.g. a flat tyre), opening of a locked door (unless a specialist locksmith is required) and four tows up to 3mi (5km) or 6mi (10km), after which you must pay by the kilometre.
- **CAA Plus** costs around $100-105 per year and includes all the above services plus towing up to 100-120mi (160-200km) and free fuel.
- **CAA Plus RV** costs around $135-150 and provides the same level of service as CAA Plus, as well as assistance with any problems you may have with a motor home (any size), camper van, pick-up truck or trailer up to a specified weight.

There are other Canadian motor service organisations in Canada, some of which are provided by automobile manufacturers, e.g. as part of an extended warranty.

> Canadian Tire (💻 www.canadiantire.ca), Canada's oldest motoring retail chain founded in 1922, is the CAA's main national roadside assistance competitor. However, you must have your vehicle towed to and repaired at a Canadian Tire outlet (if practical).

CAR & MOTORCYCLE HIRE

Car hire (rental) is common in Canada. When travelling long distances, most Canadians travel by air and hire a car on arrival (air travellers represent 80 per cent of car hire business). Airlines, charter companies, car hire companies and tour operators all offer fly-drive packages (which often include accommodation). It's usually wise to book, particularly during holiday or peak periods. Many fly-drive holiday packages (particularly when booked in Europe) include a 'free' hire car. However, fly-drive deals may not be as good value as they appear at first glance, as many contain restrictions or apply to expensive cars only. In some cases it's better to arrange a local deal yourself by calling local hire companies listed in the *Yellow Pages*. It's usually cheaper to hire a car in a city or town centre than at the airport.

The largest nationwide car hire companies in Canada are Alamo (💻 www.alamo.com), Avis (💻 www.avis.com), Budget (💻 www.budget.ca), Dollar (💻 www.dollar.com), Enterprise (💻 www.enterprise.com), Europcar (💻 www.europcar.com/car-canada.html), National (💻 www.nationalcar.ca) and Thrifty 💻 www.thrifty.com). National hire companies have offices in all major cities (open from around 8am to 10pm) and at international airports. Of the major companies, Budget and Thrifty are generally the cheapest, although all companies offer special deals, e.g. corporate rates, 24-hour rates, weekend and weekly rates, off-peak periods, holidays, extended period low rates on certain categories of vehicle, and bonus coupons for airline tickets. There are also companies that hire older cars at lower rates, such as Rent-a-Wreck (☎ 1-800-327 0116, 💻 www.rentawreck.ca).

When hiring a car, it's important to ensure that you have sufficient liability insurance (see page 226). Insurance is usually included in the basic cost, although it may be restricted to the province where you hire the car and there may be a high surcharge for inter-province travel. Check whether out-of-province insurance and collision (or loss) damage waiver (CDW/LDW) are included and, if not, how much they'll cost. You should also ask whether cover includes personal accident insurance (PAI), supplementary liability or extended protection insurance (SL/EPI) and personal effects cover (PEC), which are automatically included in most private policies but may be excluded (or severely limited) from hire policies. CDW alone can cost as much as $20 per day!

Hire cars are graded into classes or sizes by their body size, not engine capacity, e.g. sub-compact (the smallest), compact, mid-size and full size. Some companies also offer luxury models, convertibles (roadsters) and sports cars, four-wheel drive 'off-road' vehicles/SUVs, mini-vans (seven passengers) and mini-buses (up to 11 passengers). Note that with the exception of off-road vehicles, all hire vehicles usually have automatic transmission. You can also hire a motor home, e.g. from Cruise Canada (🖳 www.cruisecanada.com).

Motorcycle hire is available from a number of companies such as H-C Travel (🖳 www.hctravel.com), where the minimum hire period is usually seven days. The cost of hiring a medium-size motorbike is from around $200 per day or $1,200 a week, so depending on the length of your trip it may be cheaper to buy a bike and sell it when you no longer need it. The most powerful bikes may only be rented to those aged over 30.

Many factors influence the cost of car hire, including the day of the week (it's often cheaper at weekends because most hires are by business travellers on working days), the season (the most expensive period is July and August), the size of the town and, in the tourist season, the popularity of the local attractions. Weekend rates are usually cheaper and may include the Friday and Monday either side of the weekend. It's possible to haggle over rates with some companies, most of which also offer discounts for long-term hire; weekly rates usually work out around 10 per cent lower per day than daily rates.

Most companies have a standard daily rate plus mileage, while others offer a flat 'unlimited mileage' daily rate that works out cheaper if you're travelling long distances. A sub-compact costs from around $60 per day and a compact around $70 per day, both with unlimited mileage. With limited mileage, daily rates are around $10 per day cheaper plus 10¢ to 20¢ per mile above 100 or 150 'free' miles (160 to 240km) per day.

Most hire companies insist on payment with a major credit card and won't accept cash (Budget is a rare exception). This is so that they can trace you if you steal or damage a car and also because they can deduct extra charges from credit cards without obtaining prior approval. The estimated cost of the hire is deducted or 'blocked off' your card's credit limit as soon as you drive off, therefore you should ensure that this doesn't leave you short of credit during a trip.

☑ SURVIVAL TIP

When paying by credit card, check that you aren't charged for unauthorised extras or for something that you've already paid for, such as fuel.

Your own car insurance may cover you when driving a hire car, although you must usually carry collision insurance (see page 181) on your own policy or your insurer won't cover damage to a hire car if you decline CDW. If you pay for a hire with a major credit card (e.g. American Express or a Gold MasterCard/Visa card), your card company may provide CDW cover, but check the extent of cover provided, as most pay the excess (deductible) only after your insurance company pays a claim. If you decline CDW, you're responsible for all damage to a car (however caused) and must pay a large security deposit with a credit card or travellers' cheques.

Most hire companies won't rent to anyone under 21 and with some companies the age limit is 25. Those that do rent to people under 25 may levy a 'young driver' surcharge of around $30 per day. If you have a foreign licence, you usually need an International Driver's Permit (IDP), which must normally be used in conjunction with your foreign licence (it may not be accepted on its own). If a number of drivers are planning to drive a vehicle, they must all have an IDP.

PARKING

Parking in Canadian towns and cities can be a problem. Streets often have restricted parking, or parking is prohibited altogether and, if you park illegally, the authorities won't hesitate to tow your car away. Parking regulations may vary with the area of a city, the time of day, the day of the week and even the season. In some towns there are special parking regulations during rush-hours on major thoroughfares, where no parking is permitted on one or both sides of the street during certain times; this may also include streets with parking meters in town centres, where there's usually no parking anywhere during rush hours, i.e. between 6 and 10am and 3 to 6pm. On some streets there are parking restrictions at certain times only (shown on signs), e.g. between 9 and 11am Mondays to Thursdays.

Parking on some streets is prohibited during certain hours on some days for street cleaning; if you park during these periods, your car will be impounded. If you don't see a parking meter, don't assume that parking is free because meters tend to be set well back from the kerb so that they aren't buried by ploughed snow. In winter, some streets are designated 'snow streets', meaning you mustn't park there when snowfall exceeds a certain amount (shown on a sign), in order to leave the road free for snow ploughs. Always read all parking signs carefully. A yellow or red painted kerb also indicates that parking is forbidden.

Apart from the obvious illegal parking spots, such as across entrances and at bus stops, be careful not to park within 15 feet (5m) of a fire hydrant, often indicated by a large gap between parked cars, or your car will be towed away. Other restricted areas are in front of fire and ambulance stations and schools. Some city centre areas are also designated 'towaway' zones, where all illegally parked cars are impounded. If your car is towed away, it costs from around $110 ($80 for the tow and $30 for the parking fine) to get it back. To collect your car from the pound, you must show proof of ownership, insurance card identity, registration and your driving licence.

Your car may also be clamped (called a 'tire boot' in Canada) if you park illegally in a city. Payment of fines must be made within a certain period and there may be a reduced fine if you pay within seven days, after which it can increase dramatically. Parking offences throughout Canada are recorded on computers and, if you have an outstanding ticket when you come to renew your annual licence fee, you must pay it on the spot.

Parking regulations in Canadian cities are controlled by city police and private companies, who are particularly zealous because they're paid on results and employees usually have quotas to meet. If you're in doubt about whether on-street parking is legal, don't take a chance but park in a car park.

Parking in city centres is very expensive and on-street parking (e.g. with meters) is permitted for short periods only. For example, in central Toronto, daytime parking starts at around $4 to $5 for 30 minutes and can be as much as $20 to $25 per hour, although after 6pm it's reduced to around $7 per hour. City-owned car parks (parking lots or parkades) are indicated by a green 'P' and are slightly cheaper than privately-owned car parks. In most cities, shopping complexes and hotels have underground parking. If you live in a city and don't have private parking, it can cost anything from $100 to $500 per month, which is why many city dwellers use taxis locally and hire a car for longer trips (you also don't have to dig your car out of the snow and cold-start it in winter). Privately-owned car parks usually have security patrols, although they don't take responsibility for damage or thefts from cars.

Banks, supermarkets, large shops and other establishments often provide free parking areas for customers. However, if you remain too long (e.g. over three hours) or park after hours, you may be given a ticket or your car may even be impounded. Reserved parking spaces for handicapped motorists are provided at public buildings, shopping centres and in car parks, indicated by a sign showing a wheelchair or a wheelchair symbol painted on the ground.

Parking on main roads in rural areas is forbidden and you must pull completely off the road if you wish to stop. Overnight, off-road parking is usually prohibited or restricted when towing a trailer or driving a 'recreation vehicle' (RV) or motor home, and you must use an official trailer or RV car park.

12. HEALTH

Generally, Canada is a very healthy place to live. Sanitation standards are extremely high, the water is safe to drink and food regulations are stringent. The average life expectancy of 78 for men and 83 for women is among the highest in the world, although it's significantly lower among poor and underprivileged groups and varies according to the province or territory. The infant mortality rate is a low 4.63 deaths per 1,000 live births, although this also varies, with a high of around 12 per 1,000 in the Yukon. The main causes of death for adults are heart disease and cancer. However, MRSA and similar antibiotic-resistant infections are an increasing concern in hospitals, and are estimated to be responsible for some 8,000 deaths a year.

There are no unusual health problems in Canada, although the high incidence of tuberculosis among some migrants and refugees is worrying health officials. Hay fever sufferers planning to live in southern Ontario (including the Toronto area) should note that it has one of the highest pollen counts in North America. The most common health problems for expatriates are those associated with the hustle and bustle of life in a modern society, including stress (expatriate stress is a recognised mental condition), poor diet, too much alcohol, lack of exercise and obesity.

Of increasing concern is alcohol abuse, estimated to be directly responsible for thousands of deaths per year, many caused by motor vehicle accidents. Apart from the direct and indirect loss of life, alcohol abuse costs Canadian industry billions of dollars per year in lost production due to absenteeism. It's estimated that some 10 per cent of Canadians have a drink problem. Alcoholics Anonymous has groups in all cities and large towns in Canada, where recovering alcoholics meet to encourage each other to stay sober. If you can afford to pay for private treatment, there are a number of private clinics and hospitals that specialise in providing treatment for 'chemical dependency'. Drug abuse is also prevalent and on the increase (see **Drugs** on page 208).

Like many other western countries, Canada has an ageing population and faces an increasing burden on its health service. An ambitious plan to extend health care to include free prescription drugs (Pharmacare) has had to be shelved, and a plan to save money by cutting the number of hospital beds in favour of a 'home care' scheme met with public opposition. Although modern medical and surgical techniques make it safer and more comfortable to be treated at home, the public perception is that quality healthcare is best measured by the number of hospital beds available. An additional problem facing the authorities is the number of doctors and nurses who move to the US, where their skills are better rewarded and working conditions less stressful.

If you aren't entitled to free public healthcare (see below), you should ensure that you have adequate health insurance, generally considered to be a minimum of $500,000 per year (see **Health Insurance** on page 52). When calculating how much insurance you require, bear in mind that Canadian medical fees are comparable to those in the US (which are among the highest in the world) and some prescription drugs can be even more expensive. If you're planning long-term residence, it's wise to have a thorough medical examination, including a dental and optical check before you arrive, and, if you've been putting off elective medical or dental treatment, e.g. a 'nose job' or having your teeth capped, it's advisable to have it done before arriving in Canada.

Canada is one of the world's leading countries regarding the provision of facilities for the physically disabled, particularly for those who are wheelchair bound. Most public buildings are wheelchair-accessible, including tourist offices, museums and art galleries, as are many restaurants, public toilets, major hotels and motels. Canada's airlines provide special boarding and disembarkation services for the disabled and many car rental agencies provide special cars with hand controls (which must be booked in advance). Reserved parking is available for disabled drivers in the major cities and towns. If you require general information about any health matter, you should contact Health Canada (AL 0900C2, Ottawa, Canada K1A OK9, 💻 www.hc-sc.gc.ca) or a regional office (listed in telephone books).

Among the many books on health in Canada are the *Canadian Healthcare Sourcebook: The Direct Link to the Vital Social and Medical Support Services in Canada* (Canadian Newspaper Services) and *The Canadian Consumer's Guide to Health Care* by Sharon Lindenburger (McGraw-Hill Ryerson). A number of magazines are also dedicated to health matters, including *Canadian health* (💻 www.canadian-health.ca) and *Canadian Health & Lifestyle* (💻 www.healthandlifestyle.ca).

PUBLIC HEALTH SERVICE

Canada spends a relatively high around 11 per cent of its gross domestic product (GDP) on healthcare, higher than the average for OECD countries, but lower than the 16 per cent in the States. Unlike the US, however, where healthcare is sparse or non-existent for the poor and unemployed, Canada has a government-sponsored health insurance scheme (unofficially called Medicare) that provides 'free' basic healthcare to Canadian citizens, permanent residents and refugees. Canada's public healthcare system is funded by both the federal government, and by provincial and territorial governments. The main source of revenue is taxation, i.e. personal and corporate income taxes (in some provinces, sales tax is also used).

In some provinces you must contribute, while in others it's 'free', i.e. paid for by general taxes rather than direct payments. (Foreign students lost their right to free healthcare in 1994 and must now have private health insurance before they're permitted to attend school or university.) Some provinces charge an annual healthcare premium based on annual income; for example, in Ontario those earning below $20,000 pay nothing, while others pay $300-900 per annum (those earning $25,000-36,000 pay $300 per annum and those on incomes of $38,500-48,000 pay a premium of $450). In British Columbia, under the Medical Services Plan there's a monthly contribution of $54 for one person, $96 for two people and $108 for three or more people.

Despite the free or cheap Medicare system, many people also have private health insurance (which they either pay themselves or receive as a benefit from their employers) in order to obtain treatment that isn't covered by Medicare or to obtain faster or more specialised treatment. Medicare covers Canadian residents when travelling or working anywhere in Canada outside their home province or territory; however, reimbursement for treatment abroad is only partial, and most Canadians purchase travel insurance when travelling abroad.

Medicare has increasingly become a source of controversy in Canadian politics. Although most users have positive or very positive experiences of Medicare, it has been increasingly under fire in recent years for being under-funded (funding has failed to keep pace with the rising cost of equipment, staff and drugs, and in some cases has even been reduced); staff shortages (there's an acute shortage of doctors); discrepancies between the quality of care provided in different regions (particularly between the northern territories and the major cities); long waiting lists for specialists, diagnostic tests and (particularly) elective surgery; and long waiting times in emergency rooms. Many critics believe the system is both failing and unsustainable – a criticism made of public health systems in most countries.

Eligibility & Registration

Although it's generally referred to as Medicare, the name of the public health scheme varies from province to province, as does eligibility and conditions. Coverage for services such as dental care, prescription drugs, optometric services, hearing aids, and home care, also varies by province or territory. Generally all migrant residents who will be living or working in a province or territory for a minimum of six months are entitled to register for Medicare. If you qualify for free healthcare, you should register and apply for a health card as soon as possible after your arrival by visiting the office of the provincial ministry of health in the city or town where you're living. You're required to complete an application form and provide identification such as your birth certificate, visa and passport.

If you're unable to afford Medicare premiums, there's a 'Medical Services Plan' that provides subsidies to those in financial need, ranging from 20 to 100 per cent of the cost. Subsidies are based on an individual's (or a couple's) net income for the previous year. Temporary premium assistance provides a 100 per cent subsidy to cover an unexpected financial hardship.

In some provinces you're covered immediately after arrival, while in others you aren't covered for the first three months, i.e. you must wait two months after the end of the month in which you apply for membership before cover commences. For example, if you moved to British Columbia or New Brunswick on 20th August, the month of August will count as the first month, with September and October as the following two, and cover commencing on 1st November.

For further information, contact the relevant province or territory department of health, listed in the table below.

Health Departments

Province/Territory	Contacts (☎, 💻)
Alberta	780-427 1432, www.health.alberta.ca
British Columbia	1-800-465 4911, www.hibc.gov.bc.ca
Manitoba	1-800-392 1207, www.mpi.mb.ca/health
New Brunswick	506-457 4800, www.gnb.ca/0051/0394/index-e.asp
Newfoundland & Labrador	709-729 5021, www.gov.nl.ca/health
The Northwest Territories	1-800-661 0830, www.hlthss.gov.nt.ca
Nova Scotia	902-424 5818, www.gov.ns.ca/health
Nunavut	1-867-975 5700, www.gov.nu.ca/health
Ontario	1-800-268 1153, www.health.gov.on.ca
Prince Edward Island	902-368 6130, www.gov.pe.ca/health
Quebec	418-266 7005, www.ramq.gouv.qc.ca
Saskatchewan	1-800-667 7766, www.health.gov.sk.ca
The Yukon Territory	1-800-661 0408, www.hss.gov.yk.ca

If you aren't eligible for healthcare straight away, temporary private health insurance is available (see page 217).

Medicare covers all medical services, including doctor's fees and hospital costs, but not the cost of all prescription drugs. In British Columbia you must pay for prescriptions above $600 per year – pharmacies are linked to a computerised 'Pharmanet' system which tracks how much you spend in a year on 'eligible' medicines (for details see 🖳 www.health.gov.bc.ca/pharme).

EMERGENCIES

Canadian emergency medical services are among the best in the world. Keep a record of the phone numbers of your doctor, dentist, local hospitals and clinics, ambulance service, poison control and other emergency services (fire, police) near your phone. The action to take in an emergency depends on the degree of urgency and in a life-threatening emergency you should call 911. If necessary, an ambulance will be sent, usually staffed by paramedics and equipped with cardiac, oxygen and other emergency equipment. In Alberta and British Columbia you must pay for an ambulance, while in other provinces they're free for emergencies. Each region of Canada has a poison control number, listed at the front of phone books.

> ☑ **SURVIVAL TIP**
>
> **The emergency number to call an ambulance in Canada is 911 (the same as in the US).**

If you're able, you can go to the emergency room of the nearest hospital, many of which are open 24/7 (check the location of your nearest hospital and the fastest route from your home in advance). It's wise to also check which local hospital is best equipped to deal with emergencies such as heart attacks, car accident injuries, burns and children's injuries. (Note, however, that unless your condition is critical, you could face a long wait.)

If you don't need to go to hospital but are too ill to go to a doctor's surgery, you could call your doctor for advice, although most doctors don't make house calls. However, you may be able to get someone to drive you to a doctor or a walk-in clinic. If you need urgent medical advice or medicines, you can call a local doctor, hospital or pharmacy (listed in the phone book). Police stations keep a list of doctors' and pharmacists' private phone numbers in case of emergencies.

If you have an emergency dental problem, phone your own dentist. If he doesn't provide an emergency service outside normal surgery hours, phone a dentist who does (often indicated in the *Yellow Pages*'). Most dentists use an answering service outside normal office hours and will return your call (or you'll be called by a 'stand-in' dentist). In an emergency you may be able to obtain treatment at a university or dental hospital, where a dental surgeon is on duty. Note, however, that a dentist isn't obliged to treat anyone, even in an emergency.

DOCTORS

There are excellent doctors throughout Canada. The usual way to find one is to ask your colleagues, friends, neighbours or acquaintances if they can recommend someone (but don't rely on their recommendations alone). Your employer may advise you about medical matters and large companies may have a company doctor. You can also contact your local city or provincial medical society, who can provide you with a list of local doctors. Some hospitals also maintain a list of doctors who accept new patients. Family doctors are listed alphabetically by specialism under 'Doctors and Surgeons' in the *Yellow Pages*. In small communities where there's insufficient business to support a dedicated practice, there may be no local doctors. If you wish to find a doctor who speaks a particular language, your local embassy or consulate should be able to help you.

The availability of medical services varies greatly depending on the area, and in remote areas doctors and other medical practitioners may be scarce.

It's wise to find a doctor as soon as possible after your arrival, rather than wait until you're ill, when you may have no time to choose.

You may wish to select a doctor who's part of a group practice, although you may not be able to choose the doctor you see. Before registering with a doctor, you may wish to find out the following:

- Is he or she the right sex?
- What is the doctor's age, training and medical background?
- At which local hospitals does the doctor practise (if any)?
- Is it a group practice?
- What are the office hours?
- Does he make house calls?
- Does he practise preventive or complementary (alternative) medicine?

You can check a doctor's credentials in the Canadian Medical Association's directory, available at local libraries. If you're seeking a specialist, you may wish to consult a copy of the directory for the Royal College of Physicians and Surgeons of Canada.

Doctors' office hours vary but are typically from 8.30am to 6 or 7pm, Mondays to Fridays, the office sometimes closing earlier one day per week, e.g. at 5 or 5.30pm on Fridays (it may also open on a few evenings per week). Offices are usually also open on Saturday mornings, e.g. from 8.30 to 11.30am or noon, and some doctors have Sunday office hours for emergencies. Most doctors use an answering service outside office hours, which gives you the name of the doctor on call and his phone number.

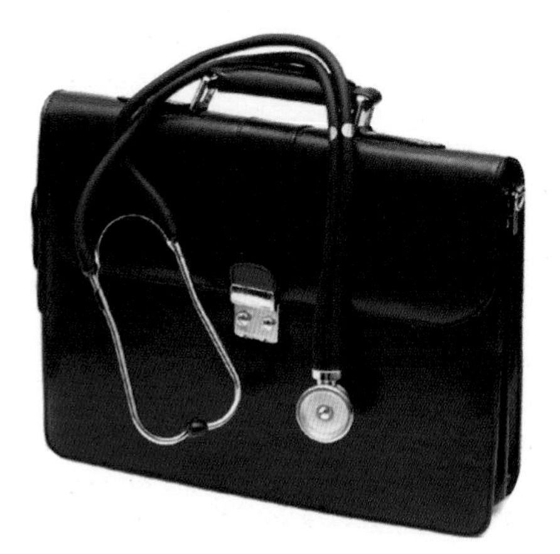

In some provinces, e.g. Ontario, many family doctor practices have created their own clinics, offering a 24-hour service if needed. Each doctor in the practice takes a turn at being 'on call' on a rotating basis and patients can also have a doctor make a home visit in extreme situations. There's no additional charge for these services, which are billed to the province in the same way as surgery visits.

All doctors operate an appointment system and you cannot just turn up during office hours and expect to be seen (unless you're going to a drop-in clinic, where appointments are unnecessary or even possible). If you're an urgent case, your doctor will usually see you immediately, but you must still phone in advance. Provided you aren't late, you generally won't need to wait to see your doctor. If you miss an appointment without giving sufficient notice, your doctor may charge you a standard fee (although unlikely).

If you don't qualify for Medicare, fees are generally around $60 for a consultation and $40 for a laboratory test. If you need to see a specialist, he'll charge up to $100 for a consultation and possibly another $75 for laboratory tests. Your doctor may wish to be paid the same day you see him in order to eliminate paperwork, although many will send you a bill. Doctors usually expect immediate payment in cash from temporary foreign residents, although some accept payment by credit card.

If you plan to live in Canada for a number of years, you should bring your medical and dental records with you (including test results, X-rays, laboratory reports, hospital records, etc.) or ask your overseas doctor to send them to your doctor in Canada. This is particularly important if you have an unusual medical history or suffer from a long-term condition because it can save considerable time and expense on tests and background studies. If you change doctors in Canada, ask your old doctor(s) to forward your medical records to your new doctor (your medical records are your property).

The cost of malpractice suits means that doctors usually err on the side of over-treatment rather than neglect and many prescribe medicines, tests and treatment that may be unnecessary or probably wouldn't be required in many other countries. If you aren't comfortable with a diagnosis, you should obtain a second opinion. If you wish to complain about professional misconduct or exorbitant fees, you should contact your provincial Ministry of Health.

In addition to conventional medicine, some medical practitioners offer alternative therapies such as acupuncture and chiropractic, although these are less common than in many other countries. Note also that alternative medicine is unregulated in Canada and isn't covered by provincial health plans.

MEDICINES & PHARMACIES

Medicines can be obtained from pharmacies, drugstores and supermarkets (many of which contain pharmacies) and may be cheaper than in other western countries (although more expensive than in the US). Chain and groups with branches throughout Canada are Shoppers Drug Mart (🖳 www.shoppersdrugmart.ca) and Pharmaplus/Rexall (🖳 www.rexall.ca). Pharmacies are packed with medicines for every ailment under the sun (hypochondriacs will think they've died and gone to heaven) and may sell over the counter medicines that are available in other countries on prescription only. However, there are strict controls on the licensing and sale of most medicines in Canada, where some medicines sold freely in other countries require a doctor's prescription. Many pharmacists keep a record of customers and the medicines dispensed to them, and you may be asked for certain details if you're a new customer.

Some items common in other countries are difficult to find in Canada, e.g. soluble aspirin (apart from Alka Seltzer); Canadians take tablets containing acetaminophen rather than paracetamol for headaches. Tablets containing codeine don't require a prescription but are kept behind the counter by pharmacists and must be requested. The brand names for the same medicines can vary from country to country and you should ask your doctor for the generic name of any medicines you take regularly. Any medicines you take with you to Canada should be accompanied by a doctor's letter explaining why you need them. Don't take non-prescribed medicines and keep medicines in their original packaging (Canadian customs officials may be suspicious of anything other than aspirin).

Provincial and territory governments provide assistance for the purchase of prescription drugs for certain groups under insurance programmes, e.g. Pharmacare. Programmes vary from province to province, but usually include seniors, provincial residents on social assistance, and some groups with specific ailments. Only in Quebec is prescription drug insurance compulsory, where it's provided through private insurance plans (e.g. group insurance or employee benefit plans) or the public health system (Régie de l'assurance maladie du Québec).

If you're visiting Canada for a limited period, you should take sufficient medicines to cover your stay, as prescription drugs can be expensive and insurance policies don't usually cover existing medical conditions (you may also be unable to obtain your usual medicine in Canada). In some provinces, pharmacists fill prescriptions from locally-registered doctors only. If you need to refill a prescription from a doctor who's resident in another province (or abroad), you must get a local doctor to write a

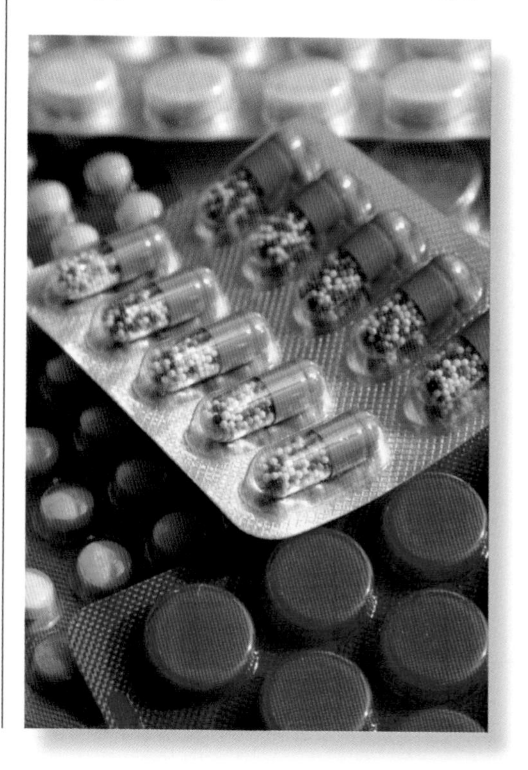

copy prescription. A hospital emergency room may refill a prescription from its own pharmacy or write a prescription that can be filled at a local pharmacy.

At least one pharmacy is open in most towns during the evenings and on Sundays for the emergency dispensing of medicines and drugs. A list is posted on the doors of pharmacies and published in local newspapers and guides. In most large cities there are pharmacies open 24/7, some of which provide a free delivery service in the local area.

Most pharmacists provide free advice regarding minor ailments, suggest appropriate medicines and also sell non-prescription medicines and drugs, toiletries, cosmetics, health foods, cleaning supplies, foodstuffs and other goods. Alternative therapies such as herbal and homeopathic medicines are popular and widely available. Health food stores sell health foods, diet foods and eternal-life-virility-youth pills and elixirs, all of which are popular in Canada.

Always use, store and dispose of unwanted drugs and medicines safely, e.g. by returning them to a pharmacist or doctor; never leave them where children can get their hands on them.

HOSPITALS & CLINICS

Canada has many excellent hospitals and clinics, including general public hospitals, special public hospitals, private hospitals and clinics, totalling over 2,000. If you're a Medicare patient, you receive free accommodation, healthcare and meals, but must usually share a 'ward' with two or three other patients (if you want a private room you must pay extra). You may need to wait for non-urgent treatment, although waiting lists are seldom longer than a few months. A general community hospital is adequate for most medical problems and usually caters for surgery, internal medicine, obstetrics and paediatrics. For more serious illnesses or major surgery, you're usually better off at a university or teaching hospital, where specialist skills are available (or in a hospital or clinic that specialises in your illness).

If you aren't eligible for Medicare, you'll be treated as a private patient, when each test, doctor's visit, pill, meal or fluff of your pillows is likely to be added to your bill. The cost of a hospital room alone is likely to exceed the cost of the most expensive hotel room and even a stay of a few days will result in a bill for thousands of dollars. If you have insufficient insurance, you may be discharged from hospital earlier than would otherwise be the case (but not if your condition is critical).

You should ensure that you have adequate hospital insurance before an emergency arises because without it, hospitalisation can be an economic disaster. If your condition is critical (life-threatening), you're usually taken to the nearest hospital, even if you have no medical insurance and are unable to pay. If you're uninsured and need non-emergency hospital treatment, you can go to the emergency room of a public hospital where, although you may have to wait, you'll be treated without advance payment.

In many areas there are private drop-in clinics or urgent care centres (known as 'doc-in-a-box' centres), e.g. Ontario has 24-hour drop-in medical clinics to help reduce the costs associated with treating after-hours emergencies in hospital emergency rooms. Typical services include treating a sprained ankle, earache or a broken arm. No appointment is necessary at a walk-in clinic, many of which are open daily. There are also private clinics which usually have a minimum charge of $35 to $75, to which must be added the cost of any special treatments or diagnostic tests. Most require immediate payment and usually accept major credit cards, although some will wait for payment from an insurance company. Public hospitals also have walk-in clinics, medical centres and emergency rooms (where there are usually long waiting times).

The admission procedure for a private hospital varies but is similar everywhere. You must report to the admissions office on arrival, where the first question you're likely to be asked is about your medical insurance or how you intend to pay for treatment. You're asked to complete a set of admission application forms, including a 'consent for treatment' form and a consent to release information to the provincial medical department. If you have insurance, you should take your certificate or proof with you. If you don't have insurance, you must pay a large deposit, which could run into thousands of dollars, or complete a financial agreement. A deposit can usually be paid in cash or personal cheque and sometimes by credit card. It's wise to check the admission procedure in advance and ask how the deposit (if applicable) should be paid. Hospital bills may need to be paid in full before you leave a hospital (but they won't keep you in for ever if you cannot pay!).

CHILDBIRTH

The traditional place to give birth in Canada is in the maternity ward of a hospital, where a stay of around three days is usual. If you wish to have your child at home, you must find a doctor and/or midwife (see below) who's willing to attend you. Some doctors are opposed to home births, particularly in cases where there could be complications, when specialists and special hospital facilities may be required. Failing this, you can engage a private midwife (a qualified nurse with special training) through an agency, who will attend you at home throughout your pregnancy and after the birth. Another option is to attend a maternity or birth centre staffed by experienced midwives, where mother and baby usually go home around 12 hours after the birth.

For hospital births, you can usually decide (with the help of your doctor or midwife) the hospital where you wish to have your baby. You aren't required to use the hospital suggested by your doctor but should book a bed as early as possible. Your doctor may refer you to an obstetrician or you can find your own (check which painkilling methods he's familiar with before choosing one).

Find out as much as possible about local hospital methods and policies on childbirth, either directly or from friends or neighbours, before booking a bed. The policy regarding a father's attendance at a birth may vary from hospital to hospital. If the presence of your husband or another person is important to you, check that it's permitted at the hospital where you plan to have your baby, and any other rules that may be in force. Birth centres usually allow family members to be present.

'Natural childbirth', which involves giving birth in a crouching position (possibly in a 'birthing pool') with minimum use of artificial aids such as an epidural, is common in Canada, and many hospitals expect mothers to attend natural childbirth lessons (they may also request the participation of the father).

Midwives are responsible for educating and supporting women and their families during the childbearing period. They can advise women before they become pregnant, in addition to providing moral, physical and emotional support throughout a pregnancy and after the birth. Your midwife may also advise you about parental education and ante-natal classes for mothers. All cities and towns have pre-natal registries (listed in the *Yellow Pages*). Information about contraception, pregnancy and abortion is also available from your family doctor.

In Canada it's usual for children to be vaccinated against diphtheria, whooping cough, tetanus, tuberculosis, polio and MMR (measles, mumps and rubella). For information, see the Public Health Agency of Canada website (💻 www.phac-aspc.gc.ca/im/index-eng.php).

Note that private health insurance policies won't pay the medical costs associated with childbirth if you were pregnant before you took out health insurance. If you have health insurance, don't forget to inform your insurance company about your new arrival.

It isn't compulsory to register a birth in Canada and there are many people whose existence has never been registered (thus depriving them of various benefits, including the right to pay taxes!). When babies are born in hospital (as most are) the parents are given a 'statement of birth' form, which should be signed by both parents and sent with a registration form to the divisional registrar at the local municipal office (forms are available from municipal offices, city halls and land registry offices). There's a fee of around $30 (it varies depending on the province) if a birth is registered within 12 months, after which period there's an additional late registration fee of around $25. Without registration, a Social Insurance Number (SIN) cannot be obtained for a child and the various tax breaks for education cannot be claimed (and you cannot obtain a passport).

Births to foreign parents may need to be reported to an embassy or consulate in order to obtain a national birth certificate and passport. If a citizen of another country has a child with a Canadian citizen (either in their native country or in Canada), Canada recognises that child as a Canadian citizen because one of the parents is Canadian (see **Citizenship** on page 307).

Abortion

Canada is one of the few countries with no legal restrictions on abortion, other than that it must be carried out by a qualified doctor. Girls as young as 12 have access to abortions without parental approval. They can be performed in hospitals by referral from your doctor or in private clinics without referral, which may charge less than hospitals if you don't have Medicare. Costs vary from province to province, some paying all costs, others none. Over 110,000 abortions are performed annually in Canada (almost a third as many as there are live births!) and, according to opinion polls, most Canadians are against legal restrictions.

For information about abortion (and the alternatives) and counselling, contact the National Abortion Federation (☏ 1-800-772 9100, 💻 www.prochoice.org/canada/index.html) and the Campaign for Life Coalition (☏ 1-800-730 5358, 💻 www.campaignlifecoalition.com).

DENTISTS

Canadian dentists use the most up-to-date equipment and techniques and provide excellent dental treatment. The best way to find a dentist is to ask your colleagues, friends or neighbours (particularly those with perfect teeth) if they can recommend someone. Your local city, county or provincial dental society can give you the names of local dentists, although it won't recommend one. Dentists are listed alphabetically in the *Yellow Pages* along with their specialities, such as general (or family) dentistry, paediatric dentistry, oral and maxillofacial surgery, endodontics, orthodontics and periodontics. Check whether a dentist provides a 24-hour emergency service, dental hygienist, and evening or Saturday business hours (many dentists have evening office hours on one day per week or open on Saturday mornings).

> Most dentists send you a postcard to remind you of a check-up every six months and may even call the day before to remind you of an appointment. If you miss a dental appointment without giving 24 hours' notice, your dentist may charge you a standard fee.

If you plan to live in Canada for a number of years, it's recommended you take a copy of your dental records with you. This is particularly important if you have an unusual dental history, when it may save you both time and money. It may pay you to have your teeth checked and (if necessary) fixed before arriving in Canada, as dental treatment, particularly cosmetic treatment, is expensive and can run into thousands of dollars.

Medicare doesn't cover non-hospital dental treatment (although children and the elderly receive subsidised treatment in some provinces) and most Canadians take out private dental insurance or are covered by schemes through their employers. Dentists may expect payment on the spot (credit cards are usually accepted), although some provide payment plans when major (i.e. expensive) treatment is necessary. In many areas there are walk-in dental clinics in health centres, department stores and shopping malls.

Personal dental insurance isn't usually worth buying – once you've paid the hefty premiums and waited the minimum three years to have your tooth capped, for instance, you might as well have saved your time and paid up front; there's usually no financial advantage.

You should obtain a written detailed quotation before starting a course of treatment (a 'rough estimate' may be just a fraction of a final bill) and an itemised bill when work is complete. If you have regular check-ups and usually have little or no treatment, you should be suspicious if a new dentist suggests that you need a lot of treatment. If this happens, obtain a second opinion before going ahead, but bear in mind that two dentists will rarely agree on the exact treatment required.

If you have a complaint that you're unable to resolve with your dentist, contact your local city or provincial dental association or the Canadian Dental Association (1815 Alta Vista Drive, Ottawa, ON K1G 3Y6, ☎ 613-523 1770, 💻 www.cda-adc.ca), which is the national professional association of Canada's 19,000 dentists.

OPTICIANS

There are three kinds of professionals providing eye care in Canada. The most highly qualified is an ophthalmologist, who's a specialist doctor trained in diagnosing and treating disorders of the eye; in addition to performing eye surgery and prescribing drugs, he may perform sight tests and prescribe glasses (spectacles) and contact lenses. You may be referred to an ophthalmologist by an optometrist or your family doctor. Optometrists are licensed to examine eyes, prescribe corrective lenses, and dispense glasses and contact lenses. They're also trained to detect eye diseases and may prescribe drugs and treatment. A Canadian optician isn't the same as an optometrist (as in some other countries) and may not examine eyes or prescribe lenses. Opticians are licensed in many provinces to fill prescriptions written by optometrists and ophthalmologists, and to fit and adjust glasses.

As with dentists, there's no need to register with an optometrist or optician. You simply make an appointment with anyone you wish, although it's wise to ask your colleagues, friends or neighbours if they can recommend someone. Opticians and optometrists are listed in the *Yellow Pages*, where they may advertise their services.

The optometrist business is competitive and, unless someone is highly recommended, you should shop around for the best deal. Prices for glasses and contact lenses vary considerably, therefore it's wise to compare costs (although make sure you're comparing similar services and products). There are many optical retail chain stores in Canada where you can have a pair of glasses made within an hour.

The prices charged for most services (glasses, lenses, contact lenses) are among the lowest in the world. For example, glasses (frames and lenses) can be purchased in Canada for $100 or less (usually inclusive of an eye examination). Note, however, that these and other special deals (e.g. 'buy one get one free') aren't necessarily good value. Always ask about extra charges for eye examinations, fittings, adjustments, lens-care kit, follow-up visits and the cost of replacement lenses (if they're expensive,

it may be worthwhile taking out insurance). Many opticians and retailers provide insurance against the accidental damage of glasses for a nominal fee.

Around one in nine Canadians wears contact lenses, two-thirds of them women. Extended-wear soft contact lenses are widely available, although medical experts warn that they should be used with caution, as they greatly increase the risk of potentially serious eye infections. Obtain advice from your doctor or an ophthalmologist before buying them.

The cost of a sight test is usually between $50 and $100. You aren't required to buy your glasses or contact lenses from the optometrist who tests your sight, who must give you your prescription at no extra charge. However, this doesn't apply to a lens-fitting prescription for contact lenses.

It's wise to have your eyes tested before your arrival in Canada and to bring a spare pair of glasses or contact lenses with you. It's also recommended that you bring a copy of your prescription, in case you need to obtain replacement glasses or contact lenses in an emergency.

You can donate your old glasses to charity by giving them to an optician or optometrist. They're sent either to Canadian charities (who give them to needy people) or overseas to developing countries.

COUNSELLING

Counselling and assistance for health and social problems is available from a variety of local community groups, volunteer organisations, national associations and self-help groups. In most provinces there are toll-free help-lines for a wide range of problems, and counselling may also be available by phone. Many colleges and educational establishments provide a counselling service for students. Look in the *Yellow Pages* under 'Social Service Organisations'. If you or a member of your family are the victims of a violent crime, the police can put you in touch with a local victim support scheme.

Problems for which help is available are numerous and include general health complaints, substance abuse (see **Drugs** below), alcoholism (e.g. Alcoholics Anonymous) and alcohol-related problems, gambling, dieting (e.g. Weight Watchers), smoking, teenage pregnancy, poison control, attempted suicide and psychiatric problems, homosexual and lesbian-related problems, youth problems, parent-child problems, child abuse, family violence (e.g. battered wives), runaways, marriage and relationship problems, rape and sexually transmitted diseases (see below). Many communities also provide a range of free health services for the homeless.

In times of need, there's nearly always someone to turn to and all services are strictly confidential. In major cities, counselling may be available in your own language if you don't speak English.

> **▲ Caution**
>
> If you need help in an emergency, someone who speaks your language can usually be found and agencies such as CanTalk (💻 www.cantalk.com) can provide a translator over the phone.

SMOKING

Around 20 per cent of Canadians smoke (according to Health Canada), although the figure is dropping each year; most smokers are aged below 44, the 20 to 24 age group being the most addicted. It's long been known that smoking causes lung and other types of cancer, as well as heart disease, bronchial complaints and a variety of other life-threatening illnesses. Health warnings on cigarette packets predict dire consequences for those who smoke, particularly pregnant women ('smoking during pregnancy can result in foetal injury, premature birth and low birth weight').

There's a ban on advertising tobacco products on radio and TV and in magazines (many people believe cigarette advertisements directly target children). Many provinces also ban the retail display of tobacco products (the so-called 'shower curtain' law). As in many countries with a strong anti-smoking lobby, sponsorship by tobacco companies (e.g. for arts and sporting events) has been banned.

Smoking in indoor (and in some cases, outdoor) workplaces and public places is banned in all territories and provinces, although some jurisdictions allow specific exemptions. Smoking may also be banned in vehicles when children are present, which in Nova Scotia applies to anyone under the age of 19! Some provinces allow smoking in specially-ventilated rooms, while other don't. As an example of smoking bans, in British Columbia smoking is banned in all public spaces such as restaurants, pubs and private clubs, offices, malls, conference centres, sports arenas, community halls, government buildings and schools, and within a three-metre radius of doors, open windows and air intakes.

Most hotels have non-smoking rooms and car rental companies also have non-smoking cars. Smoking is also banned in all federal buildings, in lifts (elevators), on most public transport, including taxis, buses, undergrounds, trains and aircraft, and in most schools (although some school boards have decided that it was better for pupils to smoke on school grounds than outside the gates, where they could fall prey to drug dealers).

Before you light up in a public place, it's wise to check whether smoking is permitted. Many employers run programmes to encourage employees to quit – in fact smoking is fast becoming a career hazard, as employers may refuse to employ smokers on the grounds that their habit may lead to costlier health insurance and lost working days due to sickness (smoking is responsible for millions of sick days each year).

Canadian health and life insurance companies may offer discounts to non-smokers. Homeowner or tenant insurance costs less for non-smokers and in some cities you may find it difficult to rent an apartment if you smoke. You must be aged 18 to purchase tobacco products, and shopkeepers face fines of at least $2,000 for selling tobacco products to minors.

DRUGS

It's estimated that around 15 per cent of Canadians use illicit drugs and almost 1,000 deaths per year are attributed to their use, almost 90 per cent of them men (over 50 per cent of murders are also attributed to drug use). Drug importation and abuse is a major problem in Canada, where officials estimate it costs the country some $2bn a year for healthcare, prevention, law enforcement and lost productivity due to illness and premature death. Canada has also become a drug exporter thanks to a booming marijuana business. Officials believe marijuana now ranks as British Columbia's most lucrative agricultural product, generating annual revenue of some $6bn.

> There's a BC-based website (💻 www.bcbuddepot.com) where you can choose from over 100 varieties of marijuana plant – with names such as 'Love Potion', 'Lifesaver', 'Amnesia Haze', 'Bogglegum', 'Canna Sutra', 'God Bud' and, curiously, 'LSD'.

Although violent crime is falling in Canada (see page 310), overall crime in the last 30 years has been increasing as a direct result of drug trafficking. In the '60s, the drug trade in Canada consisted of not much more than a few hippies smoking joints. Today, it's a mega-business, and the use of cocaine, crack cocaine, heroin and various chemical cocktails has exploded in the last few decades. At the street level, the drug trade is controlled by gangs who are armed to the teeth and don't take kindly to others trying to muscle in on their territory. Drug addicts frequently turn to crime to finance their expensive habit, which explains the high incidence of thefts from homes and automobiles.

Canada has a more lenient jail policy than the US, which many believe has helped to attract drug dealers who smuggle drugs into the US, where demand and prices are higher. The Royal Canadian Mounted Police (RCMP) has launched campaigns to stem the tide and in some areas they're effective, particularly where Canadian and US customs officers have combined forces. Except for British Columbia, Nova Scotia, Ontario and Prince Edward Island, which have a 'soft' attitude to the use of marijuana, the possession or use of marijuana is illegal. For the possession of small quantities you'll probably receive a suspended sentence and no criminal record. However, for large quantities of marijuana (when it's assumed that you're a dealer) or any quantity of hard drugs (e.g. heroin, cocaine or their derivatives) offenders can expect a five-year jail sentence.

There are drug help organisations in most cities (many with toll-free lines). Look in the *Yellow Pages* under 'Drug Abuse & Addiction' or 'Social Service Organizations' or call information for the phone numbers. For example, in Toronto there's Cocaine Anonymous, the Drug Abuse Information Line, Drugs Anonymous and Narcotics Anonymous, to name but a few.

SEXUALLY TRANSMITTED DISEASES

Like most western countries, Canada has its share of sexually transmitted diseases (STDs), particularly in the major cities. Most common are syphilis and gonorrhoea, along with genital herpes and Aids. Syphilis was rare in Canada in the last decades of the 20th century, but infection rates have risen in the 21st century. Similarly, although the number of confirmed cases of Aids has fallen steadily (to a low of 255 in 2006), the number of diagnosed HIV infections has been rising and topped 2,500 in 2006. It's reckoned that about 60,000 people in Canada live with HIV (including Aids).

Most Aids victims are homosexuals, needle-sharing drug addicts, or promiscuous visitors to some African and Asian countries where the disease is endemic. Male homosexuals continue to be most at risk from Aids, with two-thirds of all reported cases in this group. Slogans in advertisements encourage Canadian women to say 'No glove, no love', but despite this only 25 per cent of Canadians always use a condom with a casual partner. Condoms are on sale at pharmacies, drugstores, some supermarkets, men's hairdressers, and vending machines in toilets in bars and other public places.

If you would like to talk to someone in confidence about Aids or other sexually transmitted diseases, there are organisations and self-help groups in all cities providing information, advice and help, including local and provincial health departments. For further information about Aids, contact the Canadian Aids Society (☎ 613-230 3580, 🖳 www.cdnaids.ca).

DEATH

Dying can be expensive in Canada, although a simple cremation without any ceremony costs as little as around $200. In stark contrast, the average 'traditional' funeral costs around $5,000 and if you opt for a pricey coffin (around $10,000), plus embalming, limousines and an elaborate headstone, you won't see much change out of $25,000. If you pay for your funeral in advance (pay now, die later), under the Funeral Directors and Establishments Act, your money is placed in a trust fund until your death or until you request its return.

In the event of the death of a resident of Canada, all interested parties must be notified (see **Chapter 20**). You need a number of copies of the 'Proof of Death' certificate, e.g. for probate for a will, pension claims, insurance companies and financial institutions. If you need to obtain a copy of a birth, marriage or death certificate, the cheapest way is to apply to the registrar in the area where it was registered. See also **Wills** on page 249.

The death of a foreigner should be reported to his country's embassy or consulate in Canada so that it can be registered in the deceased's country of birth.

13. INSURANCE

Canadians spend around $20bn per year on insurance, including cover for their homes, cars, health and lives. There are some occasions in Canada where insurance for individuals is compulsory, including third party liability car insurance (required by law throughout Canada), and title, fire and mortgage life insurance (required by lenders) for homeowners. If you rent a car or buy one on credit, your lender will also insist that you have collision and comprehensive car insurance. Canada's social insurance (social security) system includes benefits for the unemployed, the aged, the disabled and those with very low incomes. Voluntary insurance includes private pensions, disability, health, homeowner's (casualty and liability), legal, dental, travel, automobile breakdown and life insurance.

It's unnecessary to spend half your income insuring yourself against every eventuality, from the common cold to being sued for your last dime, but it's important to be covered against any event that could precipitate a major financial disaster (such as a long illness or redundancy). As with anything connected with finance, it's important to shop around when buying insurance. Just picking up a few brochures from insurance agents, or making a few phone calls or surfing the net could save you a lot of money. Regrettably, you cannot insure yourself against being uninsured or sue your insurance agent for giving you bad advice.

If you wish to make an insurance claim against a third party or someone is claiming against you, you should seek legal advice. Canadian law is unlikely to be the same as in your previous country of residence.

For information about car insurance, see page 181.

INSURANCE COMPANIES & AGENTS

Canadian insurance companies offer a wide variety of insurance and many also provide financial services. However, under federal law, financial services companies that own insurance companies aren't permitted to sell insurance themselves (except in British Columbia). While some companies are privately owned, most are owned by shareholders of stock companies, the policyholders of mutual companies or by the government. There are over 450 Canadian insurance companies and around 200 foreign companies (which have some 60 per cent of the market) licensed to operate on a branch basis.

Most insurance companies provide a range of insurance services, while others operate in certain fields only. The major insurance companies have offices or agents in most large towns throughout Canada and include Manufacturers Life Insurance Co., Sun Life Assurance Co. of Canada, Great-West Life Assurance Co. of Canada and the London Life Insurance Group, Inc. Major 'property and casualty' insurers ('property and casualty' insurance includes all types of insurance except health and life insurance) include the Co-operators General Insurance Company, Zurich Canada, and Royal and Sun Alliance.

The majority of Canadians buy their insurance through insurance brokers and agents. You're usually better off buying insurance through an independent broker who deals with a number of insurance companies, rather than through an agent who sells the policies of one insurance company only (a so-called 'captive'). Most agents provide a free analysis of your family's insurance needs, but make sure it isn't influenced by their commission earnings. Agents or companies who charge a flat fee for their advice, rather than earn commission for selling policies, are usually the most objective.

According to independent experts, most agents offer poor advice, particularly regarding life insurance, and are interested only in selling policies (any policy). Always obtain recommendations from at least three agents, but bear in mind that this will almost certainly result in wildly different recommendations. When you've found a reliable agent, it's often wise to buy all your insurance through him, although you should still obtain quotations for new insurance needs from other agents or companies. Never allow yourself to be rushed into buying insurance (experts recommend that you 'shop till you drop' when buying insurance).

When comparing policies, bear in mind that the lowest-priced policies may offer poorer value than more expensive policies and the cheaper companies may also be slow to pay claims. Ask a broker how long particular companies take to settle claims; although all insurance companies are pleased to take your money, many aren't nearly so happy to pay up! Some companies use any available loophole to avoid settling claims, particularly if they think they can prove negligence, and you may need to threaten them with litigation before they pay. If you need to make a claim, don't send original bills or documents to your insurance company unless absolutely necessary (you can usually send a certified copy). Keep a copy of all bills, documents and correspondence, and send letters by registered post. If you receive a cheque in settlement of a claim, don't bank it if you think it's insufficient, otherwise you may be deemed to have accepted it as full and final settlement.

Make sure that the insurance company you select is one with an AAA credit rating. Before making a decision, check with consumer groups, Better Business Bureaux and insurance associations such as the Consumers' Association of Canada (436 Gilmour Street, 3rd Floor, Ottawa, ON K2P 0R8, ☎ 613-238 2533, 💻 www.consumer.ca) or the Consumers Council of Canada (1910 Yonge Street 4th Floor, Toronto, ON M4S 1Z5, ☎ 416-483 2696, 💻 www.consumerscouncil.com). It's wise to select an agent who's a member of the Insurance Bureau of Canada (777 Bay Street, Suite 2400, Toronto, ON M5G 2C8, ☎ 416-362 2031, 💻 www.ibc.ca), which sets ethical and professional standards for its members.

INSURANCE CONTRACTS

Read all insurance contracts carefully before signing them. If you don't understand everything, ask a friend or colleague to 'translate' it or take legal advice. If a policy has pages of legal jargon and 'gobbledegook' in very small print, you should be suspicious, particularly as it's common practice nowadays to be as brief as possible and write contracts clearly and concisely in simple language (apart from the small print). Some provinces have laws requiring all agreements and contracts between commercial institutions and consumers to be written in plain language.

☑ SURVIVAL TIP

Be particularly wary of policy exclusions, which may demolish the very protection that you think you're paying for, and be careful how you answer questions in an insurance proposal form. Even if you unwittingly provide false information, an insurance company can refuse to pay out if you make a claim.

Before signing an insurance contract, you should shop around and take a few days to think it over – don't sign on the spot as you may regret it later. Note also the following:

- A medical report may be required for certain insurance policies, e.g. health insurance, a pension plan or life insurance;
- Most insurance policies run for a calendar year from a specified date, therefore you should ensure that this date meets your requirements;
- All premiums should be paid punctually, as late payments can result in cancellation and denial of a claim.

The Office of the Superintendent of Financial Institutions oversees and regulates the insurance industry and there's a regional office in each province. Provinces may also have their own laws and regulations governing insurance. If you require information about local provincial insurance laws or wish to make a complaint (almost 50 per cent of complaints to local Better Business Bureaux concern insurance), contact the provincial financial services government listing, which can be found in the blue pages of your local telephone directory. For general insurance information, contact the Office of the Superintendent of Financial Institutions (255 Albert Street, Ottawa, ON K1A 0H2, ☎ 1-800-385 8647, 🖳 www.osfi-bsif.gc.ca).

In addition to federal and provincial governments overseeing the industry, there are several consumer protection groups established by insurance companies. The life and health insurance industry has a policyholder protection group, The Canadian Life and Health Insurance Association (🖳 www.clhia.ca), which provides free advice to consumers in English (☎ 1-800-268 8099) and French (☎ 1-800-361 8070). The property and casualty insurance industry has a consumer protection group, the Insurance Bureau of Canada (see above).

SOCIAL INSURANCE

Federal and provincial governments share the responsibility for social insurance (the name for social security in Canada), which includes benefits for the unemployed, the aged, the disabled and those with low incomes. Social insurance contributions are compulsory for most Canadian residents and are deducted from employees' salaries by employers. You pay 4.7 per cent of your gross salary up to a maximum contribution (which is adjusted annually for inflation and is around $1,800).

Canada's federally regulated income security programmes are administered by Human Resources and Social Development Canada (HRSDC). These include the Canada Pension Plan (CPP), which replaces part of the earnings that are lost when a Canadian retires or becomes seriously disabled, in addition to providing benefits for a surviving spouse and dependant children in the event of the death of a contributor. HRSDC is also responsible for the Employment Insurance Programme and negotiates and administers international social security agreements that assist immigrants to Canada (and emigrants from Canada) to qualify for state pensions paid by Canada and other countries.

Other federal agencies involved in income security include the Canada Revenue Agency (🖳 www.cra-arc.gc.ca), which collects CPP contributions and pays child tax benefit, and Veterans Affairs Canada (🖳 www.vac-acc.gc.ca), which is responsible for pensions and allowances for veterans and their dependants.

Provincial governments are responsible for social assistance programmes which ensure minimum levels of income for those in need. The provincial and territorial authorities determine eligibility and benefits for these programmes and have jurisdiction over workers' compensation plans, which provide benefits for injury or death at work. Several provinces also provide income support to the elderly by supplementing benefits from the seniors' benefit.

As in most countries, social insurance fraud is widespread and there are periodic crackdowns; in the late '90s, fraud investigations in Ontario saved the province over $100mn and resulted in over 1,000 convictions.

Social Insurance for Children

There are a number of social insurance payments for families, including the Canada Child Tax Benefit (CCTB), the National Child

Benefit Supplement (NCBS) and the Universal Child Care Benefit (UCCB). CCTB is a non-taxable amount paid monthly to help eligible families with the cost of raising children under 18 years of age. The CCTB may include the Child Disability Benefit (CDB), a monthly benefit that provides financial assistance for qualified families caring for children with severe and prolonged mental or physical impairments. Also included with the CCTB is the National Child Benefit Supplement (NCBS), a monthly benefit for low-income families with children. The NCBS is the federal government's contribution to the National Child Benefit, a joint initiative of federal, provincial, and territorial governments, and First Nations.

To qualify for CCTB, you must meet the following conditions:

- you must live with the child, and the child must be under the age of 18;
- you must be the person who's primarily responsible for the care and upbringing of the child (this means you're responsible for such things as supervising the child's daily activities and needs, making sure the child's medical needs are met, and arranging for child care when necessary. If there's a female parent who lives with the child, she's usually considered to be this person. However, it could be the father, a grandparent, or a guardian;
- you must be a resident of Canada;
- you or your spouse or common-law partner must be a Canadian citizen, a permanent resident, a protected person, or a temporary resident who has lived in Canada for the previous 18 months.

The CCTB and NCBS is paid at the following rates (2009):

The amount you're paid depends on your family income, as shown below:

- Families with net incomes below $20,435 receive the maximum CCTB, including the full NCBS and the supplement for the third and each additional child, along with any supplement for children aged under six that's applicable (see UCCB below).
- Families with net incomes of between $20,435 and $36,378 receive the maximum basic CTB, the supplement for the third and each additional child, and a partial NCBS, along with any supplement for children under six that's applicable (see UCCB below). Families with four or more children are also entitled to a partial NCBS if their income is just above $36,378.
- One- and two-child families with net incomes between $36,378 and approximately $99,128 receive partial benefits. Larger families may also be entitled to a partial CCTB if their income is above $99,128.

To determine the amount of benefits you're entitled to, see the CRA's on-line calculator (💻 www.cra-arc.gc.ca/bnfts/clcltr/menu-eng.html). To receive the CCTB, you and your spouse or common-law partner must each file an income tax return each year, even if you have no income to report.

In addition to the CCTB and NCBS, families are also entitled to a Universal Child Care Benefit (UCCB), which is designed to help them balance work and family life by supporting their child care with direct financial help. The UCCB is for children under the age of 6 years and is paid in instalments of $100 per month, per child.

Families already receiving the Canada Child Tax Benefit (CCTB) automatically receive the UCCB, while families that don't receive

CTTB & NCBS Rates

No. of Children	Basic CCTB	NCBS	Total	Monthly Benefit
first child	$1,255	$1,945	$3,200	$266.67
second child	$1,255	$1,720	$2,975	$247.92
third & each additional child	$1,343	$1,637	$2,980	$248.33

CCTB need to apply for UCCB by submitting a Canada Child Benefits application to the Canada Revenue Agency. If you apply late you may receive up to 11 months of retrospective payments, plus a payment for the month in which the application was received. For information, see 💻 www.universalchildcare.ca/eng/home.shtml.

International Agreements & Eligibility

International social security agreements provide for those who have lived or worked in Canada and another country and who qualify for old age, retirement, disability or survivor pensions from two or more countries. Through these agreements, continuity of cover is assured during periods spent working abroad and the possibility of making double payments (contributing to two countries' schemes for the same work) is eliminated. Such protection is granted only for a limited period abroad, e.g. up to five years.

Visitors and migrants must be resident in Canada for a minimum number of years before they become eligible for benefits. However, periods of residence or contributions in Canada and other countries (with international agreements) can be combined to meet these requirements.

There's a ten-year residence requirement before a person living in Canada becomes eligible for some benefits, and a 20-year residence requirement before a person can receive some benefits outside Canada for an indefinite period. Once eligibility has been established, the benefit payable is based on your contributions to the Canada Pension Plan.

Registration & Benefits

In order to work, pay taxes and receive social security benefits and free medical care in Canada, you require a Social Insurance Number (SIN), which is a nine-digit number used as identification on all official documents, and a Social Insurance Card. On arrival in Canada you must register at your nearest Service Canada Centre (listed on 💻 www.servicecanada.gc.ca) and apply for an SIN by producing your birth certificate, passport and record of landing. If your documents are in order, you'll receive your SIN immediately and your card about ten days after your application. (If you change your name, you must apply for a replacement card in your new name, which is provided free of charge).

You can also apply for a SIN and card by post, in which case you must either download an application form from the above website or order one by phone (☎ 1-800-206 7218 – select Option 3) and send it, with the appropriate (original) documents and cheque for $10 to Service Canada (Social Insurance Registration Office, PO Box 7000, Bathurst, New Brunswick E2A 4T1). You should receive your SIN and card within 15 working days.

If you live in New Brunswick, you can apply by phone (☎ 1-888-428 0888), quoting the relevant numbers on your immigration identity document or, if you were born in New Brunswick, your birth certificate. There's no online application procedure.

The main social security benefits are detailed below; for further details, visit 💻 www.hrsdc.gc.ca.

Retirement Income

Canada's state pension system consists of Old Age Security (OAS) and the Canada Pension Plan (CPP).

Old Age Security (OAS): Most people aged over 65 in Canada qualify for an OAS pension,

which was a maximum of $516.96 per month in January 2009 (it's reviewed four times a year to reflect increases in the cost of living) and averaging $489.57 per month. In addition, if you have a low or modest income, you may qualify for the Guaranteed Income Supplement (GIS), Allowance or Allowance for the Survivor. For information, see www.rhdcc-hrsdc.gc.ca/eng/isp/oas/oastoc.shtml.

Canada Pension Plan (CPP): A CPP retirement pension is paid only to those who have contributed to the CPP. The pension is designed to replace around 25 per cent of the earnings on which a person's contributions were based. You qualify for a CPP pension if you're aged 65 or over, or you're aged between 60 and 64 and meet certain earnings requirements, i.e. you earn less than the current monthly maximum CPP retirement pension payment, which was $908.75 per month in January 2009. The amount of your CPP retirement pension is based on how much and for how long you contributed to the Plan (or to the CPP and the Quebec Pension Plan). The age at which you choose to retire also affects the amount you receive. The average monthly retirement pension was $501.82 in January 2009.

Survivor benefits are paid on the death of a CPP contributor to his surviving spouse and dependant children. To be eligible for survivor benefits, contributions must have been made to the CPP for at least three years. There are four types of benefit: Death Benefit (a lump sum of up to $2,500), a Survivors Benefit (a maximum of $506.38 per month if the survivor is under 65, $545.25 if over 65), Disability Benefit (up to $1,105.99 per month) and Children's of Deceased Contributors Benefit (maximum $213.99). For further information about the CPP, see www.rhdcc-hrsdc.gc.ca/eng/isp/cpp/cpptoc.shtml.

Many provinces have a compulsory disability insurance scheme, usually financed by workers through payroll deductions. Benefits normally begin after a seven-day waiting period or the first day of hospitalisation, and are based on wages paid during a specific 12-month base period. See also **Disability Insurance** on page 221.

A pension is normally paid from the month following the month in which you turn 65, but it isn't paid automatically and you need to make an application six months before you plan to retire or reach the age of 65. An Application Kit is available from the HRSDC (1-800-277 9914 or see the website above).

You can choose to start drawing your pension at any time between the ages of 60 and 70, but must start drawing it at the age of 70. If you choose to take it before the age of 65, it's a smaller amount than the standard payment; if you choose to take it later, it's larger. The amount payable is adjusted by 0.5 per cent for each month that a pension is started before or after your 65th birthday and is permanent, i.e. it isn't recalculated when you reach the age of 65. For example, if you start to draw your pension at the age of 60, your monthly payments are 30 per cent lower than if you had waited until the age of 65 (although by starting it sooner you receive the pension for a longer period). If you choose to wait for your pension until the age of 70, your monthly payment is 30 per cent higher than if it was taken at the age of 65.

British Pensioners

British state pensions are frozen at the prevailing rate with no annual adjustments for inflation when the recipients move to certain Commonwealth countries, including Australia, Canada, New Zealand and South Africa. This affects over 350,000 British pensioners, including tens of thousands in Canada with frozen British state pensions (which may be equivalent to just a few C$).

There are a number of information websites and forums for British pensioners in Canada including the British Pensioners Association of Western Canada (www.britishpensioners.com) and the Canadian Alliance of British Pensioners (www.britishpensions.com).

EMPLOYMENT INSURANCE

What used to be known as unemployment insurance is now officially (and optimistically) called employment insurance (EI). The federal employment insurance scheme is financed by premiums paid by employers and employees and contributions from the federal government.

EI provides temporary financial assistance to those who lose their job through no fault of their own, e.g. those who are made redundant – if you quit or are fired from a job you don't qualify. Those who are sick, pregnant, or caring for a newborn or adopted child, as well as those who must care for a family member who's seriously ill with a significant risk of death, may also qualify for EI.

To qualify for EI benefits, applicants must show that they were employed for between 420 and 700 hours in the previous year (although it's sometimes up to 910 hours), depending on the provincial unemployment rate. To receive benefits you must file a claim stating that you're unemployed and willing to work, and must be registered at a Human Resource Centre. It's possible to apply for EI online (see website below).

After a waiting period of two weeks (new claims only) you're eligible to receive 55 per cent of your average weekly insured earnings up to an annual maximum insurable income of $42,300, which was a maximum of $447 per week in spring 2009. The number of weeks for which benefits are paid varies with the length of your previous employment, your previous employment insurance claims, and the national and regional unemployment rate.

For further information, see Service Canada (www.servicecanada.gc.ca/eng/sc/ei/index.shtml).

MEDICARE

Canada has a national healthcare system (widely known as Medicare) that's administered by federal and provincial governments. The Canadian government used to pay half of Medicare's operating costs, but this has been reduced to a third, the remainder being paid by the provinces. Medical services are paid for by various taxes and in some provinces direct contributions are also made by individuals. Medicare is available to all permanent residents of Canada who are registered under the national health insurance programme. To qualify for Medicare, you must obtain an official health card from the province where you live.

Medicare pays for most general medical services, although exactly what's covered varies from province to province. In all provinces, basic hospital charges and doctors' fees are covered, but not services that aren't medically necessary (such as cosmetic surgery). Some provinces provide cover for non-medical services, such as prescription drugs and medical apparatus.

> ☑ **SURVIVAL TIP**
>
> **It's important that you know exactly what's covered in your province of residence and to take out private health insurance to cover any additional services required.**

For further information, see **Public Health Service** on page 198.

PRIVATE HEALTH INSURANCE

It's important to check whether your family will be eligible for Medicare (see above) before you arrive in Canada because holiday or travel health policies won't cover you if you come to Canada to live or work. You may be able to extend your present health insurance policy rather than take out a new one. It's best to arrange cover before you arrive in Canada, although if you arrive without health insurance you can obtain temporary cover from a number of Canadian companies such as Blue Cross (🖳 www.bluecross.ca) and Industrial Alliance (🖳 www.inalco.com).

If you're living or working in Canada and aren't covered by Medicare or a company policy, it's extremely risky not to have private health insurance for your family because you could be faced with some very high medical bills. When deciding on the kind and extent of health insurance, make sure that it covers all your family's present and possible future health needs before you receive a large bill.

When changing employers or leaving Canada, you should ensure that you have continuous health insurance. If you and your family are covered by a company health plan, your insurance may cease after your last official day of employment. If you're planning to change your health insurance, ensure that no important benefits are lost, e.g. existing medical conditions usually won't be covered. When changing health insurance companies, it's wise to inform your old company if you have any outstanding bills for which they're liable.

As the cost of Medicare continues to rise and federal and provincial governments reduce the cover, an increasing number of Canadians are turning to private insurance (called extended health cover) to cover them for non-insured hospital and medical expenses. Over a third of Canadians have extended health cover and they spend several billion dollars per year on private health insurance, which typically covers the cost of private hospital rooms, special duty nursing, paramedic services and eye treatment.

Some employers provide free or low-cost group insurance for employees to supplement procedures and costs that aren't covered by Medicare. It's voluntary, however, and few companies pay 100 per cent of premiums; there may also be a qualification period (e.g. six months). Some companies offer 'no-frills' insurance for basic medical expenses, while others offer comprehensive plans, although few cover all medical expenses. Most plans offer a range of medical 'packages' (see below), plus optional or supplementary packages such as dental, optical, maternity and disability insurance.

▲ Caution

Never assume that an Canadian employer will take care of your health insurance requirements in Canada, but check and get it in writing. If you need to pay your own premiums, it will make a big hole in your salary.

Major Medical

A standard health insurance policy is called 'major medical' and includes doctors', surgeons' and anaesthetists' fees; outpatient prescription drugs; consultations with specialists; hospital accommodation and meals; operations or other treatment (e.g. physiotherapy, radiotherapy and chemotherapy); X-rays and diagnostic tests; maternity care (after a 12-month qualification period); medicines, X-rays and dressings while in hospital; physical and mental health treatment; substance abuse treatment; and home nursing and extended care facilities.

Options

All health plans offer options or supplements that vary from policy to policy. Options that aren't usually included in a standard health plan (particularly a direct-pay one) include dental care, maternity and baby care, routine physical examinations, eye and ear examinations, hospice care for the terminally ill, intensive care, disability and organ transplants. A basic plan also usually excludes extras for hospital in-patients such as a phone, TV or visitors' meals.

Existing Conditions

Treatment of any medical condition for which you've already received medical attention or which existed before the start of the policy are called 'pre-existing' and may not be covered. This includes childbirth if you were pregnant when you took out health insurance (however, comprehensive medical insurance usually covers complications associated with childbirth, such as a Caesarean section). Check that regular maternity charges are covered as 'any illness'. Some policies don't cover childbirth in a hospital, but cover the cost of a birth centre (see **Childbirth** on page 204).

Families

Insurance provided by an employer often offers different levels of cover for families and single people. Children over 18 may not be included in a family policy. Few employers offer free comprehensive cover (i.e. pay all medical bills) for employees and their families, although there are a few exceptions such as companies who transfer employees to Canada. If you're offered a job in Canada, check the extent of the health insurance cover provided.

Travellers

If you do a lot of overseas travelling, ensure that your health plan covers you outside Canada (most do). All bills, particularly those received for treatment outside Canada, must include precise details of all treatment and prescriptions received. Terms such as 'Dental Treatment' or 'Consultation' are insufficient. It's also helpful if bills are written in English or French, although this obviously isn't possible in all countries.

Premiums & Payment

Private health insurance can be expensive, depending on the policy or cover you select. A typical personal health option, covering two or more people in one family, costs from $75 to $250 per month, increasing as options and family members are added. Premiums for men are usually lower than for women, although the highest premiums are usually for babies under two years old.

Most policies have an annual excess (deductible), typically $100 to $500 for an individual and $500 to $1,000 for a family. This is the amount you must pay towards your total medical bills in any year before your insurance company starts paying. Consider taking a higher excess if you're young and/or in good health, e.g. $1,000, rather than paying higher premiums, and avoid buying excess cover, i.e. more than you need or something you don't need. Some policies also levy an excess on a variety of services, e.g. $10 for each routine visit to a doctor, 20 per cent of ambulance costs, and 20 per cent or $1,000 per hospital admission (in-patient). There may also be a maximum limit on the amount an insurer will pay in any one year, e.g. $100,000 (which most experts consider to be inadequate), and a lifetime maximum such as $1mn. Many insurers require a second opinion or a pre-admission review on non-emergency surgery and may penalise you (e.g. up to $1,000) if you don't follow the rules.

With some plans, premiums increase if you make frequent claims. If you have a long-term illness or a poor medical history, you may be unable to obtain health insurance at any price (although some provinces operate a provincial insurance scheme for those who have been rejected for cover by at least two insurance companies). If you or a member of your family contracts a serious, expensive or chronic disease, you may find that your health insurance is cancelled or that your premiums rocket. Some insurance companies settle bills directly with doctors or hospitals and send you a bill for your contribution, while others require you to pay medical bills and apply for reimbursement. File all claims promptly because some insurers reject claims that aren't filed within a certain period of treatment.

You may qualify for low-cost group insurance through a professional association or other organisation. However, don't assume that group rates are lower than a direct-pay plan, as some organisations 'earn' huge commissions.

Retirees can obtain a low-cost policy from the Canadian Association of Retired Persons

(CARP, 💻 www.carp.ca), which has branches (chapters) in over 20 cities.

Students

Full-time students in Canadian colleges or universities may be eligible for Medicare, depending on the province, so check with your provincial Medicare office. If you aren't eligible, you may be able to pay a college infirmary fee entitling you to receive infirmary treatment. Students' families aren't covered by a student's college infirmary fee and must be covered privately. You can also buy low cost accident insurance, which is recommended and may be compulsory. All Canadian colleges and universities provide foreign students with information about compulsory and recommended health insurance before their arrival in Canada.

DENTAL INSURANCE

Only certain groups, such as children and the elderly, are eligible for subsidised dental treatment in some provinces. For example, Nova Scotia and Newfoundland provide free dental care for children, while Alberta provides free cover for those aged over 65. Approximately 20 per cent of the population (ranging from below 5 per cent in the Maritime provinces to over 40 per cent in British Columbia) has some form of dental care provided through private insurers.

Dental insurance is often provided by employer health insurance plans and may be part of a comprehensive medical and dental plan or a separate dental plan offered in addition to medical cover. Often employers offer separate dental cover that can be linked to a choice of medical plans. Some two-thirds of workers in medium and large companies participate in an employer dental plan, around half of whom are required to contribute towards their own dental treatment costs and two-thirds towards those of their families. Dental benefits may be available under foreign health insurance policies or international health schemes (although they're usually optional).

Dental plans usually cover preventive and restorative treatment and most also cover orthodontic expenses, particularly for children. Preventive care typically includes examinations, cleaning and X-rays, while restorative treatment includes fillings, periodontal and endodontic care, prosthetics and crowns. Preventive care is typically covered at between 80 and 100 per cent; fillings, surgery endodontics and periodontics are covered at 60 to 80 per cent; and expensive inlays, crowns, prosthetics and orthodontia at 50 per cent. Under some plans, members are offered a reimbursement based on a schedule of cash allowances for restorative work, such as fillings and crowns. The percentage of dental expenses paid by a plan may be increased annually, provided that you're examined regularly by a dentist.

Some plans require members to pay a fixed contribution, e.g. $15 for preventive care, or an annual excess, e.g. $75 per year. Most plans have an annual maximum benefit, e.g. $2,000 per year, and orthodontic services usually also have a lifetime maximum of around $10,000. Treatment above a certain cost, e.g. $200, usually needs pre-authorisation.

LONG-TERM HEALTH CARE INSURANCE

Private nursing homes can cost over $3,000 per month, although government nursing homes are less expensive (but usually have long waiting lists). Homecare providers, who may include private registered nurses, cost around $50 an hour, while less skilled care such as assistance with eating or light housework costs around $25 an hour. Very few health insurance policies cover the cost of long-term healthcare, which usually includes nursing care, 'custodial care' (i.e. care in a nursing home or hospice) and home healthcare. Many Canadians therefore take out long-term healthcare (or nursing-home) insurance policies, although some employers offer long-term care policies as an employee benefit. By the year 2020, it's estimated that one in five Canadians will be aged over 65 and, with an expected shortage of federal nursing homes, long-term insurance may be a good option.

Always check exactly what's covered and under what circumstances benefits apply. The majority of long-term care plans have severe restrictions covering hospital admissions, level of care, length of cover, custodial care, cancellation provisions, and exclusions such as Alzheimer's and Aids. Many people discover that they aren't covered for nursing home care when it's too late, and policies with these restrictions should be avoided. Some policies claim to cover you for everything at any age without a medical examination or an exhaustive questionnaire about your medical history, which allows the insurance company to claim that virtually any ailment you contract was pre-existing and therefore not covered! Choose a policy where you're evaluated first and complete a medical questionnaire before agree to a policy (called 'front-end underwriting').

> ☑ **SURVIVAL TIP**
>
> **As with disability insurance, the longer the waiting period before you collect on a policy, the lower the premiums. For example, if you pay for the first 20 or 30 days (or longer) in a nursing home, your premiums are reduced.**

DISABILITY INSURANCE

Disability or 'income protection' insurance provides you with a weekly or monthly income when you're unable to work. Federal disability benefits are unlikely to be sufficient to meet your financial commitments, therefore you may need to top these up with a private disability insurance policy that guarantees you a fixed income each week or month, or a percentage of your salary when you're ill for a long period or permanently disabled. Note that the possibility of being disabled between the ages of 35 and 60 is much greater than the chance of dying.

There are two kinds of disability insurance: Short-term and long-term. Short-term disability policies pay benefits for a limited period only, e.g. up to two years, while long-term cover may continue payments until you return to work or reach retirement age (e.g. 65), or even longer. Some employers provide long-term disability insurance (where payments usually begin after six months of disability and continue until retirement age or for a specific number of years) and/or short-term disability insurance, which pays your salary for a limited number of weeks, depending on your length of service.

When shopping for disability insurance, make sure that the policy cannot be cancelled, that it has a guaranteed renewal to ensure that you can retain cover after an injury or illness without an increase in premiums, and that the benefits are index-linked. It's also wise to obtain a clause guaranteeing benefits if you return to work part-time while recovering from a disability. You should carefully consider the definition of disability used by the insurer. While contracts may contain unique definitions, 'total disability' pays out only if you're unable to work at all, while 'own (or regular) occupation' considers you disabled if you're unable to work at your usual job (far preferable). Even within this definition, beware of policies that won't pay for mental or nervous disorders, or disabilities arising from alcohol abuse or smoking. Like all forms of insurance, disability insurance must be reviewed and updated regularly to reflect your changing requirements.

All disability policies specify a qualifying period before benefit payments begin, e.g. three to six months. The longer you wait for your disability insurance to pay out, the lower your monthly premiums will be. Usually you can choose when payments start, e.g. 30, 60 or 90 days, or even one year after a disability or the onset of an illness. Your employer may, for example, pay your salary for a period, in which case you can choose to defer payments from your disability insurance for this period.

The longer the period for which you require cover and the higher the monthly income you require, the higher your monthly premiums will be. Therefore by reducing the amount of monthly income or terminating payments after you reach retirement age, you can lower your premiums. Needless to say, the younger you are, the lower your premiums. Non-smokers may also pay lower premiums.

Many professional organisations offer low-cost policies, typically around $14 to $20 per month for benefits of $3,000 per month. The maximum amount that can be insured is usually calculated as a percentage (e.g. 60 to 75 per cent) of your net monthly earnings, because you need to replace your after-tax income only (benefits from a disability policy aren't taxed). Depending on your age and profession, some insurance companies may require you to have a medical examination or to obtain a report from your family doctor.

PRIVATE PENSION PLANS

Canadians can save privately for their retirement through two kinds of authorised tax-assisted plans: the Registered Pension Plan (RPP, 💻 www.cra-arc.gc.ca/E/pub/tg/t4099/) and the Registered Retirement Savings Plan (RRSP, 💻 www.cra-arc.gc.ca/tx/ndvdls/tpcs/rrsp-reer/rrsps-eng.html). Both plans permit limited tax-free deductions from gross income. Note, however, that payments received from these plans are included in your income, unless they're transferred to another plan within certain time limits.

There are essentially two kinds of RPP: defined benefit plans and money purchase plans. With a defined benefit plan the employer or sponsor pays a fixed sum or percentage of your income for each year of service. A money purchase plan provides whatever pension income the accumulated contributions and return on investment in the plan will buy.

Most plans require contributions to be made by both the employer and the employee. An individual is allowed to contribute 18 per cent of his earned income or the RRSP maximum, whichever is lower. The maximum annual RRSP contribution in 2009 was $21,000 (increasing to $22,000 in 2010).

Under the Home Buyer's Plan (HBP), first-time homebuyers or those who have not been homeowners for five years can withdraw up to $25,000 from their RRSP to purchase a home in Canada, with no income tax payable on the amount withdrawn. However, the amount withdrawn under an HBP must be repaid over a 15-year period as of the second calendar year following the withdrawal, i.e. each year you must repay one fifteenth of the total amount you withdrew. The repayments aren't considered to be contributions to your RRSP and aren't tax deductible.

There are many useful books on how to save for your retirement, including *RRSPs and Other Retirement Strategies* by Steven G. Kelman (Globe and Mail Personal Finance Library series), *Make The Most Of What You've Got: The Canadian Guide to Managing Retirement Income* by Sandra E. Foster (John Wiley & Sons) and *The Pension Strategy for Canadians*, by Andrew Springett (Insomniac Press).

A useful resource is *Benefits Canada* digital magazine (💻 www.benefitscanada.com), which is dedicated to pension investment and employee benefits.

HOUSEHOLD INSURANCE

If you buy a home in Canada, you must take out household insurance, which covers the building and its contents (contents only for condominium owners and tenants of rented property) for 'direct loss' or damage caused by insured perils, which may be stated individually or described as 'all risks'. Theft insurance applies only when a building is ready for occupation, and vacant buildings aren't normally insured for longer than 30 days.

Homeowner's insurance cover on your home should begin as soon as you become the legal owner or tenant, even if the property is still under construction. A homeowner's policy can even cover building materials on or adjacent to your property. Insurance covers outbuildings on your land such as a garage, barn, pool house or workshop, which are automatically covered for 20 per cent of the insured value of your home: for example. if your home is insured for $300,000, any outbuildings are insured for a total of $60,000.

Contents insurance is limited to between 70 and 80 per cent of your home's insurance value: for example, if your home is insured for $300,000, your contents are insured for $210,000 to $240,000. Homeowner's policies usually limit third party liability to around $25,000. If any of these amounts is too low, you can buy additional insurance (see **Liability Insurance** below). There's usually an excess of $500 for each claim, although this may be as low as $200 with some companies. By paying an extra premium of around $40, you can have a lower excess.

If you own or rent a second home (e.g. a summer or winter holiday home), you can add it to the homeowner's policy for your principal home or buy a separate policy, but your liability cover doesn't extend to your second home.

It's important to ensure that you're comparing like with like when evaluating different policies. All policies contain maximum dollar limits, which may vary between insurance companies. The amount you should insure your home for isn't the current market value, but its replacement value, i.e. the cost of rebuilding the property should it be totally destroyed (this is less than the market value of your home because it excludes the value of the land). It's wise for a home to be insured on a guaranteed replacement cost basis, whereby if it costs more to rebuild than provided for in the policy, the insurance company pays for it. Guaranteed replacement cost covers such contingencies as increases in the cost of materials and labour, but not additional costs to conform to new building codes, e.g. if a frame dwelling has to be replaced with a brick one.

Many insurers insist that you insure your home for at least 80 per cent of the replacement cost. If you insure for less than 80 per cent, you receive a pro rata settlement of any claim, however small. For example, if you insure for 50 per cent of the replacement cost, you receive only 50 per cent of the value of a claim.

If you're buying your home with a mortgage, your lender will insist that it's covered by a homeowner's insurance policy. When the mortgage is paid off, it's wise to continue the insurance cover, as many people lose their homes each year in Canada as a result of natural disasters such as landslips, forest fires and floods.

All agents and insurance companies provide information and free advice and will usually inspect your home to assess your insurance needs (if they won't, go elsewhere). Note, however, that a comprehensive assessment should be performed by a professional appraiser, who will charge a fee.

The following types of homeowner's insurance policy are offered by most companies, although some companies don't use the standard 'HO' categories:

Basic Policy (HO-1)

The basic homeowner's policy insures your home and possessions against losses caused by the 11 'common perils': Fire or lightning, windstorm or hail, explosion, riot or civil commotion, aircraft, vehicles, smoke, vandalism or malicious mischief, theft, glass breakage and volcanic eruption. The basic policy is inadequate for most homeowners.

Broad Policy (HO-2)

The 'broad' homeowner's policy insures your home and possessions against losses caused by the 11 'common perils' listed above and a

further six perils. These include falling objects; weight of ice, snow or sleet; failure of, overflow from or freezing of a steam or hot water heating system, air-conditioning or automatic fire protective sprinkler system; accidental discharge or overflow of water or steam from a plumbing, heating, air-conditioning or automatic fire protective sprinkler system; freezing of plumbing or household appliances; and sudden and accidental damage from an 'artificially generated electrical current' created by appliances, devices, fixtures and wiring.

All-risk Policy (HO-3)

An all-risk policy protects your home against all the perils included in an HO-2 policy, plus any other perils not specifically excluded by the policy. Your possessions, however, have the same cover as with an HO-2 policy. This is the most popular form of policy and provides the most extensive protection, including everything except flood, earthquake, war, nuclear accident and certain other specified risks. You can usually insure against extra risks such as floods or earthquakes for an extra – very large – premium, although this can be done only with special insurance companies. An HO-3 policy also provides protection for loss of use, i.e. when your home becomes uninhabitable and you're required to find alternative accommodation and incur additional living expenses.

Renter's Policy (HO-4)

A renter's policy (tenant's insurance) provides the same protection as an HO-2 policy for your possessions and, most importantly, damage caused by you to the property you're renting. It doesn't cover the building itself, which must be insured by the landlord.

Comprehensive Policy (HO-5)

A comprehensive policy covers everything, including your possessions, on an all-risk basis, with the exception of any specific exclusions listed in the policy. The best policies include insurance against damage to glass (windows, patio doors, etc.), although you may have to pay extra for accidental damage, e.g. when your son blasts a baseball through a window, and you should expect your premium to rise the following year. It's the best kind of policy and the most expensive.

Condominium & Co-op Policy (HO-6)

This policy is for owners of a condominium or co-op dwelling. It covers possessions and improvements but excludes the building itself, which is separately insured by the condominium or co-op association.

Premiums & Claims

The cost of homeowner's insurance varies widely depending on the value of your home and its location, i.e. the province and neighbourhood.

Premiums depend on a range of considerations, such as whether your home is constructed of bricks/concrete or wood (wood-frame homes cost more to insure) and how far it is from a fire hydrant.

> **☑ SURVIVAL TIP**
>
> **Owners of houses vulnerable to subsidence (e.g. those built on clay) and those living in areas liable to flooding are likely to have to pay much higher homeowner's insurance premiums (if you live in a flood plain, you should have a sump pump and call the fire department if there's a flood).**

If you have extra security, such as high security door and window locks, a monitored intruder alarm system, fire extinguishers, sprinklers or smoke alarms, you usually receive a discount. You may also receive a discount if you're aged over 55, work for a particular organisation, qualify for an 'affinity' discount through an organisation such as a credit union or alumni association, or if your family are all non-smokers. You can also reduce your premium by accepting a higher deductible (see above).

Another way to save money is to carry some of the financial risk yourself with a 'named perils' policy that covers only specified risks (such as fire). If you find a comprehensive policy too expensive and a 'named perils' policy too risky, a compromise is a so-called 'broad'

policy (not to be confused with an HO-2, also known as a Broad Policy – see above) that provides comprehensive cover on buildings and 'named perils' cover on contents.

The premium for the same level of cover from different companies can vary by as much as 100 per cent, so shop around and obtain at least three estimates, but make sure that all quotes are for the same level of cover. Always ask your insurer what isn't covered and what it costs to include it. Many insurance companies allow you to pay your insurance premium in monthly instalments.

Homeowner's insurance must usually be renewed annually; bear in mind that insurance companies are continually updating their policies, therefore you must ensure that a policy still provides the cover you require when you receive the renewal notice. If you're about to move to a new home, ask your insurer if your current policy covers your contents at both locations and while they're in transit. It's your responsibility to ensure that your level of cover is adequate, particularly if you carry out expensive home improvements that substantially increase the value of your home.

If you've suffered a loss for which you're insured, inform your insurance agent or broker about it as soon as possible. If you have a burglary or theft, the police must also be informed. You're required to provide information about the circumstances of the claim as well as reasonable evidence to justify the amount claimed. Your insurer will want to know exactly what was stolen or damaged, when you acquired it and what you paid for it. A claims adjuster may be appointed to investigate a claim. You should take reasonable steps to protect against further damage. For example, if a pipe has burst, you should shut off the water supply. Don't dispose of damaged goods without first obtaining your insurer's approval. In some cases your insurer may arrange assistance for temporary repairs, such as covering a damaged roof or boarding over a broken window. If you have replacement cost cover, some insurers provide an immediate cash advance, which is adjusted when you provide proof of replacement purchase.

Bear in mind that, if you make a claim, you may have to wait months for it to be settled. Generally the larger the claim, the longer you must wait for your money, although in an emergency a company may make an interim payment. If you're dissatisfied with the amount offered, don't accept it and try to negotiate a higher figure or take legal advice.

In the event of an insurer going bust, the Property and Casualty Insurance Compensation Corporation (PACICC, ☎ 1-888-564 9199 or 416-364 8677, 💻 www.pacicc.com) will consider claims under most policies issued by homeowner's insurance companies. The maximum recovery from PACICC is $250,000 for losses arising from a single occurrence. PACICC will also refund 70 per cent of the unused premium (maximum $1,000) from the date of an insurer's collapse until the policy's expiry date.

CONTENTS INSURANCE

Contents insurance is usually offered as part of a homeowner's insurance policy (see above), which includes insurance for your furniture, clothing, electrical and electronic equipment, and household appliances. However, owners of condominiums and tenants of rented property aren't required to insure the building and may take out insurance for contents only.

Possessions aren't usually insured for their replacement value (new for old) in Canada, but for their 'actual cash value', i.e. their cost minus depreciation.

You can, however, buy replacement-cost insurance, although policies often include limits and are more expensive. When contents insurance is included in your homeowner's insurance policy, you usually have no choice between replacement value and actual cash value insurance. Note also that a basic contents policy may not include such items as credit cards (and their fraudulent use), cash, musical instruments, jewellery, valuables, sports equipment and bicycles, for which you may need to take out extra cover. A basic policy doesn't usually include accidental damage caused by you or members of your family to your own property or your home freezer contents (in the event of a breakdown or power failure).

When insuring your possessions, don't buy more insurance than you need; unless you have valuable possessions, insurance may cost more than replacing them. You may be better off insuring just a few valuable items, rather than everything. To calculate the amount of insurance you require, make an inventory of your possessions containing descriptions, purchase prices and dates, and their location in your home. Keep the list and all receipts in a safe place (such as a safety deposit box) and add new purchases to the list and make adjustments to your insurance cover as and when necessary. There are maximum limits on cover for individual items in a standard homeowner's policy (listed in contracts).

High-value possessions (called 'scheduled property') such as works of art, furs and jewellery, aren't fully covered by a standard policy and should be insured separately for their full value or through a basic policy clause (rider). For these items you must purchase extra insurance and have them appraised and listed as 'scheduled' items on your policy. You're charged a premium per $100 of coverage for the replacement cost. It's advisable to take photographs of such items, which can help with identification if they're stolen. The cost of insuring high-value items varies with the area and the local crime rate. A policy may also insure your possessions if they're stolen from somewhere other than your home, e.g. a car or hotel room.

LIABILITY INSURANCE

Liability insurance is the homeowner's version of third party insurance for car owners. It covers you for damage caused either at your home or elsewhere to other people such as visitors or employees, or to your neighbours (e.g. by your son kicking a football through a neighbour's window and smashing his collection of rare porcelain). Cover doesn't apply to injuries sustained by you or by members of your immediate household nor, if you operate a business at home, to injuries sustained by employees or people visiting you for work purposes. If you operate a business from home you must inform your insurance company, otherwise a claim will be refused.

Liability insurance is usually included in a homeowner's policy (see below), but can be purchased separately if you don't require homeowner's insurance or consider the liability insurance provided by your homeowner's policy inadequate. Homeowner's policies usually limit liability claims to around $25,000, although most companies offer optional extra cover. Considering the low cost of liability insurance and the high cost of law suits, most experts recommend $250,000 to be the minimum cover necessary, and most Canadians purchase cover of $500,000 or $1mn.

Many people take out a personal liability 'umbrella' policy to extend the cover of their homeowner's and car insurance policies, and usually include protection against claims arising from business activities and other 'injuries', such as slander. An umbrella policy provides cover in addition to the amount covered by a basic policy and isn't a replacement for these policies.

If you own or rent a second home (e.g. a summer or winter holiday home), you can add it to the homeowner's policy for your principal home or buy a separate policy, but your liability cover doesn't extend to your second home.

HOLIDAY & TRAVEL INSURANCE

Holiday and travel insurance is recommended for anyone who doesn't wish to risk having his holiday or travel spoiled by financial problems. The following information applies to Canadian residents travelling within Canada and abroad and to those visiting Canada on holiday.

Caution

Nobody should go abroad (and certainly not over the border into the US) without travel and health insurance!

Travel insurance is available from many sources, including travel agents, insurance brokers, banks, automobile clubs and transport companies (airline, rail and bus). Package holiday companies and tour operators also offer travel insurance policies. You can also buy 24-hour accident insurance and flight insurance at major airports, although it's expensive and doesn't offer the best cover. Before taking out travel insurance, carefully consider the range and level of cover you require and compare policies.

Short-term holiday and travel insurance policies may include insurance against holiday cancellation or interruption; missing your flight; departure delay at the start and end of a holiday (a common occurrence); delayed, lost or damaged baggage; lost or stolen personal effects and money; medical expenses and accidents (including evacuation home); flight cancellation; personal liability and legal expenses; and default or bankruptcy, e.g. the tour operator or airline goes bust.

The cost of travel insurance varies considerably depending on your destination. Many companies have different rates for different areas, e.g. North America, Europe and worldwide. Premiums may also be increased for those aged over 65 or 70. Generally the longer the period covered, the cheaper the daily cost, although the maximum period is usually limited, e.g. six months or a year. With some policies an excess of around $50 or $100 must be paid for each claim. For those who travel abroad frequently, whether on business or pleasure, an annual travel policy provides much better value but may have restrictions on the length of trips, e.g. 90 days.

Make sure that your travel insurance includes personal liability (e.g. $1mn or $2mn) and repatriation expenses. If your travel insurance expires while you're visiting Canada, you can buy further insurance from an insurance agent, although this won't include repatriation expenses. Flight insurance and comprehensive travel insurance is available from insurance desks at most airports, including travel accident, personal accident, worldwide medical expenses and in-transit baggage.

If you need to make a claim, you should provide as much documentary evidence as possible. Although travel insurance companies eagerly take your money, they aren't always so keen to settle claims, and you may need to persevere before they pay up. Always be persistent and make a claim irrespective of any small print, as this may be unreasonable and therefore invalid in law.

100
SIR ROBERT L. BORDEN PREMIER MINISTRE / PRIME MINISTER 1911-1920
ÉMISSION DE 2004 / ISSUE OF 2004

14. FINANCE

Canada is one of the richest countries in the world, with a GDP in 2007 of $1.27 trillion and GDP per capita of around $38,600. Almost 70 per cent of GDP is generated by services, less than 30 per cent by industry and a mere 2 per cent by agriculture. In terms of gross national product (GNP), Canada ranks around eighth in the world and has a similar standard of living to the US and the wealthiest European countries. Basic bank rate and consumer loan rates have fallen steadily in the last decade and the Bank of Canada cut its benchmark lending rate to just 0.5 per cent in March 2009.

In the late 20th century, Canada was one of the few countries in the world with a balanced budget, and it entered the new millennium with high levels of job creation and economic growth. However, the rest of the developed world, Canada experienced a slowdown in 2008-09, but less so than its neighbour, the US. The economy contracted at an annualized rate of 3.4 per cent in the fourth quarter of 2008, and in the first-quarter of 2009 by a projected 4.8 per cent. Canada's annual rate of inflation was just 1.2 per cent in March 2009.

Despite the widespread use of credit and charge cards (the average Canadian has three), which account for around half of all payments, almost the same number are made in cash, with just 5 per cent by cheque. In some circles, your financial status may be calculated by the number of credit cards you carry, although newcomers may find it difficult to obtain even one. If you have an international credit card issued by a foreign bank, it's wise to retain it until you've replaced it in Canada. Surprisingly, over 20 per cent of Canada's economy is estimated to be 'underground', with transactions made in cash in order to evade the attention of the tax authorities.

When you arrive to take up residence or employment in Canada, make sure you have sufficient funds to last you until your first payday. Don't, however, carry a lot of cash. During the first few weeks, you'll find a major credit card (e.g. MasterCard or Visa) invaluable, without which you'll need to prepay many bills, including hotel and car rental bills.

Personal finance is one of Canada's favourite subjects and there are numerous books on the subject, including *Personal Finance for Canadians* by Elliot J. Currie et al (Pearson Education), *Personal Finance For Canadians For Dummies* by Eric MBA Tyson & Tony Martin (For Dummies) and *Your Money or Your Life* by Vicki Robin (Penguin), plus personal finance magazines such as the *Financial Post* (www.financialpost.com) and *Money Sense* (www.moneysense.ca). See also **Social Insurance** and **Private Pension Plans** in **Chapter 13**.

> For details of goods and services and provincial sales taxes, see **Sales Tax** on page 292.

CANADIAN CURRENCY

The unit of currency is the Canadian dollar, which is divided into 100 cents (¢). Canadian coins are minted in values of 1¢ (penny), 5¢ (nickel), 10¢ (dime), 25¢ (quarter) and 50¢ (half-dollar, which is rarely seen nowadays), one dollar and two dollars. The penny is copper, the 5, 10, 25 and 50 cent coins are silver-coloured (an amalgam of silver and copper), the $1 coin is 11-sided and gold-coloured, and the $2 coin has a nickel outer rim and an aluminium-bronze centre. There are also silver dollars and a $1 pure gold coin, the Maple Leaf, the price (and value) of which fluctuate with the price of gold and silver.

All coins have an image of Queen Elizabeth II on one side. The $1 coin has a bird (the loon) on the reverse and is called a 'loonie', while the two-dollar coin (which has a polar bear on the reverse) is called a 'twoonie' (known as the Queen with the bear behind!). The quarter is the most useful coin and you should carry some with you for parking meters, bus and underground fares, road tolls, payphones, baggage lockers, vending machines, etc.

Banknotes (bills) are printed in denominations of $5 (blue), $10 (purple), $20 (green), $50 (red), $100 (brown) and $1,000 (purple). Canada no longer has a $1 bill; the $2 bill (red), although still legal tender, is no longer printed and quickly disappeared. All Canadian notes are the same size but depict different Canadian luminaries: $5 (Sir Wilfred Laurier, Canada's second prime minister), $10 (Sir John A. MacDonald, Canada's father of confederation and first prime minister), $20 (Queen Elizabeth II), $50 (William Lyon MacKenzie, Canada's

third prime minister), $100 (Sir Robert Borden, Canada's eighth prime minister).

If you're unfamiliar with Canadian bills, you should stick to low denominations ($5 to $20) and check them carefully to avoid errors, when receiving bills in change and when spending them. Bills above $20 are often regarded with suspicion and may not be accepted by everyone.

The US$ is Canada's 'intervention currency' (a currency that's bought and sold by central banks when it's thought to be beneficial), and the value of the Canadian dollar is closely linked to that of the US dollar. In most places in Canada you can use US dollars, although Canadian dollars aren't accepted in the US (Americans refer to C$ as 'Monopoly money', even though it's sometimes worth more than the US$). The Canadian/US dollar conversion rate in often displayed in shops which have a sign by the cash register saying, for example, 'US currency 20 per cent', meaning that if you pay in US$, you'll be given an exchange rate of US$1 = C$1.20. Check the universal currency converter (💻 www.xe.com) for the latest bank rate (not the tourist rate).

It's wise to obtain some Canadian notes before arriving in Canada and to familiarise yourself and your family with them. It's handy to have some Canadian dollars in cash, e.g. $50 to $100 in small notes. It isn't necessary – and is a waste of money – to buy travellers' cheques these days, provided you have a debit (or credit) card with which you can obtain cash from ATMs.

IMPORTING & EXPORTING MONEY

Canada has no restrictions on the movement of funds into or out of the country, and banks, corporations and individuals can deal in foreign funds or arrange payments in any currency they choose (although if you're carrying over $10,000 in cash, securities or negotiable instruments when entering the country, it must be declared). Gold may be freely purchased by Canadian residents, who may also hold and sell it in any form. However, gold originating in the US requires a permit when re-exported to any country other than the States. Importing gold articles such as watches or jewellery is unrestricted and doesn't require a licence, but gold coins or ingots must be declared on arrival. If you're planning to transfer a large amount of money to Canada (e.g. to buy a home or business), you can fix the exchange rate in advance on payment of a deposit in order to take advantage of (what you hope is) a favourable exchange rate.

With the exception of US dollars, most shops and businesses in Canada don't accept foreign currency (including foreign currency travellers' cheques), and it's best to avoid bringing them to Canada. It can even be difficult to find a bank or other financial institution that will exchange foreign currency or foreign currency travellers' cheques, particularly in small towns. You usually receive an unfavourable exchange rate or pay a High Commission when changing money at a hotel or a *bureau de change*. If you change foreign money or foreign currency travellers' cheques, try to do so in large cities and at a bank, where increased competition usually ensures a better exchange rate. You may be asked for identification (ID) when changing foreign notes at a bank.

☑ SURVIVAL TIP

It's no longer necessary to buy travellers' cheques when travelling to Canada as all you need to obtain cash from an ATM 24/7 is an international (e.g. MasterCard or Visa) credit or debit card. However, bear in mind that when travelling anywhere, you should never rely on only one source of funds.

If you're sending money abroad, it's best to send it in local currency so that the recipient doesn't have to pay conversion charges. You can send money direct from your bank to another bank via an inter-bank transfer. Most banks have a minimum service charge for international transfers (e.g. $50), which makes it expensive for small sums. Receiving banks may also take a cut, e.g. 1 or 2 per cent of the amount transferred.

CREDIT RATING

It's difficult for new arrivals in Canada to establish a credit rating (or 'line of credit') or obtain credit without excellent references from an employer (who may need to secure any borrowing) or from a foreign bank. Newcomers must establish a new credit rating in Canada because a foreign credit rating (however good) isn't taken into account. Usually you must have been employed by the same company for at least a year and earn a minimum salary, although it can still take a number of years to establish a good credit rating. Many foreigners find that they must 'build up' their credit rating by obtaining credit from local businesses and shops. It may be even more difficult for the self-employed to obtain credit because most credit applications are geared towards employees.

You should pay all your bills promptly and never bounce cheques because it will affect your credit rating; it's also expensive and can cost you over $40 (CIBC charge a $42.50 fee). Once you've established a good credit rating, you can usually obtain far more credit than is good for you (paradoxically, the more you buy on credit, the more credit-worthy you become), and banks, finance companies, credit card companies and other financial institutions constantly tempt you with credit offers.

In Canada, everyone's credit history is maintained by private companies called credit-reporting agencies or credit bureaux, e.g. Equifax (💻 www.equifax.com/EFX_Canada), Experian (💻 www.experian.ca) and TransUnion (💻 www.transunion.ca). They collect information reported to them by banks, mortgage companies, shops and other businesses. Your credit record contains information such as judgments or liens against you or your property, bankruptcies or foreclosures, as well as the failure to pay your debts, e.g. payments on revolving charge accounts. Credit bureaux can legally report negative credit information for seven years and bankruptcy information for 14 years. The only information that can be changed in your credit report is incorrect items and items that are outside the 7 or 14-year reporting periods.

If a company denies your request for credit because of your credit report, it must (under the Credit Reporting Agencies Act) tell you and identify the bureau that provided the report. All credit bureaux are required by law to share with you any information they have on file about you. This must be provided free if you've been denied credit within the past 30 days, otherwise you can be charged a fee, e.g. between $5 and $20.

In some provinces, credit-reporting agencies are required by law to make an investigation into complaints within 30 days, erase non-verifiable items, provide free reports once a year, and provide consumers with the credit-rating scores it gives to lenders. Employers may obtain a credit report on prospective employees, particularly when they'll be in a position of trust or will be handling cash.

BANKS

Canada's banking system is dominated by the 'big five' chartered banks: Canadian Imperial Bank of Commerce, BMO Bank of Montreal, Scotiabank, Royal Bank of Canada and TD Canada Trust, which between them control 80 per cent of all banking assets. The big five have a network of several thousand branches and offer telephone and internet banking.

There are also many smaller domestic banks, including credit unions (which are increasingly popular because of their range of services, lower charges and friendly service) and *caisses populaires* in Quebec, plus many foreign banks operating in Canada. The chartered banks dominate the market for consumer credit (excluding mortgages) and make around 70 per cent of all consumer loans. The rest are made by credit unions, trust and mortgage loan companies, and life insurance companies.

> Canada's banking system is regulated by the Bank of Canada (www.bankofcanada.ca), the federal government institution that's directly responsible for the country's monetary policy.

Canadian banks are prohibited from direct participation in the insurance industry and cannot offer insurance products through their branches (except in British Columbia), although they're permitted to own, develop and manage land through property corporations, and may own property (real estate) companies.

Canadians usually do their banking with one of the chartered or foreign banks, a credit union or a trust company. To bank with a credit union you must become a member and are eligible for loans at lower interest rates than those charged by banks and you may also receive a share of the profits. Trust companies operate in much the same way as banks, except that their service is more personal. If in doubt about which to choose, ask your Canadian colleagues and acquaintances for advice – most are less than happy with their bank, therefore if someone does recommend a particular institution it's worth heeding his advice.

A wide range of accounts and services is available and it's worth shopping around. Some pay you interest when you're in credit, while others simply don't charge fees (although you must maintain a minimum balance, e.g. $1,000), and some either charge for each service (e.g. cashing a cheque or clearing a payment into your account) or levy a standard monthly 'maintenance' fee for the privilege of banking with them (see **Bank Accounts** below).

Like the rest of the world, Canadian banks have embraced electronic banking and you can pay bills, transfer money between accounts, arrange a loan or mortgage, apply for a credit card, and print account statements (thus saving the fee charged by banks) 24/7 from the comfort of your home or office. Banks also offer a range of other services including:

- **Money Orders and Drafts:** instructions to your bank to pay a specified amount to a named person or company. You must pay for a money order or draft at the time of purchase;
- **Certified Cheques:** designed for recipients who need to cash a cheque immediately or who want a guarantee that the funds are available;
- **Standing Orders and Direct Debits:** called 'pre-authorised payments', e.g. for utility bill payments;
- **Overdraft Protection:** whereby a bank allows you to overdraw your account up to an agreed amount. There's a service fee of around $5 per month for this 'service', plus interest on the amount overdrawn. The overdraft limit is determined when you sign up and may be linked to a credit card or savings account, where the amount overdrawn is debited to the card or account.

Banks also offer a range of financial products and services, including mortgages, term deposits, Canada Savings Bonds, treasury bills, retirement savings and income plans, Guaranteed Investment Certificates (GICs) and mutual funds.

When choosing a bank, it's wise to pick one that's covered by the Canadian Deposit Insurance Corporation (CDIC, 50 O'Connor Street, 17th Floor, PO Box 2340, Station D, Ottawa, ON K1P 5W5, ☎ 1-800-461 2342, 💻 www.cdic.ca). In the event of a bank failure, the CDIC guarantees 'eligible deposits' up to a maximum of $100,000 per person (principal and interest). Eligible deposits include savings and cheque (chequing) accounts, term deposits such as GICs, bonds (debentures) issued by loan companies, money orders, drafts, and travellers' cheques issued by member institutions.

The CDIC doesn't cover foreign currency deposits, term deposits that mature over five years after the date of deposit, bonds issued by banks, bonds issued by governments and corporations, treasury bills, mutual funds, stocks and investments in mortgages. Therefore, it's wise to ensure that each bank you bank with holds no more than $100,000 and that deposits are covered by the CDIC guarantee. If you wish to check a bank's financial standing before opening an account, you can contact the Bank of Canada (Public Information, 234 Wellington, Ottawa, ON K1A 0G9, ☎ 1-800-303 1282, 💻 www.bankofcanada.ca).

Drive-in (or 'drive-up') banks, where people who live in their cars can obtain cash without forsaking the comfort and security of their vehicles, were invented in the US and Canadians have embraced the concept with gusto. Some banks have automatic tellers (ATMs) at car-window height, while others have a complicated system of vacuum pipes, microphones and loudspeakers connecting you to an invisible teller. If you're unfamiliar with this method of doing business, take time to read the instructions before attempting it (or leave your car and walk!).

Banking Hours

Usual banking hours are from 9am to 5pm, Mondays to Fridays (some open until 6pm on Fridays), and from 10am to 3pm on Saturdays. All banks are closed on federal and provincial holidays. Trust companies generally have much longer business hours than chartered banks, e.g. from 8.30am until 8pm. There are full-service banks at major airports (usually with standard banking hours) and ATMs are provided in most terminals. Most Canadian banks have 24-hour ATMs (see below) at all branches for cash withdrawals and deposits or separate ATM centres. Some banks have also introduced 24-hour telephone banking in recent years and most banks provide internet banking.

Bank Accounts

There are three types of bank account in Canada: Current or cheque (chequing) accounts, savings (deposit) accounts and a combination of the two known as 'cheque-savings' accounts. Most Canadians have at least one bank account and many have a number of accounts.

Before opening an account, you should shop around among local banks and compare accounts, interest rates, services and fees.

You should take particular note of a bank's charges (see below), which have increased considerably in recent years. To avoid charges, you should never overdraw your account or accept cheques from unreliable sources, keep a minimum balance in a cheque account, use your own bank's ATMs rather than other banks', obtain overdraft protection (see below) and read your bank's 'fee-disclosure' literature.

Many Canadians are paid by cheque, either bi-weekly or monthly, which they then cash or deposit in a bank account. You can also have your salary paid directly into your bank account by direct deposit and most people choose this option (just give your account details to your employer). If you want to cash a cheque, you must take it to the branch where it was drawn or a branch of the same bank.

Cheque Accounts

The best kind of account to open initially is a cheque account, which is the usual account for day-to-day financial transactions in Canada. To open an account, simply go to the bank of your choice. You usually need a permanent address and you're asked to provide a range of personal information, including your date of birth, details of your employer, a contact number for a relative in case they cannot reach you, and at least two forms of identification (ID) which have your signature and photograph on them, such as a driving licence and a passport.

If you choose an account that pays interest, you must produce your social insurance number (SIN). You may also be asked for a reference or 'co-signer', although many banks waive this requirement in the never-ending quest for new customers. If you want to deposit a large amount of cash to open the account, you may need to sign a declaration attesting to the source of the funds.

The standard cheque account is called a 'flat fee account', of which there are various kinds. For example, TD Canada Trust offers the following accounts: Value, with a service fee of $3.95 per month including ten transactions (free if you maintain a minimum balance of $1,000); Value Plus, with a monthly service fee of $8.95 including 25 transactions (free with a balance of $2,000); Infinity, for $12.95 including unlimited transactions (free with a balance of $3,000); Select for $24.95 including unlimited transactions (free with a balance of $5,000); and Plan 60 for the over-60s. All these accounts include an internet service, phone service, branch service, monthly statements, bill paying, standing orders/direct debits (pre-authorised payments), transfers between accounts and cheque books.

All banks also offer special accounts for students at universities and colleges. These offer a guaranteed overdraft for about four years, e.g. $5,500 per year or a total of $22,000, and provide a full range of banking services, including cheques, credit and debit cards, and telephone and ATM banking. While at college (and for the first year after graduating) only the interest on the loan is payable, after which there's a 20-year repayment plan. Most banks and other financial institutions are keen to add students to their customer base (not surprisingly, as many students remain in debt for decades) and generous offers are made to new students to encourage them to open accounts.

Cheques are provided free by Canadian banks depending on your account; otherwise, they typically cost around $8 for a box of five pads of 20-25 cheques. It may be cheaper to buy your cheques from a cheque printing company (see the *Yellow Pages*). New customers can order 200 cheques for around $10 in a wide variety of designs and typefaces. Most banks offer customers the option of having their cancelled cheques returned for a fee of around $2 per month. All cheques must be printed with your name; it's also wise to have your address printed on them to avoid suspicion.

Canadian banks don't issue cheque guarantee cards, and cheques are therefore subject to far more scrutiny than in some other countries, and may be accepted only when drawn on a local or in-province bank or by a business where you're known personally. (The lack of cheque guarantee cards also means that cheque theft is common.) Most retailers have strict rules regarding the acceptance of cheques and some businesses won't accept cheques at all, e.g. petrol stations and restaurants often have signs proclaiming firmly 'NO CHEQUES'.

When paying by cheque in some shops and supermarkets, you must go to a special desk and have your cheque approved before going to the checkout. You must present identification (usually a driving licence and another form of identification such as a credit card, social insurance card, or employer or college identity card). Some shops insist that customers are issued with a store identity card before they're permitted to use personal cheques. On the other hand, in shops where you're known, you may be allowed to write a cheque for more than the amount of your bill and receive the difference in cash.

> When writing cheques, Canadians write cents as a percentage, e.g.: $107.42 is written as one hundred and seven and 42/100
>
> The date is usually written month/day/year (as in the US) and not day/month/year; for example, 12th October 2009 is written 10/12/09 (October 12th 2009) and not 12/10/09.

When you deposit a cheque in a bank, most banks require you to endorse it with your signature or an endorsement stamp. They prefer you to write on the reverse sideways at the left (perforated) end of the cheque and not lengthwise (so that there's room for the bank's stamp). If you want to endorse a cheque payable to you so that it can be paid into another account, you must write on the back 'Pay to the order of ________ (name)' and sign it (using the same form of your name entered under payee). This is called a 'third party cheque' and some banks won't accept them.

Cheque bouncing, i.e. writing a cheque for more than the balance of your account, is taken seriously in Canada, where you can be prosecuted. Banks charge various fees for bouncing cheques (usually $15 to over $40), although, more importantly, it can damage your credit rating (see above). If the payee is a company, they may also charge you a fee of $25 or $30 plus the amount of the cheque. All banks offer customers overdraft protection on certain accounts, thus protecting customers from 'inadvertently' bouncing cheques (see above).

Savings Accounts

All banks, credit unions and trust companies and various other financial institutions offer a wide range of savings (or deposit) accounts, most of which are intended for short- or medium-term saving, rather than long-term growth. Trusts generally offer a higher rate of interest than commercial banks, and brokerage houses may offer even higher rates of interest (but they don't guarantee that your money is safe). It doesn't pay to keep long-term savings in a savings account when interest rates are low (Canadian savings bonds, treasury securities and money market mutual funds pay higher interest).

Savings accounts pay interest on your balance and allow a few free transactions (e.g. two debit transactions or automatic transactions per month) and charge you for the rest. Expect to be charged 40¢ to 60¢ per transaction, and around $1 for monthly statements. Most of these accounts pay higher rates of interest for larger balances. You can also open these accounts for children under 18 ('no withdrawals allowed' is an option) and senior citizens (over 60, at preferential rates) and in US$.

When opening an account, the most important considerations are how much money you wish to save (which may be a lump sum or a monthly amount) and how quickly you need access to it in an emergency. It's wise to have your cheque and savings accounts at the same bank, so that, for example, the bank can automatically transfer surplus money from your cheque to your savings account (or money from your savings account to cover an overdraft on your cheque account), or will provide a free cheque account if you maintain a savings account with a minimum balance, e.g. $500 to $1,500. Most banks provide a range of combined cheque and savings accounts, where interest is paid on deposits, usually on a sliding scale depending on the balance.

There are two main kinds of savings account: statement savings accounts and passbook savings accounts. With a statement

savings account, you have access to funds via ATMs and receive regular monthly or quarterly statements. With a passbook savings account, all transactions are recorded in a passbook, which must be presented to the teller each time you deposit or withdraw funds.

Tax must be paid on the interest earned on a savings account, although there are tax-free savings accounts for long-term savings, such as a Registered Retirement Savings Plan (RRSP – see **Private Pension Plans** on page 222).

BANK CARDS

A bank (i.e. cash, convenience or debit) card allows you to withdraw money from your account 24/7 – sometimes without even getting out of your car. The freedom from queuing, banking hours and bank tellers (who, let it be said, are usually agreeable people) provided by bankcards is convenient, and you should think twice before opening an account not offering (lots of) local ATMs. Canadians have wholeheartedly embraced this method of banking and the country ranks second in the world for the availability of ATM machines, with around six machines per 10,000 people.

ATMs are situated in the lobbies of most banks and can also be found in shopping malls, supermarkets, department stores, airports and railway stations. When a bank is closed, you must usually insert your card in a slot at the door to gain entry to the lobby. Your bank provides you with a personal identification number (PIN) to access ATMs.

You can usually withdraw a maximum of $600 daily (provided you have the money in your account) and make deposits, transfer funds between accounts, check balances and make payments. There's no charge for using a bank card when you use an ATM at a branch of your own bank, but there's normally a charge (e.g. $1 or $2) when using an ATM at an affiliated bank. Purchases using a bankcard are free, i.e. the transaction is free, the goods aren't!

ATMs are linked by computers into networks, allowing customers of different banks to draw cash from machines in major cities across the world. All banks have their own network of ATMs and most are linked with others in Canada and abroad (Cirrus or Plus). Cirrus (owned by MasterCard) is the largest North American network, with some 800,000 ATMs, while Plus (affiliated with Visa) is the second-largest. If you do a lot of travelling, you may wish to have cheque or savings accounts with different banks with different ATM networks, thus allowing you to use a wider range of ATMs in Canada and abroad.

When using ATMs to withdraw cash abroad, you receive the wholesale bank rate, which is a better rate than you can get over the counter anywhere. If possible, you should use a (debit) bankcard that allows you to tap into a cheque or savings account, rather than a credit card, which incurs interest on cash advances and a hefty fee. However, don't rely solely on ATMs to obtain cash because they can be fickle things and may not accept your card or may even 'swallow' it. Sometimes your card may be rejected by a machine at one bank and be accepted by a machine at another bank.

It's sensible not to keep a lot of money in an account for which you have a bankcard and never to have (or carry) a bankcard for a savings account with a large balance. Don't use ATMs in 'high risk' areas at night because muggings occasionally occur. If you lose your bankcard, you must notify the issuing bank immediately so that they can cancel it.

CREDIT & CHARGE CARDS

Over 600 institutions in Canada issue credit and charge cards, including American Express (Amex), Diners Club, Discover, MasterCard and Visa. There are over 50mn in circulation in Canada with a combined debt of well over

$20bn. Before issuing a credit card, companies require an assurance that you won't disappear owing them a fortune, and they'll check your bank, employer and credit bureaux to ensure that you're credit worthy (see **Credit Rating** above).

It's difficult for newcomers to obtain credit cards, even when they have excellent references or have previously held credit cards in another country. New arrivals should present a letter of introduction from their bank manager in their home country regarding their banking status. A credit card company may offer you only a pre-paid card, whereby you deposit money with the credit card company and use the card to spend it! It may also be possible to obtain a card from an offshore bank that can be paid in Canadian dollars. If your application is approved, you usually receive your card within two to four weeks. You can apply for a MasterCard or Visa card from your bank, but American Express and Diners Club applications must be made direct to the card companies.

You can obtain as many credit cards as you wish, although you should bear in mind the annual fees, e.g. $50 to $100 for charge cards. The annual fees for MasterCard and Visa cards vary considerably, e.g. from zero to around $75, the average being around $30. Cards with annual fees often charge lower interest rates than those without. The only two things that matter when obtaining credit cards are the card's annual fee and its interest rate, so shop around for the best deal you can find. If you pay off the balance each month, you should choose a card with no annual fee and other benefits.

Interest on the balance outstanding after the monthly payment date is levied at a high annual rate set by the issuing bank, which is usually three or four times the current savings rate (now much higher, as real interest rates have fallen dramatically in the last few years). However, as a response to the demand for lower interest rates, many banks have lowered their rates, although the average is still up to 20 percentage points above what banks pay to borrow money. Most cards have a grace period of 20 to 30 days for repayment, and charge fees (or increase interest rates) for late payments and for exceeding credit limits.

▲ Caution

Many banks charge interest on credit cards from the purchase date, not from the first billing date. Therefore, even if you pay off the total owed each month, you'll still incur interest charges.

When using a credit card in Canada, you may be subject to a more rigorous check than in other countries. For example, you may be asked for further identification (e.g. a driving licence). On the other hand, many businesses are extremely lax about checking signatures, which makes it easy for crooks to use stolen cards. Keep all receipts and check them against your credit card statements, because dishonest sales clerks may add a digit or two to their copy of the sales receipt.

You can use MasterCard and Visa cards to obtain cash from ATMs and banks displaying the MasterCard or Visa symbol, and can also obtain cash advances at ATMs and participating banks worldwide. However, take care when relying on ATMs, as they can gobble up your card leaving you plastic-less (and possibly short of funds), and banks charge dearly for cash withdrawals.

American Express and Diners Club cards allow you to cash personal cheques, buy travellers' cheques for limited sums, and provide free travel, car rental collision damage waiver (CDW) insurance and baggage insurance. Many Visa cards and MasterCards also provide free travel accident insurance and some cards provide a free 90-day insurance against accidental damage to purchases, extended warranties and price protection schemes. In addition to standard bank cards, most banks issue 'gold' and 'platinum' cards (they've even turned to jewel names such as 'emerald') offering additional services and extra 'status', although there's usually a fee of $75 to $150 per year and the cards are seldom worth the extra cost.

Some card companies participate in bonus schemes such as a 'frequent flyer' scheme, where cardholders earn air miles each time they use their cards, or a 'bonus' system such as Visa's 'rewards' scheme, where customers receive points each time they use their cards that are exchangeable for credits on travel, goods and discounts at department stores. Often a number of air miles or points are awarded just for signing up with a card company. The General Motors card offers holders a 5 per cent rebate on purchases to spend on GM vehicles, although you may get a better deal without a card (and GM could be bust by the time you read this!).

If you lose a credit card or it's stolen, report it immediately to the police and the issuing office (e.g. a bank or store) or phone the 24-hour, toll-free number provided by the card company, e.g. American Express (☎ 1-905-474 9380), MasterCard (☎ 1-800-555 1507) and Visa (☎ 1-800-847 2911 or 1-800-983 8472).

Note the name of the person to whom you reported the loss and the date and time of the call, and confirm the loss as soon as possible in writing. If you report the loss before the card is used, the card company cannot hold you responsible for any subsequent charges. If a thief uses your card before you report it, your liability is usually limited to $50. You can register all your credit cards with a credit card security company, whereby if your cards are stolen, one phone call to the club ensures that all your cards are cancelled and that new cards are issued. Needless to say, you should keep a list of the numbers (and security telephone numbers) for all your credit cards.

MORTGAGES

Mortgages (home loans) in Canada are available from a number of sources, including commercial banks, mortgage banks, insurance companies, builders and developers, and government agencies. By law, Canadian financial institutions cannot lend more than 75 per cent of the market value of a property (although this is under review), which means that if you want to buy a $200,000 home, you must find a deposit of at least $50,000. Lenders evaluate a property and check your credit rating (see above), employment history, income, assets, residence and liabilities.

It's advisable to check your own credit rating before applying for a mortgage, in case it could adversely affect your application, because your credit history must usually be perfect to qualify for a mortgage. New immigrants can obtain mortgages but may have to pay a deposit (down payment) of at least 35 per cent and make the first year's mortgage payments in advance. It's often difficult or more expensive to raise finance for a Canadian property from lenders in other countries.

☑ SURVIVAL TIP

For those who cannot afford the 25 per cent deposit required by most lenders in Canada, the federal government provides mortgages insured by the Central Mortgage and Housing Corporation (CMHC 💻 www.cmhc-schl.gc.ca). The CMHC was established in 1945 as a Crown Corporation to administer federal participation in housing as prescribed under the National Housing Act. Mortgage insurance provided by CMHC allows lenders to borrow up to 90 or 95 per cent of a home's value.

The maximum amount a lender will lend you depends on your income. Most lenders insist that a mortgage is no more than three times your annual salary or that monthly repayments are no more than 30 per cent of your gross monthly income. When calculating how large a mortgage you can afford, take into account the purchase (closing) costs, which average 3 to 5 per cent of the price of a property and depend on its location, cost and other factors. 'Non-income status' mortgages of 65 to 70 per cent with no proof of income or tax returns are also available, although borrowers usually require large cash reserves.

The traditional Canadian mortgage period is 25 or 30 years, although lenders also offer 10- to 20-year fixed-rate mortgages, requiring a higher deposit and/or higher monthly repayments than a 25-year mortgage. If you can afford the repayments, a 10- or 15-year mortgage can save you a considerable sum in interest compared with a 30-year mortgage. A 15-year mortgage is usually offered at a slightly lower interest rate (e.g. a 0.25 to 0.75 percentage point reduction) than a 30-year mortgage, meaning you make even greater savings. It can take up to 90 days to arrange a mortgage, depending on its complexity.

Types of Mortgage

There are essentially two basic kinds of mortgage in Canada: 'open' mortgages, which allow you to pay off your mortgage at any time without penalty, and 'closed' mortgages, where there's a penalty for early redemption. A mortgage may be 'closed' for a limited time, e.g. anything from six months to ten years.

Mortgages can have a fixed or variable rate of interest. With fixed-rate mortgages, the monthly repayments and the interest rate are fixed for an agreed period. Even when you fix your interest rates for 1, 2, 3 or 5 years, lending institutions allow you to make some additional payments, e.g. up to an additional 20 per cent per annum, without incurring any penalties, which are deducted from the principal, thus saving a lot of interest. A fixed-rate mortgage offers stability, although interest rates are initially higher than with a variable-rate mortgage and you run the risk that they'll remain higher. A fixed-rate mortgage isn't assumable, e.g. a buyer cannot take over the seller's original below-market rate mortgage. If your income is fixed or rises slowly, you're generally better off with a fixed-rate mortgage, although some people don't qualify because their income is too low.

With a variable-rate mortgage the interest rate is adjusted over the life of the mortgage, although the monthly repayments usually remain the same. If there are large fluctuations in interest rates, the monthly repayments may change each year. Because it involves greater risk, a variable-rate mortgage is usually available at a lower interest rate than a fixed-rate mortgage. You should choose a mortgage with a ceiling or cap on the rate of interest that can be charged (irrespective of how high the index goes), which can be an annual or 'lifetime' limit, i.e. over the full period of the mortgage.

Wide fluctuations in interest rates can cause 'negative amortisation' (where the balance on the loan increases instead of reduces, despite the fact that you're making maximum monthly payments). Variable-rate mortgages are a good choice for someone who expects his future income to rise sufficiently to offset the

possible higher repayments. When comparing the cost of variable mortgages with fixed-rate mortgages, bear in mind that an increase of just 1 per cent in the interest rate increases your repayments and overall debt considerably.

Mortgage interest rates vary slightly from bank to bank and from region to region, but typical rates for 25-year mortgages of the principal types in spring 2009 were: three-year closed 4.75 per cent, five-year closed 5.45 per cent and variable open one year 7.3 per cent (for current rates, see ☎ www.canadamortgage.com/ratesshow/showrates.cfm).

Whatever kind of mortgage you choose, it's sensible to investigate all the options available, taking into account your present and probable future income. Generally, the more money you can put down as a deposit, the more choice you have. When interest rates plunge, as happened in 2008-09, many borrowers (not surprisingly) wish to refinance their mortgage. However, this is generally only worthwhile when the interest rate on your mortgage is at least 2 per cent higher than the prevailing market rate, although it also depends on the size of your mortgage. Bear in mind that it can take months to refinance a loan and you must take into account changing interest rates and all associated costs and other payments. Refinancing costs usually range from 4.5 to 5 per cent of your mortgage value.

Getting the Best Deal

The sort of mortgage deal you're able to negotiate depends on several factors, not least the state of the housing and money markets. Lenders usually charge a fee for granting a mortgage, expressed as a number of points, each of which is equal to 1 per cent of the loan amount. You can sometimes get a mortgage with no points. Alternatively, you can purchase points and lower your interest rates. Points can increase the up-front cost of your mortgage considerably, but can lower your long-term costs if you stay in a house for ten years or more.

To attract new customers, lenders may offer inducements such as below-market interest rates (or no interest for the first year), loans of over 30 years, discounts, rebates and gifts ('giveaways'), most of which don't provide real savings or long-term advantages. Always shop around for the best deal you can find, including all costs.

If you're buying a property in Alberta, you may be able to take over (assume) the existing mortgage from the owner without having to go through the usual qualification process. You take on the mortgage payments and pay the vendor the difference between the balance of the mortgage and the sale price, thus saving yourself a great deal of hassle and delay.

You can employ a local mortgage search company, which uses a computerised network to find the best mortgage deal. Using the services of an independent mortgage broker (for a small fee) is another way to find a good mortgage deal.

Many books are published about mortgages in Canada, including *Mortgages For Dummies* by Eric MBA Tyson & Ray Brown (For Dummies) and *Your First Home: The Proven Path to Home Ownership*, by Gary Keller et al (McGraw-Hill), and the *Homeowner's Manual* published by the CMHC (www.cmhc-schl.gc.ca/en).

INCOME TAX

If you're resident in Canada (see **Tax Residence** below), you must pay federal and provincial income tax. Non-residents are taxed at a standard rate of 25 per cent on their Canadian source gross income, e.g. from employment or a business. If there's a double-taxation treaty between Canada and the country where you're resident (or earn an income), this usually prevents you having to pay tax twice on the same income.

When you arrive in Canada (or depart from the country) during the tax year – which is the same as the calendar year – you may be taxed as a part-time resident, when you can claim a pro-rata portion of any tax credits to which you're normally entitled. Treaties also cover short-stay visitors, teachers and professors, employees of foreign governments, trainees, students and apprentices, and also apply to capital gains tax. Information about income tax for non-residents is contained in information circular 77-16, *Non-Resident Income Tax*.

Federal income tax is levied on the worldwide income of Canadian citizens and resident expatriates (known as 'aliens'), and on certain kinds of Canadian income (including deferred profit-sharing plan payments and death benefits) earned by non-resident expatriates.

In addition to Canadian taxes, you may also be liable for taxes in your home country, although citizens of most countries are exempt from paying taxes in their home country when they spend a minimum period abroad, e.g. a year. If you're in doubt about your tax liability in your home country or country of domicile, check with your country's embassy in Canada (see **Appendix A**).

Canadian taxes are determined by the Department of Finance (known as 'Finance Canada'), but the agency responsible for the administration of federal tax laws and the collection of taxes is the Canada Revenue Agency (CRA, www.cra-arc.gc.ca). Federal income tax was introduced in 1917 as a temporary measure under the Income War Tax Act to finance Canada's participation in World War I.

Not surprisingly, the tax wasn't repealed after the war and in 1949 the federal government officially removed 'war' from the act's title and it became the Income Tax Act. The act has been amended many times, most notably in 1972, when the tax base was broadened and a capital gains tax was introduced (see below).

☑ SURVIVAL TIP

All provinces except Quebec levy a provincial income tax (see page 307) through the federal tax programme, which means that you aren't required to file a separate return for provincial income tax; Quebec residents must file separate federal and Quebec income tax returns.

The calculation of an individual's tax is a two-step process. First, your income liable to federal income tax is calculated. You may deduct from this amount whatever personal tax credits are available and a tax credit for dividend income. The result is your 'basic federal tax payable'. Provincial income tax (except for Quebec) is then calculated by applying the appropriate provincial rate to the 'basic federal tax payable' for the tax year.

In Canada, your employer usually deducts income tax from your pay, while those with business or property income usually pay their income taxes by instalments throughout the year. The Canadian tax system is based on self-assessment, which requires less bureaucracy than in many other countries but puts the onus on individuals to declare their income correctly. The Declaration of Taxpayer Rights (printed on the back of the *General Income Tax Guide*) outlines your rights when dealing with the CRA.

Although the CRA are usually helpful, they have sweeping powers and aren't slow to use them if they suspect somebody of fraud. Tax fraud is a major crime in Canada, where it's estimated to cost over $20bn per year. The CRA carries out random checks and can demand a full-scale inspection or audit of any taxpayer at any time. The CRA processes returns, looking for obvious errors and discrepancies, and also runs them through a computer programme to select some for auditing. The selection criteria are a secret, but generally the wealthier you are, the greater your chance of being audited. The 'field audit' is the main tool in the department's audit programme and can take from a few hours to several weeks, depending on the nature of the examination and/or the size and complexity of the taxpayer's income (the process is described in publication IC71-14R3, *The Tax Audit*). If you're selected for an audit, you can have professional representation at an interview or have someone represent you in your absence.

If you're found to owe additional tax, you must pay interest from the date payment was due, although when a CRA error was responsible for a delay you may be entitled to a reduction of interest. The CRA attempts to resolve tax disputes through an administrative appeals system. If you disagree with your tax bill after an audit of your tax return, you're entitled to an independent review of your case, although you should start the process with the appeals officer at your local tax office. The CRA recommends that you keep all tax documents for at least six years after filing a return.

Reducing your tax burden is a national sport and an obsession in Canada, where a wealth of tax books, magazines and free advice in financial magazines and newspapers is published, particularly during the months and weeks leading up to April 30th (tax filing day). The best-selling tax guides include *J.K. Lasser's Your Income Tax* by J. K. Lasser Institute (Wiley), *Make Sure It's Deductible* by Evelyn Jacks (McGraw-Hill), *Tax Tips for Canadians For Dummies* by Christie Henderson & Campbell Lawless (For Dummies) and *Tax Tips and Tax Shelters for Canadians* by Vlad Trkulja (Insomniac Press). Many tax guides (and computer programmes) are updated annually (the cost isn't tax deductible!).

The Canada Revenue Agency (CRA) publishes numerous free publications on a range of subjects, including a *General Income Tax Guide*, *Taxpayer Rights*, *Telefile – Filing Your Return by Telephone*, *General Income Tax and Benefits* and *Non-Residents and Temporary Residents of Canada*. You can order CRA publications and tax forms direct from the CRA (www.cra-arc.gc.ca).

Tax Residence

The Canadian Income Taxes Act doesn't define income tax residence, but anyone who resides in Canada for 183 days or more in a year is considered a resident and is taxed on his worldwide income for the full year. Tax residence isn't dependent on your status as a citizen or immigrant or on your domicile, but may be determined on 'residential ties'. For example, you're considered to be tax resident if any of the following applies:

- Your spouse and children live in Canada and you habitually visit them;
- You maintain a purchased or rented property which is used by you and your family when you visit Canada;
- You have other property such as a car or furniture that remain in Canada;
- You have 'social ties' such as a Canadian driving licence, bank account, credit cards or health insurance with a Canadian province.

If you're in doubt about your residence status, you should complete tax form NR74, Determination of Residency Status (Entering Canada), downloadable from www.cra-arc.gc.ca/e/pbg/tf/nr74/readme.html. Additional information about tax residence is contained in bulletin IT221R3-CONSOLID, Determination of an Individual's Residence Status, available from the Canada Revenue Agency (Client Services Directorate, 400 Cumberland Street, Ottawa, ON K1A 0L8, www.cra-arc.gc.ca).

Information about tax residence is contained in a *Newcomers to Canada* pamphlet available from local tax offices or Canada Revenue Agency.

Tax Withholding

Employees with no income other than their salary have their income tax withheld (deducted) from their salary by their employer, who pays it to the CRA. Employers must provide employees with a T4 form by the end of February, which details their total salary in the previous year and the amount of tax withheld (plus other withheld items such as Canada Pension Plan or employment insurance contributions). You must enter these figures on your tax return.

Self-employed people or those who receive over 25 per cent of their income from sources other than a wage or salary (e.g. investments or rents) must complete an additional 'business and professional income statement' and pay tax on their income every three months, on 15th March, June, September and December.

Federal Income Tax

Canada has four scales of federal income tax, rates depending on the type of income, as shown in the table below. Although these may seem low compared with other industrial nations, provincial income tax must be added (see below), bringing the top rate of income tax to around 50 per cent in some provinces.

Federal Tax Rates

Income Band Income	Capital Gains	Eligible Dividends*	Small Business Dividends	Other
up to $10,100	-	-	-	-
$10,100 to $40,726	7.5%	5.75%	3.08%	15%
$40,726 to $81,452	11%	4.4%	10.83%	22%
$81,452 to $126,264	13%	10.2%	15.83%	26%
Over $126,264	14.50%	14.55%	19.58%	29%

* Eligible dividends are those designated as such by public corporations and foreign private corporations (CCPCs) resident in Canada and subject to Canadian corporate income tax.

Provincial/Territory Tax Rates

Province/Territory	Tax Rate	Income Amount
Alberta	10%	all income
British Columbia	5.06%	first $35,716
	7.7%	next $35,717
	10.5%	next $10,581
	12.29%	next $17,574
	14.7%	amount over $99,588
Manitoba	10.8%	first $31,000
	12.75%	next $36,000
	17.4%	amount over $67,000
New Brunswick	10.12%	first $35,707
	15.48%	next $35,708
	16.8%	next $44,690
	17.95%	amount over $116,105
Newfoundland & Labrador	7.7%	first $31,061
	12.8%	next $31,060
	15.5%	amount over $62,121
Northwest Territories	5.9%	first $36,885
	8.6%	next $36,887
	12.2%	next $46,164
	14.05%	amount over $119,936
Nova Scotia	8.79%	first $29,590
	14.95%	next $29,590
	16.67%	next $33,820
	17.5%	amount over $93,000
Nunavut	4%	first $38,832
	7%	next $38,832
	9%	next $48,600
	11.5%	amount over $126,264
Ontario	6.05%	first $36,848
	9.15%	next $36,850
	11.16%	amount over $73,698
Prince Edward Island	9.8%	first $31,984
	13.8%	next $31,985
	16.7%	amount over $63,969
Quebec	16%	first $38,385
	20%	next $38,385
	24%	amount over $76,770
Saskatchewan	11%	first $40,113
	13%	next $74,497
	15%	amount over $114,610
The Yukon Territory	7.04%	first $38,832
	9.68%	next $38,832
	11.44%	next $48,600
	12.76%	amount over $126,2

You aren't taxed on the first $10,100 of your income (known as the 'federal basic personal amount'). The tax rates for regular income for employees is shown under 'Other Income' in the table above.

Provincial Income Tax

Each province and territory levies personal income tax at different rates and has a different 'basic personal amount', which makes it difficult to compare tax rates between them, although tax for all provinces (except Quebec) and territories is calculated the same way as federal tax. The tables below show the tax rates for each provincial/territory for 2009, which must be added to the federal tax rates above.

Credits & Deductions

Deductions are used to reduce taxable income, while non-refundable credits are used to reduce the amount of tax payable. This means that although you can use credits to reduce or eliminate federal tax, any unused portion isn't refunded. Credits are calculated by multiplying eligible amounts by 15 per cent (the same as the lowest personal tax rate).

There are a few deductions allowed when calculating your employment income. These include employee contributions to a registered pension plan (up to a specified maximum amount), travelling and certain other expenses of commissioned salesmen, certain travelling expenses of other employees, and union or professional fees. Interest may be claimed as a deduction in the year that it's paid, provided the money was borrowed for the purpose of earning income. Other carrying costs such as investment counselling fees and accounting costs are deductible. Personal interest such as the interest on mortgages or charge accounts isn't deductible.

Other deductions include contributions to RRSPs, certain childcare expenses, moving expenses for relocation within Canada and maintenance (alimony) payments. Capital gains (see below) are generally included in gross income at a rate of 50 per cent (this applies to individuals, estates and trusts, but not to corporations).

If you move home within Canada to start a job or business or as a student, you may be able to deduct your moving expenses. However, students can only deduct the expenses incurred to move to Canada from abroad if they're attending a full-time course at a college, university or other institution providing post-secondary education, and have received a scholarship, bursary, fellowship or research grant to attend that institution. Information is provided in *Claim for Moving Expenses* (form T1-M).

If you pay maintenance or other support payments, you may be able to deduct the amount paid, even if your former spouse doesn't live in Canada. Details are provided in an *Alimony or Maintenance* pamphlet available from tax offices. You must withhold tax on maintenance paid or credited to a non-resident of Canada, unless stated otherwise in a tax treaty.

An individual is allowed to deduct a number of 'personal tax credits' on his Personal Tax Credits Return (form TD1). These include a 'spousal amount' (depending on your spouse's income), an 'age amount' and a 'senior supplementary amount' (if you're over 65), a 'disability amount', a 'caregiver amount', an 'infirm dependant amount', a 'pension income amount' and a 'child amount' (see below). You may also deduct certain medical, adoption and education expenses, charitable donations, employment insurance (EI) contributions and contributions to a Canada/Quebec Pension Plan. As with tax rates, the amounts and limits of these credits and deductions have a federal element and a province/territory element. There are no joint allowances or married couples' allowances. However, for some tax deductions and credits, a family's income is combined to determine their entitlement.

If you have children under 18 years of age, you're eligible for a tax credit for each child (be sure to complete federal tax form TD1).

Quebec, Saskatchewan and the Yukon provide additional credits, and Nova Scotia, Nunavut and Prince Edward Island provide credits for children under six. For further information, obtain a copy of the pamphlet, *Your Child Tax Benefit*, from your local tax office. To apply for the child tax benefit you must complete a *Canada Child Tax Benefit Application* (form RC66) as soon as possible after you arrive in Canada or when a child is born or begins to live with you.

Income from a self-employed business or property is similar to that for a corporation, business income generally being computed on the accrual basis of accounting (whereby income is reported when earned and expenses when incurred) as opposed to the cash basis (which reports income when received and expenses when paid). Interest and other charges that were incurred to acquire business assets or investment property can usually be deducted, although there's a limit on the deduction of vehicle and home office expenses. Deductions for business meals and entertainment expenses are limited to 50 per cent of expenditure.

Tax Return

Individuals resident in Canada (unless exempt) must file a tax return for the previous tax year (1st January to 31st December) by 30th April, when main post offices remain open until midnight to date stamp tax returns (if you owe tax and are a day late filing, you're charged interest). Individuals aren't permitted to establish a different tax year end, although corporations are. Corporations must file annual tax returns, although individuals need to file only if they owe taxes or if they're eligible to claim tax credits, such as the child tax credit or a sales tax credit (see **Sales Tax** on page 292). There are no joint tax returns for married couples and families.

If the CRA doesn't send you the necessary forms and information automatically, they're available from tax service offices, Government of Canada Info-centers and post offices. The standard set of forms is called a 'general income tax package'. There's a 'simplified tax package' for those who don't require the full package, such as pensioners, employees (see below) and others with straightforward tax situations, and those with no income to declare or tax to pay but who want to claim child tax benefit or other entitlements. You must use the tax package for the province or territory where you were resident on December 31st of the relevant tax year.

☑ SURVIVAL TIP

If you were a non-resident and earned income from employment in a particular province or territory in Canada, you should use the tax package for that province or territory.

The CRA identifies you by your Social Insurance Number (SIN), which you must enter on your tax return and use in any correspondence. It's important that you quote this number correctly, as the CRA uses it to update your record of earnings for your contributions to the Canada Pension Plan (CPP) or the Quebec Pension Plan (QPP). Your SIN is also used to determine your eligibility for child tax benefit and goods and services tax (GST) credit. Even if you have no income to report or tax to pay, you may be eligible for a GST credit or other provincial or territorial tax credits, but you must file an income tax return to apply for them. You also need to give your SIN to anyone who prepares a tax information slip (such as a T3, T4, T5 or T600 slip) for you. If you fail to provide your SIN, your return will be sent back with the omission highlighted.

However you choose to file your return, you should start by gathering all the documents required to complete it correctly. You can employ an accountant or another tax professional to complete your tax return, in which case you should make sure that you provide him with all the relevant documents. The best way to find a qualified professional is through a recommendation from a friend, relative or business associate (they're also listed in the *Yellow Pages*). As with all professional services, the size of the fee is determined by the complexity of your return and the number of forms prepared, but the average person with an uncomplicated tax situation usually pays between $100 and $200.

The most appropriate professional isn't necessarily the least expensive one but the one who best meets your requirements. You should be wary of using anyone other than a reputable company or professional to complete your return, as anyone can set themselves up as a tax 'expert' in Canada. Whoever you choose, most tax consultants are incapable of completing totally error-free returns. You can authorise a representative to obtain information on your tax matters by completing an individual consent form (T1013).

Some accountants and tax advisers (preparers) offer a facility called Efile that allows you to file your tax return electronically. The CRA is in favour of this, as it improves accuracy, reduces costs and facilitates the processing of returns and payments (including refunds). Even if you prepare your own return, you can take it to an Efile service provider to submit it electronically. For more information, see the Efile Association of Canada's website (💻 www.efile.ca). If you have a home or office computer, you may prefer to complete your own tax return using a programme (the cost of which isn't tax deductible) such as Timeworks' *Easy Tax* or *Turbotax* (the top seller), Intuit Canada's *QuickTax*, Softkey's *HomeTax*, CanTax's *CanTax T1* or *GriffTax* from Colin Griffiths & Associates. Tax programmes are designed for people who already know something about taxes or who are willing to learn.

The CRA operates a system of volunteers during the tax filing period to assist taxpayers with preparing federal and provincial tax returns. Some 15,000 volunteers across the country attend training sessions at local tax offices and assist nearly 300,000 people with their returns. Income tax returns, schedules, guides, supplementary guides, pamphlets and other common documents are available in large print, Braille, and on audiocassette and DVD that can be used with voice synthesisers. For those who are deaf or hard of hearing, or have a speech impairment, a 'teletypewriter' (TTY) service is available (☎ 1-800-665 0354). The CRA also maintains an automated Tax Information Phone Service (TIPS, ☎ 1-800-267 6999, in English and French.), which provides general and personal tax information (instructions for using TIPS are contained in your income tax package).

If you're filing a paper return, you must submit all original documents, receipts and T4 slips, but make sure that you keep a copy. Your return, guide explanations, and the forms and schedules themselves tell you when to attach other supporting documents such as certificates, forms, schedules or official receipts. If you're using Efile, you must include your Efile service provider on all your supporting documents. It's important to ensure that all your paperwork and supporting documentation is in order when filing your return; if you make a claim without the required documentation it may be disallowed or could delay the processing of your return. Even if you don't need to attach certain supporting documents to your return, or you're using Efile, you must retain them in case your return is reviewed (audited).

Make sure that you file the return on time, even if slips or receipts are missing. If you know that you won't be able to get a slip by the due date, attach a note stating which slips are missing, the payer's name and address and what you're doing to obtain the slips. Generally, you should keep your supporting documents and a copy of your return, the related notice of assessment and any notice of reassessment for six years. These will also help you complete your return in the following year.

No extensions beyond the filing date of 30th April are given and you must file your tax return on time or pay a penalty. Penalties start at a minimum of 5 per cent of the tax due, plus another 1 per cent for each month you're late. If you cannot pay the full amount due by April 30th, send as much as you can and file your tax form on time anyway (the CRA will contact you to arrange a payment schedule). However, the penalty may be waived if you file your return late due to circumstances beyond your control (if this is the case, include a letter with your return stating why it has been filed late).

Failure to report an amount on your return may also result in a penalty and if you do this more than once within a four-year period, you may have to pay another penalty. Information is provided in *Guidelines for the Cancellation and Waiver of Interest and Penalties* (Circular 92-2). If you discover that you've made a mistake after filing your return (particularly one which will result in a refund!) or a mistake on a return made in the previous three years, you can file an *Amended Income Tax Return* (form T1-ADJ) for each year that you're changing.

PROPERTY TAX

Property tax is levied annually on property owners in all provinces to help pay for local services such as healthcare, primary and secondary education, police and fire services, libraries, public transport, waste disposal, highways and road safety, trading standards and social services. Tax rates are fixed by communities and are expressed as an amount per $100 or $1,000 (the 'millage' rate) of the assessed value of a property. For example, if your home is valued at $200,000 and your local tax rate is $15 per $1,000 value, your annual property tax bill will be $3,000.

The rating method varies considerably with the province, county and municipality, and there may be many different rates within a single province (e.g. British Columbia has around 1,400 tax rates in its 70 jurisdictions). Property taxes on a house of average value vary from zero in areas where houses valued below a certain amount are exempt to over $5,000 per year in high value communities. In a recent survey, taxes were highest in Winnipeg, Regina and Montreal, averaging over 2 per cent of a home's market value, and lowest in Saint John (New Brunswick) and Vancouver at less than 1 per cent.

> Middle-income families have been particularly hard hit by increases in property taxes in recent years. In some provinces, a portion of property tax is reimbursed to senior citizens, and blind and disabled people with low incomes.

One way to reduce your property tax is to appeal against your property value assessment, which may cut your local tax bill by as much as 10 per cent. Check your property record card at your local assessor's office. If you find that your assessment is based on incorrect or incomplete information, ask the assessor for a review. Tax appeal deadlines vary with the province or city. If you appeal against your property value, be prepared to back it up with some convincing evidence, e.g. lower assessments on similar properties and incorrect details, particularly wrong property and land dimensions. If necessary, hire a professional appraiser. Note that the assessor and tax board are permitted a margin for error, which may be as much as 15 per cent!

There are many books to help you reduce your property taxes, including *Challenge Your Taxes: Homeowners Guide to Reducing Property Taxes* by Jim Lumley (John Wiley) and *How To Reduce Your Property Tax: A Comprehensive Guide to Property Taxes in the US and Canada* by Frank J Adler (Harper Collins).

Taxes are usually assessed annually on 1st January but in many provinces, you receive the bill at the end of June, requiring you to pay six months in arrears and six months in advance. However, many provinces are converting to a monthly payment system.

CAPITAL GAINS TAX

Capital gains tax (CGT) was introduced in Canada in 1972, partly to finance the social security system. A capital gain is the difference between the cost price and the sale price of an asset, less any allowable deductions for buying, improvement (e.g. maintenance for real estate) and selling costs. Gains from the sale of a principal residence aren't liable for capital gains tax.

Capital gains tax in Canada is payable on the profit made on the sale of items such as antiques, shares/stocks, bonds, valuable metals (e.g. gold), a tract of land or a second home. The rates of capital gains tax differ both in the cases of individuals and corporations. Where income is earned in the form of a capital gain, only 50 per cent (the inclusion rate) of the gain is included in an individual's income for tax purposes – the other half isn't taxed.

Capital gains may arise whenever you sell or otherwise dispose of (e.g. lease, exchange or lose) an asset, i.e. when:

- You give assets other than cash as a gift;
- Shares or other securities in your name are converted or cancelled;
- You settle or cancel a debt owed to you;
- You transfer certain assets to a trust;
- Assets are stolen, destroyed or expropriated;
- An option that you hold to buy or sell goods expires;
- You change all or part of an asset's use;
- You leave Canada.

Capital losses can usually only be used to reduce or eliminate capital gains but cannot be used to reduce other income. If you have capital losses that cannot be used in the current year, you can carry back the losses to any of the three preceding taxation years. Capital losses can also be carried forward indefinitely. However, the only time they can be used to reduce other income is in the year of a taxpayer's death or the immediately preceding year, when half of the capital loss can be used to reduce other income.

Capital gains made by individuals are taxed as income, but at different rates from other kinds of income. Federal capital gains tax is levied at the rates shown in the table below.

In addition to federal capital gain tax, all provinces and territories also levy capital gain tax at varying rates. See province/territory tax departments for information.

Subject to tax treaty statutes, non-residents must pay tax on capital gains arising from the disposition of taxable Canadian property. This includes land situated in Canada, shares in Canadian private corporations, shares in Canadian public corporations in certain circumstances, property used in a business operated by a non-resident in Canada, an interest in a partnership in which over 50 per cent of the assets consist of taxable Canadian property, interests in certain trusts resident in Canada, and shares in a non-resident corporation or an interest in a non-resident trust, if more than 50 per cent of the value of the corporation or trust is derived from Canadian property.

INHERITANCE & GIFT TAX

Canada has no estate, inheritance, gift or succession taxes. On death there's a deemed

Federal Capital Gains Tax

Income Band	Tax Rate	Tax on band	Cumulative Tax
up to $10,100	-	-	
10,100 to $40,726	7.5%	$2,297	$2,297
$40,726 to $81,452	11%	$4,480	$6,777
$81,452 to $126,264	13%	$5,826	$12,603
Over $126,264	14.50%		

disposition of assets (see **Wills** below) and tax must be paid by the estate on capital gains that arise as a result of those dispositions (see **Capital Gains Tax** above).

WILLS

It's an unfortunate fact of life, but you're unable to take your worldly goods with you when you take your final bow – even if you plan to come back in a later life. Therefore, it's preferable to leave them to someone or something you love rather than to the CRA, or leave a mess which everyone will fight over (unless that's your intention!). A surprising number of people in Canada die intestate, i.e. without making a will, meaning that their estates are distributed according to local provincial law rather than as they may have wished. The biggest problem with leaving no will is the delay in winding up an estate (while perhaps searching for a will), which can cause considerable hardship and distress at an already stressful time.

If you don't have a will, most provinces in Canada divide your estate according to an established formula. Typically, two-thirds of your estate goes to your spouse and the remainder is divided between your children. When someone dies, the estate's assets cannot be distributed until probate (the official proving of a will) has been granted. Couples who aren't married are considered in most provinces to be married if they've cohabited for a certain period, which can be as little as six months.

With a little forethought, you can sidestep probate for some assets. If, for example, you name a beneficiary for your life insurance, RRSPs and RRIFs, they can be paid in the event of your death without a will. Other assets, such as bank accounts, stocks and property, may be owned jointly with right of survivorship, which means that they pass to the surviving partner automatically. In the case of a surviving spouse, the transfer won't be taxed (see **Inheritance & Gift Tax** above); in all other cases it's treated by the CRA as a sale of assets and there may be income tax or capital gains tax to pay.

You may wish to calculate the approximate tax liability in advance and buy sufficient 'first-to-die' term life insurance to cover it (although specific bequests of personal property should be detailed in a will). If you own a business, estate planning is more complicated and may require the creation of a trust or a separate will. Consult your lawyer and accountant. You can also minimise taxes by transferring property to your heirs, particularly if you haven't used your capital gains tax exemption (see **Capital Gains Tax** above). If you intend to make gifts to grandchildren, you should be aware that interest and dividends earned on financial gifts made to children aged under 18 who are close relatives are attributed to the donor and taxed accordingly. However, any capital gains tax is payable by the beneficiary.

All adults should make a will, irrespective of the value of their assets. If your circumstances change dramatically, e.g. you get married, you must make a new will because marriage automatically revokes any existing wills. Husbands and wives should make separate wills. Similarly, if you separate or are divorced, you should consider making a new will, but should ensure that you have only one valid will. You should review your will every few years to make sure that it still fits your wishes and circumstances.

A change of province may necessitate changing your will to comply with (or take advantage of) local law.

Once you've accepted that you're mortal, you'll find that making a will isn't a complicated or lengthy process. You can draw up your own will (which is better than none), although it's recommended you obtain legal advice from an experienced estate planning and probate lawyer. The fee for a straightforward will is around $250 for an individual and $350 for a couple.

Many provinces provide fill-in-the-blanks will forms costing around $5 that are designed for parents or married couples with modest estates. They help you to leave your estate to your children or spouse, allow you to give money to one other person or charity, and usually allow you to name a guardian and an executor. You normally need two witnesses (to your signature, not the contents of the will) who cannot be either a beneficiary or your spouse, although some provinces allow 'self-proved' handwritten wills.

There are a number of books about wills and probate available, including *The Complete Idiots Guide to Wills and Estates for Canadians* by Edward Olkovich and Steve Maple (Prentice Hall) and probate guides for BC and Ontario published by the Self-Counsel Press (💻 www.self-counsel.com/ca).

If you're a foreign national and don't want your estate to be subject to Canadian law, you may be eligible to have your will interpreted under the law of another country. In this case, you should employ a lawyer who's conversant with the law of both countries. If you don't specify in your will that the law of another country applies to your estate, Canadian law applies.

Your bank or lawyer usually acts as the executor of your will, but you should ideally visit a few banks and lawyers and compare fees. These may vary considerably depending on the size of your estate but all tend to include a percentage of your total estate plus hourly charges. It's best to make your beneficiaries the executors, who can then instruct a lawyer after your death if they require legal assistance; see *So You've Been Appointed Executor* by Tom Carter (Self-Counsel Press). Note that wills become part of the public record after probate.

Keep a copy of your will in a safe place (e.g. a bank) and another copy with your solicitor or the executors of your estate. You should keep information regarding bank accounts and insurance policies with your will(s), but don't forget to tell someone where they are!

COST OF LIVING

No doubt you'd like to know how far your Canadian dollars will stretch and how much money (if any) you'll have left after paying your bills. Canadians enjoy one of the highest standards of living in the world, although it has been fairly stagnant for many people in the last decade or so. Surprisingly, around 10 per cent of the population live below the official 'poverty' level, which, in the interest of political correctness, is now called the Low Income Cut-off or LICO.

Canada has traditionally been considered a relatively inexpensive country and this is still true compared with many other Western countries. However, the cost of housing in the major cities, energy, transport, insurance, recreation, clothing and food (to name just a few things) have all risen in recent years, and it's no longer an inexpensive country, particularly if you live in Toronto or Vancouver. The strength of the Canadian dollar in recent years has also increased the cost of living.

The cost of living in Canada has increased considerably for all income levels in the last decade, although incomes have increased much faster for the rich than the poor, and for most people in 'middle Canada' life has become much more expensive – in common with most other countries. The cost of living varies depending on where and how you live and it's difficult to calculate an average cost of living, even for those living in the same city. Apart from the cost of accommodation, goods and services, you should also take into account the level of local taxes (income, property and sales taxes) and the cost of education.

> Most newcomers, particularly those from the UK and Western Europe, find the cost of living in Canada is lower than in their home country.

Canadian housing is particularly inexpensive compared with other developed nations – the average house price in Canada is around seven times the average annual wage. Prices are highest in Ontario and Alberta (seven to eight times the average wage) and Vancouver (eleven times the average wage). Europeans will generally find that food, dining out and most forms of recreation, petrol (gasoline) and power (but you'll use more power to heat your home in winter) are cheaper in Canada.

In the Mercer 2008 Cost of Living Survey of 140 cities (💻 www.mercer.com/costofliving), no Canadian cities featured in the top 50, with Toronto in 54th position (with a cost of living some 30 per cent lower than London), Vancouver (64), Calgary (66), Montreal (72), and Ottawa (85). The survey found that Canadian cities have lower living costs than most other locations in the developed world. In 2008, Toronto, Vancouver and Calgary were at lower positions in the table than they were in 2006, indicating that they have become less expensive compared with other cities. On the other hand, Calgary, Montreal and Ottawa had a lower cost of living in 2006 than in 2008.

Other selected rankings were: Moscow (1), Tokyo (2), London (3), Copenhagen (6), Paris (12), Sydney (15), Dublin (16 – along with Rome), New York City (22 – the only US city in the top 50), Amsterdam (25), Madrid (28), Melbourne (36), Berlin (38), Brussels (39), Hamburg (50th), Los Angeles (55), Birmingham UK (66 – equal with Calgary), Glasgow (69), Auckland, San Francisco (78) and Chicago (84).

Note, however, that with the huge fluctuations in exchange rates in the last year (since the survey was conducted), the world has been turned upside down and the US and Euro countries have become significantly more expensive (while London, for example, has become much cheaper). The cost of living in rural areas is, not surprisingly, lower than in the major cities (particularly housing).

Canada's consumer price index (CPI), issued by Statistics Canada (💻 www.statcan.gc.ca), gives an indication of how prices have risen (or fallen) over the past year (the inflation rate). The CPI, which sceptics believe stands for 'con people incessantly', is calculated from a basket of basic goods and services. Canada's annual rate of inflation was just 1.2 per cent in March 2009. While Canadians paid less for gasoline and vehicles in 2009 than they did a year previously, they paid more for food and shelter.

Food costs rose 7.9 per cent from March 2008 to March 2009 – the largest increase since November 1986, including large increases for fresh vegetables (26 per cent) and fresh fruit (19.3 per cent), while costs for non-alcoholic beverages were up more than 10 per cent and cereal products up 11 per cent. Statistics Canada also pointed out that there was a 12-month price increase of 54.9 per cent for potatoes, largely as a result of poor harvests in Canada that led to tighter supplies. While there are no signs that food price pressures will subside anytime soon, it's clear that the downward price pressures from most other goods in the RPI basket (due to weakening domestic demand) have begun to outweigh rising costs.

The prices of staple foods in Canada is provided on the Relocate Canada website (💻 http://relocatecanada.com/foodprice.html) and Living in Canada (💻 www.livingin-canada.com/food-prices-canada.html), which will give you a rough guide to food costs. However, bear in mind that prices vary considerably across the country and from city to city. A survey in October 2008 by the Heart and Stroke Foundation (💻 www.heartandstroke.ca) found that fresh food was too expensive for almost half of all Canadians – it also found startling discrepancies in the cost of basic healthy food, not only from province to province, but also from city to city in the same province.

Nevertheless, even in the most expensive cities, the cost of living in Canada needn't be astronomical. If you shop wisely, compare prices and services before buying and don't live too extravagantly, you may be pleasantly surprised at how little you can live on.

A guide to the cost of living in Canada is shown on the government, Going to Canada, website (💻 www.goingtocanada.gc.ca – Move to Canada/Cost of Living in Canada). The Economic Research Institute website (💻 www.erieri.ca) contains a number of assessment tools including a salary assessor that allows you to compare the salaries of over 5,500 positions in Canada and the US, plus a relocation assessor that compares the cost of living in Canadian cities and thousands of worldwide locations.

52

15. LEISURE

Canada is a vast country (the second-largest in the world), stretching some 5,000mi (almost 8,000km) from the Atlantic to the Pacific, and is famous for its natural beauty. It encompasses some of the most dramatic landscapes in the world, from the majesty of the Rockies to the frozen splendour of the Arctic, interspersed with a profusion of huge lakes, raging rivers, dense forests, and endless plains and prairies. It's a nature and sports lovers' paradise, offering some of the best skiing, fishing, boating, hunting, flying, hiking and climbing (to name but a few activities) in the world. Getting away from it all isn't difficult in Canada, which has areas of wilderness bigger than most countries!

Canada also has some of North America's great cities, boasting the dramatic setting of Vancouver, the grandeur of Toronto, the French-Canadian chic of Montreal and Quebec City, and the tranquillity of the capital, Ottawa. Canada offers something for everyone and, not surprisingly, the country is one of the top ten tourist destinations in the world, attracting millions of visitors each year.

Canadians believe in working and playing hard and make the most of their free time, spending around 10 per cent of their disposable income on recreation. Although admission to major attractions can be expensive, free entertainment is provided in many cities during the summer and winter, including theatrical performances; classical, military and popular music; opera, dance, puppet shows, mime, jugglers and comedians.

Although mass culture, such as films, TV and pop music are the most popular forms of entertainment, so-called 'high culture' such as classical music, ballet, opera, museums and art also flourishes. Most Canadians live within a reasonable distance of one of the major cities, where there are numerous theatres, art galleries, museums and other cultural centres. Annual spending on entertainment and performances is over $500 per household, with around 10mn theatre tickets sold annually, over 1mn for the opera, 1.5mn for dance performances and 3.5mn for concerts.

The Canada Council for the Arts (🖳 www.canadacoucil.ca) spends millions of dollars each year supporting the arts, although in the last decade there's been a gradual shift from the literary arts of book and poetry writing to the performing arts, which now receive some two-thirds of funding. Nevertheless, tickets for the theatre, opera, orchestral concerts and even comedy shows in Canada aren't cheap (often between $60 and $110). Montreal is generally the most expensive and Calgary and Edmonton the least expensive. Canada is populated by peoples from a multitude of cultures, backgrounds and heritages, which is reflected in the diversity and boundless energy displayed in the arts.

Canadians don't let the long, harsh winters put a stop to their fun, and most cities stage winter festivals which may include dog-sled races, events celebrating the fur-trappers and early explorers, ice-skating, ice-sculpture, and almost anything else you can think of connected with snow and ice (plus of course a wide range of winter sports). The Winter Carnival in Quebec City has been described as 'New Orleans' Mardi Gras on ice', with sculptures, parades, a canoe race across the frozen St. Lawrence river, an ice hotel and copious quantities of a local drink called Caribou (a mixture of whiskey and red wine). Other major events include a Winterlude festival in Ottawa held over several weekends in February; a Festival of Lights in Niagara, Montreal and Vancouver; a First Nations Storytelling Festival in mid-January in Saskatchewan; and events celebrating the return of the sun in January in the Northwest Territories after a month of total darkness.

Open-air events at other times of the year include a Tulip Festival held in May in Quebec, including concerts, parades and a flotilla on the canal, with floral sculptures, floral tapestries and garden displays. Vancouver hosts a four-day (or rather night) firework festival called the Symphony of Fire at the end of July, and there's a similar event in Toronto in August. In Alberta, the mid-summer International Jazz Festival and dozens of similar high-profile events have made Edmonton Canada's festival city, while in July Calgary is home to the celebrated (ten-day) Stampede (where crazed horses try to unseat even crazier riders), billed as 'the greatest outdoor show on earth'.

Tickets for virtually every important event (theatre, music, sport, etc.) can be purchased through ticket agencies such as Ticketmaster (💻 www.ticketmaster.ca). Reduced price tickets are often available for local events on the day of performances. The 'Arts and Leisure' section of local newspapers and local arts and entertainment newspapers and magazines (often free) contain information about current and forthcoming shows, ticket prices and availability. Information about local events and entertainment is also available from tourist offices, libraries and town halls. Entertainment newspapers and magazines are published in all major cities, including *Toronto Life* magazine (💻 www.torontolife.com), *The Georgia Strait* (Vancouver, 💻 www.straight.com) and *Jam!* (💻 http://jam.canoe.ca). All major newspapers provide entertainment news and many have weekly guides on Fridays, e.g. the *Globe & Mail* 'Weekend' sections.

Montreal, Toronto and Vancouver have large gay and lesbian communities with clubs, bars, support groups, specialised bookshops, newspapers and magazines, including *Xtra* (Toronto, 💻 www.xtra.ca/public/toronto.aspx), *Fugues* (Montreal, 💻 www.fugues.com), *Wayves* (Halifax, 💻 http://wayves.ca), *Xtra West* (Vancouver, 💻 www.xtra.ca/public/vancouver.aspx) and *Capital Xtra* (Ottawa, 💻 www.xtra.ca/public/ottawa.aspx). Toronto and Vancouver have Gay Pride days with parades and other celebrations that attract large crowds. In the major cities, the traditional Halloween fancy-dress parties have been adopted by the gay community, which holds famously wild parties at their nightclubs.

The main purpose of this chapter (and indeed the whole book) is to provide information that isn't usually found in other books. General tourist information is available in dozens of Canadian travel books that cover the whole country or concentrate on a particular city or region. Among the best general travel guides are *Let's Go: Canada*, *Lonely Planet Canada*, *Rough Guide Canada* and *Fodor's Canada* (see **Appendix B** for a list). For information about sports facilities see **Chapter 16**.

TOURIST INFORMATION

Tourist information is generally provided at provincial or territorial level, although the Canadian Tourism Commission (CTC, #1400-1055, Dunsmuir Street, Box 49230, Vancouver, BC V7X 1L2, ☎ 604-638 8300, 💻 www.canadatourism.com) promotes

Canada internationally and provides general information. There's at least one provincial tourist office in each province, usually in the capital city, and others at major tourist attractions. Offices have toll-free phone numbers, listed in the blue section of the local *Yellow Pages* under 'Tourism' or 'Travel' (with the exception of Alberta and Northwest Territories, where numbers are listed under 'Economic development and tourism').

Tourist offices provide a wealth of free information, including maps, campsite and accommodation guides, and information about local attractions and special events scheduled for the coming year. Most provincial offices provide detailed information regarding special events or sports, but they don't generally keep much information about any given area, for which you need to contact the nearest city tourist office.

City and town tourist and information offices have a plethora of local information on every conceivable subject, both within their borders and in the surrounding area, all of which they'll send you on request. Brochures for many attractions are also distributed via hotels, campsites and other accommodation centres, public offices, libraries and many other outlets. Travel agents, both within Canada and abroad, can also provide details about many attractions, events and tours, as can offices of Air Canada.

> Dedicated tourist and travel websites for Canada include, 🖳 www.canadaforvisitors.com, www.canadatourism.ca, www.canadiantravelguide.net and http://pure.canada.travel/en_us/index.html.

NATIONAL PARKS

Canada's first national park, Banff, was established in 1887 (only the third worldwide), and today attracts over 5mn visitors annually. Soon to follow were Yoho, Glacier and Waterton Lakes National Parks in Western Canada, while in the east the first was St Lawrence Islands National Park in 1904. Today Canada has over 40 national parks and national park reserves covering an area of over 225,000km² (86,872mi²) or around 2 per cent of the country's land mass.

Parks provide a range of facilities including campsites (campgrounds), canoe and boat hire, and hiking trails, although all activities, that consume natural resources, such as mining, forestry, agriculture and hunting are prohibited. Some parks charge for entry (some offer multi-entry permits), while others are free for day use but charge for camping. Where applicable, you can expect to pay a fee of around $5 per person or $10 per car. Canada also has numerous provincial parks – around 550 in British Columbia alone!

The high season is July and August, when parking queues (line-ups) are interminable. The most popular parks are overcrowded from May to October, when bookings for campsites and other accommodation are essential. It's best to avoid the most popular parks in summer and to visit them in spring or autumn (fall), when many are also at their most beautiful. Many parks provide educational talks, guided tours and hikes, and other organised activities. Park superintendents and staff can tell you anything you wish to know about a park, including its history, flora and fauna, ecology and geology. At the Dinosaur Provincial Park in the 'badlands' of Alberta, park rangers take guided tours to known fossil sites and give talks in the evenings about dinosaurs. If you find a fossil, you'll get a certificate but you cannot take it home (there's a hefty fine if you do). Most parks have a visitor centre that provides free information and often stages exhibitions, films and slide presentations, and sells guide books.

For information about national parks, contact Parks Canada (Publications Unit (25 Eddy Street, Gatineau, QC K1A 0M5, ☎ 1-888-773 8888, 🖳 www.pc.gc.ca or www.parkscanada.ca) or see 🖳 www.national-parks-canada.com. Parks Canada also maintains many historic parks featuring historic sites and buildings, many of which have special programmes or events in summer. Costumed interpreters (often university students) will guide you round the site and explain, for example, the use of Victorian kitchen equipment. There are also a number of excellent books available, including National Parks of Canada by J.A. Kraulis & Kevin P. McNamee (Key Porter Books) and *National Parks of North America: Canada, United States, Mexico* (National Geographic Society).

Most cities have extensive park areas that are welcome retreats from the surrounding noise, the most famous of which is Stanley Park (1,000 acres/400ha) in Vancouver (see 🖳 http://city.vancouver.bc.ca/parks/parks/stanley). Most major cities also have botanical gardens, where entrance is often free, and many have zoos and bird sanctuaries. Entrance fees and opening times vary depending on the time of year, so check in advance.

Wildlife

Canada has a rich wildlife that includes various species of bear, beaver, buffalo (bison), over 500 species of birds, a plethora of fish, including the famous Atlantic and Pacific salmon, whales, wolves, coyote, deer, moose, elk, caribou, Rocky Mountain goats, lynx, cougars, skunks, porcupines, raccoons and chipmunks. However, bear in mind that that many of Canada's animals are (or can be) dangerous, including the seemingly-cute raccoon, which sometimes carries rabies, the normally placid moose, which charges at humans when scared, and, of course, bears.

Although there are relatively few bear attacks in Canada, they're widely reported and if you're a victim, you're likely to be seriously injured and may even be killed. Canada has four types of bear: Black, brown, grizzly and polar. All are very large and dangerous when provoked. They aren't, as many people think, slow and lumbering, although they're slow to get up speed, and are expert (and fast) tree climbers (apart from grizzlies). Bears don't just inhabit remote regions (one fatal attack took place in a car park in Banff) and if you're likely to be visiting an area inhabited by bears, you should take precautions and heed the warnings!

When camping, you should keep your food in an air-tight container and store it a good distance from your camp, preferably hung from a tree to deter other animals such as raccoons. Some campsites have bear-proof wooden cupboards where campers can store their food. On the west coast, a white or Kermode bear is known by the First Nations people as a spirit bear; it isn't a polar bear, but a genetic mutation of a black bear.

There are a number of books designed to help you survive a 'walk on the wild side', including *Wilderness Survival* by Gregory J. Davenport (Stackpole Books) and *Planning a Wilderness Trip in Canada and Alaska* by Keith Morton (Heritage House).

The biggest and most dangerous of all bears are the majestic polar bears, which may look cuddly in a zoo but are among the mightiest predators on earth (the largest males weigh up to 1,500kg/3,300lb). They live in the Arctic and sub-Arctic regions and, if you want to see them in the wild, one of the best places is Churchill (Manitoba) on the edge of Hudson Bay. Here bear-watching from huge tundra buggies is a popular pastime and the bears come right up to the buggies to inspect their occupants. The bears migrate past Churchill in October and November and earlier in the year (from June to August) when white beluga whales (a favourite prey) feed in the Bay.

You can join a whale-watching boat trip from many places along the Canadian coast, where the sights off the Atlantic coast include blue, finback, humpback, beluga and sometimes minke and right whales. In the Pacific, Californian grey whales reach Vancouver Island on their annual migration north in March and April, returning south in September and October. Orcas (or 'killer whales') can be seen in the Inside Passage between Vancouver Island and the mainland. The cheapest way to see them (and other whales) is to take a ferry between Vancouver, Victoria and Seattle

brown bear

or northwards up the Georgia Strait or Inside Passage (see www.bcferries.com). Several pods of orcas live in the San Juan Strait and can be see all year round. Whale watching trips are offered by many companies.

Alpine plants and flowers are a feature of the Rocky Mountains. A hike around a ski hill area in summer may be more accessible than most mountains thanks to the availability of ski lifts.

CAMPING & CARAVANNING

Canada has over 4,000 caravan (trailer) and chalet parks and campsites (campgrounds), both public and private. Camping in Canada encompasses everything from backpackers sleeping rough or with a 'pup' tent, to those touring in a luxury mobile home or 'recreational vehicle' (RV). Facilities at privately-owned campsites range from non-existent (sometimes not even water) to luxury cabins and cottages. All provinces with a shoreline provide seafront campsites, ranging from bare stretches of beach to luxury developments with all modern conveniences. Campsites have strict rules regarding noise (e.g. none between 11pm and 7am), alcohol (only on your site) and dogs (which must be on leads and mustn't foul the site).

A campsite usually has a fireplace (with free wood), picnic table and parking space, with toilets and running water available nearby. Higher-priced sites have caravan and RV 'hook-ups' for electricity, water and cable TV. Campsites usually have 'dumping stations' (for waste), flush or dry toilets, a children's area, a recreation room, restaurants and snack bars, laundry facilities, and may also have hot showers and camp shops, although you shouldn't rely on these being provided. Campsites often have sports facilities, which may include tennis, shuffleboard, volleyball, swimming, fishing, canoeing and boating. Many national and provincial parks have sporting campsites for hunters and fishermen, lodgings consisting of cabins or a central lodge with sleeping cabins (meals may be included). A float-plane (sea-plane) is necessary to reach some areas and a guide service is usually available.

For many Canadians, camping means using an RV or motor home or a caravan, rather than a tent. RVs equipped for a family of four can be rented throughout Canada from $600 to $900 per week. Note that you're usually prohibited from parking a motor home or caravan overnight on a public road. Tent campers are advised to avoid RV-oriented campsites, which may offer superior facilities but are plagued by noise and vehicle fumes. To RV 'campers', getting back to nature means taking all the modern conveniences of home with you, and few stray further than a few hundred feet from their vehicles.

Most national and provincial parks permit camping. You should try to arrive by 5pm or earlier (at the most popular parks queuing all night for a space on long weekends isn't unheard of). Many parks close their gates to visitors at 11pm and don't reopen them until 6am. Some sites display a 'No Vacancy' sign all summer, therefore if possible you should book well in advance. The peak season runs from mid-May to the end of September at the most popular parks, many of which have a one- or two-week limit on stays during the summer. You should book as far in advance as possible, particularly for holiday weekends.

In addition to camping facilities, many parks maintain a number of cabins and lodges which can be rented year-round and reserved six months to a year in advance. Many national parks provide wilderness camping in designated areas and have special facilities for RVs.

All campsites have minimum age limits and many won't issue permits to those aged under 18.

Campsites vary considerably, as do their fees, which usually range from $15 to $25 per night in national parks to $50 per night at privately-owned sites, depending on the popularity, season, facilities, location, tent size and the number sharing (group rates are usually available). A new trend in Canada's campsites is to charge according to the classification (size) of your RV and not by the person.

The American Automobile Association (AAA, www.aaa.com) and Canadian Automobile

Association (CAA, 💻 www.caa.ca) provide an abundance of camping information for members and jointly operate the 💻 www.koakampgrounds.com website, where campsites in both countries can be booked. Although more expensive than many others, 'Kampgrounds of America' (KOA) campsites generally provide the best facilities, including showers, electricity, flush toilets and phones, and often have swimming pools, laundrettes and shops.

Camping enthusiasts may be interested in *Camping Life* magazine (💻 www.campinglife.com). One of the best Canadian camping guides is *Woodall's Camping Guide Canada.*

AMUSEMENT PARKS

Canada is a great country for the young (and young at heart) and many leisure facilities are geared to children. Among the most popular amusement parks are the roller-coaster parks, which have a cult following among Canadians. There's even an organisation called the Coaster Enthusiasts of Canada (💻 http://cec.chebucto.org). One of the country's biggest amusement parks is Paramount's Canada's Wonderland (💻 www.canadaswonderland.com), which is a 30-minute drive from the centre of Toronto on Highway 400. In addition to the obligatory roller-coaster that lands in a pool of water, it has a climbing wall (harness mandatory!), a James Bond simulator and over 200 other attractions. One-day tickets cost from $31.49 to $46.69 (web specials) or you can buy a bargain season pass for just $70.90 (child), $87.26 (adult) or $163.63 for a family of four.

Other amusement parks include Calaway Park in Calgary, Alberta (💻 www.calawaypark.com), Western Canada's largest outdoor family amusement park; Playland (💻 www.pne.ca/playland) at the Pacific National Exhibition in Vancouver; and West Edmonton Mall (💻 www.westedmall.com/play), North America's largest shopping and entertainment centre, with a wealth of entertainments, including Galaxyland Amusement Park and World Waterpark.

MUSEUMS & ART GALLERIES

Canada has a wealth of excellent museums and art galleries. The capital region of Ottawa alone is home to 29 museums, including 12 national museums and institutions, most of which appeal to all interests and age groups. The National Gallery of Canada in Ottawa (💻 www.gallery.ca), housed in a beautiful purpose-built building, is a gem (one of the best museums/galleries in the world) and not to be missed – and what's more it's free!

Many galleries and museums contain works by a number of excellent Canadian artists. The so-called 'Group of Seven' artists (the group wasn't limited to the seven founding members) led by Tom Thompson (the others included Franklin Carmichael, A. J. Casson, Lawren Harris, A. Y. Jackson, Arthur Lismer, J. E. H. Macdonald and Frederick Varley) are famous for their paintings of the eastern Canadian lakelands. Over 2,000 of their works, as well as many by Inuit and north-west coast native artists, can be seen at the McMichael Canadian Collection at Kleinburg near Toronto. Other famous Canadian artists include Emily Carr, who painted the west coast (particularly the villages of the Haida Indians with their totems and the surrounding forest) and Paul Kane.

Native Indian art includes some paintings and prints, but the majority (and the best) consist of carvings of animals, birds, fish and native figures. Inuit carvers use bone, ivory (often from walruses), antlers and soapstone. A group of soapstone musk oxen standing in a defensive circle with the calves in the middle, displayed at Calgary airport, is in the 'once seen, never forgotten' category. The Winnipeg Art Gallery houses the world's largest collection of Inuit art, although there's also an extensive collection at the Inuit Gallery of Eskimo Art in Toronto.

> There are also many bizarre museums, including a shoes museum, a theatre museum of 'the unusual, the absurd and the ridiculous' and the History of Contraception Museum, which houses such fascinating exhibits as a recipe for an oral contraceptive consisting of dried beaver's testicle brewed in strong alcohol!

Many Canadian museums are refreshingly modern and stimulating, particularly those offering hands-on exhibits, such as the Science Centres in major cities. These bear little resemblance to the traditional image of rows of glass cases full of stuffed animals and dusty static exhibits.

Most museums are well designed and sometimes the buildings housing collections are as artistically or historically important as the collections themselves. In many cities (and shopping malls) there are commercial (contemporary) galleries, which are often well worth a visit, even if you have no intention of buying. Many rural museums are operated by local historical societies and private interests, and they often preserve local history or long-defunct local industries.

The opening hours of museums and galleries vary considerably. Many close on Mondays and open in the early evening one day per week, e.g. until 9pm, when admission may be free or fees reduced. Entrance to some galleries and museums is free at all times. Admission fees, when charged, can vary from $2.50 to $15 for adults (or more for special exhibitions), with discounts for children, senior citizens, the disabled (some have special access or provide wheelchairs) and possibly students (some also provide free entry to students on certain days or evenings).

CINEMA

Although cinemas (movie theaters) face increasing competition from TV and DVDs, the film industry is thriving in Canada, particularly in the major cities, where millions of tickets are sold each year. Vancouver is often referred to as 'Hollywood North' because many major films and TV series are filmed there, and Toronto hosts an annual International Film Festival (💻 www.tiffg.ca) in September that some claim is better than Cannes; each year, over 250 films from over 50 countries are screened in around 20 cinemas.

Among the many world-famous Canadian film stars (past and present) are Dan Ackroyd, John Candy, Jim Carrey, Michael J. Fox, Lorne Greene, Mike Myers (Austin Powers), Mary Pickford, Christopher Plummer, William Shatner and Donald Sutherland. Nevertheless, Canadian-made films account for just 5 per cent of the fare in Canadian cinemas, most of which show the latest American blockbusters. Every large city, however, has a 'review' theatre, where 'classic' films, foreign (subtitled) and really obscure releases are screened. In Ottawa, the Bytown and Mayfair theatres publish a monthly newsletter available from newsstands. In cities such as Toronto and Vancouver, where there are large ethnic populations, some cinemas specialise in Chinese and Indian films. Outside the major cities, however, it's difficult to find a cinema showing 'serious', classic, art (avant-garde), experimental or foreign-language films, or anything other than the latest blockbusters, and many cinemas are under threat of closure.

Surprisingly, films made by Canadians about Canada are easier to see abroad than in Canada, despite the best efforts of the National Film Board of Canada (NFB, 💻 www.nfb.ca), which releases a set of dramatic, animated or documentary films each year. The NFB has offices in most major Canadian cities, where films are shown regularly and videos and DVDs can be purchased.

There are large multi-screen (e.g. 12 to 18) cinemas in most Canadian cities. Cineplex Odeon (💻 www.cineplex.com) is the market leader (having absorbed most of its competitors), which has spawned an entity known as the 'Collosus' [*sic*], which is housed in a round building containing shops, fast food outlets and video arcades as well as cinema screens. Other cinema operators include AMC Theatres (💻 www.amctheatres.com), Empire

Theatres (💻 www.empiretheatres.com), Festival Cinemas (💻 www.festivalcinemas.ca) in Vancouver and Landmark Cinemas (💻 www.landmarkcinemas.com. Cinema and movie information sites include 💻 www.cinemaclock.com and www.icinema.ca

Drive-in cinemas, once popular throughout southern Canada, are rapidly disappearing; in the late '60s there were over 250 but there are now only less than 50. At a drive-in cinema you pay at the entrance and drive to a parking place, where you clip a small loudspeaker to your car window and watch the action on a gigantic screen. Obviously, drive-in cinemas operate only when it's dark and often in the summer only (they aren't popular when it's raining or snowing, except with couples who don't plan to watch the movie). One of the advantages (for smokers) is that you can smoke at drive-in movies!

A seat for a typical 'first-run' movie costs around $10, with discounts for children and senior citizens. Cinemas occasionally have cross-promotional (sponsorship) days with a charity, when if you bring a donation of non-perishable foods, admission is reduced or free. Cinemas also frequently run promotional features in conjunction with local radio stations and, if you listen carefully, you're almost assured of a free pass.

All films on general release in Canada are given a rating under the Motion Picture Code of Self-Regulation, as shown below.

Children (or adults) who look younger than their years may be asked for proof of their age, e.g. a school or student card, social insurance card or driving licence, for admittance to restricted films.

Film Classifications

Classification	Restrictions
G (general)	None
PG (parental guidance)	Some material may be inappropriate for children
PG-13	Some material may be inappropriate for children under 13
R (restricted)	Children under 18 require an accompanying parent or adult guardian

THEATRE

Theatre (theater) in Canada is alive and well with thriving professional and amateur theatre companies in the major cities and many smaller towns. Stratford Ontario is home to a world-renowned Shakespearean company and hosts a summer festival each year (most of which consists, not surprisingly, of works by Shakespeare). Amateur dramatic companies also thrive throughout the country. Much of the theatre in Quebec, particularly in Montreal, is in French. Toronto is the world's third-largest centre for English-language theatre (after New York and London).

However, theatre tickets aren't cheap (often between $60 and $150). Toronto's restored period theatre, Pantages, in the heart of the theatre district (Yonge Street) charges around $135 per ticket or even more for popular shows such as Phantom of the Opera. In Ottawa, the National Arts Centre is partly subsidised and consequently less expensive, e.g. it costs from around $30 to see a ballet. In Canadian theatres (as in older cinemas) the 'orchestra' refers to the front seats, while the upper stalls (dress circle) are called the balcony or mezzanine.

Tickets can be purchased through Ticketmaster ticket agencies or direct from box offices, either by phone or in person. Most people book tickets by phone and pay by credit card through 24-hour phone/charge card agencies, which usually add a surcharge of around $2.50 per ticket for their services. Tickets ordered by credit card can be collected from the theatre box office on production of your card. Often certain dates are reserved for charity or other special evenings. Discounted tickets are also available through various clubs and organisations.

Check performance times with the box office or in a newspaper or entertainment magazine. If you're late for a performance, you may have to wait until the interval before being permitted to take your seat, although it may be possible to watch the show on a monitor. There are usually daily evening performances from Mondays to Saturdays and matinee performances (2 or 3pm) on Wednesdays, Saturdays and Sundays. Matinee (and preview) tickets are usually cheaper than evening tickets. Like cinemas, theatres occasionally have cross-promotional (sponsorship) days with a charity, when, if you bring a donation of non-perishable foods, admission is reduced or free.

Most theatres have a number of spaces for wheelchairs, induction loops for the hard of hearing and toilets (restrooms) for wheelchair users (mention when booking). Some theatres produce Braille programmes and brochures and most allow entry to guide dogs (seeing-eye dogs) for the blind. Most theatres, city and regional, have restaurants and bars, and some have their own car parks.

There's also an abundance of free street theatre in the major cities, including a ten-day International Busker Festival in Halifax (Nova Scotia) in August which attracts street performers from all over the world. 'Fringe' theatre festivals are relatively new to Canada and are typically held in smaller communities (city suburbs or smaller towns) where 'new' performers try to attract attention from show business bosses. These are often run alongside a town's annual commemorative events.

Many communities boast their own amateur theatre groups, known as 'community theatre', which perform classic plays, ballet and even opera. Community theatre is usually of a high standard; in fact some Canadian amateur theatre companies, whether drama, comedy or musical, would put professional repertory companies to shame in some countries. However, if you're a budding Brad Pitt or Julia Roberts, don't let the high standards deter you. Community theatre companies are always on the lookout for new talent and people to assist in other areas such as costumes, lighting and stage scenery.

MUSIC & BALLET

Canada has a dynamic and varied music scene. Although they're often assumed to be American, Bryan Adams, Céline Dion, K.D.

Lang, Avril Lavigne, Gordon Lightfoot, Sarah Mclachlan, Leonard Cohen, Joni Mitchell and Anne Murray are just a few Canadian singers who enjoy worldwide fame. Contemporary popular music artists include Barenaked Ladies, Tragically Hip, Shania Twain, Alanis Morissette, Nellie Furtado, veteran pop rockers Rush and recent indie favourites Arcade Fire. In the Atlantic provinces there's a tradition of Celtic-based music, where top bands include the Barra MacNeils, the Rankin Family and the Irish Descendants. There's also a record label called First Nations that specialises in native Canadian music.

Canadians are particularly fond of jazz and Montreal hosts a world-famous jazz festival in summer, when many musicians perform in the streets and plazas for free. In fact, some of the best musical entertainment in Canada is provided free by street musicians (buskers) and free concerts are staged in the major cities. Street music caters for all tastes, including jazz, rock, folk, blues, country and classical. The club and bar music scene thrives in Canadian cities, where most clubs have a cover charge but few are restricted to members only.

Tickets for rock concerts are available from agencies such as Ticketmaster (💻 www.ticketmaster.ca) and from local music stores.

The best sources of information about forthcoming concerts are music newspapers and magazines such as the *Georgia Strait* (Vancouver) and *Now* (Toronto). Local newspapers also list forthcoming concerts and music festivals, and free music newspapers and magazines are published in some cities. There are also several internet music magazines such as Chartattack (🖳 www.chartattack.com). Information about local concerts is also available from tourist offices.

Classical music concerts and opera and ballet performances are major social events in Canada and are regularly staged by the cream of Canadian and international performers. Concerts generally have a strong following in most cities and performances are of a high (often international) standard. The main Canadian orchestras are the internationally renowned Montreal Symphony Orchestra, the National Arts Centre Orchestra, based in Ottawa, and the Symphony Orchestras of Ottawa, Toronto and Vancouver. Many smaller towns and cities also have orchestras, including Kanata and Nepean.

The leading opera companies are the Canadian Opera Company (based at the O'Keefe Centre in Toronto), the Vancouver Opera Association and *L'Opéra de Montréal*. Canada has three internationally renowned ballet companies: the Royal Winnipeg Ballet, *Les Grand Ballets Canadiens* and the National Ballet of Canada (also based at the O'Keefe Centre in Toronto), plus the *Ballet Classique de Montréal*. Major international ballet companies perform regularly in Canada, including Moscow's Bolshoi and Kirov companies, London's Royal Ballet and the Paris Opera Ballet.

Tickets for classical music, opera and ballet performances in most cities cost from $60 to $150, although when international stars are performing you can expect to pay much more. Major Canadian orchestras may hold a winter season at their local concert hall and, when not touring, an open-air summer season. All orchestras (and ballet and opera companies) offer season or series tickets, which for many music lovers is the only way to obtain tickets. Enquire early about tickets for the coming season. Forthcoming concerts are listed in music and entertainment magazines, and local newspapers print performance details and reviews. Information can also be obtained from tourist offices.

SOCIAL CLUBS

There are numerous 'social' clubs in Canada (as used here, the term refers to any group of people who get together to share an interest), and all Canadian cities and towns have a wide range of clubs. Joining a club is an excellent way to meet new people, make social and business contacts, and be accepted into the local community. In smaller towns, social life revolves around the church and social clubs, and if you aren't a member your life can be dull. There are exclusive private clubs in the major cities where the 'old boy' network thrives, such as the Chelsea club in Ottawa. There are also posh country clubs, although these usually revolve around golf or tennis, rather than being strictly social clubs.

Popular and widespread clubs and organisations include the Royal Canadian Legion, Masons, Shriners, YWCA/YMCA, Kiwanis (who hold an annual charity fundraising 'duck' race on Ottawa's Rideau Canal), Lion and Lioness, Toastmasters, Oddfellows, the Canadian Federation of University Women and Big Brothers/Sisters (a charitable organisation that pairs adults with young children whose parents have died or are divorced). There are also a number of fraternal associations and professional organisations, many of which are ethnic, political or labour-

oriented groups with a large membership and extensive facilities.

Canada also has a variety of children's groups and clubs such as the Girl Guides (including the Sparks, Brownies and Pathfinders) and the Boy Scouts (including the Beavers and Cubs).

NIGHTLIFE

The best nightlife in Canada is, not surprisingly, found in the major cities and embraces everything from ritzy clubs with expensive floor shows to sleazy back street bars and strip joints. The most popular forms of nightlife include music bars, discos and dance clubs. The most popular discos, with amazing sound and light systems, charge an entrance fee of from around $10 and as much as they can get away with for drinks ($10 for a soft drink isn't uncommon and for cocktails the sky's the limit). Most nightclubs have bouncers on the door, whose job is to 'vet' guests and remove troublemakers from the premises.

Dress codes vary considerably depending on the venue. If you're unsure, smart casual is best (black is safest). Jeans, leather, T-shirts and trainers are usually excluded, although in some establishments these may be the perfect gear (fashion dictates). If you don't look the part, you may be excluded or may feel uncomfortable when everyone else is wearing something different, so it's best to check in advance. An up-to-date guide giving a run-down of local hot-spots is a must if you want to be seen in the best places and avoid the dives. Always check who's playing, show times and cover charges, because they often change at short notice.

> Consult local newspapers and entertainment guides for the latest information.

GAMBLING

The old 'kill-joy' attitude introduced to Canada by Presbyterian Scottish immigrants has taken a long time to die out, and it's only since the early '90s that gambling of any sort has become accepted – which isn't to say that it didn't exist before then. Now Canadians and visitors can (legally) visit casinos without having to cross the border to the US, but some of the old attitudes still linger, particularly when it comes to dress codes. Some casinos merely suggest that appropriate dress is 'smart casual', while others produce a list stating 'no blue jeans, jogging outfits, cut-offs, shorts or beachwear' and one even proclaims 'no bustiers or clothing associated with organisations known to be violent' – whatever that means! Many casinos don't allow alcohol in gambling areas and all exclude anyone under the age of 18.

The most popular forms of gambling are the games red dog, roulette, stud poker, baccarat and blackjack, and the ubiquitous slot machines. If you wish to leave with your shirt, books such as *The Everything Casino Book* by George Mandos (Media Corp. Publications), *The Idiot's Guide to Gambling like a Pro* by Stanford Wong & Susan Spector (Alpha Books), and the *Unofficial Guide to Casino Gambling* by Basil Neston (Macmillan US) may help – along with a large slice of luck!

The Canadians are lottery mad and there are umpteen national and provincial lotteries each week. The two main lotteries are Lotto 649 – or 6/49 (even Lottery Canada, 🖳 www.lotterycanada.com, cannot decide which! – so called because you need to select six numbers out of 49, and Lotto Super 7 (on Fridays). To participate, you complete an entry form at a lottery kiosk in a shopping mall or convenience store, or you can play online (at 🖳 www.canadalotteryonline.com). Tickets for 649 are $3.95 each and must be purchased by 5pm on the day of the draw (which is at 6.49pm on Wednesdays and Saturdays in each province). You can also choose a 'quick pick' option, whereby a computer selects the numbers for you. Prizes vary according to the number of tickets sold, but jackpots of $5 to $20mn aren't uncommon. Instant lotteries are also popular, where you buy a 'scratch' card for $1, $2 or $5 and can win prizes of $10,000 to $50,000.

Another popular form of gambling is the Video Lottery Terminal (VLT), a machine similar to a 'one-armed bandit' but more lucrative (usually not for the player) as it's possible to pump as much as five to ten thousand dollars into a VLT in just half an hour! They're located at racetracks, in public halls, bars, Legion clubs and convenience stores (where losing your money is more convenient!). The proceeds of VLT machines go directly to the provincial government (otherwise they would be banned).

Canada has ordinary horse racing and trotting (saddle and harness horse racing) and most cities have at least one track, although very few are open in winter (it's difficult to see horses in ten-foot snowdrifts). All legal horse race betting is based on the totaliser (tote) system, where the total amount bet on a race is divided among the winners (after the organisers and Canada Revenue Agency have taken their cuts). Bets of between $1 and $1,000 can be made. The different kinds of bets are explained in the official programme, as is the form of the horses and riders. Generally bets are the same as in other countries, although the terminology may be different. Bets can be made for a win (or 'on the nose'), a place (to come second) and to show (to come third). An 'across the board' bet is a bet on a horse to win or be placed second or third. In the major cities, illegal bookies who take bets on horses and many other things (particularly professional sports) are commonplace.

BARS

Social drinking in Canada is usually done in bars, which include cocktail bars, singles' bars, music bars, piano bars, hotel lounge bars, 'artistic' bars, business bars, ethnic bars, gay bars, neighbourhood bars, working men's bars and endless other varieties. At the bottom end of the scale are dingy, mainly men's bars, with a noisy, beer-drinking, working-class clientele, while at the other extreme there are expensive cocktail bars frequented by executives and professionals having a quiet drink after a day at the office. There are also British and Irish-style pubs with a variety of imported British and Irish beers and traditional pub games such as darts or pool, and their interpretation of 'traditional pub grub' such as shepherd's pie or Irish stew. Many bars serve excellent lunches and snacks, and most serve some kind of food (expect to pay between $5 and $15 for a platter-sized serving). A trend in cities is 'sports' bars, with numerous TVs showing a variety of live sporting events.

Those who want a quiet chat over a drink, perhaps at lunch time or after work, are likely to go to a cocktail lounge. Similar to European wine bars in decor and clientele, they're the main venue for middle-class social drinkers, particularly in large cities.

> Singles bars are cocktail bars where customers pay high prices (e.g. at least $5 for a beer) for the privilege of chatting up the opposite (or same) sex. At their best they can be good fun, although many are simply 'meat markets' where casual pick-ups are common.

Many bars are noisy places (often with live music) where people go for an expensive night out to drink, listen to music or dance. Bars with live music usually have a cover charge of between $5 and $20. There are topless bars in some areas (these aren't bars without roofs).

Other bars cater particularly to homosexuals and lesbians, so check in advance if this isn't your scene (some 'straight' bars also have gay evenings on certain days of the week). To find a gay club or bar, look for 'alternative lifestyle' advertisements in local newspapers and in the *Yellow Pages*. In Ottawa, there's a weekly newspaper called *X-Press* that contains the most comprehensive listings of what's on for people of all persuasions. Toronto's Queen Street (that's its real name!) is an acknowledged area for transvestites and gays to assemble. Like Americans, Canadians aren't usually homophobic (at least in the major cities), and Ottawa, Toronto and Vancouver all stage a Gay Pride week sanctioned by the local city councils, including a parade and exhibitions of artwork by the local gay community.

Although better than American beer, Canadian beer is fairly weak (rarely more than 5 per cent by volume) unless you ask for an 'ice' beer (with a higher alcohol level) or an extra-strong beer such as Molson's XXX, which packs 7.3 per cent alcohol by volume (Canadians say the XXX means "three beers and you're outta here!"). All beer (not just 'ice' beer) is usually served ice cold – much colder than most foreigners (except Americans and Australians) are used to. The best-known Canadian brewers are Molson, Labatt's and Carling-O'Keefe, although the tastiest beers often come from small local breweries ('microbreweries') and 'brewpubs' (where beer is brewed on the premises).

Among the most popular beers are Molson's Canadian, Golden, Oktoberfest, Export, Dry and Ice; and Labatt's Blue, Extra and Dry. In Quebec and the Atlantic provinces, locals drink non-alcoholic spruce beer, although the taste takes some getting used to. Draught beer (or beer 'on tap') is sold by the glass in bars and restaurants for around $3 for a 340ml glass (just over half a pint). When in groups, Canadians tend to buy their own drinks rather than rounds.

Like many laws in Canada, licensing hours vary with the province, but most bars, pubs and lounges open at noon and close at 1 or 2am. Laws in Quebec are more liberal, allowing bars to stay open until 3 or 4am. Large cities usually have after-hours' bars that stay open for music and dancing after regular bars close (but they stop serving alcohol).

The minimum age for drinking alcohol in Alberta, Manitoba and Quebec is 18, while in the rest of Canada it's 19. The bartender is supposed to ask your age and may ask for identification (ID), but in practice this rarely happens if you look old enough. Acceptable identification usually consists of a driving licence or a provincial 'identification card', which you can obtain from your local motor licence office. Some city bars run 'designated driver schemes', whereby the designated driver of a group of people gets free non-alcoholic drinks all night (drinking and driving is a serious offence throughout Canada – see page 190).

Generally, there's a much stricter attitude towards drunkenness in Canada than in many other countries and, if you look as if you've had one too many, you're likely to be refused service and may even be asked to leave. Business drinking is modest and disciplined and drunken behaviour is socially unacceptable and regarded with contempt (and can also get you arrested or mugged if you aren't careful).

RESTAURANTS

While the backwoods areas of Canada tend to be served only by 'family' diners (where you may get steak and chips and little else), pizza parlours and other fast-food chains, the major cities contain a plethora of restaurants, cafeterias, diners, truck-stops, cafes, delicatessens ('delis'), snack bars, lunch counters, take-away restaurants (take-outs), coffee shops and street vendors.

The country's three largest cities, Toronto, Montreal and Vancouver, are all gastronomic capitals in their own right, with thriving restaurant scenes that blend Asian influences with classical and modern European styles. Canada's chefs embrace the wealth of home-grown ingredients from Canada's abundant (often organic) farms and wild sustainable fisheries, and are at the forefront of the local, seasonal food movement that has swept North America in recent years. What better to accompany your gourmet meal than a local wine? Although little known abroad, Canada is a sleeping giant of New World wines, with over 500 wineries in nine provinces. The industry has been growing for the past 25 years and is making increasingly sophisticated wines that score highly in blind tastings. Eating and drinking are central to the Canadian experience and every food culture in the world is celebrated somewhere.

The ethnic potpourri that makes up Canada's cities is most evident in the range and variety of its eating establishments, the most common of which include Chinese (most regional styles), Italian (plus pizza parlours), Japanese (particularly sushi bars), French, Jewish, Korean, Mexican (or Tex-Mex), Thai and Vietnamese. Vancouver and Toronto have a wealth of Chinese and other Asian restaurants, while Montreal (and Quebec in general) is a Mecca for gourmets and awash with fine French restaurants and bistros. In Vancouver, the trend (as well as reflecting the tastes of the many recent Asian immigrants – it has the third-largest China town in North America) is to follow the current fads from California, whether Italian, Korean or 'fusion' cooking. Canada's ethnic restaurants are one of the joys of eating out and they do more to promote international goodwill and cross-cultural exchange in a day than the United Nations does in a year!

Some of the most 'interesting' dining experiences are found in the Atlantic provinces, where Newfoundland prides itself on such bizarre dishes as cod cheeks, capelin (tiny fish which have been pickled and smoked before being pinned to fences to dry), brewis (soaked hard-tack biscuit boiled with cod), seal flipper pie, seal soup, and moose and rabbit pie. The Atlantic provinces also offer some of the best seafood in North America, including superb lobster in New Brunswick, scallops in Nova Scotia and mussels on Prince Edward Island. British Columbia is also noted for its seafood, not least its salmon, where the annual barbecues of Pacific sockeye salmon hot-smoked over alder wood aren't to be missed.

Canadian eating places are listed in the *Yellow Pages* by specialty or national cuisine and often also by area. Whatever your preference or price range, you'll find something to your taste and pocket in Canadian cities. Local restaurant guides are available in most cities and most travel guides provide recommendations at all price levels. Local free newspapers and entertainment guides in cities and towns are packed with advertisements for restaurants and watering holes, and may contain coupons and other discounts. Your Canadian friends, colleagues, neighbours and acquaintances will usually also be glad to recommend their favourite places (and tell you where to avoid).

There's also an abundance of restaurant websites, including the Canada restaurant and bar directory (💻 www.canadarestaurantbar.com), plus many guides for the major cities such as 💻 www.torontorestaurants.com and www.vancouverrestaurantguide.net.

There are also a number of magazines published for gourmets and wine lovers including Food & Drink (💻 www.fooddrink-magazine.com), Edible Toronto (💻 www.edibletoronto.com), Vine (💻 www.vinesmag.com) and Wine Access (💻 www.wineaccess.ca).

LIBRARIES

Canada is proud of its excellent public library service and there are libraries in all cities and most towns. Most libraries in cities open from 10am to 9pm during the week and 10am to 8pm on Saturdays, and many also open on Sunday afternoons particularly in the winter (e.g. 1 to 5pm), although they may shut on Mondays. In addition to books, newspapers and magazines, libraries usually offer books on tape, videos, DVDs, large print books and books in Braille.

Membership is free or cheap for local residents. The standard loan period is three weeks and there are fines for overdue items (usually from around 30¢ per day). Books in the 'reference' section may be used on-site only, although some encyclopaedias can be borrowed – but usually for one day only. University libraries are also open to the public, although non-students aren't allowed to take books home. Inter-library loans are a common practice, although you may have to pay a small surcharge, depending upon the distance involved. All libraries have various sections, including children's, juvenile, fiction, paperbacks (soft covers) and foreign books. Public libraries in major cities have business sections and sometimes there are separate business libraries. There may also be a newspaper and magazine section.

Local libraries are one of the best sources of free information about local community services and information (e.g. housing, consumer rights, money problems, voluntary work and job search skills), public transport, clubs and organisations. Many libraries have children's centres and activities such as story-telling, films, workshops and exhibitions, and some publish a monthly schedule of events for children. Most reference libraries provide coin-operated photocopiers (some central libraries have colour laser copiers) and many provide telephones and fax facilities (or machines that accept credit cards) and free internet access, although you may need to book in advance.

Nick Foligno, Ottawa Senators' hockey player'

16. SPORTS

Canadians take their sport very seriously, both as participants and as spectators. Over half the population participates regularly in some form of physical activity and those who don't play are usually keen spectators – if only armchair fans. The top spectator sports (including TV audiences) are ice hockey, baseball, football and basketball, while the most popular participant sports include swimming, hiking, cycling and running. Other popular sports are lacrosse (a Native North American game), skiing, aerial sports, boxing, golf, fishing, motor racing, softball, tennis, bowling, athletics and watersports such as sailing and boating. Working out is popular in Canada, where many people go to gyms or have equipment at home.

The cost of using private sports facilities is high in major cities such as Toronto and Vancouver, but generally inexpensive in smaller towns. Most communities have recreational parks (ball parks) with tennis courts, a running track and a swimming pool, the use of which may be free to local residents. Many towns also have an inexpensive YMCA sports centre with a swimming pool, gymnasium, training centre, tennis and squash/racketball courts, basketball and volleyball. Courses and coaching are provided in a wide range of sports. Many community schools and municipal recreation departments organise a variety of sports classes and most large corporations have indoor gymnasiums and sports teams. For those who can afford the high membership fees, there are exclusive country clubs and health and fitness centres in all areas, catering mainly for basketball, golf, handball, racketball, squash, swimming, tennis and volleyball. Most clubs provide professional coaching and training programmes.

Canada is proud of its athletes and the federal government Sports Canada scheme has three main funding programmes: The Athlete Assistance Program (AAP), the Sport Support Program (SSP) and the Hosting Program. Many professional athletes are paid huge salaries, particularly in top sports such as ice hockey, baseball and (American) football, where star players earn astronomical sums. Most of the country's highest paid athletes are US-born, however, and there are some professional teams with only one or two Canadians. Similarly, many US ice hockey teams are propelled to stardom by their Canadian players.

The big games of the year are the Grey Cup for the Canadian Football League (CFL) at around the same time as Canadian Thanksgiving, the Stanley Cup for the National Hockey League (NHL) at the end of May or early June, and baseball's World Series, which Canadians are proud to tell you was won in 1992 and 1993 by the Toronto Blue Jays. The NHL Super Bowl is also huge in Canada, being celebrated there with as much fervour as in the US. The major TV networks compete vigorously for the TV rights to top sporting events and professional sport is dominated by TV, although the frequency of commercial breaks makes watching most TV sport a frustrating experience.

Tickets for top events can be purchased through ticket agencies such as Ticketmaster but are generally best purchased at venues. Ticket prices for a hockey game are usually from around $40, although you can pay some $400 or more for a seat at a top game. In recent years, a number of vast stadiums have opened, including the Air Canada Centre in Toronto, which replaced the Maple Leaf Gardens, and Ottawa's Corel Centre. You can obtain the latest sports results by phone from the 'talking *Yellow Pages*' (the number is listed on the inside cover of *Yellow Pages*).

AERIAL SPORTS

Aerial ('sky') sports aren't as popular in Canada as they are in the US, although there are clubs for flying light aircraft, gliding, microlighting, hang-gliding, paragliding, para-sailing and ballooning in all the major cities and also in many smaller towns. Parachute jumping and sky diving are also popular, as is hot-air ballooning, although a one-hour ride in a two-man balloon costs around $250. Balloons are launched either early in the morning or just before sundown, when the winds are at their lightest. One of the largest annual balloon events in Canada is held in September in the Gatineau Hills north of Ottawa. It's a three-day festival and attracts balloonists from around the world, who come to show off their skills and amazing balloons, which may include a 150ft rabbit in a magician's hat, a bunch of carrots (these two are often seen together!), a brown bear, an eagle, tropical fish, the *Yellow Pages* directory, a castle, pink elephants, a T-Rex, the Statue of Liberty and a Mountie on a horse!

A directory of non-profit flying clubs in Alberta, British Columbia, Manitoba and Ontario is at 💻 http://flying-club.org/fc/fco_ca.asp.

BASEBALL

Although predominantly a US sport, baseball is also played in Canada but the country has only one team in the US major leagues, the Toronto Blue Jays (American League), who won the World Series Championship in 1992 and 1993. (Canada used to have two teams in the US major leagues, but in 2004 the Montreal Expos franchise moved to Washington DC.) The season runs from April to early October, when games are often played under floodlights. The Blue Jays (💻 http://toronto.bluejays.mlb.com) have their own enormous stadium, the Skydome in Toronto. There are also minor league teams in Canada, e.g. the Vancouver Canadians (💻 www.canadiansbaseball.com), who play in the Northwest League.

> In October, the top two teams in the American and National leagues compete against each other in the 'play-offs' to decide who will contest the World Series (established in 1903), played over seven games.

A baseball field is diamond-shaped, with a base at each corner. Each team of nine players takes it in turn to bat while the other team fields. One player bats, striking at the ball with a hard wooden bat, then scores runs by dashing from base to base while the fielders try to get him out by catching the ball before it touches the ground or by throwing the ball to a base before the batter reaches it. The man who throws the ball (from a raised 'pitcher's mound' in the centre of the diamond) is called the pitcher, and the man who stands behind the batter in the hope of catching the ball if he misses it (wearing a vast leather mitt and protective clothing) is called the catcher (what else?).

Obviously the game is much more complicated than that, and it usually takes foreigners some time (around ten years!) to understand baseball, which has a language all of its own, with many terms that have found their way into everyday speech, such as 'strike out' (to fail). Other terms include walk, bull pen, curve ball, shut-out, no-hitter, perfect game, chopper, foul out and many more. Niceties such as batting and run averages lead to much discussion among fans. For those seeking more information, there are numerous baseball books in libraries and bookshops. Watching a baseball game is an interesting day out, even if you haven't a clue what's going on. The crowds are hugely entertaining and fans are usually friendly and sociable.

Games usually last two to three hours and are normally played in the evening. Ticket prices have risen in recent years and start at around $20, with some tickets available on the day of the game; 'bleacher' seats (exposed to the sun and farthest away from the field) are the cheapest. When you buy a ticket for a baseball game that's 'called' (postponed), e.g. due to a 'rainout', you're entitled to a free ticket for another game (the origin of the term 'raincheck').

As with ice hockey (see below), there are also many 'farm' teams. College, high school and little league baseball (played by children from the age of seven to their teens) are hugely popular. Like professional teams, minor league teams are sponsored by companies who pay to have their name emblazoned on the players' jerseys. It costs around $100 to equip a child to play baseball, most of it going on a baseball glove (from around $50).

CANADIAN FOOTBALL

Canadian football is virtually the same as American football, the main differences being that the field is slightly larger (328 by 153ft/100 by 46.6m as opposed to 300 by 120ft/91.4 by 36.6m) and there are 12 instead of 11 players. There are only three 'downs' instead of the American four and there are other differences in the permitted movements of players and the times allowed between plays, all of which help to produce a faster and higher-scoring game, with ties often decided by last-minute efforts or even in overtime. In recent years, American football has gained popularity in Europe, where TV has brought the game to a wider international audience, while Canadian football has been struggling for media and spectator support.

Although Canadian football is played in America, it hasn't expanded as hoped. If anything, its popularity is falling due to a number of franchise failures. In 1997, one of the most popular Canadian teams, the Ottawa Rough Riders, was forced to close its doors; they were replaced by the Ottawa Renegades in 2002 who were suspended in 2006 (a new Ottawa team is expected to be formed in 2010).

The Canadian Football League (CFL, 💻 www.cfl.ca) is divided into two divisions, the West (BC Lions, Calgary Stampeders, Edmonton Eskimos, Saskatchewan Roughriders) and the East (Hamilton Tiger-Cats, Montréal Alouettes, Toronto Argonauts and Winnipeg Blue Bombers). Some teams are owned by communities and others privately. The culmination of the football season is the Grey Cup, which is televised nationally and attracts one of the biggest TV audiences of the year. The student equivalent is the Vanier Cup, administered by the Canadian Intercollegiate Athletic Union and contested by student teams organised into four leagues across the country.

Foreigners brought up on a diet of soccer or rugby may initially find Canadian football complicated, slow and boring. However, once you learn the rules and strategy (like chess, with feints to throw your opponents off guard), you'll probably find it a fascinating and exciting sport. Despite the heavy protective clothing, serious injuries are common, most caused by the widespread use of artificial turf, which has replaced safer natural grass in many stadiums. Somewhat surprisingly, the heavy physical exchanges rarely dissolve into violence and the behaviour of players is usually exemplary. Tickets for games cost between $25 and $75.

If you don't know the difference between a field goal and a field vole you may wish to read *The Complete Idiot's Guide to Understanding Football like a Pro* by Joe Theismann with Brian Tracy (Alpha Books).

CLIMBING

Those who find hiking a bit tame may like to try abseiling (rappelling), rock-climbing, mountaineering or caving (spelunking). Although experienced high-altitude mountaineers may not find Canada's mountains sufficiently demanding, they offer plenty of challenges for less experienced climbers. If you're a novice, it's wise to attend a course at a mountaineering or mountain school before heading for the hills. There are climbing schools in all the main climbing areas, providing basic to advanced ice, snow and rock climbing courses lasting from one day to several weeks. Most clubs have indoor training apparatus (e.g. a climbing wall) for aspiring mountaineers, which allow you to practise your skills and learn new techniques.

Many climbers are killed each year in Canada, with Mount Robson in British Columbia claiming the most lives. Most victims are inexperienced and reckless, and many more climbers owe their survival to rescuers who risk their own lives to rescue them.

Caution

It's extremely foolish, not to mention highly dangerous, to venture into the mountains (or caves) without an experienced guide, proper preparation, excellent physical condition, sufficient training and the appropriate equipment.

CYCLING

Cycling has enjoyed a surge in popularity in recent years, due to the interest in health and exercise and the creation of cycle tracks (bike paths) in the major cities. Sport cycling is seasonal in Canada, where the length of the season varies, depending on the province. Many Canadian cyclists use mudguards (fenders) to get through rain showers but the first snowfall shuts down the cycling season. Only some 2 per cent of Canadian adults use bicycles for transport and most cycling is done for enjoyment, exercise and competition, rather than as a means of getting from A to B.

Competitive cycling includes road and track racing, cycle speedway, time-trials, cross-country racing, touring, bicycle polo, mountain bike racing, downhill racing and bicycle moto-cross (BMX) for children. Bicycle touring is popular and many couples take to the road on tandems. The Tour du Canada (www.tourducanada.com) is Canada's premier annual cycle race organised by Cycle Canada (www.cyclecanada.com), who also organise many other races and events.

Most Canadian cities aren't particularly bicycle-friendly because the road network is dedicated to the automobile as in the US, although federal and provincial governments are trying to encourage cycling and there are programmes similar to the US 'bike path' and 'bike lane' programmes. However, most cities have a network of outlying bicycle paths where you can enjoy cycling without risking your life. Outside the cities, there's plenty of good cross-country cycling with lots of open roads, although when cycling on narrow roads you should beware of traffic.

Around 40 per cent of Canadians own a bicycle and some 1.5mn are bought annually. Mountain bikes are the sales leader, followed by 'hybrid' and city bikes and racing (road) bikes. There are three main Canadian bicycle manufacturers: Raleigh, Victoria Precision and Procycle (made under licence from Peugeot). Expensive bikes such as Trek and Cannondale are imported from the US, while the cheapest are imported from China or Taiwan (Rocky Mountain and Norco are the major importers). Ten-speed touring bikes (e.g. Bridgestone or Schwinn) are the most common, and cost from around $250 new, while a reasonable quality mountain or hybrid bike costs around $300.

Advertisements in *Pedal Magazine* (see below) tell you where to find the best prices. Buying by mail order or on the internet is common but you won't receive the same service as from a neighbourhood bicycle shop. Before buying a bicycle, you should obtain expert advice (e.g. from a specialist cycle store) and ensure that you buy a bike with the correct frame size. It's best to avoid the cheapest bikes that are sold by mass market stores (known as 'gas-pipe' bikes on account of the low quality steel tubing used to construct the frames). If you're on a tight budget and are comfortable doing your own repairs, you may wish to consider a second-hand bike. Check the classified ads in the local newspapers.

Bicycle brakes are sometimes the reverse of what's found in other countries, e.g. right-hand brake for the rear wheel and left-hand for the front wheel, and some brakes operate on the rear wheel by pedalling backwards (it's a good idea to work this out before entering the Tour du Canada!).

Most Canadian cyclists wear approved cycling helmets, which are mandatory in some provinces both on and off-road, in order to protect riders in the event of an accident.

The Canadian Cycling Association (💻 www.canadian-cycling.com) publishes *Pedal Magazine* and the *Complete Guide to Cycling in Canada*, and provides a wealth of information on touring, recreational and competitive cycling. The leading Canadian bicycle clubs include the Elbow Valley Cycle Club (Alberta, 💻 www.elbowvalleycc.org), and the Vancouver Bicycle Club (💻 www.vbc.bc.ca). See also Atlantic Pedaler (💻 www.atlanticpedaler.com), Canadian Cyclist (💻 www.canadiancyclist.com), Canada Trails (💻 www.canadatrails.ca), for MTB trails, and Momentum Planet (💻 www.momentumplanet.ca).

There are many books about cycling in Canada, including *Cycling the Great Divide* (McCoy), *Easy Cycling Around Vancouver* (Greystone Books) and *Freewheeling: The Story of Bicycling in Canada* (The Boston Mills Press). Cycle magazines include *Pedal* magazine (💻 www.pedalmag.com), with in-depth product and bicycle reviews and an annual buyer's guide, and *Vélo Mag* (💻 www.velomag.com – in French), which is devoted to touring, mountain biking and racing, and includes guides to day-long and multi-day rides in Quebec. Touring maps are available from the Canadian Cycling Association (see above) or from the Adventure Cycling Association (150 East Pine Street/PO Box 8308, Missoula, MT 59807, USA, ☎ 1-800-755 2453, 💻 www.adventurecycling.org).

FISHING

Canada's inland waterways and lakes are an angler's paradise, particularly the thousands of lakes in the north, where trout, walleye and northern pike grow to a huge size (the latter up to six feet). In the vast rivers that run north into the Arctic ocean, the Arctic char (a cousin of the salmon) is a popular quarry. In contrast, in certain rivers and waters along the Atlantic and Pacific coasts, some salmon species are becoming rare and there are strict catch limits or even fishing bans. However, not all salmon species or rivers are threatened and the rules governing catch limits change frequently, so you need to check locally to find out the current situation.

In general the fishing season extends from the thaw in mid-April until October. Angling for some fish is regulated by season, and in some areas 'catch-and-release' fishing is enforced. All regulations are precisely formulated to preserve stocks, and there are strictly enforced seasons and limits for all freshwater and some saltwater fish (although fishing for some saltwater species is unrestricted and permitted year round).

Ice fishing is also popular in many provinces, and consists of fishing through a hole in the ice from inside a 'fish-house' (a wooden hut on the ice), which isn't quite as cold as it sounds because wood-burning stoves keep you and your lunch warm. Essential equipment includes a giant 'corkscrew' to make the 'fishing hole' in the ice, thermal underwear, a balaclava, several sweaters, gloves and a fleecy 'overall'. The most popular ice-fishing lakes turn into little villages in winter, with anything up to 2,000 fish-houses.

There are fishing charter companies in all areas, many of which fly clients to private lakes to seek out their favourite catch. Most operate in northern Ontario and Quebec, but enthusiasts with several days to spare can go further afield.

Fishing in Canada is regulated either by local governments or tribes, and you must have the appropriate licence, which costs around $30 (much less than the minimum $100 fine for being caught fishing without one). Information about local fishing spots and contests is provided in local newspapers and available from local fish and game authorities, marinas, and bait and tackle stores.

There are many books on fishing, including *First Cast* by Phil Genova, *Fly Fishing for Dummies* by Peter Kaminsky and *Lake Fishing: Best of BC* by Karl Bruhn (Whitecap Books). Useful websites include www.fishingcanada.com, www.fishingincanada.com and www.sportfishingcanada.ca.

GOLF

Golf is a popular sport in Canada, where you don't need to be a millionaire to play (unless you plan to spend all day at the '19th hole'). In addition to the many expensive private golf courses and complexes, usually restricted to members or residents only, there are many public courses, ranging from 3 to 18 holes.

Membership isn't required to play on a public golf course, although it's wise to book in advance (sometimes it's mandatory). In some areas, private clubs are open to non-members ('green fee' golfers), although you usually need a handicap card and access may be restricted or barred at weekends, on federal holidays and during tournaments.

Annual membership of a Canadian 'country' or golf club costs at least $2,000 per year and can be much more. You must also find several current members to sponsor you as a new member and club privileges may need to be earned by a points system or by doing duty on a committee planning an event. You can expect to pay around $40 per round at a public course, which is invariably not as well-groomed as a private course, plus around $35 per day for an electric buggy (cart). Lessons are available at most clubs from around $40 for half an hour. Many clubs have driving ranges, practice greens, bunkers (sand traps) and a pro shop.

For information about golf in Canada, consult the relevant *Tee-Off Guide* (there are separate guides for Alberta, British Columbia and Manitoba/Saskatchewan, www.tee-off.ca) or *The Great Golf Courses of Canada* by John Gordon & Michael French (Warwick Publishing).

For further information about golf in Canada, see www.canadagolfguide.com, www.golfcanada.com, www.golfcanadaswest.com and www.golfincanada.ca.

GYMNASIUMS & HEALTH CLUBS

There are gymnasiums (gyms) and health and fitness clubs in most towns in Canada, that are often combined with sports or racket clubs (e.g. tennis and squash). In addition to fully-equipped gymnasiums, health clubs may also offer swimming pools, jogging tracks, and aerobics and keep-fit classes. Most health clubs are mixed, with a variety of membership levels depending on the facilities you wish to use, e.g. gym and exercise rooms only or gym plus squash or tennis. Most health and fitness clubs have facilities such as saunas, solariums, Jacuzzis, steam baths, whirlpools and massage, and many have a childcare service.

Some health and sports clubs operate a number of centres, e.g. city-wide or in a number of cities, and members can usually use the facilities at any centre. The cost of membership at a private club varies considerably depending on the area, the facilities provided and the local competition (some offer reduced rates for couples or family membership). Clubs are usually open seven days a week from around 6am until 9 or 10pm Mondays to Fridays, with shorter opening hours on Saturdays and Sundays (when some clubs are closed). All clubs provide a free trial and assessment and produce personal training programmes.

Many top class hotels have health clubs and swimming pools that may be open to the public, although access may be restricted to residents at certain times. Fitness classes are organised by local community schools, and some municipal swimming pools have gymnasiums and exercise facilities that can be used free of charge by local residents.

HIKING

Hiking is popular in Canada, not least because it has some of the most dramatic and unspoiled hiking country in the world. This includes millions of acres of national and provincial parks (see page 255), all with marked hiking trails, ranging from easy nature hikes to long-distance trails in the back-country. Each province and region boasts vast areas of outstanding natural beauty, the most popular being the Rockies; the wooded areas of Quebec and the Atlantic provinces are also exceptionally beautiful. Newfoundland's Gros Morne (French for 'Big Gloomy') National Park is a fascinating 500mn year old tableland of mountains with superb coastal trails, scenic waterfalls and landlocked fjords, although there are few plants due to the high magnesium levels in the rocks. Summer and early autumn are the best times to hike, because spring comes late and trails in mountainous areas are often snowbound until June or July.

If you're hiking in national or provincial parks and camping or sleeping rough, you may require a permit and should obtain information about weather conditions and general information about your planned route. In some parks and forests there's a system of hosted 'huts' for hikers, usually located around one day's hiking distance apart. Inexpensive accommodation is also available in many hiking areas in lodges and camps.

There are numerous hiking and mountain clubs in all areas, many of which maintain their own mountain lodges, publish guidebooks and produce books about local wildlife and other topics. Most parks provide free hiking and trail information, and details about accessible trails for those with mobility problems.

If you're taking a long trip, you should evaluate your fitness and equipment before you leave; once in the back-country there's no way out except on foot, so make sure that your boots are comfortable and that you understand the risks you're taking. Take a beacon (which sends out a homing signal) so you can be found even if you fall unconscious or become buried under snow. You can also 'heli-hike', although not in the National Parks, where it's forbidden. Like heli-skiing, you're taken into the wilderness by a helicopter and collected at the end of your hike (you hope!). You should leave a detailed itinerary of a long hike with someone and give them an estimated time by which you'll contact them to confirm that you're okay. If you fail to contact them within the specified period, they should alert the authorities to start looking for you.

Mountain or hill-walking shouldn't be confused with 'ordinary' hiking, as it's generally done at much higher altitudes and in more difficult terrain, and should be attempted only with an experienced leader. It can be dangerous for the untrained or inexperienced, and should be approached with much the same caution and preparation as mountain climbing.

There's currently a project to create a multi-use (walking, cycling, horseback riding, cross-country skiing and snowmobiling) trail across Canada, paid for by donations from private citizens and organisations. For a (tax deductible) donation of $50, your name goes on the roll of honour as having paid for a metre of the trail. The total length of the trail will eventually be around 11,234mi (18,078km), and in spring 2009 over 70 per cent had been completed. For more information or to make a donation contact the Trans Canada Trail Foundation (43 Westminster Avenue North, Montreal, QC H4X 1Y8, ☎ 1-800-465 3636, 💻 www.tctrail.ca).

The Sierra Club of Canada (421-1 Nicholas Street, Ottawa, ON K1N 7B7, ☎ 1-888-810 4204, 💻 www.sierraclub.ca), which is associated with the American Sierra Club, is Canada's premier hiking and environmental organisation. Members (who must 'donate' at least $20) receive the quarterly Canadian magazine *Scan*, in addition to a newsletter from their local chapter.

Orienteering, which is a combination of hiking and a treasure hunt (or competitive navigation on foot), is also popular in Canada. It's unnecessary to be super fit and is fun for the whole family. The only equipment that's required (in addition to suitable walking attire) is a detailed map and a compass. If you're an inexperienced hiker, you may wish to attend a course in backpacking and learn how to handle yourself in the wilderness. Orienteering is taught in high schools as part of gym lessons, so that students know how to use a compass and can find their way out if they get lost in the wilderness. Orienteering courses are run by a number of organisations, including Outward Bound Canada (996 Chetwynd Rd, RR#2, Burk's Falls, Ontario P0A 1C0, ☎ 1-888-688 9273, 💻 www.outwardbound.ca).

There are dozens of books about hiking in Canada, including *The Complete Guide to Walking in Canada: Includes Day-Hiking and Backpacking* by Elliott Katz (Firefly Books), *Frommer's Canada: With the Best Hiking & Outdoor Adventures* by Donald Olson & Hilary Davidson (Frommers) and *Hiking Canada's Great Divide Trail* by Dustin Lynx (Rocky Mountain Publishing).

HUNTING

Hunting is extremely popular in Canada, where it isn't the preserve of the wealthy or upper classes as in some countries. Hunting is prohibited in Canada's national and provincial parks, game reserves and adjacent areas, and guns are strictly forbidden in these areas. The game available includes bear, caribou, moose, elk, deer, wild hog, bighorn sheep, rabbit, raccoon, opossum, coyote, nutria, skunk, beaver, squirrel and game birds, e.g. partridge, pheasant, grouse, wild turkey, waterfowl, quail, goose and duck.

You can hunt big game during certain seasons only (which may be limited to a month for moose). You must generally be aged 16 or over to hunt big game, although younger people are often permitted to hunt small game. You must pass a three-day Hunter Education Course costing around $100 and obtain a hunting licence from the authorities in the province or territory where you plan to hunt. Fees usually vary with the location and the prey. You should expect to pay around $40 for a licence to hunt moose, $35 for a bear/deer licence and $20 for small game and birds. You receive a tag with your licence that must be attached to the carcass, and there are very large fines (up to $100,000) and jail sentences (up to two years) for killing an animal for which you don't have a licence. You're usually restricted to one deer or moose only.

Hunting regulations vary from province to province; links to the relevant provincial websites can be found on the website of the Wildlife Research Centre (💻 www.wildlife.com/regulations/tabid/81/default.aspx). Further information can be found on the Natural Resources Canada website (💻 www.nrcan.gc.ca), the ministry responsible for hunting in Canada.

▲ Caution

Note that some animals and birds, such as Canada Geese, are protected and there's a huge fine for killing them.

ICE HOCKEY

Ice hockey (called simply 'hockey' in Canada, where hockey played on grass is called field hockey and isn't a major sport) was invented in Canada in 1879 and is the world's fastest game and the major sporting passion of Canadians. It's so popular and the gear such a common sight that you could get on a bus wearing a goalie's pads and helmet and hardly anyone would give you a second look (but don't go into a bank with a face mask on, as they may think you're planning to rob it). Canada produces around 65 per cent of North America's ice hockey players, most of the rest coming from Europe.

The National Hockey League or NHL (💻 www.nhl.com) was formed in 1917 and in 2008 consisted of 30 teams, only six of which were Canadian. Teams are divided into two 'conferences', Western and Eastern, each of which has three divisions. Three of the Canadian teams, the Calgary Flames, Edmonton Oilers and Vancouver Canucks, play in the Northwest Division of the Western

Conference, the other three, the Montréal Canadiens, Ottawa Senators and Toronto Maple Leafs [*sic*] in the Northeast Division of the Eastern Conference.

The NHL season starts in October and finishes in May, during which teams play over 90 games, culminating in the play-offs for the Stanley Cup (played over a seven-game series). The Stanley Cup was an all-Canadian affair from 1893 to 1917, when it was strictly an amateur competition. In 1917 the National Hockey Association disbanded and the NHL was born, thus creating the 'modern' era of the Stanley Cup. In the 90 competitions from 1918 to 2008 (there was no 2005 competition because of the NHL 'lockout'), Canadian teams have won the cup 50 times, the most successful sides being the Montréal Canadiens, with 24 wins, and the Toronto Maple Leafs with 13, although no Canadian side has won since 1992.

Six players from each side are permitted on the ice at any time, but substitutions are allowed throughout a game, so players are constantly changing. There's a centre, free to roam all over the ice and the team's most important player and goal scorer, two wingmen, two defence men and a goalie (who's well padded to protect him from injury, the puck being struck at up to 130mph/210kph). The referees (there are two) call the two centres to 'centre ice' where the puck is dropped and the game begins.

Although games are meant to consist of three 20-minute periods, the clock is stopped each time there's a pause in play and games usually last around three hours. Hockey is often a violent sport, with body-checking and players striking each other with their sticks almost as often as they hit the puck (hence the joke "I went to a fight and a hockey game broke out"). Punch-ups are an integral part of the 'game', although there can be severe penalties for the guilty parties.

Tickets for NHL hockey games are expensive, starting from around $30 for ordinary games and rising to $2,000 (if you can get one) for the Stanley Cup final. They are often provided by companies as a perk for key employees and business associates.

Every school or small town has a junior team, which takes part in local leagues. Minor league or college teams are often referred to as 'farm' teams because they provide the talent for the NHL teams. There are even women's teams that play in their own amateur leagues. The first women's world championship was held in 1990 and there was a women's hockey tournament in the 1998 Winter Olympics. Canada won the gold medals for both men's and women's hockey at the 2002 Winter Olympics in Salt Lake City, the cause of much patriotic pride (the women retained their title in 2006, while the men didn't finish in the top three).

Enthusiasts may like to visit the Hockey Hall of Fame in Toronto (30 Yonge Street, Toronto, ON M5E 1X8, ☎ 416-360 7735, 💻 www.hhof.com). There's a wealth of books about hockey, including *Hockey for Dummies* for the uninitiated, the *Hockey Annual* by Murray Townsend (Warwick Publishers), which chronicles the events of the last season and speculates on forthcoming trends and player profiles, and *A Day in the Life of the NHL* (Harper Collins Press).

JOGGING & RUNNING

Competitive running has a strong following in Canada and jogging is extremely popular in the summer (jogging on snow and ice isn't as popular). There are usually marked jogging trails (many with exercise stations en route) in towns and cities, although you may have to compete for space with roller-bladers, skateboarders and cyclists. Races are organised throughout the year in all areas, from fun runs (and walks) of a few miles up to half and full marathons, mostly to raise money for charity (many are sponsored by the Dairy Bureau of Canada). It costs between $10 and $25 to enter fun runs, for which you receive a commemorative T-shirt (and aching feet!). At some events, participants are required to obtain sponsors. Ottawa hosts the National Capital Marathon each May and Toronto stages a marathon in September. There are running clubs in all major cities, most of which organise an extensive calendar of races, clinics and running classes.

Websites of interest to runners include 💻 www.canadarunningseries.com, www.runningmania.com, www.runningroom.com and www.time-to-run.com/canada.

LACROSSE

Lacrosse is Canada's official national sport, but it doesn't compare with hockey in popularity. North America's oldest organised sport, lacrosse was invented by the Algonquin Indians of the St Lawrence valley, who called it *baggataway* or *tewaarathon* and played it as part of a ceremonial religious rite, starting each game with rituals and dances. Lacrosse is more popular on the west coast, although there are some enthusiasts in parts of Ontario. It's played with a stick like a broom handle with a long thin net made from woven leather at one end in which the hard rubber ball is carried and passed between players (the original sticks were thought to look like a bishop's crozier, hence the French name 'la crosse').

A lacrosse field has boundaries set 13ft (4m) inside any obstacles, such as trees, bushes or stands, the ideal playing area being 361 by 210ft (110 by 64m). Goal lines are marked at each end of the field, 302ft (92m) apart, and there's at least 30ft (9m) of playing space behind each goal line. As no physical contact is permitted, players wear no protective headgear, facemasks or padded gloves, with the exception of the goalie. As in ice-hockey, the object is to get the ball into the opposing team's net.

A men's lacrosse team consists of ten players: Three in attack (offence), three in midfield, three defence and a goalkeeper.

Substitutions are permitted and are essential, particularly for the midfielders, who must cover a huge area. The defence and the attacking players normally restrict their play to half the field, while the goalie operates mainly in the area around the goal. Men's games consist of four, 25-minute periods known as 'quarters' and the winning team is the one that scores the most goals at the end of the game. Tied games are decided by two five-minute overtime periods, followed by 'sudden death' periods of four minutes, during which the first team to score wins the game.

Women's lacrosse teams have 12 players, including the goalkeeper; the others can play anywhere on the field. The playing time is 25 minutes each half, with a 10-minute break between halves. There's also an indoor version of lacrosse, played by a seven-person team in the same space as is occupied by an indoor (field) hockey arena.

Further information can be obtained from the Canadian Lacrosse Association (2211 Riverside Drive, Suite B-4, Ottawa, ON K1H 7X5, ☎ 613-260 2028, 💻 www.lacrosse.ca).

MOTOR SPORTS

Motor sports have a large following in Canada and attract more spectators than any other sport. Events embrace everything from single-seat 'formula' racing to stock car and drag racing. Most major events are held from spring to autumn at purpose-built tracks and occasionally on (closed) public roads. Among the most important races are the Indy races in Toronto (June) and Vancouver (September), which are part of the CART IndyCar World Series of races for single-seat cars, the North American equivalent of the international Formula One Grand Prix series.

However, the most popular form of motor racing is stock car racing, which is a professional sport and attracts many of Canada's and America's best drivers. Unlike in most other countries, Canadian stock cars aren't old wrecks but highly modified production line models capable of 200mph (321kph), and races are held at specially built tracks. Stock car racing in Canada is run under the auspices of North American Stock Car Auto Racing (NASCAR).

Other popular motor sports include demolition derbies (where the aim is simply to outlast the other cars), drag racing, where cars reach 100mph (161kph) in two or three seconds and approach a top speed of 300mph (482kph), and off-road driving, for which you can buy special (expensive) off-road vehicles.

The dates and venues of all Canadian motor sport events and racing calendars are published in various magazines, including Inside Track (💻 www.insidetracknews.com), *Performance Racing News* (💻 www.prnmag.com) and *Stock Car Racing* (💻 www.stockcarracing.com). A 'race track locator' can be found on 💻 www.na-motorsports.com/tracks, the premier motorsport website.

RACKET SPORTS

There are excellent facilities in Canada for most racket sports, particularly tennis, squash and racketball; badminton is generally played only at high school level. Most outdoor tennis courts are clay or hard (i.e. asphalt or cement), while indoor courts may be synthetic (e.g. AstroTurf) or hard. There are many public tennis courts in city parks, and many communities have municipal courts that can be used for a small fee by local residents. Courts are often available on a first-come, first-served basis and it may not be possible to book. Annual or season tickets are required in some towns and are inexpensive, e.g. from $75 per year for adults, with reductions of up to 50 per cent for senior citizens, students and juniors. Non-permit holders can play on some public courts for an hourly or daily rate.

There are numerous private tennis clubs in cities and rural areas, and some top-class hotels also have tennis courts that can be rented by non-residents. The cost of hiring a court at a private club is much higher than that of a public court. Some private tennis clubs also incorporate health and fitness clubs, where tennis membership entitles members to use all the club's facilities. Most private clubs have resident professionals and some tennis centres and clubs specialise in tennis packages and coaching by top pros. Tennis instruction is also provided at local clubs by certified trainers.

Tennis camps are held in many cities during the summer months, costing from around $150 per week. Most tennis camps and clinics are intended for reasonably fit and serious beginners or 'improvers', and aren't for those who play just a few social games of doubles each year. Whatever course of lessons you sign up for, you should ensure that they're designed to match your ability and fitness (which applies to all sports instruction).

For further information, contact the relevant governing bodies: Racquetball Canada (💻 www.racquetball.ca), Squash Canada (💻 www.squash.ca) and Tennis Canada (💻 www.tenniscanada.com).

SKIING & OTHER SNOW SPORTS

Skiing is one of the biggest participant sports in Canada, which has the most reliable skiing conditions in the world, and is one of the top destinations for experienced skiers. The Rockies are considered best for downhill skiing (good powder!), while eastern Canada, with its drier, wetter and heavier snow, is good for cross-country skiing (see below). The Canadian ski season lasts from October or mid-November until May or even June in some areas, and most resorts are extremely busy over Christmas, New Year and Easter. During these periods it's usually necessary to book well in advance (or better still, avoid them altogether). Queues (line-ups), although practically unknown in some resorts, are orderly, and staff everywhere are usually friendly and helpful (a pleasant change from some European resorts).

Most resorts provide a variety of sports and leisure facilities, including cross-country skiing, snow-cat skiing, bob-sledding, snowmobiling (see below), ice-skating, swimming (heated indoor and outdoor pools), racket sports, horse-riding, rock and ice climbing, and hot-air ballooning. Other diversions may include sleigh rides, dog-sledding, snowshoe tours, natural hot springs and snowmobile tours. Most resort hotels and inns have saunas, Jacuzzis, steam baths and hot tubs, and many have their own health clubs, fitness rooms, gymnasiums and aerobics and games rooms, all of which are usually free to residents. Most resorts lack good mountain restaurants, although there's usually no shortage of self-service cafeterias.

Skiing is less expensive in Canada than in the US, and even with rented equipment and lift passes, you should be able to have a day's skiing for no more than around $100 (unless you go to Whistler, Canada's answer to Aspen, Colorado, where the beautiful people go to ski and be seen). Canada will host the 2010 Winter Olympics, known as the Vancouver 2010 Olympic and Paralympic Winter Games (🖳 www.vancouver2010.com), for which Whistler will be the showpiece venue.

Winter ski lift passes (2008-09) cost from around $25 ($75.95 in Lake Louise and $55 in Whistler) per day for 'adults' (18 and over), from $15 for children aged around 6-12 (Lake Louise $24.95, Whistler $27) and from $20 for youths aged 13-17 and seniors aged over 65+ (Lake Louise $52.75, Whistler $47), while passes for those under five are usually free. Costs vary with the size of the skiing area and the number of lifts, and are usually lower on weekdays than at weekends. Half-day passes are also available and some resorts (e.g. Whistler) also offer late afternoon and sightseeing tickets. Package deals including transport, lodging and lift tickets for a period of several days or weeks reduce the overall cost considerably. Skis, boots and poles can be hired from around $30 per day for adults, slightly less for children under 13.

In many resorts there are special deals to attract skiers at the beginning and end of the season, sometimes including free skiing for women. Most resorts offer discounted passes (see above) for senior citizens (usually those aged between 65 and 70) and free passes for those aged 70 or over. The latest fees and special offers can be found on resort websites, e.g. 🖳 www.skibanff.com, www.skilouise.com and www.whistlerblackcomb.com.

Accommodation and amenities in the major resorts are superb, and comfort, service and attention to detail are second to none. Most resorts have a huge range of accommodation, including hotels and inns, self-catering 'aparthotels', studios, apartments and condominiums.

If you're taking your family, you may find it best to choose a resort with a centralised lift system on one mountain, making it easier to get together for lunch or at the end of the day. Most resorts have excellent facilities for children, including a wide range of non-skiing entertainments.

All major resorts have ski schools, many of which teach the Graduated Length Method (GLM), the North American equivalent of the French *ski évolutif* (which starts beginners on skis around three feet long). Most nursery and children's ski schools provide all-day supervision, although some require parents to collect their children for lunch. Many resorts provide a nursery for children aged from two months to three years and children's ski school (usually ages 3 to 12), which may include lunch and lunchtime supervision. Babysitters are also available in most resorts.

If you're an advanced skier, it's best to choose a multi-centre area of two or three resorts because even the largest Canadian ski areas are small compared with the many linked areas in Europe. Even many intermediate skiers find that they can ski most of the runs (trails) in the majority of Canadian resorts in about five days. Most resorts have a variety of graded runs for all standards, from beginner to expert. Black runs may be graded as single diamond (steep) or double diamond (help!). Many resorts also have illuminated runs for night skiing.

Skiing varies from immaculately groomed 'freeway' runs to challenging off-piste (back-country) skiing. Off-piste skiing is strictly controlled and areas are usually clearly marked. If you're an experienced off-piste skier (and rich), you can go heli-skiing in some areas, which entails renting a helicopter to reach virgin areas. You can expect to pay $3,000 or more for the helicopter, a guide and four nights' accommodation. Among the companies offering heli-skiing are Selkirk Tangiers Helicopter Skiing (Revelstoke, BC – www.selkirk-tangiers.com) and TLH Heli-Skiing (Whistler area, BC – www.tlhheliskiing.com).

Caution

Off-piste skiing is dangerous due to the risk of avalanches (particularly in the west) and all off-piste skiers must wear avalanche beacons and attend survival seminars.

Skiing in Canadian (and US) resorts is generally much more regulated than in Europe and to avoid crowding, some resorts restrict the number of passes sold. Stewards armed with walkie-talkies are posted everywhere and, if you ski recklessly you're given a warning; repeat offenders lose their ski lift passes. Not surprisingly, resort owners are keen to avoid accidents and all skiers should have personal liability insurance (in addition to accident and health insurance). Almost all lifts are chair-lifts (double, triple and quadruple) because most mountains aren't high enough to need cable cars.

The best skiing in the east is in Newfoundland (e.g. Marble Mountain, which has the highest snowfall in eastern North America at over 200ft/60m annually) and Quebec (e.g. Mont Tremblant, Mont Sainte Anne and Mont Saint Saveur). There's a wealth of resorts to choose from in the west, including Jasper, Banff and Lake Louise (all Alberta); and Blackcomb/Whistler, Big White, Sun Peaks, Cypress Mountain and Grouse Mountain (all British Columbia). The combined resort of Blackcomb and Whistler (www.whistlerblackcomb.com) is reckoned by many to be the best in North America (or the world), although its steep gradients and long runs aren't suitable for beginners. There's also good skiing in dozens of smaller resorts, and superb skiing over the border in the States.

Snowboarding has become a fashionable sport in recent years, particularly among the young, trendy set – nicknamed the 'teenage death dwarfs' by one commentator because of the danger to skiers as they hurtle down the slopes and try tricks like 'the flip'. Snowboarding is much like surfing and is said to be easier to learn than skiing; experts reckon it shouldn't take more than three days to become competent. Snowboards aren't permitted on all ski runs, although many resorts (in recognition of the potential of this market) offer special 'parks' for snowboarders. If you want to get off the beaten track, some heli-ski operators offer snowboarding packages.

Although *après-ski* entertainment in Canada isn't always up to European standards, facilities in the best resorts are excellent and most have a wide choice of restaurants and bars, particularly in Quebec, where they have a distinctly French flavour.

There are many books about skiing in North America, among the best of which are *Ski Canada – Where to Ski and Snowboard* by Patrick Twomey and *The Skiers Book of Trail Maps, USA and Canada* by Cynthia Blair & Mike Bell. Several ski magazines are published in Canada, including *Ski Canada* (🖳 www.skicanadamag.com), which provides subscribers with a discount card for equipment, passes, etc.

For further general information, contact the Canadian Ski Council, which likes to be known as 'Ski and Snowboard Canada' (PO Box 10, Collingwood, ON L9Y 3Z4 or RR3, 209554 Hwy 26 W, Unit 1, Craigleith, ON L9Y 3Z2, ☎ 705-445 9140, 🖳 www.skicanada.org).

Cross-country Skiing

Cross-country skiing is popular throughout Canada and is an inexpensive alternative to downhill skiing. A set of skis, poles and boots costs as little as $150. You can enjoy cross-country skiing in Alberta, British Columbia and Ontario (where Thunder Bay on Lake Superior has hosted the World Nordic Ski Championships), although the best cross-country skiing is to be found in the eastern provinces. New Brunswick has more than 900km (560mi) of marked trails in national and provincial parks, as well as many others maintained by hotels and small communities. Quebec also has an extensive network of trails.

Although you can enjoy cross-country skiing wherever there's sufficient snow, cross-country skiing centres are becoming increasingly popular and offer lessons, ski hire and man-made trails (a lot easier, although less adventurous than making your own). Trail maps are provided and are a necessity when you're faced with miles of trails running in all directions. Costs (including parking) are about $10 to $20 per day, although in some areas (such as the National Capital region near Ottawa) skiing is free. (However, donation boxes are provided for those who would like to contribute to the upkeep of the trails, which most people happily do.) Many trails have cabins where you can have a rest or a drink or snack. For information about cross-country skiing, visit the Cross Country Canada website (🖳 www.cccski.com).

Snowmobiling

Invented in Canada in 1922, snowmobiles are motorbikes without wheels, driven across the snow by a spinning rubber track and steered by metal skis connected to the handlebars. Modern snowmobiles are capable of speeds of up to 100mph (160kph), but if you're planning to do that sort of speed, it's wise to stick to the marked tracks (it isn't unknown for landowners to 'discourage' trespassers by stringing wires across their land at neck height!). Even at lower speeds you need to wrap up well to protect yourself from the constant high-speed blast of icy air.

> **▲ Caution**
>
> It advisable to avoid frozen lakes – fatal accidents occasionally occur when snowmobiles crash through the ice.

Snowmobiles are a standard way of getting around in winter for people who live in the 'great white north' and many Canadians also own them just for fun. There are snowmobile clubs which stage various competitions and other events throughout the winter, such as the North American Snowmobile Festival in Thetford Mines and the Provincial Snowmobile Festival in Saint-Gabriel (both in Quebec, which has a vast linked network of snowmobile trails). New Brunswick has over 3,728mi (6,000km) of 'groomed' trails and Newfoundland has an annual snowmobile endurance race, the Viking 1,000, covering over 777mi (1,250km) of untracked wilderness, and lasting for four days!

The Canadian Council of Snowmobile Organisations (🖳 www.ccso-ccom.ca) has established a set of standard hand signals (turning, slowing, snowmobile approaching, etc.) rather like those used for motorcycles. There's a wide range of snowmobile models (starting at around $10,000) from a number of manufacturers (e.g. Ski-Doo, Arctic Cat, Polaris and Yamaha), plus a huge choice of accessories for enthusiasts, such as saddlebags. You can also hire snowmobiles, although most rental agencies prefer to take you on one of their guided tours first, to see how you get on – not only are the machines expensive, but if you go off into the wilderness on your own and get into trouble, you're liable to die, and they don't want to accept the responsibility for that!

Guided tours cost around $250 per day for a standard 500cc machine; a week (with accommodation and meals) costs from $1,600 (during the first two weeks in December) to $2,250 (during high season in February and March). If you want to try a more powerful machine, it costs an additional $200 for a 600cc machine or $300 for a 700cc machine. Protective clothing is provided, but it's recommended that you also wear a T-shirt and turtle-neck pullover, 'long-john' underwear, a neck warmer or balaclava, woollen socks, sunglasses and sunscreen.

If you want to go into the mountains, you should also rent an avalanche kit, consisting of avalanche beacon/transceiver, avalanche probe, shovel and Global Positioning System (GPS) for around $30 per day. Among the many snowmobile tour companies is Great Canadian Snowmobile Tours (Box 9242, Revelstoke, BC V0E 3KO, ☎ 250-837 9594, 💻 www.snowmobilerevelstoke.com).

There are a number of magazines for aficionados, including *OSM Magazine* (💻 www.osm-mag.com) is North America's leading magazine for snowmobilers. Further information can be obtained from the CCSO (above) and numerous websites including 💻 www.snowmobilecanada.com, www.snowmobile-canada.com and www.snowmobileforum.com.

Dog-sledding

Dog-sledding has become a major sport in North America, where races attract contestants from all over the world. As well as the celebrated Iditerarod race in Alaska, there's the 1,000-mile Yukon Quest race through the Yukon and Alaska (you can read about it in the *Yukon Quest* by John Firth, published by Lost Moose Publishing). However, it isn't necessary to go quite so far to try dog-sledding, and in winter it's possible in most areas to take anything from a half-day trip to a seven-day tour. You should expect to pay around $80 (adult) or $30 (child) for a half-day trip, or up to $2,750 for a seven-day trip including accommodation.

SWIMMING

Swimming is the most popular sport (or pastime) in Canada. Private pools are quite common, particularly in the warmer areas (e.g. Western BC), where they're often a standard feature of family houses and condominium complexes. There are public heated indoor and outdoor swimming pools in most towns, and numerous beaches along Canada's thousands of miles of ocean and lake shores. Many of Canada's National Parks have supervised beaches with professional and bilingual staff; however, there are often dangerous tides, so always heed the warning signs (a red flag means danger!).

Note that lakes and rivers are generally colder than sea waters and often have dangerous rapids and whirlpools.

Many hotels and motels have indoor or outdoor pools, but these are rarely if ever supervised by a professional, indicated by 'Use at your own risk' or 'The management assumes no liability' notices.

A visit to a public pool costs from around $3 and many municipalities offer introductory swimming lessons for children and youths. The aim of many swimmers is to earn a bronze medallion, which means not only that you're a proficient swimmer, but also that you're trained in life-saving. Lessons are taught under the supervision of qualified Red Cross instructors.

Joining a swimming club costs from around $250 a year, which entitles you to exclusive use of the pool during certain times of the day/week, with appointed times for everyone from toddlers to senior citizens.

WATERSPORTS

Watersports are hugely popular in Canada and include sailing, windsurfing (also called sailboarding), waterskiing, rowing, power boating, canoeing, surfing and sub-aqua. This is hardly surprising considering Canada has thousands of lakes and rivers and a vast coastline. Boats and equipment can be hired at coastal resorts, lakes and rivers, and instruction is available for most watersports in towns and holiday areas. Sailing and powerboats, canoes and rowing boats are generally available for hire in coastal towns and on inland waterways. Jet skis or wet bikes can also be hired at many resorts, although they should be avoided by the inexperienced as they can be fatal in the wrong hands. Wetsuits are often required for surfing, windsurfing, waterskiing and sub-aqua, even in summer, and they're essential during the winter months when the water is freezing.

Canoeing & Kayaking

Canoeing and kayaking are popular on Canada's lakes, rivers and in Pacific coastal waters (the most famous venue is Algonquin Park, two hours north-west of Ottawa). Canoes are popular as a way of exploring the calmer lakes and the back-country waterways in summer and early autumn. If you lack experience (and the longer the trip, the more experience you should have of wilderness expeditions, which can involve bad weather, unfriendly wildlife and injury), it makes sense to go with an organised, supervised group. Organisations called outfitters arrange expeditions for small groups, although you must make sure that you choose one that's licensed by the local province, which means that they're experienced and carry insurance. Provincial tourist authorities can provide a list of licensed outfitters.

If you want to use a kayak (a one or two-man enclosed boat), you need some previous experience or training. Handling a kayak isn't as easy as it looks, even on a river, and for sea kayaking you need instruction in a sheltered cove before heading out into the surf (in addition to knowing the tide times, weather forecast and information about the coastal rock formations). Most coastal towns in British Columbia offer kayak hire, instruction and guided trips.

A useful book is *Canoeing, the Complete Guide to Equipment and Techniques* by Dave Harrison (Stackpole Books). Further information can be obtained from the governing body, CanoeKayak Canada (CKC, Suite 705, 2197 Riverside Drive, Ottawa, ON K1H 7X3, ☎ 613-260 1818, www.canoekayak.ca).

Sailing & Boating

Sailing is a popular summer sport, and there are sailing clubs along Canada's east and west coasts. There are also exclusive yacht clubs which social-climbers often join for the prestige and social contacts, rather than for the sailing (membership fees can be astronomical). You can hire anything from a modest sailing dinghy to an ocean-going yacht, although you need experience to hire some craft. All craft must be registered and licensed. Canada's Department of Fisheries and Oceans and the Royal Canadian Mounted Police (RCMP) are adept at ensuring that owners and users have the correct documentation and there are large fines for offenders. Always check with the coastguard before setting sail and ensure that you have the proper navigation charts because frequent and fierce storms are common in some areas.

Further information can obtained from the Canadian Yachting Association (CYA, Portsmouth Olympic Harbour, 53 Yonge Street, Kingston, ON K7M 6G4, ☎ 613-545 3044, www.sailing.sa).

Boating and sailing accidents are fairly common, and it's essential for participants, particularly children, to wear lifejackets at all times.

Sub-aqua

Scuba diving is popular in Canada, where you can receive instruction by certified diving instructors at indoor pools, costing from around $75 to $150 depending on the location. (Due to the fact that everyone is equally buoyant in water, there's great interest from organisations caring for disabled people to allow them to enjoy this sport.) Most dealers selling scuba apparatus provide on-site maintenance and support for equipment, and many offer a 'try it for free the first time' deal. Useful websites include those of Canada's oldest diving club, the Canadian Sub-Aqua Club (💻 www.cansac.ca) and *Diver* magazine (💻 www.divermag.com).

Surfing & Waterskiing

There are several types of surfing, including traditional board surfing, body surfing and 'boogie boarding' (body surfing with a short foam board). Skim boards are small oval boards used for skimming along beaches. Windsurfers (or sailboards), surfboards, bodyboards and wetsuits can be hired at most locations. Windsurfing is popular on both coasts and on the St Lawrence river near Montreal, but isn't permitted everywhere.

Waterskiing is popular on lakes and in calm coastal areas. You can hire a tow-boat and skis for a reasonable fee in many areas. Further information can be obtained from Water Ski and Wakeboard Canada (💻 www.waterski-wakeboard.ca).

Whitewater Rafting

Whitewater river rafting (or river running) is hugely popular throughout Canada, particularly on the fast rivers of British Columbia and in the Rockies, e.g. the Fraser River, and is an unforgettable experience (better than the hairiest of roller-coasters). The best (or worst, if you're terrified) time to go is in April or May, when waters are at their most turbulent due to melting snow. Experience is usually unnecessary, as the inflatable rubber, pontoon-type boats are virtually unsinkable (although you won't be if you fall out). However, not all trips are suitable for families or novices. Expect to get wet and don't be surprised if you're thrown out of the raft. It isn't recommended for poor swimmers, although life jackets are provided and mandatory. If you're inexperienced you should be accompanied by a professional guide, who will (hopefully) reduce the danger but not the thrills.

Oops!

Trips cost from $60 for half a day up to hundreds of dollars for a week-long excursion with meals. Dozens of companies organise whitewater rafting expeditions throughout Canada, and in most cases all you have to do is turn up at the riverside, find the organiser's trailer and book on the spot for the next trip.

There are a number of books published for whitewater fans, including the *Whitewater Rafting Manual: Tactics and Techniques for Great River Adventures* by Jimmie Johnson (Stackpole Books), *Whitewater Rafting in North America* by Lloyd D. Armstead (Pequot Press) and *Whitewater Rafting: An Introductory Guide* by Cecil Kuhne. You can find details of rafting destinations in Canada at 💻 www.raftingamerica.com, and a wealth of operators online, such as 💻 www.reorafting.com and www.wildwater.com.

OTHER SPORTS

Below is a selection of other popular sports and activities that are popular in Canada.

> **Athletics**
>
> Most towns and villages have local athletics (track) clubs, which hold local competitions and sports days. For information about local clubs and facilities, contact Athletics Canada (Suite B1-110 2445 St-Laurent Boulevard, Ottawa, ON K1G 6C3, ☎ 613-260 5580, 💻 www.athletics.ca).

Basketball

Although basketball was invented in Canada (in 1891 by Dr James A. Naismith, a Canadian whose name can be found adorning many streets in Canadian cities), it's principally played in the US, where the professional basketball league, the National Basketball Association (NBA) was formed in 1949. It took until 1995 for Canada to gain entry with two teams, but now there's only one, the Toronto Raptors (💻 www.nba.com/raptors), which plays in the Atlantic Division of the Eastern Conference, the other team – the Vancouver Grizzlies – having moved to Memphis in the US. The Raptors have a new stadium in the Air Canada Centre in Toronto. The NBA consists of 30 teams, divided into the Eastern and Western Conference, each of which has two divisions. Teams play a total of around 82 games during the regular season, running from November to April.

Curling

Curling is a winter sport which involves sliding a lump of polished granite (a 'rock') across a patch of ice. Each team consists of four players, known as skip (the captain), third (second in charge, who 'throws' third), second (who throws second) and lead (who throws first). The teams throw alternately, until eight rocks have been thrown, each aiming at a series of marked spots called 'buttons'. Other team members have a brush with which they sweep the ice to smooth the progress of the rock, which has an attached handle of a different colour for each team. The skill is in throwing the rock so that it veers and swerves over the lumpy ice, although as a spectator sport it's rather like watching paint dry. The main body governing curling, which is now an Olympic sport, is the Canadian Curling Association (1660 Vimont Court, Cumberland, ON K4A 4J4, ☎ 613-834 2076, 💻 www.curling.ca).

Horse Riding

Horse riding and equestrian sports have a large following throughout Canada, in both urban and rural areas. There are three types of saddle: Western or 'stock seat', the most common (and the kind you're most likely to be offered if you want to ride in the National Parks), 'hunt seat' (basically the way most Europeans ride) and 'saddle seat' (like the hunt seat, but used for specialist riding). There are also dressage and show-jumping events. Horse riding costs around $100 per hour, including an experienced guide. Lessons cost from around $25 per hour, depending on the level of teaching and on whether you sign up for a series or a single lesson. Most national and provincial parks have a network of bridle paths and riding trails, and horses can be hired in many national parks, where horse riding is an excellent way to get off the beaten track. Riding holidays are also offered at ranches throughout Canada.

Ice Skating

Ice skating is a popular indoor and outdoor sport in Canada, where major cities have skating rinks open throughout the year, although the ice is often occupied by hockey players. All rinks have skate hire and a skate sharpening service and offer lessons for individuals and groups. It's an inexpensive activity and may even be free in many smaller towns (outdoor rinks, which are mostly just frozen lakes, ponds or rivers, are also usually free). Each community in the city erects wooden barriers and fills the central space with water, regularly grooming the ice that forms for kids to skate. Some rinks hold ice-dancing evenings costing around $10 (including skate hire). Ottawa boasts that its Rideau Canal (4.8mi/7.7km) is the longest 'skating rink' in the world. Books about ice-skating include the *Skater's Edge Sourcebook: Ice Skating Resource Guide* by Alice Berman (Skaters Edge). Further information can be found on the website of Skate Canada (🖳 www.skatecanada.ca).

Roller-skating, Skateboarding & BMX Biking

Roller-skating is a popular pastime, although traditional roller-skates have been largely replaced by 'in-line' skates or rollerblades. In-line roller hockey is played by Canadian youths on the streets and some people even skate to work during the snow-free months. The cost of skates varies depending on the manufacturer (and current fashion), but you can buy used skates at 'Play it Again Sports' shops throughout Canada.

Rinks and specially designed circuits are provided in many towns for skateboarding and BMX cycles. Children can start at around seven years old, although participants of all ages should be protected against falls with crash helmets and elbow and knee pads. It's difficult to hire skateboards because they're too easily stolen, although BMX bikes can usually be hired.

snowmobiles

Rollercoaster, West Edmonton Mall, AB

17. SHOPPING

As it shares a border with the ultimate consumer society (the US), it's hardly surprising that Canada is also a major consumer nation. Newspaper, magazine and TV advertisements all exhort Canadians to spend liberally, and most do, leading to annual consumer spending of over $500bn. Shopping facilities in the major cities are the equivalent of those in the States or Europe, with most top brands and designer names available. Toronto's Yonge Street and Montreal's 'underground city' are considered to be Canada's best shopping areas, although all the major cities offer plenty of temptations to part you from your money.

Many Canadians work long hours, which leaves little time for shopping. Therefore they prefer one-stop shopping in supermarkets, department stores or suburban malls. Canada's shops (stores) and shopping centres (malls) offer a vast choice of goods in every shape, colour and size you could desire (plus many that you couldn't imagine anyone wanting!). Prices are competitive, particularly when compared with those in Europe; computer hardware and software, stereo systems, CDs, DVDs, cameras and sports equipment are particularly good value. Clothes are also good value (unless you want designer label clothes, which are as exorbitantly priced in Canada), the best bargains being in casual and winter clothing. Low prices and value aren't always the same thing, but many stores offer a 'price guarantee', which means that they'll 'meet or beat' any advertised price for goods, so it pays to comparison-shop.

In the major cities, you may find some shop assistants (store clerks) who are brusque and rude, but in general they're friendly and helpful. With few exceptions, you're refused entry if you're carrying open food or drink containers, smoking, have bare feet or aren't wearing a shirt.

Most shops accept major credit cards, although American Express is becoming unpopular with smaller shops and many won't accept it (due to the high charges). Most shops also accept Canadian or American dollar travellers' cheques (and $US) and some give change. Unlike American shops, where the offer of cash causes panic, Canadian shops are usually happy to accept it and a few may even insist on it. Cash machines (ATMs) are located in most malls, large stores and supermarkets.

Many shops provide free catalogues at various times of the year (often delivered to homes) and free shopping guides are published in most areas. If you're looking for a particular item or want to save time, check the *Yellow Pages* or online shopping sites.

You don't need to worry about returning faulty goods because the customer is 'always right' and most shops exchange goods or give refunds without question. On the rare occasions when there's a problem, a complaint to the local consumer protection agency or Better Business Bureau usually resolves the matter. See also **Consumer Associations** on page 305

Canadian shops use both Imperial and metric measures; those who are used to metric measures may find the conversion tables in **Appendix D** useful.

> **▲ Caution**
>
> Like most of the rest of the world, Canada's cities have their share of bag-snatchers and pickpockets who will empty your wallet before you even get to the shops if you don't keep a tight hold on it (wearing a money belt is recommended in some places).

Bargain Shopping

One lesson Canadians learned from the recession in the early '90s (and the latest) is that only the foolish or wealthy pay the full price and, although most goods have price labels, you stand a good chance of saving money if you comparison shop. Seasonal sales offer good bargains and many people delay making major purchases until the sales. Most stores hold sales at various times of the year, the largest of which are in January, July and October. Top department stores usually have pre-season clothing sales, e.g. autumn/winter clothes are on sale for a limited period in August or September. Sales are also common on statutory holidays such as Labour Day and Canada Day weekends, although the biggest sales traditionally start on Boxing Day (26th December).

Often 'end-of-line' reductions can be found outside the sale season and there are some items where the last of a shop's stock of a particular item can go for as little as 25 per cent of its normal price. The secret of buying at low prices is to comparison shop 'til you drop, checking prices at different stores (which can also be done online at 💻 www.canadaretail.ca and www.pricecanada.com). However, make sure that you're comparing like with like because it's easy to save money by buying inferior goods – and beware of bargains that seem too good to be true – they usually are!

The best bargains can be found at discount malls and centres, factory outlets and warehouse clubs. Discount stores and factory outlets are able to offer lower prices on branded goods because their profit margins and overheads are cut to the bone and the middleman is excluded. Factory outlet malls usually have rules stating that stores must discount merchandise at least 10 per cent below any local discount store or offer at least one-third off regular retail prices. Many discount stores operate on the 'pile 'em high and sell 'em low' principle, with no fancy displays or customer areas, no demonstrations and little customer or after-sales service – just rock-bottom prices. You should know exactly what you want when shopping at discount stores because staff don't waste time discussing products and are likely to employ the hard sell or ignore you if you're undecided.

There are also chains of discount stores in ordinary shopping malls, such as Loonie (dollar) Stores (after the colloquial name for a dollar coin), where everything in the store is under $5. A sign of the difficult times in the last few years is the number of consignment stores that have appeared everywhere, buying and selling used clothes and household goods).

Factory outlets are common in Canada, most of which are owned and operated by manufacturers, although there are also special malls dedicated to factory outlets. What is claimed to be Canada's largest factory outlet mall, The Factory Outlet Shopper, opened in 1999 at Niagara Falls (7500 Lundy's Lane, Niagara Falls, ON, L2H 1G8, ☎ 1-888-284 5781, 💻 www.canadaoneoutlets.com). Although they may sell obsolete or overstocked items, most factory outlets don't sell poor quality goods or 'seconds' (flawed or damaged goods) but quality products at bargain prices. Ask your friends and neighbours if there are any factory outlets in your area and look out for them on your travels. Designer clothes can also be purchased from factory outlets in cities.

In most cities there are also huge warehouse stores specialising in selling remainders, leftover stock, overruns and cancelled orders at reduced prices, which can cost a fraction of the normal retail price. Since the mid-'80s, 'warehouse clubs' such as Costco (💻 www.costco.ca) have become the fastest-growing retail sector in Canada. They charge an annual membership fee of from $50 (which can often be recouped in one visit) and offer huge discounts on branded goods (particularly food, with prices for bulk quantities typically 20 per cent below supermarket prices). The hackneyed slogan 'the more you spend, the more you save' is true, although discerning shoppers profit most.

Supermarkets offer discount coupons (e.g. 20¢ or 50¢ off branded items), which are either

printed in newspapers and magazines or issued as books of coupons that are delivered to local homes and available at stores.

Cutting out (clipping) coupons is a way of life for many Canadian shoppers, who can save around $20 per week by using them. In fact, prices are set in the expectation that you'll use coupons, therefore you'll pay too much if you don't use them. Some stores also accept coupons issued by their rivals.

Local newspapers, *Yellow Pages* and flyers delivered to homes contain literally hundreds of coupons from local businesses such as restaurants, fast food outlets, cinemas, hotels, car rental companies, dry cleaners and many others. Note that most coupons have an expiry date. When shopping for a 'big ticket' item such as a hi-fi system with a coupon or special offer voucher, it isn't advisable to tell the assistant (clerk) until you have verified that the goods are in stock. If he knows that you have a discount voucher, you may find that the item is suddenly 'out of stock' because your discount usually comes out of his commission.

Second-hand Goods

There's a huge market in Canada for second-hand goods, which can be purchased from special bargain shops and charity shops, at auction rooms and garage sales, and through classified advertisements in newspapers and magazines.

There's a large market in used (often called 'antique' or 'vintage') clothes in major cities, sold by consignment stores with names such as 'Second Chance' or 'Second Fiddle', which sell second-hand clothes on commission. Some of these haven't even been worn, having been purchased by shopping addicts who buy everything in sight and then never wear them. The new craze among working women is to hold 'swap meets', where they take unwanted clothes and swap them, and donate any left over to women's shelters. Charity shops (thrift stores) are also a good place to pick up inexpensive and fashionable new and second-hand clothing, donated by shops and individuals.

Another place to pick up a bargain is at a public auction, although it's usually necessary to have specialist knowledge about what you're planning to buy (particularly antiques), as you'll probably be competing with experts. Auctions are held throughout the year for everything from antiques to houses, while car auctions, which were originally open to the trade only are now open to the public. Estate and bankruptcy auction sales are frequent and a source of good bargains. Charity-run antique and craft fairs and flea markets are also good hunting grounds. These are typically organised as fund raisers and held in local schools, churches, women's clubs, town squares and on college campuses. Local auctions and fairs are widely advertised in local newspapers and through leaflets. For information about local markets, ask at your local tourist office, chamber of commerce or library.

One of the best places to obtain second-hand bargains in Canada is at private 'yard' and 'tag' sales (garage sales), an American 'invention'. Families moving house or periodically emptying their attics, store rooms and wardrobes, often sell unwanted clothes, furniture, records, books and assorted bric-a-brac in their garage or driveway or on their front lawn. Sometimes people moving abroad or across the country sell practically the entire contents of their homes. Most garage sales take place on spring or summer weekends and are advertised in local newspapers and via posters, flyers, supermarket bulletin boards, home-made street signs and word of mouth. They can be found simply by driving around neighbourhoods on a Saturday.

Yard sales are often a good place to find interesting 'Canadiana', considered junk by most

Canadians but collectible by foreigners. Prices are negotiable and items can often be bought for next-to nothing, as Canadians don't ask or expect to get much for second-hand goods. At the end of the day, anything left is practically given away. It's possible to furnish an entire apartment with items purchased at garage and estate sales. The best bargains are found in high- and middle-class areas, where some people sell their designer clothes after wearing them just a few times.

When seeking specific items, such as cameras or sports equipment, it's wise to check the classified advertisements in specialist magazines. Specialist shops often have a bulletin board where private ads are placed by customers, with detachable slips containing the vendor's phone number at the bottom. Many shopping malls and office buildings also have public bulletin boards with advertisements, and most local newspapers contain dedicated classified sections for cars, boats, household goods and miscellaneous items. A good source of furniture and household items is also expatriate club newsletters, particularly when members are returning home.

Special newspapers and magazines for bargain hunters, such as *Bargain Finder* (💻 www.buysell.com), are published in most areas, some of which have separate editions for automotive and general merchandise. Publications may be distributed free (when the advertiser pays) or advertisements may be free to private advertisers, in which case publications usually cost a couple of dollars. Advertisers are normally required to indicate their status (private or dealer) so that prospective buyers know who they're dealing with.

The online version of *Bargain Finder* (see above) are sites such as 💻 www.craigslist.com and www.usedvictoria.com, where goods can be posted free, together with a photo.

SALES TAX

The prices of goods and services are usually shown and quoted exclusive of sales taxes (although tax is sometimes included as a sales ploy to make you feel as if you're getting away without paying it). This means that, if you have only $10 in your pocket, you won't usually be able to buy something priced at $10, which will cost at least $10.50 (Alberta) and as much as $11.55 (Prince Edward Island).

There are two types of sales tax: federal goods and services tax (GST) and provincial sales tax (PST) – also know as retail sales tax (RST) in some provinces. GST – known to Canadians as the 'gouge and screw tax' – was introduced on 1st January 1991 and was reduced from 6 to 5 per cent from 1st January 2008, while PST is levied in all provinces except Alberta at varying rates (see the table below). In New Brunswick, Newfoundland and Nova Scotia, GST and PST are combined into a single' harmonised sales tax' (HST) of 13 per cent (5 per cent GST and 8 per cent PST). In Quebec, GST is known as *taux produits et services* (TPS) and PST as *taux des ventes et services Québec* (TVQ).

Sales Tax Rates

Province	HST	GST	PST	Total Tax
Alberta	-	5%	-	5%
British Columbia	-	5%	7%	12%
Manitoba	-	5%	7%	12%
New Brunswick	13%	-	-	13%
Newfoundland and Labrador	13%	-	-	13%
Nova Scotia	13%	-	-	13%
Ontario	-	5%	8%	13%
Prince Edward Island*	-	5%	10%	15.5%
Quebec *	-	5%	7.5%	12.875%
Saskatchewan	5%	5%	10%	

* In Prince Edward Island and Quebec, PST is levied on GST and is therefore effectively 10.5 per cent and 7.875 per cent respectively.

PST may apply to different goods and services depending on the province. For example, in Ontario, PST is usually 8 per cent, but is 5 per cent on lodgings, 10 per cent on entertainment and alcohol at restaurants, and 12 per cent on alcohol at retail stores. In Alberta there's a 4 per cent tax on lodgings, while in British Columbia, PST on alcohol is 10 per cent.

Sales tax is calculated on the amount paid for an item (usually minus any trade-in value, if applicable) and is paid by the buyer. It applies to almost all goods and services that are sold, leased, transferred, or otherwise provided through the production and distribution process. Sales tax not only applies to new goods and goods sold by businesses, but also to the sale of certain used products such as cars, motor homes, boats and aircraft.

Certain goods and services are exempt from sales tax, including basic food stuffs; most health, medical and dental services that are performed for medical reasons by licensed doctors or dentists; bridge, road and ferry tolls; most educational services such as university courses leading to certificates or diplomas and tutoring provided for a credit course (but not courses provided by profit-making companies); and most financial services. Some goods or services that are exempt from sales taxes in other countries aren't exempt in Canada, including newspapers and magazines, professional services, and mail order catalogue purchases.

A number of goods and services are zero-rated, which means that they've been declared taxable, but the rate has been set at zero for the time being, i.e. until the government gets desperate for money! Examples include agricultural products (e.g. wheat, grain, raw wool and unprocessed tobacco); farm livestock (with some exceptions, such as horses) and most fishery products (e.g. fish for human consumption); prescription medicines; most medical devices (e.g. hearing aids and false teeth); international passenger air travel except to the continental United States and St Pierre and Miquelon; and inbound and international freight transport subject to certain conditions.

Some provinces levy a refundable 'environment tax' on recyclable items such as drink and food cans and bottles. and plastic fruit cartons. These can be returned to the shop where you purchased them for a tax refund – which, incidentally, is one of the few chores children are happy to do!

Due to changes to the law that took effect in April 2007, visitors to Canada (i.e. non-residents) can no longer reclaim GST (or HST) on either personal goods or accommodation, even as part of a tour package.

SHOPPING HOURS

Canada's cities and large towns have long shopping hours. Many drugstores, petrol stations and convenience stores are open 24/7 in most areas, where you can even shop at 3am if you wish! On major roads, 24-hour service stations also sell food. Other shops, particularly supermarkets and drugstores, are generally open from 7.30am to 9pm. In almost all major cities, at least one chemist is open until midnight or even 24/7 (see the *Yellow Pages* for a list). In town centre (downtown) shopping areas, major shops may open from 9.30am to 6pm from Mondays to Wednesdays, 9.30am to 9pm on Thursdays and Fridays and from 9.30am to 7pm on Saturdays. Most malls open at around 10am and close at 9pm. In smaller towns, shops usually open between 9 and 10am and close at 6pm, Mondays to Saturdays. Whenever possible, avoid shopping at lunchtimes and on Saturdays, when shops are usually packed.

Sunday opening is subject to provincial and/ or municipal laws. It's rare in New Brunswick, Newfoundland, Nova Scotia and Prince Edward Island, although most other provinces have shops that are open from noon until 5pm on Sundays. Business hours on statutory holidays are usually at the discretion of individual shopkeepers, although you'll rarely find a shop open on Christmas Day. Shops usually post their holiday business hours a week or so before a holiday.

SHOPPING CENTRES

All Canadian cities and suburbs have vast indoor shopping centres, called malls (pronounced 'mawls'). The mall concept was invented in Canada and has spread throughout North America and most of the rest of the world. Many malls boast that you're under cover from the time you drive into the car park (parking lot) – a considerable advantage in a country which can be under snow for six (or more) months per year. Discount or outlet malls, comprising discount and factory outlet shops, are also common throughout Canada (see **Bargain Shopping** on page 290). The success of the mall concept has led to a change in the facilities and outlets in most town centres, which major retailers have largely abandoned.

Malls vary from enormous luxury shopping centres such as Toronto's Eaton Centre and Vancouver's Pacific Centre, to smaller centres in country towns. The average mall contains 50 to 100 shops, including many department and chain stores as well as supermarkets, clothing shops, furniture and furnishing outlets, film processing shops, jewellers, music shops, book stores, banks, laundrettes, hairdressers, opticians, restaurants, fast food outlets, and a wide selection of boutiques and specialist shops. In some malls there are car hire offices, airline booking desks and even clinics, and many contain leisure and entertainment facilities such as a skating rink, ten-pin bowling alley, cinemas, amusement arcades and art galleries.

Alberta's West Edmonton Mall (one of the world's largest) boasts its own indoor amusement park (with a roller coaster), the world's largest indoor water park with a wave pool and water slides, mini golf (a replica of the American Pebble Beach course), submarine ride, aquarium, over 100 restaurants, nightclubs, recreation centre with bowling alleys and arcades, cinemas, casino, chapel, hotels complete with several different 'theme rooms', plus over 800 shops and services (for those who actually come to shop!). As you can imagine – this place is HUGE!

MARKETS

In many cities there are farmers' or 'green' markets, where local farmers sell fresh and reasonably priced produce most days of the week, although Canadian street markets generally don't compare with those in Europe. Local fishermen also set up stalls in fishing ports. As in most countries, markets are usually the best place to shop for fresh and organic food and are a good place to buy an assortment of bread and a wider variety of cheese than you can find in most supermarkets. Most stallholders offer tastings and some shoppers get their breakfast by 'grazing' from stall to stall. Flea (i.e. junk) markets are common in major cities and specialise in clothing, jewellery, antiques and miscellaneous bric-a-brac.

In provinces with severe winters, markets may be held between spring and autumn only or may be held indoors. There are often small impromptu markets in many cities, although it's illegal to sell goods in the street without a vendor's licence.

Second-hand flea markets are common in cities and towns across Canada and are generally held in vacant buildings, in malls or (in the summer) on church lawns or in car parks.

Ask at your local tourist office, library or town hall for information about local markets.

For information about farmers' markets, see www.farmersmarketscanada.ca and http://marketplace.chef2chef.net/farmer-markets/canada.htm, which has links to provincial associations of farmers' markets such as www.bcfarmersmarket.org/directory and www.farmersmarketsontario.com. There are also websites dedicated to flea markets such as www.ontariofleamarkets.com.

DEPARTMENT & CHAIN STORES

There are excellent department and chain stores throughout Canada, many of which specialise in clothing. Department stores, as their name implies, consist of separate departments selling everything from clothes to perfume, electrical apparatus to furniture. Each floor may be dedicated to a particular kind of goods, such as ladies' or men's clothes (which are often sold through franchised boutiques) or furniture and furnishings, and they usually include restaurants, cafeterias, phones and toilets.

In a department store, the floor at street level is designated the first floor (not the ground floor), the floor below the ground floor is usually called the basement and the floor above may be called the mezzanine. The basement or lower basement may be occupied by a bargain department where reduced price or inexpensive goods are sold. Some stores, such as the Army & Navy, operate basement stores famous for their cut-price branded clothes and unbeatable prices.

The best Canadian department stores include The Bay (run by the Hudson's Bay Company) and Sears (it used to be called Sears Roebuck, which invented the shopping catalogue in the 19th century). The largest nationwide discount department stores, sometimes called mass merchandisers, include Wal-Mart and Zellers (owned by The Bay), which have branches in a number of cities, along with Fields, Holt Renfrew and Saan. Most department stores have mail order catalogues and operate a home delivery service (many will deliver goods anywhere in the world).

Chain stores, which are also often franchised, are stores with two or more branches, often located in different towns, e.g. Canadian Tire and Home Hardware. Many department stores are also chain stores. Saan is typical: having started business in 1947 in Winnipeg, it has some 142 outlets throughout Canada (it used to have 350 stores, having down-sized after filing for court protection due to financial problems). There are dozens of chain stores in Canada, selling everything from electrical items to food, books and clothes. Some are to be found country-wide while others are regional; for example, Canadian Superstore, IGA, Safeway and Save-on-Foods are dominant in the west, while in Ontario you're more likely to find Independent Grocers, Loblaws and Loeb.

Most department and chain stores accept all major credit cards, although some issue their own cards (with high interest rates). If you have a store credit card, you'll be inundated with pre-sale post, special offers and seasonal catalogues.

FOOD SHOPS & SUPERMARKETS

Most Canadians buy their food from Canada's largest supermarket chains, which include Loblaws (www.loblaw.ca), the country's largest retailer and food distributor, Sobeys (www.sobeys.ca), Metro (www.metroca) in Quebec and Ontario, and Safeway (www.safeway.ca). Many people also shop at warehouse clubs such as Costco, where large savings can be made by buying in bulk. Like department stores, supermarkets have been increasingly losing business to warehouse clubs, although the latter cannot compete with supermarkets for variety, and typically stock some 4,000 lines (many non-food) compared to a supermarket's 20,000.

The average family of four spends around $800 per month on groceries – less than in many other countries, although it has increased considerably in recent years, particularly for fruit and vegetables. A shocking survey in October 2008 carried out by the Heart and Stroke Foundation (www.heartandstroke.ca) found that fresh food was too expensive for almost half of all Canadians! Food is cheapest overall in western Canada and most expensive in the Northwest Territories, Nunavut and the Yukon, where most food must be imported. It pays to shop around for the lowest food prices – a survey by the Heart and Stroke Foundation in 2008 found startling discrepancies in the cost of basic healthy food, not only from province to province, but also from city to city and stores to stores in the same province.

The quality, variety and size of produce (fruit and vegetables) in Canadian supermarkets is excellent and often overwhelming to the newcomer. Stores are huge and packed year-round with the most exotic produce, mountains of meat and dairy products (although fresh fish isn't easy to find away from coastal areas), and convenience foods by the truckload. Canadian supermarkets invariably carry larger stocks and offer a wider variety of merchandise than their counterparts in Europe. The choice is mind-boggling, e.g. 40 or 50 flavours of tea, and countless brands of breakfast cereal, sold in boxes of different sizes.

Produce departments are self-service and fruit and vegetables aren't usually pre-packed, so you can buy as little or as much as you like. Organically-grown produce is becoming increasingly widely available. Meat is relatively inexpensive in Canada, although most meat is from animals that are 'finished' (fattened before slaughter) in vast feed-lots in order to produce large animals in the shortest possible time (a process that may include feeding them steroids and antibiotics). Meat from naturally reared livestock is also available but costs a little more. Many foreign foods and ingredients are available in supermarkets and there are also ethnic food stores and supermarkets in many neighbourhoods. Food shops in areas with a large Jewish population often have a kosher section.

Most Canadian supermarkets sell own brand (private label) foods and also have a 'generic' section, where tins and packets bear only the name of the product, statutory information (e.g. weight, ingredients, etc.) and a bar code. These may sell for as little as half (average three-quarters) the price of their name-brand counterparts (it's estimated that a family of four can save almost $2,000 per year by buying own brand items) and in some cases the product is virtually identical to the branded item and may even be produced in the same factory. When comparing different brands, ensure that the quality (grade) and quantity are the same.

All supermarkets have bargain offers on certain items to attract customers, when goods are often sold at below cost ('loss leaders') and prominently displayed, e.g. at the end of aisles. Many supermarkets have regular discount days. For example, on the first Tuesday of each month, Safeway offers 10 per cent off all purchases over $35 or offers Air Miles. Supermarkets distribute weekly flyers (advertising sheets) of special prices, on which many people rely.

Supermarket check-out assistants use scanners to scan bar codes, and purchases and prices are displayed on screens as they're scanned. Always check screens and your bill, as mistakes are sometimes made (on as many as one in ten products, according to 'thrifty shopping' expert Ian Nicholson). It's rarely necessary to take a shopping bag, as most stores provide free or inexpensive bags at the checkout, where an assistant often packs your bags and may even carry them to your car. It has become a green policy to bring re-usable bags with you

and supermarkets also sells fibre bags for $1 each. For every re-usable bag you have, they discount 3¢ from your bill (the cost of the plastic bag they would have had to supply). Some supermarkets make home deliveries (for a fee).

In some suburban areas there are few specialist food shops, so you may have little choice but to shop at a supermarket. In neighbourhoods without local supermarkets, corner stores may be open for up to 20 hours a day. It's possible to buy inexpensive, naturally-grown fruit and vegetables from local farmers or co-operatives in rural areas (including 'pick your own' farms). Many have roadside stalls or signs advertising their produce (see also **Markets** above).

There are numerous specialist food shops, gourmet food shops, markets and delicatessens in all major cities, selling every luxury food imaginable, although they're too expensive for basic foodstuffs. Larger food shops may provide catering services for anything from a small dinner party or picnic to a 100-head banquet or wedding reception, complete with crockery, glasses, furniture, flowers and staff.

For a rough guide to staple food prices in Canada, see Relocate Canada (💻 http://relocatecanada.com/foodprice.html) and Living in Canada (💻 www.livingin-canada.com/food-prices-canada.html).

CLOTHING

Most Canadians are quite conservative in their dress, eschewing the loud checked trousers and garish Bermuda shorts of their American neighbours, although they do tend to follow American fashion trends (except in Quebec, where they follow European/French fashion). The eastern provinces are generally more conservative than the central and western provinces, where people dress more casually. Whatever the style of dress, the pattern followed by most people is to dress in layers that you can take off or put on as you go from centrally heated home to the cold outdoors to an overheated shop or a car that takes a while to warm up.

If you arrive in winter from a country that doesn't have cold winters, you'll need to buy warm clothing as soon as you arrive. For any sort of outdoor winter activity you need thermal underwear (ideally made of fabric such as polypropylene which draws perspiration away from the body), woollen or thermal socks, mittens and hats, and a pair of waterproof winter boots. Most Canadians in the north wear jackets and under-vests filled with duck or goose-down that keep out the wind as well as the cold.

> Apart from the Puffa down-filled jacket, Canada's favourite garment is the humble 'blue jean' – good value at around $50 for 'top' brands such as Levi's and Wrangler (although you can pay a fortune for 'designer' jeans).

T-shirts, often with original designs and slogans, are fashionable and sold everywhere. Shops selling designs from the world's top fashion houses flourish in Canada's largest cities, including Boss, Calvin Klein, Cambridge, Chanel, Giorgio Armani, Gucci, Hardy Amies, Konen, Polo (Ralph Lauren), Manzoni, Samuelsohn and Tommy Hilfiger.

As in many countries, large department stores are the showcases for new fashions and stage fashion shows to which they invite favoured clients, i.e. those who spend lots of money. Trendy boutiques, where the emphasis is on designer clothes and chic accessories, are found everywhere. Among the most famous Canadian men's stores is Henry Singer, which has a reputation for selling high quality, classic men's clothing. The most popular mainstream clothes stores are Banana Republic, Benetton, Gap (and GapKids) and Roots Canada, while the best value specialist clothing chains include Below the Belt, Bootlegger, Stitches and Thrifty's. A popular chain of sports shops is Play It Again Sports, with over 475 outlets in the USA and Canada, selling second-hand as well as new clothing and equipment.

One of the most surprising things about shopping for quality clothes in Canada is the number of stores selling quality branded clothes at much lower prices than in other countries. However, in smaller towns the reverse may be true. Some successful clothing companies, particularly those which sell clothing for outdoor activities, sell almost

entirely by mail-order. Some of the best outlets for bargain-priced designer clothes are chains such as Hangers and Winners, which buy factory overruns and clothes that department stores cannot sell (although there may be no refunds or exchanges). Department stores also have their own outlet stores such as Sears Clearance Centre and The Bay Clearance Centre.

Although many clothes shops also sell shoes, there's a wide variety of specialist shoe stores in Canada, although most Canadian shoes are imported from the US and include Alden, Bass, Docksides, Florsheim, Hush Puppies, Mephisto, Rockport, Sebago, Selby, Sioux, Sperry and Timberland. European brands are also widely available, such as Bally and Clarks. When buying winter boots, choose those with non-slip soles as well as waterproof outers, which won't discolour from slushy ice and snow. Good children's shoes are produced by Bass, Capezio and Striderite. Shoe repairers can be found in all towns and in department stores, where repairs may be done while you wait. In most cities and towns, there are sports shoe shops selling specialist sports shoes, leisure shoes and trainers, which are good value in Canada.

The average North American (male and female) is larger than the average person in most other countries and therefore Canadian and American clothes are often cut larger. Men's shirts sometimes come in different sleeve lengths (as well as collar sizes), which is fine as long as you know the size you need. (See **Appendix D** for conversion tables between Canadian, British and continental European sizes.) Whenever possible, try clothes on before buying and don't be afraid to return them if they don't fit. Most Canadian shops exchange clothes or give a refund (if you're unsure, ask when buying) unless they were purchased during a sale, although the exchange and refund periods can vary considerably.

FURNITURE & FURNISHINGS

Canada has millions of trees and thus has a thriving furniture manufacturing industry. Home-manufactured furniture is good value and top quality furniture is often cheaper in Canada than in many other countries. There's a huge choice of traditional and contemporary designs in most price ranges, although (as with most things) quality is usually reflected in the price. A number of manufacturers and wholesalers sell directly to the public, offering large savings on store prices, although you should compare quality before buying. There are shops specialising in beds, leather furniture, and reproduction and antique furniture. Companies both manufacture and install fitted bedrooms, bathrooms and kitchens. If you want reasonably priced, good quality, modern furniture, there are a number of companies (e.g. IKEA, Leons and The Brick) selling furniture for home assembly.

Furniture and home furnishings is a competitive business in Canada, where you may be able to haggle over prices, particularly when you're spending a large amount or are paying cash. Many shops offer 'rooms-to-go' or even 'homes-to-go', where you can buy everything you need at the same time at a discounted price. Another way to save money is to wait for the sales, when prices may be reduced by as much as 50 per cent or more (see **Bargain Shopping** on page 290).

If you cannot wait and don't want to pay cash, look for an interest-free credit deal, but don't expect to get a bargain price as well. Check the advertisements in local newspapers (particularly 'home' or 'habitat' sections) and home and design magazines. All large furniture retailers publish catalogues and brochures that may be distributed to local homes. Furniture for home and office can also be rented, although it isn't cost-effective in the long term.

☑ **SURVIVAL TIP**

Second-hand furniture can be purchased from charity shops, through advertisements in local newspapers, garage sales (see Second-hand Goods above) and online auctions.

HOUSEHOLD GOODS

The electricity supply in Canada is 110/120 volts AC with a frequency of 60 Hertz (cycles) and therefore imported electrical apparatus made for a 220/240V 50 cycle supply won't work unless it has a 'dual voltage' switch or is used with a transformer (see page 107). It usually isn't worthwhile bringing electrical equipment to Canada as a wide range of Canadian and American-made items is available at reasonable prices. Don't bring a TV or DVD player made for a different market (e.g. Europe) to Canada because it won't work (see page 133).

Most new homes come complete with major appliances such as a stove and dishwasher and may also include a microwave, refrigerator and washer. Large household appliances such as cookers (stoves or ranges), refrigerators and dishwashers are usually provided in rented accommodation. Practically nobody brings large household appliances to Canada, particularly as the standard width in Canada isn't the same as in other countries, except the US.

Canadian refrigerators are huge and usually have the capacity to store a year's supply of food for a family of 14. Small appliances, such as vacuum cleaners, grills, toasters and electric irons, are inexpensive in Canada and generally good quality. Always shop around when buying large appliances and be prepared to haggle over prices, even when goods are on offer. You may wish to look for interest-free deals, but also make sure that the price is competitive. Bear in mind that some inexpensive deals don't include delivery and installation, so compare inclusive prices.

Canadian beds and bed linen such as sheets, pillowcases and quilts (comforters) aren't the same size or shape as in many other countries.

NEWSPAPERS, MAGAZINES & BOOKS

Canada has daily and weekly newspapers with morning, evening and Sunday editions, plus many free and foreign-language newspapers in the major cities. Quebec's newspapers are written in French, with some newspapers published in French and English editions. In addition to newspapers, a large number of periodicals are published in weekly, monthly, bi-monthly, quarterly or bi-annual editions. GST (see **Sales Tax** above) is levied on all newspapers, magazines and books, and although most provinces don't levy PST on newspapers or magazines, most do tax books. Canada doesn't have a genuine national press as is common in many European countries, and most newspapers are regional (city or provincial) or local. Local entertainment magazines and newspapers are published in all major cities, and free newspapers (some of which are surprisingly good) containing local community news are published in all regions and delivered to homes.

The closest Canada has to a national newspaper is the influential and respected *Globe & Mail*, a Toronto newspaper that publishes stories of interest to Canadians from coast to coast. The only other 'national' paper is the *National Post,* which incorporates the old *Financial Post.* Quality regional newspapers include the *Edmonton Journal*, the *Ottawa Citizen* and the *Vancouver Sun*; less serious 'tabloids' such as the *Edmonton Sun*, *Calgary Sun*, *Toronto Sun* and *The Province* (Vancouver) feature pictures of attractive young ladies (but not topless, which is illegal) and men, known as 'sunshine' girls' and boys. As in many western countries, the serious newspapers are usually broadsheets, while the tabloids are more interested in scandal, sex and sport (not necessarily in that order). The best Canadian newspapers are well written and compare favourably with the best European newspapers, and contain good international news coverage (unlike US newspapers).

Most Canadians read newspapers for the comics, sport, fashion, crime reports and local news, and rely on TV for 'serious' news. Major Canadian newspapers contain comprehensive sport and entertainment sections, as well as international news and foreign sports coverage. Many newspapers have magazine-format 'lifestyle' and 'home living' sections in order to compete with magazines. Most Canadian newspapers are online and can be accessed via www.world-newspapers.com/canada.html (search by province) and www.onlinenewspapers.com/canada.htm (listed A-Z by town/city).

Large city newspapers may print two editions daily (a city and rural edition) and some dailies (although not the *Globe & Mail*) also publish Sunday editions. Friday and Saturday editions are often huge and contain ten or more sections of world news, local news, sport, entertainment, finance, home and lifestyle, TV and radio programmes, comic strips, and car and property information (these sections are full of advertisements and are known as 'cat-box liners'). However, Friday and Saturday editions usually cost three times as much as other editions, therefore it may be cheaper to buy a bag of cat litter.

Weekly news magazines such as *MacLean's* (known cynically as Maclone's by those who think it's a copy of *Time*) are hugely popular and a good way to catch up on the most important Canadian and international news. Other popular Canadian magazines include *Canadian Geographic*, *Today's Parent*, *Harrowsmith Country Life*, *Now* and *Chatelaine*. If you have a taste for anarchical reportage, try *Frank Magazine*, which contains hot gossip and smutty stories. (Don't throw your old magazines away when you've finished with them – some second-hand bookshops will buy them for around a quarter of their original price.)

About a third of Canadians (i.e. those living in the major cities) have newspapers delivered to their homes. Newspapers are sold in towns from 'honour' vending machines located on street corners, in shopping malls, and at railway and bus stations. You insert the exact price (usually 50¢ to 75¢) in a slot and pull down a handle to open the door (you're trusted to take one copy only, hence 'honour'). These machines are the only place you can buy a newspaper without paying sales tax, because the machine manufacturers haven't yet figured out an easy way to cope with the few extra cents. In major cities, newspapers and magazines are sold from newsstands.

Some foreign newspapers and periodicals are available from specialist newsstands in major cities, although they're expensive and newspapers are usually a few days old (with the exception of *The New York Times* and *The Wall Street Journal,* which are available on the day of publication). Some public and university libraries keep a selection of foreign daily newspapers in their reading rooms, although they're usually old copies. Most Canadian and foreign newspapers and magazines can be purchased on subscription at huge savings over newsstand prices, and many Canadian magazines offer gifts to new subscribers.

Despite the imposition of sales tax, Canada is still one of the cheapest countries in the world in which to buy books, particularly paperbacks. There are cut-price and remainder bookstores in major cities, and most general bookstores have a bargain basement where discount books are sold. Some stores, e.g. Wal-Mart and Kmart, discount all books – typically a 25 per cent reduction. The biggest nationwide chains include Chapters-Indigo (www.chapters.indigo.ca).

In major cities there are second-hand and exchange bookshops for collectors and bargain hunters, often located near university campuses. Specialist bookshops are common, including some selling foreign-language books. Except in Quebec and New Brunswick, French-language books are available only at specialised shops in the major cities, where many bookshops are open until late evening (some until midnight) and some also open on Sundays. Many offer comfortable places to sit and read and may also have a café.

You can buy books online from a number of booksellers, including Abe Books (🖳 www.abebooks.com), who can locate books worldwide, Amazon (🖳 www.amazon.ca) and Chapters (🖳 www.chapters.indigo.ca). You can find a bookseller in a particular city or by name via the Canadian Booksellers Association website (🖳 www.cbabook.org).

There are also mail-order book clubs in Canada, most of which have introductory offers at hugely discounted prices; see 🖳 www.canadianbookclubs.com and www.canada-book-clubs.com for information. Some book clubs offer a wide range of general books, while others specialise in a particular subject, e.g. photography or computers (clubs advertise in newspapers and magazines). Many organisations and clubs run their own libraries or book exchanges, and public libraries in all towns have a wide selection of books (see page 266).

ALCOHOL & TOBACCO

The sale of alcohol (liquor) in Canada is strictly controlled in most areas, where licensing laws are set by provinces and municipalities. You can generally buy spirits (hard liquor) only at shops operated by the provincial Liquor Control Board (LCB), but wines and beers are sold in supermarkets and privately-owned beer and wine shops. Shops selling alcohol cannot open before 10am and must close no later than local bars. Government 'liquor stores' close any time between 6pm and 11pm on weekdays and Saturdays, while beer and wine shops usually close at 11pm. All shops selling alcohol are closed on Sundays. When shops are closed, you can buy beer or wine from some local bars, called off-sales, for drinking off the premises.

☑ SURVIVAL TIP

Prices vary little (if at all) in LCB stores, although in some cities prices are lower and people may travel from out of town to stock up. Sales tax (PST) on alcohol varies from province to province, so those who live near the border of a province/territory with lower PST often drive over the border to buy it.

An 'open container' law forbids the consumption of alcohol in public and it's illegal to have an open container in a vehicle, even in the boot (trunk). The minimum legal age for buying alcohol is 18 in Alberta, Manitoba and Quebec, and 19 in the rest of Canada, which are also the minimum drinking ages in bars. A retailer is supposed to ask your age and may ask for identification, although in practice this rarely happens if you look old enough. Acceptable identification usually consists of a driving licence or a Provincial Identification Card issued by the provincial Liquor Control Board (where there is one).

Canada produces some good (particularly ice wine, although it's expensive) and improving wines, but most still have some way to go reach the average quality of, for example, Californian wines. There are high import duties on foreign wine to protect the Canadian wine industry, although you can still find reasonably priced French and Californian wines. When buying Canadian wine, look for the Vintner's Quality Assurance (VQA) sign on the labels (the Canadian equivalent of the French *appellation contrôlée* system), which indicates better quality wines.

Beer is sold in 341ml and 355ml sizes, usually in packs of six (a 'six-pack' or 'half-sack') or cases of 12 ('twelve-pack') or 24 (a 'two-four'); 'supercans' are also available in 473ml or 950ml sizes. Canadian beer usually has an alcohol content of 5 or 6 per cent. In Quebec and the Atlantic provinces a non-alcoholic spruce 'beer' is made (from the sap of spruce trees) and in the fruit-growing areas of British Columbia, Ontario and Quebec you can find apple or cherry 'ciders' with variable alcohol content. The price of rye whisky (such as Canadian Club and Seagrams) and other spirits is around $25 for a 26oz bottle.

Like alcohol, the purchase and use of tobacco and tobacco products is restricted to those over the age of 18 in Alberta, Manitoba and Quebec, and 19 elsewhere. Canadian cigarettes are generally milder than American, the major brands including Player's, Craven A, DuMaurier, Matinee and Export A. You can also buy Cuban cigars, which are banned in the US.

HOME SHOPPING

Mail-order shopping is widespread in Canada, where busy lifestyles encourage people to favour the convenience of shopping by catalogue, telephone and via the internet (see below), which has overtaken mail-order shopping in the last decade. Over half of all Canadians shop from home and almost anything can be delivered overnight (although you pay extra for this service) or within a few days, from within Canada or the US.

Mail-order has a long tradition in Canada, where the mail-order catalogue was invented; and those living in remote areas have purchased the latest fashions, consumer goods and even wooden houses by post since the late 19th century. Despite increased competition from the internet, mail-order remains big business. Many Canadian companies sell their products and services exclusively via direct retailing to both corporate and private customers, particularly financial and insurance services, computers, and office equipment and supplies.

> **☑ SURVIVAL TIP**
>
> **Many stores, such as The Bay (www.hbc.com), publish catalogues and will send goods anywhere in the world, and specialist companies such as Canadian Tire (www.canadiantire.ca) and Sears (www.sears.ca) also produce elaborate catalogues.**

There's generally little risk when buying goods by mail-order in Canada, as consumer-protection laws and Canada Post's rules regarding mail-order sales are strict. If you have any doubts about a company's reputation, you should check with your provincial or local consumer protection agency or a Better Business Bureau before ordering. Keep a copy of the advertisement or offer and a record of your order, including the company's name, address and phone number, the price of items ordered, any handling or other charges, the date you posted or telephoned your order, and your method of payment.

Shopping by phone has also increased considerably in recent years, particularly with the proliferation of charge, credit and debit cards. One of the most popular methods of telephone shopping is via TV through companies such as the Shopping Channel. Cable TV shopping shows offer goods at seemingly bargain prices, some even providing a 24-hour service for insomniac shoppers. Orders are placed by phone and goods are posted to you.

You should be wary of unsolicited telemarketing sales, which have increased dramatically in recent years. A caller will try to sell direct or arrange an appointment to visit you and may offer a variety of gifts and inducements to tempt you. If you're tempted, ask for written information by post and check out the company or organisation, e.g. with a Better Business Bureau. Never give credit card or bank account details over the phone to 'cold' callers. As a general rule, it's wise to ignore all unsolicited phone calls, as you don't know whether the caller is a conman.

For further information about direct marketing, see the *Direct Marketing* newspaper (www.dmn.ca) or contact a local direct marketing organisation, such as the Direct Marketing Association of Toronto (DMAT, www.dmatoronto.org).

If you have any complaints about direct marketing, e.g. to get your name removed from mailing lists, you can contact the Canadian Marketing Association (CDMA, 1 Concorde Gate, Suite 607, Don Mills, ON M3C 3N6, ☎ 416-391 2362, www.the-cma.org) and ask to be registered on their 'don't post, don't call' service. The CDMA also deals with regulatory affairs. Other complaints can be taken up with the Office of Consumers Affairs (Industry Canada, 235 Queen Street, 6th Floor West, Ottawa, ON K1A 0H5 (☎ 613-946 2576, ✉ consumer.information@ic.gc.ca, 💻 http://consumerinformation.ca).

Duty is payable on any imported item (i.e. including anything purchased abroad by mail-order) worth over $60; to be exempt from duty, items worth under $60 must be marked as a 'gift' on the customs' declaration form.

Internet Shopping

Internet shopping has exploded in Canada in recent years and now accounts for an increasing share of purchases. Most Canadian (and American) stores (Costco, Sears, etc.) have a website where they offer online shopping and there are also online price comparison sites such as 💻 www.canadaretail.ca and www.pricecanada.com and a wealth of online shopping sites, including 💻 www.amazon.ca, www.canadaretail.ca, http://canadianinternetshopping.com, www.cybershopping.ca, www.onlineshoppers.ca and www.theshoppingchannel.com. Ebay (💻 www.ebay.ca) and eBid.net (💻 http://ca.ebid.net – auctions without fees), are popular online auctions sites.

All prices on websites selling goods to domestic buyers must include GST and PST, which must also be paid on imported goods, along with duty (if applicable), although gifts worth less than $60 and goods valued below $20 are exempt. However, alcoholic beverages, tobacco products and advertising material don't qualify for the gift exemption.

DUTY-FREE ALLOWANCES

Residents and non-residents are allowed certain exemptions from duty when bringing goods into Canada (see below). Articles exempt from duty must have been acquired for your personal or household use, must be brought with you when you enter Canada and must be declared to customs.

After your allowances have been deducted, a flat rate duty of 10 per cent is applied to the next $1,000 value of dutiable goods. The value of imported goods is based on the fair retail value of each item in the country where it was acquired and not necessarily the price paid. If you underestimate the value or misrepresent an article in your declaration, you may have to pay a penalty in addition to duty. If you're in doubt about the value of an article, declare it at the price paid. If you fail to declare an article acquired abroad, you're liable to a penalty equivalent to its value in Canada. In addition, it's subject to forfeiture and you may be liable to prosecution. If you're in doubt about whether an article should be declared, declare it and let the customs official decide.

Residents

If you're resident (even temporarily) in Canada, you're entitled to certain duty-free allowances when you travel abroad, but what you may bring into Canada duty free depends on how long you've been away, as follows:

Duty-free Allowances

Duration of Absence	Allowance
24 hours	Goods (excluding tobacco and alcohol products) worth up to $50
48 hours	Goods (including tobacco and alcohol products – see below) worth up to $400
7 days or more	Goods (including tobacco and alcohol products – see below) worth up to $750

You may claim these allowances an unlimited number of times each year, but you cannot combine them with another person's allowances. All imported goods must be declared, irrespective of whether they're within the above allowances.

When travelling abroad (including to the US), residents should take receipts for cameras, jewellery, watches, etc. with you and declare them to customs before leaving Canada, so that you aren't charged duty on them when you return. You may not bring certain goods into Canada or you may need a permit (see **Restricted Goods** on page 83).

Alcohol & Tobacco

There are specific personal exemption limits for importing alcohol and tobacco products into Canada, as shown below:

- 1.5 litres of wine **or** 1.4 litres of spirits **or** 24 x 355ml (12oz) tins or bottles (total 8.5 litres) of beer or ale for each person who's allowed to drink. You may also bring in alcohol in addition to your duty-free allowance, provided you pay the duty and that the total amount doesn't exceed the limits set by the province or territory you're entering.
- 200 cigarettes **and** 50 cigars **and** 7oz (200g) of loose tobacco for each person who's permitted to smoke.

Note that the legal age for the import of alcohol is 19 in all provinces and territories, except for Alberta, Manitoba and Quebec, where it's 18. The legal age for importing tobacco products is also 19, with the exception of Alberta, Manitoba, Northwest Territories, Nunavut, Quebec, Saskatchewan and the Yukon, where it's 18.

Visitors

Visitors can bring in personal effects without paying duty or tax, provided they don't leave them in Canada. They can also import the amounts of alcohol and tobacco products listed above.

Visitors can also bring in gifts duty and tax-free (provided they aren't alcohol or tobacco) with a value $60 or less per item. Gifts over $60 are subject to duty and tax on the amount above $60.

You should, nevertheless, declare any articles acquired abroad if they're accompanying you and you think you may have exceeded your duty-free exemption. The head of a family may make a joint declaration for all members residing in the same household and entering Canada together, and family members can combine their personal exemptions even if the articles acquired by one family member exceed his personal exemption.

RECEIPTS & WARRANTIES

When shopping in Canada you should insist on a receipt as proof of payment (this is particularly useful when an automatic alarm is activated as you're leaving a shop!). It may also be impossible to return or exchange goods without a receipt and you may also need one to return an item for repair or replacement under a warranty. You should check receipts immediately on paying (particularly in supermarkets); if you're overcharged, you cannot usually obtain redress later.

Although it isn't required by law, most shops will give a cash refund or credit on a charge account or credit card within a certain period, e.g. one to two weeks (although you may be offered only a shop credit or exchange on discounted goods). Some discount and outlet stores don't allow any returns. Shops may display their refund policy on a sign or it may be listed on your receipt.

All goods sold in Canada carry an implied warranty of 'merchantability', meaning that they must perform the function for which they were designed. If they don't, you can return them to the store where you purchased them and demand a replacement or your money back. In addition to the implied warranty, some goods carry written warranties. Although written warranties are voluntary, when provided they must (by law) be written in clear, everyday language, and the precise terms and duration must be specified at the top of the warranty document.

The period of a warranty varies considerably, e.g. from one to five years, which may be an important consideration when making a purchase. Warranties can also be full or limited; a full warranty provides you with maximum protection, although usually for a limited period. You may be offered the chance to purchase an extension warranty when you buy certain goods. These cost from $60 to $100 and aren't usually worth the money because they rarely extend beyond the natural working life of a product. Warranties may be transferable when goods are sold or given away during the warranty period. You're often asked to complete and post a warranty card confirming the date of purchase, although under a full warranty this isn't necessary. Most warranties are with the manufacturer or importer, to whom goods must usually be returned. A local or provincial consumer protection agency, Better Business Bureau or consumer association can usually advise you of your rights. When travelling abroad, it's wise to take receipts for cameras, video cameras and other expensive items with you (see Duty-free Allowances above).

CONSUMER ASSOCIATIONS

There's a number of consumers' organisations in Canada, including the Consumers Association of Canada (436 Gilmour Street, 3rd Floor, Ottawa, ON K2P 0R8, ☎ 613-238 2533, 💻 www.consumer.ca), which promotes and explains consumer rights and helps individuals to resolve disputes with retailers. The Canadian Council of Better Business Bureaus (2 St Clair Avenue East, Suite 800, Toronto, ON M4T 2T5, ☎ 416-644 4936, 💻 www.ccbbb.ca) promotes high ethical standards of business practice and provides a 'platform' for the discussion of retailer-consumer relations, as well as helping to resolve disputes.

Snowy Owl

18. ODDS & ENDS

This chapter contains miscellaneous information. Although not all topics included are of vital importance, most are of general interest to anyone living or working in Canada, including such weighty matters as tipping and toilets.

CANADIAN CITIZENSHIP

In general, anyone born in Canada automatically becomes a Canadian citizen. You may also qualify as a Canadian citizen if you were born abroad and one of your parents was Canadian at the time of your birth. If you think you may come under this category, check with your local Canadian High Commission, embassy or consulate. All others can become a Canadian citizen only through a process called naturalisation. To be eligible for naturalisation you must be aged 18 or over, be in Canada legally as a 'permanent resident', have lived in Canada for three of the past four years (except for children) and be able to understand, speak, read and write English or French. You must undergo a written 'citizenship test' of around 20 questions to demonstrate that you know about the rights and responsibilities of a citizen, and have a reasonable knowledge of Canada's geography, history and political system.

The test is in two parts: General questions about Canada and questions about the region where you live. Typical questions cover native Americans, the early explorers, railway building, when Canada became a country, who has the right to apply for a Canadian passport, what the names of the provinces are, when European settlers first came to your region, the capital city, mineral and natural resources in the region, and which political party is in power. You're given a study guide of typical questions when you apply for citizenship, with some recommended books to read to prepare for the test. The questions you may be asked and other information about naturalisation are listed in a free booklet, *How to Become a Canadian Citizen*, available from citizenship offices or the Registrar of Canada Citizenship (PO Box 10000, Sydney, NS B1P 7C1). You can even attend citizenship classes; information is also available on the internet (💻 www.cic.gc.ca/english/citizenship/index.asp).

Children don't need to have lived in Canada for three years before applying for citizenship. Parents can apply for citizenship for their children as soon as they receive permanent resident status, provided that the parents are already Canadian citizens themselves or are in the process of applying for citizenship (which means that you can submit the papers for the whole family at the same time). A separate application form is required for each child. Children (under 18) don't need to sit a written test, but if they're over 14 they must take the oath of citizenship.

The fee for the 'right to be a citizen' of Canada is $100 (which applies to the 'retention', 'resumption' or 'renunciation' of citizenship). A proof of citizenship document or a search of the citizenship records, costs $75. If an application is refused, adults receive a refund of their fee, but children don't.

You cannot become a Canadian citizen if you're under a deportation order (and shouldn't be in Canada), you've been charged with an indictable offence or have been convicted of one in the past three years, or if you've been in prison, on parole or on probation within the last four years.

Naturalisation is a legal status and therefore Canadian citizenship is conferred by a judge in a 'naturalisation ceremony', when an 'oath of citizenship' is taken. The oath is normally sworn on the bible, but if you wish to use your own holy book, you may do so (take it with you as they may not have one available). Canadian law permits dual nationality for naturalised citizens, who have virtually the same rights as native-born Canadians, but your previous country of citizenship may not allow you to retain citizenship after you've taken Canadian nationality. There's no compulsion for immigrants to become Canadian citizens and they're free to live in Canada for as long as they wish, provided that they're in the country legally and abide by the laws of the land.

Passports

Once you become a Canadian citizen you can apply for a Canadian passport, including for any children. Application forms (available from your local passport office) must be accompanied by two photographs.

The requirements regarding photographs are strict; if they aren't met, a passport won't be issued. The exact specifications can be found on the Passport Canada website (🖳 www.ppt.gc.ca – click 'Site Map' on the left, then 'Photos').

One photograph must then be signed on the reverse (along with the form) by an eligible guarantor, as listed on the form. You must also provide evidence of Canadian citizenship, any previous Canadian passport, a certificate of identity or a refugee travel document issued in the last five years, and pay the fee shown in the box below.

Passport Application Fees

Type of Passport	Age		
	16+	3-15	Under 3
24 pages	$87	$37	$22
48 pages	$92	$39	$24

The fee can be paid in cash at a passport office, by money order (postal or bank), certified cheque or bank draft payable to the Receiver General for Canada, or by a debit or credit card. If you live in an area where there's a passport office, you can submit your application in person, which takes around five days compared with ten or more for postal applications (Passport Canada offices are listed in the *Yellow Pages*). Alternatively you can post your application to Passport Canada (Foreign Affairs and International Trade Canada, Gatineau QC K1A 0G3, ☎ 1-800-567 6868 or 819-997 8338, 🖳 www.ppt.gc.ca).

CLIMATE

Due to its vast size and varied topography, ranging from temperate rainforest to tundra and permafrost, Canada's climate varies enormously. Temperatures in the southern region of the prairie provinces of Alberta, Manitoba and Saskatchewan vary from 100°F (38°C) in summer to -12°F (-24°C) in winter. In Yellowknife (Northwest Territories), the winter temperature drops to -28°F (-33°C), although the Yukon holds the record for the coldest temperature ever recorded in Canada which was -81°F (-61°C). Fortunately, not too many people live in these inhospitable areas. Not surprisingly, the northern region of some provinces and the northern territories are referred to as the Great White North, where summer (the frost-free period) lasts barely two months.

Vancouver and Victoria on the Pacific coast have the smallest annual temperature swings, while the largest variations are experienced in Ontario and Quebec, which have harsh winters and hot, humid summers. In the Atlantic provinces of New Brunswick, Newfoundland and Labrador, Prince Edward Island and Nova Scotia, spring and summer are warm and pleasant, but winter can be very cold and windy.

In winter it's cold or freezing everywhere except on the southern coast of British Columbia (e.g. Vancouver), which has the most temperate climate thanks to warm, moist Pacific Ocean airstreams. Everywhere else experiences a lot of snow, plus chilling winds and occasional ice storms, when 'snow' instantly freezes forming a thick coat of ice on everything. During a particularly severe ice storm in southern Ontario and Quebec in early 1998, power lines were brought down by the weight of the ice and the region was without electricity for several days.

If you're a keen skier you'll welcome some snow, but won't perhaps be so enthusiastic when snowdrifts make the roads impassable, engulf your home and cut you off from the outside world for days on end.

Temperatures are often reduced considerably by the wind speed. This creates what's known as the wind chill factor, where a temperature of 10°F (-12°C) combined with a wind speed of 25mph (40kph) results in a wind chill factor of -29°F (-34°C). The wind chill factor can cause temperatures to drop as low as -60°F (-51°C), when people (not surprisingly) are warned to stay at home. However, in southern Alberta there's often a warm, dry winter wind called a Chinook, which can raise winter temperatures, e.g. from below −20°C (−4°F) to as high as 10°C to 20°C (50°F to 68°F) – but don't be fooled as it doesn't last more than a few hours or days and soon turns cold again!

Canadian meteorologists are constantly on alert for severe weather patterns, and warnings are issued if a heavy snowfall or ice storm is expected and storm watches are broadcast on TV and radio (some radios have a special national weather service band).

Spring and autumn (fall) are the most pleasant seasons in Canada, but quite short in some regions and temperatures can vary considerably from week to week. Spring and autumn are warm and sunny with low humidity in most regions, although it can be very wet in some areas (particularly on the Atlantic and Pacific coasts). The Atlantic Provinces are a blaze of colour in the autumn, particularly the maple trees, and many tourists flock to see the display.

On 2nd February, Canadians celebrate 'Groundhog Day', when Wiarton Willie the groundhog is supposed to come out of his hole to check the weather. The story goes that if it's a bright sunny day and Willie sees his shadow on the ground at midday, he'll dash back down because winter is going to stay for another six weeks. There was a major fuss in 1999 when Willie died and someone started a 'Who Whacked Willie' website, which is now defunct. However, the good people of Wiarton appointed a new groundhog, known as Wee Willie Junior, in good time for the next year's tourist season (see 💻 www.wiarton-willie.org).

Average Maximum Temperatures				
City	**Winter (Jan)**	**Spring (Apr)**	**Summer (Jul)**	**Autumn (Oct)**
Calgary	-6°C (21°F)	8°C (46°F)	22°C (72°F)	10°C (50°F)
Halifax	-1°C (30°F)	9°C (48°F)	23°C (73°F)	14°C (57°F)
Montreal	-6°C (21°F)	11°C (52°F)	26°C (79°F)	13°C (55°F)
Ottawa	-6°C (21°F)	11°C (52°F)	26°C (79°F)	13°C (55°F)
St John's	0°C (32°F)	5°C (41°F)	21°C (70°F)	11°C (52°F)
Toronto	-7°C (19°F)	6°C (43°F)	21°C (70°F)	9°C (48°F)
Vancouver	5°C (41°F)	13°C (55°F)	22°C (72°F)	14°C (57°F)
Whitehorse	-16°C (3°F)	6°C (43°F)	20°C (68°F)	4°C (39°F)
Winnipeg	-14°C (7°F)	9°C (48°F)	26°C (79°F)	12°C (54°F)
Yellowknife	-25°C (-13°F)	-1°C (30°F)	21°C (70°F)	1°C (34°F)

Canadians usually overreact to extremes of climate, with freezing air-conditioning in summer and sweltering heating in winter. Because most buildings are too hot or too cold, it's often a problem knowing what to wear and many people dress in layers that they take off or put on, depending on the indoor or outdoor temperature.

The average maximum temperatures for selected cities are shown above.

Weather forecasts are provided in daily newspapers and broadcast by radio and TV stations, although the National Broadcasting Company (NBC) has terminated its 24-hour weather channel. The Weather Office (💻 www.weatheroffice.gc.ca) provides comprehensive and up-to-date regional weather information.

CRIME

Unlike its neighbour to the south, Canada has a relatively low crime rate, although illegal drugs and gang violence (not unconnected) are an increasing problem in the cities. In 2007, Quebec and Ontario (where Toronto had the second-lowest overall crime rate among all 27 metropolitan areas) had the lowest crime rates and Saskatchewan the highest, followed by British Columbia (which had the highest property crime rate). Overall the crime rate declined for the third consecutive year, continuing a downward trend since 1991, when crime peaked; violent crime also fell, with homicides falling for the second year running.

The low crime rate (some city suburbs excepted) is often cited as a reason why Canada is one of the most desirable places in the world to live. That's not to say that you should leave your valuables in an unlocked car or walk the inner city streets on your own late at night! Crime is naturally more common in the major cities and popular tourist areas, where petty thieves haunt bus and train stations, car parks and camping areas.

Prevention & Safety

Staying safe in a large city is mostly a matter of common sense. Most areas are safe most of the time, particularly when there are a lot of people around, although at night you should keep to brightly lit main streets and avoid secluded areas (best of all, take a taxi). Walk in the opposite direction to the traffic so nobody can drive alongside (curb-crawl) you at night, and walk on the outside of the pavement (sidewalk), so that you're less likely to be mugged from a doorway. Avoid parks at night and keep to a park's main paths or where there are other people during the day. When you're in an unfamiliar city, ask a policeman, taxi driver or local person if there are any unsafe neighbourhoods – and avoid them!

Most city apartments are fitted with a security system, so that you can speak to visitors before allowing them access to the building, and doors have a peephole and security chain so that you can check a caller's identity before opening the door.

Be careful who you allow into your home and always check the identity of anyone claiming to be an official or an employee of a utility or other company – check by phone with their office if you aren't expecting anybody.

Store anything of value in a home safe or a bank safety deposit box and ensure that you have adequate insurance (see **Chapter 13**). Don't make it obvious that nobody is at home by leaving tell-tale signs such as a pile of newspapers or mail. Many people leave lights, a radio or a TV on (activated by random timers) when they aren't at home, and ask their neighbours to keep an eye on their homes when they're on holiday (vacation). Many towns have 'crime watch' areas (neighbourhood watch, block watch), where residents keep an eye open for suspicious characters and report them to the local police. If you have something stolen and need to make an insurance claim, you must report the theft to the police and make a note of the crime report number for the claim form.

Guns & Other Weapons

The number of deaths caused by guns (firearms) in Canada has been on the decrease since 1991 (when 1,444 people were killed by guns – although the annual death toll was even higher before 1978), thanks largely to increasingly restrictive import and ownership legislation. However, the number of pistol (handgun) killings has remained more or less constant owing to the prevalence of pistol smuggling. In 2007, 594 people died as a result of being shot, although 'only 188' of those deaths were counted as murders (homicides) – a sixth of the gun-murder rate of the US.

Since December 2002, all guns have had to be registered, although as recently as early 2006, it was estimated that as many as 70 per cent of guns were unregistered.

Even sporting guns must be registered, licensed and declared when they're imported into Canada, and you cannot import anything except a regular sporting rifle or shotgun with a barrel at least 18.5in (470mm) long and an overall length of 26in (660mm) manufactured for sporting, hunting or competition use only. For full details contact the Canada Firearms Centre (Ottawa, ON, K1A 1M6, ☎ 1-800-731 4000, 💻 www.cfc-cafc.gc.ca).

Since 1st September 2008, when 'Bill 9' was passed, Quebec has had some of the most restrictive gun laws in Canada. Dubbed 'Anastasia's Law' in memory of 18-year-old Anastasia DeSousa, one of four students killed two years previously at Montreal's Dawson College, the bill bans guns in schools and day-care centres and on public and school transport, with fines of up to $5,000 for contraventions.

There are three classes of guns and gun licences, which are normally issued only to over-18s, but in some cases even to under-12s: non-restricted, restricted and 'prohibited'. Note, however, that 'prohibited' guns aren't actually prohibited; they simply require a 'prohibited licence'! All guns with barrels shorter than 104mm (i.e. pistols) are 'restricted'. For non-restricted and restricted weapons, you need a 'Possession and Acquisition Licence' (PAL), for which you must have passed a Canadian Firearms Safety Course (CFSC) and a Canadian Restricted Firearms Safety Course (CRFSC) respectively.

There's a long list of other weapons that you may not own or import, including tear gas, spiked wristbands and 'knuckle-dusters'.

GEOGRAPHY

Even larger than its southern neighbour the USA, Canada covers an area of 3.85mn mi² (9.97mn km²) and is, since the disintegration of the USSR, the second-largest country in the world, after China. Canada stretches around 4,800mi (7,700km) from east to west, from the Atlantic Ocean to the Pacific Ocean. The country extends around 3,000mi (4,800km) from north to south, from Pelee Island in Lake Erie to Ellesmere Island in the Arctic Ocean, and the southern border with the US is 5,525mi (8,892km) in length. The country is divided into seven main geographical regions, as follows.

The Arctic or 'Great White North'

The Arctic region comprises the Northwest Territories, Nunavut and the Yukon, and encompasses around 40 per cent of Canada's land area. North of the tree line, the Arctic is a land of harsh beauty with long, dark and freezing winters. North of the mainland is a maze of islands separated by convoluted straits and sounds, the most famous of which form the fabled Northwest Passage (the route to the Orient sought by many early explorers). The harsh climate of this remote area means that relatively few people live there and those that do usually scratch a living from the fur trade or work in mining. Dawson City (in the Yukon) was the scene of the Klondyke Gold Rush in 1898, which for a brief period was the richest gold field of all time.

Apart from the indigenous First Nations people, most inhabitants are transients, such as miners, hunters and government employees on a short tour of duty. The total population of this vast region is barely 100,000, with around half living in the two major towns of Whitehorse and Yellowknife.

After much lobbying, the eastern part of the Northwest Territories became the province of Nunavut ('our land') on 1st April 1999, with its capital at Iqaluit (population around 6,000) on the southern tip of Baffin Island.

The Atlantic Provinces-Appalachian Region

This region was the first to be settled by Europeans and takes in Canada's smallest provinces of New Brunswick, Newfoundland and Labrador, Nova Scotia and Prince Edward Island. These provinces, which are an extension of the Appalachians (an ancient mountain range), consist mainly of forested hills, low mountains and rocky coastlines, with the population mostly comprised of scattered small communities. The Grand Banks, extending 250mi (around 400km) off the coast, is one of the world's richest fishing grounds, although it has been ravaged by over-fishing in recent decade. Some 10 per cent of the population lives here, mostly relying on forestry and fishing for a living.

The Canadian Shield

The Canadian (or Laurentian) Shield is billions of years old and Canada's largest geographical feature (covering half the mainland). It extends from the region around Hudson Bay in the north stretching east to Labrador, south to Kingston on Lake Ontario and north-west as far as the Arctic Ocean. The region is rich in minerals, although it has only a thin layer of soil on a solid granite base, therefore not much grows (apart from trees) and the population is sparse.

The Cordillera

This region encompasses the Yukon and most of British Columbia, and is part of the 9,000mi (14,500km) chain of mountains stretching from Tierra del Fuego (Chile) to Alaska. It includes the highest point in Canada, Mount Logan (6,050m/19,849ft) in the St Elias Mountains in the south-west corner of the Yukon. The Cordillera is home to around 15 per cent of the population, most of whom live within 150mi (240km) of the US border. Apart from some farming and fruit production, the main industries are forestry and tourism.

The Great Lakes & St. Lawrence Lowlands

The southern areas of Ontario and Quebec, the industrial heartland of Canada, contain Canada's two largest cities, Toronto and Montreal. The region has some prime agricultural land, while the large expanses of Lakes Erie and Ontario moderate the climate and extend the number of frost-free days, permitting the cultivation of grapes, pears, peaches and other fruit. The Great Lakes and the St. Lawrence region is also sugar maple country. With rich soil, easy access to the sea via the St Lawrence Seaway and a long border with the US, this region is home to over half of Canada's population.

The Pacific Coast

The British Columbia coast in the west is indented with deep fjords, shielded from Pacific storms and bathed by warm, moist, Pacific air currents. These help provide the mildest climate in Canada, although Vancouver Island's west coast receives an exceptional amount of rain, hence it's temperate rain forest climate. The region encompasses three major mountain ranges: The Rocky Mountains, the Columbia Mountains and the Coast Mountains, and is home to Canada's oldest (Western Canadian cedars, up to 1,300 years old) and tallest (Douglas firs) trees, used as replacement masts for the ships of early explorers.

The Prairies

The southern areas of Alberta, Manitoba and Saskatchewan (also known as the Interior Plains or Heartland) are Canada's 'breadbasket' (and one of the richest grain-producing regions in the world), consisting largely of cereal fields. Around a quarter of the population is descended from migrants from Germany, Russia, the Ukraine and other eastern European countries (most of whose ancestors arrived in the early 20th century). Manitoba and Saskatchewan are home to around 7 per cent of the population, while Alberta has around 11 per cent, which has risen rapidly with the oil boom.

> Alberta has the distinction of being the source of more dinosaur bones than anywhere else in the world and boasts a world-class fossil museum at the main site, Drumheller.

Provincial & Territorial Profiles

Canada is a federation made up of ten provinces and three territories: Alberta, British Columbia, Manitoba, New Brunswick, Newfoundland and Labrador, Nova Scotia, Ontario, Prince Edward Island, Quebec and Saskatchewan, and the Northwest Territories, Nunavut and the Yukon Territory.

Alberta

Alberta is the most westerly of Canada's three Prairie Provinces (the other two are Manitoba and Saskatchewan). Alberta lies in western Canada, east of British Columbia, and is the sixth-largest province/territory, covering 255,303mi² (661,185km²). It has a population of around 3.6mn and the major cities are Calgary (1.1mn) and the capital, Edmonton (1mn). Calgary is in southern Alberta in the foothills of the Rockies and is a hilly, sprawling city 1,048m (3,440ft) above sea level. It's a cosmopolitan and modern city, a significant business centre, and an important destination for eco-tourism and winter sports, with Banff and several important mountain resorts just an hour's drive away. The G8 Summit was held in one such resort in 2002.

The city's economy is based on petroleum, with agriculture, high technology and tourism also contributing to its healthy economic growth. The climate isn't as harsh as in much of the prairies: Winters are cold, but temperatures are sometimes moderated by mild winds blowing from the Pacific Ocean; summers are warm, although only 60-90 days are frost free. Calgary's climate is semi-arid and droughts are common.

Edmonton is in southern central Alberta and sprawls over almost 270mi² (700km²), making it one of North America's largest cities by area. It's home to around one million people and is a centre of culture, education and government, and a service centre for the oilsands projects in the north of the province. Oil-related activities are important to the economy and there's a significant technology sector. Edmonton's climate is continental and the city has one of the greatest temperature ranges in Canada, with warm summers and cold or very cold winters. Thunderstorms are common in summer, but the climate is quite dry and Edmonton receives much less snow than many North American cities.

Alberta has a strong economy, the cornerstone being oil, which accounts for around a quarter of economic activity (Alberta has huge oil and natural gas reserves). Other major industries include business and commercial services, energy, finance, manufacturing, real estate, retail, transport, utilities and wholesale. Over the past 15 years, the areas that have experienced the most rapid growth include business services, electronics, food processing, machinery, petrochemicals, telecommunications, tourism and wood products.

flag of British Columbia

Alberta is sometimes regarded as a 'hick' province because, outside the cities, it's culturally and politically conservative. Nevertheless, it attracts large numbers of immigrants, many from other parts of Canada, drawn by its booming economy, low taxes and spectacular scenery, notably the Rockies (which also offer excellent skiing).

British Columbia

British Columbia is on Canada's west (Pacific) coast and is the fifth-largest province/territory, covering 364,791mi² (944,735km²), which is around four times the size of the UK. It has a population of 4.5mn, with the capital, Victoria, located on the southeast tip of Vancouver Island. The largest city is Vancouver, situated in the south-west corner of the mainland.

Many people believe that British Columbia is the most beautiful part of Canada, particularly its coastal fjords, the Rockies and Vancouver Island's temperate rain forests. The province has a wide variety of landscapes and its coasts, forests, lakes, mountains and rivers make it ideal for camping, fishing, hiking, hunting, mountaineering, rock climbing, skiing (Whistler, two hours north of Vancouver, is Canada's largest ski resort) and watersports. The province also has a strong Green (environmental) movement, vibrant artistic communities on the west coast and a booming marijuana growing 'industry'!

British Columbia's economy is diverse and includes energy (it produces some gas and oil), filming, fishing, information technology, lumber, mining, retirees, technology and tourism. People are attracted to the province by its beauty, mild climate and outdoor lifestyle, but the economy is sometimes unstable (affected by resource prices and the state of industrial relations) and the job market can be restrictive. The west coast is an earthquake zone and the experts claim that a large quake is overdue!

The capital, Victoria, is home to around 330,000 people (in the metropolitan area, 80,000 of whom live in the city) and is a tourist centre for Vancouver Island. Defence, the government sector (civil service) and retail are also important to the economy, and there's a growing technology industry. Victoria has the kindest climate of all Canada's cities, with mild, wet winters and warm, dry summers; the balmy weather is a major attraction for tourists and retirees. It's so mild that some palm and even banana species manage to flourish.

Vancouver's metropolitan area is home to around 2.1mn people (some 600,000 live in the city) and one of British Columbia's major attractions, regularly voted one of the best cities in which to live in the world. It has all the facilities and attractions you would expect from a major city, as well as easy access to the Pacific Ocean and the Pacific Coast Range, and is Canada's largest port. The international trade passing through the port is important to the city's economy, as are banking and finance, filming, high technology, natural resource-related industries and tourism.

Vancouver prides itself on the wealth of natural beauty within its metropolitan area, including Stanley Park, which is one of North America's largest urban parks. It's a relaxed city with breathtaking views, an outdoor lifestyle and a lively cultural scene. Vancouver also boasts the second-largest Chinatown in North America (after San Francisco's) and the second-warmest climate of Canada's major cities (after nearby Victoria on Vancouver Island), although because of its coastal location and mountainous surrounds, it's a city of micro-climates. Much of the city is fairly wet, but not as wet as is commonly supposed, although winters can be depressingly grey and damp. Vancouver's many attractions have drawn tens of thousands of people to live in the city and helped to drive up accommodation costs (much of the housing is apartments rather than houses), making them the most expensive in Canada.

Vancouver has been described as an 'interesting' blend of wealth and poverty. It also has Canada's highest crime rate.

Manitoba

Manitoba is the most easterly of the three Prairie Provinces (the others are Alberta and Saskatchewan), in the longitudinal centre of Canada; Saskatchewan is to the west and Ontario to the east. Manitoba is the eighth-largest province/territory, covering 250,134mi^2 (647,797km^2), with a population of around 1.2mn, some 700,000 of whom live in the capital, Winnipeg. Manitoba has a coastline on Hudson Bay and lakes cover around 15 per cent of the surface area, which is generally flat and low-lying.

Manitoba is an affordable, friendly place to live, but its economy is small and lacks diversity. Farming is important (particularly wheat production), as are mining and tourism, especially bear-watching, hunting and fishing. Churchill, a port on Hudson Bay, has one of the world's largest and most accessible polar bear populations, an increasingly popular tourist attraction.

Winnipeg is known as the 'Gateway to the West' and plays a prominent role in agriculture, education, finance, manufacturing and transportation. The city lies near the geographic centre of North America and is one of the coldest large cities in the world (it's sometimes called 'Winterpeg'), but it receives a lot of sunshine throughout the year. Owing to the city's flatness and high snowfall, it's subject to flooding, which is sometimes severe; it also has an unfortunate reputation as the mosquito capital of North America. As if these dubious distinctions weren't enough, Winnipeg also has Canada's second-highest crime rate (after Vancouver) and around twice that of Toronto.

New Brunswick

New Brunswick is one of Canada's three Maritime Provinces (Nova Scotia and Prince Edward Island are the others – also called the Maritimes) situated in the extreme southeast of coastal Canada. It's the eleventh-largest province/territory, covering 28,152mi^2 (72,908km^2), and is home to around 750,000 people. New Brunswick is Canada's only official bilingual province (English and French), with around a third of the population French-speaking.

New Brunswick lies in the Appalachian mountain range; much of the province is gently rolling hills, around 80 per cent of which is forested. There are fewer urban dwellers in New Brunswick than the Canadian average – around 50 per cent rather than 80 per cent. The capital is Fredericton (pop. 86,000) – smaller than both Moncton and Saint John – a quiet, conservative city in the west-central part of the province. Set inland from the coast, Fredericton experiences more extreme temperatures than most cities in Atlantic Canada. It's New Brunswick's artistic, cultural and educational centre, and home to two universities, which, along with the provincial government, are important employers (the city is also developing an IT industry).

New Brunswick has a mixed economy: Service-based industries include education, finance, healthcare and insurance, and there's some heavy industry and transportation. The rural economy relies on farming (especially potatoes – McCain, of oven chips fame, originated here), fishing (particularly lobster and scallops), forestry and mining. Tourism is increasing in importance and New Brunswick is looking for more immigrants to boost the labour force and counterbalance its ageing population.

Newfoundland & Labrador

This Atlantic coast province is made up of two parts, Newfoundland and Labrador, together covering 156,465mi² (405,212km²), making it Canada's tenth-largest province/territory. The former is a large, rocky island (it's Canada's fourth-largest island and the world's fifteenth-largest) sitting in the mouth of the Saint Lawrence River; the latter is a thinly populated region of the mainland to the northwest of Newfoundland. The province has a population of around 507,000, almost all of whom live in Newfoundland; only some 35,000 people live in Labrador, many of them Cree and Inuit, who suffer a depressingly high incidence of alcohol abuse and suicide.

The province has a wild, isolated feel and, despite its maritime setting, experiences severe weather; much of Newfoundland's interior is tundra, and icebergs regularly float past its beaches. The capital, St. John's, which is on the southeast tip of the island, is attractive but famously wet and foggy. It receives less sunshine than any other provincial/territorial capital and can become snow-bound in winter. St. John's is the most easterly city in North America and the second-largest city in Atlantic Canada (after Halifax in Nova Scotia), and is thought to be the oldest city in English-speaking North America. As a result of its isolation, Newfoundland has its own dialect, which can be difficult for outsiders to penetrate, and a distinctive Celtic air.

Its people tend to identify more with their province than with their country, even more so than in Quebec. Newfoundland has its own time zone, separated from the rest of the North American east coast by a half hour (rather than the usual one-hour difference).

The chronic over-fishing of the North Atlantic's cod stocks has had a disastrous effect on this maritime province but there are signs of economic improvement, particularly as a result of offshore oil reserves. These might create the jobs necessary to win back some of the many locals who've moved elsewhere in Canada. Tourism is also being touted as a source of employment. Newfoundland and Labrador is one of only two provinces/territories (the other is Saskatchewan) where the population has fallen over the last decade or so.

Northwest Territories

This large territory in northern Canada is east of the Yukon and west and south of Nunavut (Canada's other two territories). It covers 452,513mi² (1,171,918km²), making it the third-largest province/territory, but is home to a mere 43,000 people, many of them indigenous. This is isolated frontier country, with long, freezing winters and short, warm, mosquito-plagued summers. It's an expensive place to live (partly because of the cost of shipping in supplies), but there's a strong sense of community.

The economy is largely based on the territory's huge natural resources, particularly diamonds, gold and natural gas. Yellowknife is the capital, home to around half the territory's population. It lies on the north shore of the huge Great Slave Lake and has a dry, sub-arctic climate. Yellowknife has the feel of a frontier mining outpost, and is a government town and service centre for the territory's mines.

Nova Scotia

Nova Scotia (which is Latin for 'New Scotland') is on Canada's south-east coast and is the second-smallest province/territory (after Prince Edward Island), encompassing 21,346mi² (55,283km²). Despite this, it's the most populated of the three Maritime Provinces (New Brunswick and Prince Edward Island are the other two), home to 940,000 people. The northern part of Nova Scotia is Cape Breton Island, but much of the province is a peninsula jutting out into the Atlantic Ocean, with many beaches and estuaries. Nowhere in Nova Scotia is more than 37mi (60km) from the sea. Outside of the capital, Halifax, much of the province is rural and wooded, scattered with picturesque coastal villages.

Nova Scotia's economy has traditionally been resource-based, but over the past couple of decades it has diversified and film production, music-related industries, technology and tourism have become more significant. However, fishing, forestry and mining are still important and there's some agriculture, although it's restricted by the tough climate in most of the province. Housing in Nova Scotia is generally affordable.

Halifax is the capital of Nova Scotia, a large, cosmopolitan city with a historic feel. It has an important comedy festival and an attractive harbour front that draws many tourists. It's the largest population centre in Canada's Atlantic region (with around 375,000 inhabitants) and the cultural and economic centre of Canada's east coast. It sits on Nova Scotia's Atlantic coast and, like most of the province, has unpredictable weather. The provincial government is Halifax's largest employer and the port is also important (the province is a major beer exporter), while offshore oil and gas reserves have boosted the economy in recent decades.

Niagara Falls, Ontario, ON

Nunavut

This massive territory in the far north of Canada is the country's largest province/territory, covering 808,244mi² (2,093,190km²), which is about the size of Western Europe; if it was a country, Nunavut would be the world's thirteenth-largest. Despite its huge size, Nunavut has Canada's smallest provincial/territorial population, a mere 31,000 people, 85 per cent of whom are indigenous, mainly Inuit. It became a separate territory in 1999 (having previously been part of the Northwest Territories), although its boundaries were established six years previously.

Nunavut means 'our land' in Inuktitut, the language of the Inuit.

Nunavut is a remote, inaccessible region. Arctic tundra covers most of it, except for a small area of the south-west, which manages to sustain taiga forest. The territory's capital is Iqaluit (formerly Frobisher Bay) on the south side of Baffin Island in the east of Nunavut. It was chosen as the capital in a territorial referendum and its population is only some 60 per cent Inuit, lower than in other parts of the territory.

Iqaluit's climate is Arctic, with long, freezing cold winters and short summers, which are too cool to allow tree growth, with average temperatures below freezing for eight months of the year. As a result, most of the buildings are functional, designed to retain heat and withstand the harsh climate, rather than built for aesthetic reasons. It's a tough, isolated environment, and boredom and loneliness are common problems. Several diamond and gold mining projects are currently under consideration and, if approved, will create more employment.

Ontario

Ontario is in east-central Canada and is the fourth-largest province/territory, covering 415,629mi² (1,076,395km²). It's Canada's most populous region, home to around 13mn people or almost 40 per cent of the population. To the north lies Hudson Bay, to the east Quebec and to the west Manitoba. Ontario's capital is Toronto (Canada's largest city) and the province also boasts Ottawa, Canada's capital city. Ontario's urban areas are known for being liberal and progressive, but the province's rural areas are much more conservative.

The relatively temperate area of the Great Lakes-Saint Lawrence Valley in the south of the province is the most populated region of Ontario. All parts of the province have snowy winters, but winters in the south are rather shorter and less severe than in the north. The south of Ontario has hot, humid summers.

Ontario has around 250,000 lakes and over 62,000mi (100,000km) of rivers. This abundance of water means that it's well endowed with hydroelectric energy, which has been a boon to the economy, as have excellent transport links to the US. The latter have made manufacturing an important industry, notably chemicals, electrical products, food, iron, machinery, motor vehicles, paper and steel. Toronto is the centre of Canada's banking and financial services industries and a significant port; IT is also an important source of jobs and wealth.

Ontario is a popular tourist destination and visitor income is important in rural areas, with watersports and wilderness pursuits attracting summer visitors, and hunting and snowmobiling drawing visitors in winter. Tourism is a significant part of the economy of Ontario's southern border towns and cities, which attract a lot of cross-border visitors from the US. In northern Ontario, lumber and mining are important activities, with the traditional crafts of the (mainly) native peoples who live there.

Toronto lies on the north-west shore of Lake Ontario and is the largest city in Canada (around 5.1mn people) and the fifth-largest in North America (after Mexico City, New York City, Los Angeles and Chicago). It's part of the Golden Horseshoe, a densely populated region of Ontario which contains over 8mn people or a quarter of Canada's population. Toronto is an important city with international influence and is one of the world's most cosmopolitan, where over 40 per cent of residents were born outside Canada. It's also one of the safest cities in North America.

Toronto's climate is moderated by the waters of Lake Ontario and is one of the mildest and least snowy in the east, although this is relative – its winters are severe to many foreigners. Summers are warm or hot. Like most large cities, Toronto has strengths and weaknesses: It has excellent museums and a vibrant performing arts scene, some impressive architecture (the famous CN Tower is the world's tallest free-standing land structure) and an extensive bicycle culture. However, homelessness is a problem, the traffic can be heavy, air quality is sometimes poor, housing is expensive and many people find the sprawling suburbs uninspiring. Ottawa is Canada's capital and its fourth-largest city, with 1.1mn inhabitants. It's an attractive, friendly, low-crime, bilingual city with generally affordable housing, situated on the eastern border (with Quebec) of Ontario.

Ottawa has the dubious distinction of being the world's second-coldest capital city (after Ulan Bator in Mongolia). Ice storms are common, but summers are warm and humid, if sometimes short. The city is also prey to earthquakes (usually minor), which strike on average every three years. Federal government and high technology are Ottawa's major employers.

Prince Edward Island

Situated in the Gulf of Saint Lawrence off Canada's south-east coast, Prince Edward Island is one of the three Maritime provinces (New Brunswick and Nova Scotia are the others; Prince Edward Island lies to the north). It's Canada's smallest province/territory, covering a mere 2,185mi^2 (5,660km^2), with a population of around 140,000, making it the province/territory with the highest density of population (around 25 people per km^2 compared with the Canadian average of a mere 3 per km^2). The province is named after Prince Edward Augustus, Duke of Kent and Strathearn, and the father of Queen Victoria.

Around half the island is forested and much of the rest is given over to farming – it's sometimes called the 'Garden Province'. Potatoes are the most important crop, the island contributing about a third of Canada's total production. As well as agriculture, tourism is important to the economy, the island attracting over 1mn visitors annually (*Anne of Green Gables* was written here). The main attractions are the province's beaches, coves, golf courses and its opportunities for eco-tourism. Fishing also contributes to the economy, especially shellfish. The 8-mi (13-km) Confederation Bridge connects the west end of the island to New Brunswick. Winters on Prince Edward Island are milder than in much of Canada, while summers are fresh and breezy. It's quite wet throughout the year and the island receives less sunshine than the Canadian average.

The capital and largest city is Charlottetown (its metropolitan area is home to around 60,000 people), built around a natural harbour on the south coast and retaining many attractive Victorian buildings. It's the wealthiest city in Atlantic Canada, the economy being dominated by the public sector, although education, healthcare, technology and tourism are also important.

Quebec

Quebec is situated in eastern Canada and is the second-largest province/territory, covering 595,434mi^2 (1,542,056km^2), which is around three times the size of France. The population of 7.75mn makes it the second most populous province/territory (after Ontario), although much of the centre and north is sparsely populated. The far north is arctic or sub-arctic, with mainly Inuit inhabitants. The majority of Quebec's population live in the Saint Lawrence River Valley in the south of the province, many of them in Quebec City, the province's capital, and Montreal, its largest city. The Saint Lawrence River Valley is fertile and well suited to agriculture, the major products being dairy foods, *foie gras*, fruit, livestock, maple syrup and vegetables. North of the Saint Lawrence River Valley, the land is dominated by coniferous forests, lakes and rivers, where hydroelectricity, lumber, paper and pulp dominate the economy.

Quebec's official language is French – it's the only Canadian province/territory where English isn't an official language. The great majority of French Canadians live in Quebec, which has a stronger sense of identity than most of Canada, with its own legal code and immigration rules and high taxation. The province is generally informal and vibrant, with a high quality of life.

The capital, Quebec City, lies in southeast Quebec, northeast

Old Quebec

of Montreal. It's home to around 715,000 people and is an attractive, historic city (North America's only walled city), known for its Winter Carnival. It's full of restaurants and has a wealth of cultural activities (art galleries abound), and attracts a lot of tourists who are important to its economy. Housing is generally affordable, but prices are rising.

Montreal is in south Quebec and is Canada's second-largest city, with 3.6mn inhabitants in the wider metropolitan area (half of them live in the city), making it the world's second-largest French-speaking metropolitan area (after Paris), although many of its inhabitants are bilingual (unlike Paris). Montreal is the most densely populated city in Canada and a gay-friendly place. It plays host many international events and festivals, including the Montreal Jazz Festival and the Montreal World Film Festival, and is a vibrant, cosmopolitan city, the cultural centre of Quebec.

Montreal is renowned for its lively nightlife and attractive city parks, and has quite a low crime rate, but its climate isn't to everybody's taste.

Montreal is situated where several climatic regions meet and, as a result, has marked seasonal and even day-to-day weather variations, a feature of life in the city. It's wet, with rainfall spread fairly evenly throughout the year, and the city spends a lot of money clearing snow in winter. The wind chill factor often makes winter days seem even colder than they are, while in summer, heatwaves and high humidity are common.

Montreal is a centre of commerce, finance and industry, as well as a major port and the world's largest inland port. It's also an important rail city, the eastern terminus of the Canadian Pacific Railway. The main industries include clothing manufacturing, education, electrical items, fabric, high technology, pharmaceuticals and tobacco. Montreal is also a significant player in the aerospace and defence industries, as well as a popular film location, able to 'feel' European or American. The economy is quite healthy, although this means that house prices are catching up with Canada's most expensive cities, and in the last few decades some businesses have moved their head offices from Montreal to Toronto in response to Quebec's separatist movement.

Saskatchewan

Saskatchewan is the middle of Canada's three prairie provinces (Alberta lies to the west, Manitoba to the east) and covers 251,385mi^2 (651,036km^2), making it the seventh-largest province/territory. It's named after the Cree word for 'fast-moving river', and has a population of around 1mn, most of whom live in the southern half of the province; the north is thinly populated but attracts many visitors, drawn by the canoeing and fishing opportunities. Regina is the capital city (population around 195,000) and Saskatoon the largest city, with 234,000 inhabitants. Saskatchewan is a welcoming province with cheap housing and is anxious to attract new investment and immigrants. Along with Newfoundland and Labrador, it's the only province whose population has dropped over the past dozen years.

Saskatchewan's economy has traditionally been dependent on agriculture, particularly wheat, with which the province is still closely associated. Agriculture remains important, as do fishing, forestry (especially in the north) and hunting, but they're not as central as they once were. Mining is of huge significance: Saskatchewan is the world's largest potash exporter and supplier of uranium. Finance, insurance and real estate are also major contributors to the province's economy, as are education, healthcare and social services.

The capital, Regina, has an unprepossessing location – on a flat, treeless plain – but it's a pleasant city and an important commercial and cultural centre. It has a dry climate, with cold winters and warm summers, although summer nights are usually cool. Saskatoon, the province's largest city, is sometimes called the City of Bridges, due to its seven river crossings. It's one of the world's foremost agricultural biotechnology centres, and potash and uranium-related businesses are important to the city's economy; food processing and IT are also significant. Saskatoon has warm summers and very cold winters, and is one of Canada's sunniest cities.

The Yukon Territory

The Yukon is a territory in the far north-west of Canada, covering 186,286mi^2 (482,443km^2), making it the ninth-largest province/territory. Its population is a mere 33,000, around 25,000 of whom live in the capital, Whitehorse. Archaeologists claim to have found evidence of North America's oldest inhabitants in the Old Crow area of the Yukon, the finds having been carbon-dated to around 40,000 BC, although the evidence is disputed by many scholars.

The Yukon's economy has traditionally consisted mainly of mining, especially asbestos, copper, gold, lead, silver and zinc, with the famous Klondike Gold Rush of the 1890s flooding the territory with prospectors. Tourism is also important, with visitors attracted by the Yukon's scenic beauty and opportunities for outdoor leisure activities. The manufacturing of clothing, furniture and handicrafts is important, as is hydroelectricity, although fishing and trapping have dwindled in importance. The territory's largest employer, however, is the government sector. The capital, Whitehorse, is located in the south-west of the Yukon, and is named after the Whitehorse rapids.

Whitehorse is a functional government town, with a good range of facilities, and was host to the Canadian Winter Games in 2007. Like much of the Yukon, it has a dry, sub-arctic climate, and is Canada's driest city, being in the rain shadow of the Coast Mountains. Its winters are milder than in some of Canada's prairie cities and, despite its cold climate, Whitehorse has been ranked as having one of Canada's most comfortable climates (although it's bottom of the list – most of the others are in mild British Columbia).

GOVERNMENT

Canada is a confederation of provinces and was officially created as a country on 1st July 1867 from the provinces now known as Ontario, Quebec, New Brunswick and Nova Scotia. The other provinces and territories joined the confederation between then and 1949, when Newfoundland and Labrador was the last to join (apart from Nunavut, which was created on 1st April 1999). 1st July is celebrated annually as the federal holiday, Canada Day. Canada is a constitutional monarchy, with Queen Elizabeth II as the constitutional head of state. Except when in Canada, she delegates her (mainly ceremonial) duties to her Canadian representatives, the Governor General (GG) and the provincial representatives called Lieutenant Governors. In theory, the Prime Minister (PM) and the cabinet advise the Queen, but in practical terms the country is run by the elected federal and provincial governments.

The GG, who's a Canadian citizen, is appointed by the Queen on the advice of the PM and acts on the cabinet's advice, giving royal assent to bills passed in parliament, summoning, opening and closing parliament, and dissolving it before an election. In 1982, a new Constitution Act was passed which included the 'Canada Charter of Rights and Freedoms' which defines and protects the personal rights and basic freedoms of Canadian citizens and residents (before this

Parliament Building, Ottowa, ON

province/territory flags

date, changes to the Canadian Constitution had to be approved by the British government).

Canada is a democracy with three levels of government (federal, provincial and municipal), each elected by popular vote. The Canadian system of government is based on the British constitution and has a House of Commons and a Senate (roughly equivalent to the British House of Lords). The House of Commons has around 300 members, from which the Cabinet is mostly drawn (ministers may also be appointed from the Senate). Federal elections must be held every five years (or sooner), when the Prime Minister (and head of government) is chosen by the members of the political party with the most members of the House of Commons. The Senate consists of 105 senators appointed by the Prime Minister and the Governor General. Senators must retire at the age of 75 and aren't allowed to introduce financial bills or defeat constitutional amendments (although they can delay them from becoming law).

Each house has specific duties. For example, the Senate's duties include confirming laws initiated by the House of Commons, but it cannot initiate bills to spend public money or raise taxes. It has three basic functions: To review government bills, to investigate (via committees) major social and economic issues, and to provide a national forum for debating public issues and regional concerns. The House of Commons mainly exists to introduce and discuss legislation (bills) that may eventually become law. Each bill has several readings, the first of which is just a simple reading with no debate. Then it's printed and distributed to Members before having a second reading and moving to committee stage. After this it goes back to the house, with or without amendments, for a vote on whether to make it law. The federal government is responsible for national defence, foreign policy, trade and commerce, currency, banking, criminal law, fisheries, shipping, postal services, some social benefits and taxation.

There's no system of proportional representation in Canada, which has many political parties, large and small.

The major parties are the Liberals (or Grits), the Progressive Conservatives (PC or Tories), the New Democratic Party (NDP) and the Reform Party. Parties promoting Quebec independence are the *Bloc Québécois* (federally) and the *Parti Québécois* (provincially). On a scale from right wing to left wing, the national parties line up as follows: Reform, PC, Liberal and NDP. There are also fringe parties such as the Green Party and the Natural Law Party.

Provincial & Territorial

Each province has its own government, organised in the same way as the federal parliament. The territories have seats in the federal House of Commons, but are administered by the federal government. Those elected to the legislature are called Members of the Legislative Assembly (MLA), Members of the National Assembly (MNA), Members of Provincial Parliament (MPP) or Members of the House of Assembly (MHA), depending on the province or territory.

The provinces have a large degree of autonomy, which includes raising their own provincial taxes and drafting provincial laws with regard to trade and commerce, education, provincial highways and driving, marriage, divorce, licensing, firearms, social services (e.g. health and welfare), wages and criminal justice. Provincial governments are also responsible for civil and some criminal law, property rights, vehicle and marriage licensing, municipal institutions and working conditions. The responsibility for immigration and agriculture is shared between the federal and provincial governments.

Local

Each province is made up of a number of municipalities, each with its own separate local government (council) that passes local by-laws in its community. Its responsibilities include primary and secondary education; police, fire and ambulance services; courts and jails; libraries; health and welfare; public transport subsidies; parks and recreation; waste disposal; highways and road safety (including snow removal); and trading standards. The council is headed by a mayor and other elected representatives, usually called councillors. Around 4,700 municipal governments report to their provincial government and have no formal contact with the federal government. Southern Ontario and southern Quebec are divided into counties, which comprise a number of municipalities.

Voting

You must be a Canadian citizen, aged over 18 and on the list of electors in order to vote in Canada. The 'electoral roll' used to be compiled by enumerators who called on households to check who was eligible to vote, but it's now up to individuals to ensure that they're on the list and receive their 'elector information card' (which confirms that a person is on the list of electors and tells him where and when to vote). If you haven't been given a card or there are errors on it, you should contact Elections Canada (☏ 1-800 463 6868, 🖳 www.elections.ca) or a local office.

> On polling day, you simply take your card to your local polling station, obtain a voting paper from the polling officer and cast your vote by placing an X in the box next to the name of your favoured candidate, before putting the paper in the ballot box. Voting in Canada is by secret ballot.

LEGAL SYSTEM

The Canadian legal system is based on federal law, augmented by provincial laws and local by-laws. Most rights and freedoms enjoyed by Canadians are enshrined in the Canadian Charter of Rights and Freedoms (which became part of the constitution in 1982). Canadian law and the constitution apply to everyone in Canada, irrespective of citizenship or immigration status, and even illegal immigrants have the same basic legal rights as a Canadian citizen.

Under the Canadian constitution, each province has the right to make its own laws in certain areas and you shouldn't automatically assume that the law is the same in different provinces. In most of Canada (Quebec being, as usual, the exception) laws are a mixture of statute and common law. Common law is particularly valid in the case of civil law, which is based on precedent and deals with private matters between individuals, such as property disputes or business transactions. In Quebec, there's a written *Code Civil* (based on French Napoleonic Law) that contains general principles and rules for different types of cases. Unlike common law, the judge looks at this written code for guidance before considering precedents set by earlier judgements, but although the principles are different, the decisions reached are generally much the same.

Provincial courts deal with most types of criminal offence, small claims (private disputes involving limited amounts of money) and youth and family courts. Judges at this level are appointed by the province. The next highest level is the superior court, with judges appointed by the federal government, which handle serious criminal and civil cases. Above this level is the provincial Court of Appeal. A separate system of federal courts operates alongside provincial courts and deals with cases arising under the Canadian constitution or any federal law or treaty. These include claims against the federal government and such matters as patents, copyright and maritime law. The federal court is based in Ottawa, but judges may sit across the country. Federal court judges may also act as arbitrators under the Unemployment Insurance Act and in certain cases involving agriculture.

At the top of the legal system is the Supreme Court of Canada, which consists of a Chief Justice and eight other judges appointed by the federal cabinet. Three of these judges must come from Quebec and three traditionally also come from Ontario, two from Western Canada and one from the Atlantic Provinces. Cases may be referred to the supreme court only if the court itself agrees (although this doesn't apply to certain cases, such as criminal cases where an acquittal has been set aside by a provincial court of appeal), the idea being to restrict its deliberations to matters of public importance or those that raise important questions of law. The Supreme Court sits in Ottawa for three sessions each year (winter, spring and autumn) and has recently begun to use tele-conferencing to permit presentations from other parts of the country. Information about the Supreme Court of Canada is available at www.scc-csc.gc.ca. There's also a Tax Court of Canada that sits in major cities across the country.

The courts are administered by an official who's known variously as the 'registrar', 'clerk' or 'administrator of the court'. His duties include informing the legal profession of court procedures, signing orders and judgements, issuing summonses and collecting court costs. Jury management is usually dealt with by a sheriff or bailiffs. In addition to formal courts, some minor matters are heard by a judge sitting 'in chambers', and in Ontario, Family Law Commissions deal with some divorce cases and other family law matters. In some cities there are judicial officers who can act as judges in certain circumstances, such as assessing penalties under summary convictions on criminal code offences or issuing search warrants. In the north and in some provinces, official judges take part in 'circle courts', where the judge, police, social workers, tribal officials, victims and the convicted person, sit in a circle to consider an appropriate sentence and restitution.

There's no Canadian equivalent of the US 'Miranda' law that requires arresting officers to recite your rights to you. You do, however, have the right to remain silent, the right to have a lawyer present during questioning and the right to have a free legal aid lawyer if you cannot afford one. It's wise to say nothing until you've spoken with a lawyer. If you're arrested, you're entitled to call your lawyer and if you don't have one, the police officer must give you the number of the legal aid office and allow you to call them. You must be allowed to talk to your lawyer alone and must be brought before a court within 24 hours or released.

An area where Canada differs considerably from its US neighbour is in the matter of private litigation. Obviously, people and companies do go to court to settle their differences, but suing large corporations in the hope that a sympathetic jury will award you millions of dollars is rare in Canada.

The provinces also have a Small Claims Court to resolve relatively simple disputes concerning money or property, e.g. with a neighbour, merchant or customer, for amounts of up to $25,000, without the necessity of hiring a lawyer. The maximum claim varies according to the province: $5,000 in Newfoundland and Labrador, $6,000 in New Brunswick, $7,000 in Quebec, $8,000 in Prince Edward Island, $10,000 in Ontario and Manitoba, and $25,000 in Alberta, British Columbia, Nova Scotia and Saskatchewan.

Small claims courts are designed to be an easier and less expensive way to resolve disputes than in higher courts, with a simplified procedure, no strict pleadings' requirements, no formal discovery process and parties costs usually limited. In general, disputes involving title to land, slander, libel, bankruptcy, false imprisonment or malicious prosecution must be handled in a superior court, and cannot be determined in small claims courts.

Many social service agencies provide free legal assistance to immigrants, although some may serve the nationals of a particular country or religion only. There are help lines and agencies offering free legal advice in most towns and cities, many working with legal aid societies (offering free advice and referral on legal matters), Better Business Bureaux (dealing with consumer-related complaints, shopping services, etc.) and departments of consumer affairs (which also handle consumer complaints).

MARRIAGE & DIVORCE

To get married in Canada, the bride and groom must usually be aged at least 18, or 16 if they have parental consent, although the ages vary depending on the province. In most provinces,

marriage licences are issued by local city or county clerks and an application must usually be made in the municipality where the woman lives. Common law marriages don't require a licence and carry the same legal status as official marriages after six months. They consist of a man and woman living together as man and wife. Gay common law marriages are quite common and in 1999, the Supreme Court ruled that 'a same sex couple is still a couple', thus giving them full legal status.

Canada has a high divorce rate, with some 70,000 couples getting divorced each year (around half the marriage rate). Once you've been separated from your spouse for a year, you can file (petition) for a divorce and if your spouse doesn't raise any objections within one month, the petition is rubber-stamped and you're free to marry again (this is known as an 'uncontested divorce'). If you anticipate any objections, you should consult a divorce lawyer. Due to the high probability of divorce in Canada, many potential marriage partners insist on a (decidedly unromantic) marriage contract or prenuptial agreement, limiting a spouse's claims in the event of a divorce.

Foreigners living in Canada who are married, divorced or widowed should have a valid marriage licence, divorce papers or death certificate. These are necessary to confirm your marital status with the authorities, e.g. to receive certain legal or social insurance benefits. Foreigners married abroad come under the marriage laws of the country where they were married.

Like most things in Canada, marriage and divorce laws vary from province to province. If you're contemplating either and need to know the law, a series of books covering a number of provinces (including Alberta, British Columbia and Ontario) is published by the Self-Counsel Press.

MILITARY SERVICE

There's no draft (conscription) in Canada and no requirement to register for military service because all members of the armed forces (💻 www.forces.gc.ca) are volunteers. Canada's armed forces have decreased from a high of 112,000 in 1986 to the 2008 level of 62,000 regulars and 25,000 reserves (including 4,000 Canadian Rangers). Women are allowed to serve in combat roles in the military, although prejudice is rife, which has been highlighted in recent years by a number of high-profile lawsuits against the military for sexual harassment and other abuses.

NATIONAL ANTHEM & FLAG

The National Anthem, 'O Canada', was composed in 1880 by Calixa Lavallée (the French lyrics were written by Sir Adolphe-Basile Routhier). The English lyrics were originally composed by Mr. Justice Robert Stanley Weir in 1908, but there have been many versions over the years. The latest official English version was agreed in 1968 by a special joint committee of the Senate and the House of Commons.

The national flag of a red maple leaf on a white background with red sidebars (representing the two ocean boundaries) was instituted in 1965 after a design competition. The sidebars are red, rather than blue, because part of the reason for the new flag was to show independence from Britain and

Canadian Anthem

English	French
O Canada! Our home and native land!	Ô Canada! Terre de nos aïeux,
True patriot love in all thy sons command.	Ton front est ceint de fleurons glorieux!
With glowing hearts we see thee rise,	Car ton bras sait porter l'épée,
The true North strong and free.	Il sait porter la croix!
From far and wide,	Ton histoire est une épopée
O Canada, we stand on guard for thee.	Des plus brillants exploits.
God keep our land glorious and free!	Et ta valeur, de foi trempée,
O Canada, we stand on guard for thee.	Protégera nos foyers et nos droits;
O Canada, we stand on guard for thee.	Protégera nos foyers et nos droits.

France, both of which have red, white and blue in their national flags. Each province and territory also has its own flag.

PETS

All animals and birds imported into Canada are subject to health, quarantine, agriculture, wildlife and customs requirements and prohibitions, as are pets taken out of Canada and returned. Pets excluded from entry must be exported or destroyed. Dogs and cats under three months of age can be imported from the US without documentation, as can 'seeing eye' and other trained dogs from any country, provided they accompany you on arrival and are in good health.

Dogs and cats over three months old can be imported from the US provided that you obtain a certificate signed and dated by a veterinarian showing that the animal has been vaccinated against rabies not less than 30 days or more than 180 days before its importation. The certificate must identify the animal by breed, age, sex, colouring and any distinguishing marks. Pets also require a veterinary certificate of health issued no more than five days prior to shipment.

For animals other than dogs and cats from the US and animals of any kind from other countries, you should check the regulations with Animal Health (Canadian Food Inspection Agency, ☎ 613-225 2342, 💻 www.inspection.gc.ca).

Cats or dogs imported from countries considered by the veterinary Director General of Canada to be rabies-free (such as the UK), either originating from that country or having been quarantined in that country for at least six months, may not require a rabies certificate, provided they have a general health certificate.

Birds from countries other than the USA can only be imported as excess baggage via Air Canada and require an import permit. The import of birds is also subject to control by the Canadian Wildlife Service (💻 www.cws-scf.ec.gc.ca) and CITES export and import permits may be required for certain species.

Pets from outside the USA must be shipped by air to Canada in an International Air Transport Association (IATA) approved container, available from pet shipping agents. It's advisable to use a company that's experienced in exporting and transporting animals abroad, such as Par Air Services in the UK (☎ +44-1206-330332, 💻 www.parair.co.uk).

Note also the following:

- Don't let your pets run free and don't allow your children to play with or approach strange or wild animals because they could have rabies. If a child is bitten by an unknown animal, he may require a series of anti-rabies injections.
- Always shop around and compare veterinarian fees. You can take out health insurance for less than $1 per day for a dog and under 50¢ per day for a cat, which

covers veterinary bills and replacement of your pet due to its death from accident or illness.

- In most municipalities, dogs must have licences and some also require cats to be licensed. Some communities levy a higher licence fee for un-neutered animals and may require you to hold a breeder's licence if an animal isn't neutered. In some municipalities, animals must be tattooed or have a microchip inserted under their skin so that they can be traced when lost. Proof of vaccination against rabies may be required in order to obtain a licence. Check with your local town hall or city clerk.
- Most communities require dogs to be kept on leads in municipal parks and for the owner to clear up after them. Take a 'poop-scoop' and a plastic bag with you when walking your dog and 'stoop and scoop' when your dog does his business. This is taken seriously and there are large fines for those who don't comply, which accounts for the lack of 'canine waste' on the streets.
- There are severe penalties for cruelty to animals in Canada, although animal rights campaigners claim that cruelty laws are inadequate.
- With the exception of seeing-eye and hearing guide dogs, which may travel on trains and buses free of charge, dogs aren't allowed on public transport or in most restaurants and shopping malls.
- Your vet will arrange to collect and cremate the body of a dead pet (for a fee), although you can bury a dead pet in your garden (yard) in some areas.
- Don't forget that the ground is frozen in winter! There are many commercial pet cemeteries in Canada, where the pets of the rich and famous are given a send-off befitting their pampered position in life.
- Many apartments and rented accommodation have regulations forbidding the keeping of dogs and other animals (cats are sometimes okay) and finding accommodation that accepts dogs is difficult in most cities. The number of cats and dogs per residence may also be limited, and large animals such as horses may be prohibited (particularly in condos).

Most major cities and towns have animal hospitals and clinics, and individuals and humane societies in many areas run sanctuaries for injured or orphaned wild animals and abandoned pets. Many cities and towns have animal shelters where you can get a stray dog or cat free of charge; the policy is generally to retain all animals for adoption for as long as it takes to find them a new home.

For further information about keeping pets in Canada, contact Canada's Society for the Prevention of Cruelty to Animals (SPCA, www.spca.com).

POLICE

Canada's national police force is the world-famous Royal Canadian Mounted Police (RCMP), affectionately known as the Mounties. Its motto isn't, as many people think, 'they always get their man', but *'Maintiens le Droit'* (uphold the right). The distinguished uniform of red jacket, breeches and broad hat is now worn only for ceremonial purposes and the only horses in use these days are those employed by the 32-strong musical riding team based at its headquarters in Rockliffe, Ottawa. There are no physical limitations for recruits, who no longer need to be at least 5ft 10in (1.78m) tall and have perfect vision. The only requirement is passing some physical tests and having good mental health.

As in many police forces, the pay isn't exceptional and in the last decade many officers have defected to municipal police forces or private security companies.

> One benefit of being in the RCMP is that when you're in ceremonial uniform you get your photograph taken a lot and if you're a man, you'll apparently be in great demand from women suffering from what's known as 'scarlet fever'.

With the exception of Ontario and Quebec, the RCMP is the only provincial/territorial police force. Large cities in other provinces have their own regional forces and smaller communities have a local police force that's responsible for crime and road traffic offences. Canada also has an anti-terrorist force, the Canadian Security and Intelligence Service (CSIS).

All police are armed, and in crime-prone, inner-city areas they wear bullet-proof vests and carry pepper sprays (they also use rubber bullets in riot situations). In general, Canadian police officers are civil and polite. However, if you're stopped by a police officer, either in a car or when walking, don't make any sudden movements and keep your hands where they can be seen. Some police officers may interpret any movement as an attempt to reach a concealed weapon. Always remain courteous and helpful. It may not do any harm to emphasise that you're a foreigner or to tell the officer you're a visitor or newcomer. See also **Crime** and **Legal System** above.

POPULATION

The population of Canada in spring 2009 was estimated to be around 33.6mn by Statistics Canada, of which almost a third were of British origin. A further quarter of Canadians are descendants of the original French settlers, most of whom live in Quebec, although there are also large numbers in New Brunswick (which is officially bilingual), Ontario and Manitoba. Canada is one of the most ethnically-diverse countries in the world, with some 50 per cent of the population with an ethnic origin other than British or French. Canada's third-largest ethnic group is Irish, while other major groups include German, Italian, Ukrainian, Dutch, Polish, Greek and Scandinavian.

In recent decades, there has been an influx of immigrants from Asia, particularly Chinese, and to a lesser extent Latin Americans and people from the Caribbean. Toronto and Vancouver are among the world's most cosmopolitan cities, with large Chinese communities, while in other areas there are German, East European, African and Caribbean communities. Canada has over 35 ethnic groups with at least 100,000 members each, of which ten have over 1mn.

For an up to date estimate of the Canadian population, see Canada's 'population clock' from Statistics Canada (💻 www.statcan.gc.ca/edu/clock-horloge/edu06f_0001-eng.htm).

There are also around 350,000 'Native or Aboriginal Indians' (First Nations – those who aren't Inuit or Métis), 30,000 Inuit and some 400,000 *Métis*, the name used to denote those of mixed Native American and European blood. Collectively, they comprise around 4 per cent of the population. The majority of Native Canadians live in the Yukon, Northwest Territories, Nunavut and Ontario, although each province has some Native Canadian communities.

Ontario is the most populous province and is home to almost 40 per cent of Canadians (almost 13mn), over 80 per cent of whom live in the urban areas between Kingston and Windsor (along the Great Lakes that make up the southern border), followed by Quebec (7.75mn), British Columbia (4.4mn) and Alberta (3.6mn). Population growth is highest in Western Canada, where the provinces of Saskatchewan, Alberta, British Columbia and Yukon all have growth rates higher than the national average (in 2008, Alberta's population growth was running at almost twice the national average). In the east, only Prince Edward Island has outpaced the national average growth in recent years.

Some 80 per cent of Canadians live in urban areas, around a third in the major cities and their suburbs, while only some 2mn (around 7 per cent) live in genuine rural areas. Canada's largest cities (metropolitan area) are Toronto with 5.1mn inhabitants, Montreal (3.6mn), Vancouver (2.1mn), Ottawa, the capital, (1.1mn), Calgary (1.1mn), Edmonton (1mn), Quebec City

(716,000), Winnipeg (695,000) and Hamilton (693,000). The population density is one of the lowest in the world, with just three people per km^2 or just over one person per square mile.

RELIGION

There's no official religion in Canada and it doesn't play a large part in Canadian life. Most Canadians are Christian (at least nominally), fairly evenly divided between Roman Catholics (of French descent) and Protestants (of British descent), but many other religions are also represented. There are many Jewish people in Montreal, Toronto and Winnipeg, and Vancouver has the highest concentration of Sikhs outside the Punjab. The large Chinese population in Toronto is mainly Buddhist. There are also small pockets of rural traditional sects such as Mennonites, Hutterites and Doukhobors.

Church attendance has steadily diminished since the '50s and a general lack of interest in religion by the children of immigrant families has lead to some domestic strife. Most of the First Nations population list themselves as Catholic thanks to Jesuit missionaries, although there has been something of a revival of ancient customs and beliefs in recent years. In recent years, many Native Americans (and immigrants) have turned to belief systems based on the natural world and the legends of their ancestors (as evidenced by the huge popularity of the fantasy books written by the Canadian author Charles de Lint).

Although the influence of religion has declined in most western societies in the latter part of the 20th century and the early 21st century (the US is a notable exception), churches and religious meeting places representing a multitude of faiths can be found throughout Canada. In smaller towns and communities, churches are often the main centres of social and community life and most organise a wide range of social activities, including sports events, dances, coffee hours, dinners and suppers, discussion groups and outings. Many also run nursery schools and after-school and youth programmes for older children. Many charities and social activities are administered by church and religious groups, including homeless shelters, canteens, workshops for the disabled, youth centres, special schools

and many other projects. If you want to know how poorer people live, you need only ask a minister in any major city.

For information about local religious centres and service times, contact your local library or phone religious centres for information (listed in the *Yellow Pages* under 'religious organisations' or 'churches'). Some religious centres conduct services in a number of languages. In some areas, a church directory is published and local religious services are also usually listed in tourist guides and published in local newspapers, where a whole page may be devoted to church and religious news.

SOCIAL CUSTOMS

All countries have their own particular social customs and Canada is no exception. Good manners, politeness and consideration for others are considered important by Canadians, although they're generally informal in their relationships and won't be too upset if you break the social rules – provided that your behaviour isn't too outrageous. As a foreigner, you may be forgiven if you accidentally insult your host, but you may not be invited again!

The following are a few common Canadian social customs:

- Canadians often greet total strangers, particularly in small towns and communities. This may vary from a formal "Good morning" to a more casual "Hi"; it's considered polite to respond likewise. Canadians often reply "You're welcome" or something similar when somebody thanks them and they may think you're impolite if you don't do likewise.
- It isn't usual to ask people personal questions such as their age or how much they paid for things – both are considered rude (unlike in the US, where such questions are commonplace).

☑ SURVIVAL TIP

If you're interested in learning more about Canada's culture and customs, you'll find our sister publication, *Culture Wise Canada*, indispensible.

- It isn't advisable to ask a Canadian whether he's American, which may be taken as an insult. Canadians don't usually refer to the USA as America (as in North America), but call it the States or the US.
- When introduced to someone, it's common to follow the cue of the person performing the introduction, e.g. if someone is introduced as Bill, you can usually call him Bill. Canadians generally dislike formality or any sort of social deference due to age or position, and most quickly say, "Please call me Paul (or Paula)". To Canadians, informality shows no lack of respect. Due to the rise of women's liberation in Canada (which inevitably found its way over the US border), women may be introduced with the title 'Ms' (pronounced 'Mizz') and some women object to the title 'Miss' or 'Mrs'. However, in conversation most Canadians don't use names or titles at all. As a consequence of the diverse religions in Canada, Canadians refer to 'first' or 'given' names, rather than 'Christian' names.

  After you've been introduced to someone, you usually say something like "Pleased to meet you" or "My pleasure" and shake hands with a firm grip (although more common among men). If someone asks, "How are you?" it's normal to reply "Fine thanks" (even if you feel dreadful). When saying goodbye, it isn't customary in Canada to shake hands again, except in business meetings. Among friends in Quebec, it's common for men to kiss women on one or both cheeks. Men don't usually kiss or embrace each other in Canada, although this depends on their nationality or ethnic origin (and sexual orientation).
- Canadians don't usually have inherited titles (e.g. Sir or Lord) but do defer to people with a professional title that has been earned. These include foreign diplomats (e.g. Sir), members of the Senate (Senator), judges, medical doctors and others with a doctorate, military officers (e.g. General, Colonel, even when retired), professors, priests and other religious ministers (e.g. Father, Rabbi, Reverend).
- If you're invited to dinner, it's customary to take along a small present of flowers, chocolates or a bottle of wine (but nothing too extravagant or ostentatious). Flowers can be tricky because to some people carnations mean bad luck, chrysanthemums are for cemeteries and roses signify love. If you stay with someone as a house guest for a few days, it's customary to give your host or hostess a small gift when you leave. Potluck suppers are popular in some parts of Canada, where guests or couples bring enough food to feed themselves and all the dishes are then placed on a large table and you help yourself to whatever you fancy. If you bring something unusual or extra spicy, you should tell your host so that other people can be warned.
- Most Canadians don't smoke and smoking without asking permission is considered rude in confined public places – if you can somewhere where smoking isn't banned – and totally unacceptable in someone's home.
- Although many foreigners have the impression that Canadians are relaxed and casual in their dress, they often have strict dress codes, particularly in the workplace. Some offices have introduced

a 'dress-down' day, one day per week (usually Friday), when employees may wear casual attire (presentable blue jeans are permissible, but shorts or anything scruffy aren't). Formal social invitations usually state what dress is appropriate ('business attire' means jacket and tie for men and a dress or business suit for women). If you're in any doubt, it's perfectly acceptable to ring your hostess and ask what you should wear. Black or dark clothes are usually worn at funerals in Canada.

- Guests are normally expected to be punctual, with the exception of certain society parties, when late arrival is *de rigueur* (provided that you don't arrive after the celebrity guest). It's usual to arrive half an hour to an hour after the official start of a dance. You should, however, never be late for funerals, weddings, the theatre and other public performances, sports events, lectures and business appointments, to name but a few.
- Invitations to cocktail parties or receptions may state 5 to 7pm, in which case you may arrive at any time between these hours. Dinner invitations are often phrased as 8 for 8.30pm. This means you should arrive at 8pm for drinks and dinner will be served (usually promptly) at 8.30pm. Arriving late for dinner is considered impolite, although you must also never arrive early (unless you plan to help with the cooking).
- Some families say grace before meals, so you should follow your host's example before tucking in. If you're confused by a multitude of knives, forks and spoons, don't panic but just copy what your neighbour is doing (the rule is to start at the outside and work in).
- Don't overstay your welcome. This becomes obvious when your host starts looking at his watch, talking about his early start the next day, yawning, or in desperation, falling asleep.

TIME ZONES

Canada is divided into six time zones, shown on the map below.

Four of these are the same as the time zones of the US, the 'extra' zones being AST and NST. PST is eight hours behind GMT and NST three-and-a-half hours behind. The following table shows the time in each zone when it's noon in Vancouver.

Canadian Time Zones

Zone/Province	Time
Pacific Standard Time (PST)	noon
Mountain Standard Time (MST)	1pm
Central Standard Time (CST)	2pm
Eastern Standard Time (EST)	3pm
Atlantic Standard Time (AST)	4pm
Newfoundland and Labrador Standard Time (NST)	4.30pm

Canada operates a 'daylight saving' scheme, when each province except Saskatchewan moves its clocks forward one hour on the last Sunday in April and returns them to standard time on the last Sunday in October. When telling the time, Canadians say 'twenty to three' or two forty, while 'twenty after three' is 'twenty minutes ***past*** three' or three twenty. Times are commonly written with a colon, e.g. 2:40 or 3:20. Canadians don't generally use the 24-hour clock.

TIPPING

Tipping in Canada is similar to the US, although Canadians have a reputation as poor tippers and some don't tip (or tip very little) and don't mind being thought cheap – they like to think they're being thrifty (there's a local joke that goes "What's the difference between a canoe and a Canadian? A canoe tips!"). In Canada, tips are generally given only to people in service jobs such as bartenders, restaurant staff, cab drivers and redcaps, and not to all and sundry as south of the border.

Many restaurant owners and other employers exploit the practice of tipping by paying starvation wages in the certain knowledge that employees can supplement their wages with tips. If you don't tip a waiter he may not starve, but he'll certainly struggle to survive on his meagre salary. In general, a service charge isn't included in the bill in restaurants and you're expected to tip the waiter, waitress and bartenders around 15 per cent, depending on the class of establishment.

If a service charge is included it should be shown on the menu and bill. Restaurant tips can be included in credit card payments or given as cash. The total on credit card counterfoils is often left blank (even when service is included in the price) to encourage you to leave a tip. Some bills even include separate boxes for gratuities, but don't forget to fill in the total before signing it. Most restaurant staff prefer you to leave a cash tip because tips included in credit card payments aren't always passed on to staff.

Most people give the door attendant or superintendent of their apartment block a tip (or 'sweetener') for extra services, usually ranging from a few dollars up to $20, depending on the services provided. Christmas is generally a time for giving tips to all and sundry, e.g. your door attendant, newspaper boy, parking attendant, hairdresser, laundryman, handyman, etc. The size of a tip depends on how often someone has served you, the quality and friendliness of service, and how wealthy you are. Generally tips range from a few dollars up to $50 or more for the superintendent of your apartment block (it pays to be nice to him), which is usually placed inside a Christmas card. If you're unsure who or how much to tip, ask your neighbours, friends or colleagues for advice (who will all tell you something different!).

TOILETS

Some Canadians find the word 'toilet' distasteful and use a myriad of 'genteel' terms such as restroom, powder room, washroom, bathroom, ladies' or men's room, and even 'comfort station' to refer to their toilets (never 'water closet'). When inquiring about a toilet, most people ask for the restroom/bathroom or the men's or ladies' room. Take care when using public toilets, as it isn't always easy to tell from the (often stylised) sign on the door whether it's the ladies' or men's room. Public toilets can be found in most public buildings, restaurants and other public places.

Separate toilets are usually provided for men and women. There's usually no charge for using them, although you shouldn't expect to stroll in off the street and be allowed to use a restroom in a private building such as an office block.

Bars and restaurants may try to deter non-customers with intimidating signs such as 'Restrooms for Patrons Only', although you can usually get away with using the toilet in a busy bar and many people use the facilities in large hotels. Some toilets in large hotels and restaurants have an attendant, when it's customary to 'tip' around 50¢. Some toilets provide nappy (diaper) changing facilities or facilities for nursing mothers (nursing isn't usually performed in public in Canada).

Many shopping centres (malls) have special toilets for the disabled, as do airports and major railway stations, although most public toilets for motorists aren't accessible to disabled drivers.

19. THE CANADIANS

Who are the Canadians? What are they like? Let's take a candid and totally prejudiced look at the Canadian people, tongue firmly in cheek, and hope they forgive my flippancy or that they don't read this bit (which is why it's hidden away at the back of the book!). The typical Canadian is polite, hard-working, law-abiding, classless, unpretentious, generous, friendly, independent, liberal, cheerful, a good skier, proud, compassionate, an animal lover, reserved, dull, helpful, practical, introverted, conservative, a city dweller, fair, prosperous, a 'nice guy', peace-loving, an environmentalist, indefinable, honest, an immigrant, polite, respectful, a humanitarian, healthy, unassuming, an outdoorsman, cautious, democratic, modest, boring, loyal, relaxed, convivial, honourable, informal, tolerant, decisive, tough, pragmatic, well-educated, determined, sporting, hospitable, cosmopolitan, patriotic, mean, stoic, a hockey fan – and definitely NOT an American.

You may have noticed that the above list contains a few contradictions, which is hardly surprising as there's no such thing as a typical Canadian and few people conform to the popular stereotype (whatever that is). Canada is one of the most cosmopolitan and multicultural countries in the world (Toronto and Vancouver are among the world's most cosmopolitan cities) and a nation of foreigners (except for a few hundred thousand Native Americans and Inuit) who often have little in common with one another. However, despite its diverse racial mix, Canada isn't a universal melting pot and has been called a cultural mosaic, where the country's multicultural approach emphasises the different backgrounds and cultures of its people. (Canadians are remarkably tolerant towards immigrants, who are warmly welcomed.)

Canadians are one of the most difficult peoples to categorise and the country has been described as not so much a nation as a collection of different peoples on a continental scale. For a nation that's made up almost entirely of immigrants, it's hardly surprising that many Canadians have an identity crisis and spend a lot of time pondering 'The Canadian Question'. (As good an answer as any to the eternal question, "What is a Canadian?" is probably "A person who knows how to make love in a canoe.").

Canadians pride themselves on their lack of class-consciousness and don't have the same caste distinctions and pretensions common in the old world. Canada isn't, however, a classless society and status is as important there as it is anywhere else, although it's usually based on money and character rather than birthright. Canada generally has no class or 'old school tie' barriers to success and almost anyone, however humble his origins, can fight his way to the top of the heap (although colour barriers aren't always so easy to overcome). However, although it doesn't have an aristocracy, old money and political alliances are important in the east, and there are still a number of barriers that even vast amounts of new money cannot breach. Despite the fact that the majority of Canadians are misplaced Britons, French and other Europeans on the wrong side of the Atlantic (plus an influx of Asians in recent decades), modern Canada has, not surprisingly, more in common with the US than with Britain or Europe.

However, apart from lifestyle, Canadians have little in common with Americans and, indeed, are at pains to emphasise the differences between themselves and their southern neighbours ('south of the border' in Canada means the USA, not Mexico). Canadians don't like being mistaken for Americans, who they see as arrogant, brash, vulgar and successful ('if you've got it, flaunt it' isn't the Canadian way – Canadians are increasingly playing down their 'wealth' – they even forgo designer bags for nondescript carriers with no logos).

It doesn't help that the US is Canada's biggest trading partner and has a huge influence on the Canadian economy; in a much quoted speech in 1969, then Prime Minister Pierre Trudeau remarked that "Living next to the US is like sleeping with an elephant. No matter how friendly and even-tempered the beast, one is affected by every twitch and grunt". One sure way of making yourself unpopular with Canadians is to call them Americans. It's best to refer to the States or the US when you mean the USA, and North America when you mean the continent. So as not to be confused with Yanks when travelling, Canadians often wear a maple leaf badge or stick huge Canadian flags on their luggage to let people know where they are from.

Although they're often assumed to be Americans, many Canadians enjoy (or have enjoyed) worldwide fame, including Dan Ackroyd, Bryan Adams, Paul Anka, Elizabeth Arden, Margaret Atwood, Saul Bellow, Raymond Burr, John Candy, Jim Carrey, Leonard Cohen, Michael J. Fox, Glenn Gould, J. K. Galbraith, Lorne Greene, Wayne Gretsky, Arthur Hailey, Jack Kerouac, K. D. Lang, Gordon Lightfoot, Raymond Massey, Joni Mitchell, Anne Murray, Mike Myers, Mary Pickford, Christopher Plummer, William Shatner, David Steinberg, Donald Sutherland and Neil Young, to name but a few. However, most don't (or didn't) complain too vociferously when being taken for Americans as it's good for business and helps to be accepted in the US.

Canada also gave the world Trivial Pursuit (not many people know that), instant mashed potatoes, the gas mask, the parka, baby cereal, the electron microscope, the zip, the snowmobile (no surprise there), the paint roller, Greenpeace (founded in Vancouver in 1970), the push-up bra, insulin, the chocolate bar, Ghostbusters, the paint roller, ice hockey and basketball (a real surprise – and a sore point with Americans). Canada is proud of its contribution to space exploration in terms of the Canadarm, a shuttle remote manipulator system used on the Space Shuttle. The world would be a much poorer place without Canadians (and zips).

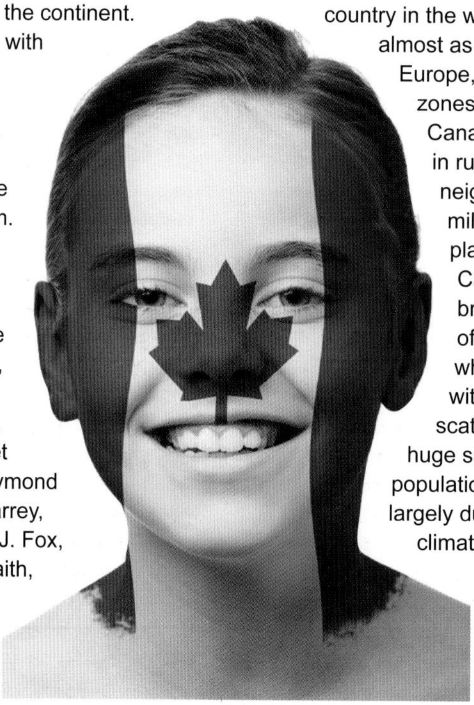

You may have noticed that Canada is a very large country (it takes a week just to drive across it); so large in fact that Canadians coined a new word to describe it: HUMONGOUS. It's the second-largest country in the world (after China) and almost as large as the whole of Europe, with six different time zones. The more you see of Canada the bigger it gets and in rural areas your nearest neighbours are likely to be miles away. The interior plains or the prairies are Canada's (and the world's) bread basket, consisting of hundreds of miles of wheat fields interspersed with vast forests and a few scattered towns. Despite it huge size, Canada has a small population of just 33.6mn people, largely due to its inhospitable climate.

The weather is a topical subject of conversation in Canada, which is surprising considering that most of the year it's either bloody freezing or as hot as hell, with little in between (with the exception of Vancouver, which is really part of the US). For most of the year much of Canada is frozen solid and most of the time is spent indoors trying to keep warm or cool (which is why they invented Trivial Pursuit). However, unlike most Americans, Canadians revel in their winters and turn (and tame) the weather to their advantage. They love the outdoor life and have a thriving winter sports industry, and spend the summers hiking, camping, hunting, fishing and boating (and trying to avoid being eaten by bears). The outdoors has a major influence on the lives of most Canadians, although most live in cities. They are passionate conservationists and schemes to protect the environment and recycling abound.

If you wonder what Canadians get up to during the long winters, judging by the low birth-rate it isn't sex (immigration is encouraged in order to compensate for the low birth-rate). Canadians are fairly broad-minded when it comes to sex and nudity, and some provinces have 'topless' laws which make it discriminatory to forbid women to go topless in any place where men can go without a shirt. This hasn't, however, led to a surfeit of women baring their breasts in public, but simply to many places (such as sports stadiums) banning topless men (and hence women). There also aren't a lot of topless bars with male 'hosts'.

> While on the subject of sex, you may be interested to know that (according to one survey) the average Canadian makes love 102 times per year (how do they know these things – surely they don't believe what people tell them?).

Canadians are apparently thoughtful lovers and rate highest in the league for considering their partner's satisfaction more important than their own and ninth in the list of countries considered good lovers. Naturally the French are top in this respect (it must have been a French survey) – the statistics don't mention French Canadians, who no doubt consider themselves French in this regard! Like Americans, Canadians are tolerant of homosexuals and many cities have 'Gay Pride' days, when parades and other celebrations attract large crowds, including straights (or as they're called by gays, 'breeders').

Life in Canada isn't always a bed of roses, however, and it has 'a few' problems, although they're relatively minor compared with those faced by most other countries. These include the treatment and rights of its indigenous peoples such as the Inuit (who used to be known as Eskimos) and Native Americans, who are now collectively referred to in politically correct terms as 'First Nations' people. In recent years, the Canadian government has moved away from its paternalistic attitude and in 1999 'granted' the Inuit around 800,000 square miles (2mn km^2) of the Northwest Territories as a separate and autonomous territory called Nunavut ('our land').

However, although the deal included the eviction of all non-Inuit-owned businesses, put federal agencies under Inuit control and included payments totalling $500mn plus interest, it isn't as generous as it seems. In return, the Inuit had to renounce claims of direct ownership of most of the territory, especially the offshore gas and oil exploration areas (as John Paul Getty said, "The meek shall inherit the earth, but not the mineral rights"). This agreement has also opened a can of worms, with other native groups now pressing for similar deals, and what started as orderly protests have become barricaded roads and armed confrontations in some areas.

Other problems (common to many countries) include inadequate infrastructure in the major cities (which is put under huge strain by the influx of migrants); crime (particularly gang warfare) and drug use; deteriorating health and social services; the rising cost of living; climate change and conservation; increasing poverty and homelessness; and unemployment and other problems caused by the recession and credit crunch.

Canada's other major concern is the acrimonious debate over the future of Quebec. There's a historic animosity between French-Canadians and English speakers dating back to the beginning of the 17th century, when the French were instrumental in opening up North America. They were involved in a running war with the British that culminated in the defeat of the French forces at Quebec City in 1759, following which 'New France' was ceded to Britain in 1763. Despite its defeat, the Province of Quebec remained a stronghold of French nationalism and some 200 years later in the early '60s the French-Canadians, fed up with their almost second-class citizen status in a country dominated by Anglo-Saxons, formed a separatist movement to demand that Quebec become a separate state. The campaign forced referendums (or 'neverendums' as they're called) on the question of Quebec separation in 1980 and 1995, both of which were only narrowly defeated (in 1995, just 52 per cent voted to remain part of Canada), although a more recent poll of *Québécois* showed that over 75 per cent want to remain part of Canada.

The average English-speaking Canadian has a jaundiced view of the *Québécois* and the French language, which many believe has more influence than it merits. In an effort to appease French-Canadians, the French language has become the first language of Quebec and Canada has become officially bilingual. To the immense irritation of the rest of Canada, all official documents and much other printed matter must be dual-language, most of the civil service speaks only French, and the dreaded 'language police' have garnered the sort of power that enables them to force Chinese businesses in Chinatown to remove their Chinese signs. Outside Quebec, many Canadians cannot wait to see the back of the *Québécois*, if only "so we won't need to have our soup can labels printed in French". Irritation also involves government money disappearing into Quebec coffers as another form of appeasement. Of one thing you can be sure, the separation issue is unlikely to go away.

Now for the good bit. Canada is one of the most open, liberal, stable and tolerant societies in the world. It has a thriving economy with political stability, abundant natural resources, a skilled workforce, steady population growth, and substantial domestic and foreign capital investment. It's renowned for its beauty, outdoor lifestyle, unspoilt environment, rich flora and fauna, healthy diet, friendly people, creativity, open spaces, sports facilities, cultural diversity, freedom, good transportation, quality education and healthcare, excellent local government and things that work.

> Canadians have more freedom from government interference than the people of most countries, to do, say and act any way they like. They place a high value on hard work, fairness, honesty and order, which help make Canada one of the least corrupt, safest and most civilised countries in the world.

Canadians are family oriented, which is one of the most important foundations in their lives, and it's a caring society where the community comes before the individual. This is highlighted by the abundance of charitable and voluntary organisations in Canada that do invaluable work (both nationally and internationally), supported by a veritable army of millions of voluntary workers.

Despite the shock of the recession, Canadians have strong faith in themselves and are optimistic about the future (although less so). Although immigrants may criticise some aspects of Canadian life, most feel privileged to live there and are proud to call themselves Canadians, and very few seriously consider leaving. In fact, immigrants from a vast range of backgrounds firmly believe that Canada is the promised land and a great place to live and raise a family. This is borne out by the United Nations' 'quality of life' survey that consistently ranks Canada in the number one position, based on criteria such as the standard of healthcare, educational achievement, wealth, life expectancy and standard of living. It may not be everyone's idea of paradise (particularly if you hate the cold), but Canada certainly has a good claim to be the best country in the world. For vitality and *joie de vivre* Canada has few equals, and for those fortunate enough to secure a residence permit it's a (promised) land where you can turn your dreams into reality.

Long Live Canada! *Vive le Canada! O Canada!*

20. MOVING HOUSE OR LEAVING CANADA

When moving house or leaving Canada there are many things to be considered and a 'million' people to inform. The checklists contained in this chapter will make the task easier and hopefully help prevent an ulcer or nervous breakdown (only divorce and bereavement cause more stress than moving house), provided of course that you don't leave everything to the last minute. See also Moving House and Relocation Consultants in Chapter 5.

MOVING HOUSE WITHIN CANADA

When moving house within Canada, particularly when changing provinces, the following matters should be considered:

- Give notice to your employer or inform him of your new address.
- If you live in rented accommodation you must give your landlord the necessary notice, as specified in your lease. If you don't give sufficient notice, you must pay the rent until the end of your lease or for the full notice period.
- If you aren't moving into permanent accommodation, book temporary accommodation and have it confirmed in writing.
- Inform the following:
  - your utility companies, e.g. electricity, gas and water companies. Make sure any security deposits are returned if you're moving to a new area.
  - your phone company, preferably at least two weeks in advance. If you're moving home and remaining in the same code area you may be able to retain your existing number. Don't forget to have your line disconnected when moving, otherwise the new owners or tenants will be able to make calls at your expense.
  - your insurance companies (for example health, car, homeowner's, life, etc.), banks, stockbroker and other financial institutions, credit card and loan companies, lawyer and accountant, and local businesses where you have accounts. Make sure you have valid insurance if you're moving to another province.
  - your doctor, dentist and other health practitioners. Health records should be transferred to your new doctor and dentist, if applicable. Contact your vet for information and health records for your pets and any special transportation requirements.
  - all regular correspondents. These may include subscriptions, social and sports clubs, church and other organisations, professional and trade journals, not forgetting your friends and relatives.

- your family's schools. If applicable, arrange for schooling in your new community. Try to give a term's notice and obtain a copy of any relevant school reports or records from your children's current schools.

- Arrange to have your post redirected (see **Change of Address** on page 119). This should be arranged two to four weeks before moving.
- If you're moving to another province and have a Canadian driving licence or Canadian registered car, inform your local motor licence office as soon as possible after moving. Give your automobile association (see page 192) your new address.
- Return any library books or anything borrowed.
- Book a moving company well in advance to transport your furniture and personal effects to your new home. If you have just a few items of furniture to move you may prefer to do your own move, in which case you may need to rent a vehicle or trailer. Keep a record of all moving expenses for tax purposes.
- Arrange for a cleaning or decorating company for rented accommodation, if necessary.
- If renting, contact your landlord or the letting agency to have your security deposit returned.
- Cancel newspaper and other regular home deliveries.
- If necessary, arrange for someone to look after your children and pets during the move.
- Ask yourself (again): "Is it really worth all this trouble?"

LEAVING CANADA

Before leaving Canada permanently or for an indefinite period, the following matters should be considered in addition to those listed above under **Moving House**:

- Check that your family's passports are valid.
- Check whether there are any special requirements (e.g. visas, permits or inoculations) for entry into your destination country by contacting the local embassy or consulate in Canada. A Canadian exit permit or visa isn't required.
- If you're shipping household and personal effects, find out the exact procedure from the local embassy of your destination country. Special forms may need to be completed before arrival. If you've been living in Canada for less than a year, you're required to re-export all imported personal effects, including furniture and vehicles (if you sell them you should pay duty). Contact an international shipping company well in advance to arrange shipment of your furniture and personal effects.

> Notify any utility companies well in advance if you need to get a security deposit returned.

- You must pay your federal and provincial taxes for the current year in the normal way before leaving Canada (see **Chapter 14**). If you're leaving Canada permanently and are a member of a company pension plan (or have a private pension plan), you should receive a lump sum payment in lieu of a pension. Contact your company personnel office, local Canada Revenue Agency office or pension company for information.

  As a non-resident, you may be subject to a withholding tax of 25 per cent on interest, dividends, rents, royalties, alimony, pension benefits and certain payments from retirement savings plans, old age social insurance benefits and the net income from a business in Canada. If you've been employed temporarily in Canada, you must ensure that the Canada Revenue Agency is aware that you're no longer a resident, otherwise you could continue to receive tax demands.
- Arrange to sell anything you aren't taking with you (home, car, furniture, etc.). If you have a Canadian-registered car that you're exporting, check the procedure and cost (e.g. shipping, tax and import duty) of exporting it, and make arrangements for its shipment. Depending on your destination, your pets may require special inoculations or may be required to go into quarantine for a period. If you're taking your pets with you by air, you'll need to arrange their transportation. Make arrangements well in advance.

- Arrange health, travel and other insurance as necessary (see **Chapter 13**).
- Depending on your destination, arrange health and dental checks for your family before leaving Canada. Obtain a copy of your family's health and dental records and a statement from your health insurance company stating your present level of cover.
- Settle any loans, leases or instalment contracts and pay all outstanding bills (allow plenty of time because some companies may be slow to respond).
- Check whether you're entitled to a rebate on your car registration and car and other insurance. Obtain a letter from your Canadian car insurance company stating your 'good-driver' discount.
- Sell your house, apartment or other property, or arrange to let it through a friend or an agent (see **Chapter 5**).
- Check whether you require an international driver's permit or a translation of your Canadian or foreign driving licence for your country of destination.
- Give friends and business associates an address, phone number and email address where you can be contacted abroad.
- If you're travelling by air, allow yourself plenty of time to get to the airport, register your luggage and clear security and immigration.
- Buy a copy of *Living and Working in* ******** by Survival Books before leaving Canada. If we haven't published it yet, drop us a line and we will get started on it right away!

Have a safe journey!

Inukshuk - Inuit stone landmark

APPENDICES

APPENDIX A: USEFUL ADDRESSES

Embassies & High Commissions

The list below includes the majority of foreign embassies and High Commissions (for Commonwealth countries) in the capital, Ottawa. Many countries also have consulates in other cities, e.g. Montreal, Toronto and Vancouver, which are listed in phone books. For countries that don't have representation in Canada, contact the embassy in Washington DC, USA. Further details of embassies and High Commissions in Canada can be found on the Foreign Affairs and International Trade Canada website (💻 www.international.gc.ca).

Algeria: 500 Wilbrod Street, Ottawa, ON K1N 6N2 (☎ 613-789 8505, 💻 www.embassyalgeria.ca).

Argentina: 81 Metcalfe Street, Suite 700, Ottawa, ON K1P 6K7 (☎ 613-236 2351, 💻 www.argentina-canada.net).

Australia: 50 O'Connor Street, Suite 710, Ottawa, ON K1P 6L2 (☎ 613-236 0841, 💻 www.ahc-ottawa.org).

Austria: 445 Wilbrod Street, Ottawa, ON K1N 6M7 (☎ 613-789 1444, 💻 www.bmeia.gv.at/en/embassy/ottawa.html).

Bangladesh: 340 Albert Street, Suite 1250, Ottawa, ON K2P 2L6 (☎ 613-236 0138, 💻 www.bdhc.org).

Belgium: 360 Albert Street, Suite 820, Ottawa, ON K1R 7X7 (☎ 613-236 7267, 💻 www.diplomabe.bc/ottawa).

Chile: 50 O'Connor Street, Suite 1413, Ottawa, ON K1P 6L2 (☎ 613-235 4402, 💻 www.chile.ca).

China: 515 St. Patrick Street, Ottawa, ON K1N 5H3 (☎ 613-789 3434, 💻 www.chinaembassycanada.org/eng).

Colombia: 360 Albert Street, Suite 1002, Ottawa, ON K1R 7X7 (☎ 613-230 3760, 💻 www.embajadacolombia.ca/en).

Cote D'Ivoire: 9 Marlborough Avenue, Ottawa, ON K1N 8E6 (☎ 613-236 9919, 💻 http://ambaci-ottawa.org).

Croatia: 229 Chapel Street, Ottawa, ON K1N 7Y6 (☎ 613-562 7820, 💻 www.croatiaemb.net).

Czech Republic: 251 Cooper Street, Ottawa, ON K2P 0G2 (☎ 613-562 3875, 💻 www.mfa.cz/ottawa).

Denmark: 47 Clarence Street, Suite 450, Ottawa, ON K1N 9K1 (☎ 613-562 1811, 💻 www.ambottawa.um.dk/en).

Egypt: 454 Laurier Avenue East, Ottawa, ON K1N 6R3 (☎ 613-234 4931, 💻 www.mfa.gov.eg/missions/canada/ottawa/embassy/en-gb).

Ethiopia: 151 Slater Street, Suite 210, Ottawa, ON K1P 5H3 (☎ 613-235 6637, 💻 www.ottawa.ethiopianembassy.net/index.htm).

Finland: 55 Metcalfe Street, Suite 850, Ottawa, ON K1P 6L5 (☎ 613-288 2233, 💻 www.finland.ca).

France: 42 Sussex Drive, Ottawa, ON K1M 2C9 (☎ 613-789 1795, 💻 www.ambafrance-ca.org).

Germany: 1 Waverley Street, Ottawa, ON K2P 0T8 (☎ 613-232 1101, 💻 www.ottawa.diplo.de).

India: 10 Springfield Road, Ottawa, ON K1M 1C9 (☎ 613-744 3751, 💻 www.hciottawa.ca).

Indonesia: 55 Parkdale Avenue, Ottawa, ON K1Y 1E5 (☎ 613-724 1100, 💻 www.indonesia-ottawa.org).

Ireland: 130 Albert Street, Suite 1105, Ottawa, ON K1P 5G4 (☎ 613-233 6281, 💻 www.embassyofireland.ca).

Israel: 50 O'Connor Street, Ottawa, ON K1P 6L2 (☎ 613-567 6450, 💻 www.embassyofisrael.ca).

Japan: 255 Sussex Drive, Ottawa, ON K1N 9E6 (☎ 613-241 8541, 💻 www.ca.emb-japan.go.jp).

Kenya: 415 Laurier Avenue East, Ottawa, ON K1N 6R4 (☎ 613-563 1773, 💻 www.kenyahighcommission.ca).

Korea (South): 150 Boteler Street, 5th Floor, Ottawa, ON K1N 5A6 (☎ 613-244 5010, 💻 http://can-ottawa.mofat.go.kr/eng/am/can-ottawa/main/index.jsp).

Latvia: 350 Sparks Street, Suite 1200, Ottawa, ON K1R 7S8 (☎ 613-238 6014, 💻 www.ottawa.am.gov.lv/en).

Lebanon: 640 Lyon Street, Ottawa, ON K1S 3Z5 (☎ 613-236 5825, 💻 www.lebanonembassy.ca).

Mexico: 45 O'Connor Street, Suite 1000, Ottawa, ON K1P 1A4 (☎ 613-233 8988, 💻 www.sre.gob.mx/canadaingles).

Morocco: 38 Range Road, Ottawa, ON K1N 8J4 (613-236 7391, www.ambamaroc.ca).

New Zealand: 99 Bank Street, Suite 727, Ottawa, ON K1P 6G3 (613-238 5991, www.nzembassy.com/canada).

Norway: 150 Melcalfe Street, Suite 1300, Ottawa, ON K2P 1P1 (613-238 6571, www.emb-norway.ca).

Paraguay: 151 Slater Street, Suite 501, Ottawa, ON K1P 5H3 (613-567 1283, www.paraguayembassy.ca).

Poland: 443 Daly Avenue, Ottawa, ON K1N 6H3 (613-789 0468, www.polishembassy.ca).

Russia: 285 Charlotte Street, Ottawa, ON K1N 8L5 (613-235 4341, www.rusembcanada.mid.ru).

Spain: 74 Stanley Avenue, Ottawa, ON K1M 1P4 (613-747 2252, www.maec.es/subwebs/embajadas/ottawa/en/home/paginas/home.aspx).

Sri Lanka: 333 Laurier Avenue, Ottawa, ON K1P 1C1 (613-233 8449, www.srilankahcottawa.org).

Thailand: 180 Island Park Drive, Ottawa, ON K1Y 0A2 (613-722 4444, www.magma.ca/~thaiott/mainpage.htm).

Trinidad and Tobago: 200 First Avenue, Ottawa, ON K1S 2G6 (613-232 2418, www.ttmissions.com).

Ukraine: 310 Somerset Street, Ottawa, ON K2P 0J9 (613-230 2961, www.ukremb.ca/canada/en/news/top.htm).

United Kingdom: 80 Elgin Street, Ottawa, ON K1P 5K7 (613-237 1530, www.britainincanada.org).

United States of America: 490 Sussex Drive, Ottawa, ON K1N 1G8 (613-238 5335, http://ottawa.usembassy.gov/content/index.asp).

Uruguay: 130 Albert Street, Suite 1905, Ottawa, ON K1P 5G4 (613-234 2727, http://embassyofuruguay.ca/).

Miscellaneous

Association of Canadian Travel Agents (ACTA), 350 Sparks Street, Suite 510, Ottawa, ON K1R 7S8 (613-237 3657, www.acta.ca).

Association of Universities and Colleges of Canada, 350 Albert Street, Suite 600, Ottawa, ON K1R 1B1 (613-563 1236, www.aucc.ca).

Bank of Canada, Public Information, 234 Wellington, Ottawa, ON K1A 0G9 (1-800-303 1282, www.bankofcanada.ca).

Canada Mortgage and Housing Corporation, 700 Montreal Road, Ottawa, ON K1A 0P7 (☏ 613-748 2000, 💻 www.cmhc-schl.gc.ca/en/co/reho).

Canada Revenue Agency, Client Services Directorate, 400 Cumberland Street, Ottawa, ON K1A 0L8 (☏ 1-800-267 6999, 💻 www.cra-arc.gc.ca).

Canadian Association of Independent Schools, 12 Bannockburn Avenue, Toronto, ON M5M 2M8 (☏ 416-780 1779, 💻 www.cais.ca).

Canadian Council of Better Business Bureaus, 2 St Clair Avenue East, Suite 800, Toronto, ON M4T 2T5 (☏ 416-644 4936, 💻 www.ccbbb.ca).

Canadian Franchise Association, 5399 Eglinton Avenue West, Suite 116, Toronto, ON M9C 5K6 (☏ 1-800-665 4232 or 416-695 2896, 💻 www.cfa.ca).

Canadian Human Rights Commission, National Office, 344 Slater Street, 8th Floor, Ottawa, ON K1A 1E1 (☏ 613-995 1151, 💻 www.chrc-ccdp.ca).

Canadian Real Estate Association (CREA), 200 Catherine Street, 6th Floor, Ottawa, ON K2P 2K9 (☏ 613-237 7111, 💻 www.crea.ca).

Canadian Tourism Commission, #1400-1055, Dunsmuir Street, Box 49230, Vancouver, BC V7X 1L2 (☏ 604-638 8300, 💻 www.canadatourism.com).

Canadian Transportation Agency, 15 Eddy Street, Gatineau, Quebec, K1A 0N9 (☏ 1-888-222 2592, 💻 www.cta-otc.gc.ca).

Consumers' Association of Canada, 436 Gilmour Street, 3rd Floor, Ottawa, ON K2P 0R8 (☏ 613-238 2533, 💻 www.consumer.ca).

Consumers Council of Canada, 1910 Yonge Street, 4th Floor, Toronto, ON M4S 1Z5 (☏ 416-483 2696, 💻 www.consumerscouncil.com).

Forum for International Trade Training (FITT), 116 Lisgar Street, Suite 300, Ottawa, ON K2P 0C2 (☏ 613-230 3553, 💻 www.fitt.ca).

Greyhound Canada, 877 Greyhound Way SW, Calgary, AB T3C 3V8 (☏ 1-800-661 8747, 💻 www.greyhound.ca).

Health Canada, AL 0900C2, Ottawa, Canada K1A OK9 (💻 www.hc-sc.gc.ca).

Human Resources and Skills Development Canada, 140 Promenade du Portage, Phase IV, Hull, QC K1A 0J9 (💻 www.hrsdc.gc.ca).

Insurance Bureau of Canada, 777 Bay Street, Suite 2400, Toronto, ON M5G 2C8 (☏ 416-362 2031, 💻 www.ibc.ca).

Job Bank, Employment Information Services, Service Canada, 140 Promendade du Portage, Phase IV, 5th Floor, Box 511, Hull, QC K1A OJ9 (💻 www.jobbank.gc.ca).

Natural Resources Canada, 580 Booth, Ottawa, ON K1A 0E4 (☏ 613-995 0947, 💻 www.nrcan.gc.ca).

Office of Consumers Affairs, Industry Canada, 235 Queen Street, 6th Floor West, Ottawa, ON K1A 0H5 (☎ 613-946 2576, 💻 http://consumerinformation.ca).

Passport Canada, Foreign Affairs and International Trade Canada, Gatineau QC K1A 0G3 (☎ 1-800-567 6868 or 819-997 8338, 💻 www.ppt.gc.ca).

Parks Canada, Publications Unit, 25 Eddy Street, Gatineau, QC K1A 0M5 (☎ 1-888-773 8888, 💻 www.pc.gc.ca or www.parkscanada.ca).

Status of Women Canada, MacDonald Building, 123 Slater Street, 10th Floor, Ottawa, ON K1P 1H9 (☎ 613-995 7835, 💻 www.swc-cfc.gc.ca).

Transport Canada, 330 Sparks Street, Tower C, Place de Ville, Ottawa, ON K1A 0N5 (☎ 613-990 2309, 💻 www.tc.gc.ca).

VIA Rail Canada, PO Box 8116, Station 'A', Montreal, PQ H3C 3N3 (☎ 1-800-681 2561, 💻 www.viarail.ca).

Links to Canadian government departments can be found at 💻 http://canada.gc.ca/depts/major/depind-eng.html and links to provincial and territorial governments at 💻 http://canada.gc.ca/othergov-autregouv/prov-eng.html.

bald eagle

APPENDIX B: FURTHER READING

Newspapers & Magazines

Listed below is a small selection of the hundred of newspapers and magazines published in Canada. For a complete list of Canadian newspapers, see www.world-newspapers.com/canada.html (search by province) or www.onlinenewspapers.com/canada.htm (listed A-Z by town/city). For information about (and to subscribe to) Canadian magazines, see http://magazinescanada.ca.

British Columbia Magazine (www.bcmag.ca). Quarterly travel magazine.

Calgary Herald (www.calgaryherald.com). Daily newspaper.

Calgary Sun (www.calgarysun.com). Daily newspaper.

Canada Employment Weekly (www.mediacorp.com).

Canadian Business (www.canadianbusiness.com). Monthly business magazine.

Canadian Living (www.canadianliving.com). Monthly women's home and lifestyle magazine.

Edmonton Journal (www.edmontonjournal.com). Daily newspaper.

The Gazette (www.montrealgazette.com). Daily newspaper for Montreal.

The Globe and Mail (www.theglobeandmail.com). Daily newspaper.

The Halifax Daily News (www.halifaxnewsnet.ca). Daily newspaper.

Maclean's Magazine (www.blog.macleans.ca). Weekly current affairs magazine.

Moving To Magazines (www.movingto.com). Home moving guides to Alberta, Montreal, Southwest Ontario, Ottawa, Saskatchewan, Toronto, Vancouver and Winnipeg.

National Post (www.nationalpost.com). Daily newspaper.

Ottawa Citizen (www.ottawacitizen.com). Daily Newspaper.

The Province (www.theprovince.com). Daily newspaper.

Toronto Life (www.torontolife.com). Monthly lifestyle magazine.

Vancouver Magazine (www.vanmag.com). Monthly lifestyle magazine.

The Vancouver Sun (www.vancouversun.com). Daily newspaper.

The Windsor Star (www.windsorstar.com). Daily newspaper.

Winnipeg Free Press (www.winnipegfreepress.com). Daily newspaper.

Books

In the list below, the publication title is followed by the author's name and the publisher (in brackets). Some titles may be out of print, but you may still be able to find a copy in a bookshop or library, or from a second-hand bookseller.

Culture

Blame Canada!: 'South Park' and Contemporary Culture, Toni Johnson-Woods (Continuum)

Canada and the British World: Culture, Migration, and Identity, Phillip A. Buckner & R. Douglas Francis (UBC)

Canada – The Culture, Bobby D. Kalman (Crabtree)

Culture Wise Canada, Graeme Chesters & Sally Jennings (Survival Books)

How to be a Canadian, Will & Ian Ferguson (Douglas & McIntyre)

The Indians of Canada: Their Manners and Customs, John McLean (Asian Educational Services)

Language, Culture and Values in Canada at the Dawn of the 21st Century, André LaPierre (Carleton University Press)

So you want to be Canadian, Kerry Colburn & Rob Sorensen (Chronicle)

Why We Act Like Canadians, Pierre Berton (McClelland & Stewart)

Food & Drink

Flavours of Canada, Anita Stewart & Robert Wigington (Raincoast)

Cooking Collections: Canadian Feasts from Land & Sea (Centax)

The Definitive Canadian Wine and Cheese Cookbook, Gurth Pretty & Tony Aspler (Whitecap)

Canadian Wine for Dummies, Tony Apier & Barbara Leslie (John Wiley)

The New Canadian Basics Cookbook, Carol Ferguson & Murray McMillan (Penguin)

Nothing More Comforting: Canada's Heritage Food, D. Duncan (Dundurn Group)

History

A Brief History of Canada, Roger Riendeau (Fitzhenry & Whiteside)

Canada: A People's History Volume 2, Pierre Turgeon & Don Gillmor (McClelland & Stewart)

Canadian History for Dummies, Will Ferguson (John Wiley)

A History of the Peoples of Canada, J. M. Bumstead (OUP)

An Illustrated History of Canada, Craig Brown (Key Porter)

The Penguin History of Canada, Kenneth McNaught (Penguin)

A Short History of Canada, Desmond Morton (McClelland & Stewart)

A Social History of Canada, George Woodcock (Penguin)

The Story of Canada, Janet Lunn & Christopher Moore (Lester Publishing)

A Traveller's History of Canada, Robert Bothwell (Cassell)

Literature

Anne of Green Gables, Lucy Maud Montgomery (Puffin Books)

Canadian Literature in English! 1 and 2, W. J. Keith (Porcupine's Quill)

The Colony of Unrequited Dreams, Wayne Johnston (Vintage Canada)

The Diviners, Margaret Laurence (McClelland & Stewart)

A History of Canadian Literature, W. H. New ((McGill-Queen's University Press)

Jade Peony, Wayson Choy (Douglas & McIntyre)

Joshua Then and Now, Mordechai Richler (McClelland & Stewart)

Of Girls and Women, Alice Munro (Penguin)

The Shipping News, E. Annie Proulx (Fourth Estate/Collier MacMillan)

Surfacing, Margaret Atwood (Virago/Fawcett)

White Fang, Jack London (Penguin)

Living & Working

Buying, Owning & Selling a Home in Canada, Margaret Kerr & Joann Kurtz (Wiley)

How to Move to Canada: A Primer for Americans, Terese Loeb Kreuzer & Carol Bennett (St Martin's Griffin)

How to Start a Small Business in Canada, Tariq Nadeem (Self-Help)

Start Your Own Business in Canada, James Stephenson & Rieva Levonsky (Entrepreneurs Press)

Working in Canada, Walter Johnson (Black Rose)

Outdoor Life

The Adventure Guide to Canada, P. Hobbs (Hunter Publishing)

The Complete Guide to Walking in Canada, Elliot Katz (Firefly)

The Good Life: Up the Yukon Without a Paddle, Dorian Amos (Eye)

A Handbook of the Canadian Rockies, Ben Gadd (Corax)

Hiking Canada's Great Divide, Dustin Lynx (Rocky Mountain)

The National Geographic Traveller Canada (AA Publishing)

The Outdoor Traveller's Guide to Canada, David Dunbar (Stewart, Tabori & Chang)

The Last Wilderness, P. Browning (Hutchinson)

People

The Big Picture: What Canadians Think about almost Anything, Allan R. Gregg (Macfarlane, Walter & Ross)

Canada – The People, Bobby D. Kalman (Crabtree)

The Canadian Atlas: Our Nation, Environment, and People (Reader's Digest)

The Canadians, George Woodcock (Fitzhenry & Whiteside)

The Eskimos and Aleuts, Don Dumond (Thames & Hudson)

Native People Native Lands: Canadian Indians, Inuit and Metis, B.A. Cox (McGill-Queen's University Press)

The People of New France (Themes in Canadian Social History), Alan Greer (UTP)

A People's Dream: Aboriginal Self-government in Canada?, Daniel Russell (UBC)

Xenophobe's Guide to the Canadians, Vaughn Roste (Oval)

Why We Act Like Canadians, Pierre Berton (McClelland & Stewart)

Tourist Guides

In addition to the national tourist guides listed below, there are numerous regional, provincial and city guides.

Baedeker Canada (AA/Baedeker)

Birnbaum's Canada, Alexandra Mayes Birnbaum (Harper-Perennial)

Blue Guide Canada (A & C Black)

Canada (DK Eyewitness Travel Guides), Hugh Thompson (DK Publishing)

Canada: 25 Ultimate Experiences (Rough Guides)

Discover Canada (Berlitz)

Fodor's Canada (Fodor's)

Frommer's Canada, Hilary Davidson, et al (Frommers)

Insight Guide: Canada (APA Publications)

Let's Go: USA and Canada (Pan)

Lonely Planet Canada, Andrea Schulte-Peevers, et al (Lonely Planet)

Michelin Green Guide Canada (Michelin)

The Rough Guide to Canada, Phil Lee, Tim Jepson, et al (Rough Guides)

Miscellaneous

1001 Questions about Canada, John R. Colombo (Doubleday)

Canada – Flying High, Jim Wark & Erin McCloskey (White Star)

Canada – A Portrait (Statistics Canada)

Canada from A to Z, Bobby D. Kalman (Crabtree)

Canada Year Book (Statistics Canada)

Canadian Encyclopaedia (McClelland & Stewart)

Canadian World Almanac and Book of Facts (Global Press)

***City to City (**also called **'O Canada! Travels in an Unknown Country')**, Jan Morris (Harper Collins)

A Day in the Life of Canada, Rick Smolen (Collins)

Destination Canada, Harold Mante (Windsor Books)

The Government of Canada, Robert MacGregor Dawson (University of Toronto Press)

Trans Canada Rail Guide, Melissa Graham (Trailblazer)

The Truth About Canada, Mel Hurtig (Emblem)

APPENDIX C: USEFUL WEBSITES

Below is a list of useful websites (by subject in alphabetical order) for readers wishing to learn more about Canada and Canadians.

Business

Canada Business (www.cbsc.org): Government website covering all aspects of business in Canada.

Canadian Business (www.canadianbusiness.com): Everything you need to know about Canadian business.

Canada Business Directory (www.cdnbusinessdirectory.com).

Canada Franchise Association (www.cfa.ca).

Doing Business with Canada (www.canadainternational.gc.ca/ci-ci/commerce_canada/index.aspx): Government website for those wishing to do business with Canada.

Invest in Canada (http://investincanada.gc.ca): Government website for investors.

Culture

Bella Online (www.bellaonline.com/site/canadianculture): Canadian culture site.

British Council Canada (www.britishcouncil.org/canada.htm). The UK's agency for international and cultural relations.

Canadians.ca (www.canadians.ca): Famous Canadians and more.

Canadian Culture (www.canadianculture.com): Canada's networking resource directory.

Canadian Cultural Web Directory (www.artscanadian.com).

Civilization.ca (www.civilization.ca): Information about the archaeology and history of Canada's Aboriginal peoples.

Culture-Canada (www.culture-canada.ca): A multicultural website.

Culture, Heritage and Recreation (www.culturecanada.gc.ca/index_e.cfm): Government programs and services.

Culture Online: Made in Canada (www.culture.ca/english.jsp): Website of the Department of Canadian Heritage.

Culturescope.ca (www.culturescope.ca): Canadian cultural observatory, which disseminates cultural policy and research information in Canada and abroad.

The Greatest Canadian (www.cbc.ca/greatest): Great Canadians, as chosen by Canadians in a CBC poll.

Shaw (http://members.shaw.ca/kcic1/index.html): Miscellaneous information about Canada and the Canadians.

Education

Association of Universities and Colleges of Canada (www.auccca): The voice of Canada's universities.

Canlearn (www.canlearn.ca): Source of interactive and comprehensive information and services designed to help individuals save, plan and pay for lifelong learning opportunities.

Canada Education Association (www.cea-ace.ca): An organisation dedicated to improving education in Canada.

Education Canada (www.educationcanada.com): Canada's '#1 online source for teaching and other education jobs'.

Education@Canada (www.educationcanada.cmec.ca): International gateway to education in Canada.

Government

Canada International (www.canadainternational.gc.ca): Contains links to government services, information and resources for immigrants.

Canada Revenue Agency (www.cra-arc.gc.ca): The Canadian tax office.

Citizenship and Immigration Canada (www.cic.gc.ca): Government website devoted to immigration and citizenship information.

Environment Canada (www.ec.gc.ca): Government information about the environment.

Government of Canada (http://canada.gc.ca/home.html): Information about services offered by the government to Canadians, non-Canadians and businesses.

Health Canada (www.hc-sc.gc.ca): Government information on all aspects of healthcare.

Human Resources and Skills Development Canada (HRSDC, www.hrsdc.gc.ca): Information on a vast number of subjects to 'improve Canadians' quality of life.'

Government of Canada – Prime Minister (💻 www.pm.gc.ca): The website of Canada's Prime Minister.

Library and Archives Canada (💻 www.collectionscanada.gc.ca/amicus): What's on at Canada's many national collections.

Passport Canada (💻 www.ppt.gc.ca): Information about passports.

Statistics Canada (💻 www.statcan.gc.ca): Government statistics on all aspects of Canada and Canadian life.

The Weather Office (💻 www.weatheroffice.ec.gc.ca): Environment Canada's weather information website.

Living & Working

BuyitCanada.com (💻 www.buyitcanada.com): A directory, divided into provinces and cities, with links to websites about everything from apartment rentals and the arts to immigration lawyers and utilities.

Canadian Relocation Systems (💻 http://relocatecanada.com): A guide for people relocating within or moving to Canada, with information about life, services and prices throughout the country.

Council of Canadians (💻 www.canadians.org): Canada's largest citizens' organisation, with members and chapters across the country.

Immigration.ca (💻 www.immigration.ca): The website of the extravagantly named Canadian Citizenship and Immigration Resource Center, a legal firm specialising in immigration.

Living in Canada (💻 www.livingin-canada.com): Information about emigration to Canada.

Moving in Canada (💻 www.movingincanada.com): A comprehensive guide to life in Canada's various provinces, cities and towns.

SOS Canada 2000 (💻 http://soscanada2000.com): A country and migration guide to Canada.

Media

Canada.com (💻 www.canada.com): A comprehensive network, with news and information about everything Canadian, from careers to shopping.

Canadian Broadcasting Corporation (💻 www.cbc.ca): Information about CBC's radio and television output as well as coverage of the arts, business, news, sports and much else.

Canadian Magazine Publishers Association (💻 www.cmpa.ca): Information and subscriptions to all Canadian magazines.

Canadian Newspaper Association (💻 www.cna-acj.ca).

Canadian Newspapers (💻 www.onlinenewspapers.com/canada.htm and www.world-newspapers.com/canada.html): Links to all Canadian newspapers.

Cyberpresse.ca (💻 www.cyberpresse.ca): News in French.

Radio-locator (💻 www.radio-locator.com): Find online radio stations throughout Canada.

Miscellaneous

About Canada (💻 www.canada.gc.ca/acanada/viewcategory.htm?lang=eng): General information from the Government of Canada.

Atlas of Canada (💻 http://atlas.nrcan.gc.ca/site/index.html): An atlas from Natural Resources Canada.

Bank of Canada (💻 www.bankofcanada.ca): Contains a wealth of financial information, including exchange rates.

Canada411 (💻 www.canada411.ca): Online *Yellow Pages*.

Canada Council for the Arts (💻 www.canadacouncil.ca): Supporting the arts and art organisations across Canada.

Canada Online (💻 http://canadaonline.about.com): General information from About.com.

Canada Post (💻 www.canadapost.ca): Comprehensive information about Canada's postal services and prices.

Canadian Atlas (💻 www.canadiangeographic.ca/atlas): Canadian Geographic's atlas of Canada.

Canadian Automobile Association (CAA, 💻 www.caa.ca).

Canadian Beer Index (💻 www.realbeer.com/canada): Site dedicated to Canada's favourite tipple.

Canada History (💻 www.canadahistory.com): Good online overview of Canada from prehistory to the present.

The Canadian Council for the Arts (💻 www.canadacouncil.ca): Information about dance, music, theatre, the visual arts and writing.

The Canadian Encyclopedia (💻 www.thecanadianencyclopedia.com): The most comprehensive and authoritative source of information on all things Canadian.

Canadian Favourites (💻 http://canadianfavourites.com): A website celebrating Canadian food.

FactsCanada.ca (💻 www.factscanada.ca): Contains information and news about all aspects of Canada.

Inuit Art of Canada (💻 www.inuitartofcanada.com): Authorised by the Canadian government to promote and distribute Inuit art.

The National Hockey League (💻 www.nhl.com): Information about all aspects of Canada's beloved hockey.

Neil's Garage (💻 www.neilyoung.com): The website of Canada's most respected and influential musician, Neil Young.

Parks Canada (💻 www.pc.gc.ca): Government body that manages national parks, historical sites, archaeology, and marine conservation.

The Royal Canadian Geographic Society (💻 www.rcgs.org): The RCGC is dedicated to imparting a broader knowledge of Canada — its people and places, its natural and cultural heritage and its environmental, social and economic challenges.

Royal Society of Canada (💻 www.rsc.ca): Academies of arts, humanity and sciences, since 1882.

Virtual Museum of Canada (💻 www.virtualmuseum.ca/english/index_flashft.html).

The Weather Network (💻 www.theweathernetwork.com): Voted the number weather site by Canadians.

Wikipedia (💻 http://en.wikipedia.org/wiki/canada): The Canada pages of the free online encyclopaedia.

Wines of Canada (💻 www.winesofcanada.com): A website devoted to Canada's wine industry and its over 500 wineries.

Travel & Tourism

CampSource.ca (💻 www.campsource.ca): A guide to camping resources in Canada.

Canada Events (💻 www.canadaevents.ca): What's on across Canada.

Canada.Travel (💻 www.canada.travel): The official travel guide to Canada.

Canadian Tourism Commission (💻 www.canadatourism.com): Comprehensive information and links about all aspects of life in Canada.

Fish and Hunt Canada (💻 www.fishandhuntcanada.com): The best fishing and hunting trips in Canada.

Trail Canada (💻 www.trailcanada.com): All you need to know about travel and holidays in Canada.

Transport Canada (💻 www.tc.gc.ca): The government website about everything to do with travel in Canada.

Trail Canada (💻 www.trailcanada.com): Comprehensive travel guide.

Train Travel in Canada (💻 www.seat61.com/canada.htm).

Via Rail (💻 www.viarail.ca): Canada's railway company.

Wikitravel Canada (💻 http://wikitravel.org/en/canada): Canada travel guide from Wikitravel (part of Wikipedia).

APPENDIX D: WEIGHTS & MEASURES

Canada uses the metric system of measurement. Those who are more familiar with the imperial system will find the tables on the following pages useful. Some comparisons shown are only approximate, but are close enough for most everyday uses.

In addition to the variety of measurement systems used, clothes sizes often vary considerably with the manufacturer – as we all know only too well! Try all clothes on before buying and don't be afraid to return something if, when you try it on at home, you decide it doesn't fit (most shops will exchange goods or give a refund).

Women's Clothes										
Continental	34	36	38	40	42	44	46	48	50	52
UK	8	10	12	14	16	18	20	22	24	26
US	6	8	10	12	14	16	18	20	22	24

Pullover's												
	Women's						Men's					
Continental	40	42	44	46	48	50	44	46	48	50	52	54
UK	34	36	38	40	42	44	34	36	38	40	42	44
US	34	36	38	40	42	44		sm	med		lg	xl

Men's Shirts										
Continental	36	37	38	39	40	41	42	43	44	46
UK/US	14	14	15	15	16	16	17	17	18	-

Men's Underwear						
Continental	5	6	7	8	9	10
UK	34	36	38	40	42	44
US	sm		med		lg	xl

NB: sm = small, med = medium, lg = large, xl = extra large

Children's Clothes						
Continental	92	104	116	128	140	152
UK	16/18	20/22	24/26	28/30	32/34	36/38
US	2	4	6	8	10	12

Children's Shoes															
Continental	18	19	20	21	22	23	24	25	26	27	28	29	30	31	32
UK/US	2	3	4	4	5	6	7	7	8	9	10	11	11	12	13
Continental	33	34	35	36	37	38									
UK/US	1	2	2	3	4	5									

Shoes (Women's & Men's)												
Continental	35	36	37	37	38	39	40	41	42	42	43	44
UK	2	3	3	4	4	5	6	7	7	8	9	9
US	4	5	5	6	6	7	8	9	9	10	10	11

Weight

Imperial	Metric	Metric	Imperial
1oz	28.35g	1g	0.035oz
1lb*	454g	100g	3.5oz
1cwt	50.8kg	250g	9oz
1 ton	1,016kg	500g	18oz
2,205lb	1 tonne	1kg	2.2lb

Area

British/US	Metric	Metric	British/US
1 sq. in	0.45 sq. cm	1 sq. cm	0.15 sq. in
1 sq. ft	0.09 sq. m	1 sq. m	10.76 sq. ft
1 sq. yd	0.84 sq. m	1 sq. m	1.2 sq. yds
1 acre	0.4 hectares	1 hectare	2.47 acres
1 sq. mile	2.56 sq. km	1 sq. km	0.39 sq. mile

Capacity			
Imperial	**Metric**	**Metric**	**Imperial**
1 UK pint	0.57 litre	1 litre	1.75 UK pints
1 US pint	0.47 litre	1 litre	2.13 US pints
1 UK gallon	4.54 litres	1 litre	0.22 UK gallon
1 US gallon	3.78 litres	1 litre	0.26 US gallon

NB: An American 'cup' = around 250ml or 0.25 litre.

Length			
British/US	**Metric**	**Metric**	**British/US**
1in	2.54cm	1cm	0.39in
1ft	30.48cm	1m	3ft 3.25in
1yd	91.44cm	1km	0.62mi
1mi	1.6km	8km	5mi

Temperature	
°Celsius	**°Fahrenheit**
0	32 (freezing point of water)
5	41
10	50
15	59
20	68
25	77
30	86
35	95
40	104
50	122

Temperature Conversion

Celsius to Fahrenheit: multiply by 9, divide by 5 and add 32. (For a quick and approximate conversion, double the Celsius temperature and add 30.)

Fahrenheit to Celsius: subtract 32, multiply by 5 and divide by 9. (For a quick and approximate conversion, subtract 30 from the Fahrenheit temperature and divide by 2.)

NB: The boiling point of water is 100°C / 212°F. Normal body temperature (if you're alive and well) is 37°C / 98.6°F.

Power			
Kilowatts	**Horsepower**	**Horsepower**	**Kilowatts**
1	1.34	1	0.75

Oven Temperature		
Gas	**Electric**	
	°F	**°C**
-	225–250	110–120
1	275	140
2	300	150
3	325	160
4	350	180
5	375	190
6	400	200
7	425	220
8	450	230
9	475	240

Air Pressure	
PSI	**Bar**
10	0.5
20	1.4
30	2
40	2.8

bison

INDEX

A

B

C

D

E

F

G

H

I

J/K

Q/R

S

T

U

V

W

Y

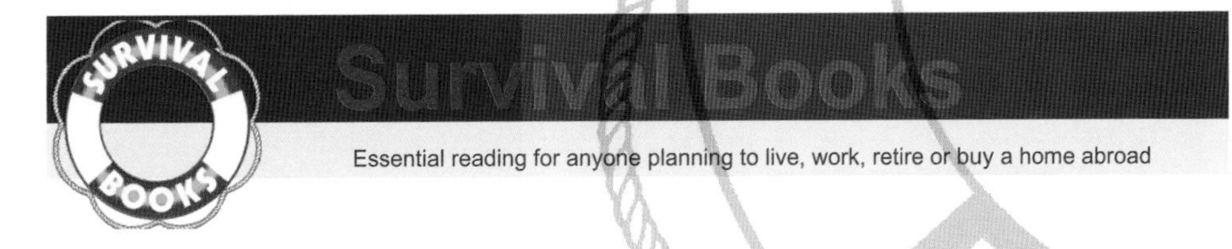

Survival Books was established in 1987 and by the mid-'90s was the leading publisher of books for people planning to live, work, buy property or retire abroad.

From the outset, our philosophy has been to provide the most comprehensive and up-to-date information available. Our titles routinely contain up to twice as much information as other books and are updated frequently. All our books contain colour photographs and some are printed in two colours or full colour throughout. They also contain original cartoons, illustrations and maps.

Survival Books are written by people with first-hand experience of the countries and the people they describe, and therefore provide invaluable insights that cannot be obtained from official publications or websites, and information that is more reliable and objective than that provided by the majority of unofficial sites.

Survival Books are designed to be easy – and interesting – to read. They contain a comprehensive list of contents and index and extensive appendices, including useful addresses, further reading, useful websites and glossaries to help you obtain additional information as well as metric conversion tables and other useful reference material.

Our primary goal is to provide you with the essential information necessary for a trouble-free life or property purchase and to save you time, trouble and money.

We believe our books are the best – they are certainly the best-selling. But don't take our word for it – read what reviewers and readers have said about Survival Books at the front of this book.

Living and Working Series

Our Living and Working guides are essential reading for anyone planning to spend a period abroad – whether it's an extended holiday or permanent migration – and are packed with priceless information designed to help you avoid costly mistakes and save both time and money.

Living and Working guides are the most comprehensive and up-to-date source of practical information available about everyday life abroad. They aren't, however, simply a catalogue of dry facts and figures, but are written in a highly readable style – entertaining, practical and occasionally humorous.

Our aim is to provide you with the comprehensive practical information necessary for a trouble-free life. You may have visited a country as a tourist, but living and working there is a different matter altogether; adjusting to a new environment and culture and making a home in any foreign country can be a traumatic and stressful experience. You need to adapt to new customs and traditions, discover the local way of doing things (such as finding a home, paying bills and obtaining insurance) and learn all over again how to overcome the everyday obstacles of life.

All these subjects and many, many more are covered in depth in our Living and Working guides – don't leave home without them.

The Expats' Best Friend!

Culture Wise Series

Our **Culture Wise** series of guides is essential reading for anyone who wants to understand how a country really 'works'. Whether you're planning to stay for a few days or a lifetime, these guides will help you quickly find your feet and settle into your new surroundings.
Culture Wise guides:

- Reduce the anxiety factor in adapting to a foreign culture
- Explain how to behave in everyday situations in order to avoid cultural and social gaffes
- Help you get along with your neighbours
- Make friends and establish lasting business relationships
- Enhance your understanding of a country and its people.

People often underestimate the extent of cultural isolation they can face abroad, particularly in a country with a different language. At first glance, many countries seem an 'easy' option, often with millions of visitors from all corners of the globe and well-established expatriate communities. But, sooner or later, newcomers find that most countries are indeed 'foreign' and many come unstuck as a result. **Culture Wise** guides will enable you to quickly adapt to the local way of life and feel at home, and – just as importantly – avoid the worst effects of culture shock.

Culture Wise – The Wise Way to Travel

The essential guides to Culture, Customs & Business Etiquette

Other Survival Books

The Best Places to Buy a Home in France/Spain: Unique guides to where to buy property in Spain and France, containing detailed regional profiles and market reports.

Buying, Selling and Letting Property: The best source of information about buying, selling and letting property in the UK.

Earning Money From Your French Home: Income from property in France, including short- and long-term letting.

Investing in Property Abroad: Everything you need to know and more about buying property abroad for investment and pleasure.

Life in the UK - Test & Study Guide: essential reading for anyone planning to take the 'Life in the UK' test in order to become a permanent resident (settled) in the UK.

Making a Living: Comprehensive guides to self-employment and starting a business in France and Spain.

Renovating & Maintaining Your French Home: The ultimate guide to renovating and maintaining your dream home in France.

Retiring in France/Spain: Everything a prospective retiree needs to know about the two most popular international retirement destinations.

Running Gîtes and B&Bs in France: An essential book for anyone planning to invest in a gîte or bed & breakfast business.

Rural Living in France: An invaluable book for anyone seekingthe 'good life', containing a wealth of practical information about all aspects of French country life.

Shooting Caterpillars in Spain: The hilarious and compelling story of two innocents abroad in the depths of Andalusia in thelate '80s.

For a full list of our current titles, visit our website at www.survivalbooks.net

PHOTO

www.dreamstime.com

Pages 1 © Dan Bannister ,16 © Kuzma, 19 © Medaphoto, 24 © Ondacaracola, 26 © Tatianatatiana, 28 © Maigi, 41 © Michaelmill, 42 © Fred II, 45 © Inspireme, 51 © Michaelmill, 53 © Jamey Ekins, 62 © Albln, 65 © Monkeybusinessimages, 66 © Fotomy, 69 © Andresr, 70 © Pressmaster, 72 © Rido, 74 © Rido, 76 © Devonyu, 78 © Argironeta, 81 © Mhryciw, 87 © Uniqueglen, 88 © Kwest19, 94 © Reefer, 97 © Ulga, 100 © Ramone, 103 © Norman Pogson, 105 © Billm2, 106 © Jackrussell, 111 © Elenathewise, 112 © Peteklinger, 114 © Laroach, 116 © Tupungato, 119 © Tupungato, 120 © Diego.cervo, 122 © Elliotwestacott, 129 © Galoff, 132 © Saniphoto, 135 © Kyolshin, 137 © Ekychan, 139 © Petarneychev, 140 © Katseyephoto, 143 © Monkeybusinessimages, 145 © Jgfoto, 146 © Sumnergraphicsinc, 149 © Arekmalang, 150 © Andresr, 153 © Monkeybusinessimages, 156 © Cybernesco, 159 © Tim Pohl, 160 © Bradcalkins, 165 © Paha_l, 167 © Fer737ng, 169 © Wayne Stadler, 171 © Gvictoria, 172 © Taylorjackson, 177 © Tupungato, 178 © Actinicblue, 181 © Kvv515kvv, 187 © Fotogeek, 196 © Diego.cervo, 198 © Kurhan, 201 © Elnur, 202 © Stevemcsweeny, 206 © Fotograf77, 209 © Thevinman, 213 © Fmatte, 215 © Howard Sandler, 219 © Andresr, 228 © Devonyu, 230 © Igenkin, 249 © Philipdyer, 252 © Deb22, 254 © Sumeetw, 256 © Iamcdn, 258 © Misscanon, 261 © Spanishalex, 262 © Yuri_arcurs, 265 © Maceofoto, 267 © Dmitryp, 268 © Alphababy, 271 © Sprokop. 273 © Assignments, 274 © Molka, 277 © Katsephoto, 283 © Mschalke, 285 © Rafter, 287 © Uniqueglen, 288 © Fallsview, 294 © Lafucina, 296 © Starfotograf, 298 © Bruno1998, 300 © Anniecounie, 303 © Yuri-arcurs,

CREDITS

305 © Lumix2004,309 © Bcbounders, 311 ©Vadkoz, 312 © Outdoorsman, 314 © Tupungato, 317 © Hsandler, 319 © Jf123, 322 © Jewhyte, 325 © Litwinphotography, 327 © Graphicphoto, 329 © Avalvo, 333 © Zanskar, 334 © Leloft1911, 336 © Perrush, 339 © Brad Calkins, 340 © Filtv, 343 © Onepony, 344 © Elenaray, 365 © Wulfespirit, 382 © Awcnz62, 382 © Erickn, 383 © Nsilcock, 383 © Elkeflorida

www.shutterstock.com

Pages 14 © Jason Kasumovic, 31 © Pedro Nogueira, 33 © Feng Yu, 37 © Zsott Nyulaszi, 47 © Andresr, 61 © Mike Norton, 82 © Jovan Nikolic, 98 © V.J. Matthew, 110 © fotosav, 126 © Cloki, 130 © Rui Vale de Sousa, 175 © Oksana Perkins, 185 © Oksana Perkins, 189 © Avalon Imaging, 191 © terekov igor, 195 © David P. Lewis, 210 © Oksana Perkins, 220 © Andresr, 223 © Steve Rosset, 225 © Emilia Stasiak, 226 © Zoran Vukmanov Simokov, 234 © SandraG, 236 © Fancy, 239 © Maximus I, 240 © Rui Vale de Sousa, 251 © objectsforall, 278 © Larry St. Pierre, 280 © Richard Avner, 291 © Elena Kalistratova, 306 © rieke photos, 349 © Nick Biemans, 366 © Hannamariah, 374 © Hannamariah, 382 © Dmitry Pichugin, 383 © Yury Zaporozhchenko

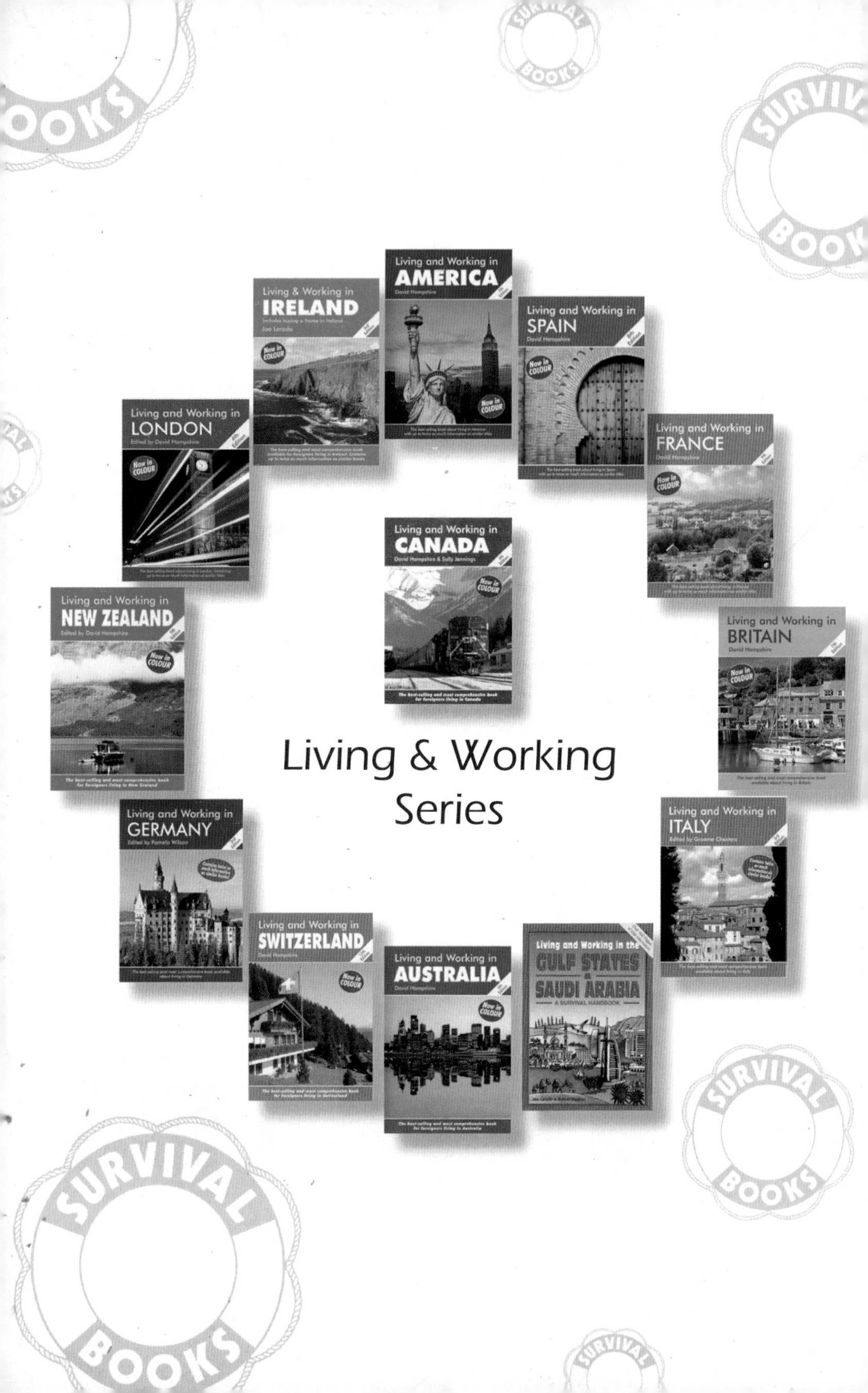

Living and Working in
AMERICA
Living & Working in
IRELAND
Living and Working in
SPAIN
Living and Working in
LONDON
Living and Working in
FRANCE
Living and Working in
CANADA
Living and Working in
NEW ZEALAND
Living and Working in
BRITAIN
Living & Working
Series
Living and Working in
GERMANY
Living and Working in
ITALY
Living and Working in
SWITZERLAND
Living and Working in
AUSTRALIA
Living and Working in the
GULF STATES
&
SAUDI ARABIA
A SURVIVAL HANDBOOK
SURVIVAL
BOOKS